VMR® STAN

USE

CARS, VANS, TRUCKS & SPORT UTILITIES 1988 - 2001

Volume 9, Number 3 | ISSN: 1069-8779 | ISBN: 1-883899-44-3

Publisher	John A. Iafolla
Editor	John A. Iafolla
Statistics Editor	Sandra A. Brown
Office Manager	Linda Mekulsia
Circulation Director	Michael A. Gerardo
Production Director	Kelly J. Hulitzky

Printed in the USA
CBN: 10231 0943RT

VMR International, Inc.
41 No. Main St.
No. Grafton, MA 01536 USA

www.vmrintl.com

Customer Support:
** MUST HAVE CURRENT BOOK **
(800) 867-4685 (M-F 10am-4pm EST)
Fax: (508) 839-6266

HOW TO USE THIS GUIDE

UNDERSTAND THE TERMS USED IN CAR BUYING AND SELLING

Base Equipment Levels - VMR has based all prices for all vehicles on the same level of equipment: **Automatic transmission, air conditioning, power steering, power brakes, and am/fm stereo** are included in all pricing unless specifically indicated otherwise. If a vehicle is not listed, or if there is no price listed, market data was not available at time of printing.

Wholesale - The price a seller should expect to receive from a dealer in a sale or trade. It assumes that the vehicle is in good mechanical condition, clean and well maintained. Reconditioning or repair costs should be deducted.

Retail - The maximum a buyer should expect to pay a dealer. The vehicle needs no mechanical attention and is clean, showing only normal wear for its age. Any reconditioning or repair costs should be deducted. VMR recommends that you bargain towards the midpoint (or better) of the wholesale and retail price. This should still leave enough profit to satisfy a dealer. Keep in mind that dealers usually ask for more (often much more) than they will take and that many dealer price guides tend to be on the high side of the market.

Condition - All prices in this guide assume that the vehicle is "clean" and in good mechanical condition. For vehicles not up to this standard, reconditioning or repair costs should be deducted. Vehicles over 2 years old in superior condition usually command a premium, typically around 5%.

Availability - Refers to supply and demand. If particularly "hot" and in great demand with a limited supply, you can expect to pay a premium for the vehicle. This variable can also be affected by seasonal and geographic factors. Local classifieds can give you a feel of the availability of a particular model.

Regional Considerations - There are no great differences in values between different areas of the country. Some imports may be priced slightly higher on the west coast, and four-wheel drive vehicles command a little more in the snow belt. In both cases, the premium is less than 5%.

Private sale - A sale between two individuals. No dealer is involved. If buying from a private party, you should try to pay close to wholesale.

"Demo" Vehicles - Vehicles that have not been sold and were used soley as dealer "demonstration" models. Dealers may try to price these as discounted new vehicles. They are used vehicles and should be priced as such.

"Salvage" Vehicles - Vehicles that have a salvage title due to body or frame work, water damage, or other serious conditions, should be valued less than prices in this guide. It is illegal in most states to sell a salvage-titled vehicle without disclosing it to the buyer. Some states issue rebuilder or flood titles as well. VMR does not recommend purchasing these types of vehicles. VMR offers a free lemon check at its website (www.vmrintl.com) for cars and trucks manufactured from 1981-up. Have the vehicle id number (VIN) ready. You may also order a full vehicle history report that will disclose any insurance claims on the vehicle.

DO YOUR HOMEWORK

Find out what it's worth - Use the VMR guide to determine the wholesale and retail value of a vehicle. Be sure to add or deduct for options or packages listed with each car or on the van and truck option table on page 4. (**Canada:** All pricing is US$. Convert to CAN$ at the current exchange rate.)

Adjust for mileage - VMR has three mileage charts, depending on the wholesale value of the vehicle. Be sure to add or deduct for mileage.

EQUIPMENT LEVELS FOR CARS

Standard and optional equipment pricing is one of the most important parts of buying or selling a used car. Many consumers pay extra for "options" that are actually part of a vehicle's standard equipment. Vehicle Market Research International (VMR) has done extensive research on equipment levels for this guide, so the consumer knows exactly what he or she should be paying for.

Unless indicated otherwise, the price for each model of each vehicle includes: **automatic transmission, air conditioning, power brakes, power steering, and am-fm stereo.** You must adjust the price in this guide if this equipment is not present on the vehicle or if other options are on the vehicle. The dollar amounts to be added or deducted are listed with each vehicle.

If equipment is not listed in the Add or Deduct sections of each model it is either standard or does not affect its value. **DO NOT ADD OR DEDUCT FOR EQUIPMENT THAT IS NOT LISTED WITH THE MODEL.**

If equipment is not standard on a model and affects its value it will be listed in a table of factory-installed equipment that follows the model. Use these tables to add to the price if the vehicle has the option and deduct if it does not.

The following example summarizes how to price optional equipment :

Model listings show drive wheels and engine specifications

ANYCAR	FWD/ 2.3L-I4 (110hp)	WS	Rtl
GL	4Dr Sdn	5000	6525
GL	2Dr Cpe	4900	6400
GLS	4Dr Sdn	5900	7450
GLS	2Dr Cpe	5825	7375
LX	4Dr Sdn	5700	7200
Add:			
3.0 Liter V6 (std GLS)		350	350
Air bag-driver		200	200
Cassette (GL)		50	50
Cruise ctrl		100	100
Pwr dr locks (std LX)		100	100
Pwr windows		125	125
Deduct:			
No air cond		550	550
Manual trans		500	500

Current values for vehicles with standard VMR equipment levels

V6 engine is standard on GLS - add only to GL and LX

Add cassette price only to GL model

Power dr locks are standard on the LX - add only to GL and GLS

Add values for all other options to GL, LX and GLS

Deduct value from all models if equipped with manual trans or does not have A/C

Loaded vehicles - Vehicles equipped with lots of *minor options* ("gadgets and toys") may be worth slightly more than the values listed in this guide.

Dealer or owner-installed options - If you determine that an option was installed by the dealer or the owner, it should be carefully inspected and usually valued at less than a similar manufacturer-installed option.

EQUIPMENT LEVELS FOR VANS, SPORT UTILITY VEHICLES AND LIGHT TRUCKS

Unless specifically indicated otherwise, Van, Sport Utility and Light Truck prices in this guide include: **automatic transmission, air conditioning, power steering, power brakes, am-fm stereo and 2-wheel drive.**

If the vehicle has one (or more) of the features listed below, you must add the value(s) to the price in this guide. You must deduct if the vehicle has a manual transmission or does not have air conditioning or power steering.

EQUIPMENT	2001	2000	1999	1998	1997	1996	1995	1994	1993	1992	OLDER
Auto transmission (Deduct if no)											
Compact Pkps/Spt Utes	525	500	425	375	275	225	150	125	100	-	-
All other	675	600	525	450	375	300	250	200	150	100	75
A/C - Vans & Sport Utes (Deduct if no)	750	725	650	575	525	450	375	325	250	175	100
A/C - Cargo vans & Pickups (Deduct if no)	700	650	550	475	425	375	300	225	150	125	75
Power steering (Deduct if no)	250	225	200	175	150	125	100	75	50	25	-
Power Door Locks	175	150	125	100	75	50	50	25	25	-	-
Power Seat	150	125	100	75	50	25	50	25	-	-	-
Power Windows	200	175	175	150	125	100	75	75	50	25	-
Cruise Control	200	175	150	125	100	75	75	50	25	-	-
CD Player	200	175	150	100	75	50	25	-	-	-	-
Extended Van-Full size	350	300	275	225	200	175	150	125	100	75	75
11/12/15 Passenger seating (Large Vans)	375	325	300	250	200	150	125	100	75	50	50
Sliding rear window	150	125	100	100	75	50	25	-	-	-	-
Leather seats	400	350	300	250	200	150	100	75	50	-	-
Dual A/C	350	325	275	250	225	175	150	125	100	50	-
Sunroof-manual	225	200	200	175	150	125	100	75	50	25	25
Sunroof-power	425	400	375	325	275	225	200	150	100	75	50
Tilt wheel	175	150	125	100	75	50	25	-	-	-	-
Sunscreen/Prvcy Glass	375	325	300	250	200	175	125	100	75	75	50
4-bucket seating (minivans)	250	225	200	175	125	100	100	75	75	50	-
HD towing pkg	275	250	225	200	175	150	125	100	50	25	25
454,460 V8	725	700	650	575	450	400	325	275	250	175	125
Diesel engine (V8)	1,850	1,725	1,650	1,550	1,400	1,250	975	825	750	600	450
1-ton (over 3/4 ton)	600	550	500	450	400	350	275	250	200	150	100
Dual rear wheels	950	875	775	700	625	525	400	350	275	200	150
Crew Cab (over ext cab)	900	850	750	675	600	500	400	350	275	200	150

VMR *Standard Used Car Prices* is the result of careful analysis and research of passenger vehicles and their current values. The publisher does not assume responsibility for errors of omission or commission.

MILEAGE ADJUSTMENT TABLE Group I: current wholesale value under $12,500

Mileage	2001	2000	1999	1998	1997	1996	1995	1994	1993	1992	1991	older
0 to 10,000	475	775	1075	1500	1750	2050	2300	2575	2800	3025	3150	3275
10,001 to 15,000		550	800	1250	1575	1850	2075	2350	2550	2750	2850	2975
15,001 to 22,500	250	275	650	1075	1425	1700	1825	2125	2300	2475	2575	2675
22,501 to 30,000	475		500	875	1175	1525	1650	1925	2100	2250	2350	2450
30,001 to 37,500	775	250	300	675	950	1225	1450	1625	1900	2025	2100	2175
37,501 to 45,000	975	400		475	800	1050	1300	1425	1675	1775	1850	1925
45,001 to 52,500	1175	650	275	275	600	850	1050	1300	1525	1625	1700	1775
52,501 to 60,000	1475	975	500		250	650	850	975	1225	1375	1425	1475
60,001 to 67,500	1850	1225	900	275		200	650	725	1050	1150	1200	1250
67,501 to 75,000	2250	1475	1200	700	275		250	425	800	950	1000	1050
75,001 to 82,500	2625	1725	1500	1050	725	250		225	475	675	700	725
82,501 to 90,000	3000	2000	1750	1300	1050	650	250		275	475	500	525
90,001 to 105,000	3350	2250	2100	1625	1475	1175	675	250		250	250	275
105,001 to 120,000	3625	2475	2300	1950	1700	1475	1075	600	225			100
120,001 to 135,000	3850	2650	2525	2350	2050	1900	1550	1075	550			
Over 135,000	4475	3025	2850	2650	2325	2175	1850	1500	1050	500	225	

Shaded numbers should be deducted from a vehicle's value. Non-shaded numbers should be added. Maximum addition or deduction should not exceed 60% of a vehicle's value.

MILEAGE ADJUSTMENT TABLE Group II: current whlsle value $12,500 - $25,000

Mileage	2001	2000	1999	1998	1997	1996	1995	1994	1993	1992	1991	older
0 to 10,000	650	1350	1700	1975	2375	2800	3100	3425	3775	4050	4200	4275
10,001 to 15,000		975	1350	1750	2000	2475	2725	3075	3400	3575	3725	3800
15,001 to 22,500	400	575	1075	1575	1800	2225	2375	2775	3025	3225	3350	3425
22,501 to 30,000	675		850	1350	1575	2000	2100	2350	2650	2875	3000	3050
30,001 to 37,500	1075	450	600	1000	1350	1700	1850	2125	2375	2625	2725	2775
37,501 to 45,000	1475	775		750	1075	1450	1625	1925	2100	2225	2325	2375
45,001 to 52,500	2075	1125	425		800	1150	1425	1750	1900	2050	2125	2175
52,501 to 60,000	2650	1475	900	450	575	900	1150	1425	1700	1800	1875	1925
60,001 to 67,500	3100	1925	1300	850		625	825	1200	1450	1525	1575	1600
67,501 to 75,000	3650	2375	1575	1275	425		650	950	1200	1250	1350	1475
75,001 to 82,500	4350	2950	2025	1775	800	400		750	950	1025	1075	1100
82,501 to 90,000	5000	3375	2400	2225	1150	725	425		750	850	875	900
90,001 to 105,000	5500	3775	2800	2550	1550	1150	800	400		500	525	525
105,001 to 120,000	6000	4350	3275	2925	2025	1600	1350	875	450		225	225
120,001 to 135,000	6725	5000	3825	3450	2700	2400	2025	1400	775			
Over 135,000	8075	5750	4425	4025	3450	3000	2625	2375	1175	800	250	

Shaded numbers should be deducted from a vehicle's value. Non-shaded numbers should be added. Maximum addition or deduction should not exceed 60% of a vehicle's value.

MILEAGE ADJUSTMENT TABLE

Group III: current wholesale value over $25,000

Mileage	2001	2000	1999	1998	1997	1996	1995	1994	1993	1992	1991	older
0 to 10,000	1050	1775	2300	2700	3050	3400	3950	4200	4625	5050	5200	5350
10,001 to 15,000		1100	1800	2150	2450	3050	3475	3825	4200	4550	4675	4825
15,001 to 22,500	625	600	1450	1825	2150	2675	3100	3300	3650	4100	4275	4400
22,501 to 30,000	900		1100	1550	1825	2300	2725	3000	3275	3600	3750	3875
30,001 to 37,500	1300	700	775	1175	1550	1975	2400	2600	2850	3125	3250	3350
37,501 to 45,000	1950	1125		900	1325	1750	2100	2300	2500	2750	2850	2925
45,001 to 52,500	2625	1750	675		975	1425	1775	2025	2275	2475	2575	2650
52,501 to 60,000	3225	2475	1275	425	700	1150	1450	1750	1975	2175	2250	2325
60,001 to 67,500	3875	3100	1700	900		750	1125	1400	1625	1850	1925	1975
67,501 to 75,000	4450	3700	2525	1900	700		800	1125	1375	1525	1575	1625
75,001 to 82,500	5025	4250	3025	2650	1250	700		850	1100	1250	1300	1350
82,501 to 90,000	5775	4900	3500	3225	2375	1150	675		900	1025	1075	1100
90,001 to 105,000	6650	5525	4125	3925	2975	2300	1350	650		625	650	675
105,001 to 120,000	7575	6625	5025	4600	3500	3025	2500	1325	550		400	400
120,001 to 135,000	8700	7550	6125	5850	4275	3625	3250	2375	1200			
Over 135,000	9925	8675	7175	6850	5050	4275	3900	3200	2150	1050	500	

Shaded numbers should be deducted from a vehicle's value. Non-shaded numbers should be added. Maximum addition or deduction should not exceed 60% of a vehicle's value.

Subscriptions:

1-800-867-4685

ACURA

2001 — WS / Ret

CL — FWD/3.2L-V6 (225hp)

Model	WS	Ret
Base 2dr Sdn		
Type S (260hp) 2dr Sdn		

INTEGRA — FWD/1.8L-I4 (140hp)

Model	WS	Ret
GS 4dr Sdn	15750	18450
GS 2dr Hbk	15625	18325
GS-R (5sp) 4dr Sdn	16900	19700
GS-R (5sp) 2dr Hbk	16775	19550
LS 4dr Sdn	15275	17925
LS 2dr Hbk	15150	17800
Type-R 2dr Hbk		

Deduct:
- Manual (not GS-R,R) 675

NSX — RWD/3.0L-V6 (290hp)

Model	WS	Ret
6sp/auto 2dr Cpe		
T- 6sp/auto 2dr Cpe		

RL — FWD/3.5L-V6 (210hp)

Model	WS	Ret
3.5 4dr Sdn	29400	32675

Add:
- Navigation System 800

TL — FWD/3.2L-V6 (225hp)

Model	WS	Ret
3.2 4dr Sdn	23225	26525

Add:
- Navigation System 800

2000 — WS / Ret

INTEGRA — FWD/1.8L-I4 (140hp)

Model	WS	Ret
GS 4dr Sdn	13425	15925
GS 2dr Hbk	13300	15800
GS-R (5sp) 4dr Sdn	14175	16750
GS-R (5sp) 2dr Hbk	14050	16600
LS 4dr Sdn	12925	15400
LS 2dr Hbk	12800	15250
Type-R 2dr Hbk	16775	19550

Deduct:
- Manual (not GS-R,R) 525

NSX — RWD/3.0L-V6 (290hp)

Model	WS	Ret
6sp/auto 2dr Cpe		
T- 6sp/auto 2dr Cpe		

RL — FWD/3.5L-V6 (210hp)

Model	WS	Ret
3.5 4dr Sdn	26925	30225

Add:
- Navigation System 875

TL — FWD/3.2L-V6 (225hp)

Model	WS	Ret
3.2 4dr Sdn	20475	23550

Add:
- Navigation System 875

1999 — WS / Ret

CL — FWD/2.3L-I4 (150hp)

Model	WS	Ret
2.3CL 2dr Cpe	14400	17000
3.0CL (200hp-6cyl) 2dr Cpe	15675	18375

Deduct:
- 5spd manual 525

INTEGRA — FWD/1.8L-I4 (140hp)

Model	WS	Ret
GS 4dr Sdn	12350	14775
GS 2dr Hbk	12225	14650
GS-R (5sp) 4dr Sdn	13325	15825
GS-R (5sp) 2dr Hbk	13175	15525
LS 4dr Sdn	11900	14300
LS 2dr Hbk	11800	14175

Deduct:
- No air cond 500
- Manual (not GS-R,R) 425

NSX — RWD/3.0L-V6 (290hp)

Model	WS	Ret
6sp/auto 2dr Cpe	56775	62025
T- 6sp/auto 2dr Cpe	59425	64850

RL — FWD/3.5L-V6 (210hp)

Model	WS	Ret
3.5 4dr Sdn	24225	27325

Add:
- Navigation System 725

TL — FWD/3.2L-V6 (225hp)

Model	WS	Ret
3.2 4dr Sdn	19000	21950

Add:
- Navigation System 725

1998 — WS / Ret

CL — FWD/2.3L-I4 (150hp)

Model	WS	Ret
2.3CL 2dr Cpe	12075	14475
3.0CL (200hp-6cyl) 2dr Cpe	13350	15850

Add:
- Leather Seats 250

Deduct:
- 5spd manual 425

INTEGRA — FWD/1.8L-I4 (140hp)

Model	WS	Ret
GS 4dr Sdn	11200	13525
GS 2dr Hbk	11100	13425
GS-R (5sp) 4dr Sdn	11550	13900
GS-R (5sp) 2dr Hbk	11450	13800
LS 4dr Sdn	10200	12450
LS 2dr Hbk	10125	12375
RS 2dr Hbk	9400	11600
Type R (5sp) 2dr Hbk	14450	17050

Add:
- Alloy wheels (RS) 100
- Leather seats (std GS) 200

Deduct:
- No air cond 425
- Manual (not GS-R,R) 350

NSX — RWD/3.0L-V6 (290hp)

Model	WS	Ret
6sp/auto 2dr Cpe	48050	52700
T- 6sp/auto 2dr Cpe	49900	54675

RL — FWD/3.5L-V6 (210hp)

Model	WS	Ret
3.5 4dr Sdn	18050	20725

Add:
- Bose Audio w/CD changer 200
- Traction Control 350
- Navigation System 600
- Heated Seats 125

TL — FWD/2.5L-I5 (176hp)

Model	WS	Ret
2.5 4dr Sdn	14150	16725
3.2 (6cyl) 4dr Sdn	15775	18475

1997 — WS / Ret

CL — FWD/2.2L-I4 (145hp)

Model	WS	Ret
2.2CL 2dr Cpe	9650	11850
3.0CL (6cyl) 2dr Cpe	11250	13575

Deduct:
- 5spd manual 350

INTEGRA — FWD/1.8L-I4 (140hp)

Model	WS	Ret
GS 4dr Sdn	9550	11750
GS 2dr Hbk	9450	11650
GS-R (5sp) 4dr Sdn	9900	12125
GS-R (5sp) 2dr Hbk	9800	12025
LS 4dr Sdn	8675	10800
LS 2dr Hbk	8575	10700
RS 2dr Hbk	7900	9975
Type R (5sp) 2dr Hbk	12675	15125

Add:
- Alloy wheels (RS,LS) 75
- Leather seats 175

Deduct:
- No air cond 350
- Manual (not GS-R,R) 300

NSX — RWD/3.0L-V6 (290hp)

Model	WS	Ret
6sp/auto 2dr Cpe	41050	45825
T- 6sp/auto 2dr Cpe	42700	47625

RL — FWD/3.5L-V6 (210hp)

Model	WS	Ret
3.5 4dr Sdn	15100	17575

Add:
- Bose Audio w/CD changer 175
- Traction Control 300
- Navigation System 500

TL — FWD/2.5L-I5 (176hp)

Model	WS	Ret
2.5 4dr Sdn	11200	13525
3.2 (6cyl) 4dr Sdn	12675	15125

Add:
- Leather Seats 200
- Moonroof-pwr 250
- Traction Control 250

1996 — WS / Ret

INTEGRA — FWD/1.8L-I4 (142hp)

Model	WS	Ret
GS-R (5sp) 4dr Sdn	8250	10350
GS-R (5sp) 2dr Hbk	8175	10275
LS 4dr Sdn	7250	9275
LS 2dr Hbk	7175	9175
RS 4dr Sdn	6675	8650
RS 2dr Hbk	6575	8525
SE 4dr Sdn	7975	10050
SE 2dr Hbk	7900	9975

Add:
- Alloy wheels (std GS-R,SE) 50
- Leather seats 150

Deduct:
- No air cond 275
- Man trans (not GS-R) 250

NSX — RWD/3.0L-V6 (270hp)

Model	WS	Ret
5sp/auto 2dr Cpe	36850	41325

RL — FWD/3.5L-V6 (210hp)

Model	WS	Ret
3.5 4dr Sdn	13050	15525

Add:
- Bose Audio w/CD changer 150
- Traction Control 250
- Navigation System 400

TL — FWD/2.5L-I5 (176hp)

Model	WS	Ret
2.5 4dr Sdn	9275	11450
3.2 (6cyl) 4dr Sdn	10575	12850

Add:
- Leather Seats 175
- Moonroof-pwr 200
- Traction Control 225

1995 — WS / Ret

INTEGRA — FWD/1.8L-I4 (142hp)

Model	WS	Ret
GS-R (5sp) 4dr Sdn	7100	9100
GS-R (5sp) 2dr Hbk	7050	9050
LS 4dr Sdn	5950	7850
LS 2dr Hbk	5875	7775
RS 4dr Sdn	5425	7300
RS 2dr Hbk	5350	7200

SE 4dr Sdn	6550	8500
SE 2dr Hbk	6475	8425

Add:
- Alloy wheels (std GS-R,SE) . . . 50
- Leather seats . . . 125

Deduct:
- No air cond . . . 250
- Man trans (not GS-R) . . . 225

LEGEND FWD/3.2L-V6 (200hp)

GS (230hp) 4dr Sdn	11750	14125
L 4dr Sdn	9925	12150
L (230hp) 2dr Cpe	10875	13175
LS 4dr Sdn	11100	13425
LS (230hp) 2dr Cpe	12050	14450

Add:
- Leather seats (L only) . . . 150

Deduct:
- Manual trans . . . 250

NSX RWD/3.0L-V6 (270hp)

5sp/auto 2dr Cpe	34600	38875

1994 WS Ret

INTEGRA FWD/1.8L-I4 (142hp)

	WS	Ret
GS-R (5sp) 2dr Hbk	5700	7600
LS 4dr Sdn	4900	6700
LS 2dr Hbk	4825	6625
RS 4dr Sdn	4500	6275
RS 2dr Hbk	4450	6225

Add:
- Alloy wheels (std GS-R) . . . 25
- Leather seats . . . 125

Deduct:
- No air cond . . . 225
- Man trans (not GS-R) . . . 200

LEGEND FWD/3.2L-V6 (200hp)

	WS	Ret
GS 4dr Sdn	10275	12525
L 4dr Sdn	8400	10500
L (230hp) 2dr Cpe	9325	11500
LS 4dr Sdn	9400	11600
LS (230hp) 2dr Cpe	10275	12525

Add:
- Leather seats (L only) . . . 125

Deduct:
- Manual trans . . . 225

NSX RWD/3.0L-V6 (252hp)

	WS	Ret
5sp/auto 2dr Cpe	27650	31625

VIGOR FWD/2.5L-I5 (176hp)

	WS	Ret
GS 4dr Sdn	6550	8500
LS 4dr Sdn	5800	7700

Deduct:
- Manual trans . . . 225

1993 WS Ret

INTEGRA FWD/1.8L-I4 (140hp)

	WS	Ret
GS 4dr Sdn	4375	6125
GS 2dr Hbk	4325	6075
GS-R (5sp) 2dr Hbk	4550	6325
LS 4dr Sdn	3925	5650
LS 2dr Hbk	3875	5600
RS 4dr Sdn	3350	4925
RS 2dr Hbk	3300	4850

Add:
- Alloy wheels . . . 25
- Cassette . . . 25
- Leather seats . . . 100

Deduct:
- No air cond . . . 200
- Man trans (not GS-R) . . . 175

LEGEND FWD/3.2L-V6 (230hp)

	WS	Ret
Base 4dr Sdn	6425	8375
L 4dr Sdn	6975	8975
L (230hp) 2dr Cpe	8125	10200
LS 4dr Sdn	7725	9775
LS (230hp) 2dr Cpe	8875	11025

Add:
- Leather seats (L only) . . . 125

Deduct:
- Manual trans . . . 200

NSX RWD/3.0L-V6 (270hp)

	WS	Ret
5sp/auto 2dr Cpe	23975	27325

VIGOR FWD/2.5L-I5 (176hp)

	WS	Ret
GS 4dr Sdn	4975	6800
LS 4dr Sdn	4500	6275

Deduct:
- Manual trans . . . 200

1992 WS Ret

INTEGRA FWD/1.8L-I4 (140hp)

	WS	Ret
GS 4dr Sdn	3650	5250
GS 2dr Hbk	3600	5175
GS-R (5sp) 2dr Hbk	3875	5600
LS 4dr Sdn	3175	4725
LS 2dr Hbk	3175	4725
RS 4dr Sdn	2700	4175
RS 2dr Hbk	2700	4175

Add:
- Alloy wheels . . . 25
- Cassette . . . 25

Deduct:
- No air cond . . . 175
- Man trans (not GS-R) . . . 175

LEGEND FWD/3.2L-V6 (200hp)

	WS	Ret
Base 4dr Sdn	5250	7100
L 4dr Sdn	5700	7600
L 2dr Cpe	6700	8675
LS 4dr Sdn	6325	8275
LS 2dr Cpe	7275	9300

Add:
- Leather seats (L) . . . 75

Deduct:
- Manual trans . . . 200

NSX RWD/3.0L-V6 (270hp)

	WS	Ret
5sp/auto 2dr Cpe	21750	24925

VIGOR FWD/2.5L-I5 (176hp)

	WS	Ret
GS 4dr Sdn	4025	5750
LS 4dr Sdn	3625	5225

Deduct:
- Manual trans . . . 200

1991 WS Ret

INTEGRA FWD/1.8L-I4 (130hp)

	WS	Ret
GS 4dr Sdn	3150	4700
GS 2dr Hbk	3100	4650
LS 4dr Sdn	2825	4325
LS 2dr Hbk	2775	4250
RS 4dr Sdn	2550	4000
RS 2dr Hbk	2500	3950

Add:
- Alloy wheels (std GS) . . . 25

Deduct:
- No air cond . . . 175
- Manual trans . . . 150

LEGEND FWD/3.2L-V6 (200hp)

	WS	Ret
Base 4dr Sdn	5000	6825
L 4dr Sdn	5250	7100
L 2dr Cpe	6500	8450
LS 4dr Sdn	5625	7500
LS 2dr Cpe	6800	8775

Add:
- Leather seats (L only) . . . 75

Deduct:
- Manual trans . . . 175

NSX RWD/3.0L-V6 (270hp)

	WS	Ret
5sp/auto 2dr Cpe	21700	24875

1990 WS Ret

INTEGRA FWD/4.0L-I4 (130hp)

	WS	Ret
GS 4dr Sdn	2575	4025
GS 2dr Hbk	2550	4000
LS 4dr Sdn	2300	3500
LS 2dr Hbk	2275	3475
RS 4dr Sdn	2075	3250
RS 2dr Hbk	2075	3250

Add:
- Alloy wheels (std GS) . . . 25

Deduct:
- No air cond . . . 150
- Manual trans . . . 125

LEGEND FWD/2.7L-V6 (160hp)

	WS	Ret
Base 4dr Sdn	2775	4250
Base 2dr Cpe	3100	4650
L 4dr Sdn	3025	4550
L 2dr Cpe	3350	4925
LS 4dr Sdn	3350	4925
LS 2dr Cpe	3650	5250

Add:
- Leather seats (std LS) . . . 50
- Sunroof-pwr (Base only) . . . 100

Deduct:
- Manual trans . . . 150

1989 WS Ret

INTEGRA FWD/1.6L-I4 (118hp)

	WS	Ret
LS 4dr Hbk	1725	2850
LS 2dr Hbk	1700	2825
RS 4dr Hbk	1600	2700
RS 2dr Hbk	1575	2675

Add:

Deduct:
- No air cond . . . 100
- Manual trans . . . 100

LEGEND FWD/2.7L-V6 (160hp)

	WS	Ret
Base 4dr Sdn	2100	3275
Base 2dr Cpe	2375	3800
L 4dr Sdn	2325	3750
L 2dr Cpe	2575	4025
LS 4dr Sdn	2575	4025
LS 2dr Cpe	2775	4250

Add:
- Leather seats (std LS) . . . 25
- Sunroof-pwr (Base only) . . . 75

Deduct:
- Manual trans . . . 125

1988 WS Ret

INTEGRA FWD/1.6L-I4 (118hp)

	WS	Ret
LS 4dr Hbk	1050	1975
LS 2dr Hbk	1025	1950
LS Spec Edit 2dr Hbk	1075	2000
RS 4dr Hbk	950	1675
RS 2dr Hbk	925	1650

Add:

Deduct:
- No air cond . . . 100
- Manual trans . . . 50

LEGEND FWD/2.7L-V6 (161hp)

	WS	Ret
Base 4dr Sdn	1925	3075
Base 2dr Cpe	2125	3300
L 4dr Sdn	2025	3200
L 2dr Cpe	2225	3425
LS 4dr Sdn	2200	3400
LS 2dr Cpe	2400	3850

Add:
Sunroof-pwr . . . 50
Leather seats (L) . . . 25

Deduct:
Manual trans . . . 75

ALFA ROMEO

1995 WS Ret

164 RWD/3.0L-V6 (210hp)

	WS	Ret
L 4dr Sdn	9450	11650
Quadrifoglio (5sp) 4dr Sdn	10875	13300

Add:
CD player . . . 75

Deduct:
Manual trans (not Q) . . . 250

1994 WS Ret

164 RWD/3.0L-V6 (210hp)

	WS	Ret
L 4dr Sdn	8375	10475
Quadrifoglio (5sp) 4dr Sdn	9825	12175

Add:
CD player . . . 50

Deduct:
Manual trans (not Q) . . . 225

SPIDER (5sp) RWD/2.0L-I4 (120hp)

	WS	Ret
Base 2dr Cnv	7800	9850
Veloce 2dr Cnv	8700	10825

Add:
Alloy wheels (std Veloce) . . . 25
CD player (std Veloce) . . . 50
Removable hardtop . . . 250

Deduct:
No air cond . . . 225

1993 WS Ret

164 RWD/3.0L-V6 (183hp)

	WS	Ret
L 4dr Sdn	5300	7150
S (5sp) 4dr Sdn	6150	8075

Add:
Leather seats (std S) . . . 125

Deduct:
Manual trans (not S) . . . 200

SPIDER (5sp/auto) RWD/2.0L-I4 (120hp)

	WS	Ret
Base 2dr Cnv	6600	8575
Veloce 2dr Cnv	7650	9700

Add:
Alloy wheels (std Veloce) . . . 25
CD player . . . 50
Removable hardtop . . . 225

Deduct:
No air cond . . . 200

1992 WS Ret

164 RWD/3.0L-V6 (183hp)

	WS	Ret
L 4dr Sdn	4500	6275
S (5sp) 4dr Sdn	5275	7125

Add:
Leather seats (std S) . . . 75

Deduct:
Manual trans (not S) . . . 200

SPIDER (5sp/auto) RWD/2.0L-I4 (120hp)

	WS	Ret
Base 2dr Cnv	5950	7850
Veloce 2dr Cnv	6925	8925

Add:
Alloy wheels (std Veloce) . . . 25
CD player . . . 25
Removable hardtop . . . 200

Deduct:
No air cond . . . 175

1991 WS Ret

164 RWD/3.0L-V6 (183hp)

	WS	Ret
Base 4dr Sdn	2575	4025
L 4dr Sdn	3200	4750
S (5sp) 4dr Sdn	3725	5425

Add:
Alloy wheels (Base only) . . . 25
Lthr sport seats (Base) . . . 75
Recaro seats (S only) . . . 125
Sunroof-pwr . . . 125

Deduct:
Manual trans (not S) . . . 175

SPIDER (5sp/auto) RWD/2.0L-I4 (120hp)

	WS	Ret
Base 2dr Cnv	5100	6950
Veloce 2dr Cnv	5750	7650

Add:
Alloy wheels (Base only) . . . 25
Removable Hardtop . . . 175

Deduct:
No air cond . . . 175

1990 WS Ret

SPIDER (5spd) RWD/2.0L-I4 (115hp)

	WS	Ret
Graduate 2dr Cnv	4475	6250
Quadrifoglio 2dr Cnv	4975	6800
Veloce 2dr Cnv	4750	6525

Add:

Deduct:
No air cond . . . 125

1989 WS Ret

MILANO RWD/2.5L-V6 (154hp)

	WS	Ret
3.0L 4dr Sdn	2600	3975
Gold 4dr Sdn	2375	3725
Platinum 4dr Sdn	2475	3850

Add:
Sunroof-pwr . . . 75

SPIDER (5spd) RWD/2.0L-I4 (115hp)

	WS	Ret
Graduate 2dr Cnv	4125	5750
Quadrifoglio 2dr Cnv	4525	6175
Veloce 2dr Cnv	4325	5950

Add:

Deduct:
No air cond . . . 100

1988 WS Ret

MILANO RWD/2.5L-V6 (154hp)

	WS	Ret
Gold 4dr Sdn	1850	2925
Platinum 4dr Sdn	1925	3025
Verde 4dr Sdn	2875	4275

Add:
Sunroof-pwr . . . 50

SPIDER (5spd) RWD/2.0L-I4 (115hp)

	WS	Ret
Graduate 2dr Cnv	3475	4950
Quadrifoglio 2dr Cnv	3800	5400
Veloce 2dr Cnv	3675	5175

Add:

Deduct:
No air cond . . . 75

AUDI

2001 WS Ret

A4 FWD/1.8L-I4 (170hp)

	WS	Ret
1.8T 4dr Sdn	22525	25275
1.8T Quattro AWD 4dr Sdn	24050	26875
1.8T Avant AWD 4dr Wgn	25100	28000
2.8 (6cyl) 4dr Sdn	24850	27725
2.8 Quattro (6cy/AWD) 4sd	26050	29000
2.8 Avant (6cyl/AWD) Wgn	27125	30125

Add:
Bose audio . . . 300
Moonroof-pwr . . . 475
CD Changer . . . 325
Navigation sys . . . 525
Sport pkg (incls 17" 10-spke whls) 375

Deduct:
Manual trans . . . 750
No leather . . . 425

A6 AWD/2.8L-V6 (200hp)

	WS	Ret
2.7 Quattro (AWD/V6) 4sd	33950	37075
4.2 Quattro (AWD/V8) 4sd	38650	42025
Avant Quattro (AWD) Wgn	29550	32500
Base 2.8 4dr Sdn	25950	28900
Quattro (AWD) 4dr Sdn	28475	31575

Add:
Bose audio . . . 300
Third seat (wgn) . . . 550
Moonroof-pwr . . . 550
6-disc CD changer (trunk) . . . 425
Navigation sys . . . 625
Wheels-polished (4.2) . . . 275
Sport pkg . . . 450

Deduct:
No Leather . . . 475

A8 AWD/4.2L-V8 (310hp)

4.2 Quattro 4dr Sdn . . .
4.2 Quattro L 4dr Sdn . . .

Add:
17" polished alum. whls . . . 525
Navigation sys . . . 675
Warm weather pkg . . . 825
Suede&leather trim . . . 1350

S4 AWD/1.8L-I4 (170hp)

AWD Turbo 4dr Sdn . . .
AWD Turbo 4dr Wgn . . .

Add:
Bose audio . . . 300
Moonroof-pwr . . . 475
CD Changer . . . 325
Navigation sys . . . 525
Sport pkg (incls 17" 10-spk whls) 375
Quattro system (AWD) . . . 2325

Deduct:
Manual trans . . . 750
No leather . . . 425

S8 FWD/4.2L-V8 (360hp)

Quattro 4dr Sdn . . .

TT FWD/1.8L-I4 (180hp)

Base 2dr Cnv . . .
Base 2dr Cpe . . .
Quattro (225hp) 2dr Cnv . . .
Quattro (225hp) 2dr Cpe . . .

2000

2000	WS	Ret
A4 FWD/1.8L-I4 (150hp)		
1.8T 4dr Sdn	19000	21525
2.8 (6cyl) 4dr Sdn	21250	23925
Avant 1.8T (AWD) 4dr Wgn	20050	22650
Avant 2.8 (6cyl/AWD)	23525	26325

Add:
- Bose audio . . . 225
- Moonroof-pwr . . . 375
- Leather seats . . . 325
- CD Changer . . . 250
- Navigation sys . . . 400
- Sport pkg (incls 16" 10-spk whls) 275
- Quattro system (AWD) . . . 1825

Deduct:
- Manual trans . . . 575
- No leather . . . 325

A6 AWD/2.8L-V6 (200hp)	WS	Ret
2.7 Quattro (AWD/V6 4sd	31575	34625
4.2 Quattro (AWD/V8 4dr Sdn...		
Avant Quattro (AWD) Wgn	28800	31900
Base 2.8 4dr Sdn	25250	28150
Quattro (AWD) 4dr Sdn	27725	30775

Add:
- Bose audio . . . 225
- Third seat (wgn) . . . 425
- Moonroof-pwr . . . 425
- 6-disc CD changer (trunk) . . . 325
- Navigation sys . . . 500
- Wheels-polished (4.2) . . . 225
- Sport pkg . . . 350

Deduct:
- No Leather . . . 375

A8 AWD/4.2L-V8 (310hp)	WS	Ret
4.2 Quattro 4dr Sdn	41300	45650
4.2 Quattro L 4dr Sdn		

Add:
- 17" polished alum. whls . . . 400
- Navigation sys . . . 525
- Warm weather pkg . . . 650
- Suede & leather trim . . . 1050

S4 AWD/1.8L-I4 (150hp)	WS	Ret
4dr Sdn..................		

Add:
- Bose audio . . . 225
- Moonroof-pwr . . . 375
- Leather seats . . . 325
- CD Changer . . . 250
- Navigation sys . . . 400
- Sport pkg (incls 16" 10-spk whls) 275
- Quattro system (AWD) . . . 1825

Deduct:
- Manual trans . . . 575
- No leather . . . 325

TT FWD/1.8L-I4 (180hp)	WS	Ret
Base 2dr Cpe	23925	27275
Quattro (225hp) 2dr Cpe	26225	29775

Add:
- Bose audio w/CD changer . . . 350
- Performance pkg w/17" wheels 350
- Quattro AWD system . . . 1625

1999

1999	WS	Ret
A4 FWD/1.8L-I4T (150hp)		
1.8T 4dr Sdn	16025	18375
2.8 (6cyl) 4dr Sdn	18125	20600
Avant 1.8T (AWD) 4dr Wgn	16950	19350
Avant 2.8 (6cyl/AWD Wgn	20225	22825

Add:
- Bose audio w/CD . . . 250
- Moonroof-pwr . . . 300
- Leather seats . . . 275
- Sport pkg (incl 16" whls) . . . 225
- Quattro system (AWD) . . . 1500

Deduct:
- Manual trans . . . 475
- Vinyl Seats . . . 275

A6 AWD/2.8L-V6 (200hp)	WS	Ret
Avant Quattro (AWD) Wgn	24875	27750
Base 4dr Sdn	21850	24550
Quattro (AWD) 4dr Sdn	23900	26725

Add:
- Bose audio w/CD changer . . . 275
- Third seat (wgn) . . . 350
- Leather seats . . . 300
- Moonroof-pwr . . . 350
- Solar pkg w/pwr rear shade . . . 500
- Wheels-16" alloy . . . 150

Deduct:
- Cloth seats . . . 300

A8 FWD/3.7L-V8 (230hp)	WS	Ret
Base 4dr Sdn	29425	33025
Quattro (4.2L/AWD) 4sd	35350	39325

Add:
- 17" polished alum. whls . . . 325
- Solar pkg w/pwr rear shades . . 525
- Suede & leather trim . . . 850

1998

1998	WS	Ret
A4 FWD/1.8L-I4 (150hp)		
1.8T 4dr Sdn	13200	15375
2.8 (6cyl) 4dr Sdn	15025	17325
Avant 2.8 (6cyl) 4dr Wgn	15850	18200

Add:
- Bose audio w/CD . . . 200
- Moonroof-pwr . . . 250
- Leather seats . . . 225
- Quattro system (AWD) . . . 1250

Deduct:
- Manual trans . . . 400
- Vinyl Seats . . . 225

A6 FWD/2.8L-V6 (200hp)	WS	Ret
Base 4dr Sdn	16750	19350
Base 4dr Wgn	18775	21500
Quattro (AWD) 4dr Sdn	20100	22925
Quattro (AWD) 4dr Wgn	22125	25100

Add:
- Bose audio w/CD changer . . . 225
- Leather seats . . . 250
- Moonroof-pwr . . . 300
- Solar pkg w/pwr rear shade . . . 425

Deduct:
- Manual trans . . . 400
- Vinyl Seats . . . 225

A8 FWD/3.7L-V8 (230hp)	WS	Ret
Base 4dr Sdn	27425	31075
Quattro (4.2L/AWD) 4sd	32525	36275

Add:
- 17" polished alum. whls . . . 275
- Solar pkg w/pwr rear shades . . 425

CABRIOLET FWD/2.8L-V6 (172hp)	WS	Ret
2dr Cnv	18850	21575

Add:
- CD changer . . . 225
- 16" wheels . . . 125

Deduct:
- Manual Roof . . . 600
- Cloth seats . . . 250

1997

1997	WS	Ret
A4 FWD/2.8L-I4 (190hp)		
1.8T 4dr Sdn	10325	12350
2.8 (6cyl) 4dr Sdn	11900	14000

Add:
- Bose audio w/CD . . . 175
- Moonroof-pwr . . . 200
- Leather seats . . . 175
- Quattro system (AWD) . . . 1025

Deduct:
- Manual trans . . . 325

A6 FWD/2.8L-V6 (172hp)	WS	Ret
Base 4dr Sdn	13325	15525
Base 4dr Wgn	15075	17375
Quattro (AWD) 4dr Sdn	15125	17425
Quattro (AWD) 4dr Wgn	16975	19375

Add:
- Bose audio w/CD . . . 175
- Leather seats . . . 200
- Moonroof-pwr . . . 250

Deduct:
- Manual trans . . . 325

A8 FWD/3.7L-V8 (230hp)	WS	Ret
Base 4dr Sdn	21600	24775
Quattro (AWD) 4dr Sdn	26225	29775

Add:
- 17" polished alum. whls . . . 225
- Warm weather pkg. . . . 350

CABRIOLET FWD/2.8L-V6 (172hp)	WS	Ret
2dr Cnv	15350	17850

Add:
- CD changer . . . 175
- 16" wheels . . . 100

Deduct:
- Manual Roof . . . 500

1996

1996	WS	Ret
A4 FWD/2.8L-V6 (172hp)		
Base 4dr Sdn	9925	11925
Quattro (AWD) 4dr Sdn	11100	13150

Add:
- Bose audio w/CD . . . 150
- Sunroof-pwr . . . 175
- Leather seats . . . 150

Deduct:
- Manual trans . . . 275

A6 FWD/2.8L-V6 (172hp)	WS	Ret
Base 4dr Sdn	10000	12000
Base 4dr Wgn	11350	13425
Quattro (AWD) 4dr Sdn	11825	13925
Quattro (AWD) 4dr Wgn	13400	15600

Add:
- Bose audio w/CD . . . 150
- Leather seats . . . 175
- Sunroof-pwr . . . 200

CABRIOLET FWD/2.8L-V6 (172hp)	WS	Ret
2dr Cnv	12550	14850

Add:
- CD changer . . . 150

1995

1995	WS	Ret
90 FWD/2.8L-V6 (172hp)		
Base 4dr Sdn	6600	8400
Quattro (5sp-AWD) 4dr Sdn	7650	9500
Quattro Spt (5sp-AWD) 4sd	7825	9700
Sport 4dr Sdn	6800	8600

Add:
- Pwr seat . . . 25
- Sunroof-pwr . . . 150
- Leather seats . . . 150

Deduct:
- Man trans (not Qttro) . . . 250

A6 FWD/2.8L-V6 (172hp)	WS	Ret
Base 4dr Sdn	7825	9700

Base 4dr Wgn 9025 10975
Quattro (AWD) 4dr Sdn 9400 11350
Quattro (AWD) 4dr Wgn .. 10700 12750

Add:
CD changer 150
Integrated phone 75
Leather seats 150
Bose audio 75

CABRIOLET FWD/2.8L-V6 (172hp)

2dr Cnv 10600 12750

Add:
CD changer 150

S6 AWD/2.2L-I5 (227hp)

Quattro (5sp) 4dr Sdn 14275 16525
Quattro (5sp) 4dr Wgn.... 15300 17600

Add:
CD changer 150

1994 WS Ret

100 FWD/2.8L-V6 (172hp)

CS 4dr Sdn 7700 9550
CS Quattro (AWD) 4dr Sdn. 8475 10375
CS Quattro (AWD) 4dr Wgn 9525 11500
S 4dr Sdn.............. 6300 8075
S 4dr Wgn 7225 9050
S4 (AWD/Turbo--5sp) 4sd. 11925 14025

Add:
CD changer 125
Integrated phone 75
Leather seats (S only) 125

Deduct:
Manual trans 225

90 FWD/2.8L-V6 (172hp)

CS 4dr Sdn 6625 8425
CS Quattro (5sp-AWD) 4sd. 7250 9075
S 4dr Sdn.............. 5400 7125

Add:
CD changer 125
Sunroof-pwr (S only) 150
Leather seats (S only) 125

Deduct:
Man trans (not Qttro) 225

CABRIOLET FWD/2.8L-V6 (172hp)

2dr Cnv 9100 11050

Add:
CD changer 125

V8 QUATTRO AWD/4.2L-V8 (276hp)

Sedan 4dr Sdn.......... 12625 14775

Deduct:
Manual trans 225

1993 WS Ret

100 FWD/2.8L-V6 (172hp)

Base 4dr Sdn........... 4450 6100
CS 4dr Sdn 5800 7550
CS Quattro (AWD) 4dr Sdn. 7050 8875
CS Quattro (AWD) 4dr Wgn 8075 9950
S 4dr Sdn.............. 4875 6550
S4 (AWD/Turbo-5sp) 4sd . 10575 12600

Add:
CD changer 125
Integrated phone 50
Leather seats (S only) 125

Deduct:
Manual trans 200

90 FWD/2.8L-V6 (172hp)

CS 4dr Sdn 4550 6200
CS Quattro (5sp-AWD) 4sd. 5400 7125
S 4dr Sdn.............. 4025 5650

Add:
CD changer 100
Sunroof-pwr (S only) 125

Deduct:
Man trans (not Qttro) 200

V8 QUATTRO AWD/4.2L-V8 (276hp)

Sedan 4dr Sdn 10875 12925

Deduct:
Manual trans 225

1992 WS Ret

100 FWD/2.8L-V6 (172hp)

Base 4dr Sdn 3625 5100
CS 4dr Sdn 4650 6300
CS Quattro (AWD) 4dr Sdn 5725 7475
CS Quattro (AWD) 4dr Wgn 6350 8125
S 4dr Sdn 4050 5675
S4 (AWD/Turbo-5sp) 4sd .. 8575 10475

Add:
CD changer 100
Integrated phone 50
Leather seats 100

Deduct:
Manual trans 200

80 FWD/2.3L-I5 (130hp)

Base 4dr Sdn 2750 4150
Quattro (5sp-AWD) 4dr Sdn 3275 4750

Add:
CD changer 75
Sunroof-pwr 125

Deduct:
Man trans (not Qttro) 200

V8 QUATTRO AWD/2.3L-V8 (130hp)

Sedan 4dr Sdn 8300 10200

Deduct:
Manual trans 200

1991 WS Ret

100 FWD/2.3L-I5 (130hp)

Base 4dr Sdn 4000 5625
Quattro (5sp-AWD) 4dr Sdn 4650 6300

Add:
Bose audio 50
Leather seats 75
Power seats 25

Deduct:
Man trans (not Qttro) 175

200 AWD/2.2L-I5 (162hp)

Quattro (5sp-Turbo) 4dr Sdn 5450 7175
Quattro (5sp-Turbo) 4dr Wgn 5650 7400
Turbo (FWD) 4dr Sdn 4750 6400

Deduct:
Man trans (not Qttro) 175

80 FWD/2.3L-I5 (130hp)

Base 4dr Sdn 2775 4175
Quattro (5sp-AWD) 4dr Sdn 3050 4500

Add:
ABS brakes 50
Sunroof-manual 25

Deduct:
Man trans (not Qttro) 175

90 FWD/2.3L-I5 (130hp)

Base 4dr Sdn 3325 4800
Quattro (5sp-AWD) 4dr Sdn 3525 5000
Quattro (5sp-AWD) 2dr Cpe 3475 4950

Add:
Leather seats 50
Pwr seat 25

Deduct:
Man trans (not Qttro) 175

V8 QUATTRO AWD/3.6L-V8 (240hp)

Sedan 4dr Sdn........... 6700 8500

Deduct:
Manual trans 175

1990 WS Ret

100 FWD/2.3L-I5 (130hp)

Base 4dr Sdn 3475 4950
Quattro (5sp-AWD) 4dr Sdn. 4025 5650

Add:
Bose audio 50
Leather seats 50

Deduct:
Man trans (not Qttro) 150

200 AWD/2.2L-I5 (162hp)

Quattro (5sp-Tbo) 4dr Sdn.. 4500 6150
Quattro (5sp-Tbo) 4dr Wgn . 4675 6325
Turbo (FWD) 4dr Sdn...... 3950 5550

Deduct:
Man trans (not Qttro) 150

80 FWD/2.0L-I4 (108hp)

Base 4dr Sdn 2350 3700
Quattro (5sp-AWD) 4dr Sdn. 2625 4000

Add:
ABS 25
Sport pkg 25
Sunroof-manual 25

Deduct:
Man trans (not Qttro) 150

90 FWD/2.3L-I5 (130hp)

Base 4dr Sdn 2800 4200
Quattro (5sp-AWD) 4dr Sdn. 3000 4425
Quattro (5sp-AWD) 2dr Cpe. 2900 4325

Add:
Leather seats 50

Deduct:
Man trans (not Qttro) 150

V8 QUATTRO AWD/3.6L-V8 (240hp)

Sedan 4dr Sdn........... 5175 6875

Deduct:
Manual trans 150

1989 WS Ret

100 FWD/2.3L-I5 (130hp)

Base 4dr Sdn 2275 3425
Base 4dr Wgn............ 2375 3725
E 4dr Sdn 2200 3325
Quattro (5sp-AWD) 4dr Sdn. 2500 3875

Add:
ABS brakes 25
Air bag-driver 25
Leather seats 25

Deduct:
Man trans (not Qttro) 100

200 AWD/2.2L-I5 (162hp)

Quattro (5sp-AWD) 4dr Sdn. 3425 4900
Quattro (5sp-AWD) 4dr Wgn 3500 4975
Turbo (FWD) 4dr Sdn...... 2850 4250

Add:
Leather seats (Base only) 25

Deduct:
Man trans (not Qttro) 100

80 FWD/2.0L-I4 (108hp)

Base 4dr Sdn 1575 2625
Quattro (5sp-AWD) 4dr Sdn. 1700 2775

Add:
- ABS brakes . . . 25
- Sunroof-pwr . . . 50

Deduct:
- Man trans (not Qttro) . . . 100

90 FWD/2.3L-I5 (130hp)

Model	WS	Ret
Base 4dr Sdn	1975	3075
Quattro (5sp-AWD) 4dr Sdn	2125	3250

Add:

Deduct:
- Man trans (not Qttro) . . . 100

1988 WS Ret

5000 FWD/2.2L-I5 (162hp)

Model	WS	Ret
CS 4dr Sdn	1750	2825
CS Quattro (5sp-AWD) 4sd	2125	3250
CS Quattro (5sp-AWD) Wgn	2325	3675
S 4dr Sdn	1200	2100
S 4dr Wgn	1425	2350
S Quattro (5sp-AWD) 4sd	1725	2800

Add:
- ABS brakes (std CS) . . . 25
- Leather seats . . . 25
- Sunroof-pwr (std CS) . . . 50

Deduct:
- Man trans (not Qttro) . . . 75

80 FWD/2.0L-I4 (108hp)

Model	WS	Ret
Base 4dr Sdn	1375	2300
Quattro (5sp-AWD) 4dr Sdn	1475	2400

Add:
- ABS brakes . . . 25
- Sunroof-pwr . . . 50

Deduct:
- Man trans (not Qttro) . . . 75

90 FWD/2.3L-I5 (130hp)

Model	WS	Ret
Base 4dr Sdn	1650	2700
Quattro (5sp-AWD) 4dr Sdn	1825	2900

Add:

Deduct:
- Man trans (not Qttro) . . . 75

BMW

2001 WS Ret

3-SERIES AWD/2.5L-I6 (170hp)

Model	WS	Ret
325xi (AWD) 4dr Sdn	26875	30175
325i 4dr Sdn	25825	29050
325iT 4dr Wgn	27975	31350
325xiT (AWD) 4dr Wgn	29225	32475
325Ci 2dr Cnv	28325	31725
325Ci 2dr Cpe	26150	29400
330i (3.0L/225hp) 4dr Sdn	29550	33150
330xi (3.0L/AWD) 4dr Sdn	31200	34925
330i (3.0L/225hp) 2dr Cnv		
330Ci (3.0L/225hp) Cpe	29875	33175
M3 (6sp/3.2L-335hp) 2dr Cnv		
M3 (6sp/3.2L-335hp) 2dr Cpe		

Add:
- Harmon Kardon sound . . . 450
- Navigation sys . . . 525
- Wood trim . . . 225
- Sport pkg (incl 17" Star-spk whls) 525
- Moonroof-pwr . . . 575
- Hardtop (conv) . . . 2200

Deduct:
- Wheel covers . . . 300
- No leather . . . 450
- No CD . . . 200

5-SERIES RWD/2.5L-I6 (184hp)

Model	WS	Ret
525i 4dr Sdn	32575	35975
525iT 4dr Wgn		
530i (3.0L/225hp) 4dr Sdn		
540i (282hp V8) 4dr Sdn		
540iT (282hp V8) 4dr Wgn		
M5 (6sp/5.0L-400hp 4sd	65375	70500

Add:
- Premium HiFi audio . . . 450
- Navigation system . . . 600
- Sport Pkg (incl 17" Cross Spks) . 675
- Moonroof-pwr (std 540) . . . 550
- Wood trim . . . 225
- Self-leveling susp. (T) . . . 275

Deduct:
- Manual trans . . . 1000
- No leather (528) . . . 550
- No CD . . . 300

7-SERIES RWD/4.4L-V8 (282hp)

Model	WS	Ret
740i 4dr Sdn		
740iL 4dr Sdn		
750iL (326hp V12) 4dr Sdn		

Z3 RWD/2.5L-I6 (184hp)

Model	WS	Ret
2.5 (2.5L/184hp) 2dr Rds		
3.0 (3.0L-225hp) 2dr Cpe	26350	29900
3.0 (3.0L-225hp) 2dr Rds	28325	32025
M (3.2L-315hp) 2dr Cpe		
M (3.2L-315hp) 2dr Rds		

Add:
- Lthr seats (2.3L) . . . 450
- Power roof (conv) . . . 1175
- Harmon Kardon sound (2.3) . . . 475
- 17" whls (2.8 cnv) . . . 525

Deduct:
- No CD player . . . 200

Z8 RWD/5.0L-V8 (394hp)

Model	WS	Ret
2dr Rds		

2000 WS Ret

3-SERIES RWD/2.5L-I6 (170hp)

Model	WS	Ret
323i 4dr Sdn	22475	25475
323i 4dr Wgn	28125	31500
323i 2dr Cnv	25950	29175
323Ci 2dr Cpe	21950	24900
328i 4dr Sdn	26150	29675
328i 2dr Cnv		
328Ci 2dr Cpe	25625	28825

Add:
- Harmon Kardon sound . . . 350
- Navigation sys . . . 400
- Wood trim . . . 175
- Sport pkg(incl V- or Star-spk whls 400
- Moonroof-pwr . . . 450
- Hardtop (conv) . . . 1700

Deduct:
- Wheel covers . . . 250
- No leather . . . 350
- No CD . . . 175

5-SERIES RWD/2.8L-I6 (193hp)

Model	WS	Ret
528i 4dr Sdn	30675	34025
528iT 4dr Wgn	31425	34825
540i (282hp V8) 4dr Sdn	35625	39600
540iT (282hp V8) 4dr Wgn		
M5 (6sp/5.0L-400hp 4sd	57175	61825

Add:
- Premium HiFi audio . . . 350
- Navigation system . . . 475
- Wheels-17in alloy . . . 525
- Moonroof-pwr (std 540) . . . 425
- Wood trim . . . 175
- Self-leveling susp. (T) . . . 225

Deduct:
- Manual trans . . . 775
- No leather (528) . . . 425
- No CD . . . 250

7-SERIES RWD/4.4L-V8 (282hp)

Model	WS	Ret
740i 4dr Sdn	39800	43625
740iL 4dr Sdn	41800	45750
750iL (326hp V12) 4dr Sdn	52200	57125

Add:
- Navigation System . . . 525
- Self leveling susp. (std 750) . . 350

Z3 RWD/2.3L-I6 (170hp)

Model	WS	Ret
2.3 2dr Rds	18600	21525
2.8 (2.8L-193hp) 2dr Cpe	22650	25900
2.8 (2.8L-193hp) 2dr Rds	23000	26275
M (3.2L-240hp) 2dr Cpe	28225	31925
M (3.2L-240hp) 2dr Rds	30400	34075

Add:
- Lthr seats (2.3L) . . . 350
- Power roof . . . 925
- Harmon Kardon sound (2.3) . . 375
- 17" whls (na 2.3 cnv) . . . 400

Deduct:
- No CD player . . . 175

Z8 RWD/5.0L-V8 (394hp)

Model	WS	Ret
2dr Rds		

1999 WS Ret

3-SERIES RWD/2.8L-I6 (190hp)

Model	WS	Ret
323i 4dr Sdn	19525	22300
323i 2dr Cnv	24250	27375
323is 2dr Cpe	18225	20925
328i 4dr Sdn	22850	26125
328i 2dr Cnv	27800	31150
328is 2dr Cpe	21550	24475

Add:
- Harmon Kardon sound . . . 300
- Lthr seats (std 328 Cnv) . . . 300
- Sport pkg (incl 16" spoked alloys) 325
- Cruise ctrl (ti, 323 sdn) . . . 125
- Moonroof-pwr . . . 375
- Hardtop (conv) . . . 1400

Deduct:
- Man trans (not Cnv) . . . 450
- Wheel covers . . . 200
- No CD . . . 125

5-SERIES RWD/2.8L-I6 (193hp)

Model	WS	Ret
528i 4dr Sdn	26800	30100
528iT 4dr Wgn	28575	32000
540i (282hp V8) 4dr Sdn	31350	35075
540iT (282hp V8) 4dr Wgn		

Add:
- Premium HiFi audio . . . 300
- Navigation system . . . 400
- Wheels-17in alloy . . . 425
- Moonroof-pwr (std 540) . . . 350

Deduct:
- Manual trans . . . 650
- Vinyl seats (528) . . . 350
- No CD . . . 200

7-SERIES RWD/4.4L-V8 (282hp)

Model	WS	Ret
740i 4dr Sdn	35475	39050
740iL 4dr Sdn	37325	41025
750iL (326hp V12) 4dr Sdn	47325	52025

Add:
- Navigation System . . . 425
- Self leveling susp. (std 750) . . 300

Deduct:
- No CD player . . . 225

M3 RWD/3.2L-I6 (240hp)

Model	WS	Ret
5spd/AT 2dr Cnv	28475	31875
5spd/AT 2dr Cpe	26625	29900

Add:
- Harmon Kardon w/CD chngr . . 250

Forged alloys	475
Cruise ctrl	100
Sunroof-pwr	350
Pwr seat	150
Hardtop (conv)	1500

Deduct:

No Cruise	125

Z3 — RWD/2.3L-I6 (170hp)

2.5 2dr Rds	17600	20450
2.8 (2.8L-193hp) 2dr Rds	21550	24725
M (3.2L-240hp) 2dr Cpe		
M (3.2L-240hp) 2dr Rds	28075	31775

Add:

Lthr seats (1.9L)	300
Power roof	750
Harmon Kardon sound	300
17" wheels (2.8L)	325

Deduct:

No CD player	125

1998 WS Ret

3-SERIES — RWD/1.9L-I4 (138hp)

318i 4dr Sdn	14825	17275
318ti 2dr Hbk	12275	14550
323i (6cyl) 2dr Cnv	21375	24275
323is (6cyl) 2dr Cpe	16925	19525
328i (6cyl) 4dr Sdn	19275	22050
328i (6cyl) 2dr Cnv	25150	28325
328is (6cyl) 2dr Cpe	19225	21975

Add:

Harmon Kardon sound	250
Lthr seats (std 325 Cnv)	250
Sport pkg (incls 16" alloys)	275
Cruise ctrl (ti)	100
Sunroof-pwr	300
Hardtop (conv)	1175

Deduct:

Man trans (not Cnv)	375
Wheel covers	175

5-SERIES — RWD/2.8L-I6 (190hp)

528i 4dr Sdn	23525	26575
540i (282hp V8) 4dr Sdn	27425	30750

Add:

Premium HiFi audio	250
Navigation system	325
17in wheels	350

Deduct:

Manual trans	525
Vinyl seats (528)	300
No CD	150

7-SERIES — RWD/4.4L-V8 (282hp)

740i 4dr Sdn	29325	32575
740iL 4dr Sdn	30900	34275
750iL (326hp V12) 4dr Sdn	39475	43325

Add:

Navigation System	350
Self leveling susp. (std 750)	250

Deduct:

No CD player	175

M3 — RWD/3.2L-I6 (240hp)

5spd/AT 4dr Sdn	24350	27475
5spd/AT 2dr Cpe	24350	27475

Add:

Harmon Kardon w/CD chngr	200
Forged alloys	375
Cruise ctrl	75
Pwr seat	125
Hardtop (conv)	1225

Z3 — RWD/1.9L-I4 (138hp)

1.9L 2dr Rds	17475	20325
2.8L (6cyl) 2dr Rds	20975	24100
M (6cyl) 2dr Rds	25525	29000

Add:

Lthr seats (1.9L)	250
Power roof	625
Harmon Kardon sound	250
17" wheels (2.8L)	275

1997 WS Ret

3-SERIES — RWD/1.9L-I4 (138hp)

318i 4dr Sdn	12500	14800
318i 2dr Cnv	17725	20375
318iS 2dr Cpe	12750	15050
318ti 2dr Hbk	10325	12475
328i (6cyl) 4dr Sdn	16575	19150
328i (6cyl) 2dr Cnv	21800	24750
328iS (6cyl) 2dr Cpe	16575	19150

Add:

Harmon Kardon sound	200
Traction control	175
Lthr seats (std 325 Cnv)	200
Sport pkg (incls 16" alloys)	225
Cruise ctrl (ti)	50
Sunroof-pwr	250
Hardtop (Cnv)	1025

Deduct:

Man trans (not Cnv)	300
Wheel covers	125

5-SERIES — RWD/2.8L-I6 (190hp)

528i 4dr Sdn	20000	22825
540i (8cyl) 4dr Sdn	23500	26550

Add:

Premium HiFi audio	200
Navigation system	275

Deduct:

Manual trans	450
Cloth seats (528)	250

7-SERIES — RWD/4.4L-V8 (282hp)

740i 4dr Sdn	25050	28225
740iL 4dr Sdn	26500	29775
750iL (12cyl) 4dr Sdn	34275	37775

Add:

Navigation System	300
Self leveling susp. (std 750)	200

Deduct:

No CD player	150
Cloth seats	250

8-SERIES — RWD/5.4L-V12 (322hp)

840Ci (8cyl) 2dr Cpe	31400	34800
850Ci 2dr Cpe	36925	40600

M3 — RWD/3.2L-I6 (240hp)

5-speed 4dr Sdn	21125	24025
5-speed 2dr Cpe	21125	24025

Add:

Lthr seats	175
Harmon Kardon sound	175
Forged alloys	325
Cruise ctrl	50
Wood interior	50
Pwr seat	100

Z3 — RWD/1.9L-I4 (138hp)

1.9L 2dr Rds	15350	18025
2.8L 2dr Rds	18525	21450

Add:

Traction control (1.9L)	225
Lthr seats (1.9L)	200
Harmon Kardon sound	225
17" wheels (2.8L)	225

1996 WS Ret

3-SERIES — RWD/1.9L-I4 (138hp)

318i 4dr Sdn	10400	12550
318i 2dr Cnv	15625	18125
318iS 2dr Cpe	11150	13350
318ti 2dr Hbk	8850	10875
328i (6cyl) 4dr Sdn	13900	16300
328iC (6cyl) 2dr Cnv	19300	22075
328iS (6cyl) 2dr Cpe	14450	16875

Add:

CD changer	175
Traction control	150
Lthr seats (std 325 Cpe,Cnv)	175
Sport pkg (incls 16" whls)	175
Hardtop (Cnv)	900

Deduct:

Man trans (not Cnv)	275
Wheel covers	100

7-SERIES — RWD/4.4L-V8 (282hp)

740iL 4dr Sdn	23500	26550
750iL (12cyl) 4dr Sdn	30400	33725

Add:

CD changer (std 750)	175
Self leveling susp. (std 750)	150

8-SERIES — RWD/5.4L-V12 (322hp)

840Ci (8cyl) 2dr Cpe	26600	29875
850Ci 2dr Cpe	31375	34775

M3 — RWD/3.2L-I6 (240hp)

5-speed 2dr Cpe	17625	20275

Add:

Luxury pkg	425
Premium sound	150
Forged alloys	250
Cruise ctrl	25

Z3 — RWD/1.9L-I4 (138hp)

5-speed 2dr Rds	13700	16225

Add:

Traction control	200

Deduct:

Cloth seats	150

1995 WS Ret

3-SERIES — RWD/1.8L-I4 (138hp)

318i 4dr Sdn	8675	10700
318i 2dr Cnv	12325	14600
318iS 2dr Cpe	8900	10950
318ti 2dr Hbk	8100	10075
325i (6cyl) 4dr Sdn	11600	13825
325iC (6cyl) 2dr Cnv	15600	18100
325iS (6cyl) 2dr Cpe	11750	14000

Add:

CD changer	150
Traction control	125
Lthr seats (std 325 Cpe,Cnv)	150
Sport pkg (incls 16in alloys)	150

Deduct:

Man trans (not Cnv)	250

5-SERIES — RWD/2.5L-I6 (189hp)

525i 4dr Sdn	12275	14550
525iT 4dr Wgn	13275	15625
530i (8cyl) 4dr Sdn	13625	16000
540i (8cyl) 4dr Sdn	14925	17375

Add:

CD changer	150
Leather seats (525)	150
Sunroof-dual pwr (525iT)	250
Traction control	325
Wood trim	50

Deduct:

Man trans (not M5)	325

7-SERIES — RWD/4.0L-V8 (282hp)

740i 4dr Sdn	16875	19475
740iL 4dr Sdn	18775	21500
750iL (12cyl) 4dr Sdn	24700	27850

Add:

CD changer (std 750)	150

Traction control (740)	375	

8-SERIES RWD/5.4L-V12 (322hp)

Model	WS	Ret
840Ci (8cyl) 2dr Cpe	23050	26075
850Ci 2dr Cpe	27375	30700
Add:		
Electronic damping	350	

M3 RWD/3.0L-V6 (240hp)

Model	WS	Ret
5-speed 2dr Cpe	15750	18275
Add:		
Luxury pkg	400	
Forged alloys	250	
Deduct:		
Cloth seats	125	

1994 — WS — Ret

3-SERIES RWD/1.8L-I4 (138hp)

Model	WS	Ret
318i 4dr Sdn	7450	9400
318iC 2dr Cnv	10775	12950
318iS 2dr Cpe	7750	9700
325i (6cyl) 4dr Sdn	9900	12000
325iC (6cyl) 2dr Cnv	13675	16050
325iS (6cyl) 2dr Cpe	9825	11925
Add:		
CD changer	125	
Cruise ctrl (318 only)	25	
Leather seats (318,325 4dr)	125	
Sport pkg	100	
Deduct:		
Man trans (not Cnv)	225	

5-SERIES RWD/2.5L-I6 (189hp)

Model	WS	Ret
525i 4dr Sdn	10125	12250
525iT 4dr Wgn	10950	13125
530i (8cyl) 4dr Sdn	11175	13375
540i (8cyl) 4dr Sdn	12225	14500
Add:		
CD changer	125	
Leather seats (525iT only)	150	
Sunroof-dual pwr (525iT)	225	
Traction control	300	
Wood trim	50	
Deduct:		
Man trans (not M5)	300	

7-SERIES RWD/4.0L-V8 (282hp)

Model	WS	Ret
740i 4dr Sdn	11925	14175
740iL 4dr Sdn	13425	15775
750iL (12cyl) 4dr Sdn	16500	19075
Add:		
CD changer (std 750)	125	
Traction control (740)	350	

8-SERIES RWD/5.0L-V12 (296hp)

Model	WS	Ret
840Ci (8cyl) 2dr Cpe	20175	23000
850Ci 2dr Cpe	23875	26950
850CSi (6-spd) 2dr Cpe	27800	31150

1993 — WS — Ret

3-SERIES RWD/1.8L-I4 (138hp)

Model	WS	Ret
318i 4dr Sdn	6000	7825
318iS 2dr Cpe	6600	8475
325i (6cyl) 4dr Sdn	8225	10225
325iC (6cyl) 2dr Cnv	9950	12075
325iS (6cyl) 2dr Cpe	8525	10550
Add:		
CD changer	125	
Cruise ctrl (318 only)	25	
Leather seats (4dr only)	125	
Sport pkg	50	
Deduct:		
Man trans (not Cnv)	200	

5-SERIES RWD/2.5L-I6 (189hp)

Model	WS	Ret
525i 4dr Sdn	8850	10875
525iT 4dr Wgn	9225	11275
535i 4dr Sdn	9825	11925
Add:		
CD changer	125	
Integrated phone	50	
Leather seats (525iT only)	125	
Sunroof-dual pwr (525iT)	175	
Traction control	250	
Deduct:		
Man trans (not M5)	275	

7-SERIES RWD/4.0L-V8 (282hp)

Model	WS	Ret
740i 4dr Sdn	10025	12150
740iL 4dr Sdn	11400	13625
750iL (12cyl) 4dr Sdn	13750	16125
Add:		
CD changer (std 750)	125	
Integrated phone (std 750)	50	

850Ci RWD/5.0L-V12 (296hp)

Model	WS	Ret
Coupe 2dr Cpe	19125	21875
Deduct:		
Manual trans	275	

1992 — WS — Ret

3-SERIES RWD/1.8L-I4 (134hp)

Model	WS	Ret
318i (5sp) 4dr Sdn	5025	6800
318iC (5sp) 2dr Cnv	6100	7950
318iS (5sp) 2dr Cpe	5300	7100
325i (6cyl) 4dr Sdn	6875	8775
325iC (6cyl) 2dr Cnv	7875	9850
325iS (6cyl) 2dr Cpe	7075	8975
Add:		
Leather seats (4dr only)	75	
Deduct:		
Manual trans (325)	200	

5-SERIES RWD/2.5L-I6 (189hp)

Model	WS	Ret
525i 4dr Sdn	7525	9475
535i 4dr Sdn	8300	10300
M5 (5sp) 4dr Sdn	14000	16400
Add:		
Leather seats	100	
Wood & lthr pkg	100	
Deduct:		
Man trans (not M5)	250	

7-SERIES RWD/3.5L-I6 (208hp)

Model	WS	Ret
735i 4dr Sdn	8425	10425
735iL 4dr Sdn	9000	11050
750iL (12cyl) 4dr Sdn	11275	13475
Add:		
CD Changer (std 750)	100	

850i RWD/5.0L-V12 (296hp)

Model	WS	Ret
Coupe 2dr Cpe	16225	18775
Deduct:		
Manual trans	250	

1991 — WS — Ret

3-SERIES RWD/1.8L-I4 (168hp)

Model	WS	Ret
318i 4dr Sdn	3225	4725
318iC 2dr Cnv	5225	7000
318iS 2dr Cpe	3200	4700
325i (6cyl) 4dr Sdn	4575	6275
325iX (6cyl-AWD) 4dr Sdn	5325	7125
325iC (6cyl) 2dr Cnv	7050	8950
325i (6cyl) 2dr Cpe	4575	6275
325iX (6cyl-AWD) 2dr Cpe	5275	7050
Add:		
CD changer	75	
Leather seats	75	
Sport pkg (incls lthr)	325	
Sunroof-man (318 only)	25	
Sunroof-pwr (325 only)	125	
Deduct:		
Manual trans	175	

5-SERIES RWD/2.5L-I6 (189hp)

Model	WS	Ret
525i 4dr Sdn	6375	8250
535i 4dr Sdn	7850	9825
M5 (5sp) 4dr Sdn	14550	16975
Add:		
CD changer	75	
Integrated phone	25	
Leather seats (525 only)	75	
Deduct:		
Man trans (not M5)	225	

7-SERIES RWD/3.5L-I6 (208hp)

Model	WS	Ret
735i 4dr Sdn	7250	9175
735iL 4dr Sdn	7725	9675
750iL (12cyl) 4dr Sdn	10325	12475
Add:		
CD changer (std 750)	75	
Integrated phone	25	

850i RWD/5.0L-V12 (296hp)

Model	WS	Ret
Coupe 2dr Cpe	13975	16375
Deduct:		
Manual trans	225	

M3 RWD/2.3L-I4 (192hp)

Model	WS	Ret
(5sp) 2dr Cpe	8575	10600

1990 — WS — Ret

3-SERIES RWD/2.5L-I6 (134hp)

Model	WS	Ret
325i 4dr Sdn	3550	5075
325iX (AWD) 4dr Sdn	4375	6075
325iC 2dr Cnv	6250	8100
325i 2dr Cpe	3550	5075
325iS 2dr Cpe	3675	5225
325iX (AWD) 2dr Cpe	4325	6025
Add:		
Sunroof-pwr	100	
Leather seats	50	
Deduct:		
Manual trans	150	

5-SERIES RWD/2.5L-I6 (168hp)

Model	WS	Ret
525i 4dr Sdn	5125	6900
535i 4dr Sdn	6425	8300
Add:		
CD player	25	
Leather seats (525 only)	50	
Deduct:		
Manual trans	200	

7-SERIES RWD/3.5L-I6 (208hp)

Model	WS	Ret
735i 4dr Sdn	6000	7825
735iL 4dr Sdn	6425	8300
750iL (12cyl) 4dr Sdn	7875	9850
Add:		
CD player (735 only)	25	
Integrated phone	25	

M3 RWD/2.3L-I4 (192hp)

Model	WS	Ret
(5sp) 2dr Cpe	7200	9125

1989 — WS — Ret

3-SERIES RWD/2.5L-I6 (168hp)

Model	WS	Ret
325i 4dr Sdn	3325	4900
325iX (5sp-AWD) 4dr Sdn	4100	5825
325iC 2dr Cnv	5225	7075
325i 2dr Cpe	3300	4850
325iS 2dr Cpe	3400	4975
325iX (5sp-AWD) 2dr Cpe	4075	5800
Add:		
Hardtop (Convertible)	300	

Deduct:
Manual trans 125

5-SERIES RWD/2.5L-I6 (168hp)

	WS	Ret
525i 4dr Sdn	4650	6425
535i 4dr Sdn	5075	6925

Add:
CD player 25

Deduct:
Manual trans 175

6-SERIES RWD/3.5L-I6 (208hp)

	WS	Ret
635CSi 2dr Cpe	7075	9075

Add:
CD player 25

Deduct:
Manual trans 175

7-SERIES RWD/3.5L-I6 (208hp)

	WS	Ret
735i 4dr Sdn	5350	7200
735iL 4dr Sdn	5600	7475
750iL (12cyl) 4dr Sdn	5950	7850

Add:
CD player 25

M3 RWD/2.3L-I4 (192hp)

	WS	Ret
(5sp) 2dr Cpe	6250	8175

1988 WS Ret

3-SERIES RWD/2.7L-I6 (127hp)

	WS	Ret
325 4dr Sdn	3025	4550
325i 4dr Sdn	3075	4625
325i 2dr Cnv	4075	5800
325 2dr Cpe	2725	4200
325iS 2dr Cpe	2850	4350
325iX (5sp-AWD) 2dr Cpe	3350	4925

Add:
Hardtop (Convertible) 250

Deduct:
Man trans (not iX) 75

5-SERIES RWD/2.7L-I6 (127hp)

	WS	Ret
528e 4dr Sdn	2300	3500
535i 4dr Sdn	2625	4100
535is 4dr Sdn	2650	4125
M5 (5sp) 4dr Sdn	8150	10250

Add:
Lthr seats (528e only) 25

Deduct:
Man trans (not M5) 125

6-SERIES RWD/3.5L-I6 (208hp)

	WS	Ret
635CSi 2dr Cpe	6350	8300
M6 (5sp) 2dr Cpe	11375	13725

Deduct:
Man trans (not M6) 150

7-SERIES RWD/3.5L-I6 (208hp)

	WS	Ret
735i 4dr Sdn	4525	6300
750iL (12cyl) 4dr Sdn	4725	6500

Deduct:
Manual trans 150

M3 RWD/2.3L-I4 (192hp)

	WS	Ret
(5sp) 2dr Cpe	5100	6950

BUICK

2001 WS Ret

CENTURY FWD/3.1L-V6 (175hp)

	WS	Ret
Custom 4dr Sdn	11175	13250
Limited 4dr Sdn	12700	14850

Add:
CD player 250
Cassette (std Ltd) 175
Lthr seats (std Ltd) 400
Special Edit. trim 325
Pwr seat (std Ltd) 200
Moon roof-pwr 475
Aluminum wheels 200

Deduct:
No cruise 175

LESABRE FWD/3.8L-V6 (205hp)

	WS	Ret
Custom 4dr Sdn	14075	16325
Limited 4dr Sdn	15875	18225

Add:
CD player 250
CD changer 350
GT pkg (incls 16in alloys) 475
Leather seats 400
Premium sound 100
Wheels-16" alum 225

PARK AVENUE FWD/3.8L-V6 (205hp)

	WS	Ret
Base 4dr Sdn	20100	22700
Ultra (240hp SC V6) 4sd.	22475	25200

Add:
CD player (std Ultra) 250
CD changer 350
Moon roof-pwr 575
Chrome wheels 250

REGAL FWD/3.8L-V6 (200hp)

	WS	Ret
GS (240hp SC V6) 4dr Sdn	13500	15700
LS 4dr Sdn	11750	13850

Add:
CD changer 375
CD player (std GS) 225
Leather seats (std GS) 400
Monsoon audio 175
Chrome wheels 250
16" Alum wheels (std GS) 200
Sunroof-pwr 500

Deduct:
Manual seat 200

2000 WS Ret

CENTURY FWD/3.1L-V6 (175hp)

	WS	Ret
Custom 4dr Sdn	9575	11550
Limited 4dr Sdn	11050	13100

Add:
CD player 175
Cassette 150
Lthr seats (std Ltd) 300
Special Edit. trim 250
Pwr seat 150
Moon roof-pwr 350
Aluminum wheels 175

Deduct:
No cruise 150

LESABRE FWD/3.8L-V6 (205hp)

	WS	Ret
Custom 4dr Sdn	12650	14800
Limited 4dr Sdn	14400	16650

Add:
CD player 175
Cassette (std Ltd) 150
CD changer 275
GT pkg (incls 16in alloys) 375
Leather seats 300
Premium sound 75
Pwr seat (std Ltd) 150
Wheels-16" alum 175

PARK AVENUE FWD/3.8L-V6 (205hp)

	WS	Ret
Base 4dr Sdn	15650	17975
Ultra (240hp SC V6) 4sd.	18075	20550

Add:
CD player 175
CD changer 275
Leather seats (std Ultra) 325
Moon roof-pwr 450
Chrome wheels 200

REGAL FWD/3.8L-V6 (200hp)

	WS	Ret
GS (240hp SC V6) 4dr Sdn	12550	14700
LS 4dr Sdn	10900	12950

Add:
CD changer 275
CD player 175
Leather seats (std GS) 300
Monsoon audio 125
Chrome wheels 200
Alum. wheels (std GS) 175
Sunroof-pwr 400

Deduct:
Manual seat 150

1999 WS Ret

CENTURY FWD/3.1L-V6 (175hp)

	WS	Ret
Custom 4dr Sdn	8350	10250
Limited 4dr Sdn	9775	11750

Add:
CD player 150
Cassette 100
Leather seats 250
Pwr seat 125
Moon roof-pwr 300
Aluminum wheels 125

Deduct:
No cruise 100

LESABRE FWD/3.8L-V6 (205hp)

	WS	Ret
Custom 4dr Sdn	9975	11975
Limited 4dr Sdn	11575	13675

Add:
CD player 150
Cassette (std Ltd) 100
GT pkg (incls 16in alloys) 300
Leather seats 250
Premium sound 50
Pwr seat (std Ltd) 125
Alum wheels (std Ltd) 125

PARK AVENUE FWD/3.8L-V6 (205hp)

	WS	Ret
Base 4dr Sdn	13300	15500
Ultra (240hp SC V6) 4dr Sdn	15500	17825

Add:
CD player 150
CD changer 225
Leather seats (std Ultra) 275
Moon roof-pwr 375
Chrome wheels 150

REGAL FWD/3.8L-V6 (200hp)

	WS	Ret
GS (240hp SC V6) 4dr Sdn	11775	13875
LS 4dr Sdn	10225	12225

Add:
CD changer 225
CD player 150
Leather seats (std GS) 250
Monsoon audio 100
Pwr seat (std GS) 125
Chrome wheels 150
Alum. wheels (std LS) 125
Sunroof-pwr 325

RIVIERA FWD/3.8L-V6 (240hp)

	WS	Ret
2dr Cpe	14850	17125

Add:
3.8L Supercharged V6 600
Moonroof-pwr 375
Chrome wheels 150

1998 WS Ret

CENTURY FWD/3.1L-V6 (160hp)

	WS	Ret
Custom 4dr Sdn	7550	9400
Limited 4dr Sdn	8725	10650

Add:
CD player 125

Cassette 75
Leather seats 200
Pwr seat 75
Moon roof-pwr 250
Aluminum wheels 100

Deduct:
No cruise 75

LESABRE FWD/3.8L-V6 (205hp)

Model		
Custom 4dr Sdn	8625	10550
Limited 4dr Sdn	10025	12025

Add:
CD player 125
Cassette 75
GT pkg (incls 16in alloys) 250
Leather seats 200
Premium sound 25
Pwr seat (std Ltd) 75
Alum wheels (std Ltd) 100

PARK AVENUE FWD/3.8L-V6 (205hp)

Model		
Base 4dr Sdn	11400	13475
Ultra 4dr Sdn	13300	15500

Add:
CD player 125
CD changer 200
Leather seats (std Ultra) 225
Moon roof-pwr 300
Chrome wheels 125

REGAL FWD/3.8L-V6 (240hp)

Model		
GS 4dr Sdn	10375	12400
LS 4dr Sdn	9000	10925

Add:
CD changer 200
CD player 125
Leather seats (std GS) 200
Premium sound 25
Pwr seat (std GS) 75
Chrome wheels 125
Special wheels (std GS) 100
Sunroof-pwr 275

RIVIERA FWD/3.8L-V6 (240hp)

Model		
2dr Cpe	12225	14350

Add:
3.8L Supercharged V6 500
Moonroof-pwr 300
Chrome wheels 125

SKYLARK FWD/3.1L-V6 (155hp)

Model		
Custom 4dr Sdn	5025	6725

Add:
Cruise ctrl 75
Pwr windows 75

1997 WS Ret

CENTURY FWD/3.1L-V6 (160hp)

Model	WS	Ret
Custom 4dr Sdn	6750	8550
Limited 4dr Sdn	7825	9700

Add:
CD player 100
Cassette 50
Leather seats 175
Pwr seat 50
Moon roof-pwr 200
Aluminum wheels 75

Deduct:
No cruise 50

LESABRE FWD/3.8L-V6 (205hp)

Model	WS	Ret
Custom 4dr Sdn	7225	9050
Limited 4dr Sdn	8450	10350

Add:
CD player 100
Cassette 50
Cruise ctrl (std Ltd) 50
GT pkg (incls 16in alloys) 200
Leather seats 175
Premium sound 25
Pwr seat (std Ltd) 50
Alum wheels (std Ltd) 75

PARK AVENUE FWD/3.8L-V6 (205hp)

Model	WS	Ret
Base 4dr Sdn	9950	11950
Ultra 4dr Sdn	11650	13750

Add:
CD player 100
Delco/Bose audio 150
Leather seats (std Ultra) 175
Moon roof-pwr 250
Chrome wheels 100

REGAL FWD/3.8L-V6 (195hp)

Model	WS	Ret
GS 4dr Sdn	8950	10875
LS 4dr Sdn	7725	9575

Add:
3.8 Liter V6 (std GS) 150
CD player 100
Leather seats 175
Premium sound 25
Pwr seat 50
Special wheels (std GS) 75
Sunroof-pwr 225

RIVIERA FWD/3.8L-V6 (205hp)

Model	WS	Ret
2dr Cpe	10150	12150

Add:
3.8L Supercharged V6 425
Leather seats 175
Sunroof-pwr 250
Chrome wheels 100

SKYLARK FWD/2.4L-I4 (150hp)

Model	WS	Ret
Custom 4dr Sdn	4225	5850
Custom 2dr Cpe	4100	5725
Gran Sport (6cyl) 4dr Sdn	5350	7075
Gran Sport (6cyl) 2dr Cpe	5250	6975
Limited 4dr Sdn	4900	6575
Limited 2dr Cpe	4775	6425

Add:
3.1 Liter V6 (std GS) 250
Cassette (Custom) 25
CD player 75
Cruise ctrl (Custom) 50
Pwr seat 25
Pwr windows (Custom) 50
Leather Seats 150
Moonroof-pwr 175

1996 WS Ret

CENTURY FWD/3.1L-V6 (160hp)

Model	WS	Ret
Custom 4dr Sdn	4300	5925
Limited 4dr Sdn	4475	6125
Special 4dr Sdn	3925	5525
Special 4dr Wgn	4375	6000

Add:
Cassette (Base) 25
CD player 75
Cruise ctrl (Base) 50
Leather seats 150
Luggage rack (Wgn) 25
Pwr seat 25
Third seat (wgn 25
Special wheels 50

Deduct:
2.2 Liter 4cyl 175

LESABRE FWD/3.8L-V6 (205hp)

Model	WS	Ret
Custom 4dr Sdn	5700	7450
Limited 4dr Sdn	6825	8625

Add:
CD player 75
Cassette (std Ltd) 25
Cruise ctrl (std Ltd) 50
GT pkg (incls 16in alloys) 175
Leather seats 150
Premium sound 25
Pwr seat (std Ltd) 25
Special wheels (std Ltd) 50

PARK AVENUE FWD/3.8L-V6 (205hp)

Model	WS	Ret
Base 4dr Sdn	7225	9050
Ultra 4dr Sdn	8675	10600

Add:
CD player 75
Delco/Bose audio 125
Leather seats (std Ultra) 150
GT pkg (incls 16in alloys) 50
Sunroof-pwr 200

REGAL FWD/3.1L-V6 (160hp)

Model	WS	Ret
Custom 4dr Sdn	5125	6825
Custom 2dr Cpe	5025	6725
Gran Sport 4dr Sdn	6250	8025
Gran Sport 2dr Cpe	6150	7925
Limited 4dr Sdn	5800	7550

Add:
3.8 Liter V6 (std GS) 125
Olympic Gold Trim 25
CD player 75
Leather seats 150
Premium sound 25
Pwr seat 25
Special wheels (std GS) 50
Sunroof-pwr 175

RIVIERA FWD/3.8L-V6 (205hp)

Model	WS	Ret
2dr Cpe	7775	9650

Add:
3.8L Supercharged V6 350
Leather seats 150
Sunroof-pwr 200

ROADMASTER RWD/5.7L-V8 (260hp)

Model	WS	Ret
Base 4dr Sdn	7700	9550
Estate 4dr Wgn	8850	10775
Limited 4dr Sdn	8775	10700

Add:
CD player 75
Leather seats 150
Special wheels 50
Vinyl roof-Landau 125

SKYLARK FWD/2.4L-I4 (150hp)

Model	WS	Ret
Custom 4dr Sdn	3400	4875
Custom 2dr Cpe	3275	4750
Gran Sport (6cyl) 4dr Sdn	4425	6075
Gran Sport (6cyl) 2dr Cpe	4350	5975
Limited 4dr Sdn	4025	5650
Limited 2dr Cpe	3900	5500

Add:
3.1 Liter V6 (std GS) 200
Cassette (Custom) 25
CD player 50
Cruise ctrl (Custom) 25
Pwr seat 25
Pwr windows (Custom) 50
Leather Seats 150
Olympic Gold Trim 25
Moonroof-pwr 150

1995 WS Ret

CENTURY FWD/3.1L-V6 (160hp)

Model	WS	Ret
Custom 4dr Sdn	3525	5000
Special 4dr Sdn	3175	4625
Special 4dr Wgn	3575	5050

Add:
Cassette 25
CD player 50
Cruise ctrl 25
Leather seats 125
Luggage rack (Wgn) 25
Pwr seat 25
Pwr windows 50
Special wheels 50

Deduct:
- 2.2 Liter 4cyl . . . 175

LESABRE — FWD/3.8L-V6 (170hp)

Model	WS	Ret
Custom 4dr Sdn	4450	6100
Limited 4dr Sdn	5400	7125

Add:
- CD player . . . 50
- Cassette (std Ltd) . . . 25
- Cruise ctrl (std Ltd) . . . 25
- GT pkg (incls 16in alloys) . . . 150
- Leather seats . . . 125
- Premium sound . . . 25
- Pwr seat (std Ltd) . . . 25
- Special wheels (std Ltd) . . . 50

PARK AVENUE — FWD/3.8L-V6 (205hp)

Model	WS	Ret
Base 4dr Sdn	5800	7550
Ultra 4dr Sdn	7125	8950

Add:
- CD player . . . 50
- Delco/Bose audio . . . 125
- Leather seats (std Ultra) . . . 150
- GT pkg (incls 16in alloys) . . . 50
- Sunroof-pwr . . . 200

REGAL — FWD/3.1L-V6 (160hp)

Model	WS	Ret
Custom 4dr Sdn	4300	5925
Custom 2dr Cpe	4175	5800
Gran Sport 4dr Sdn	5250	6975
Gran Sport 2dr Cpe	5150	6850
Limited 4dr Sdn	4850	6525

Add:
- 3.8 Liter V6 (std GS) . . . 100
- Cassette (std GS) . . . 25
- CD player . . . 50
- Cruise ctrl . . . 25
- Leather seats . . . 125
- Premium sound . . . 25
- Pwr seat . . . 25
- Special wheels (std GS) . . . 50
- Sunroof-pwr . . . 175

RIVIERA — FWD/3.8L-V6 (205hp)

Model	WS	Ret
2dr Cpe	6225	8000

Add:
- 3.8L Supercharged V6 . . . 325
- CD player . . . 50
- Leather seats . . . 125
- Leather seats . . . 150
- Sunroof-pwr . . . 200

ROADMASTER — RWD/5.7L-V8 (260hp)

Model	WS	Ret
Base 4dr Sdn	5450	7175
Estate 4dr Wgn	6500	8300
Limited 4dr Sdn	6400	8175

Add:
- CD player . . . 50
- Leather seats . . . 125
- Premium sound (std Ltd) . . . 25
- Special wheels . . . 50
- Vinyl roof-Landau . . . 125

SKYLARK — FWD/2.3L-I4 (150hp)

Model	WS	Ret
Custom 4dr Sdn	2600	3975
Custom 2dr Cpe	2500	3875
Gran Sport (6cyl) 4dr Sdn	3525	5000
Gran Sport (6cyl) 2dr Cpe	3475	4950
Limited 4dr Sdn	3150	4600
Limited 2dr Cpe	3050	4500

Add:
- 3.1 Liter V6 (std GS) . . . 175
- Cassette (Custom) . . . 25
- CD player . . . 50
- Cruise ctrl (Custom) . . . 25
- Pwr seat . . . 25
- Pwr windows (Custom) . . . 25
- Tilt wheel (Custom) . . . 25

Deduct:
- No air cond . . . 250

1994 — WS — Ret

CENTURY — FWD/3.1L-V6 (160hp)

Model	WS	Ret
Custom 4dr Sdn	3050	4500
Special 4dr Sdn	2800	4200
Special 4dr Wgn	3150	4600

Add:
- Cassette . . . 25
- CD player . . . 50
- Cruise ctrl . . . 25
- Leather seats . . . 125
- Luggage rack (Wgn) . . . 25
- Pwr seat . . . 25
- Pwr windows . . . 25
- Special wheels . . . 25

Deduct:
- 2.2 Liter 4cyl . . . 150

LESABRE — FWD/3.8L-V6 (170hp)

Model	WS	Ret
Custom 4dr Sdn	3650	5150
Limited 4dr Sdn	4425	6075

Add:
- CD player . . . 50
- Cassette (std Ltd) . . . 25
- Cruise ctrl (std Ltd) . . . 25
- GT pkg (incls 16in alloys) . . . 150
- Leather seats . . . 125
- Pwr seat (std Ltd) . . . 25
- Special wheels (std Ltd) . . . 25

PARK AVENUE — FWD/3.8L-V6 (170hp)

Model	WS	Ret
Base 4dr Sdn	4825	6500
Ultra 4dr Sdn	5900	7650

Add:
- CD player . . . 50
- Delco/Bose audio . . . 100
- Leather seats (std Ultra) . . . 125
- GT pkg (incls 16in alloys) . . . 50
- Sunroof-pwr . . . 175

REGAL — FWD/3.1L-V6 (160hp)

Model	WS	Ret
Custom 4dr Sdn	3625	5100
Custom 2dr Cpe	3525	5000
Gran Sport 4dr Sdn	4425	6075
Gran Sport 2dr Cpe	4350	5975
Limited 4dr Sdn	4125	5750

Add:
- 3.8 Liter V6 (std GS) . . . 75
- Cassette (std GS) . . . 25
- CD player . . . 50
- Cruise ctrl . . . 25
- Leather seats . . . 125
- Pwr seat . . . 25
- Special wheels (std GS) . . . 25
- Sunroof-pwr . . . 150

ROADMASTER — RWD/5.7L-V8 (260hp)

Model	WS	Ret
Base 4dr Sdn	4450	6100
Estate 4dr Wgn	5250	6975
Limited 4dr Sdn	5175	6875

Add:
- CD player . . . 50
- Leather seats . . . 125
- Special wheels . . . 25
- Vinyl roof-Landau . . . 100

SKYLARK — FWD/2.3L-I4 (115hp)

Model	WS	Ret
Custom 4dr Sdn	2100	3225
Custom 2dr Cpe	2000	3100
Gran Sport (6cyl) 4dr Sdn	2825	4225
Gran Sport (6cyl) 2dr Cpe	2800	4200
Limited 4dr Sdn	2550	3925
Limited 2dr Cpe	2475	3850

Add:
- 3.1 Liter V6 (std GS) . . . 175
- Cassette . . . 25
- CD player . . . 25
- Cruise ctrl (Custom) . . . 25
- Pwr seat . . . 25
- Pwr windows (Custom) . . . 25
- Special wheels (std GS) . . . 25

Deduct:
- No air cond . . . 225

1993 — WS — Ret

CENTURY — FWD/3.3L-V6 (160hp)

Model	WS	Ret
Custom 4dr Sdn	2325	3675
Custom 4dr Wgn	2625	4000
Custom 2dr Cpe	2275	3425
Limited 4dr Sdn	2475	3850
Special 4dr Sdn	2225	3350
Special 4dr Wgn	2500	3875

Add:
- Air bag (Special only) . . . 100
- Cassette . . . 25
- CD player . . . 50
- Cruise ctrl . . . 25
- Leather seats . . . 100
- Pwr seat . . . 25
- Pwr windows . . . 25
- Special wheels . . . 25

Deduct:
- 2.2 Liter 4cyl . . . 125

LESABRE — FWD/3.8L-V6 (110hp)

Model	WS	Ret
Custom 4dr Sdn	3225	4675
Limited 4dr Sdn	3900	5500

Add:
- CD player . . . 50
- Cassette . . . 25
- Cruise ctrl . . . 25
- GT pkg (incls 16in alloys) . . . 125
- Leather seats . . . 100
- Pwr seat . . . 25
- Special wheels . . . 25

PARK AVENUE — FWD/3.8L-V6 (170hp)

Model	WS	Ret
Base 4dr Sdn	4050	5675
Ultra 4dr Sdn	4850	6525

Add:
- CD player . . . 50
- Delco/Bose audio . . . 75
- Leather seats (std Ultra) . . . 100
- GT pkg (incls 16in alloys) . . . 25
- Sunroof-pwr . . . 150

REGAL — FWD/3.1L-V6 (140hp)

Model	WS	Ret
Custom 4dr Sdn	2775	4175
Custom 2dr Cpe	2700	4100
Gran Sport 4dr Sdn	3475	4950
Gran Sport 2dr Cpe	3450	4925
Limited 4dr Sdn	3175	4625
Limited 2dr Cpe	3125	4575

Add:
- 3.8 Liter V6 (std GS) . . . 75
- ABS brakes (std Ltd,GS) . . . 100
- Cassette (std GS) . . . 25
- CD player . . . 50
- Cruise ctrl . . . 25
- Leather seats . . . 100
- Pwr seat . . . 25
- Pwr windows . . . 25
- Special wheels (std GS) . . . 25
- Sunroof-pwr . . . 150

RIVIERA — FWD/3.8L-V6 (170hp)

Model	WS	Ret
Coupe 2dr Cpe	4700	6350

Add:
- CD player . . . 50
- Delco/Bose audio . . . 75
- Leather seats . . . 100
- Sunroof-pwr . . . 150

ROADMASTER — RWD/5.7L-V8 (180hp)

Model	WS	Ret
Base 4dr Sdn	3725	5325
Estate 4dr Wgn	4425	6075
Limited 4dr Sdn	4350	5975

Add:
- CD player . . . 50
- Leather seats . . . 100
- Special wheels . . . 25

SKYLARK FWD/2.3L-I4 (115hp)

Custom 4dr Sdn	1800	2875
Custom 2dr Cpe	1725	2800
Gran Sport (6cyl) 4dr Sdn	2475	3850
Gran Sport (6cyl) 2dr Cpe	2425	3800
Limited 4dr Sdn	2175	3300
Limited 2dr Cpe	2100	3225

Add:
- 3.3 Liter V6 (std GS) . . . 150
- Cassette . . . 25
- CD player . . . 25
- Cruise ctrl . . . 25
- Pwr seat . . . 25
- Pwr windows . . . 25
- Special wheels (std GS) . . . 25

Deduct:
- No air cond . . . 200

1992 WS Ret

CENTURY FWD/2.5L-V6 (160hp)

Custom 4dr Sdn	1900	3000
Custom 4dr Wgn	2125	3250
Custom 2dr Cpe	1875	2975
Limited 4dr Sdn	2000	3100
Limited 4dr Wgn	2225	3350
Special 4dr Sdn	1800	2875

Add:
- Cassette . . . 25
- CD player . . . 25
- Cruise ctrl . . . 25
- Leather seats . . . 75
- Pwr dr locks . . . 25
- Pwr windows . . . 25
- Special wheels . . . 25

Deduct:
- 4cyl . . . 125

LESABRE FWD/3.8L-V6 (170hp)

Custom 4dr Sdn	2625	4000
Limited 4dr Sdn	3125	4575

Add:
- ABS brakes (std Ltd) . . . 75
- Cassette . . . 25
- CD player . . . 25
- Cruise ctrl . . . 25
- GT pkg (incls 16" wheels) . . . 100
- Leather seats . . . 75
- Pwr dr locks . . . 25
- Pwr seat . . . 25
- Pwr windows . . . 25
- Special wheels . . . 25

PARK AVENUE FWD/3.8L-V6 (170hp)

Base 4dr Sdn	3300	4775
Ultra 4dr Sdn	3950	5550

Add:
- CD player . . . 25
- Delco/Bose audio . . . 50
- Lthr seats (std Ultra) . . . 75
- Sunroof-pwr . . . 150

REGAL FWD/3.1L-V6 (140hp)

Custom 4dr Sdn	2325	3675
Custom 2dr Cpe	2250	3375
Gran Sport 4dr Sdn	2875	4275
Gran Sport 2dr Cpe	2825	4225
Limited 4dr Sdn	2650	4050
Limited 2dr Cpe	2600	3975

Add:
- 3.8 Liter V6 (std GS) . . . 50
- ABS brakes (std Ltd,GS) . . . 75
- Cassette (std GS) . . . 25
- CD player . . . 25
- Cruise ctrl . . . 25
- Leather seats . . . 75
- Pwr dr locks . . . 25
- Pwr seat . . . 25
- Pwr windows . . . 25
- Special wheels (std GS) . . . 25
- Sunroof-pwr . . . 125

Deduct:
- No air cond . . . 200

RIVIERA FWD/3.8L-V6 (170hp)

Coupe 2dr Cpe	3800	5400

Add:
- CD player . . . 25
- Delco/Bose audio . . . 50
- Leather seats . . . 75
- Sunroof-pwr . . . 150

ROADMASTER RWD/5.7L-V8 (180hp)

Base 4dr Sdn	2950	4375
Estate 4dr Wgn	3550	5025
Limited 4dr Sdn	3450	4925

Add:
- CD player . . . 25
- Cruise ctrl . . . 25
- Integrated phone . . . 50
- Leather seats . . . 75
- Special wheels . . . 25

SKYLARK FWD/2.3L-I4 (120hp)

Base 4dr Sdn	1500	2425
Base 2dr Cpe	1450	2375
Gran Sport (6cyl) 4dr Sdn	2000	3100
Gran Sport (6cyl) 2dr Cpe	1950	3050

Add:
- 3.3 Liter V6 (std GS) . . . 125
- CD player . . . 25
- Cruise ctrl . . . 25
- Pwr windows . . . 25
- Special wheels (std GS) . . . 25

Deduct:
- No air cond . . . 175

1991 WS Ret

CENTURY FWD/3.3L-V6 (160hp)

Custom 4dr Sdn	1675	2725
Custom 4dr Wgn	1925	3025
Custom 2dr Cpe	1625	2675
Limited 4dr Sdn	1800	2875
Limited 4dr Wgn	2050	3150
Special 4dr Sdn	1550	2475

Add:
- Cassette . . . 25
- CD player . . . 25
- Cruise ctrl . . . 25
- Leather seats . . . 50
- Pwr dr locks . . . 25
- Pwr windows . . . 25
- Special wheels . . . 25
- Third seat (Wgn) . . . 25

Deduct:
- 4cyl . . . 100

LESABRE FWD/3.8L-V6 (165hp)

Base 2dr Cpe	1875	2975
Custom 4dr Sdn	2025	3125
Limited 4dr Sdn	2450	3825
Limited 2dr Cpe	2400	3775

Add:
- ABS brakes . . . 50
- Cassette . . . 25
- Cruise ctrl . . . 25
- Leather seats . . . 50
- Pwr dr locks . . . 25
- Pwr windows . . . 25
- Special wheels . . . 25

PARK AVENUE FWD/3.8L-V6 (170hp)

Base 4dr Sdn	2725	4125
Ultra 4dr Sdn	3225	4675

Add:
- CD player . . . 25
- Delco/Bose audio . . . 50
- Lthr seats (std Ultra) . . . 50
- Sunroof-pwr . . . 125

REATTA FWD/3.8L-V6 (170hp)

Coupe 2dr Cpe	6025	7775
Roadster 2dr Cnv	8700	10625

Add:
- CD player . . . 25
- Integrated phone . . . 125
- Sunroof-pwr . . . 125

REGAL FWD/3.1L-V6 (135hp)

Custom 4dr Sdn	1975	3075
Custom 2dr Cpe	1900	3000
Gran Sport 4dr Sdn	2550	3925
Gran Sport 2dr Cpe	2500	3875
Limited 4dr Sdn	2325	3675
Limited 2dr Cpe	2275	3425

Add:
- 3.8 Liter V6 . . . 50
- Cassette . . . 25
- Cruise ctrl . . . 25
- Leather seats . . . 50
- Pwr dr locks . . . 25
- Pwr windows . . . 25
- Spcl wheels (std GS,GT) . . . 25
- Sunroof-pwr . . . 100

RIVIERA FWD/3.8L-V6 (170hp)

Coupe 2dr Cpe	3175	4625

Add:
- CD player . . . 25
- Delco/Bose audio . . . 50
- Leather seats . . . 50
- Special wheels . . . 25
- Sunroof-pwr . . . 125

ROADMASTER RWD/5.0L-V8 (170hp)

Estate 4dr Wgn	3075	4525

Add:
- CD player . . . 25
- Integrated phone . . . 25
- Leather seats . . . 50

SKYLARK FWD/2.5L-I4 (110hp)

Base 4dr Sdn	1425	2350
Base 2dr Cpe	1375	2300
Custom 4dr Sdn	2000	3100
Custom 2dr Cpe	1950	3050
Gran Sport 2dr Cpe	1725	2800
Luxury Edit 4dr Sdn	2100	3225

Add:
- 2.3 Liter Quad4 4cyl . . . 25
- 3.3 Liter V6 . . . 100
- ABS brakes . . . 50
- Pwr windows . . . 25
- Special wheels (std GS) . . . 25
- Sunroof-manual . . . 25

Deduct:
- No air cond . . . 175

1990 WS Ret

CENTURY FWD/3.3L-V6 (160hp)

Custom 4dr Sdn	1275	2175
Custom 4dr Wgn	1475	2400
Custom 2dr Cpe	1225	2125
Limited 4dr Sdn	1375	2300
Limited 4dr Wgn	1575	2625

Add:
- Leather seats . . . 25
- Pwr windows . . . 25
- Special wheels . . . 25

Deduct:
- 4cyl . . . 75

ELECTRA — FWD/3.8L-V6 (165hp)

Model	WS	Ret
Limited 4dr Sdn	1750	2825
T-Type 4dr Sdn	1850	2925

Add:
- Cabriolet roof . . . 25
- CD player . . . 25
- Delco/Bose . . . 50
- Leather seats . . . 25
- Sunroof-pwr . . . 100

LESABRE — FWD/3.8L-V6 (165hp)

Model	WS	Ret
Base 2dr Cpe	1325	2250
Custom 4dr Sdn	1475	2400
Estate (8cyl-RWD) 4dr Wgn	1775	2850
Limited 4dr Sdn	1775	2850
Limited 2dr Cpe	1725	2800

Add:
- ABS Brakes . . . 25
- Leather seats . . . 25
- Pwr windows . . . 25
- Special wheels . . . 25

PARK AVENUE — FWD/3.8L-V6 (165hp)

Model	WS	Ret
Base 4dr Sdn	2050	3150
Ultra 4dr Sdn	2500	3875

Add:
- ABS (std Ultra) . . . 25
- CD player . . . 25
- Delco/Bose audio . . . 50
- Lthr seats (std Ultra) . . . 25
- Sunroof-pwr . . . 100

REATTA — FWD/3.8L-V6 (165hp)

Model	WS	Ret
Coupe 2dr Cpe	4100	5725
Roadster 2dr Cnv	6425	8200

Add:
- CD player . . . 25
- Sunroof-pwr . . . 100

REGAL — FWD/3.1L-V6 (135hp)

Model	WS	Ret
Custom 2dr Cpe	1650	2700
Gran Sport 4dr Sdn	2075	3200
Limited 2dr Cpe	1925	3025

Add:
- 3.8 Liter V6 . . . 25
- ABS brakes . . . 25
- Leather seats . . . 25
- Premium sound . . . 150
- Pwr windows . . . 25
- Spcl wheels (std GS) . . . 25
- Sunroof-pwr . . . 75

RIVIERA — FWD/3.8L-V6 (165hp)

Model	WS	Ret
Coupe 2dr Cpe	2450	3825

Add:
- CD player . . . 25
- Delco/Bose audio . . . 50
- Leather seats . . . 25
- Special wheels . . . 25
- Sunroof-pwr . . . 100

SKYLARK — FWD/2.5L-I4 (110hp)

Model	WS	Ret
Base 4dr Sdn	1150	2050
Base 2dr Cpe	1075	1975
Custom 4dr Sdn	1625	2675
Custom 2dr Cpe	1600	2650
Gran Sport 2dr Cpe	1400	2325
Luxury Edit 4dr Sdn	1650	2700

Add:
- 2.3 Liter Quad 4 4cyl . . . 25
- 3.3 Liter V6 . . . 75

Deduct:
- No air cond . . . 150

1989 — WS — Ret

CENTURY — FWD/3.3L-V6 (155hp)

Model	WS	Ret
Custom 4dr Sdn	1025	1925
Custom 4dr Wgn	1175	2075
Custom 2dr Cpe	1000	1700
Estate 4dr Wgn	1150	2050
Limited 4dr Sdn	1100	2000

Add:

Deduct:
- 4cyl . . . 50
- No air cond . . . 125

ELECTRA — RWD/3.8L-V6 (157hp)

Model	WS	Ret
Estate (8cyl-RWD) 4dr Wgn	1925	3025
Limited 4dr Sdn	1425	2350
T-Type 4dr Sdn	1450	2375

Add:
- Cabriolet roof . . . 25
- CD Player . . . 25
- Delco/Bose audio . . . 25
- Lthr seats (std Ultra) . . . 25
- Sunroof-pwr . . . 75

LESABRE — FWD/3.8L-V6 (157hp)

Model	WS	Ret
Base 2dr Cpe	1075	1975
Custom 4dr Sdn	1175	2075
Estate (8cyl-RWD) 4dr Wgn	1350	2275
Limited 4dr Sdn	1425	2350
Limited 2dr Cpe	1400	2325
T-Type 2dr Cpe	1450	2375

Add:
- Leather seats . . . 25

PARK AVENUE — FWD/3.8L-V6 (155hp)

Model	WS	Ret
Base 4dr Sdn	1625	2675
Ultra 4dr Sdn	1975	3075

Add:
- Delco/Bose audio . . . 25
- Lthr seats (std Ultra) . . . 25
- Sunroof-pwr . . . 75

REATTA — FWD/3.8L-V6 (157hp)

Model	WS	Ret
Coupe 2dr Cpe	3675	5175

Add:
- Sunroof-pwr . . . 75

REGAL — FWD/2.8L-V6 (130hp)

Model	WS	Ret
Custom 2dr Cpe	1300	2200
Gran Sport 2dr Cpe	1600	2650
Limited 2dr Cpe	1525	2450

Add:
- Leather seats . . . 25
- Sunroof-pwr . . . 50

RIVIERA — FWD/3.8L-V6 (157hp)

Model	WS	Ret
Coupe 2dr Cpe	1800	2875

Add:
- Delco/Bose audio . . . 25
- Leather seats . . . 25
- Sunroof-pwr . . . 75

SKYHAWK — FWD/2.0L-I4 (90hp)

Model	WS	Ret
Base 4dr Sdn	850	1525
Base 4dr Wgn	850	1525
Base 2dr Cpe	775	1300

Add:

Deduct:
- No air cond . . . 75
- Manual trans . . . 100

SKYLARK — FWD/2.5L-I4 (110hp)

Model	WS	Ret
Custom 4dr Sdn	1250	2150
Custom 2dr Cpe	1225	2125
Limited 4dr Sdn	1300	2200
Limited 2dr Cpe	1250	2150

Add:
- 2.3 Liter Quad4 4 cyl . . . 25
- 3.3 Liter V6 . . . 50
- SE pkg . . . 100

Deduct:
- No air cond . . . 100
- Manual trans . . . 100

1988 — WS — Ret

CENTURY — FWD/2.8L-V6 (125hp)

Model	WS	Ret
Custom 4dr Sdn	825	1500
Custom 4dr Wgn	950	1650
Custom 2dr Cpe	800	1475
Estate 4dr Wgn	925	1625
Limited 4dr Sdn	875	1550
Limited 2dr Cpe	825	1500

Add:
- Leather seats . . . 25

Deduct:
- 4cyl . . . 50
- No air cond . . . 100

ELECTRA — FWD/3.8L-V6 (165hp)

Model	WS	Ret
Base 4dr Sdn	1100	2000
Estate (8cyl-RWD) 4dr Wgn	1600	2650
T-Type 4dr Sdn	1125	2025

Add:
- Delco/Bose audio . . . 25
- Leather seats . . . 25
- Sunroof-pwr . . . 50

LESABRE — FWD/3.8L-V6 (150hp)

Model	WS	Ret
Base 2dr Cpe	775	1300
Custom 4dr Sdn	850	1525
Estate (8cyl-RWD) 4dr Wgn	1000	1700
Limited 4dr Sdn	1075	1975
Limited 2dr Cpe	1025	1925
T-type 2dr Cpe	1100	2000

Add:
- Delco/Bose . . . 25
- Leather seats . . . 25

PARK AVENUE — FWD/3.8L-V6 (165hp)

Model	WS	Ret
Sedan 4dr Sdn	1225	2125

Add:
- Delco/Bose audio . . . 25
- Leather seats . . . 25
- Sunroof-pwr . . . 50

REATTA — FWD/3.8L-V6 (165hp)

Model	WS	Ret
Coupe 2dr Cpe	1775	2850

Add:
- Sunroof-pwr . . . 50

REGAL — FWD/2.8L-V6 (125hp)

Model	WS	Ret
Custom 2dr Cpe	1050	1950
Limited 2dr Cpe	1200	2100

Add:
- Leather seats . . . 25

Deduct:
- No air cond . . . 100

RIVIERA — FWD/3.8L-V6 (165hp)

Model	WS	Ret
Base 2dr Cpe	1400	2325
T-Type 2dr Cpe	1525	2450

Add:
- Delco/Bose audio . . . 25
- Lthr seats (std T-type) . . . 25
- Sunroof-pwr . . . 50

SKYHAWK — FWD/2.0L-I4 (96hp)

Model	WS	Ret
Base 4dr Sdn	600	1100
Base 4dr Wgn	625	1125
Base 2dr Cpe	550	1050

Add:

Deduct:
- No air cond . . . 50
- Manual trans . . . 50

SKYLARK — FWD/2.3L-I4 (150hp)

Model	WS	Ret
Custom 4dr Sdn	925	1625
Custom 2dr Cpe	925	1625
Limited 4dr Sdn	1000	1700

Limited 2dr Cpe 925 1625

Add:
- 2.3 Liter Quad 4 25
- 3.0 Liter V6 50
- Sunroof-pwr 25

Deduct:
- No air cond 75
- Manual trans 75

CADILLAC

2001 WS Ret

CATERA RWD/3.0L-V6 (200hp)

Sport 4dr Sdn 20475 23550

Add:
- Bose Audio w/CD 400
- Sport pkg (incl 17" whls) 400
- Moonroof-pwr 575
- Wheels-chrome 250

Deduct:
- No leather 450

DEVILLE FWD/4.6L-V8 (275hp)

Base 4dr Sdn 24975 28425
DHS 4dr Sdn 26900 30500
DTS (300hp) 4dr Sdn 28425 32150

Add:
- CD changer 400
- Seats-adaptive 325
- Navigation System 1025
- Night vision 400
- Moonroof-pwr 575
- Wheels-chrome 250

Deduct:
- Cloth seats 525
- No CD player 200

ELDORADO FWD/4.6L-V8 (275hp)

ESC 2dr Cpe 26850 30450
ETC (300hp) 2dr Cpe 29275 32850

Add:
- CD changer 425
- Bose audio w/CD 400
- Moonroof-pwr 575
- Wheels-chrome 275

Deduct:
- Cloth seats 525
- No CD player 200

SEVILLE FWD/4.6L-V8 (275hp)

SLS 4dr Sdn 25750 29250
STS (300hp) 4dr Sdn 28275 31975

Add:
- CD changer 425
- Bose audio (std STS) 250
- Seat pkg (incls adaptive seats) 1100
- Moonroof-pwr 575
- Wheels-chrome 275

Deduct:
- No CD player 200

2000 WS Ret

CATERA RWD/3.0L-V6 (200hp)

Sport 4dr Sdn 18825 21775

Add:
- Bose Audio w/CD 300
- Sport pkg 300
- Moonroof-pwr 450
- Wheels-chrome 200

Deduct:
- No leather 350

DEVILLE FWD/4.6L-V8 (275hp)

Base 4dr Sdn 22475 25725
DHS 4dr Sdn 24375 27775
DTS (300hp) 4dr Sdn 24950 28400

Add:
- CD changer (Base) 300
- Seats-adaptive 250
- Lthr seats (Base) 350
- Night vision 300
- Moonroof-pwr 450
- Wheels-chrome 200

Deduct:
- Cloth seats 400
- No CD player 175

ELDORADO FWD/4.6L-V8 (275hp)

ESC 2dr Cpe 21625 24800
ETC (300hp) 2dr Cpe 24025 27400

Add:
- CD changer 325
- Bose audio w/CD 300
- Moonroof-pwr 450
- Wheels-chrome 225

Deduct:
- Cloth seats 400
- No CD player 175

SEVILLE FWD/4.6L-V8 (275hp)

SLS 4dr Sdn 23600 26925
STS (300hp) 4dr Sdn 26050 29575

Add:
- CD changer 325
- Bose audio (std STS) 200
- Seat pkg (incls adaptive seats) 850
- Moonroof-pwr 450
- Wheels-chrome 225

Deduct:
- No CD player 175

1999 WS Ret

CATERA RWD/3.0L-V6 (200hp)

Sport 4dr Sdn 15425 18100
Sport 4dr Sdn 15425 18100

Add:
- Bose Audio w/CD 250
- Leather seats 250
- Moonroof-pwr 375
- Wheels-chrome 150

DEVILLE FWD/4.6L-V8 (275hp)

Base 4dr Sdn 17125 19925
Concours 4dr Sdn 19525 22525
d'Elegance 4dr Sdn 18900 21850

Add:
- CD changer 275
- Lthr seats (std Concours) 300
- Moonroof-pwr 375
- Wheels-chrome 150

Deduct:
- Cloth seats 325
- No CD player 125

ELDORADO FWD/4.6L-V8 (275hp)

Base 2dr Cpe 19975 23025
Touring (300hp) 2dr Cpe 22150 25375

Add:
- CD changer 275
- Bose audio w/CD 250
- Lthr seats (std Touring) 275
- Moonroof-pwr 375
- Wheels-chrome 175

Deduct:
- Cloth seats 325
- No CD player 125

SEVILLE FWD/4.6L-V8 (275hp)

SLS 4dr Sdn 20700 23800
STS (300hp) 4dr Sdn 22950 26225

Add:
- CD changer 275
- Bose audio (std STS) 150
- Seat pkg (incls adaptive seats) 700
- Moonroof-pwr 375
- Wheels-chrome 175

Deduct:
- No CD player 125

1998 WS Ret

CATERA RWD/3.0L-V6 (200hp)

Sport 4dr Sdn 11750 14125

Add:
- Bose Audio w/CD 200
- Leather seats 200
- Moonroof-pwr 300
- Wheels-chrome 125

DEVILLE FWD/4.6L-V8 (275hp)

Base 4dr Sdn 14275 16850
Concours 4dr Sdn 16375 19125
d'Elegance 4dr Sdn 15800 18500

Add:
- CD changer 225
- Lthr seats (std Concours) 250
- Moonroof-pwr 300
- Wheels-chrome 125

ELDORADO FWD/4.6L-V8 (275hp)

Base 2dr Cpe 16200 18925
Touring 2dr Cpe 17975 20850

Add:
- CD changer 225
- Bose audio w/CD 200
- Lthr seats (std Touring) 225
- Moonroof-pwr 300
- Wheels-chrome 150

SEVILLE FWD/4.6L-V8 (275hp)

SLS 4dr Sdn 17400 20225
STS 4dr Sdn 19175 22150

Add:
- CD changer 225
- Bose audio (std STS) 125
- Moonroof-pwr 300
- Wheels-chrome 150

1997 WS Ret

CATERA RWD/3.0L-V6 (200hp)

Sport 4dr Sdn 9975 12200

Add:
- Bose Audio 175
- Leather seats 175
- Moonroof-pwr 250
- Wheels-chrome 100

DEVILLE FWD/4.6L-V8 (275hp)

Base 4dr Sdn 11825 14200
Concours 4dr Sdn 13700 16225
d'Elegance 4dr Sdn 13250 15750

Add:
- CD changer 175
- Lthr seats (std Concours) 200
- Moonroof-pwr 250
- Wheels-chrome 100

ELDORADO FWD/4.6L-V8 (275hp)

Base 2dr Cpe 14375 16975
Touring 2dr Cpe 15950 18675

Add:
- CD changer 175
- Bose audio 100
- Lthr seats (std Touring) 175
- Moonroof-pwr 250
- Wheels-chrome 125

SEVILLE FWD/4.6L-V8 (275hp)

SLS 4dr Sdn 14375 16975
STS 4dr Sdn 15850 18550

Add:
- CD changer 200

Bose audio	100
Leather seats (std STS)	200
Moonroof-pwr	250
Wheels-chrome	125

1996 — WS / Ret

DEVILLE — FWD/4.6L-V8 (274hp)

	WS	Ret
Base 4dr Sdn	9350	11525
Concours 4dr Sdn	11000	13325
Add:		
CD changer	150	
Lthr seats (std Concours)	175	
Sunroof-pwr	200	
Wheels-chrome	50	

ELDORADO — FWD/4.6L-V8 (275hp)

	WS	Ret
Base 2dr Cpe	11050	13375
Touring 2dr Cpe	13550	16075
Add:		
CD changer	150	
Lthr seats (std Touring)	150	
Sunroof-pwr	200	
Wheels-chrome	75	

FLEETWOOD — RWD/5.7L-V8 (260hp)

	WS	Ret
Base 4dr Sdn	10775	13075
Add:		
Brougham pkg	350	
CD player	75	
Leather seats	150	
Sunroof-pwr	200	

SEVILLE — FWD/4.6L-V8 (275hp)

	WS	Ret
SLS 4dr Sdn	11200	13525
STS 4dr Sdn	12500	14950
Add:		
Delco/Bose (includes CD)	250	
Leather seats (std STS)	175	
Sunroof-pwr	200	
Wheels-chrome	75	

1995 — WS / Ret

DEVILLE — FWD/4.9L-V8 (200hp)

	WS	Ret
Base 4dr Sdn	7475	9500
Concours 4dr Sdn	8825	10975
Add:		
CD player	75	
Lthr seats (std Concours)	150	
Sunroof-pwr	200	
Wheels-chrome	50	

ELDORADO — FWD/4.6L-V8 (275hp)

	WS	Ret
Base 2dr Cpe	8825	10975
Touring 2dr Cpe	9875	12100
Add:		
CD player	75	
Lthr seats (std Touring)	150	
Sunroof-pwr	200	
Wheels-chrome	50	

FLEETWOOD — RWD/5.7L-V8 (260hp)

	WS	Ret
Base 4dr Sdn	8500	10625
Add:		
Brougham pkg	325	
CD player	75	
Leather seats	150	
Sunroof-pwr	200	

SEVILLE — FWD/4.6L-V8 (275hp)

	WS	Ret
SLS 4dr Sdn	8975	11125
STS 4dr Sdn	10050	12300
Add:		
Delco/Bose (includes CD)	225	
Leather seats (std STS)	150	
Sunroof-pwr	200	
Wheels-chrome	50	

1994 — WS / Ret

DEVILLE — FWD/4.9L-V8 (200hp)

	WS	Ret
Base 4dr Sdn	6350	8300
Concours 4dr Sdn	7350	9375
Add:		
CD player	50	
Lthr seats (std Concours)	125	
Sunroof-pwr	175	
Wheels-chrome	25	

ELDORADO — FWD/4.6L-V8 (270hp)

	WS	Ret
Base 2dr Cpe	7150	9150
Touring 2dr Cpe	7975	10050
Add:		
CD player	50	
Lthr seats (std Touring)	125	
Sunroof-pwr	175	
Wheels-chrome	50	

FLEETWOOD — RWD/5.7L-V8 (260hp)

	WS	Ret
Base 4dr Sdn	6950	8950
Add:		
Brougham pkg	300	
CD player	50	
Leather seats	125	
Sunroof-pwr	175	

SEVILLE — FWD/4.6L-V8 (270hp)

	WS	Ret
SLS 4dr Sdn	7200	9200
STS 4dr Sdn	8125	10200
Add:		
Delco/Bose (includes CD)	200	
Leather seats (std STS)	125	
Sunroof-pwr	175	
Wheels-chrome	50	

1993 — WS / Ret

ALLANTE — FWD/4.6L-V8 (295hp)

	WS	Ret
Roadster 2dr Cnv	17825	20700
Add:		
Removable hardtop	925	

DEVILLE — FWD/4.9L-V8 (200hp)

	WS	Ret
Base 4dr Sdn	4450	6225
Base 2dr Cpe	4350	6100
Add:		
CD player	50	
Delco/Bose audio	100	
Lthr seats (Std Touring)	125	
Roof-Cabrio/Phaeton/Padded	150	
Sunroof-pwr	150	
Touring pkg	450	

ELDORADO — FWD/4.9L-V8 (200hp)

	WS	Ret
Base 2dr Cpe	6150	8075
Add:		
CD player	50	
Delco/Bose audio	100	
Lthr seats (std Touring)	100	
Sunroof-pwr	150	
Touring pkg	450	

FLEETWOOD — RWD/5.7L-V8 (185hp)

	WS	Ret
Base 4dr Sdn	5475	7350
Add:		
Brougham pkg	250	
CD player	50	
Leather seats	100	
Sunroof-pwr	150	

SEVILLE — FWD/4.9L-V8 (200hp)

	WS	Ret
Base 4dr Sdn	5900	7875
STS 4dr Sdn	6550	8600
Add:		
Delco/Bose (includes CD)	175	
Leather seats (std STS)	125	
Sunroof-pwr	150	

SIXTY SPECIAL — FWD/4.9L-V8 (200hp)

	WS	Ret
60S 4dr Sdn	5125	6975
Add:		
CD player	50	
Delco/Bose audio	100	
Leather seats	125	
Sunroof-pwr	150	

1992 — WS / Ret

ALLANTE — FWD/4.5L-V8 (200hp)

	WS	Ret
Roadster 2dr Cnv	12350	14775
Add:		
Removable hardtop	900	

Brougham — RWD/5.0L-V8 (170hp)

	WS	Ret
Base 4dr Sdn	4500	6275
Add:		
5.7 Liter V8	50	
CD player	25	
d'Elegance	375	
Leather seats	75	
Sunroof-pwr	150	
Wire wheels	50	

DEVILLE — FWD/4.9L-V8 (200hp)

	WS	Ret
Coupe 2dr Cpe	3525	5100
Sedan 4dr Sdn	3600	5175
Add:		
CD player	25	
Delco/Bose audio	50	
Lthr seats (Std Touring)	100	
Roof-Cabrio/Phaeton/Padded	125	
Sunroof-pwr	150	
Touring pkg	450	

ELDORADO — FWD/4.9L-V8 (200hp)

	WS	Ret
Coupe 2dr Cpe	4900	6700
Add:		
CD player	25	
Delco/Bose audio	50	
Lthr seats (std Touring)	75	
Sunroof-pwr	150	
Touring pkg	450	

FLEETWOOD — FWD/4.9L-V8 (200hp)

	WS	Ret
Coupe 2dr Cpe	3975	5700
Sedan 4dr Sdn	4050	5775
Sixty Special 4dr Sdn	4525	6300
Add:		
CD player	25	
Delco/Bose audio	50	
Leather seats	100	
Sunroof-pwr	150	

SEVILLE — FWD/4.9L-V8 (200hp)

	WS	Ret
Base 4dr Sdn	4875	6675
STS 4dr Sdn	5300	7150
Add:		
Delco/Bose (includes CD)	175	
Leather seats (std STS)	100	
Sunroof-pwr	150	

1991 — WS / Ret

ALLANTE — FWD/4.5L-V8 (200hp)

	WS	Ret
Roadster 2dr Cnv	11025	13350
Add:		
Integrated phone	25	
Removeable hardtop	700	

Brougham — RWD/5.0L-V8 (170hp)

	WS	Ret
Base 4dr Sdn	3850	5575
Add:		
5.7 Liter V8	50	
CD player	25	
d'Elegance	275	
Delco/Bose audio	50	
Leather seats	75	

- Special wheels 25
- Sunroof-pwr 125

DEVILLE FWD/4.9L-V8 (200hp)

Model	WS	Ret
Coupe 2dr Cpe	3250	4800
Sedan 4dr Sdn	3300	4850

Add:
- Cabriolet roof 100
- CD player 25
- Delco/Bose audio 50
- Leather seats 75
- Roof-Cabrio/Phaetn/Vinyl 75
- Special wheels 25
- Sunroof-pwr 125

ELDORADO FWD/4.9L-V8 (200hp)

Model	WS	Ret
Coupe 2dr Cpe	4150	5900

Add:
- Biarritz(incl Cabrio rf) 400
- Delco/Bose audio 50
- Leather seats 75
- Roof-Cabrio/Padded vinyl 75
- Special wheels 25
- Sunroof-pwr 125
- Touring pkg 425

FLEETWOOD FWD/4.9L-V8 (200hp)

Model	WS	Ret
Coupe 2dr Cpe	3575	5150
Sedan 4dr Sdn	3625	5225
Sixty Special 4dr Sdn	4025	5750

Add:
- CD player 25
- Delco/Bose audio 50
- Lthr seats (std 60S) 75
- Sunroof-pwr 125

SEVILLE FWD/4.9L-V8 (200hp)

Model	WS	Ret
Base 4dr Sdn	3525	5100
STS 4dr Sdn	3900	5625

Add:
- CD player 25
- Delco/Bose audio 50
- Leather seats (std STS) 75
- Phaeton roof 50
- Sunroof-pwr 125

1990 WS Ret

ALLANTE FWD/4.5L-V8 (200hp)

Model	WS	Ret
Roadster 2dr Cnv	10700	13000

Add:
- Integrated phone 25

BROUGHAM RWD/5.0L-V8 (140hp)

Model	WS	Ret
Sedan 4dr Sdn	3025	4550

Add:
- CD player 25
- d'Elegance 250
- Delco/Bose audio 50
- Leather seats 50
- Special wheels 25
- Sunroof-pwr 100

DEVILLE FWD/4.5L-V8 (180hp)

Model	WS	Ret
Coupe 2dr Cpe	2675	4150
Sedan 4dr Sdn	2675	4150

Add:
- ABS brakes 25
- CD player 25
- Delco/Bose audio 50
- Leather seats 50
- Special wheels 25
- Spring edit pkg 300
- Sunroof-pwr 100
- Vinyl roof-Cabrio/Padded 50

ELDORADO FWD/4.5L-V8 (180hp)

Model	WS	Ret
Coupe 2dr Cpe	3275	4825

Add:
- ABS brakes 25
- Biarritz(incl Cabrio rf) 350
- CD player 25
- Delco/Bose audio 50
- Lthr seats(std Biarritz) 50
- Sunroof-pwr 100
- Touring pkg 350
- Vinyl roof-Cabrio/Padded 50

FLEETWOOD FWD/4.5L-V8 (180hp)

Model	WS	Ret
Coupe 2dr Cpe	2875	4375
Sedan 4dr Sdn	2925	4425
Sixty Special 4dr Sdn	3175	4725

Add:
- CD player 25
- Delco/Bose audio 50
- Leather seats (std 60S) 50
- Sunroof-pwr 100

SEVILLE FWD/4.5L-V8 (180hp)

Model	WS	Ret
Base 4dr Sdn	2900	4400
STS 4dr Sdn	3225	4775

Add:
- ABS brakes (std STS) 25
- Delco/Bose audio 50
- Leather seats (std STS) 50
- Phaeton roof 50
- Sunroof-pwr 100

1989 WS Ret

ALLANTE FWD/4.5L-V8 (200hp)

Model	WS	Ret
Roadster 2dr Cnv	8200	10300

BROUGHAM RWD/5.0L-V8 (140hp)

Model	WS	Ret
Sedan 4dr Sdn	2275	3475

Add:
- CD player 25
- d'Elegance 225
- Delco/Bose audio 25
- Formal roof 25
- Leather seats 25
- Special wheels 25
- Sunroof-pwr 75

DEVILLE FWD/4.5L-V8 (155hp)

Model	WS	Ret
Coupe 2dr Cpe	2150	3350
Sedan 4dr Sdn	2175	3375

Add:
- CD Player 25
- Delco/Bose 25
- Leather seats 25
- Special wheels 25
- Sunroof-pwr 75
- Vinyl roof-Cabrio/Formal 25

ELDORADO FWD/4.5L-V8 (155hp)

Model	WS	Ret
Coupe 2dr Cpe	2500	3950

Add:
- Biarritz(incl Cabrio rf) 300
- CD Player 25
- Delco/Bose 25
- Leather seats 25
- Sunroof-pwr 75

FLEETWOOD FWD/4.5L-V8 (155hp)

Model	WS	Ret
Coupe 2dr Cpe	2300	3500
Sedan 4dr Sdn	2325	3750
Sixty Special 4dr Sdn	2525	3975

Add:
- CD player 25
- Delco/Bose 25
- Sunroof-pwr 75

SEVILLE FWD/4.5L-V8 (155hp)

Model	WS	Ret
Base 4dr Sdn	2325	3750
STS 4dr Sdn	2650	4125

Add:
- CD Player 25
- Delco/Bose 25
- Leather seats 25
- Phaeton roof 25
- Sunroof-pwr 75

1988 WS Ret

ALLANTE FWD/4.1L-V8 (170hp)

Model	WS	Ret
Roadster 2dr Cnv	7450	9300

BROUGHAM RWD/5.0L-V8 (140hp)

Model	WS	Ret
Sedan 4dr Sdn	1800	2875

Add:
- d'Elegance 175
- Delco/Bose audio 25
- Leather seats 25
- Sunroof-pwr 50

CIMARRON FWD/2.8L-V6 (125hp)

Model	WS	Ret
Sedan 4dr Sdn	950	1650

Add:
- Delco/Bose audio 25

Deduct:
- Manual trans 75

DEVILLE FWD/4.5L-V8 (155hp)

Model	WS	Ret
Coupe 2dr Cpe	1700	2775
Sedan 4dr Sdn	1675	2725

Add:
- Cabriolet roof 25
- Delco/Bose audio 25
- Leather seats 25
- Special wheels 25
- Sunroof-pwr 50
- Touring pkg 100

ELDORADO FWD/4.5L-V8 (155hp)

Model	WS	Ret
Coupe 2dr Cpe	1950	3050

Add:
- Biarritz 250
- Delco/Bose 25
- Leather seats 25
- Sunroof-pwr 50

FLEETWOOD FWD/4.5L-V8 (155hp)

Model	WS	Ret
d'Elegance 4dr Sdn	1925	3025
Sixty Special 4dr Sdn	1875	2975

Add:
- Delco/Bose audio 25
- Leather seats 25
- Sunroof-pwr 50

SEVILLE FWD/4.5L-V8 (1555hp)

Model	WS	Ret
Base 4dr Sdn	1900	3000
Elegante 4dr Sdn	2100	3225
STS 4dr Sdn	2125	3250

Add:
- Delco/Bose audio 25
- Leather seats 25
- Phaeton roof 25
- Sunroof-pwr 50

CHEVROLET

2001 WS Ret

CAMARO RWD/3.8L-V6 (200hp)

Model	WS	Ret
Base 2dr Cnv		
Base 2dr Cpe	12775	14925
Z/28 (8cyl) 2dr Cnv		
Z/28 (8cyl) 2dr Cpe	17525	20175

Add:
- Cruise ctrl (std conv) 200
- 12-disc CD changer 400
- Pwr dr locks (std conv) 200
- Pwr seat (std Z conv) 150
- Pwr windows (std conv) 175
- Alum wheels (Base) 200
- Leather seats 400
- T-tops 775
- SS pkg 1900

Deduct:
- Manual trans 650
- No CD player 225

CAVALIER — FWD/2.2L-I4 (115hp)

Model	WS	Ret
Base 4dr Sdn	7575	9425
Base 2dr Cpe	7450	9300
LS 4dr Sdn	8475	10375
Z/24 2dr Cnv		
Z/24 2dr Cpe	10000	12000

Add:
- 2.4L 4cyl-150hp (LS) 375
- Cassette (Base) 200
- CD player (Base) 200
- Cruise control (Base) 200
- Pwr windows (std Z/24) 175
- Sunroof-pwr 500
- Tilt wheel (Base) 100
- Pwr dr locks (std Z/24) 200
- Wheels-alum (std Z/24) 175

Deduct:
- No air cond 725
- Manual trans 625

CORVETTE — RWD/5.7L-V8 (345hp)

Model	WS	Ret
C5 2dr Cnv		
C5 Z06 (385hp) 2dr Cpe		
C5 2dr Htp		

IMPALA — FWD/

Model	WS	Ret
Base 4dr Sdn	11950	14050
LS 4dr Sdn	14000	16225

Add:
- ABS brakes (std LS) 300
- 3.8L-V6/200hp (std LS) 425
- CD player 225
- Lthr seats 400
- Pwr seat (std LS) 200
- Moonroof-pwr 450
- Wheels-alum (std LS) 200

Deduct:
- No cassette 200
- No cruise ctrl 200

LUMINA — FWD/3.1L-V6 (175hp)

Model	WS	Ret
Base 4dr Sdn	9100	11050

Add:
- ABS brakes 325
- Pwr Seat 200
- CD player 225
- Lthr seats 325

MALIBU — FWD/3.1L-V6 (170hp)

Model	WS	Ret
Base 4dr Sdn	9250	11200
LS 4dr Sdn	10475	12500

Add:
- CD player 250
- Cassette (std LS) 200
- Cruise ctrl (std LS) 200
- Lthr seats 400
- Pwr dr locks (std LS) 200
- Pwr seat (std LS) 200
- Pwr windows (std LS) 175
- Sunroof-pwr 450
- Wheels-alum (std LS) 200

Deduct:
- 2.4L (4cyl-150hp) 475

METRO — FWD/1.3L-I4 (79hp)

Model	WS	Ret
LSi (1.3L 4cyl) 4dr Sdn		

MONTE CARLO — FWD/3.8L-V6 (200hp)

Model	WS	Ret
LS 2dr Cpe	12125	14250
SS (3.8L 200hp) 2dr Cpe		

Add:
- CD player 250
- Wheels-alum (std SS) 275
- Leather seats 325
- Pwr seat 150
- Moonroof-pwr 450

Deduct:
- No cruise 175

PRIZM — FWD/1.8L-I4 (125hp)

Model	WS	Ret
Base 4dr Sdn	8625	10550
LSi 4dr Sdn	9400	11350

Add:
- ABS brakes 375
- Cassette (std LSi) 150
- CD Player 250
- Cruise ctrl (std LSi) 200
- Leather seats 275
- Pwr dr locks (std LSi) 200
- Pwr windows (std LSi) 175
- Sunroof-pwr 425
- Tilt wheel (std LSi) 100
- Wheels-alloy 175

Deduct:
- Manual trans 675

2000 — WS Ret

CAMARO — RWD/3.8L-V6 (200hp)

Model	WS	Ret
Base 2dr Cnv	13900	16125
Base 2dr Cpe	11375	13450
Z/28 (8cyl) 2dr Cnv	16950	19550
Z/28 (8cyl) 2dr Cpe	14575	17000

Add:
- Cruise ctrl (std Z conv) 150
- 12-disc CD changer 300
- Pwr dr locks (std Z conv) 150
- Pwr seat (std Z conv) 75
- Pwr windows 150
- Alum wheels (Base) 175
- Leather seats 300
- T-tops 600
- SS pkg 1475

Deduct:
- Manual trans 500
- No CD player 175

CAVALIER — FWD/2.2L-I4 (115hp)

Model	WS	Ret
Base 4dr Sdn	7150	8975
Base 2dr Cpe	7025	8850
LS 4dr Sdn	8075	9950
Z/24 2dr Cnv	10325	12350
Z/24 2dr Cpe	8725	10650

Add:
- 2.4L 4cyl-150hp (LS) 275
- Cassette (Base 150
- CD player (std Z24) 175
- Cruise control (Base) 150
- Pwr windows (std Z/24) 150
- Sunroof-pwr 375
- Tilt wheel (Base) 75
- Pwr dr locks (std Z/24) 150
- Wheels-alum (std Z/24) 150

Deduct:
- No air cond 550
- Manual trans 475

CORVETTE — RWD/5.7L-V8 (345hp)

Model	WS	Ret
C5 2dr Cnv	36625	40275
C5 2dr Cpe	31375	34775
C5 2dr Htp	30275	33600

Add:
- CD changer 325
- Roof-dual lift-off pnls 675
- Roof-transparent 475
- Suspension-F45 525
- Z51 handling pkg 325
- Wheels-magnesium 425

Deduct:
- No CD player 175

IMPALA — FWD/

Model	WS	Ret
Base 4dr Sdn	9925	11925
LS 4dr Sdn	11925	14025

Add:
- ABS brakes (std LS) 225
- 3.8L-V6 (200hp) 325
- CD player 175
- Lthr seats 300
- Pwr seat (std LS) 150
- Moonroof-pwr 350
- Wheels-alum (std LS) 175

Deduct:
- No cassette 150
- No cruise ctrl 150

LUMINA — FWD/3.1L-V6 (160hp)

Model	WS	Ret
Base 4dr Sdn	7950	9825

Add:
- ABS brakes 250
- Pwr Seat 150
- CD player 175
- Lthr seats 250
- Wheels-16" alum 175

MALIBU — FWD/3.1L-V6 (170hp)

Model	WS	Ret
Base 4dr Sdn	8350	10250
LS 4dr Sdn	9575	11550

Add:
- CD player 200
- Cassette (std LS) 150
- Cruise ctrl (std LS) 150
- Lthr seats 300
- Pwr dr locks (std LS) 150
- Pwr seat (std LS) 150
- Pwr windows (std LS) 150
- Sunroof-pwr 350
- Wheels-alum (std LS) 175

Deduct:
- 2.4L (4cyl-150hp) 375

METRO — FWD/1.3L-I4 (79hp)

Model	WS	Ret
Base (5sp) 2dr Hbk		
LSi (1.3L 4cyl) 4dr Sdn	5450	7175
LSi (1.3L 4cyl) 2dr Hbk		

Add:
- ABS brakes 225
- Pwr dr locks 100
- CD player 175
- Cassette 150

Deduct:
- Man trans (not Base) 400
- No air cond 475
- No radio 125

MONTE CARLO — FWD/3.8L-V6 (200hp)

Model	WS	Ret
LS 2dr Cpe	12125	14250
SS (3.8L 200hp) 2dr Cpe	13525	15725

Add:
- CD player 200
- Wheels-alum (std SS) 200
- Leather seats 250
- Pwr seat 100
- Moonroof-pwr 350

Deduct:
- No cruise 150

PRIZM — FWD/1.8L-I4 (120hp)

Model	WS	Ret
Base 4dr Sdn	7275	9100
LSi 4dr Sdn	8025	9900

Add:
- ABS brakes 275
- Cassette (std LSi) 75
- CD Player 175
- Cruise ctrl (std LSi) 150
- Leather seats 200
- Pwr dr locks (std LSi) 150
- Pwr windows (std LSi) 150
- Sunroof-pwr 325
- Tilt wheel (std LSi) 75
- Wheels-alloy 150

Deduct:
- No air cond 600
- Manual trans 525

1999 — WS / Ret

CAMARO — RWD/3.8L-V6 (200hp)

Model	WS	Ret
Base 2dr Cnv	12900	15075
Base 2dr Cpe	10975	13025
Z/28 (8cyl) 2dr Cnv	15875	18400
Z/28 (8cyl) 2dr Cpe	13750	16125

Add:

CD player	150
Cruise ctrl	125
Delco/Bose audio	225
Pwr dr locks	125
Pwr seat	50
Pwr windows	100
Alum wheels (Base)	125
Leather seats	250
T-tops	500
SS pkg (Z)	1325

Deduct:

Manual trans	400

CAVALIER — FWD/2.2L-I4 (115hp)

Model	WS	Ret
Base 4dr Sdn	6075	7850
Base 2dr Cpe	5950	7700
LS 4dr Sdn	6900	8725
RS 2dr Cpe	6475	8275
Z/24 2dr Cnv	9975	11975
Z/24 2dr Cpe	8100	9975

Add:

2.4L 4cyl-150hp (LS)	225
Cassette (std RS,Z/24)	125
CD player	125
Cruise control (Base)	125
Pwr windows (std Z/24)	100
Sunroof-pwr	325
Tilt wheel (Base)	50
Pwr dr locks (std Z/24)	125
Wheels-alum (std Z/24)	100

Deduct:

No air cond	450
Manual trans	400

CORVETTE — RWD/5.7L-V8 (345hp)

Model	WS	Ret
C5 2dr Cnv	32425	35825
C5 2dr Cpe	28350	31750
C5 2dr Htp	26800	30100

Add:

CD changer	275
Roof-dual lift-off pnls	550
Roof-transparent	400
Suspension-F45	425
Z51 handling pkg	275

Deduct:

No CD player	125

LUMINA — FWD/3.1L-V6 (160hp)

Model	WS	Ret
Base 4dr Sdn	7525	9375
LS 4dr Sdn	8450	10350
LTZ (3.8L 200hp) 4dr Sdn	8800	10725

Add:

3.8L 6cyl-200hp (std LTZ)	325
ABS brakes (Base)	225
Cassette (Base)	125
CD player	150
Lthr seats	225
Pwr seat	125
Wheels-alum (Base)	150

MALIBU — FWD/3.1L-V6 (150hp)

Model	WS	Ret
Base 4dr Sdn	7300	9125
LS 4dr Sdn	8400	10300

Add:

CD player	150
Cassette (std LS)	125
Cruise ctrl (std LS)	125
Lthr seats	250
Pwr dr locks (std LS)	125
Pwr seat (std LS)	125
Pwr windows (std LS)	100
Sunroof-pwr	300
Wheels-alum (std LS)	125

Deduct:

2.4L (4cyl-150hp)	300

METRO — FWD/1.3L-I3 (79hp)

Model	WS	Ret
Base (5sp) 2dr Hbk	3775	5375
LSi (1.3L 4cyl) 4dr Sdn	4625	6275
LSi (1.3L 4cyl) 2dr Hbk	4250	5875

Add:

ABS brakes	175
Pwr dr locks	50
CD player	150
Cassette	125

Deduct:

Man trans (not Base)	325
No air cond	400

MONTE CARLO — FWD/3.1L-V6 (160hp)

Model	WS	Ret
LS 2dr Cpe	8400	10300
Z34 (3.8L 200hp) 2dr Cpe	9675	11650

Add:

CD player	150
Wheels-alum (std Z34)	175
Leather seats	225
Pwr seat	75
Moonroof-pwr	300

Deduct:

No cruise	100

PRIZM — FWD/1.8L-I4 (120hp)

Model	WS	Ret
Base 4dr Sdn	6475	8275
LSi 4dr Sdn	7175	9000

Add:

ABS brakes	225
Cassette (std LSi)	50
CD Player	150
Cruise ctrl (std LSi)	125
Leather seats	175
Pwr dr locks (std LSi)	125
Pwr windows	100
Sunroof-pwr	275
Tilt wheel (std LSi)	50
Wheels-alloy	100

Deduct:

No air cond	500
Manual trans	425

1998 — WS / Ret

CAMARO — RWD/3.8L-V6 (200hp)

Model	WS	Ret
Base 2dr Cnv	11500	13575
Base 2dr Cpe	9400	11350
Z/28 (8cyl) 2dr Cnv	14300	16725
Z/28 (8cyl) 2dr Cpe	11625	13850

Add:

CD player	125
Cruise ctrl	75
Delco/Bose audio	200
Pwr dr locks	75
Pwr seat	50
Pwr windows	75
Alum wheels (Base)	100
Leather seats	200
T-tops	425
SS pkg (Z)	1175

Deduct:

Manual trans	350

CAVALIER — FWD/2.4L-I4 (115hp)

Model	WS	Ret
Base 4dr Sdn	5050	6750
Base 2dr Cpe	4950	6650
LS 4dr Sdn	5750	7500
RS 2dr Cpe	5375	7100
Z/24 2dr Cnv	8550	10450
Z/24 2dr Cpe	6800	8600

Add:

2.4L 4cyl-155hp (LS)	200
Cassette (std RS,Z/24)	75
CD player	100
Cruise control (Base)	75
Pwr windows (std Z/24)	75
Sunroof-pwr	275
Tilt wheel (Base)	25
Pwr dr locks (std Z/24)	75
Wheels-alum (std Z/24)	75

Deduct:

No air cond	375
Manual trans	325

CORVETTE — RWD/5.7L-V8 (345hp)

Model	WS	Ret
C5 2dr Cnv	29475	32750
C5 2dr Cpe	25150	28325

Add:

CD changer	225
Roof-dual lift-off pnls	450
Roof-transparent	325
Suspension-F45	350
Z51 handling pkg	225

LUMINA — FWD/3.1L-V6 (160hp)

Model	WS	Ret
Base 4dr Sdn	6050	7800
LS 4dr Sdn	6850	8650
LTZ (3.8L/200hp) 4dr Sdn	6950	8775

Add:

ABS brakes (Base)	175
Cassette (Base)	75
CD player	125
Cruise ctrl (Base)	75
Lthr seats	175
3.8L 6cyl-200hp	300
Pwr seat	75
Pwr windows (Base)	100
Wheels-alum (Base)	125

MALIBU — FWD/3.1L-V6 (150hp)

Model	WS	Ret
Base 4dr Sdn	6550	8350
LS 4dr Sdn	7525	9375

Add:

CD player	125
Cassette (std LS)	100
Cruise ctrl (std LS)	75
Lthr seats	200
Pwr dr locks (std LS)	75
Pwr seat (std LS)	75
Pwr windows (std LS)	75
Sunroof-pwr	250
Wheels-alum (std LS)	100

Deduct:

2.4L (4cyl-150hp)	250

METRO — FWD/1.0L-I3 (55hp)

Model	WS	Ret
Base (5sp) 2dr Hbk	3025	4450
LSi (4cyl) 4dr Sdn	3825	5425
LSi (4cyl) 2dr Hbk	3475	4950

Add:

ABS brakes	150
Pwr dr locks	50
CD player	125
Cassette	100

Deduct:

Man trans (not Base)	275
No air cond	325

MONTE CARLO — FWD/3.8L-V6 (200hp)

Model	WS	Ret
LS 2dr Cpe	7275	9100
Z34 2dr Cpe	8450	10350

Add:

CD player	125
Cruise ctrl (std Z34)	100
Wheels-alum (std Z34)	150
Leather seats	175
Pwr seat	50
Moonroof-pwr	250

PRIZM — FWD/1.8L-I4 (120hp)

Model	WS	Ret
Base 4dr Sdn	5575	7300
LSi 4dr Sdn	6200	7975

Add:

Option	
ABS brakes	200
Cassette (Base only)	50
CD Player	125
Cruise ctrl (Base only)	75
Leather seats	150
Pwr dr locks (std LSi)	75
Pwr windows	75
Sunroof-pwr	225
Tilt wheel (std LSi)	25
Wheels-alloy	75

Deduct:

Option	
No air cond	425
Manual trans	350

1997 — WS Ret

CAMARO — RWD/3.8L-V6 (200hp)

Model	WS	Ret
Base 2dr Cnv	9375	11325
Base 2dr Cpe	7725	9575
RS 2dr Cnv	10350	12375
RS 2dr Cpe	8650	10575
SS (8cyl) 2dr Cnv	21125	24250
SS (8cyl) 2dr Cpe	17875	20750
Z/28 (8cyl) 2dr Cnv	11575	13800
Z/28 (8cyl) 2dr Cpe	9925	12025

Add:

Option	
CD player	100
Cruise ctrl	50
Delco/Bose audio	150
Pwr dr locks	50
Pwr seat	25
Pwr windows	50
Alum wheels (Base)	75
Leather seats	175
T-tops	350
30th Anniv (Wht w/orange)	575
4-whl disc brks (std Z28,SS)	100

Deduct:

Option	
No air cond	350
Manual trans	300
No Cassette	25

CAVALIER — FWD/2.2L-I4 (120hp)

Model	WS	Ret
Base 4dr Sdn	4150	5775
Base 2dr Cpe	4050	5675
LS 4dr Sdn	4775	6425
LS 2dr Cnv	6000	7750
RS 2dr Cpe	4425	6075
Z/24 2dr Cpe	5725	7475

Add:

Option	
Cassette (std Z/24)	50
CD player	75
Cruise control	50
Pwr windows	50
Sunroof-pwr	225
Tilt wheel (std Z/24)	25
Pwr dr locks	75
Wheels-alum (std Z/24)	50

Deduct:

Option	
No air cond	325
Manual trans	275

CORVETTE — RWD/5.7L-V8 (345hp)

Model	WS	Ret
C5 2dr Cpe	22950	25975

Add:

Option	
CD changer	175
Roof-transparent	275
Suspension-F45 adj	300
Z51 handling pkg	175

LUMINA — FWD/3.lL-V6 (160hp)

Model	WS	Ret
Base 4dr Sdn	4925	6625
LS 4dr Sdn	5650	7400
LTZ 4dr Sdn	5725	7475

Add:

Option	
ABS brakes (Base)	150
Cassette (Base)	50
CD player	100
Cruise ctrl (Base)	50
Lthr seats	150
3.4L DOHC 6cyl-215hp	425
Pwr seat	50
Pwr windows (Base)	75
Wheels-alum (Base)	100

MALIBU — FWD/3.1L-V6 (155hp)

Model	WS	Ret
Base 4dr Sdn	5625	7350
LS 4dr Sdn	6500	8300

Add:

Option	
CD player	100
Cassette (std LS)	50
Cruise crtl (std LS)	50
Pwr windows (std LS)	50
Pwr dr locks (std LS)	50
Pwr windows (std LS)	50
Wheels-alum (std LS)	75

Deduct:

Option	
2.4L (4cyl-150hp)	225

MONTE CARLO — FWD/3.1L-V6 (160hp)

Model	WS	Ret
LS 2dr Cpe	6075	7850
Z34 2dr Cpe	7150	8975

Add:

Option	
CD player	100
Cruise ctrl (std Z34)	75
Wheels-alum (std Z34)	100
Leather seats	150
Pwr seat	25
Sunroof-pwr	200

1996 — WS Ret

BERETTA — FWD/3.1L-V6 (160hp)

Model	WS	Ret
Base 2dr Cpe	3150	4600
Z-26 2dr Cpe	4350	5975

Add:

Option	
Cassette (std Z26)	25
CD player	50
Cruise ctrl	25
Pwr windows	50
Wwheels-16" alloys	50
Sunroof-manual	50
Tilt wheel (std Z26)	25

Deduct:

Option	
4cyl	175
No air cond	275
Manual trans	225

CAMARO — RWD/3.8L-V6 (200hp)

Model	WS	Ret
Base 2dr Cnv	7775	9650
Base 2dr Cpe	6250	8025
RS 2dr Cnv	8600	10525
RS 2dr Cpe	7100	8925
SS (8cyl) 2dr Cnv	18000	20875
SS (8cyl) 2dr Cpe	16000	18725
Z/28 (8cyl) 2dr Cnv	9600	11700
Z/28 (8cyl) 2dr Cpe	7975	9950

Add:

Option	
CD player	75
Cruise ctrl	25
Delco/Bose audio	125
Pwr dr locks	25
Pwr seat	25
Pwr windows	50
Special wheels (base)	50
Leather seats	150
T-tops	275
4whl disc brks(std Z28)	50

Deduct:

Option	
No air cond	300
Manual trans	250
No Cassette	25

CAPRICE — RWD/4.3L-V8 (200hp)

Model	WS	Ret
Base 4dr Sdn	7075	8900
Base 4dr Wgn	8175	10075

Add:

Option	
5.7 Liter V8	175
CD player	75
Cruise ctrl	50
Delco/Bose audio	125
Leather seats	150
Pwr seat	25
Pwr windows	50
Special wheels	50

CAVALIER — FWD/2.2L-I4 (120hp)

Model	WS	Ret
Base 4dr Sdn	3375	4850
Base 2dr Cpe	3275	4750
LS 4dr Sdn	3950	5550
LS 2dr Cnv	4500	6150
Z/24 2dr Cpe	4750	6400

Add:

Option	
Cassette (std Z/24)	25
CD player	50
Cruise control	25
Pwr windows	50
Special wheels (std Z24)	50
Sunroof-pwr	175
Tilt wheel (std Z/24)	25
Pwr dr locks	25

Deduct:

Option	
No air cond	250
Manual trans	225

CORSICA — FWD/3.1L-V6 (155hp)

Model	WS	Ret
Base 4dr Sdn	2825	4225

Add:

Option	
Cassette	25
CD player	50
Cruise ctrl	25
Pwr windows	50
Sunroof-manual	50
Tilt wheel	25

Deduct:

Option	
4cyl	175
No air cond	275
Manual trans	250

CORVETTE — RWD/5.7L-V8 (300hp)

Model	WS	Ret
Collector Edit. 2dr Cnv	25800	29300
Collector Edit. 2dr Cpe	21975	25175
Coupe 2dr Cpe	16275	18650
Gran Sport 2dr Cnv	30250	33900
Gran Sport 2dr Cpe	23525	26850
Roadster 2dr Cnv	19950	22525

Add:

Option	
5.7L LT4 (std Gran Sport)	500
CD player	75
Delco/Bose	125
Removable hardtop (Cnv)	350
Roof-transparent (Cpe)	225
Suspension-FX3 adj	100
Z07 handling pkg	175

IMPALA SS — RWD/5.7L-V8 (260hp)

Model	WS	Ret
Touring Sdn 4dr Sdn	13400	15600

Add:

Option	
CD player	100

LUMINA — FWD/3.1L-V6 (160hp)

Model	WS	Ret
Base 4dr Sdn	3700	5200
LS 4dr Sdn	4350	5975

Add:

Option	
ABS brakes (std LS)	150
Cassette (std LS)	25
CD player	75
Cruise ctrl	50
3.4L DOHC V6	350
Pwr seat	25
Pwr windows (std LS)	50
Alloy wheels	75

MONTE CARLO — FWD/3.1L-V6 (160hp)

Model	WS	Ret
LS 2dr Cpe	4925	6625
Z34 2dr Cpe	5900	7650

Add:

Option	
CD player	75

- Cruise ctrl (std Z34) 50
- Alloy wheels (std Z34) 75
- Leather seats 125
- Pwr seat 25
- Sunroof-pwr 175

1995 — WS / Ret

BERETTA — FWD/3.1L-V6 (155hp)

Model	WS	Ret
Base 2dr Cpe	2550	3925
Z-26 2dr Cpe	3675	5175

Add:
- Cassette (std Z26) 25
- CD player 50
- Cruise ctrl (std Z26) 25
- Pwr windows 25
- Special wheels 25
- Sunroof-manual 50
- Tilt wheel (std Z26) 25

Deduct:
- 4cyl 175
- No air cond 250
- Manual trans 200

CAMARO — RWD/3.4L-V6 (160hp)

Model	WS	Ret
Base 2dr Cnv	6125	7900
Base 2dr Cpe	4700	6350
Z/28 (8cyl) 2dr Cnv	7775	9650
Z/28 (8cyl) 2dr Cpe	6375	8150

Add:
- CD player 50
- Cruise ctrl 25
- Delco/Bose audio 125
- Pwr dr locks 25
- Pwr seat 25
- Pwr windows 25
- Special wheels (std Z28) 50
- T-tops 275

Deduct:
- No air cond 275
- Manual trans 225

CAPRICE — RWD/4.3L-V8 (200hp)

Model	WS	Ret
Base 4dr Sdn	4900	6575
Base 4dr Wgn	5850	7600

Add:
- Cassette 25
- CD player 50
- Cruise ctrl 25
- Delco/Bose audio 125
- Leather seats 125
- Pwr seat 25
- Pwr windows 50
- Special wheels 50

CAVALIER — FWD/2.2L-I4 (120hp)

Model	WS	Ret
Base 4dr Sdn	2575	3950
Base 2dr Cpe	2525	3900
LS 4dr Sdn	3000	4425
LS 2dr Cnv		
Z/24 2dr Cpe	3525	5000

Add:
- Cassette (std Z/24) 25
- CD player 50
- Cruise control 25
- Pwr windows 25
- Special wheels (std Z24) 25
- Sunroof-pwr 175
- Tilt wheel (std Z/24) 25
- Pwr dr locks 25

Deduct:
- No air cond 225
- Manual trans 200

CORSICA — FWD/3.1L-V6 (155hp)

Model	WS	Ret
Base 4dr Sdn	2200	3325

Add:
- Cassette 25
- CD player 50
- Cruise ctrl 25
- Pwr windows 25
- Sunroof-manual 50
- Tilt wheel 25

Deduct:
- 4cyl 150
- No air cond 250
- Manual trans 225

CORVETTE — RWD/5.7L-V8 (300hp)

Model	WS	Ret
Coupe 2dr Cpe	14350	16600
Pace Car Edit. 2dr Cnv		
Roadster 2dr Cnv	17200	19625
ZR1 2dr Cpe	29075	32650

Add:
- CD player (std ZR1) 75
- Delco/Bose (std ZR1) 125
- Integrated phone 75
- Removable hardtop (Cnv) 325
- Roof-transparent (Cpe) 200
- Susp-FX3 adj (not ZR1) 75
- Z07 handling pkg (not ZR1) 150

IMPALA SS — RWD/5.7L-V8 (260hp)

Model	WS	Ret
Touring Sdn 4dr Sdn	11200	13275

Add:
- CD player 75

LUMINA — FWD/3.1L-V6 (160hp)

Model	WS	Ret
Base 4dr Sdn	3025	4450
LS 4dr Sdn	3550	5025

Add:
- ABS brakes (std LS) 125
- Cassette (std LS) 25
- CD player 50
- Cruise ctrl 25
- Delco/Bose audio 125
- 3.4L DOHC V6 325
- Pwr seat 25
- Pwr windows (std LS) 50
- Integrated child seat 25
- Moonroof-pwr 175
- Wheels-alum 50

MONTE CARLO — FWD/3.1L-V6 (160hp)

Model	WS	Ret
LS 2dr Cpe	4150	5775
Z34 2dr Cpe	4950	6650

Add:
- CD player 75
- Cruise ctrl (std Z34) 50
- Alloy wheels (std Z34) 75
- Leather seats 100

1994 — WS / Ret

BERETTA — FWD/3.IL-V6 (155hp)

Model	WS	Ret
Base 2dr Cpe	2075	3200
Z-26 2dr Cpe	2925	4350

Add:
- Cassette (std Z26) 25
- CD player 25
- Cruise ctrl 25
- Pwr windows 25
- Special wheels 25
- Sunroof-manual 25

Deduct:
- 4cyl (ohv only) 150
- No air cond 250
- Manual trans 200

CAMARO — RWD/3.4L-V6 (160hp)

Model	WS	Ret
Base 2dr Cnv	5250	6975
Base 2dr Cpe	4075	5700
Z/28 (8cyl) 2dr Cnv	6700	8500
Z/28 (8cyl) 2dr Cpe	5375	7100

Add:
- CD player 50
- Cruise ctrl 25
- Delco/Bose audio 100
- Pwr dr locks 25
- Pwr seat 25
- Pwr windows 25
- Special wheels (std Z28) 25
- T-tops 250

Deduct:
- No air cond 250
- Manual trans 200

CAPRICE — RWD/4.3L-V8 (200hp)

Model	WS	Ret
Base 4dr Sdn	3875	5475
Base 4dr Wgn	4725	6375
LS 4dr Sdn	4600	6250

Add:
- Cassette (std LS) 25
- CD player 50
- Cruise ctrl (std LS) 25
- Delco/Bose audio 100
- Integrated phone 50
- Leather seats 125
- Pwr dr locks (std LS) 25
- Pwr seat 25
- Pwr windows (std LS) 25
- Special wheels (std LS) 25

CAVALIER — FWD/2.2L-I4 (120hp)

Model	WS	Ret
RS 4dr Sdn	1775	2850
RS 4dr Wgn	2025	3125
RS 2dr Cnv	2700	4100
RS 2dr Cpe	1725	2800
VL 4dr Sdn	1525	2450
VL 2dr Cpe	1475	2400
Z/24 (6cyl) 2dr Cnv	3975	5600
Z/24 (6cyl) 2dr Cpe	2875	4275

Add:
- 3.1L V6 engine (Std Z24) 175
- Cassette (std Z/24) 25
- CD player 25
- Cruise control 25
- Pwr windows (std Cnv) 25
- Special wheels (std Z24) 25
- Sunroof-manual 25

Deduct:
- No air cond 225
- Manual trans 175

CORSICA — FWD/3.IL-V6 (155hp)

Model	WS	Ret
LT 4dr Sdn	1800	2875

Add:
- Cassette 25
- CD player 25
- Cruise ctrl 25
- Pwr windows 25
- Sunroof-manual 25

Deduct:
- 4cyl 150
- No air cond 250
- Manual trans 200

CORVETTE — RWD/5.7L-V8 (300hp)

Model	WS	Ret
Coupe 2dr Cpe	12750	14900
Roadster 2dr Cnv	15275	17575
ZR1 2dr Cpe	25200	28650

Add:
- CD player (std ZR1) 50
- Delco/Bose (std ZR1) 100
- Integrated phone 75
- Leather seats (std ZR1) 125
- Removable hardtop (Cnv) 300
- Transparent roof (Cpe) 100
- Susp-FX3 adj (not ZR1) 75
- Z07 handling pkg (not ZR1) 150

IMPALA SS — RWD/4.3L-V8 (200hp)

Model	WS	Ret
Touring Sdn 4dr Sdn	9825	11800

Add:
- CD player 50

LUMINA — FWD/3.1L-V6 (140hp)

Model	WS	Ret
Base 4dr Sdn	2275	3425
Base 2dr Cpe	2200	3325
Eurosport 4dr Sdn	2825	4225

Model	WS	Ret
Eurosport 2dr Cpe	2800	4200
Z34 2dr Cpe	3825	5425

Add:
- ABS brakes (std Euro,Z34) 125
- Cassette (std 3.4 Sdn,Z34) 25
- CD player 50
- Cruise ctrl (std Z34) 25
- Delco/Bose audio 100
- Euro 3.4 (incls DOHC V6) 725
- Pwr seat 25
- Pwr windows (std Euro cpe, Z34) 25

Deduct:
- 4cyl 150
- No air cond 250

1993 WS Ret

BERETTA FWD/3.1L-V6 (175hp)

Model	WS	Ret
Base 2dr Cpe	1575	2625
GT 2dr Cpe	2200	3325
GTZ (4cyl,5sp) 2dr Cpe	2600	3975

Add:
- Cassette 25
- CD player 25
- Cruise ctrl 25
- Pwr dr locks 25
- Pwr windows 25
- Spcl wheels (Base only) 25
- Sunroof-manual 25

Deduct:
- 4cyl (not GTZ) 125
- No air cond 200
- Man trans (not GTZ) 175

CAMARO RWD/3.4L-V6 (160hp)

Model	WS	Ret
RS 2dr Cpe	3525	5000
Z/28 (8cyl) 2dr Cpe	4450	6100

Add:
- CD player 50
- Cruise ctrl 25
- Delco/Bose audio 75
- Pwr dr locks 25
- Pwr seat 25
- Pwr windows 25
- Special wheels (std Z28) 25
- T-tops 225

Deduct:
- No air cond 200
- Manual trans 175

CAPRICE RWD/5.0L-V8 (170hp)

Model	WS	Ret
Base 4dr Sdn	3175	4625
Base 4dr Wgn	3925	5525
LS 4dr Sdn	3950	5550

Add:
- Cassette 25
- CD player 50
- Cruise ctrl 25
- Delco/Bose audio 75
- Leather seats 100
- LTZ pkg 175
- Pwr dr locks (std LS) 25
- Pwr seat 25
- Pwr windows (std LS) 25
- Special wheels (std LTZ) 25

CAVALIER FWD/2.2L-I4 (110hp)

Model	WS	Ret
RS 4dr Sdn	1575	2625
RS 4dr Wgn	1700	2775
RS 2dr Cnv	2250	3375
RS 2dr Cpe	1550	2475
VL 4dr Sdn	1350	2275
VL 4dr Wgn	1525	2450
VL 2dr Cpe	1350	2275
Z/24 (6cyl) 2dr Cnv	3275	4750
Z/24 (6cyl) 2dr Cpe	2625	4000

Add:
- 3.1L V6 engine (Std Z24) 150
- Cassette 25
- CD player 25
- Cruise control 25
- Pwr windows (std Cnv) 25
- Special wheels (std Z24) 25
- Sunroof-manual 25

Deduct:
- No air cond 175
- Manual trans 175

CORSICA FWD/3.IL-V6 (140hp)

Model	WS	Ret
LT 4dr Sdn	1450	2375

Add:
- Cassette 25
- CD player 25
- Cruise ctrl 25
- Pwr dr locks 25
- Pwr windows 25
- Special wheels 25
- Sunroof-manual 25

Deduct:
- 4cyl 125
- No air cond 200
- Manual trans 175

CORVETTE RWD/5.7L-V8 (300hp)

Model	WS	Ret
Coupe 2dr Cpe	12225	14350
Roadster 2dr Cnv	14275	16525
ZR1 2dr Cpe	27675	31325

Add:
- CD player (std ZR1) 50
- Delco/Bose (std ZR1) 75
- Integrated phone 50
- Leather seats (std ZR1) 100
- Removable hardtop (Cnv) 275
- Transparent roof (Cpe) 75

LUMINA FWD/3.IL-V6 (140hp)

Model	WS	Ret
Base 4dr Sdn	1900	3000
Base 2dr Cpe	1825	2900
Eurosport 4dr Sdn	2375	3725
Eurosport 2dr Cpe	2375	3725
Z34 2dr Cpe	3200	4650

Add:
- ABS brakes (std Euro,Z34) 100
- Cassette (std 3.4 Sdn,Z34) 25
- CD player 50
- Cruise ctrl (std Z34) 25
- Delco/Bose audio 75
- Euro 3.4 (incls DOHC V6) 650
- Pwr seat 25
- Pwr windows 25
- Tilt wheel (std Z34) 25

Deduct:
- 4cyl 125
- No air cond 225

1992 WS Ret

BERETTA FWD/2.2L-V6 (140hp)

Model	WS	Ret
Base 2dr Cpe	1375	2300
GT 2dr Cpe	1825	2900
GTZ (4cyl,5sp) 2dr Cpe	2225	3350

Add:
- CD player 25
- Cruise ctrl 25
- Pwr dr locks 25
- Pwr windows 25
- Spcl wheels (Base only) 25
- Sunroof-manual 25

Deduct:
- 4cyl (ohv only) 125
- No air cond 175
- Man trans (not GTZ) 150

CAMARO RWD/5.0L-V8 (170hp)

Model	WS	Ret
RS 2dr Cnv	3900	5500
RS 2dr Cpe	2825	4225
Z/28 2dr Cnv	4700	6350
Z/28 2dr Cpe	3575	5050

Add:
- 5.0L TPI V8 (std Z28) 175
- 5.7 Liter V8 (Z28 only) 200
- Cassette 25
- CD player 25
- Cruise ctrl 25
- Delco/Bose audio 50
- Leather seats 50
- Pwr dr locks 25
- Pwr windows 25
- Special wheels (std Z28) 25
- T-tops 200

Deduct:
- 6cyl 125
- No air cond 200
- Manual trans 175

CAPRICE RWD/5.0L-V8 (170hp)

Model	WS	Ret
Base 4dr Sdn	2350	3700
Base 4dr Wgn	3000	4425
Caprice Classic 4dr Sdn	3025	4450

Add:
- Cassette 25
- CD player 25
- Cruise ctrl 25
- Delco/Bose audio 50
- Integrated phone 50
- Leather seats 75
- LTZ pkg 150
- Pwr dr locks (std Classic) 25
- Pwr seat 25
- Pwr windows(std Classic) 25
- Special wheels (std LTZ) 25

CAVALIER FWD/2.2L-I4 (110hp)

Model	WS	Ret
RS 4dr Sdn	1300	2200
RS 4dr Wgn	1425	2350
RS 2dr Cnv	1900	3000
RS 2dr Cpe	1275	2175
VL 4dr Sdn	1150	2050
VL 4dr Wgn	1225	2125
VL 2dr Cpe	1125	2025
Z/24 (6cyl) 2dr Cnv	2800	4200
Z/24 (6cyl) 2dr Cpe	2200	3325

Add:
- 3.1L V6 engine (Std Z24) 125
- CD player 25
- Cruise ctrl 25
- Pwr dr locks 25
- Pwr windows (std Cnv) 25
- Special wheels (std Z24) 25
- Sunroof-manual 25

Deduct:
- No air cond 175
- Manual trans 150

CORSICA FWD/3.1L-V6 (140hp)

Model	WS	Ret
LT 4dr Sdn	1175	2075

Add:
- CD player 25
- Cruise ctrl 25
- Pwr dr locks 25
- Pwr windows 25
- Special wheels 25
- Sunroof-manual 25

Deduct:
- 4cyl 100
- No air cond 175
- Manual trans 175

CORVETTE RWD/5.7L-V8 (300hp)

Model	WS	Ret
Coupe 2dr Cpe	10675	12700
Roadster 2dr Cnv	12525	14675
ZR1 2dr Cpe	22825	25575

Add:
- CD player (std ZR1) 25
- Delco/Bose (std ZR1) 50
- Integrated phone 50
- Leather seats (std ZR1) 75
- Removable hardtop (Cnv) 250

Transparent roof (Cpe) 75

LUMINA FWD/3.1L-V6 (140hp)

Base 4dr Sdn	1600	2650
Base 2dr Cpe	1550	2475
Eurosport 4dr Sdn	2000	3100
Eurosport 2dr Cpe	2025	3125
Z34 2dr Cpe	2775	4175

Add:
ABS brakes(std Euro,Z34) 75
Cassette (std Z34) 25
CD player 25
Cruise ctrl (std Z34) 25
Delco/Bose audio 50
Euro 3.4 (incls DOHC V6) . . . 500
Pwr dr locks 25
Pwr seat 25
Pwr windows 25

Deduct:
4cyl 125
No air cond 200

1991 WS Ret

BERETTA FWD/3.1L-V6 (140hp)

Base 2dr Cpe	1075	1975
GT 2dr Cpe	1425	2350
GTZ (4cyl,5sp) 2dr Cpe	1575	2625

Add:
CD player 25
Pwr windows 25
Special wheels (Base) 25
Sunroof-manual 25

Deduct:
4cyl (ohv only) 150
No air cond 175
Man trans (not GTZ) 150

CAMARO RWD/5.0L-V8 (170hp)

RS 2dr Cnv	3400	4875
RS 2dr Cpe	2425	3800
Z/28 2dr Cnv	4025	5650
Z/28 2dr Cpe	3025	4450

Add:
5.7 Liter V8 (Z28) 175
Cassette 25
CD player 25
Leather seats 25
Pwr windows 25
T-tops 175

Deduct:
No air cond 175
Manual trans 150

CAPRICE RWD/5.0L-V8 (170hp)

Base 4dr Sdn	1750	2825
Base 4dr Wgn	2200	3325
Caprice Classic 4dr Sdn	2225	3350

Add:
Cassette 25
CD player 25
Cruise ctrl 25
Delco/Bose audio 50
Integrated phone 25
Leather seats 50
Pwr dr locks (std Clsc) 25
Pwr windows (std Clsc) 25
Special wheels 25

CAVALIER FWD/2.2L-I4 (95hp)

RS 4dr Sdn	925	1625
RS 4dr Wgn	1050	1950
RS 2dr Cnv	1425	2350
RS 2dr Cpe	875	1550
VL 4dr Sdn	800	1475
VL 4dr Wgn	900	1600
VL 2dr Cpe	750	1275
Z/24 (6cyl) 2dr Cpe	1550	2475

Add:
3.1 Liter V6 (std Z24) 100
CD player 25
Pwr windows (std Cnv) 25
Sunroof-manual 25

Deduct:
No air cond 150
Manual trans 125

CORSICA FWD/3.1L-V6 (140hp)

LT 4dr Hbk	1025	1925
LT 4dr Sdn	975	1675

Add:
3.1 Liter V6 100
CD player 25
Pwr windows 25
Special wheels 25
Sunroof-manual 25

Deduct:
4cyl 150
No air cond 175
Manual trans 150

CORVETTE RWD/5.7L-V8 (245hp)

Coupe 2dr Cpe	10150	12150
Roadster 2dr Cnv	11925	14025
ZR1 2dr Cpe	21400	24325

Add:
CD player (std ZR1) 25
Delco/Bose (std ZR1) 50
Leather seats (std ZR1) 50
Removable hardtop (Cnv) 225
Transparent roof (Cpe) 50

LUMINA FWD/3.1L-V6 (140hp)

Base 4dr Sdn	1325	2250
Base 2dr Cpe	1250	2150
Eurosport 4dr Sdn	1650	2700
Eurosport 2dr Cpe	1650	2700
Z34 2dr Cpe	1925	3025

Add:
Cassette (std Z34) 25
Cruise ctrl (std Z34) 25
Delco/Bose audio 50
Pwr dr locks 25
Pwr windows 25

Deduct:
4cyl 100
No air cond 175

1990 WS Ret

BERETTA FWD/3.1L-V6 (135hp)

Base 2dr Cpe	900	1600
GT 2dr Cpe	1175	2075
GTZ (4cyl,5sp) 2dr Cpe	1200	2100

Add:
Sunroof-manual 25

Deduct:
4cyl (ohv only) 125
No air cond 150
Man trans (not GTZ) 100

CAMARO RWD/5.0L-V8 (170hp)

IROC-Z 2dr Cnv	3675	5175
IROC-Z 2dr Hbk	2675	4075
RS 2dr Cnv	3175	4625
RS 2dr Hbk	2200	3325

Add:
5.7 Liter V8 (IROC) 175
CD player 25
Delco/Bose audio 50
Leather seats 25
T-tops 150

Deduct:
6cyl 75
No air cond 150
Manual trans 100

CAPRICE RWD/5.0L-V8 (170hp)

Base 4dr Sdn	1175	2075
Classic 4dr Sdn	1475	2400
Classic Brghm 4dr Sdn	1700	2775
Classic Brghm LS 4dr Sdn	1850	2925
Classic 4dr Wgn	1550	2475

Add:
Leather seats 25
Pwr windows 25
Special wheels 25

CAVALIER FWD/2.2L-I4 (95hp)

Base 4dr Sdn	600	1100
Base 4dr Wgn	700	1225
Base 2dr Cpe	575	1075
RS 4dr Sdn	700	1225
RS 4dr Wgn	775	1300
RS 2dr Cpe	675	1200
VL 4dr Sdn	625	1125
VL 4dr Wgn	725	1250
VL 2dr Cpe	600	1100
Z/24 2dr Cpe	1250	2150

Add:
3.1 liter 6cyl 50
Sunroof-manual 25

Deduct:
No air cond 125
Manual trans 100

CELEBRITY FWD/3.IL-V6 (135hp)

Wagon 4dr Wgn	1025	1925

Add:
Eurosport 25
Pwr windows 25
Special wheels 25

Deduct:
4cyl 75
No air cond 150

CORSICA FWD/3.1L-V6 (135hp)

LT 4dr Hbk	875	1550
LT 4dr Sdn	850	1525
LTZ 4dr Sdn	1125	2025

Add:
CL trim 25

Deduct:
4cyl 75
No air cond 150
Manual trans 125

CORVETTE RWD/5.7L-V8 (245hp)

Coupe 2dr Cpe	9675	11650
Roadster 2dr Cnv	11450	13525
ZR1 2dr Cpe	20275	23100

Add:
CD player (std ZR1) 25
Delco/Bose (std ZR1) 50
Leather seats (std ZR1) 50
Removable hardtop (Cnv) . . . 225
Transparent roof (Cpe) 50

LUMINA FWD/3.1L-V6 (135hp)

Base 4dr Sdn	1050	1950
Base 2dr Cpe	1025	1925
Eurosport 4dr Sdn	1300	2200
Eurosport 2dr Cpe	1300	2200

Add:
Pwr windows 25
Special wheels (Euro) 25

Deduct:
4cyl 75
No air cond 150

1989 WS Ret

BERETTA FWD/2.8L-V6 (125hp)

Base 2dr Cpe	725	1250

Model	WS	Ret
GT 2dr Cpe	950	1650

Add:

Deduct:
- 4cyl . . . 50
- No air cond . . . 100
- Manual trans . . . 100

CAMARO — RWD/5.0L-V8 (170hp)

Model	WS	Ret
IROC 2dr Cnv	3150	4600
IROC 2dr Hbk	2200	3325
RS 2dr Cnv	2675	4075
RS 2dr Hbk	1725	2800

Add:
- 5.0L TPI V8 (IROC-Z) . . . 50
- 5.7 Liter V8 . . . 150
- Delco/Bose audio . . . 25
- Leather seats . . . 25
- T-tops . . . 100

Deduct:
- 6cyl . . . 50
- No air cond . . . 125
- Manual trans . . . 100

CAPRICE — RWD/5.0L-V8 (170hp)

Model	WS	Ret
Base 4dr Sdn	925	1625
Classic 4dr Sdn	1175	2075
Classic Brghm 4dr Sdn	1325	2250
Classic Brghm LS 4dr Sdn	1475	2400
Classic 4dr Wgn	1175	2075

Add:
- Leather seats . . . 25

CAVALIER — FWD/2.0L-I4 (90hp)

Model	WS	Ret
Base 4dr Sdn	500	975
Base 4dr Wgn	575	1075
Base 2dr Cpe	475	950
RS 4dr Sdn	575	1075
RS 4dr Wgn	625	1125
RS 2dr Cpe	550	1050
VL 2dr Cpe	450	925
Z/24 2dr Cnv	1725	2800
Z/24 2dr Cpe	1025	1925

Add:
- 2.8 Liter V6 (std Z24) . . . 50

Deduct:
- No air cond . . . 100
- Manual trans . . . 100

CELEBRITY — FWD/2.8L-V6 (125hp)

Model	WS	Ret
Sedan 4dr Sdn	725	1250
Wagon 4dr Wgn	775	1300

Add:
- Eurosport pkg . . . 25
- Sunroof-pwr . . . 50

Deduct:
- 4cyl . . . 50
- No air cond . . . 125

CORSICA — FWD/2.8L-V6 (130hp)

Model	WS	Ret
Base 4dr Hbk	675	1200
Base 4dr Sdn	625	1125
LTZ 4dr Sdn	900	1600

Add:

Deduct:
- 4cyl . . . 50
- No air cond . . . 100
- Manual trans . . . 100

CORVETTE — RWD/5.7L-V8 (240hp)

Model	WS	Ret
Coupe 2dr Cpe	8700	10625
Roadster 2dr Cnv	10300	12325

Add:
- Delco/Bose . . . 25
- Leather seats . . . 25
- Removable glass roof . . . 50
- Removable hardtop (Cnv) . . . 225

1988 — WS / Ret

BERETTA — FWD/2.0L-V6 (90hp)

Model	WS	Ret
Base 2dr Cpe	600	1100
GT 2dr Cpe	700	1225

Add:

Deduct:
- 4cyl . . . 50
- No air cond . . . 75
- Manual trans . . . 50

CAMARO — RWD/5.0L-V8 (170hp)

Model	WS	Ret
Base 2dr Cnv	2200	3325
Base 2dr Cpe	1250	2150
IROC-Z 2dr Cnv	2475	3850
IROC-Z 2dr Cpe	1525	2450

Add:
- 5.0L TPI V8 (RS,IROC) . . . 50
- 5.7 Liter V8 (IROC) . . . 125
- T-tops . . . 75

Deduct:
- 6cyl . . . 50
- No air cond . . . 100
- Manual trans . . . 75

CAPRICE — RWD/5.0L-V8 (170hp)

Model	WS	Ret
Base 4dr Sdn	900	1600
Classic 4dr Sdn	1025	1925
Classic Brghm 4dr Sdn	1150	2050
Classic Brghm LS 4dr Sdn	1200	2100
Classic 4dr Wgn	1075	1975

Add:
- Leather seats . . . 25

Deduct:
- 6cyl . . . 75
- No air cond . . . 125

CAVALIER — FWD/2.0L-I4 (90hp)

Model	WS	Ret
Base 4dr Sdn	450	925
Base 4dr Wgn	500	975
Base 2dr Cpe	425	900
RS 4dr Sdn	475	950
RS 2dr Cpe	450	925
VL 2dr Cpe	350	800
Z/24 2dr Cnv	1475	2400
Z/24 2dr Cpe	800	1475

Add:
- 2.8 Liter V6 (std Z24) . . . 50

Deduct:
- No air cond . . . 50
- Manual trans . . . 50

CELEBRITY — FWD/2.8L-V6 (125hp)

Model	WS	Ret
Coupe 2dr Cpe	525	1000
Sedan 4dr Sdn	550	1050
Wagon 4dr Wgn	600	1100

Add:
- Eurosport pkg . . . 25

Deduct:
- 4cyl . . . 50
- No air cond . . . 100
- Manual trans . . . 75

CORSICA — FWD/2.0L-V6 (90hp)

Model	WS	Ret
Base 4dr Sdn	500	975

Add:

Deduct:
- 4cyl . . . 50
- No air cond . . . 75
- Manual trans . . . 75

CORVETTE — RWD/5.7L-V8 (240hp)

Model	WS	Ret
Coupe 2dr Cpe	8050	9925
Roadster 2dr Cnv	9625	11600

Add:
- Delco/Bose . . . 25
- Leather seats . . . 25
- Transparent roof (Cpe) . . . 25

MONTE CARLO — RWD/5.0L-V8 (150hp)

Model	WS	Ret
LS 2dr Cpe	2050	3150
SS 2dr Cpe	3150	4700

Add:
- T-tops . . . 75

Deduct:
- 6cyl . . . 50
- No air cond . . . 100

NOVA — FWD/1.6L-I4 (74hp)

Model	WS	Ret
Base 4dr Hbk	500	975
Base 4dr Sdn	500	975
Twin-Cam 4dr Sdn	775	1300

Add:
- CL pkg . . . 25
- Cruise ctrl . . . 25

Deduct:
- No air cond . . . 50
- Manual trans . . . 50

SPECTRUM — FWD/1.5L-I4 (70hp)

Model	WS	Ret
Base 4dr Sdn	175	600
Base 2dr Hbk	175	600
Express 2dr Hbk	125	525
Turbo 4dr Sdn	175	600

Add:

Deduct:
- No air cond . . . 50
- Manual trans . . . 50

SPRINT (5sp) — FWD/1.0L-I3 (48hp)

Model	WS	Ret
Base 4dr Hbk	250	675
Base 2dr Hbk	225	650
Metro 2dr Hbk	250	675
Turbo 2dr Hbk	250	675

Add:
- Automatic trans . . . 25

Deduct:
- No air cond . . . 50

CHRYSLER

2001 — WS / Ret

300 — FWD/3.5L-V6 (253hp)

Model	WS	Ret
M 4dr Sdn	18525	21025

Add:
- Sunroof-pwr . . . 550
- 4-disc CD changer . . . 350
- Performance Handling . . . 400
- Wheels-chrome . . . 375

CONCORDE — FWD/2.7L-V6 (200hp)

Model	WS	Ret
LX 4dr Sdn	12400	14550
LXi 4dr Sdn	14600	16875

Add:
- CD player (LX) . . . 225
- Moonroof-pwr . . . 500
- Leather seats (LX) . . . 400
- Wheels-chrome (LXi) . . . 350
- Wheels-alum (LX) . . . 250

Deduct:
- No ABS . . . 325

LHS — FWD/3.5L-V6 (253hp)

Model	WS	Ret
Touring 4dr Sdn	17525	19975

Add:
- Sunroof-pwr . . . 550
- 4-disc CD changer . . . 400
- Wheels-chrome . . . 375

PT CRUISER — FWD/2.4L-I6 (150hp)

Model	WS	Ret
Base 4dr Wgn	14225	16475

Deduct:

Manual trans	850	
Manual locks	200	
No cruise ctrl	200	

SEBRING FWD/2.7L-V6 (200hp)

LX 4dr Sdn	12475	14625
LX 2dr Cnv	14575	16850
LX 2dr Cpe	12075	14200
LXi 4dr Sdn	14375	16625
LXi 2dr Cnv	16275	18650
LXi 2dr Cpe	13375	15575

Add:

ABS brakes (std Ltd.)	325	
CD player (LX)	225	
CD changer	425	
Sunroof-pwr	475	
Pwr seat (LX)	200	
Wheels-alum (LX,JX)	225	
Wheels-chrome	325	

Deduct:

2.4L-I4 (150hp)	650	
Vinyl seats	375	
Manual trans	625	
No Cassette	175	

2000 WS Ret

300 FWD/3.5L-V6 (253hp)

M 4dr Sdn	16950	19350

Add:

Moonroof-pwr	425	
4-disc CD changer	275	
Performance Handling	300	
Wheels-chrome	275	

Deduct:

Cloth seats	400	

CIRRUS FWD/2.5L-V6 (168hp)

LX (4cyl) 4dr Sdn	7225	9050
LXi 4dr Sdn	9100	11050

Add:

ABS brakes (std LXi)	225	
CD changer	250	
Premium audio	125	
Pwr seat	150	
Moonroof-pwr	375	

CONCORDE FWD/2.7L-V6 (200hp)

LX 4dr Sdn	11800	13900
LXi 4dr Sdn	13975	16200

Add:

CD player (LX)	175	
Moonroof-pwr	400	
Infinity audio (LX)	250	
Leather seats (LX)	300	
Wheels-alum (LX)	175	

Deduct:

No ABS	250	

LHS FWD/3.5L-V6 (253hp)

Touring 4dr Sdn	16350	18725

Add:

Moonroof-pwr	425	
4-disc CD changer	300	
Wheels-chrome	275	

SEBRING FWD/2.5L-V6 (163hp)

JX 2dr Cnv	11525	13600
JXi 2dr Cnv	12800	14975
LX 2dr Cpe	10575	12600
LXi (3.0L V6) 2dr Cpe	11825	13925

Add:

ABS brakes (Cpe)	250	
CD player	175	
CD changer	325	
Sunroof-pwr	350	
Pwr seat (LX)	150	
Wheels-alum (LX,JX)	175	

Deduct:

2.0L/2.4L-I4 (140/150hp)	500	
Vinyl seats	275	
Manual trans	475	
No Cassette	150	

1999 WS Ret

300 FWD/

M 4dr Sdn	14725	17000

Add:

Moonroof-pwr	350	
Wheels-chrome	225	

Deduct:

Cloth seats	325	

CIRRUS FWD/2.5L-V6 (168hp)

LXi 4dr Sdn	8775	10700

Add:

CD changer	225	
Pwr seat	125	
Leather seats	225	
Moonroof-pwr	300	

CONCORDE FWD/2.7L-V6 (200hp)

LX 4dr Sdn	10250	12250
LXi 4dr Sdn	12200	14325

Add:

CD player (LX)	150	
Moonroof-pwr	325	
Infinity audio (LX)	200	
Leather seats	250	
Wheels-alum (LX)	150	

Deduct:

No ABS brakes	250	

LHS FWD/

Touring 4dr Sdn.	13750	15975

Add:

Moonroof-pwr	350	
4-disc CD changer	225	
Wheels-chrome	225	

SEBRING FWD/2.5L-V6 (163hp)

JX 2dr Cnv	11400	13475
JXi 2dr Cnv	12600	14700
LX 2dr Cpe	9825	11800
LXi 2dr Cpe	10975	12900

Add:

ABS brakes (LX)	225	
Cruise ctrl (LX)	125	
Pwr dr locks (LX)	125	
Pwr windows (LX)	125	
Leather seats (std JXi)	225	
Sunroof-pwr	300	
Pwr seat (LX)	125	
CD player	150	
CD changer	275	
Wheels-16in alum (LX,JX)	150	

Deduct:

2.0L/2.4L-I4 (140/150hp)	425	
Vinyl seats	225	
Manual trans	400	
No Cassette	100	

1998 WS Ret

CIRRUS FWD/2.5L-V6 (168hp)

LXi 4dr Sdn	7675	9525

Add:

CD player	125	
CD changer	200	
Pwr seat	75	
Leather seats	200	
Moonroof-pwr	250	

Deduct:

2.4L (4cyl-150hp)	250	

CONCORDE FWD/3.2L-V6 (225hp)

LX 4dr Sdn	8825	10750
LXi 4dr Sdn	10525	12550

Add:

ABS brakes (LX)	200	
CD player	125	
Moonroof-pwr	275	
Infinity audio (LX)	175	
Leather seats	200	
Wheels-alum (LX)	125	

Deduct:

No ABS brakes	200	

SEBRING FWD/2.5L-V6 (163hp)

JX 2dr Cnv	9850	11850
JXi 2dr Cnv	10825	12875
LX 2dr Cpe	8475	10375
LXi 2dr Cpe	9475	11450

Add:

ABS brakes (LX,JX)	175	
Cruise ctrl (LX,JX)	75	
Pwr dr locks (LX,JX)	75	
Pwr windows (std LXi)	100	
Leather seats (std JXi)	200	
Sunroof-pwr	250	
Pwr seat (LX, JX)	75	
CD player	125	
CD changer	225	
16" alum whls (LX,JX)	125	

Deduct:

2.0L(4cyl-140hp)	350	
2.4L(4cyl-150hp)	350	
Manual trans	325	
No Cassette	75	

1997 WS Ret

CIRRUS FWD/2.4L-V6 (150hp)

LX 4dr Sdn	5625	7350
LXi 4dr Sdn	6500	8300

Add:

CD player	75	
CD changer	175	
Pwr seat (std LXi)	50	
Leather seats (std LXi)	150	
Wheels-alum (std LXi)	75	

Deduct:

2.4L (4cyl-150hp)	225	

CONCORDE FWD/3.5L-V6 (214hp)

LX 4dr Sdn	6400	8175
LXi 4dr Sdn	7825	9700

Add:

ABS brakes	150	
CD player	75	
Moonroof-pwr	225	
Infinity audio (LX)	125	
Leather seats	175	
Wheels-alum (LX)	100	

Deduct:

No ABS brakes	175	

LHS FWD/3.5L-V6 (214hp)

Touring 4dr Sdn	7800	9675

SEBRING FWD/2.0L-V6 (140hp)

JX 2dr Cnv	8650	10575
JXi 2dr Cnv	9850	11850
LX 2dr Cpe	7200	9025
LXi 2dr Cpe	8100	9975

Add:

ABS brakes (LX,JX)	150	
Cruise ctrl (LX,JX)	75	
Pwr dr locks (LX,JX)	75	
Pwr windows (std LXi)	75	
Leather seats (std JXi)	150	
Sunroof-pwr	200	
Pwr seat	75	
Infinity audio (LX,JX)	50	

- CD player 100
- CD changer 175
- 16" alum whls (LX,JX) 75

Deduct:
- 2.0L(4cyl-140hp) 275
- 2.4L(4cyl-150hp) 275
- Manual trans 275
- No Cassette 50

1996 WS Ret

CIRRUS FWD/2.4L-V6 (150hp)

	WS	Ret
LX 4dr Sdn	4650	6300
LXi 4dr Sdn	5425	7150

Add:
- Cd player 50
- Pwr seat (std LXi) 50
- Leather seats (std LXi) 125
- Alloy wheels (std LXi) 50

Deduct:
- 2.4 Liter 4cyl 175

CONCORDE FWD/3.3L-V6 (161hp)

	WS	Ret
LX 4dr Sdn	5325	7050
LXi 4dr Sdn	6625	8425

Add:
- 3.5L DOHC V6 (LX) 225
- CD player 50
- Moonroof-pwr 175
- Infinity audio (LX) 100
- Leather seats 150
- Pwr seat (LX) 25
- Wheels-alloy (LX) 75

NEW YORKER FWD/3.5L-V6 (214hp)

	WS	Ret
Base 4dr Sdn	4900	6575
LHS 4dr Sdn	6375	8150

Add:
- CD player 50
- Infinity audio 100
- Leather seats 150
- Special wheels 50
- Moonroof-pwr 175

SEBRING FWD/2.5L-V6 (155hp)

	WS	Ret
JX 2dr Cnv	6975	8800
JXi 2dr Cnv	8000	9875
LX 2dr Cpe	5525	7250
LXi 2dr Cpe	6350	8125

Add:
- 16in alloys (LX,JX) 50
- Cruise ctrl (LX,JX) 25
- Pwr dr locks (LX,JX) 25
- Pwr windows (std LXi) 50
- Leather seats (std JXi) 125
- Sunroof-pwr 175
- Pwr seat 25
- Infinity audio (LX,JX) 25
- CD player 75
- CD changer 150

Deduct:
- 4cyl 250
- Manual trans 225
- No Cassette 25

1995 WS Ret

CIRRUS FWD/2.5L-V6 (162hp)

	WS	Ret
LX 4dr Sdn	4000	5625
LXi 4dr Sdn	4600	6250

Add:
- Cd player 50
- Pwr seat (std LXi) 50
- Leather seats (std LXi) 125
- Integrated child seat 25

CONCORDE FWD/3.3L-V6 (161hp)

	WS	Ret
Base 4dr Sdn	4525	6175

Add:
- 3.5L DOHC V6 200
- CD player 75
- Moonroof-pwr 175
- Infinity audio 125
- Leather seats 125
- Power seat 25
- Hdlng Grp (incls 16" alloys) 150

LEBARON FWD/3.0L-V6 (141hp)

	WS	Ret
GTC 2dr Cnv	3675	5175

Add:
- ABS brakes 125
- CD player 50
- Cruise ctrl 25
- Leather seats 125
- Premium sound 25
- Pwr dr locks 25
- Pwr seat 25
- Aluminum whls 50

Deduct:
- 2.5 Liter 4cyl 150
- No air cond 275
- Manual trans 250

NEW YORKER FWD/3.5L-V6 (214hp)

	WS	Ret
Base 4dr Sdn	4125	5750
LHS 4dr Sdn	5225	6950

Add:
- CD player 50
- Infinity audio 125
- Leather seats 125
- Special wheels 50
- Moonroof-pwr 175

SEBRING FWD/2.5L-V6 (140hp)

	WS	Ret
LX 2dr Cpe	4775	6425
LXi 2dr Cpe	5500	7225

Add:
- 16in alloys (std LXi) 50
- Cruise ctrl (std LXi) 25
- Pwr dr locks (std LXi) 25
- Pwr windows (std LXi) 50
- Leather seats 125
- Sunroof-pwr 150
- Pwr seat 25
- Infinity audio 25
- Cd player 50

Deduct:
- 4cyl 225
- Manual trans 200
- No Cassette 25

1994 WS Ret

CONCORDE FWD/3.3L-V6 (161hp)

	WS	Ret
Sedan 4dr Sdn	3175	4625

Add:
- 3.5L DOHC V6 175
- CD player 50
- Infinity audio 100
- Leather seats 125
- Power dr locks 25
- Power seat 25
- Power windows 50
- Touring grp (incl 16" whls) 150

LEBARON FWD/3.0L-V6 (141hp)

	WS	Ret
GTC 2dr Cnv	2925	4350
Landau 4dr Sdn	2500	3875
LE 4dr Sdn	2150	3275

Add:
- ABS brakes 125
- Cassette (std Landau,Cnv) 25
- CD player 50
- Cruise ctrl (std Sdn) 25
- Leather seats 125
- Pwr dr locks (std Landau) 25
- Pwr seat 25
- Special whls 25

Deduct:
- 2.5 Liter 4cyl 150
- No air cond 250
- Manual trans 225

NEW YORKER FWD/3.5L-V6 (214hp)

	WS	Ret
Base 4dr Sdn	2775	4175
LHS 4dr Sdn	3750	5350

Add:
- Infinity audio (incls. CD) 100
- Leather seats 125
- Special wheels (std LHS) 50
- Sunroof-pwr 150

1993 WS Ret

CONCORDE FWD/3.3L-V6 (153hp)

	WS	Ret
Sedan 4dr Sdn	2675	4075

Add:
- 3.5L DOHC V6 175
- Infinity audio 75
- Leather seats 100
- Power dr locks 25
- Power seat 25
- Power windows 50
- Touring grp (incl 16" whls) 125

IMPERIAL FWD/3.8L-V6 (150hp)

	WS	Ret
Sedan 4dr Sdn	2900	4325

Add:
- Infinity audio (incls CD) 100
- Leather seats 100

LEBARON FWD/3.0L-V6 (141hp)

	WS	Ret
Base 2dr Cnv	2450	3825
Base 2dr Cpe	1875	2975
GTC 2dr Cnv	3150	4600
GTC 2dr Cpe	2475	3850
Landau 4dr Sdn	2350	3700
LE 4dr Sdn	2025	3125
LX 2dr Cnv	2900	4325
LX 2dr Cpe	2200	3325

Add:
- ABS brakes 100
- Cassette (std Landau,LX Cnv) 25
- CD player 50
- Cruise ctrl (std LX,Sdn) 25
- Leather seats (std LX Cnv) 100
- Premium sound 25
- Pwr dr locks (std LX) 25
- Pwr seat 25
- Pwr windows (std Cpe&Cnv) 25
- Special whls (std GTC) 25

Deduct:
- 2.5 Liter 4cyl 125
- No air cond 225
- Manual trans 200

NEW YORKER FWD/3.3L-V6 (147hp)

	WS	Ret
Fifth Ave 4dr Sdn	2800	4200
Salon 4dr Sdn	2475	3850

Add:
- ABS brakes 100
- Integrated phone 50
- Infinity audio 75
- Leather seats 100
- Special wheels 25

1992 WS Ret

IMPERIAL FWD/3.8L-V6 (150hp)

	WS	Ret
Sedan 4dr Sdn	2475	3850

Add:
- Infinity 10 spkr audio 75
- Leather seats 75

LEBARON FWD/3.0L-V6 (141hp)

	WS	Ret
Base 4dr Sdn	1675	2725
Base 2dr Cnv	2125	3250
Base 2dr Cpe	1575	2625
GTC 2dr Cnv	2650	4050
GTC 2dr Cpe	2050	3150

	WS	Ret
Landau 4dr Sdn	1900	3000
Premium LX 4dr Sdn	1800	2875
Premium LX 2dr Cnv	2450	3825
Premium LX 2dr Cpe	1825	2900

Add:
- ABS brakes . . . 75
- Cassette (std Landau) . . . 25
- CD player . . . 25
- Cruise ctrl (std LX) . . . 25
- Lthr seats (std LX Cnv) . . . 75
- Pwr dr locks . . . 25
- Pwr seat . . . 25
- Pwr windows . . . 25
- Spcl whls (Base,LX cpe) . . . 25
- Sunroof-manual . . . 25

Deduct:
- 2.5 Liter 4cyl . . . 100
- No air cond . . . 200
- Manual trans . . . 200

NEW YORKER — FWD/3.3L-V6 (147hp)

	WS	Ret
Fifth Ave 4dr Sdn	2300	3450
Salon 4dr Sdn	1950	3050

Add:
- ABS brakes . . . 75
- Cassette . . . 25
- Cruise ctrl . . . 25
- Integrated phone . . . 50
- Infinity audio . . . 50
- Leather seats . . . 75
- Pwr dr locks . . . 25
- Pwr seat . . . 25
- Special wheels . . . 25
- Sunroof-pwr . . . 150

1991 — WS Ret

IMPERIAL — FWD/3.8L-V6 (147hp)

	WS	Ret
Sedan 4dr Sdn	2250	3375

Add:
- Infinity audio . . . 50
- Leather seats . . . 50

LEBARON — FWD/3.0L-V6 (141hp)

	WS	Ret
Base 4dr Sdn	1500	2425
GTC 2dr Cnv	2200	3325
GTC 2dr Cpe	1600	2650
Highline 2dr Cnv	1800	2875
Highline 2dr Cpe	1350	2275
Premium LX 2dr Cnv	2025	3125
Premium LX 2dr Cpe	1500	2425

Add:
- 2.5L 4cyl Turbo (Base) . . . 50
- 3.0L V6 (Base Cpe, Cnv) . . . 100
- ABS brakes . . . 50
- Cassette . . . 25
- CD player . . . 25
- Cruise ctrl . . . 25
- Perf pkg (GTC-incls Turbo) . . . 175
- Infinity audio . . . 50
- Leather seats . . . 50
- Pwr dr locks . . . 25
- Pwr windows . . . 25
- Special wheels (std GTC) . . . 25
- Sunroof-manual . . . 25

Deduct:
- 2.5 Liter 4cyl . . . 75
- No air cond . . . 175
- Manual trans . . . 175

NEW YORKER — FWD/3.3L-V6 (147hp)

	WS	Ret
Fifth Ave 4dr Sdn	2025	3125
Salon 4dr Sdn	1750	2825

Add:
- ABS brakes . . . 50
- Infinity audio . . . 50
- Integrated phone . . . 25
- Leather seats . . . 50
- Special wheels . . . 25
- Sunroof-pwr . . . 100

TC MASERATI — FWD/3.0L-V6 (141hp)

	WS	Ret
Convertible 2dr Cnv	7625	9575

1990 — WS Ret

IMPERIAL — FWD/3.3L-V6 (147hp)

	WS	Ret
Sedan 4dr Sdn	1925	3025

Add:
- Infinity audio . . . 50
- Leather seats . . . 25

LEBARON — FWD/3.0L-V6 (142hp)

	WS	Ret
Base 4dr Sdn	1200	2100
GT 2dr Cnv	1825	2900
GT 2dr Cpe	1350	2275
GTC (4cyl Turbo) 2dr Cnv	1775	2850
GTC (4cyl Turbo) 2dr Cpe	1300	2200
Highline 2dr Cnv	1475	2400
Highline 2dr Cpe	1100	2000
Premium 2dr Cnv	1625	2675
Premium 2dr Cpe	1200	2100

Add:
- Leather seats . . . 25
- Pwr windows (std Prem Cnv) . . . 25
- Special whls (std GT,GTC) . . . 25
- Sunroof-manual . . . 25

Deduct:
- 2.5 Liter 4cyl . . . 75
- No air cond . . . 150
- Manual trans . . . 150

NEW YORKER — FWD/3.3L-V6 (147hp)

	WS	Ret
Fifth Ave 4dr Sdn	1625	2675
Landau 4dr Sdn	1525	2450
Salon 4dr Sdn	1350	2275

Add:
- ABS brakes . . . 25
- Infinity audio . . . 50
- Lthr seats (std Mark Cross) . . . 25
- Mark Cross pkg . . . 175
- Special wheels . . . 25
- Sunroof-pwr . . . 75

TC MASERATI — FWD/3.0L-V6 (142hp)

	WS	Ret
3.0 Liter V6 2dr Cnv	6550	8425
Twin-cam 2dr Cnv	6675	8550

1989 — WS Ret

CONQUEST — RWD/2.6L-I4 (188hp)

	WS	Ret
TSi 2dr Hbk	1675	2725

Add:
- Leather seats . . . 25
- Sunroof-pwr . . . 50

Deduct:
- No air cond . . . 100
- Manual trans . . . 100

FIFTH AVENUE — RWD/5.2L-V8 (140hp)

	WS	Ret
Sedan 4dr Sdn	1175	2075

Add:
- Leather seats . . . 25
- Sunroof-pwr . . . 75

LEBARON — FWD/2.5L-I4 (100hp)

	WS	Ret
GT 2dr Cnv	1475	2400
GT 2dr Cpe	1100	2000
GTC 2dr Cnv	1550	2475
GTC 2dr Cpe	1150	2050
GTS Turbo 4dr Hbk	1100	2000
Highline 4dr Hbk	875	1550
Highline 2dr Cnv	1200	2100
Highline 2dr Cpe	850	1525
Premium 4dr Hbk	1150	2050
Premium 2dr Cnv	1325	2250
Premium 2dr Cpe	975	1675

Add:
- 2.5L Turbo (Base,Prem) . . . 50
- Leather seats . . . 25
- Sunroof-pwr . . . 50

Deduct:
- No air cond . . . 125
- Manual trans . . . 125

NEW YORKER — FWD/3.0L-V6 (141hp)

	WS	Ret
Base 4dr Sdn	1100	2000
Landau 4dr Sdn	1175	2075

Add:
- Infinity audio . . . 25
- Lthr seats (std Mrk Crs) . . . 25
- Mark Cross pkg . . . 150
- Special wheels . . . 25
- Sunroof-pwr . . . 50

TC MASERATI — FWD/2.2L-I4 (200hp)

	WS	Ret
Convertible 2dr Cnv	5400	7200

1988 — WS Ret

CONQUEST — RWD/2.6L-I4 (176hp)

	WS	Ret
TSi 2dr Hbk	1425	2350

Add:
- Sunroof-pwr . . . 50

Deduct:
- No air cond . . . 100
- Manual trans . . . 50

FIFTH AVENUE — RWD/5.2L-V8 (140hp)

	WS	Ret
Sedan 4dr Sdn	950	1650

Add:
- Leather seats . . . 25
- Sunroof-pwr . . . 50

LEBARON — FWD/2.2L-I4 (97hp)

	WS	Ret
Base 4dr Sdn	575	1075
GTS Highline 4dr Hbk	600	1100
GTS Premium 4dr Hbk	625	1125
Highline 2dr Cnv	925	1625
Highline 2dr Cpe	575	1075
Premium 2dr Cnv	975	1675
Premium 2dr Cpe	625	1125
Town & Country 4dr Wgn	950	1650

Add:
- 2.2 Liter 4cyl Turbo . . . 25
- Lthr seats (std Mark Crss) . . . 25
- Mark Cross pkg . . . 25
- Sunroof-pwr . . . 50

Deduct:
- No air cond . . . 100
- Manual trans . . . 75

NEW YORKER — FWD/3.0L-V6 (136hp)

	WS	Ret
Base 4dr Sdn	900	1600
Landau 4dr Sdn	975	1675
Turbo 4dr Sdn	850	1525

Add:
- Lthr seats (std Mrk Crs) . . . 25
- Mark Cross pkg . . . 100
- Sunroof-pwr . . . 50

DAIHATSU

1992 — WS Ret

CHARADE (5sp) — FWD/1.3L-I4 (80hp)

	WS	Ret
SE 4dr Sdn	575	1075
SE 2dr Hbk	450	925
SX (Auto) 4dr Sdn	750	1275

Deduct:
- 3cyl . . . 25
- No air cond . . . 150

1991 — WS — Ret

CHARADE (5sp) FWD/1.3L-I4 (80hp)

	WS	Ret
SE 4dr Sdn	450	925
SE 2dr Hbk	350	800
SX (Auto) 4dr Sdn	600	1100
Deduct:		
No air cond	125	

1990 — WS — Ret

CHARADE (5sp) FWD/1.3L-I4 (80hp)

	WS	Ret
SE 4dr Sdn	300	750
SE 2dr Hbk	225	650
SX 4dr Sdn	400	850
SX 2dr Hbk	350	800
Deduct:		
3cyl	25	
No air cond	100	

1989 — WS — Ret

CHARADE (5sp) FWD/1.0L-I3 (153hp)

	WS	Ret
CES 2dr Hbk	150	575
CLS 2dr Hbk	200	625
CLX 2dr Hbk	75	475
Deduct:		
No air cond	75	

DAEWOO

2001 — WS — Ret

LANOS FWD/1.6L-I4 (105hp)

- S 4dr Sdn
- S 2dr Hbk
- Sport 2dr Hbk

LEGANZA FWD/2.2L-I4 (131hp)

- CDX 4dr Sdn
- SE 4dr Sdn
- SX 4dr Sdn

NUBIRA FWD/2.0L-I4 (129hp)

- CDX 4dr Sdn
- CDX 4dr Wgn
- SE 4dr Sdn

2000 — WS — Ret

LANOS FWD/1.6L-I4 (105hp)

	WS	Ret
S 4dr Sdn	5400	7075
S 2dr Hbk	5050	6750
SE 2dr Hbk	5500	7175
SX 4dr Sdn	6000	7800

LEGANZA FWD/2.2L-I4 (131hp)

	WS	Ret
CDX 4dr Sdn	8300	10150
SE 4dr Sdn	6850	8700
SX 4dr Sdn	7500	9350

NUBIRA FWD/2.0L-I4 (129hp)

	WS	Ret
CDX 4dr Sdn	6700	8500
CDX 4dr Wgn	7125	8975
SE 4dr Sdn	5425	7200

DODGE

2001 — WS — Ret

INTREPID FWD/2.7L-V6 (200hp)

- Base 4dr Sdn
- ES 4dr Sdn
- R/T (3.5L/242hp) 4dr Sdn

NEON FWD/2.0L-I4 (132hp)

- ES 4dr Sdn
- R/T (150hp/5sp) 4dr Sdn
- SE 4dr Sdn

STRATUS FWD/2.7L-V6 (200hp)

- ES 4dr Sdn
- R/T 2dr Cpe
- SE 4dr Sdn
- SE 2dr Cpe

VIPER RWD/8.0L-V10 (450hp)

- GTS 2dr Cpe
- RT/10 2dr Cnv

2000 — WS — Ret

AVENGER FWD/2.5L-V6 (163hp)

	WS	Ret
Base 2dr Cpe		
ES 2dr Cpe		
Add:		
ABS brakes	250	
CD player (std ES)	175	
Moonroof-pwr	375	
Infinity audio	150	
Leather seats (std ES)	325	
Deduct:		
2.0L-I4 (140hp)	450	
Manual trans	475	
No air cond	625	
No cassette	150	

INTREPID FWD/2.7L-V6 (200hp)

	WS	Ret
Base 4dr Sdn	10000	12000
ES 4dr Sdn	12025	14150
R/T (3.5L/242hp) 4dr Sdn		
Add:		
ABS brakes (std R/T)	350	
3.2L-V6 (225hp)	325	
CD changer	300	
CD player (std R/T)	175	
Premium sound (std R/T)	175	
Leather seats	325	
Pwr seat (std ES)	150	

NEON FWD/2.0L-I4 (132hp)

	WS	Ret
ES 4dr Sdn	7975	9850
Highline 4dr Sdn	7000	8825
Add:		
ABS brakes	275	
Alum wheels	175	
4-disc CD changer	275	
CD player	175	
Cruise ctrl	150	
Pwr windows (std ES)	150	
Pwr dr locks (std ES)	75	
Leather seats	200	
Sunroof-pwr	325	
Deduct:		
No air cond	550	
Manual trans	500	

STRATUS FWD/2.5L-I4 (168hp)

	WS	Ret
ES (2.5L-V6/168hp) 4dr Sdn	9650	11625
SE 4dr Sdn	8300	10200
Add:		
ABS brakes (std ES)	250	
CD player	175	
CD changer	275	
Leather seats (std ES)	325	
Pwr dr locks (std ES)	150	
Pwr seat	150	
Pwr windows (std ES)	175	
Sunroof-pwr	375	
Deduct:		
Manual trans	575	

VIPER RWD/8.0L-V10 (450hp)

- GTS 2dr Cpe
- RT/10 2dr Cnv

1999 — WS — Ret

AVENGER FWD/2.5L-V6 (163hp)

	WS	Ret
Base 2dr Cpe	9250	11175
ES 2dr Cpe	10800	12725
Add:		
2.5L-V6 (163hp)	350	
16" alum whls (Base)	175	
CD player	150	
Cruise ctrl (std ES)	100	
Infinity audio	100	
Leather seats	275	
Pwr dr locks	100	
Pwr seat	125	
Pwr windows	125	
Sunroof-pwr	325	
ABS brakes	225	
Deduct:		
2.0L-I4 (140hp)	375	
Manual trans	400	
No air cond	525	
No cassette	125	

INTREPID FWD/2.7L-V6 (200hp)

	WS	Ret
Base 4dr Sdn	8400	10300
ES (3.2L/225hp) 4dr Sdn	10275	12300
Add:		
ABS brakes (std ES)	275	
CD changer	250	
CD player	150	
Infinity spkrs	125	
Leather seats	275	
Pwr seat (std ES)	125	
16in wheels (std ES)	150	

NEON FWD/2.0L-I4 (132hp)

	WS	Ret
Competition (5sp) 4dr Sdn	5400	7100
Competition (5sp) 2dr Cpe	5400	7100
Highline 4dr Sdn	5625	7350
Highline 2dr Sdn	5550	7275
R/T (5sp) 4dr Sdn	5825	7575
R/T (5sp) 2dr Sdn	5800	7525
Add:		
ABS brakes	225	
Alum wheels (Highline)	150	
Cassette	125	
CD player	150	
Cruise ctrl	125	
Premium sound	50	
Pwr dr locks	50	
Leather seats	175	
Pwr windows	100	
Sunroof-pwr	275	
Tilt wheel	50	
Deduct:		
No air cond	450	
Manual trans	425	

STRATUS FWD/2.4L-I4 (150hp)

	WS	Ret
Base 4dr Sdn	7000	8825
ES (2.5L-V6/168hp) 4dr Sdn	8250	10150
Add:		
ABS brakes (std ES)	225	
CD player	150	
CD changer	225	
Leather seats	275	
Pwr dr locks (std ES)	100	
Pwr seat	125	
Pwr windows (std ES)	125	
Sunroof-pwr	325	
Deduct:		
Manual trans	475	

VIPER — RWD/8.0L-V10 (450hp)

Model	WS	Ret
GTS 2dr Cpe	51000	55800
RT/10 2dr Cnv	49700	54300

Add:
- Hardtop (Rds) . . . 1150
- Competition group . . . 3900

Deduct:
- No air cond . . . 1525

1998 — WS Ret

AVENGER — FWD/2.5L-V6 (163hp)

Model	WS	Ret
Base 2dr Cpe	8000	9875
ES 2dr Cpe	9600	11575

Add:
- 2.5L-V6 (163hp) . . . 300
- 16" alum whls (Base) . . . 150
- CD player . . . 125
- Cruise ctrl (std ES) . . . 75
- Infinity audio . . . 75
- Leather seats . . . 225
- Pwr dr locks . . . 75
- Pwr seat . . . 75
- Pwr windows . . . 100
- Sunroof-pwr . . . 250
- ABS brakes . . . 200

Deduct:
- 2.0L-I4 (140hp) . . . 300
- Manual trans . . . 325
- No air cond . . . 425
- No cassette . . . 75

INTREPID — FWD/2.7L-V6 (200hp)

Model	WS	Ret
Base 4dr Sdn	7350	9200
ES 4dr Sdn	8925	10850

Add:
- ABS brakes (std ES) . . . 250
- CD changer . . . 200
- CD player . . . 125
- Infinity spkrs . . . 100
- Leather seats . . . 225
- Pwr seat (std ES) . . . 75
- 16in wheels (std ES) . . . 100

NEON — FWD/2.0L-I4 (132hp)

Model	WS	Ret
Competition (5sp) 4dr Sdn	4475	6125
Competition (5sp) 2dr Cpe	4475	6125
Highline 4dr Sdn	4700	6350
Highline 2dr Cpe	4650	6300
R/T (5sp) 4dr Sdn	4950	6700
R/T (5sp) 2dr Cpe	4950	6700

Add:
- ABS brakes . . . 200
- Alum wheels (Highline) . . . 100
- Cassette . . . 75
- CD player . . . 125
- Cruise ctrl . . . 75
- Premium sound . . . 25
- Pwr dr locks . . . 50
- Leather seats . . . 150
- Pwr windows . . . 75
- Sunroof-pwr . . . 225
- Tilt wheel . . . 25

Deduct:
- No air cond . . . 375
- Manual trans . . . 350

STRATUS — FWD/2.4L-I4 (150hp)

Model	WS	Ret
Base 4dr Sdn	5350	7075
ES (2.5L-V6/168hp) 4dr Sdn	6450	8225

Add:
- 2.5L (6cyl-164hp) . . . 300
- ABS brakes (std ES) . . . 175
- CD player . . . 100
- CD changer . . . 200
- Leather seats . . . 225
- Pwr dr locks (std ES) . . . 75
- Pwr seat . . . 75
- Pwr windows (std ES) . . . 100
- Sunroof-pwr . . . 250

Deduct:
- Manual trans . . . 400

VIPER — RWD/8.0L-V10 (450hp)

Model	WS	Ret
GTS 2dr Cpe	43875	48425
RT/10 2dr Cnv	42500	46950

Add:
- Hardtop (Rds) . . . 950

Deduct:
- No air cond . . . 1275

1997 — WS Ret

AVENGER — FWD/2.0L-V6 (140hp)

Model	WS	Ret
Base 2dr Cpe	6700	8500
ES 2dr Cpe	8125	10000

Add:
- ABS brakes (std ES) . . . 175
- 16" alum whls (std ES) . . . 100
- CD player . . . 100
- Cruise ctrl (std ES) . . . 50
- Infinity audio . . . 50
- Leather seats . . . 175
- Pwr dr locks . . . 50
- Pwr seat . . . 50
- Pwr windows . . . 75
- Sunroof-pwr . . . 225

Deduct:
- Manual trans . . . 275
- No air cond . . . 350
- No cassette . . . 50

INTREPID — FWD/3.3L-V6 (161hp)

Model	WS	Ret
Base 4dr Sdn	5075	6775
ES 4dr Sdn	6525	8325

Add:
- ABS brakes (std ES) . . . 200
- 3.5L-V6/214hp (std ES) . . . 250
- CD player . . . 100
- Infinity audio . . . 175
- Leather seats . . . 175
- Pwr seat (std ES) . . . 50

NEON — FWD/2.0L-I4 (132hp)

Model	WS	Ret
Base 4dr Sdn	3200	4650
Base 2dr Cpe	3150	4600
Highline 4dr Sdn	3625	5100
Highline 2dr Cpe	3575	5050
Sport 4dr Sdn	4250	5875
Sport 2dr Cpe	4250	5875

Add:
- ABS brakes . . . 150
- Competition pkg . . . 50
- Alum wheels . . . 75
- Cassette . . . 50
- CD player . . . 100
- Cruise ctrl . . . 50
- Premium sound . . . 25
- Pwr dr locks . . . 25
- Leather seats . . . 100
- Pwr windows . . . 50
- Sunroof-pwr . . . 175
- Tilt wheel . . . 25

Deduct:
- No air cond . . . 325
- Manual trans . . . 275

STRATUS — FWD/2.4L-I4 (150hp)

Model	WS	Ret
Base 4dr Sdn	4250	5875
ES 4dr Sdn	5200	6900

Add:
- 2.5L (6cyl-164hp) . . . 250
- ABS brakes (std ES) . . . 150
- CD player . . . 75
- Premium sound . . . 25
- Leather seats . . . 175
- Pwr dr locks (std ES) . . . 50
- Pwr seat . . . 50
- Pwr windows (std ES) . . . 75
- Sunroof-pwr . . . 225

Deduct:
- Manual trans . . . 325

VIPER — RWD/8.0L-V10 (450hp)

Model	WS	Ret
GTS 2dr Cpe	41675	46050
Roadster 2dr Cnv	39125	43375

Add:
- Hardtop (Rds) . . . 800
- Blue Clearcoat (GTS) . . . 475

Deduct:
- No air cond . . . 1050

1996 — WS Ret

AVENGER — FWD/2.0L-I4 (140hp)

Model	WS	Ret
Base 2dr Cpe	4775	6425
ES (6cyl) 2dr Cpe	6050	7800

Add:
- ABS brakes (std ES) . . . 150
- Alloy wheels (Base) . . . 75
- CD player . . . 75
- Cruise ctrl (std ES) . . . 50
- Infinity audio . . . 25
- Leather seats . . . 150
- Pwr dr locks . . . 50
- Pwr seat . . . 25
- Pwr windows . . . 50
- Sunroof-pwr . . . 175

Deduct:
- Manual trans . . . 225
- No air cond . . . 300
- No cassette . . . 25

INTREPID — FWD/3.3L-V6 (161hp)

Model	WS	Ret
Base 4dr Sdn	4175	5800
ES 4dr Sdn	5425	7150

Add:
- ABS brakes (std ES) . . . 150
- 3.5L-V6/214hp (std ES) . . . 225
- CD player . . . 75
- Infinity audio . . . 150
- Leather seats . . . 150
- Pwr seat (std ES) . . . 25
- Special wheels (Base) . . . 50

Deduct:
- No air cond . . . 300

NEON — FWD/2.0L-I4 (132hp)

Model	WS	Ret
Base 4dr Sdn	2400	3775
Highline 4dr Sdn	2750	4150
Highline 2dr Cpe	2725	4125
Sport 4dr Sdn	3325	4800
Sport 2dr Cpe	3325	4800

Add:
- ABS brakes . . . 150
- Aluminum wheels . . . 50
- Competition pkg . . . 25
- Cassette . . . 25
- CD player . . . 75
- Cruise ctrl . . . 25
- Premium sound . . . 25
- Pwr dr locks (std Sport) . . . 25
- Leather seats . . . 75
- Pwr windows . . . 50
- Sunroof-pwr . . . 150
- Tilt wheel (std Sport) . . . 25

Deduct:
- No air cond . . . 250
- Manual trans . . . 225

STEALTH — FWD/3.0L-V6 (164hp)

Model	WS	Ret
Base 2dr Cpe	7450	9300
R/T 2dr Cpe	8800	10725
R/T Turbo (6sp-AWD) 2dr Cpe	12550	14700

Add:
- ABS brakes (std R/T Turbo) . . . 150
- CD player . . . 75
- Cruise ctrl (Base only) . . . 25
- Leather seats . . . 125

Premium sound		25
Pwr dr locks (std R/T Turbo)		25
Pwr windows (std R/T Turbo)		50
Chrome wheels		50
Sunroof-pwr		175
Deduct:		
No air cond		300
Manual trans		250

STRATUS — FWD/2.0L-I4(132hp)

Base 4dr Sdn	3250	4725
ES 4dr Sdn	4100	5725
Add:		
2.5L (6cyl-162hp)		200
ABS brakes (std ES)		150
Integrated child seat		25
CD player		50
Premium sound		25
Leather seats		150
Pwr dr locks (std ES)		50
Pwr seat		25
Pwr windows (std ES)		50
Sunroof-pwr		175
Deduct:		
Manual trans		275
2.0L (4cyl-132hp)		200

VIPER — RWD/8.0L-V10(415hp)

GTS 2dr Cpe	37900	42050
Roadster 2dr Cnv	36250	40275
Add:		
Hardtop		650
Deduct:		
No air cond		875

1995 — WS — Ret

AVENGER — FWD/2.0L-I4(140hp)

	WS	Ret
Base 2dr Cpe	3800	5400
ES (6cyl) 2dr Cpe	4725	6375
Add:		
ABS brakes (std ES)		125
CD player		50
Cruise ctrl (std ES)		25
Infinity audio		25
Leather seats		150
Pwr dr locks		25
Pwr seat		25
Pwr windows		50
Deduct:		
Manual trans		200
No air cond		275
No cassette		25

INTREPID — FWD/3.3L-V6(161hp)

	WS	Ret
Base 4dr Sdn	3150	4600
ES 4dr Sdn	4025	5650
Add:		
ABS brakes (std ES)		125
Cassette (std ES)		25
CD player		50
Cruise ctrl (std ES)		25
Infinity audio		125
Leather seats		150
Pwr dr locks		25
Pwr seat		25
Pwr windows		50
Special wheels (Base)		50
3.5L DOHC 6cyl		225
Integrated child seat		25
Deduct:		
No air cond		275

NEON — FWD/2.0L-I4(132hp)

	WS	Ret
Base 4dr Sdn	1825	2900
Highline 4dr Sdn	2150	3275
Highline 2dr Cpe	2100	3225
Sport 4dr Sdn	2625	4000
Sport 2dr Cpe	2625	4000
Add:		
ABS brakes (std Sport)		125
Alum wheels (std Sport0		50
Competition pkg		25
Cassette		25
CD player		50
Cruise ctrl		25
Premium sound		25
Pwr dr locks (std Sport)		25
Leather seats		75
Pwr windows		25
Sunroof-manual		50
Tilt wheel (std Sport)		25
Deduct:		
No air cond		225
Manual trans		200

SPIRIT — FWD/2.5L-I4(100hp)

	WS	Ret
Base 4dr Sdn	2150	3275
Add:		
3.0 Liter 6cyl		175
CD player		50
Pwr dr locks		25
Pwr seat		25
Pwr windows		50
Deduct:		
No air cond		275

STEALTH — FWD/3.0L-V6(164hp)

	WS	Ret
Base 2dr Cpe	5925	7675
R/T 2dr Cpe	7150	8975
R/T Turbo (6sp-AWD) Cpe	10475	12500
Add:		
ABS brakes (std R/T Turbo)		150
CD player		50
Cruise ctrl (Base only)		25
Leather seats		125
Premium sound		25
Pwr dr locks (std R/T Turbo)		25
Pwr windows (std R/T Turbo)		25
Chrome wheels		50
Sunroof-manual		50
Deduct:		
No air cond		275
Manual trans		225

STRATUS — FWD/2.0L-I4(132hp)

	WS	Ret
Base 4dr Sdn	2700	4100
ES (6cyl) 4dr Sdn	3550	5025
Add:		
ABS brakes (std ES)		125
Integrated child seat		25
CD player		50
Premium sound		25
Leather seats		150
Pwr dr locks (std ES)		25
Pwr seat		25
Pwr windows (std ES)		50
Deduct:		
Manual trans		250

VIPER — RWD/8.0L-V10(400hp)

	WS	Ret
Roadster 2dr Cnv	31150	34875
Deduct:		
No air cond		800

1994 — WS — Ret

COLT — FWD/1.5L-I4(92hp)

	WS	Ret
Base 4dr Sdn	1600	2650
Base (5sp) 2dr Cpe	1075	1975
ES 4dr Sdn	1925	3025
ES 2dr Cpe	1650	2700
Add:		
ABS brakes		125
Cassette		25
Cruise ctrl		25
Pwr dr locks		25
Pwr windows		25
Special wheels		25
Deduct:		
No air cond		225
Manual steering		25
Manual trans		200

INTREPID — FWD/3.3L-V6(161hp)

	WS	Ret
Base 4dr Sdn	2325	3675
ES 4dr Sdn	3025	4450
Add:		
ABS brakes		125
Cassette (std ES)		25
CD player		50
Cruise ctrl (std ES)		25
Infinity audio		125
Leather seats		125
Pwr dr locks		25
Pwr seat		25
Pwr windows		25
Special wheels (Base)		25
3.5L 24V 6cyl		200
Deduct:		
No air cond		250

SHADOW — FWD/2.2L-I4(93hp)

	WS	Ret
Base 4dr Hbk	1325	2250
Base 2dr Hbk	1250	2150
ES 4dr Hbk	1775	2850
ES 2dr Hbk	1725	2800
Add:		
2.5L 4cyl (Base Hbk)		75
3.0 Liter V6		175
ABS brakes		100
Cassette		25
CD player		50
Cruise ctrl		25
Pwr dr locks		25
Power seat		25
Pwr windows (std Cnv)		25
Special wheels		25
Sunroof-manual		25
Deduct:		
No air cond		225
Manual trans		200

SPIRIT — FWD/2.5L-I4(100hp)

	WS	Ret
Base 4dr Sdn	1550	2475
Add:		
3.0 Liter 6cyl		175
ABS brakes		125
Cassette		25
CD player		50
Cruise ctrl		25
Pwr dr locks		25
Pwr seat		25
Pwr windows		25
Deduct:		
No air cond		250
Manual trans		225

STEALTH — FWD/3.0L-V6(164hp)

	WS	Ret
Base 2dr Cpe	4450	6100
R/T 2dr Cpe	5475	7200
R/T Turbo (6sp-AWD) 2dr	8400	10300
Add:		
ABS brakes (std Turbo)		125
Cassette (Base)		25
CD player		50
Cruise ctrl (std Turbo)		25
Leather seats		100
Pwr dr locks (std Turbo)		25
Pwr windows (std Turbo)		25
Chrome wheels		25
Sunroof-manual		50
Deduct:		
No air cond		250
Manual trans		200

VIPER — RWD/8.0L-V10(400hp)

	WS	Ret
Roadster 2dr Cnv	27625	31275

Deduct:
No air cond 725

1993 WS Ret

COLT FWD/1.5L-I4 (92hp)

	WS	Ret
Base 4dr Sdn	1150	2050
Base (5sp) 2dr Hbk	875	1550
GL 4dr Sdn	1225	2125
GL 2dr Hbk	1100	2000

Add:
ABS brakes 100
Cassette 25
Cruise ctrl 25
Pwr dr locks 25
Pwr windows 25
Special wheels 25

Deduct:
No air cond 175
Manual steering 25
Manual trans 175

DAYTONA FWD/2.5L-I4 (100hp)

	WS	Ret
Base 2dr Hbk	1600	2650
ES 2dr Hbk	1850	2925
IROC R/T (Turbo) 2dr Hbk	2300	3650
IROC (6cyl) 2dr Hbk	2425	3800

Add:
3.0L 6cyl (std IROC) 150
ABS brakes 100
Cassette 25
CD player 50
Cruise ctrl 25
Leather seats 75
Premium sound 25
Pwr dr locks 25
Pwr seat 25
Pwr windows 25
Spcl whls (std ES,IROC) 25

Deduct:
No air cond 200
Manual trans 175

DYNASTY FWD/3.0L-V6 (141hp)

	WS	Ret
Base 4dr Sdn	1775	2850
LE 4dr Sdn	2075	3200

Add:
ABS brakes 100
Cassette 25
Cruise ctrl 25
Infinity audio 75
Leather seats 100
Pwr dr locks 25
Pwr seat 25
Pwr windows 25
Special wheels 25
Sunroof-pwr 150

Deduct:
2.5 Liter 4cyl 125
No air cond 225

INTREPID FWD/3.3L-V6 (153hp)

	WS	Ret
Base 4dr Sdn	1975	3075
ES 4dr Sdn	2600	3975

Add:
3.5L 24V 6cyl 150
ABS brakes 100
Cassette 25
CD player 50
Cruise ctrl 25
Infinity audio 100
Leather seats 100
Pwr dr locks 25
Pwr seat 25
Pwr windows 25
Special wheels (Base) 25

Deduct:
No air cond 225

SHADOW FWD/2.2L-I4 (93hp)

	WS	Ret
Base 4dr Hbk	1150	2050
Base 2dr Cnv	1875	2975
Base 2dr Hbk	1075	1975
ES 4dr Hbk	1475	2400
ES 2dr Cnv	2275	3425
ES 2dr Hbk	1450	2375

Add:
2.5L 4cyl (Base Hbk) 75
3.0 Liter V6 150
ABS brakes 100
Cassette 25
CD player 50
Cruise ctrl 25
Pwr dr locks 25
Power seat 25
Pwr windows (std Cnv) 25
Special wheels 25
Sunroof-manual 25

Deduct:
No air cond 175
Manual trans 175

SPIRIT FWD/2.5L-I4 (100hp)

	WS	Ret
Base 4dr Sdn	1250	2150
ES 4dr Sdn	1550	2475

Add:
3.0 Liter 6cyl 150
ABS brakes 100
Cassette 25
CD player 50
Cruise ctrl (std ES) 25
Pwr dr locks 25
Pwr seat 25
Pwr windows 25

Deduct:
No air cond 225
Manual trans 200

STEALTH FWD/3.0L-V6 (164hp)

	WS	Ret
Base 2dr Cpe	3750	5350
ES 2dr Cpe	4050	5675
R/T 2dr Cpe	4625	6275
R/T Turbo (AWD) 2dr Cpe	6875	8675

Add:
ABS brakes (std R/T) 125
Cassette (std R/T) 25
CD player 50
Cruise ctrl (std R/T) 25
Leather seats 75
Pwr dr locks (std R/T) 25
Pwr windows (std R/T) 25
Spcl wheels (Base only) 25
Sunroof-manual 50

Deduct:
No air cond 200
Manual trans 175

VIPER RWD/8.0L-V10 (400hp)

	WS	Ret
Roadster 2dr Cnv	26200	29750

1992 WS Ret

COLT FWD/1.5L-I4 (92hp)

	WS	Ret
Base 2dr Hbk	725	1250
GL 2dr Hbk	925	1625

Add:

Deduct:
No air cond 175
Manual trans 150

DAYTONA FWD/2.5L-I4 (100hp)

	WS	Ret
Base 2dr Hbk	1350	2275
ES 2dr Hbk	1550	2475
IROC R/T (Turbo) 2dr Hbk	1925	3025
IROC (6cyl) 2dr Hbk	1925	3025

Add:
3.0L 6cyl (Base,ES) 125
ABS brakes (std R/T) 75
Cassette 25
CD player 25
Cruise ctrl 25
Leather seats 50
Pwr dr locks 25
Pwr windows 25
Special whls (std ES,IROC) . . . 25

Deduct:
No air cond 175
Manual trans 150

DYNASTY FWD/3.0L-V6 (141hp)

	WS	Ret
Base 4dr Sdn	1525	2450
LE 4dr Sdn	1775	2850

Add:
ABS brakes 75
Cassette 25
Cruise ctrl 25
Infinity audio 50
Leather seats 75
Pwr dr locks 25
Pwr seat 25
Pwr windows 25
Special wheels 25
Sunroof-pwr 150

Deduct:
2.5 Liter 4cyl 100
No air cond 200

MONACO FWD/3.0L-V6 (150hp)

	WS	Ret
ES 4dr Sdn	1175	2075
LE 4dr Sdn	975	1675

Add:
ABS brakes 75
Cassette (std ES) 25
Cruise ctrl 25
Jensen audio 25
Leather seats 75
Pwr dr locks 25
Pwr seat 25
Pwr windows 25
Special wheels 25

Deduct:
No air cond 200

SHADOW FWD/2.2L-I4 (93hp)

	WS	Ret
America 4dr Hbk	750	1275
America 2dr Hbk	700	1225
ES 4dr Hbk	1175	2075
ES 2dr Cnv	1800	2875
ES 2dr Hbk	1125	2025
Highline 4dr Hbk	975	1675
Highline 2dr Cnv	1575	2625
Highline 2dr Hbk	925	1625

Add:
2.5 Liter 4cyl (std ES) 50
2.5 Liter 4cyl turbo 100
3.0 Liter V6 125
Cassette 25
Cruise ctrl 25
Pwr windows (std Cnv) 25
Special wheels (std ES) 25
Sunroof-manual 25
Sunroof-pwr 75

Deduct:
No air cond 175
Manual trans 150

SPIRIT FWD/2.5L-I4 (100hp)

	WS	Ret
Base 4dr Sdn	1125	2025
ES 4dr Sdn	1450	2375
LE 4dr Sdn	1300	2200
R/T (5sp-Turbo) 4dr Sdn	1775	2850

Add:
2.5L 4cyl turbo (std ES) 100
3.0 Liter 6cyl (Base,LE) 125
ABS brakes 75
Cassette (std ES,R/T) 25
CD player 25

Cruise ctrl (Base only)	25
Leather seats	75
Pwr dr locks	25
Pwr seat	25
Pwr windows	25
Spcl wheels (std ES,R/T)	25
Deduct:	
No air cond	200
Man trans (not R/T)	200

STEALTH
FWD/3.0L-V6 (164hp)

	WS	Ret
Base 2dr Cpe	3400	4875
ES 2dr Cpe	3675	5175
R/T Turbo (AWD) 2dr Cpe.	5525	7250
R/T 2dr Cpe	4275	5900
Add:		
ABS brakes (std R/T)	75	
Cassette (std R/T)	25	
CD player	25	
Cruise ctrl (std R/T)	25	
Leather seats	50	
Pwr dr locks (std R/T)	25	
Pwr windows (std R/T)	25	
Spcl wheels (Base only)	25	
Sunroof-manual	25	
Deduct:		
No air cond	200	
Manual trans	175	

VIPER
RWD/8.0L-V10 (400hp)

	WS	Ret
Roadster 2dr Cnv	38750	42975

1991 — WS — Ret

COLT
FWD/1.5L-I4 (92hp)

	WS	Ret
Base 2dr Hbk	575	1075
GL 2dr Hbk	750	1275
Vista 4dr Wgn	1175	2075
Add:		
4-wheel drive	175	
Pwr windows	25	
Deduct:		
No air cond	150	
Man trans (not 4WD)	125	

DAYTONA
FWD/2.5L-I4 (100hp)

	WS	Ret
Base 2dr Hbk	1150	2050
ES 2dr Hbk	1275	2175
IROC (6cyl) 2dr Hbk	1625	2675
Shelby 2dr Hbk	3625	5375
Add:		
2.5L turbo (std Shelby)	50	
3.0 Liter V6 (std IROC)	100	
Cassette	25	
CD player	25	
Leather seats	25	
Pwr windows	25	
Special whls (std IROC)	25	
Sunroof-manual	25	
Deduct:		
No air cond	175	
Manual trans	150	

DYNASTY
FWD/3.0L-V6 (141hp)

	WS	Ret
Base 4dr Sdn	1275	2175
LE 4dr Sdn	1500	2425
Add:		
ABS brakes	50	
Cassette	25	
Cruise ctrl	25	
Infinity audio	50	
Integrated phone	25	
Leather seats	50	
Pwr dr locks	25	
Pwr windows	25	
Special wheels	25	
Sunroof-pwr	100	
Deduct:		
2.5 Liter 4cyl	100	
No air cond	175	

MONACO
FWD/3.0L-V6 (150hp)

	WS	Ret
ES 4dr Sdn	975	1675
LE 4dr Sdn	800	1475
Add:		
ABS brakes	50	
Cassette (std ES)	25	
CD player	25	
Cruise ctrl	25	
Leather seats	50	
Pwr dr locks	25	
Pwr windows	25	
Special wheels (std ES)	25	
Sunroof-pwr	100	
Deduct:		
No air cond	175	

SHADOW
FWD/2.2L-I4 (93hp)

	WS	Ret
America 4dr Hbk	600	1100
America 2dr Hbk	550	1050
ES 4dr Hbk	975	1675
ES 2dr Cnv	1550	2475
ES 2dr Hbk	925	1625
Highline 4dr Hbk	800	1475
Highline 2dr Cnv	1300	2200
Highline 2dr Hbk	775	1300
Add:		
2.5 Liter 4cyl Turbo	50	
Pwr windows (std Cnv)	25	
Special wheels (std ES)	25	
Sunroof-manual	25	
Deduct:		
No air cond	150	
Manual trans	125	

SPIRIT
FWD/2.5L-I4 (100hp)

	WS	Ret
Base 4dr Sdn	925	1625
ES (Turbo) 4dr Sdn	1200	2100
LE 4dr Sdn	1125	2025
R/T (5sp-Turbo) 4dr Sdn	1625	2675
Add:		
2.5L 4cyl Turbo (std ES)	50	
3.0 Liter V6 (Base,LE)	100	
ABS brakes	50	
Cassette (std ES,R/T)	25	
Cruise ctrl (Base only)	25	
Pwr dr locks	25	
Pwr windows	25	
Special wheels (std R/T)	25	
Sunroof-manual	25	
Deduct:		
No air cond	175	
Man trans (not R/T)	175	

STEALTH
FWD/3.0L-V6 (164hp)

	WS	Ret
Base 2dr Cpe	2800	4200
ES 2dr Cpe	3025	4450
R/T 2dr Cpe	3550	5025
R/T Turbo (AWD) 2dr Cpe	4575	6225
Add:		
ABS brakes (std R/T)	50	
Cassette (std R/T)	25	
CD player	25	
Integrated phone	25	
Leather seats	25	
Pwr windows (std R/T)	25	
Spcl wheels (Base only)	25	
Deduct:		
No air cond	175	
Manual trans	125	

1990 — WS — Ret

COLT
FWD/1.5L-I4 (75hp)

	WS	Ret
Base (4sp) 2dr Hbk	500	975
DL 4dr Wgn	775	1300
GL 2dr Hbk	600	1100
GT 2dr Hbk	750	1275
Vista 4dr Wgn	975	1675
Add:		
4-wheel drive	150	
GT pkg	125	
Deduct:		
No air cond	125	
Man trans (not Base,4WD)	125	

DAYTONA
FWD/2.5L-I4 (100hp)

	WS	Ret
Base 2dr Hbk	925	1625
ES 2dr Hbk	1075	1975
ES Turbo 2dr Hbk	1175	2075
Shelby Turbo 2dr Hbk	1250	2150
Add:		
Leather seats	25	
Spcl wheels (Base only)	25	
Sunroof-manual	25	
T-tops	150	
Deduct:		
No air cond	150	
Manual trans	125	

DYNASTY
FWD/3.3L-V6 (141hp)

	WS	Ret
Base 4dr Sdn	1100	2000
LE 4dr Sdn	1275	2175
Add:		
ABS brakes	25	
Infinity audio	50	
Pwr windows	25	
Special wheels	25	
Sunroof-pwr	75	
Deduct:		
2.5 Liter 4cyl	75	
No air cond	150	

OMNI
FWD/2.2L-I4 (93hp)

	WS	Ret
Hatchback 4dr Hbk	500	975
Add:		
Deduct:		
No air cond	125	
Manual trans	125	

SHADOW
FWD/2.2L-I4 (93hp)

	WS	Ret
Hatchback 4dr Hbk	500	975
Hatchback 2dr Hbk	475	950
Add:		
2.5 Liter 4cyl Turbo	50	
ES trim	75	
Infinity sound	25	
Sunroof-manual	25	
Deduct:		
No air cond	125	
Manual trans	125	

SPIRIT
FWD/2.5L-I4 (100hp)

	WS	Ret
Base 4dr Sdn	775	1300
ES (Turbo) 4dr Sdn	1050	1950
LE 4dr Sdn	950	1650
Add:		
2.5L 4cyl Turbo (std ES)	50	
3.0 Liter V6 (Base,LE)	75	
Pwr windows	25	
Special wheels (std ES)	25	
Sunroof-manual	25	
Deduct:		
No air cond	150	
Manual trans	150	

1989 — WS — Ret

ARIES
FWD/2.2L-I4 (93hp)

	WS	Ret
America 4dr Sdn	600	1100
America 2dr Cpe	575	1075
Add:		
Deduct:		
No air cond	100	
Manual trans	100	

COLT FWD/1.5L-I4 (81hp)

Base (4sp) 2dr Hbk	350	800
DL 4dr Wgn	525	1000
E (5sp) 2dr Hbk	425	900
GT 2dr Hbk	525	1000
Vista 4dr Wgn	825	1500
Add:		
4-wheel drive	100	
Turbo pkg (5spd)	50	
Deduct:		
No air cond	75	
Man trans (not Base,4WD)	75	

DAYTONA FWD/2.5L-I4 (96hp)

Base 2dr Hbk	625	1125
ES 2dr Hbk	675	1200
ES Turbo 2dr Hbk	725	1250
Shelby Turbo 2dr Hbk	825	1500
Add:		
2.2L Turbo II	150	
Leather seats	25	
Sunroof-manual	25	
T-tops	100	
Cass. (Base,ES)	25	
Deduct:		
No air cond	100	

DIPLOMAT RWD/5.2L-V8 (140hp)

Salon 4dr Sdn	500	975
SE 4dr Sdn	600	1100
Add:		
Sunroof-pwr	50	
Deduct:		
No air cond	125	

DYNASTY FWD/3.0L-V6 (141hp)

Base 4dr Sdn	750	1275
LE 4dr Sdn	800	1475
Add:		
Infinity audio	25	
Sunroof-pwr	50	
Deduct:		
2.5 Liter 4cyl	75	
No air cond	125	

LANCER FWD/2.2L-I4 (93hp)

Base 4dr Hbk	625	1125
ES Turbo 4dr Sdn	725	1250
Shelby 4dr Sdn	1	1
Add:		
2.5L 4cyl Turbo (Base)	50	
Leather seats	25	
Sunroof-pwr	50	
Deduct:		
No air cond	125	
Manual trans	125	

OMNI AMERICA FWD/2.2L-I4 (93hp)

Hatchback 4dr Hbk	400	850
Add:		
Deduct:		
No air cond	75	
Manual trans	75	

SHADOW FWD/2.2L-I4 (93hp)

Hatchback 4dr Hbk	425	900
Hatchback 2dr Hbk	400	850
Add:		
2.5 Liter 4cyl Turbo	50	
ES trim	50	
Deduct:		
No air cond	75	
Manual trans	75	

SPIRIT FWD/2.5L-I4 (100hp)

Base 4dr Sdn	700	1225
ES (Turbo) 4dr Sdn	825	1500
LE 4dr Sdn	750	1275
Add:		
2.5 Liter 4cyl Turbo	50	
Deduct:		
No air cond	125	
Manual trans	125	

1988 — WS Ret

600 FWD/2.2L-I4 (97hp)

Base 4dr Sdn	425	900
SE 4dr Sdn	450	925
Add:		
2.2 Liter 4cyl Turbo	25	
Deduct:		
No air cond	100	

ARIES FWD/2.2L-I4 (97hp)

America 4dr Sdn	475	950
America 4dr Wgn	500	975
America 2dr Cpe	475	950
Add:		
Deduct:		
No air cond	75	
Manual trans	75	

COLT FWD/1.5L-I4 (68hp)

Base (4sp) 2dr Hbk	275	725
DL 4dr Sdn	375	825
DL 4dr Wgn	375	825
DL 2dr Hbk	350	800
E 4dr Sdn	325	775
E (5sp) 2dr Hbk	300	750
Premier 4dr Sdn	425	900
Vista 4dr Wgn	725	1250
Add:		
4cyl turbo	25	
4-wheel drive	50	
Deduct:		
No air cond	50	
Man trns (not Bse,E Hb,4WD)	50	

DAYTONA FWD/2.5L-I4 (100hp)

Base 2dr Hbk	450	925
Pacifica 2dr Hbk	600	1100
Shelby Z 2dr Hbk	600	1100
Add:		
2.2L Turbo (Base only)	25	
T-tops	75	
Deduct:		
No air cond	100	
Manual trans	50	

DIPLOMAT RWD/5.2L-V8 (140hp)

Base 4dr Sdn	425	900
Salon 4dr Sdn	400	850
SE 4dr Sdn	425	900
Add:		
Sunroof-pwr	50	
Deduct:		
No air cond	100	

DYNASTY FWD/3.0L-V6 (136hp)

Base 4dr Sdn	625	1125
Premium 4dr Sdn	675	1200
Add:		
Leather seats	25	
Sunroof-pwr	50	
Deduct:		
4cyl	50	
No air cond	100	

LANCER FWD/2.2L-I4 (97hp)

Base 4dr Hbk	475	950
ES 4dr Hbk	500	975
Shelby 4dr Hbk	1575	2625
Add:		
2.2L 4cyl Turbo(Base,ES)	25	
Leather seats	25	
Sunroof-pwr	50	
Deduct:		
No air cond	100	
Manual trans	75	

OMNI AMERICA FWD/2.2L-I4 (97hp)

America 4dr Hbk	350	800
Add:		
Deduct:		
No air cond	50	
Manual trans	50	

SHADOW FWD/2.2L-I4 (97hp)

Hatchback 4dr Hbk	350	800
Hatchback 2dr Hbk	350	800
Add:		
2.2 Liter Turbo	25	
ES trim	50	
Deduct:		
No air cond	50	
Manual trans	50	

EAGLE

1998 — WS Ret

TALON FWD/2.0L-I4 (210hp)

Base 2dr Hbk	8475	10375
ESi 2dr Hbk	9175	11125
TSi Turbo AWD 2dr Hbk	12325	14450
TSi Turbo 2dr Hbk	10825	12875
Add:		
ABS brakes	200	
CD player	125	
Cruise ctrl (std AWD)	75	
Leather seats	175	
Pwr dr locks (std AWD)	75	
Pwr windows (std AWD)	75	
Pwr seat	50	
Sunroof-pwr	250	
16in alum wheels (ESi)	100	
Deduct:		
No air cond	425	
No cassette	75	
Manual trans	325	

1997 — WS Ret

TALON FWD/2.0L-I4 (205hp)

Base 2dr Hbk	6400	8175
ESi 2dr Hbk	7675	9525
TSi Turbo AWD 2dr Hbk	10550	12575
TSi Turbo 2dr Hbk	9125	11075
Add:		
ABS brakes	150	
CD player	100	
Cruise ctrl (std AWD)	50	
Leather seats	150	
Pwr dr locks (std AWD)	50	
Pwr windows (std AWD)	50	
Pwr seat	25	
Sunroof-pwr	200	
Deduct:		
No air cond	350	
No cassette	50	
Manual trans	275	

VISION FWD/3.5L-V6 (214hp)

ESi 4dr Sdn	5250	6975
TSi 4dr Sdn	6675	8475
Add:		
ABS brakes (std TSi)	175	
Infinity audio	175	
CD player	100	
Leather seats	175	

Sunroof-pwr 225
Pwr seat (std TSi) 50

1996 — WS Ret

SUMMIT — AWD/1.8L-I4 (113hp)

Model	WS	Ret
AWD 4dr Wgn	4025	5650
DL 4dr Wgn	3225	4675
DL 2dr Sdn	1850	2925
ESi 4dr Sdn	2725	4125
ESi 2dr Sdn	1900	3000
LX 4dr Sdn	2475	3850
LX 4dr Wgn	3675	5175

Add:
ABS brakes . . . 125
Cassette . . . 25
Cruise ctrl . . . 25
Luggage rack (Wgn) . . . 25
Pwr dr locks (std LX Wgn) . . . 25
Pwr windows . . . 50
Wheel upgrade . . . 50
Tilt wheel (std Wgn) . . . 25

Deduct:
No air cond . . . 250
Manual steering . . . 25
Manual trans . . . 225

TALON — FWD/2.0L-I4 (140hp)

Model	WS	Ret
Base 2dr Hbk	5400	7125
ESi 2dr Hbk	6050	7800
TSi Turbo AWD 2dr Hbk	8575	10475
TSi Turbo 2dr Hbk	7350	9200

Add:
ABS brakes . . . 150
CD player . . . 75
Cruise ctrl (std AWD) . . . 25
Leather seats . . . 125
Pwr dr locks (std AWD) . . . 25
Pwr windows (std AWD) . . . 50
Pwr seat . . . 25
Sunroof-pwr . . . 175

Deduct:
No air cond . . . 275
No cassette . . . 25
Manual trans . . . 225

VISION — FWD/3.3L-V6 (161hp)

Model	WS	Ret
ESi 4dr Sdn	4225	5850
TSi 4dr Sdn	5550	7275

Add:
ABS brakes (std TSi) . . . 150
Infinity audio . . . 150
CD player . . . 75
Integrated child seat . . . 25
Leather seats . . . 150
Sunroof-pwr . . . 175
Pwr seat (std TSi) . . . 25

1995 — WS Ret

SUMMIT — AWD/1.5L-I4 (92hp)

Model	WS	Ret
AWD 4dr Wgn	3575	5050
DL 4dr Wgn	2650	4050
DL 2dr Sdn	1625	2675
ESi 4dr Sdn	2475	3850
LX 4dr Sdn	2275	3425
LX 4dr Wgn	3250	4725

Add:
ABS brakes . . . 100
Cassette . . . 25
Cruise ctrl . . . 25
Luggage rack (Wgn) . . . 25
Pwr dr locks (std LX Wgn) . . . 25
Pwr windows . . . 25
Special wheels . . . 25

Deduct:
No air cond . . . 225
Manual steering . . . 25
Manual trans . . . 200

TALON — FWD/2.0L-I4 (140hp)

Model	WS	Ret
ESi 2dr Hbk	4200	5825
TSi Turbo AWD 2dr Hbk	6425	8200
TSi Turbo 2dr Hbk	5575	7300

Add:
ABS brakes . . . 125
CD player . . . 50
Cruise ctrl (std AWD) . . . 25
Leather seats . . . 100
Pwr dr locks (std AWD) . . . 25
Pwr windows . . . 25
Sunroof-pwr . . . 150

Deduct:
No air cond . . . 250
Manual steering . . . 25
Manual trans . . . 200

VISION — FWD/3.3L-V6 (161hp)

Model	WS	Ret
ESi 4dr Sdn	3150	4600
TSi 4dr Sdn	4150	5775

Add:
ABS brakes (std TSi) . . . 150
Infinity audio . . . 125
CD player . . . 50
Integrated child seat . . . 25
Leather seats . . . 125
Moonroof-pwr . . . 175
Pwr seat (std TSi) . . . 25
Special wheels (std TSi) . . . 50

1994 — WS Ret

SUMMIT — FWD/1.5L-I4 (92hp)

Model	WS	Ret
(AWD) 4dr Wgn	2650	4050
DL 4dr Sdn	1425	2350
DL 4dr Wgn	1950	3050
DL 2dr Sdn	750	1275
ES 4dr Sdn	1875	2975
ES 2dr Sdn	1450	2375
ESi 4dr Sdn	1975	3075
ESi 4dr Wgn	2450	3825
LX 4dr Sdn	1600	2650
LX 4dr Wgn	2350	3700

Add:
ABS brakes . . . 75
Cassette . . . 25
Cruise ctrl . . . 25
Pwr dr locks (std LX Wgn) . . . 25
Pwr windows . . . 25
Special wheels . . . 25

Deduct:
No air cond . . . 225
Manual steering . . . 25
Manual trans . . . 200

TALON — FWD/1.8L-I4 (92hp)

Model	WS	Ret
DL 2dr Hbk	2150	3275
ES 2dr Hbk	2575	3950
TSi Turbo AWD 2dr Hbk	4175	5800
TSi Turbo 2dr Hbk	3475	4950

Add:
ABS brakes . . . 125
Cassette (DL only) . . . 25
CD player . . . 50
Cruise ctrl . . . 25
Leather seats . . . 75
Pwr dr locks . . . 25
Pwr windows . . . 25
Spcl wheels (std TSi 4WD) . . . 25
Sunroof-man . . . 75

Deduct:
No air cond . . . 225
Manual steering . . . 25
Manual trans . . . 200

VISION — FWD/3.3L-V6 (161hp)

Model	WS	Ret
ESi 4dr Sdn	2350	3700
TSi 4dr Sdn	3125	4575

Add:
ABS brakes (std TSi) . . . 125
CD player . . . 50
Leather seats . . . 125
Pwr seat (std TSi) . . . 25
Special wheels (std TSi) . . . 25

1993 — WS Ret

SUMMIT — AWD/1.5L-I4 (92hp)

Model	WS	Ret
AWD 4dr Wgn	2275	3425
DL 4dr Sdn	1175	2075
DL 4dr Wgn	1725	2800
DL 2dr Sdn	600	1100
ES 4dr Sdn	1350	2275
ES 2dr Sdn	950	1650
LX 4dr Wgn	2075	3200

Add:
ABS brakes . . . 75
Cassette . . . 25
Cruise ctrl . . . 25
Pwr dr locks . . . 25
Pwr windows . . . 25
Special wheels . . . 25

Deduct:
No air cond . . . 175
Manual steering . . . 25
Manual trans . . . 175

TALON — FWD/1.8L-I4 (92hp)

Model	WS	Ret
DL 2dr Hbk	1825	2900
ES 2dr Hbk	2200	3325
TSi Turbo AWD 2dr Hbk	3675	5175
TSi Turbo 2dr Hbk	2950	4375

Add:
ABS brakes . . . 100
Cassette (DL only) . . . 25
CD player . . . 50
Cruise ctrl . . . 25
Leather seats . . . 75
Pwr dr locks . . . 25
Pwr windows . . . 25
Spcl wheels (std TSi 4WD) . . . 25
Sunroof-man . . . 50

Deduct:
No air cond . . . 200
Manual steering . . . 25
Manual trans . . . 175

VISION — FWD/3.3L-V6 (153hp)

Model	WS	Ret
ESi 4dr Sdn	2000	3100
TSi 4dr Sdn	2675	4075

Add:
ABS brakes (std TSi) . . . 100
Cassette (std TSi) . . . 25
CD player . . . 50
Cruise ctrl (std TSi) . . . 25
Leather seats . . . 100
Pwr dr locks (std TSi) . . . 25
Pwr seat . . . 25
Pwr windows . . . 25
Special wheels (std TSi) . . . 25

1992 — WS Ret

PREMIER — FWD/3.0L-V6 (150hp)

Model	WS	Ret
ES 4dr Sdn	1400	2325
ES Limited 4dr Sdn	1625	2675
LX 4dr Sdn	900	1600

Add:
ABS brakes . . . 75
Cassette (LX only) . . . 25
CD player . . . 25
Cruise ctrl (LX only) . . . 25
Leather seats . . . 75
Pwr dr locks (LX only) . . . 25
Pwr seat . . . 25
Pwr windows (std Ltd) . . . 25
Special wheels (std Ltd) . . . 25

SUMMIT AWD/1.5L-I4 (92hp)

Model	WS	Ret
AWD 4dr Wgn	1925	3025
Base 4dr Sdn	750	1275
Base 2dr Hbk	650	1150
DL 4dr Wgn	1525	2450
ES 4dr Sdn	875	1550
ES 2dr Hbk	650	1150
LX 4dr Wgn	1775	2850

Add:
- ABS brakes . . . 50
- Cruise ctrl . . . 25
- Pwr dr locks . . . 25
- Pwr windows . . . 25
- Special wheels . . . 25

Deduct:
- No air cond . . . 175
- Manual trans . . . 150

TALON FWD/2.0L-I4 (135hp)

Model	WS	Ret
Base 2dr Hbk	1600	2650
TSi Turbo AWD 2dr Hbk	2625	4000
TSi Turbo 2dr Hbk	2350	3700

Add:
- ABS brakes . . . 75
- Cassette . . . 25
- CD player . . . 25
- Cruise ctrl . . . 25
- Leather seats . . . 50
- Pwr dr locks . . . 25
- Pwr windows . . . 25
- Spcl wheels(std TSi 4WD) . . . 25
- Sunroof-man . . . 50

Deduct:
- No air cond . . . 175
- Manual trans . . . 150

1991 WS Ret

PREMIER FWD/3.0L-V6 (150hp)

Model	WS	Ret
ES 4dr Sdn	1150	2050
ES Limited 4dr Sdn	1325	2250
LX 4dr Sdn	700	1225

Add:
- ABS brakes . . . 50
- Cassette (std LX only) . . . 25
- Cruise ctrl (LX only) . . . 25
- Leather seats (std Ltd) . . . 50
- Pwr dr locks (LX only) . . . 25
- Pwr windows (std Ltd) . . . 25
- Special wheels (std Ltd) . . . 25

SUMMIT FWD/1.5L-I4 (92hp)

Model	WS	Ret
Base 4dr Sdn	550	1050
Base 2dr Hbk	525	1000
ES 4dr Sdn	700	1225
ES 2dr Hbk	575	1075

Add:
- Pwr windows . . . 25
- Special wheels . . . 25

Deduct:
- No air cond . . . 150
- Manual trans . . . 125

TALON FWD/2.0L-I4 (135hp)

Model	WS	Ret
Base 2dr Hbk	1350	2275
TSi Turbo AWD 2dr Hbk	2225	3350
TSi Turbo 2dr Hbk	1975	3075

Add:
- ABS brakes . . . 50
- Cassette . . . 25
- CD player . . . 25
- Leather seats . . . 25
- Pwr windows . . . 25
- Special wheels (std AWD) . . . 25
- Sunroof-manual . . . 25

Deduct:
- No air cond . . . 175
- Manual trans . . . 125

1990 WS Ret

PREMIER FWD/3.0L-V6 (150hp)

Model	WS	Ret
ES 4dr Sdn	875	1550
ES Limited 4dr Sdn	1100	2000
LX 4dr Sdn	525	1000

Add:
- CD player . . . 25
- Leather seats (std Ltd) . . . 25
- Pwr windows (std Ltd) . . . 25
- Special wheels (std Ltd) . . . 25
- Sunroof-pwr . . . 75

Deduct:
- No air cond . . . 150

SUMMIT FWD/1.5L-I4 (81hp)

Model	WS	Ret
Base 4dr Sdn	375	825
DL 4dr Sdn	475	950
ES 4dr Sdn	625	1125
LX 4dr Sdn	550	1050

Add:

Deduct:
- No air cond . . . 125
- Manual trans . . . 125

TALON FWD/2.0L-I4 (135hp)

Model	WS	Ret
Base 2dr Hbk	1200	2100
TSi Turbo AWD 2dr Hbk	1650	2700
TSi Turbo 2dr Hbk	1550	2475

Add:
- ABS brakes . . . 25
- Leather seats . . . 25
- Sunroof-manual . . . 25

Deduct:
- No air cond . . . 150
- Manual trans (Base only) . . . 125

1989 WS Ret

MEDALLION FWD/2.2L-I4 (103hp)

Model	WS	Ret
DL 4dr Sdn	200	625
DL 4dr Wgn	250	675
LX 4dr Sdn	250	675
LX 4dr Wgn	325	775

Add:
- Sunroof-pwr . . . 25

Deduct:
- No air cond . . . 100
- Manual trans . . . 100

PREMIER FWD/3.0L-V6 (150hp)

Model	WS	Ret
ES 4dr Sdn	700	1225
ES Limited 4dr Sdn	850	1525
LX 4dr Sdn	450	925

Add:
- Sunroof-pwr . . . 25

Deduct:
- No air cond . . . 100
- Manual trans . . . 100

SUMMIT FWD/1.5L-I4 (81hp)

Model	WS	Ret
DL 4dr Sdn	400	850
LX 4dr Sdn	425	900

Add:

Deduct:
- No air cond . . . 75
- Manual trans . . . 75

1988 WS Ret

EAGLE 4WD/4.2L-I6 (112hp)

Model	WS	Ret
4-wheel drive 4dr Wgn	775	1300

Add:

Deduct:
- No air cond . . . 75

MEDALLION FWD/2.2L-I4 (103hp)

Model	WS	Ret
DL 4dr Sdn	150	575
DL 4dr Wgn	175	600
LX 4dr Sdn	175	600

Add:

Deduct:
- No air cond . . . 75
- Manual trans . . . 75

PREMIER FWD/2.5L-V6 (111hp)

Model	WS	Ret
ES 4dr Sdn	475	950
LX 4dr Sdn	325	775

Add:
- Sunroof-pwr . . . 25

Deduct:
- 4cyl . . . 25
- No air cond . . . 100

FORD

2001 WS Ret

CROWN VICTORIA RWD/4.6L-V8 (220hp)

Model	WS	Ret
Base 4dr Sdn	14075	16325
LX 4dr Sdn	15575	17900

Add:
- 4.6L V8-235hp w/dual exh . . . 325
- Handling pkg w/16" alloys . . . 325
- Sport pkg w/bucket seats . . . 375
- CD player . . . 250
- CD changer (incls prem sound) 475
- Premium sound . . . 200
- Traction ctrl . . . 250
- Leather seats . . . 425
- Pwr seat (std LX) . . . 200

ESCORT FWD/2.0L-I4 (110hp)

Model	WS	Ret
Base 4dr Sdn	7275	9100
ZX2 (130hp) 2dr Cpe	7575	9425

Add:
- ABS brakes . . . 325
- Cruise ctrl . . . 200
- CD changer . . . 200
- Pwr dr locks . . . 200
- Pwr windows . . . 175
- Wheels-chrome . . . 175
- Sunroof-pwr . . . 425
- Tilt wheel . . . 100
- Leather seats . . . 325

Deduct:
- No air cond . . . 725
- Manual trans . . . 650

Focus FWD/2.0L-I4 (110hp)

Model	WS	Ret
LX 4dr Sdn	8500	10400
SE 4dr Sdn	9675	11650
SE 4dr Wgn	10250	12250
ZTS 4dr Sdn	10925	13100
ZX3 2dr Hbk	8600	10525

Add:
- 2.0L-I4 (130hp) (SE) . . . 350
- ABS brakes (std ZTS) . . . 300
- Cruise ctrl . . . 200
- Leather seats . . . 300
- Tilt wheel (std ZTS) . . . 150
- Pwr windows (std ZTS) . . . 200
- Pwr dr locks (std SE,ZTS) . . . 175
- Wheels-alloy (LX) . . . 225
- Sony Ltd Edition (SE) . . . 450

Deduct:
- No air cond . . . 800
- Manual trans . . . 650
- No CD . . . 175

MUSTANG RWD/3.8L-V6 (190hp)

Model	WS	Ret
Base (6cyl) 2dr Cnv		
Base (6cyl) 2dr Cpe		

	WS	Ret
Bullitt 2dr Cpe		
Cobra (5sp) 2dr Cnv		
Cobra (5sp) 2dr Cpe		
GT 2dr Cnv	17525	20375
GT 2dr Cpe	14375	16625

Add:

ABS brakes (Base)	300
Cruise ctrl (Base)	200
Leather seats (std Cobra,Bullitt)	300
Mach 460 w/CD chngr (std Cobra)	275
Pwr seat (std Cobra)	150
Traction ctrl (std Cobra)	250
Wheels-17in alloy (std Cobra)	275

Deduct:

Man trans (6cyl only)	675

TAURUS FWD/3.0L-V6 (155hp)

	WS	Ret
LX 4dr Sdn	9900	12000
SE 4dr Sdn	10850	13025
SE 4dr Wgn	12575	14875
SEL (200hp) 4dr Sdn	11975	14225
SES 4dr Sdn	10900	13075

Add:

3.0L-V6 (200hp)(std SEL)	450
ABS brakes (LX,SE sdn)	375
Alum wheels (LX)	200
Chrome wheels	250
Cassette (LX)	200
CD player (LX,SE)	200
Cruise ctrl (LX)	175
Mach audio	425
Leather seats	400
Pwr seat (LX,SE sdn)	200
Sunroof-pwr	550
Third seat (wgn)	175

Deduct:

No ABS brakes	300

2000 WS Ret

CONTOUR FWD/2.5L-V6 (170hp)

	WS	Ret
SE 4dr Sdn	7575	9425
SE Sport 4dr Sdn	8100	9975
SVT (200hp/5sp) 4dr Sdn	11175	13250

Add:

ABS brakes (std SVT)	225
CD player (std SVT)	175
Premium sound	75
Pwr seat (std SVT)	75
Moonroof-pwr (std SVT)	350
Lthr seats (std SVT)	300
Traction control	150

Deduct:

Manual trans (not SVT)	575
No air cond	650
2.0L-I4 (125hp)	325

CROWN VICTORIA RWD/4.6L-V8 (200hp)

	WS	Ret
Base 4dr Sdn	12000	14125
LX 4dr Sdn	13475	15675

Add:

4.6L V8-215hp w/dual exh	250
Handling pkg w/16" alloys	250
CD player	175
CD changer (incls prem sound)	375
Premium sound	150
Traction ctrl	200
Leather seats	325
Pwr seat (std LX)	150

ESCORT FWD/2.0L-I4 (110hp)

	WS	Ret
Base 4dr Sdn	6400	8175
ZX2 (130hp) 2dr Cpe	6675	8475

Add:

ABS brakes	250
Cruise ctrl	150
CD player	150
Pwr dr locks	150
Pwr windows	150
Wheels-chrome	150
Sunroof-pwr	325
Tilt wheel	75
Leather seats	250

Deduct:

No air cond	550
Manual trans	500
Manual steering	150

Focus FWD/2.0L-I4 (110hp)

	WS	Ret
LX 4dr Sdn	8025	9900
SE 4dr Sdn	9200	11150
SE 4dr Wgn	9750	11725
ZTS 4dr Sdn	10400	12550
ZX3 2dr Hbk	8100	9975

Add:

2.0L-I4 (130hp) (SE)	275
ABS brakes (std ZTS)	225
Cruise ctrl	150
Leather seats	250
Tilt wheel (std ZTS)	100
Pwr windows (std ZTS)	150
Pwr dr locks (std SE,ZTS)	125
Wheels-alloy (LX)	175
Sony Ltd Edition (SE)	350

MUSTANG RWD/3.8L-V6 (190hp)

	WS	Ret
Base (6cyl) 2dr Cnv	13375	15575
Base (6cyl) 2dr Cpe	11150	13225
Cobra (5sp) 2dr Cnv		
Cobra (5sp) 2dr Cpe		
GT 2dr Cnv	15825	18525
GT 2dr Cpe	13500	15700

Add:

ABS brakes (Base)	225
Cruise ctrl (std Cobra)	150
Leather seats (std Cobra)	250
Mach 460 sound (std Cobra)	225
Pwr seat (std Cobra)	75
Traction ctrl (std Cobra)	200
Wheels-17in alloy (std Cobra)	225

Deduct:

Man trans (6cyl only)	525

TAURUS FWD/3.0L-V6 (155hp)

	WS	Ret
LX 4dr Sdn	8950	10875
SE 4dr Sdn	9900	11900
SE 4dr Wgn	11600	13700
SEL (200hp) 4dr Sdn	10575	12600
SES 4dr Sdn	9900	11900

Add:

3.0L-V6 (200hp)(std SEL)	350
ABS brakes (std SEL)	275
Alum wheels (LX)	175
Chrome wheels	200
Cassette (LX)	150
CD changer	275
Cruise ctrl (LX)	150
Mach audio	325
Leather seats	300
Pwr seat (std SES,SEL)	150
Sunroof-pwr	425
Third seat (wgn)	150

Deduct:

ABS delete (SEL)	225

1999 WS Ret

CONTOUR FWD/2.0L-I4 (125hp)

	WS	Ret
LX 4dr Sdn	6225	8000
SE 4dr Sdn	6925	8750
SVT (200hp/5sp) 4dr Sdn	9300	11250

Add:

2.5L 170hp V6	375
CD player	150
ABS brakes (std SVT)	200
Cassette (LX)	125
Cruise ctrl (LX)	125
Premium sound	50
Pwr dr locks (LX)	125
Pwr seat (std SVT)	50
Pwr windows (LX)	125
Sunroof-pwr (std SVT)	300
Leather seats (std SVT)	250
Wheels-alloy (std SVT)	125
Traction control	125

Deduct:

Manual trans (not SVT)	475
No air cond	550

CROWN VICTORIA RWD/4.6L-V8 (200hp)

	WS	Ret
Base 4dr Sdn	10225	12225
LX 4dr Sdn	11550	13650

Add:

4.6L V8-215hp w/dual exh	225
CD player	150
CD changer (incls prem sound)	300
Premium sound	125
Leather seats	275
Pwr seat (std LX)	125
Wheels-alloy	150
Traction ctrl	150

ESCORT FWD/2.0L-I4 (110hp)

	WS	Ret
LX 4dr Sdn	5150	6850
SE 4dr Sdn	5825	7575
SE 4dr Wgn	6250	8025
ZX2 Cool 2dr Cpe	5475	7200
ZX2 Hot 2dr Cpe	5800	7550

Add:

ABS brakes	225
Cassette (std SE,Hot)	50
Cruise ctrl	125
CD player	125
Pwr dr locks (std wgn)	125
Pwr windows (std wgn)	100
Wheels-alum (std wgn)	100
Sunroof-pwr	275
Tilt wheel	50
Luggage rack (wgn)	50
Leather seats	225
Sport pkg (incls tach)	50

Deduct:

No air cond	450
Manual trans	425
Manual steering	125

MUSTANG RWD/4.6L-V8 (260hp)

	WS	Ret
Base (6cyl) 2dr Cnv	14650	16925
Base (6cyl) 2dr Cpe	10725	12775
Cobra (5sp) 2dr Cnv	19525	22300
Cobra (5sp) 2dr Cpe	17425	20050
GT 2dr Cnv	16925	19725
GT 2dr Cpe	12850	15025

Add:

ABS brakes (Base)	200
Cruise ctrl (std Cobra)	125
Leather seats (std Cobra)	200
Mach 460 sound (std Cobra)	175
Pwr seat (std Cobra)	50
Traction ctrl (std Cobra)	150
Wheels-17in alloy (std Cobra)	175
35th Anniv pkg (incls 17" wheels)	1100

Deduct:

Man trans (6cyl only)	425

TAURUS FWD/3.0L-V6 (145hp)

	WS	Ret
LX 4dr Sdn	7400	9250
SE 4dr Sdn	8250	10150
SE 4dr Wgn	9850	11850
SHO 4dr Sdn	12275	14400

Add:

3.0L-V6 (185/200hp)	300
ABS brakes (std SHO)	225
Alum wheels (std SHO)	125
Chrome wheels	150
Cassette (LX)	125
CD changer (std SHO)	225
Cruise ctrl (LX)	100
Mach audio	275
Leather seats (std SHO)	250

- Pwr dr locks (LX) 100
- Pwr seat (std SHO) 125
- Sunroof-pwr 350
- Third seat (wgn) 100

1998 — WS / Ret

CONTOUR — FWD/2.0L-I4 (125hp)

Model	WS	Ret
GL 4dr Sdn	5025	6725
LX 4dr Sdn	5175	6875
SE 4dr Sdn	5675	7425

Add:
- 2.5L 170hp V6 (std SE) 300
- CD player 125
- Cassette (Base) 75
- Cruise ctrl (LX) 75
- Premium sound 25
- Pwr dr locks (LX) 75
- Pwr seat (std SVT) 50
- Pwr windows (LX) 100
- Sunroof-pwr (std SVT) 250
- Leather seats (std SVT) 200
- Alloy wheels (LX) 100
- Traction control 175

Deduct:
- Manual trans (not SVT) 400
- No air cond 450

CROWN VICTORIA — RWD/4.6L-V8 (200hp)

Model	WS	Ret
Base 4dr Sdn	8825	10750
LX 4dr Sdn	10025	12025

Add:
- 4.6L V8-215hp w/dual exh . . . 175
- ABS brakes 200
- Cassette (std LX) 75
- CD player 125
- Premium sound 75
- Leather seats 225
- Pwr seat (std LX) 75
- Alloy wheels 125

ESCORT — FWD/2.0L-I4 (110hp)

Model	WS	Ret
LX 4dr Sdn	4325	5950
SE 4dr Sdn	4875	6550
SE 4dr Wgn	5250	6975
ZX2 2dr Cpe	4700	6350

Add:
- ABS brakes 175
- Cassette 50
- Cruise ctrl 75
- CD player 75
- Pwr dr locks 75
- Pwr windows 75
- Alum wheels 75
- Sunroof-pwr 225
- Tilt wheel 25
- Luggage rack (wgn) 25
- Sport pkg (incls tach) 50

Deduct:
- No air cond 375
- Manual trans 350
- Manual steering 75

MUSTANG — RWD/4.6L-V8 (225hp)

Model	WS	Ret
Base (6cyl) 2dr Cnv	11075	13125
Base (6cyl) 2dr Cpe	9050	11000
Cobra (5sp) 2dr Cnv	16950	19550
Cobra (5sp) 2dr Cpe	14850	17300
GT 2dr Cnv	12950	15425
GT 2dr Cpe	10950	13000

Add:
- ABS brakes (std Cobra) 200
- Cruise ctrl (std Cobra) 75
- Leather seats 75
- Mach 460 sound 150
- Pwr seat (std Cobra) 50
- Polished alum whls (GT) 125

Deduct:
- No air cond 425
- Man trans (6cyl only) 350
- No Cassette 50

TAURUS — FWD/3.0L-V6 (145hp)

Model	WS	Ret
LX 4dr Sdn	6250	8025
SE 4dr Sdn	6975	8800
SE 4dr Wgn	8325	10225
SHO 4dr Sdn	10650	12675

Add:
- 3.0L 200hp 24V V6 250
- ABS brakes (std SHO) 200
- Alum wheels (std SHO) 100
- Chrome wheels 125
- Cassette 75
- CD changer 200
- Cruise ctrl (LX) 75
- Mach audio 225
- Leather seats (std SHO) 200
- Pwr dr locks (LX) 75
- Pwr seat (std SHO) 75
- Sunroof-pwr 300
- Third seat (wgn) 75

1997 — WS / Ret

ASPIRE (5sp) — FWD/1.3L-I4 (63hp)

Model	WS	Ret
Base 4dr Hbk	2625	4000
Base 2dr Hbk	2350	3700

Add:
- ABS brakes 125
- Automatic trans 275
- Cassette 25
- Dlx interior 25

CONTOUR — FWD/2.0L-I4 (125hp)

Model	WS	Ret
Base 4dr Sdn	3875	5475
GL 4dr Sdn	4025	5650
LX 4dr Sdn	4475	6125
SE (6cyl) 4dr Sdn	5400	7125

Add:
- 2.5L 24V DOHC V6 (std SE) . . 250
- CD player 100
- Cassette (Base) 50
- Cruise ctrl 50
- Premium sound 25
- Pwr dr locks 50
- Pwr seat 25
- Pwr windows 75
- Sunroof-pwr 200
- Leather seats 175
- Alloy wheels (std SE) 75
- Traction control 150
- Tilt wheel 25

Deduct:
- Manual trans 325
- No air cond 375

CROWN VICTORIA — RWD/4.6L-V8 (190hp)

Model	WS	Ret
Base 4dr Sdn	6800	8600
LX 4dr Sdn	7750	9625

Add:
- 4.6L V8 w/dual exh 150
- ABS brakes 175
- Cassette (std LX) 50
- CD player 100
- Cruise ctrl (std LX) 50
- Leather seats 175
- Pwr seat (std LX) 50
- Alloy wheels (std LX) 75

ESCORT — FWD/2.0L-I4 (110hp)

Model	WS	Ret
Base 4dr Sdn	3275	4750
LX 4dr Sdn	3850	5450
LX 4dr Wgn	4175	5800

Add:
- ABS brakes 150
- Cassette 25
- Cruise ctrl 50
- CD player 50
- Pwr dr locks 50
- Pwr windows 50
- Alum wheels 50
- Sunroof-pwr 175
- Tilt wheel 25
- Luggage rack (wgn) 25
- Sport pkg (incls tach) 25

Deduct:
- No air cond 325
- Manual trans 275
- Manual steering 75

MUSTANG — RWD/4.6L-V8 (215hp)

Model	WS	Ret
Base (6cyl) 2dr Cnv	9075	11025
Base (6cyl) 2dr Cpe	7325	9175
Cobra (5sp) 2dr Cnv	14550	16975
Cobra (5sp) 2dr Cpe	12575	14875
GT 2dr Cnv	10850	13150
GT 2dr Cpe	8950	10875

Add:
- ABS brakes (std Cobra) 150
- CD player 100
- Cruise ctrl (std Cobra) 50
- Leather seats 50
- Mach 460 sound 125
- Pwr dr locks (std Cnv,Cobra) . . . 50
- Pwr seat (std Cobra) 25
- Pwr windows(std Cnv,Cobra) . . 50
- Alum wheels-15" (Base) 100
- Alloy wheels-17" (GT) 125

Deduct:
- No air cond 350
- Man trans (6cyl only) 300
- No Cassette 25

PROBE — FWD/2.5L-V6 (164hp)

Model	WS	Ret
Base 2dr Hbk	5025	6725
GT (6cyl) 2dr Hbk	6450	8225

Add:
- ABS brakes 175
- CD player 100
- Cruise ctrl 50
- Leather seats 150
- Premium sound 25
- Pwr dr locks 50
- Pwr seat 25
- Pwr windows 50
- Alum wheels (std GT) 75
- Sunroof-power 250
- Tilt wheel 25

Deduct:
- No air cond 350
- Man trans (not GT) 275
- No Cassette 25

TAURUS — FWD/3.0L-V6 (145hp)

Model	WS	Ret
G 4dr Sdn	4475	6125
GL 4dr Sdn	4775	6425
GL 4dr Wgn	5425	7150
LX 4dr Sdn	6100	7875
LX 4dr Wgn	6700	8500
SHO 4dr Sdn	8325	10225

Add:
- ABS brakes (std SHO) 175
- Alum wheels (G,GL) 75
- Chrome wheels 75
- Cassette (std LX,SHO) 50
- CD changer 150
- Cruise ctrl (std SHO) 50
- Mach audio 175
- Leather seats (std SHO) 175
- Pwr dr locks (std LX,SHO) . . . 50
- Pwr seat (std LX,SHO) 50
- Sunroof-pwr 250
- Third seat (wgn) 50

THUNDERBIRD — RWD/3.8L-V6 (145hp)

Model	WS	Ret
LX 2dr Cpe	6475	8275

Add:
- 4.6 Liter SOHC-V8 300
- ABS brakes 225
- CD player 100
- Pwr seat 50
- Leather seats 150

Chrome alum wheels	75
Moonroof-pwr	225

1996 WS Ret

ASPIRE (5sp) FWD/1.3L-I4 (63hp)

	WS	Ret
Base 4dr Hbk	1875	2975
Base 2dr Hbk	1600	2650

Add:

ABS brakes	125
Automatic trans	225
Cassette	25

CONTOUR FWD/2.0L-I4 (125hp)

	WS	Ret
GL 4dr Sdn	3350	4825
LX 4dr Sdn	3725	5325
SE (6cyl) 4dr Sdn	4475	6125

Add:

2.5L 24V DOHC V6 (std SE)	200
CD player	75
Cassette (Base)	25
Cruise ctrl	25
Premium sound	25
Pwr dr locks	25
Pwr seat	25
Pwr windows	50
Sunroof-pwr	175
Leather seats	150
Alloy wheels (std SE)	50
Traction control	125

Deduct:

Manual trans	275
No air cond	300

CROWN VICTORIA RWD/4.6L-V8 (190hp)

	WS	Ret
Base 4dr Sdn	5250	6975
LX 4dr Sdn	6125	7900

Add:

4.6L V8 w/dual exh	125
ABS brakes	150
Cassette (std LX)	25
CD player	75
Cruise ctrl (std LX)	50
Leather seats	150
Pwr seat (std LX)	25
Special wheels (std LX)	50

ESCORT FWD/1.9L-I4 (88hp)

	WS	Ret
Base 2dr Hbk	2275	3425
GT (1.8L-127hp) 2dr Hbk	3500	4975
LX 4dr Hbk	2900	4325
LX 4dr Sdn	2925	4350
LX 4dr Wgn	3225	4675
LX 2dr Hbk	2750	4150

Add:

Cassette (std GT)	25
Cruise ctrl	25
Luggage rack (Wgn)	25
CD player	50
Pwr dr locks	25
Pwr windows	50
Special wheels (std GT)	50
Sunroof-pwr	150
Tilt wheel	25

Deduct:

No air cond	250
Manual trans	225
Manual steering	50

MUSTANG RWD/4.6L-V8 (215hp)

	WS	Ret
Base (6cyl) 2dr Cnv	7225	9050
Base (6cyl) 2dr Cpe	6100	7875
Cobra (5sp) 2dr Cnv	13725	16100
Cobra (5sp) 2dr Cpe	10475	12625
GT 2dr Cnv	8775	10925
GT 2dr Cpe	7575	9425

Add:

ABS brakes (std Cobra)	150
CD player	75
Cruise ctrl (std Cobra)	25
Leather seats	25
Mach 460 sound	75
Pwr dr locks (std Cnv,Cobra)	25
Pwr seat (std Cobra)	25
Pwr windws (std Cnv,Cobra)	50
Cast alum. wheels (Base)	75
Alloy wheels-17in (GT)	100

Deduct:

No air cond	275
Man trans (6cyl only)	250
No Cassette	25

PROBE FWD/2.5L-V6 (164hp)

	WS	Ret
GT (6cyl) 2dr Hbk	5175	6875
SE 2dr Hbk	3950	5550

Add:

ABS brakes	150
CD player	75
Cruise ctrl	25
Leather seats	125
Premium sound	25
Pwr dr locks	25
Pwr seat	25
Pwr windows	50
Alum wheels (std GT)	50
Sunroof-power	200
Tilt wheel	25

Deduct:

No air cond	275
Man trans (not GT)	225
No Cassette	25
Base trim (SE)	75

TAURUS FWD/3.0L-V6 (145hp)

	WS	Ret
G 4dr Sdn	3550	5025
GL 4dr Sdn	3875	5475
GL 4dr Wgn	4450	6100
LX 4dr Sdn	4975	6675
LX 4dr Wgn	5500	7225
SHO 4dr Sdn	7275	9100

Add:

ABS brakes (std SHO)	150
Cassette (G)	25
CD changer	125
Cruise ctrl (std SHO)	50
JBL audio	150
Leather seats (std SHO)	150
Pwr dr locks (std LX,SHO)	50
Pwr seat (std LX,SHO)	25
Integrated child seat	25
Wheel upgrade (G,GL)	50
Sunroof-pwr	200
Third seat (wgn)	50

THUNDERBIRD RWD/3.8L-V6 (145hp)

	WS	Ret
LX 2dr Cpe	4900	6575

Add:

4.6 Liter SOHC-V8	250
ABS brakes	175
CD player	75
Pwr seat	25
Leather seats	150
Chrome alum wheels	50
Sunroof-pwr	200

1995 WS Ret

ASPIRE (5sp) FWD/1.3L-I4 (63hp)

	WS	Ret
Base 4dr Hbk	1250	2150
Base 2dr Hbk	1125	2025
SE 2dr Hbk	1400	2325

Add:

ABS brakes	100
Automatic trans	200
Cassette	25
CD player	50
Sport pkg	25
Sunroof-manual	50
Wheels-aluminum	25

CONTOUR FWD/2.0L-I4 (125hp)

	WS	Ret
GL 4dr Sdn	2600	3975
LX 4dr Sdn	2900	4325
SE (6cyl) 4dr Sdn	3600	5075

Add:

2.5L 24V DOHC V6 (std SE)	200
CD player	50
Cassette (Base)	25
Cruise ctrl	25
Premium sound	25
Pwr dr locks	25
Pwr seat	25
Pwr windows	25
Moonroof-pwr	150
Leather seats	125
Alloy wheels (std SE)	50
Traction control	125

Deduct:

Manual trans	250
No air cond	275

CROWN VICTORIA RWD/4.6L-V8 (190hp)

	WS	Ret
Base 4dr Sdn	4125	5750
LX 4dr Sdn	4775	6425

Add:

4.6L V8 w/dual exh	100
ABS brakes	125
Cassette	25
CD player	50
Cruise ctrl (std LX)	25
Integrated phone	100
JBL audio	150
Leather seats	150
Pwr seat (std LX)	25
Special wheels (std LX)	50

ESCORT FWD/1.9L-I4 (127hp)

	WS	Ret
Base 2dr Hbk	1625	2675
GT (1.8L-127hp) 2dr Hbk	2600	3975
LX 4dr Hbk	2100	3225
LX 4dr Sdn	2150	3275
LX 4dr Wgn	2425	3800
LX 2dr Hbk	1975	3075

Add:

Cassette (std GT)	25
Cruise ctrl	25
Luggage rack (Wgn)	25
Premium sound	25
Pwr dr locks	25
Pwr windows	25
Special wheels (std GT)	50
Sunroof-pwr	150
Tilt wheel	25

Deduct:

No air cond	225
Manual trans	200
Manual steering	25

MUSTANG RWD/5.0L-V8 (215hp)

	WS	Ret
Base (6cyl) 2dr Cnv	6275	8050
Base (6cyl) 2dr Cpe	5050	6750
Cobra (5sp) 2dr Cnv	13175	15350
Cobra (5sp) 2dr Cpe	11150	13225
GT 2dr Cnv	7625	9475
GT 2dr Cpe	6300	8075
GTS 2dr Cpe	8350	10250
R-Model 2dr Cpe	23150	25925

Add:

Cassette	25
CD player	50
Cruise ctrl	25
Leather seats	25
Mach 460 sound	75
Pwr dr locks (std Cnv,GT)	25
Pwr seat	25
Pwr windows (std Cnv,GT)	25
Wheels-cast alum (Base)	50
Wheels-17in alloy	75
ABS brakes	125

Deduct:
No air cond 250
Man trans (6cyl only) 225

PROBE FWD/2.0L-I4 (118hp)

Base 2dr Hbk	2825	4225
GT (6cyl) 2dr Hbk	3950	5550

Add:
ABS brakes 125
Cassette 25
CD player 50
Cruise ctrl 25
Leather seats 100
Premium sound 25
Pwr dr locks 25
Pwr seat 25
Pwr windows 25
Alum wheels (std GT) 50
Sunroof-power 175
Tilt wheel 25

Deduct:
No air cond 250
Man trans (not GT) 200

TAURUS FWD/3.0L-V6 (140hp)

GL 4dr Sdn	2775	4175
GL 4dr Wgn	3375	4850
LX 4dr Sdn	3625	5100
LX 4dr Wgn	4175	5800
SE 4dr Sdn	2900	4325
SHO 4dr Sdn	4625	6275

Add:
3.8L V6 (std SE,LX Wgn) 100
ABS brakes (std SHO) 150
Cassette (std SHO) 25
CD player 50
Cruise ctrl (std SHO) 25
JBL audio 150
Leather seats 125
Pwr dr locks (std LX,SHO) 25
Pwr seat (std LX,SHO) 25
Pwr windows (std LX,SHO) . . . 50
Special wheels (GL only) 50
Sunroof-pwr 175
Third seat (GL Wgn) 25

Deduct:
No air cond 275
Manual trans (SHO) 250

THUNDERBIRD RWD/3.8L-V6 (140hp)

LX 2dr Cpe	3900	5500
SC (230hp/SC) 2dr Cpe	5925	7675

Add:
4.6 Liter OHC-V8 225
ABS brakes (std SC) 125
CD player 50
Integrated phone 50
JBL audio 150
Leather seats 125
Special wheels (std SC) 50
Sunroof-pwr 175

Deduct:
Manual trans (SC) 250

1994 WS Ret

ASPIRE (5sp) FWD/1.3L-I4 (64hp)

Base 4dr Hbk	1075	1975
Base 2dr Hbk	925	1625
SE 2dr Hbk	1175	2075

Add:
ABS brakes 75
Automatic trans 175
Cassette 25
CD player 50
Sport pkg 25
Sunroof-manual 25
Wheels-aluminum 25

CROWN VICTORIA RWD/4.6L-V8 (190hp)

Base 4dr Sdn	3525	5000
LX 4dr Sdn	4075	5700

Add:
4.6L V8 w/dual exh 75
ABS brakes 125
Cassette 25
CD player 50
Cruise ctrl 25
Integrated phone 75
JBL audio 125
Leather seats 125
Pwr dr locks 25
Pwr seat (std LX) 25
Special wheels 25

ESCORT FWD/1.9L-I4 (127hp)

Base 2dr Hbk	1400	2325
GT (1.8L-127hp) 2dr Hbk	2225	3350
LX 4dr Hbk	1800	2875
LX 4dr Sdn	1850	2925
LX 4dr Wgn	2050	3150
LX 2dr Hbk	1700	2775

Add:
Cassette (std GT) 25
Cruise ctrl 25
Pwr dr locks 25
Pwr windows 25
Special wheels (std GT) 25
Sunroof-pwr 125

Deduct:
No air cond 225
Manual trans 200
Manual steering 25

MUSTANG RWD/5.0L-V8 (215hp)

Cobra (5sp) 2dr Cnv	12075	14200
Cobra (5sp) 2dr Cpe	9325	11275
GT 2dr Cnv	6575	8375
GT 2dr Cpe	5275	7000
LX (6cyl) 2dr Cnv	5450	7175
LX (6cyl) 2dr Cpe	4250	5875

Add:
Cassette 25
CD player 50
Cruise ctrl 25
Leather seats 25
Mach 460 sound 50
Pwr dr locks (std Cnv,GT) 25
Pwr seat 25
Pwr windows (std Cnv) 25
Special wheels (Base) 50
Wheels 17" alloys 50

Deduct:
No air cond 225
Man trans (6cyl only) 200

PROBE FWD/2.0L-I4 (118hp)

Base 2dr Hbk	2375	3725
GT (6cyl) 2dr Hbk	3325	4800
SE 2dr Hbk	2750	4150

Add:
ABS brakes 125
Cassette (std SE) 25
CD player 50
Cruise ctrl (std SE) 25
Leather seats 75
Pwr dr locks (std SE) 25
Pwr seat 25
Pwr windows (std SE) 25
Special wheels (Base) 25
Sunroof-power 175
Tilt wheel (std SE) 25

Deduct:
No air cond 225
Man trans (not GT) 200

TAURUS FWD/3.0L-V6 (140hp)

GL 4dr Sdn	2275	3425
GL 4dr Wgn	2750	4150
LX 4dr Sdn	2950	4375
LX 4dr Wgn	3425	4900
SHO 4dr Sdn	3900	5500

Add:
3.8L V6 (std LX Wgn) 75
ABS brakes (std SHO) 125
Cassette (std SHO) 25
CD player 50
Cruise ctrl (std SHO) 25
JBL audio 125
Leather seats 125
Pwr dr locks (std LX,SHO) 25
Pwr seat (std LX,SHO) 25
Pwr windows (std LX,SHO) . . . 25
Special wheels (GL only) 25
Sunroof-pwr 175
Third seat (GL Wgn) 25

Deduct:
No air cond 250
Manual trans (SHO) 225

TEMPO FWD/2.3L-I4 (96hp)

GL 4dr Sdn	1575	2625
GL 2dr Cpe	1525	2450
LX 4dr Sdn	1875	2975

Add:
3.0 Liter V6 175
Air bag-driver 125
Cassette 25
Cruise ctrl 25
Pwr dr locks (std LX) 25
Pwr seat 25
Pwr windows 25

Deduct:
No air cond 225
Manual trans 200

THUNDERBIRD RWD/3.8L-V6 (140hp)

LX 2dr Cpe	3325	4800
SC (215hp/SC) 2dr Cpe	5150	6850

Add:
4.6 Liter OHC-V8 200
ABS brakes (std SC) 125
CD player 50
Integrated phone 50
JBL audio 125
Leather seats 125
Special wheels (std SC) 25
Sunroof-pwr 175

Deduct:
Manual trans (SC) 225

1993 WS Ret

CROWN VICTORIA RWD/V.6L-V8 (190hp)

Base 4dr Sdn	2775	4175
LX 4dr Sdn	3200	4650

Add:
4.6L V8 w/dual exh 75
ABS brakes 100
Air bag-passenger 75
Cassette 25
Cruise ctrl 25
Integrated phone 75
JBL audio 100
Leather seats 100
Pwr dr locks 25
Pwr seat (std LX) 25
Special wheels 25

ESCORT FWD/1.9L-I4 (88hp)

Base 2dr Hbk	1050	1950
GT (1.8L-122hp) 2dr Hbk	1675	2725
LX 4dr Hbk	1325	2250
LX 4dr Sdn	1350	2275
LX 4dr Wgn	1500	2425
LX 2dr Hbk	1250	2150
LX-E (1.8L-122hp) 4dr Sdn	1650	2700

Add:

Cassette (std GT,LX-E)	25
Cruise ctrl	25
Pwr dr locks	25
Pwr windows	25
Special wheels (std GT)	25
Sunroof-pwr	100

Deduct:

No air cond	175
Manual trans	175
Manual steering	25

FESTIVA (5sp) FWD/1.3L-I4 (63hp)

Model		
GL 2dr Hbk	775	1300
L 2dr Hbk	525	1000

Add:

Automatic trans	175
Cassette	25
Sport pkg (GL)	25
Sunroof-manual	25

Deduct:

No air cond	175

MUSTANG RWD/5.0L-V8 (205hp)

Model		
Cobra (5sp) 2dr Hbk	5725	7475
GT 2dr Cnv	5150	6850
GT 2dr Hbk	4250	5875
LX 5.0L 2dr Cnv	4625	6275
LX (4cyl) 2dr Cnv	3875	5475
LX 5.0L 2dr Cpe	3825	5425
LX (4cyl) 2dr Cpe	2900	4325
LX 5.0L 2dr Hbk	3750	5350
LX (4cyl) 2dr Hbk	2825	4225

Add:

Cassette	25
CD player	50
Cruise ctrl	25
Leather seats	25
Pwr dr locks (std Cnv)	25
Pwr seat	25
Pwr windows (std Cnv)	25
Special wheels (LX 4cyl)	50
Sunroof-manual	50

Deduct:

No air cond	200
Man trans (4cyl only)	175

PROBE FWD/2.0L-I4 (115hp)

Model		
Base 2dr Hbk	1950	3050
GT (6cyl) 2dr Hbk	2775	4175

Add:

ABS brakes	100
Cassette	25
CD player	50
Cruise ctrl	25
Leather seats	75
Pwr dr locks	25
Pwr seat	25
Pwr windows	25
Special wheels (std GT)	25
Sunroof-power	150
Tilt wheel	25

Deduct:

No air cond	200
Man trans (not GT)	175

TAURUS FWD/3.0L-V6 (140hp)

Model		
GL 4dr Sdn	1775	2850
GL 4dr Wgn	2175	3300
LX 4dr Sdn	2325	3675
LX 4dr Wgn	2675	4075
SHO 4dr Sdn	3000	4425

Add:

3.8L V6 (std LX Wgn)	75
ABS brakes (std SHO)	125
Air bag-passenger	50
Cassette (std SHO)	25
CD player	50
Cruise ctrl (std SHO)	25
JBL audio	100
Leather seats	100
Pwr dr locks (std LX,SHO)	25
Pwr seat (std LX,SHO)	25
Pwr windows (std LX,SHO)	25
Special wheels (GL only)	25
Sunroof-pwr	150
Third seat (Wgn)	25

Deduct:

No air cond	225
Manual trans (SHO)	225

TEMPO FWD/2.3L-I4 (96hp)

Model		
GL 4dr Sdn	1250	2150
GL 2dr Cpe	1175	2075
LX 4dr Sdn	1525	2450

Add:

3.0 Liter V6	150
Air bag-driver	100
Cassette	25
Cruise ctrl	25
Pwr dr locks (std LX)	25
Pwr seat	25
Pwr windows	25

Deduct:

No air cond	200
Manual trans	175

THUNDERBIRD RWD/3.8L-V6 (215hp)

Model		
LX 2dr Cpe	2525	3900
SC (215hp/SC) 2dr Cpe	3700	5200

Add:

5.0 Liter V8	175
ABS brakes (std SC)	125
CD player	50
JBL audio	100
Leather seats	100
Special wheels (std SC)	25
Sunroof-pwr	150

Deduct:

Manual trans (SC)	200

1992 WS Ret

CROWN VICTORIA RWD/4.6L-V8 (190hp)

Model	WS	Ret
Base 4dr Sdn	2225	3350
LX 4dr Sdn	2525	3900
Touring 4dr Sdn	2700	4100

Add:

4.6L V8 w/dual exh.	50
ABS brakes (std Touring)	75
Air bag-passenger	25
Cassette	25
Cruise ctrl (std Trng)	25
Integrated phone	50
JBL audio	75
Leather seats	75
Pwr dr locks	25
Pwr seat	25
Pwr windows	25
Spcl wheels (std Trng)	25

ESCORT FWD/1.9L-I4 (88hp)

Model	WS	Ret
GT 2dr Hbk	1425	2350
LX 4dr Hbk	1125	2025
LX 4dr Sdn	1150	2050
LX 4dr Wgn	1275	2175
LX 2dr Hbk	1075	1975
LX-E (1.8L-122hp) 4dr Sdn.	1400	2325
Pony 2dr Hbk	875	1550

Add:

Cruise ctrl	25
Pwr dr locks	25
Pwr windows	25
Sunroof-pwr	75

Deduct:

No air cond	175
Manual trans	150
Manual steering	25

FESTIVA (5sp) FWD/1.3L-I4 (63hp)

Model	WS	Ret
GL 2dr Hbk	625	1125
L 2dr Hbk	450	925

Add:

Automatic trans	150
Sunroof-manual	25

Deduct:

No air cond	175

MUSTANG RWD/5.0L-V8 (225hp)

Model	WS	Ret
GT 2dr Cnv	4525	6175
GT 2dr Hbk	3675	5175
LX (4cyl) 2dr Cnv	3300	4775
LX 5.0L 2dr Cnv	3950	5550
LX (4cyl) 2dr Cpe	2475	3850
LX 5.0L 2dr Cpe	3225	4675
LX (4cyl) 2dr Hbk	2425	3800
LX 5.0L 2dr Hbk	3175	4625

Add:

Cassette	25
Cruise ctrl	25
Leather seats	25
Pwr dr locks (std Cnv)	25
Pwr windows (std Cnv)	25
Special wheels (LX 4cyl)	25
Sunroof-manual	25

Deduct:

No air cond	175
Man trans (4cyl only)	175

PROBE FWD/2.2L-I4 (110hp)

Model	WS	Ret
GL 2dr Hbk	1625	2675
GT (Turbo) 2dr Hbk	2400	3775
LX (6cyl) 2dr Hbk	1850	2925

Add:

ABS brakes	75
Cassette	25
CD player	25
Cruise ctrl	25
Leather seats	50
Pwr dr locks	25
Pwr windows	25
Special wheels	25
Sunroof-manual	25

Deduct:

No air cond	175
Man trans (not GT)	150

TAURUS FWD/3.0L-V6 (140hp)

Model	WS	Ret
GL 4dr Sdn	1450	2375
GL 4dr Wgn	1775	2850
L 4dr Sdn	1250	2150
L 4dr Wgn	1600	2650
LX 4dr Sdn	1900	3000
LX 4dr Wgn	2200	3325
SHO (5sp-220hp) 4dr Sdn	2475	3850

Add:

3.8L V6 (std LX Wgn)	50
ABS brakes (std SHO)	75
Air bag-passenger	25
Cassette	25
CD player	25
Cruise ctrl (std SHO)	25
JBL audio	75
Leather seats	75
Pwr dr locks (std LX,SHO)	25
Pwr seat (std LX,SHO)	25
Pwr windows (std LX,SHO)	25
Special wheels (std SHO)	25
Sunroof-pwr	100
Third seat (Wgn)	25

Deduct:

No air cond	200

TEMPO FWD/2.3L-I4 (96hp)

Model	WS	Ret
GL 4dr Sdn	1050	1950
GL 2dr Cpe	975	1675
GLS (6cyl) 4dr Sdn	1200	2100

GLS (6cyl) 2dr Cpe	1150	2050
LX 4dr Sdn	1200	2100

Add:
- 3.0 Liter V6 (std GLS) . . . 125
- Air bag-driver . . . 50
- Cruise ctrl . . . 25
- Pwr dr locks (std LX) . . . 25
- Pwr windows . . . 25

Deduct:
- No air cond . . . 175
- Manual trans . . . 175

THUNDERBIRD — RWD/3.8L-V6 (140hp)

Base 2dr Cpe	1975	3075
LX 2dr Cpe	2175	3300
SC 2dr Cpe	3175	4625
Sport (V8) 2dr Cpe	2425	3800

Add:
- 5.0 Liter V8 (std Sport) . . . 150
- ABS brakes (std SC) . . . 75
- Cassette (Base only) . . . 25
- CD player . . . 25
- Cruise ctrl (std LX) . . . 25
- JBL audio . . . 75
- Leather seats . . . 75
- Pwr dr locks (std LX) . . . 25
- Pwr seat . . . 25
- Special wheels (std SC) . . . 25
- Sunroof-pwr . . . 100

Deduct:
- Manual trans (SC) . . . 175

1991 — WS — Ret

CROWN VICTORIA — RWD/5.0L-V8 (150hp)

	WS	Ret
Base 4dr Sdn	1950	3050
Base 4dr Wgn	2000	3100
Cntry Squre LX 4dr Wgn	2225	3350
Country Squire 4dr Wgn	2050	3150
LX 4dr Sdn	2100	3225
LX 4dr Wgn	2150	3275

Add:
- 5.7 Liter V8 . . . 50
- Brougham roof . . . 25
- Cassette . . . 25
- Cruise ctrl . . . 25
- Integrated phone . . . 25
- Leather seats . . . 50
- Pwr dr locks . . . 25

ESCORT — FWD/1.9L-I4 (88hp)

GT 2dr Hbk	1000	1700
LX 4dr Hbk	800	1475
LX 4dr Wgn	925	1625
LX 2dr Hbk	750	1275
Pony 2dr Hbk	550	1050

Add:
- Sunroof-pwr . . . 50

Deduct:
- No air cond . . . 150
- Manual trans . . . 125
- Manual steering . . . 25

FESTIVA (5sp) — FWD/1.3L-I4 (63hp)

GL 2dr Hbk	525	1000
L 2dr Hbk	425	900

Add:
- Automatic trans . . . 100
- Sunroof-manual . . . 25

Deduct:
- No air cond . . . 150

MUSTANG — RWD/5.0L-V8 (225hp)

GT 2dr Cnv	3650	5150
GT 2dr Hbk	2800	4200
LX (4cyl) 2dr Cnv	2675	4075
LX 5.0L 2dr Cnv	3325	4800
LX (4cyl) 2dr Cpe	2100	3225
LX 5.0L 2dr Cpe	2500	3875
LX (4cyl) 2dr Hbk	2100	3225
LX 5.0L 2dr Hbk	2500	3875

Add:
- Cassette . . . 25
- Leather seats . . . 25
- Pwr windows (std Cnv) . . . 25
- Spcl wheels (std GT,5.0) . . . 25
- Sunroof-manual . . . 25

Deduct:
- No air cond . . . 175
- Man trans (4cyl only) . . . 150

PROBE — FWD/2.2l-I4 (110hp)

GL 2dr Hbk	1325	2250
GT (Turbo) 2dr Hbk	1700	2775
LX (6cyl) 2dr Hbk	1575	2625

Add:
- ABS brakes . . . 50
- Cassette . . . 25
- CD player . . . 25
- Leather seats . . . 25
- Pwr windows . . . 25
- Special wheels (std GT) . . . 25
- Sunroof-manual . . . 25

Deduct:
- No air cond . . . 175
- Man trans (not GT) . . . 125

TAURUS — FWD/3.2L-V6 (140hp)

GL 4dr Sdn	1150	2050
GL 4dr Wgn	1400	2325
L 4dr Sdn	1025	1925
L 4dr Wgn	1275	2175
LX 4dr Sdn	1375	2300
LX 4dr Wgn	1600	2650
SHO (5sp-220hp) 4dr Sdn	2125	3250

Add:
- 3.8L V6 (std LX Wgn) . . . 50
- ABS brakes (std LX, SHO) . . . 50
- Cassette (std SHO) . . . 25
- CD player . . . 25
- Cruise ctrl (std SHO) . . . 25
- JBL audio . . . 50
- Leather seats . . . 50
- Pwr dr locks(std LX,SHO) . . . 25
- Pwr windows (std LX,SHO) . . . 25
- Special wheels (std SHO) . . . 25
- Sunroof-pwr . . . 100
- Third seat (Wgn) . . . 25

Deduct:
- 4cyl . . . 100
- No air cond . . . 175

TEMPO — FWD/2.3L-I4 (98hp)

AWD 4dr Sdn	1200	2100
GL 4dr Sdn	900	1600
GL 2dr Cpe	850	1525
GLS 4dr Sdn	1025	1925
GLS 2dr Cpe	975	1675
L 4dr Sdn	825	1500
L 2dr Cpe	775	1300
LX 4dr Sdn	1050	1950

Add:
- Air bag-driver . . . 50
- Pwr windows . . . 25

Deduct:
- No air cond . . . 175
- Manual trans . . . 150

THUNDERBIRD — RWD/3.8L-V6 (140hp)

Base 2dr Cpe	1725	2800
LX 2dr Cpe	1950	3050
SC 2dr Cpe	2575	3950

Add:
- 5.0 Liter V8 . . . 125
- ABS brakes (std SC) . . . 50
- Cassette (std LX) . . . 25
- CD player . . . 25
- Cruise ctrl (std LX) . . . 25
- JBL audio . . . 50
- Leather seats . . . 50
- Pwr dr locks (std LX) . . . 25
- Special wheels (std SC) . . . 25
- Sunroof-pwr . . . 100

Deduct:
- Manual trans (SC) . . . 150

1990 — WS — Ret

CROWN VICTORIA — RWD/5.0L-V8 (150hp)

	WS	Ret
Base 4dr Sdn	1550	2475
Base 4dr Wgn	1575	2625
Cntry Squire LX 4dr Wgn	1725	2800
Country Squire 4dr Wgn	1575	2625
LX 4dr Sdn	1650	2700
LX 4dr Wgn	1675	2725

Add:
- 5.7L V8 . . . 25
- Brougham roof . . . 25
- Leather seats . . . 25
- Special wheels . . . 25

ESCORT — FWD/1.9L-I4 (90hp)

GT (5sp) 2dr Hbk	675	1200
LX 4dr Hbk	525	1000
LX 4dr Wgn	600	1100
LX 2dr Hbk	500	975
Pony 2dr Hbk	425	900

Add:

Deduct:
- No air cond . . . 125
- Manual trans . . . 125

FESTIVA (5sp) — FWD/1.3L-I4 (63hp)

L 2dr Hbk	375	825
L Plus 2dr Hbk	425	900
LX 2dr Hbk	500	975

Add:
- Automatic trans . . . 50

Deduct:
- No air cond . . . 125

MUSTANG — RWD/5.0L-V8 (225hp)

GT 2dr Cnv	3325	4800
GT 2dr Hbk	2675	4075
LX (4cyl) 2dr Cnv	2525	3900
LX 5.0L 2dr Cnv	3050	4500
LX (4cyl) 2dr Cpe	1975	3075
LX 5.0L 2dr Cpe	2375	3725
LX (4cyl) 2dr Hbk	2000	3100
LX 5.0L 2dr Hbk	2375	3725

Add:
- Leather seats . . . 25
- Sunroof-manual . . . 25

Deduct:
- No air cond . . . 150
- Man trans (4cyl only) . . . 125

PROBE — FWD/2.2L-I4 (110hp)

GL 2dr Hbk	1075	1975
GT (Turbo) 2dr Hbk	1325	2250
LX (6cyl) 2dr Hbk	1200	2100

Add:
- ABS brakes . . . 25
- CD player . . . 25
- Leather seats . . . 25
- Special wheels (GL only) . . . 25
- Sunroof-manual . . . 25

Deduct:
- No air cond . . . 150
- Man trans (not GT) . . . 125

TAURUS — FWD/3.0L-V6 (140hp)

GL 4dr Sdn	925	1625
GL 4dr Wgn	1100	2000
L 4dr Sdn	800	1475

Model	WS	Ret
L 4dr Wgn	1000	1700
LX 4dr Sdn	1125	2025
LX 4dr Wgn	1300	2200
SHO (5sp-220hp) 4dr Sdn	1725	2800

Add:
- 3.8L V6 (std LX Wgn) . . . 25
- ABS brakes (std SHO) . . . 25
- CD player . . . 25
- JBL audio . . . 50
- Leather seats . . . 25
- Pwr windows (std LX,SHO) . . . 25
- Special wheels (std SHO) . . . 25
- Sunroof-pwr . . . 75

Deduct:
- 4cyl . . . 75
- No air cond . . . 150

TEMPO — FWD/2.3L-I4 (98hp)

Model	WS	Ret
AWD 4dr Sdn	1000	1700
GL 4dr Sdn	750	1275
GL 2dr Cpe	750	1275
GLS 4dr Sdn	850	1525
GLS 2dr Cpe	825	1500
LX 4dr Sdn	875	1550

Add:

Deduct:
- No air cond . . . 150
- Manual trans . . . 125

THUNDERBIRD — RWD/3.8L-V6 (140hp)

Model	WS	Ret
Base 2dr Cpe	1525	2450
LX 2dr Cpe	1650	2700
SC 2dr Cpe	2125	3250

Add:
- ABS brakes (std SC) . . . 25
- CD player . . . 25
- JBL audio . . . 50
- Leather seats . . . 25
- Special wheels (std SC) . . . 25
- Sunroof-pwr . . . 75

Deduct:
- Manual trans (SC) . . . 125

1989 — WS Ret

CROWN VICTORIA — RWD/5.0L-V8 (150hp)

Model	WS	Ret
Base 4dr Sdn	1175	2075
Base 4dr Wgn	1200	2100
Cntry Squire LX 4dr Wgn	1375	2300
Country Squire 4dr Wgn	1250	2150
LX 4dr Sdn	1300	2200
LX 4dr Wgn	1325	2250
S 4dr Sdn	1000	1700

Add:
- Leather seats . . . 25

ESCORT — FWD/1.9L-I4 (90hp)

Model	WS	Ret
GT (5sp) 2dr Hbk	500	975
LX 4dr Hbk	425	900
LX 4dr Wgn	475	950
LX 2dr Hbk	400	850
Pony 2dr Hbk	325	775

Add:

Deduct:
- No air cond . . . 75
- Manual trans . . . 75

FESTIVA (5sp) — FWD/1.3L-I4 (58hp)

Model	WS	Ret
L 2dr Hbk	300	750
L Plus 2dr Hbk	350	800
LX 2dr Hbk	400	850

Add:
- Automatic trans . . . 25

Deduct:
- No air cond . . . 75

MUSTANG — RWD/5.0L-V8 (225hp)

Model	WS	Ret
GT 2dr Cnv	2725	4125
GT 2dr Hbk	2250	3375
LX (4cyl) 2dr Cnv	2075	3200
LX 5.0L 2dr Cnv	2525	3900
LX (4cyl) 2dr Cpe	1575	2625
LX 5.0L 2dr Cpe	1950	3050
LX (4cyl) 2dr Hbk	1625	2675
LX 5.0L 2dr Hbk	1950	3050

Add:
- Leather seats . . . 25
- Sunroof-manual . . . 25

Deduct:
- No air cond . . . 100
- Man trans (4cyl only) . . . 100

PROBE — FWD/2.2L-I4 (110hp)

Model	WS	Ret
GL 2dr Hbk	850	1525
GT (Turbo) 2dr Hbk	1075	1975
LX 2dr Hbk	1000	1700

Add:
- Sunroof-manual . . . 25

Deduct:
- No air cond . . . 100
- Man trans (not GT) . . . 100

TAURUS — FWD/3.0L-V6 (140hp)

Model	WS	Ret
GL 4dr Sdn	725	1250
GL 4dr Wgn	900	1600
L 4dr Sdn	600	1100
L 4dr Wgn	800	1475
LX 4dr Sdn	900	1600
LX 4dr Wgn	1050	1950
SHO (5sp-220hp) 4dr Sdn	1400	2325

Add:
- 3.8 Liter V6 . . . 25
- JBL audio . . . 25
- Leather seats . . . 25
- Sunroof-pwr . . . 50

Deduct:
- 4cyl . . . 50
- No air cond . . . 125

TEMPO — FWD/2.3L-I4 (98hp)

Model	WS	Ret
AWD 4dr Sdn	825	1500
GL 4dr Sdn	550	1050
GL 2dr Cpe	550	1050
GLS 4dr Sdn	625	1125
GLS 2dr Cpe	600	1100
LX 4dr Sdn	675	1200

Add:

Deduct:
- No air cond . . . 100
- Manual trans . . . 100

THUNDERBIRD — RWD/3.8L-V6 (140hp)

Model	WS	Ret
Base 2dr Cpe	1225	2125
LX 2dr Cpe	1325	2250
SC 2dr Cpe	1675	2725

Add:
- CD player . . . 25
- JBL audio . . . 25
- Leather seats . . . 25
- Sunroof-pwr . . . 50

Deduct:
- Manual trans (SC) . . . 100

1988 — WS Ret

CROWN VICTORIA — RWD/5.0L-V8 (150hp)

Model	WS	Ret
Base 4dr Sdn	975	1675
Base 4dr Wgn	1000	1700
Cntry Squire LX 4dr Wgn	1075	1975
Country Squire 4dr Wgn	1025	1925
LX 4dr Sdn	1025	1925
LX 4dr Wgn	1050	1950
S 4dr Sdn	850	1525

Add:
- Leather seats . . . 25

ESCORT — FWD/1.9L-I4 (90hp)

Model	WS	Ret
EXP 2dr Cpe	475	950
GL 4dr Hbk	300	750
GL 4dr Wgn	325	775
GL 2dr Hbk	275	725
GT (5sp) 2dr Hbk	300	750
Pony 2dr Hbk	275	725

Add:

Deduct:
- No air cond . . . 50
- Manual trans . . . 50

FESTIVA (5sp) — FWD/1.3L-I4 (58hp)

Model	WS	Ret
L 2dr Hbk	200	625
L Plus 2dr Hbk	200	625
LX 2dr Hbk	200	625

Add:
- Automatic trans . . . 25

Deduct:
- No air cond . . . 50

MUSTANG — RWD/5.0L-V8 (225hp)

Model	WS	Ret
GT 2dr Cnv	2350	3700
GT 2dr Hbk	1900	3000
LX (4cyl) 2dr Cnv	1950	3050
LX 5.0L 2dr Cnv	2200	3325
LX (4cyl) 2dr Cpe	1500	2425
LX 5.0L 2dr Cpe	1700	2775
LX (4cyl) 2dr Hbk	1550	2475
LX 5.0L 2dr Hbk	1725	2800

Add:
- T-tops . . . 75

Deduct:
- No air cond . . . 100
- Man trans (4cyl only) . . . 50

TAURUS — FWD/3.0L-V6 (140hp)

Model	WS	Ret
GL 4dr Sdn	525	1000
GL 4dr Wgn	600	1100
L 4dr Sdn	475	950
L 4dr Wgn	550	1050
LX 4dr Sdn	650	1150
LX 4dr Wgn	700	1225
MT-5 (4cyl,5sp) 4dr Sdn	275	725

Add:
- 3.8 Liter V6 . . . 25
- Leather seats . . . 25
- Sunroof-pwr . . . 50

Deduct:
- 4cyl (except MT5) . . . 50
- No air cond . . . 100

TEMPO — FWD/2.3L-I4 (98hp)

Model	WS	Ret
AWD 4dr Sdn	575	1075
GL 4dr Sdn	475	950
GL 2dr Cpe	450	925
GLS 4dr Sdn	475	950
GLS 2dr Cpe	450	925
LX 4dr Sdn	500	975

Add:

Deduct:
- No air cond . . . 75
- Manual trans . . . 75

THUNDERBIRD — RWD/3.8L-V6 (140hp)

Model	WS	Ret
Base 2dr Cpe	950	1650
LX 2dr Cpe	1000	1700
Sport (8cyl) 2dr Cpe	1100	2000
Turbo Coupe 2dr Cpe	1000	1700

Add:
- 5.0 Liter V8 (std Sport) . . . 50
- Leather seats . . . 25

Sunroof-pwr	50	

GEO

1997 WS Ret

METRO FWD/1.0L-I3 (55hp)

	WS	Ret
Base (5sp) 2dr Hbk	1450	2375
LSi (4cyl) 4dr Sdn	2550	3925
LSi (4cyl) 2dr Hbk	2100	3225
Add:		
1.3 Liter 4cyl (std 4dr)	150	
ABS brakes	125	
Pwr dr locks	25	
CD player	75	
Cassette	50	
Deduct:		
Man trans (not Base)	225	
No air cond	275	

PRIZM FWD/1.6L-I4 (100hp)

	WS	Ret
Base 4dr Sdn	4325	5950
LSi 4dr Sdn	4750	6400
Add:		
1.8 Liter 4cyl	150	
ABS brakes	150	
Cassette	25	
CD Player	100	
Cruise ctrl	50	
Leather seats	100	
Pwr dr locks	50	
Pwr windows	50	
Sunroof-pwr	175	
Tilt wheel (std LSi)	25	
Wheels-alloy	50	
Deduct:		
No air cond	350	
Manual trans	300	

1996 WS Ret

METRO FWD/1.0L-I3 (55hp)

	WS	Ret
Base (4cyl) 4dr Sdn	1850	2925
Base (5sp) 2dr Hbk	1175	2075
LSi (4cyl) 4dr Sdn	2125	3250
LSi 2dr Hbk	1650	2700
Add:		
1.3 Liter 4cyl (std 4dr)	125	
ABS brakes	125	
Pwr dr locks	25	
CD player	50	
Deduct:		
Man trans (not Base)	200	
No air cond	225	

PRIZM FWD/1.6L-I4 (105hp)

	WS	Ret
Base 4dr Sdn	3575	5050
LSi 4dr Sdn	3975	5600
Add:		
1.8 Liter 4cyl	125	
ABS brakes	150	
Cassette	25	
CD Player	75	
Cruise ctrl	25	
Leather seats	75	
Pwr dr locks	25	
Pwr windows	50	
Sunroof-pwr	150	
Tilt wheel (std LSi)	25	
Wheels-alloy	50	
Deduct:		
No air cond	275	
Manual steering	25	
Manual trans	250	

1995 WS Ret

METRO Ba/1.0L-I3 (55hp)

	WS	Ret
Base 4dr Sdn	1550	2475
Base (5sp) 2dr Hbk	975	1675
LSi (4cyl) 4dr Sdn	1750	2825
LSi 2dr Hbk	1350	2275
Add:		
1.3 Liter 4cyl (std 4dr)	100	
ABS brakes	75	
Pwr dr locks	25	
CD player	50	
Deduct:		
Man trans (not Base)	175	
No air cond	200	

PRIZM Ba/1.6L-I4 (105hp)

	WS	Ret
Base 4dr Sdn	2850	4250
LSi 4dr Sdn	3175	4625
Add:		
1.8 Liter 4cyl	150	
ABS brakes	150	
Cassette	25	
CD Player	50	
Cruise ctrl	25	
Pwr dr locks	25	
Pwr windows	25	
Sunroof-pwr	150	
Tilt wheel (std LSi)	25	
Wheels-alloy	25	
Deduct:		
No air cond	250	
Manual steering	25	
Manual trans	225	

1994 WS Ret

METRO FWD/1.0L-I3 (52hp)

	WS	Ret
Base 4dr Hbk	900	1600
Base 2dr Hbk	775	1300
XFi (5sp) 2dr Hbk	425	900
Add:		
Cassette	25	
Deduct:		
Man trans (not XFi)	175	
No air cond	200	

PRIZM FWD/1.6L-I4 (105hp)

	WS	Ret
Base 4dr Sdn	2250	3375
LSi 4dr Sdn	2475	3850
Add:		
1.8 Liter 4cyl	125	
ABS brakes	125	
Cassette	25	
CD Player	50	
Cruise ctrl	25	
Pwr dr locks	25	
Pwr windows	25	
Sunroof-pwr	125	
Wheels-alloy	25	
Deduct:		
No air cond	225	
Manual steering	25	
Manual trans	200	

1993 WS Ret

METRO FWD/1.0L-I3 (55hp)

	WS	Ret
Base 4dr Hbk	700	1225
Base 2dr Hbk	550	1050
LSi 4dr Hbk	900	1600
LSi 2dr Cnv	1100	2000
LSi 2dr Hbk	800	1475
XFi (5sp) 2dr Hbk	325	775
Add:		
Cassette	25	
Deduct:		
Man trans (not XFi)	150	
No air cond	150	

PRIZM FWD/1.6L-I4 (105hp)

	WS	Ret
Base 4dr Sdn	1925	3025
LSi 4dr Sdn	2100	3225
Add:		
ABS brakes	100	
Cassette	25	
CD Player	50	
Pwr dr locks	25	
Pwr windows	25	
Sunroof-pwr	100	
Deduct:		
No air cond	200	
Manual steering	25	
Manual trans	175	

STORM FWD/1.6L-I4 (90hp)

	WS	Ret
2+2 2dr Cpe	1175	2075
GSi 2dr Cpe	1600	2650
Add:		
Alloy wheels	25	
Cassette	25	
Deduct:		
No air cond	175	
Manual trans	175	

1992 WS Ret

METRO FWD/1.0L-I3 (52hp)

	WS	Ret
Base 4dr Hbk	450	925
Base 2dr Hbk	375	825
LSi 4dr Hbk	575	1075
LSi 2dr Cnv	925	1625
LSi 2dr Hbk	500	975
XFi (5sp) 2dr Hbk	300	750
Add:		
Deduct:		
Man trans (not XFi)	125	
No air cond	150	

PRIZM FWD/1.6L-I4 (102hp)

	WS	Ret
Base 4dr Sdn	1375	2300
GSi 4dr Sdn	1800	2875
Add:		
LSi trim (Base only)	75	
Pwr dr locks	25	
Pwr windows	25	
Sunroof-pwr	75	
Deduct:		
No air cond	175	
Manual trans	175	

STORM FWD/1.6L-I4 (95hp)

	WS	Ret
2+2 2dr Cpe	975	1675
Base 2dr Hbk	925	1625
GSi 2dr Cpe	1300	2200
Add:		
Alloy wheels (std GSi)	25	
Deduct:		
No air cond	175	
Manual trans	150	

1991 WS Ret

METRO FWD/1.0L-I3 (55hp)

	WS	Ret
Base 4dr Hbk	350	800
Base 2dr Hbk	300	750
LSi 4dr Hbk	475	950
LSi 2dr Cnv	725	1250
LSi 2dr Hbk	425	900
XFi (5sp) 2dr Hbk	225	650
Add:		
Deduct:		
No air cond	125	

Man trans (not XFi) 100

PRIZM FWD/1.6L-I4 (102hp)

Model	WS	Ret
Base 4dr Hbk	1200	2100
Base 4dr Sdn	1150	2050
GSi 4dr Hbk	1575	2625
GSi 4dr Sdn	1500	2425

Add:
LSi trim (Base only) 50
Pwr windows 25
Sunroof-pwr 50

Deduct:
No air cond 175
Manual trans 150

STORM FWD/1.6L-I4 (95hp)

Model	WS	Ret
2+2 2dr Cpe	825	1500
Base 2dr Hbk	800	1475
GSi 2dr Cpe	1125	2025

Add:

Deduct:
No air cond 150
Manual trans 125

1990 WS Ret

METRO FWD/1.0L-I3 (49hp)

Model	WS	Ret
Base 4dr Hbk	300	750
Base 2dr Hbk	275	725
LSi 4dr Hbk	375	825
LSi 2dr Hbk	350	800
XFi (5sp) 2dr Hbk	175	600

Add:

Deduct:
Man trans (not XFi) 100
No air cond 100

PRIZM FWD/1.6L-I4 (102hp)

Model	WS	Ret
Base 4dr Hbk	1025	1925
Base 4dr Sdn	1000	1700
GSi 4dr Hbk	1175	2075
GSi 4dr Sdn	1150	2050

Add:
LSi trim (Base only) 50
Sunroof-pwr 50

Deduct:
No air cond 150
Manual trans 125

STORM FWD/1.6L-I4 (95hp)

Model	WS	Ret
2+2 Sport 2dr Cpe	725	1250
GSi Sport 2dr Cpe	950	1650

Add:

Deduct:
No air cond 125
Manual trans 125

1989 WS Ret

METRO FWD/1.0L-I3 (55hp)

Model	WS	Ret
Base (5sp) 2dr Hbk	150	575
LSi 4dr Hbk	300	750
LSi 2dr Hbk	275	725

Add:

Deduct:
No air cond 75
Man trans (not Base) 50

SPECTRUM FWD/1.5L-I4 (70hp)

Model	WS	Ret
Base 4dr Sdn	450	925
Base 2dr Hbk	375	825

Add:

Deduct:
No air cond 75
Manual trans 75

HONDA

2001 WS Ret

ACCORD FWD/2.3L-I4 (150hp)

Model	WS	Ret
DX (135hp) 4dr Sdn	11375	13600
EX 4dr Sdn	16350	18900
EX 2dr Cpe	16350	18900
LX 4dr Sdn	13650	16025
LX 2dr Cpe	13550	15925
VP (135hp) 4dr Sdn	12625	14925

Add:
3.0L-V6 (200hp) 600
ABS brakes (std EX) 375
Leather seats 425
Pwr seat 175
Wheels-alloy (std EX) 200

Deduct:
No air cond 825
Manual trans 750

CIVIC FWD/1.7L-I4 (115hp)

Model	WS	Ret
DX 4dr Sdn	9800	11900
DX 2dr Cpe	9625	11725
EX (127hp) 4dr Sdn	12125	14400
EX (127hp) 2dr Cpe	11975	14225
GX (CNG 4cyl) 4dr Sdn		
HX (117hp-5sp/CVT) 2dr Cpe	10625	12775
LX 4dr Sdn	11175	13375

Add:
Cassette (Honda)(DX) 125

Deduct:
No air cond 725
Man trans 650
No CD 175

INSIGHT FWD/1.0L-I3 (73hp)

Gas/Electric 2dr Hbk . . . .

PRELUDE FWD/2.2L-I4 (200hp)

Base 2dr Cpe . . . .
Type SH (5sp) 2dr Cpe . . . .

S2000 RWD/2.0L-I4 (240hp)

Model	WS	Ret
2-seat 2dr Cnv	25700	29775

2000 WS Ret

ACCORD FWD/2.3L-I4 (150hp)

Model	WS	Ret
DX (135hp) 4dr Sdn	10325	12475
EX 4dr Sdn	15175	17650
EX 2dr Cpe	15175	17650
LX 4dr Sdn	12525	14825
LX 2dr Cpe	12425	14700

Add:
3.0L-V6 (200hp) 475
ABS brakes (std EX) 275
CD player (std EX) 200
Leather seats 325
Pwr seat 125
Wheels-alloy (std EX) 175

Deduct:
No air cond 650
Manual trans 575

CIVIC FWD/1.6L-I4 (106hp)

Model	WS	Ret
CX 2dr Hbk	7725	9675
DX 4dr Sdn	9075	11125
DX 2dr Cpe	8925	10975
DX 2dr Hbk	8550	10575
EX (127hp) 4dr Sdn	11275	13475
EX (127hp) 2dr Cpe	11100	13300
HX (115hp-5sp/CVT) 2dr Hbk	9450	11525
LX 4dr Sdn	10325	12475
Si (160hp) 2dr Cpe	12925	15400
VP 4dr Sdn	8225	10300

Add:
ABS brakes (std EX sdn) 275
CD player (std EX,Si) 175
Cassette (Honda) 75

Deduct:
No air cond 550
Man trans (not HX) 500

INSIGHT FWD/1.0L-I3 (73hp)

Gas/Electric 2dr Hbk . . . .

PRELUDE FWD/2.2L-I4 (200hp)

Model	WS	Ret
Base 2dr Cpe	15400	18075
Type SH (5sp) 2dr Cpe	17200	20025

Deduct:
Manual trans (Base) 525

S2000 RWD/2.0L-I4 (240hp)

Model	WS	Ret
2-seat 2dr Cnv	23625	27475

1999 WS Ret

ACCORD FWD/2.3L-I4 (150hp)

Model	WS	Ret
DX (135hp) 4dr Sdn	9375	11450
EX 4dr Sdn	13875	16250
EX 2dr Cpe	13875	16250
LX 4dr Sdn	11400	13625
LX 2dr Cpe	11300	13500

Add:
3.0L-V6 (200hp) 375
ABS brakes (std EX) 225
CD player (std EX) 150
Leather seats 275
Pwr seat 100
Wheels-alloy (std EX) 125

Deduct:
No air cond 525
Manual trans 475

CIVIC FWD/1.6L-I4 (106hp)

Model	WS	Ret
CX 2dr Hbk	7275	9200
DX 4dr Sdn	8475	10475
DX 2dr Cpe	8325	10325
DX 2dr Hbk	8000	9975
EX (127hp) 4dr Sdn	10550	12700
EX (127hp) 2dr Cpe	10400	12550
HX (115hp-5sp/CVT) 2dr Hbk	8825	10850
LX 4dr Sdn	9650	11750
Si (5sp/160hp) 2dr Cpe	11850	14100

Add:
ABS brakes (std EX sdn) 225
CD player (std EX,Si) 125
Cassette (Honda) 50

Deduct:
No air cond 450
Man trans (not HX) 425

PRELUDE FWD/2.2L-I4 (200hp)

Model	WS	Ret
Base 2dr Cpe	14050	16600
Type SH (5sp) 2dr Cpe	15100	18100

Deduct:
Manual trans (Base) 425

1998 WS Ret

ACCORD FWD/2.3L-I4 (150hp)

Model	WS	Ret
DX (135hp) 4dr Sdn	8575	10700
EX 4dr Sdn	12400	14825
EX 2dr Cpe	12400	14825
LX 4dr Sdn	10325	12600
LX 2dr Cpe	10250	12500

Add:
3.0L-200hp V6 325
ABS brakes (std EX) 200
Alloy wheels (std EX) 100

Leather seats	225	
Pwr seat	75	

Deduct:

No air cond	450	
Manual trans	400	

CIVIC — FWD/1.6L-I4 (106hp)

Model	WS	Ret
CX 2dr Hbk	6500	8450
DX 4dr Sdn	7550	9600
DX 2dr Cpe	7450	9475
DX 2dr Hbk	7150	9150
EX (127hp) 4dr Sdn	9275	11450
EX (127hp) 2dr Cpe	9125	11300
HX (115hp-5sp/CVT) 2dr Hbk	7850	9925
LX 4dr Sdn	8525	10650

Add:

- ABS brakes (std EX sdn) 200
- Alloy wheels (std HX) 75
- Cassette (Honda) 50

Deduct:

- No air cond 375
- Man trans (not HX) 350

PRELUDE — FWD/2.2L-I4 (195hp)

Model	WS	Ret
Base 2dr Cpe	12925	15400
Type SH (5sp) 2dr Cpe	14375	16975

Deduct:

- Manual trans (Base) 350

1997 — WS Ret

ACCORD — FWD/2.2L-I4 (130hp)

Model	WS	Ret
DX 4dr Sdn	7225	9250
EX (145hp) 4dr Sdn	10400	12675
EX (145hp) 4dr Wgn	10800	13100
EX (145hp) 2dr Cpe	10425	12700
LX 4dr Sdn	8700	10825
LX 4dr Wgn	9200	11375
LX 2dr Cpe	8500	10625
Special Edit. 4dr Sdn	9350	11525
Special Edit. 2dr Cpe	9150	11325

Add:

- 2.7L V6 250
- ABS brakes (std EX) 175
- Alloy wheels (std EX) 75
- Leather seats 175
- Pwr seat 50

Deduct:

- No air cond 375
- Manual trans 325

CIVIC — FWD/1.6L-I4 (106hp)

Model	WS	Ret
CX 2dr Hbk	5625	7500
DX 4dr Sdn	6550	8500
DX 2dr Cpe	6425	8375
DX 2dr Hbk	6250	8175
EX (127hp) 4dr Sdn	8125	10200
EX (127hp) 2dr Cpe	8000	10075
HX (115hp-5sp/CVT) 2dr Hbk	6875	8850
LX 4dr Sdn	7525	9550

Add:

- ABS brakes (std EX sdn) 150
- Alloy wheels (std HX) 50
- Cassette (Honda) 25

Deduct:

- No air cond 325
- Man trans (not HX) 275

DEL SOL — FWD/1.6L-I4 (106hp)

Model	WS	Ret
S 2dr Cpe	7800	9850
Si (127hp) 2dr Cpe	8750	10875
VTEC (160hp/5sp) Cpe	9725	11950

Deduct:

- No air cond 325

PRELUDE — FWD/2.2L-I4 (195hp)

Model	WS	Ret
Base 2dr Cpe	10775	13075
Type SH (5sp) 2dr Cpe	12050	14450

Deduct:

- Manual trans (Base) 300

1996 — WS Ret

ACCORD — FWD/2.2L-I4 (130hp)

Model	WS	Ret
Anniv. Edit. 4dr Sdn	8275	10375
DX 4dr Sdn	5700	7600
EX (145hp) 4dr Sdn	8475	10600
EX (145hp) 4dr Wgn	8375	10475
EX (145hp) 2dr Cpe	8475	10600
LX 4dr Sdn	7025	9025
LX 4dr Wgn	7425	9450
LX 2dr Cpe	6825	8800

Add:

- 2.7L V6 225
- ABS brakes (std EX) 150
- Alloy wheels (std EX) 50
- Leather seats 150
- Pwr seat 25

Deduct:

- No air cond 300
- Manual trans 275

CIVIC — FWD/1.6L-I4 (106hp)

Model	WS	Ret
CX (5sp) 2dr Hbk	3600	5175
DX 4dr Sdn	5100	6950
DX 2dr Cpe	5000	6825
DX 2dr Hbk	4750	6525
EX (127hp) 4dr Sdn	6500	8450
EX (127hp) 2dr Cpe	6375	8325
HX (115hp-5sp) 2dr Hbk	5300	7150
LX 4dr Sdn	5925	7825

Add:

- ABS brakes 150
- Alloy wheels (std HX) 50
- Cassette 25

Deduct:

- No air cond 250
- Man trans (not HX) 225

DEL SOL — FWD/1.6L-I4 (106hp)

Model	WS	Ret
S 2dr Cpe	6300	8250
Si (127hp) 2dr Cpe	7200	9200
VTEC (160hp/5sp) Cpe	8025	10100

Deduct:

- No air cond 250

PRELUDE — FWD/2.2L-I4 (135hp)

Model	WS	Ret
S 2dr Cpe	7700	9750
Si (2.3L-160hp) 2dr Cpe	9100	11275
VTEC (190hp/5sp) 2dr Cpe	10675	12975

Add:

- Alloy wheels (S) 50

Deduct:

- Manual trans (S,Si) 250

1995 — WS Ret

ACCORD — FWD/2.2L-I4 (130hp)

Model	WS	Ret
DX 4dr Sdn	4700	6475
EX (145hp) 4dr Sdn	6975	8975
EX (145hp) 4dr Wgn	7300	9325
EX (145hp) 2dr Cpe	6875	8850
LX 4dr Sdn	5750	7650
LX 4dr Wgn	6125	8050
LX 2dr Cpe	5575	7450

Add:

- 2.7L V6 200
- ABS brakes 150
- Alloy wheels (Std EX) 50
- Leather seats 150

Deduct:

- No air cond 275
- Manual trans 250

CIVIC — FWD/1.5L-I4 (70hp)

Model	WS	Ret
CX (70hp-5sp) 2dr Hbk	2875	4375
DX 4dr Sdn	4250	6000
DX 2dr Cpe	4150	5900
DX 2dr Hbk	3950	5675
EX (1.6L-125hp) 4dr Sdn	5475	7350
EX (1.6L-125hp) 2dr Cpe	5375	7250
LX 4dr Sdn	4700	6475
Si (1.6L-125hp/5sp) 2dr Hbk	4850	6650
VX (92hp/5sp) 2dr Hbk	4175	5925

Add:

- ABS brakes 125
- Alloy wheels 25
- Cassette 25

Deduct:

- No air cond 225
- Manual trans (DX,LX,EX) 200

DEL SOL — FWD/1.5L-I4 (102hp)

Model	WS	Ret
S 2dr Cpe	4875	6675
Si (1.6L-125hp) 2dr Cpe	5625	7500
VTEC (1.6L-160hp/5s Cpe	6325	8275

Deduct:

- No air cond 225

PRELUDE — FWD/2.2L-I4 (135hp)

Model	WS	Ret
S 2dr Cpe	6175	8100
SE (2.3L-160hp) 2dr Cpe	7600	9650
Si (2.3L-160hp) 2dr Cpe	7250	9275
VTEC (190hp/5sp) 2dr Cpe	8425	10525

Add:

- Alloy wheels (S) 50

Deduct:

- Manual trans 250

1994 — WS Ret

ACCORD — FWD/2.2L-I4 (130hp)

Model	WS	Ret
DX 4dr Sdn	4300	6050
DX 2dr Cpe	4225	5975
EX (145hp) 4dr Sdn	6175	8100
EX (145hp) 4dr Wgn	6400	8350
EX (145hp) 2dr Cpe	6025	7950
LX 4dr Sdn	5025	6850
LX 4dr Wgn	5350	7200
LX 2dr Cpe	4900	6700

Add:

- ABS brakes 125
- Alloy wheels (Std EX) 25
- Leather seats 125

Deduct:

- No air cond 250
- Manual trans 225

CIVIC — FWD/1.5L-I4 (70hp)

Model	WS	Ret
CX (70hp/5sp) 2dr Hbk	2500	3950
DX 4dr Sdn	3675	5275
DX 2dr Cpe	3575	5150
DX 2dr Hbk	3375	4950
EX (1.6L-125hp) 4dr Sdn	4725	6500
EX (1.6L-125hp) 2dr Cpe	4650	6425
LX 4dr Sdn	4125	5850
Si (1.6L-125hp/5sp) 2dr Hbk	4250	6000
VX (92hp/5sp) 2dr Hbk	3725	5425

Add:

- ABS brakes 125
- Alloy wheels 25
- Cassette 25

Deduct:

- No air cond 225
- Manual trans (DX,LX,EX) 200

DEL SOL — FWD/1.5L-I4 (102hp)

Model	WS	Ret
S 2dr Cpe	4325	6075
Si (1.6L-125hp) 2dr Cpe	4950	6775
VTEC (1.6L-160hp/5s Cpe	5550	7425

Deduct:
No air cond 225

PRELUDE FWD/2.2L-I4 (135hp)

S 2dr Cpe.	5425	7300
Si (2.3L-160hp) 2dr Cpe	6175	8100
Si 4WS (2.3L-160hp) Cpe	6625	8600
VTEC (190hp/5sp) 2dr Cpe.	7175	9175

Add:
Alloy wheels (S) 25

Deduct:
No air cond 225
Manual trans 200

1993 WS Ret

ACCORD FWD/2.2L-I4 (125hp)

10th Anniv 4dr Sdn	4450	6225
DX 4dr Sdn	3550	5125
DX 2dr Cpe	3450	5025
EX (140hp) 4dr Sdn.	4575	6350
EX (140hp) 4dr Wgn	4825	6625
EX (140hp) 2dr Cpe.	4475	6250
LX 4dr Sdn.	4000	5725
LX 4dr Wgn	4300	6050
LX 2dr Cpe.	3900	5625
SE 4dr Sdn	5100	6950
SE 2dr Cpe	5050	6900

Add:
Alloys (Std EX, Anniv) 25

Deduct:
No air cond 225
Manual trans 200

CIVIC FWD/1.5L-I4 (102hp)

CX (70hp/5sp) 2dr Hbk	1775	2900
DX 4dr Sdn	2625	4100
DX 2dr Cpe	2575	4025
DX 2dr Hbk	2425	3875
EX (1.6L-125hp) 4dr Sdn	3500	5075
EX (1.6L-125hp) 2dr Cpe	3425	5000
LX 4dr Sdn.	3000	4500
Si (1.6L-125hp/5sp) 2dr Hbk	3125	4675
VX (92hp/5sp) 2dr Hbk	2625	4100

Add:
Alloy wheels 25
Cassette 25

Deduct:
No air cond 175
Manual trans (DX,LX,EX) 175

DEL SOL FWD/1.5L-I4 (102hp)

S 2dr Cpe.	3325	4900
Si (1.6L-125hp) 2dr Cpe	3825	5525

Deduct:
No air cond 175

PRELUDE FWD/2.2L-I4 (135hp)

S 2dr Cpe.	4525	6300
Si (2.3L-160hp) 2dr Cpe	5050	6900
Si 4WS (2.3L-160hp) Cpe	5375	7250
VTEC (190hp/5sp) 2dr Cpe.	5925	7825

Add:
Alloy wheels (std Si) 25

Deduct:
No air cond 200
Manual trans 175

1992 WS Ret

ACCORD FWD/2.2L-I4 (125hp)

DX 4dr Sdn	3075	4625
DX 2dr Cpe	2950	4450
EX (140hp) 4dr Sdn.	3975	5700
EX (140hp) 4dr Wgn	4200	5950
EX (140hp) 2dr Cpe.	3900	5625
LX 4dr Sdn	3425	5000
LX 4dr Wgn	3700	5300
LX 2dr Cpe	3325	4900

Add:
Alloy wheels (std EX) 25

Deduct:
No air cond 200
Manual trans 200

CIVIC FWD/1.5L-I4 (70hp)

CX (70hp/5sp) 2dr Hbk	1550	2525
DX 4dr Sdn	2275	3475
DX 2dr Hbk	2100	3275
EX (1.6L-125hp) 4dr Sdn	3025	4550
LX 4dr Sdn	2600	4075
Si (1.6L-125hp/5sp) 2dr Hbk	2650	4125
VX (92hp/5sp) 2dr Hbk	2225	3425

Add:
Alloy wheels 25

Deduct:
No air cond 175
Manual trans (DX,LX,EX) 150

PRELUDE FWD/2.2L-I4 (135hp)

S 2dr Cpe	3875	5600
Si (2.3L-160hp) 2dr Cpe	4375	6125
Si 4WS (2.3L-160hp) Cpe.	4625	6400

Add:
Alloy wheels (std Si) 25

Deduct:
No air cond 175
Manual trans 175

1991 WS Ret

ACCORD FWD/2.2L-I4 (125hp)

DX 4dr Sdn	2525	3975
DX 2dr Cpe	2425	3875
EX (140hp) 4dr Sdn	3325	4900
EX (140hp) 4dr Wgn	3525	5100
EX (140hp) 2dr Cpe	3300	4850
LX 4dr Sdn	2800	4275
LX 4dr Wgn	3000	4500
LX 2dr Cpe	2700	4175
SE 4dr Sdn	3525	5100

Add:
Alloy wheels (DX, LX) 25

Deduct:
No air cond 175
Manual trans 175

CIVIC FWD/1.5L-I4 (70hp)

4WD (1.6L-108hp) 4dr Wgn	2300	3500
Base 4dr Wgn	2000	3175
Base (70hp/4sp) 2dr Hbk	1275	2225
DX 4dr Sdn	1850	3000
DX 2dr Hbk	1675	2800
EX (1.6L-108hp) 4dr Sdn	2275	3475
LX 4dr Sdn	2125	3300
Si (1.6L-108hp/5sp) 2dr Hbk	2050	3225

Deduct:
No air cond 150
Manual trans (not Si,Base) 125

CRX FWD/1.5L-I4 (92hp)

Base 2dr Hbk	2000	3175
HF (62hp/5sp) 2dr Hbk	1825	2975
Si (1.6L-108hp/5sp) 2dr Hbk	2225	3425

Add:
Alloy wheels (std Si) 25

Deduct:
No air cond 150
Man trans (Base only) 125

PRELUDE FWD/2.0L-I4 (135hp)

Si 2.0 2dr Cpe	3150	4700
Si (2.1L-140hp) 2dr Cpe	3375	4950
Si 4WS (2.1L-140hp) Cpe	3525	5100

Add:
Alloy wheels (2.0 only) 25

Deduct:
No air cond 175
Manual trans 150

1990 WS Ret

ACCORD FWD/2.2L-I4 (125hp)

DX 4dr Sdn.	2075	3250
DX 2dr Cpe.	2000	3175
EX (140hp) 4dr Sdn	2775	4250
EX (140hp) 2dr Cpe	2700	4175
LX 4dr Sdn	2325	3750
LX 2dr Cpe	2225	3425

Add:
Alloy whls (DX,LX only) 25

Deduct:
No air cond 150
Manual trans 150

CIVIC FWD/1.5L-I4 (70hp)

4WD (1.6L-108hp) 4dr Wgn.	2000	3175
Base 4dr Wgn.	1775	2900
Base (70hp/4sp) 2dr Hbk	1100	2025
DX 4dr Sdn.	1600	2700
DX 2dr Hbk.	1450	2425
EX (1.6L-108hp) 4dr Sdn	1925	3075
LX 4dr Sdn	1800	2925
Si (1.6L-108hp/5sp) 2dr Hbk	1750	2875

Deduct:
No air cond 125
Manual trans (not Si,Base) . . . 125

CRX FWD/1.5L-I4 (92hp)

Base 2dr Hbk	1700	2825
HF (62hp/5sp) 2dr Hbk.	1550	2525
Si (1.6L-108hp/5sp) 2dr Hbk	1875	3025

Add:

Deduct:
No air cond 125
Man trans (Base only) 125

PRELUDE FWD/2.0L-I4 (140hp)

S 2dr Cpe.	2525	3975
Si 2.0 (135hp) 2dr Cpe.	2700	4175
Si (2.1L-140hp) 2dr Cpe.	2850	4350
Si 4WS (2.1L-140hp) Cpe	3025	4550

Add:
Alloy wheels (2.0) 25

Deduct:
No air cond 150
Manual trans 125

1989 WS Ret

ACCORD FWD/2.0L-I4 (98hp)

DX 4dr Sdn.	1450	2425
DX 2dr Cpe.	1400	2375
DX 2dr Hbk.	1375	2350
LX 4dr Sdn	1500	2475
LXi (120hp) 4dr Sdn.	1700	2825
LXi (120hp) 2dr Cpe.	1650	2775
LXi (120hp) 2dr Hbk.	1625	2725
SEi (120hp) 4dr Sdn.	1825	2975
SEi (120hp) 2dr Cpe.	1775	2900

Add:

Deduct:
No air cond 125
Manual trans 125

CIVIC FWD/1.5L-I4 (70hp)

4WD (1.6L-108hp) 4dr Wgn.	1450	2425
Base 4dr Wgn.	1225	2175

Base (70hp/4sp) 2dr Hbk	950	1675
DX 4dr Sdn	1175	2125
DX 2dr Hbk	1050	1975
LX 4dr Sdn	1300	2250
Si (1.6L-108hp/5sp) 2dr Hbk	1250	2200

Add:

Deduct:
No air cond . . . 75
Manual trans (not Si,Bse Hbk) . . 75

CRX FWD/1.5L-I4 (70hp)

Base 2dr Hbk	1325	2275
HF (62hp/5sp) 2dr Hbk	1225	2175
Si (1.6L-108hp/5sp) 2dr Hbk	1550	2525

Add:

Deduct:
No air cond . . . 75
Man trans (Base only) . . . 75

PRELUDE FWD/2.0L-I4 (104hp)

S 2dr Cpe	1575	2675
Si (135hp) 2dr Cpe	1775	2900
Si 4WS (135hp) 2dr Cpe	1850	3000

Add:

Deduct:
No air cond . . . 125
Manual trans . . . 100

1988 WS Ret

ACCORD FWD/2.0L-I4 (98hp)

	WS	Ret
DX 4dr Sdn	1150	2100
DX 2dr Cpe	1125	2075
DX 2dr Hbk	1125	2075
LX 4dr Sdn	1225	2175
LXi (120hp) 4dr Sdn	1400	2375
LXi (120hp) 2dr Cpe	1350	2300
LXi (120hp) 2dr Hbk	1325	2275

Add:

Deduct:
No air cond . . . 100
Manual trans . . . 75

CIVIC FWD/1.5L-I4 (70hp)

	WS	Ret
4WD (1.6L-105hp/6sp 4dr Wgn	1200	2150
Base 4dr Wgn	1050	1975
Base (70hp/4sp) 2dr Hbk	775	1325
DX 4dr Sdn	975	1700
DX 2dr Hbk	875	1600
LX 4dr Sdn	1125	2075

Add:

Deduct:
No air cond . . . 50
Man trans (not Bse Hbk,4WD) . . 50

CRX FWD/1.5L-I4 (92hp)

	WS	Ret
DX 2dr Hbk	1125	2075
HF (62hp/5sp) 2dr Hbk	1025	1950
Si (1.6L-105hp/5sp) 2dr Hbk	1325	2275

Add:

Deduct:
No air cond . . . 50
Man trans (DX only) . . . 50

PRELUDE FWD/2.0L-I4 (104hp)

	WS	Ret
S 2dr Cpe	1375	2350
Si (135hp) 2dr Cpe	1550	2525
Si 4WS (135hp) 2dr Cpe	1600	2700

Add:

Deduct:
No air cond . . . 100
Manual trans . . . 50

HYUNDAI

2001 WS Ret

ACCENT FWD/1.6L-I4 (105hp)

	WS	Ret
GL 4dr Sdn	6975	8800
GS 2dr Hbk	6625	8425
L (5sp) 2dr Hbk	5850	7600

Add:
Pwr dr locks . . . 150
Alloy wheels . . . 175
CD Player . . . 225
Pwr windows . . . 175
Sunroof-manual . . . 200

Deduct:
No air cond . . . 725
Manual trans (not L) . . . 600

ELANTRA FWD/2.0L-I4 (140hp)

	WS	Ret
GLS 4dr Sdn	8625	10550
GT 4dr Hbk		

Add:
ABS brakes . . . 375
Alloy wheels (std GT) . . . 175
CD player (std GT) . . . 200
Cruise ctrl . . . 150
Moonroof-power . . . 450

Deduct:
No air cond . . . 725
Manual trans . . . 650

SONATA FWD/2.4L-I4 (149hp)

	WS	Ret
Base 4dr Sdn	9825	11800
GLS (6cyl) 4dr Sdn	11500	13575

Add:
ABS brakes . . . 375
CD player (std GLS) . . . 250
Leather seats . . . 350
Sunroof-pwr . . . 475

Deduct:
Manual trans . . . 750

TIBURON FWD/2.0L-I4 (140hp)

	WS	Ret
Base 2dr Cpe	10475	12500

Add:
ABS brakes . . . 300
CD player . . . 250
Leather seats . . . 350
Sunroof-pwr . . . 450

Deduct:
Manual trans . . . 725
No Air Cond . . . 775

XG300 FWD/3.0L-V6 (192hp)

	WS	Ret
Luxury 4dr Sdn	14375	16625

Add:
8-Disc CD changer . . . 350
Moonroof-pwr . . . 625
CD player (std GLS) . . . 250
Leather seats . . . 350
Sunroof-pwr . . . 475
Traction ctrl . . . 175

2000 WS Ret

ACCENT FWD/1.5L-I4 (92hp)

	WS	Ret
GL 4dr Sdn	6100	7875
GS 2dr Hbk	5725	7475
L (5sp) 2dr Hbk	4975	6675

Add:
Pwr dr locks . . . 100
Alloy wheels . . . 150
CD Player . . . 175
Pwr windows . . . 150
Sunroof-manual . . . 150

Deduct:
No air cond . . . 550
Manual trans (not L) . . . 475

ELANTRA FWD/2.0L-I4 (140hp)

	WS	Ret
GLS 4dr Sdn	7150	8975
GLS 4dr Wgn	7750	9625

Add:
ABS brakes . . . 275
Alloy wheels . . . 150
CD player . . . 175
Cruise ctrl . . . 75
Moonroof-power . . . 350

Deduct:
No air cond . . . 550
Manual trans . . . 500

SONATA FWD/2.4L-I4 (149hp)

	WS	Ret
Base 4dr Sdn	8350	10250
GLS (6cyl) 4dr Sdn	10100	12100

Add:
ABS brakes . . . 275
CD player (std GLS) . . . 175
Leather seats . . . 275
Sunroof-pwr . . . 375
Traction ctrl . . . 100

Deduct:
Manual trans . . . 575

TIBURON FWD/2.0L-I4 (140hp)

	WS	Ret
Base 2dr Cpe	9025	10975

Add:
ABS brakes . . . 250
CD player . . . 175
Leather seats . . . 275
Sunroof-pwr . . . 350

Deduct:
Manual trans . . . 575
No Air Cond . . . 600

1999 WS Ret

ACCENT FWD/1.5L-I4 (92hp)

	WS	Ret
GL 4dr Sdn	5000	6700
GS 2dr Hbk	4675	6325
L (5sp) 2dr Hbk	4000	5625

Add:
ABS brakes . . . 175
Alloy wheels (std GSi) . . . 100
CD Player . . . 150
Pwr windows . . . 100
Sunroof-manual . . . 125

Deduct:
No air cond . . . 450
Manual trans (not L) . . . 400

ELANTRA FWD/2.0L-I4 (140hp)

	WS	Ret
GL 4dr Sdn	5900	7650
GL 4dr Wgn	6375	8150
GLS 4dr Sdn	6650	8450
GLS 4dr Wgn	7075	8900

Add:
ABS brakes . . . 225
Alloy wheels . . . 100
CD player . . . 125
Cruise ctrl . . . 50
Premium sound . . . 50
Sunroof-power . . . 300

Deduct:
No air cond . . . 450
Manual trans . . . 425

SONATA FWD/2.4L-I4 (149hp)

	WS	Ret
Base 4dr Sdn	6450	8225
GL 4dr Sdn	7125	8950
GLS (6cyl) 4dr Sdn	8050	9925

Add:
ABS brakes . . . 225
Alloy wheels (std GLS) . . . 125
CD player (std GLS) . . . 150
Cruise ctrl (std GLS) . . . 100

Option	Value
Leather seats	225
Sunroof-pwr	300
Traction ctrl	50

Deduct:

Option	Value
Manual trans	475

TIBURON — FWD/2.0L-I4 (140hp)

Model	WS	Ret
Base 2dr Cpe	7375	9225
FX 2dr Cpe	8600	10525

Add:

Option	Value
ABS brakes	200
CD player	150
Cruise ctrl	100
Leather seats	225
Sunroof-pwr	300
Wheels-alloy	125

Deduct:

Option	Value
Manual trans	475
No Air Cond	500

1998 — WS Ret

ACCENT — FWD/1.5L-I4 (92hp)

Model	WS	Ret
GL 4dr Sdn	4025	5650
GS 2dr Hbk	3750	5350
GSI 2dr Hbk	4275	5900
L (5sp) 2dr Hbk	3150	4600

Add:

Option	Value
ABS brakes	150
Alloy wheels (std GSi)	75
CD Player	75
Cassette	50
Sunroof-manual	100

Deduct:

Option	Value
No air cond	375
Manual trans (not L)	325

ELANTRA — FWD/1.8L-I4 (130hp)

Model	WS	Ret
Base 4dr Sdn	4350	5975
Base 4dr Wgn	4700	6350
GLS 4dr Sdn	4950	6650
GLS 4dr Wgn	5325	7050

Add:

Option	Value
ABS brakes	200
Alloy wheels	75
CD player	100
Cruise ctrl	50
Premium sound	50
Sunroof-power	250

Deduct:

Option	Value
No air cond	375
Manual trans	350

SONATA — FWD/2.0L-I4 (137hp)

Model	WS	Ret
Base 4dr Sdn	4650	6300
GL 4dr Sdn	5225	6950
GLS (6cyl) 4dr Sdn	6025	7775

Add:

Option	Value
3.0 Liter V6 (GL)	250
ABS brakes	200
Alloy wheels (std GLS)	100
CD player	125
Cruise ctrl (std GLS)	75
Leather seats	200
Sunroof-pwr	250

Deduct:

Option	Value
Manual trans	400

TIBURON — FWD/2.0L-I4 (140hp)

Model	WS	Ret
Base 2dr Cpe	6000	7750
FX 2dr Cpe	7050	8875

Add:

Option	Value
Alloy wheels (std FX)	100
CD player	125
Cruise ctrl	75
Leather seats	200
Sunroof-pwr	250

Deduct:

Option	Value
Manual trans	400
No Air Cond	400

1997 — WS Ret

ACCENT — FWD/1.5L-I4 (92hp)

Model	WS	Ret
GL 4dr Sdn	2775	4175
GS 2dr Hbk	2525	3900
GT 2dr Hbk	3000	4425
L (5sp) 2dr Hbk	1975	3075

Add:

Option	Value
ABS brakes	100
Alloy wheels (std GT)	50
CD Player	50
Cassette	25
Sunroof-manual	50

Deduct:

Option	Value
No air cond	325
Manual steering (GS,GL)	50
Manual trans (not L)	275

ELANTRA — FWD/1.8L-I4 (130hp)

Model	WS	Ret
Base 4dr Sdn	3850	5450
Base 4dr Wgn	4250	5875
GLS 4dr Sdn	4450	6100
GLS 4dr Wgn	4750	6400

Add:

Option	Value
ABS brakes	150
Alloy wheels	50
Cassette (std GLS)	50
CD player	75
Cruise ctrl	25
Premium sound	25
Sunroof-power	200

Deduct:

Option	Value
No air cond	325
Manual trans	275

SONATA — FWD/2.0L-I4 (137hp)

Model	WS	Ret
Base 4dr Sdn	3875	5475
GL 4dr Sdn	4375	6000
GLS (6cyl) 4dr Sdn	5075	6775

Add:

Option	Value
3.0 Liter V6 (GL)	200
ABS brakes	175
Alloy wheels (std GLS)	75
CD player	100
Cruise ctrl (std GLS)	50
Leather seats	150
Sunroof-pwr	200

Deduct:

Option	Value
Manual trans	325

TIBURON — FWD/1.8L-I4 (130hp)

Model	WS	Ret
Base 2dr Cpe	5075	6775
FX 2dr Cpe	6025	7775

Add:

Option	Value
Alloy wheels (std FX)	75
CD player	100
Cruise ctrl	50
Leather seats	150
Sunroof-pwr	200

Deduct:

Option	Value
Manual trans	325
No Air Cond	325

1996 — WS Ret

ACCENT — FWD/1.5L-I4 (92hp)

Model	WS	Ret
Base 4dr Sdn	2325	3675
Base 2dr Hbk	2100	3225
GT 2dr Hbk	2525	3900
L (5sp) 2dr Hbk	1625	2675

Add:

Option	Value
ABS brakes	100
Alloy wheels (std GT)	50
Cassette	25
Sunroof-manual	25

Deduct:

Option	Value
No air cond	250
Manual steering	25
Manual trans	225

ELANTRA — FWD/1.8L-I4 (130hp)

Model	WS	Ret
Base 4dr Sdn	2225	3350
Base 4dr Wgn	2575	3950
GLS 4dr Sdn	2725	4125
GLS 4dr Wgn	3075	4525

Add:

Option	Value
ABS brakes	150
Alloy wheels	50
Cassette (std GLS)	25
CD player	50
Cruise ctrl	25
Premium sound	25
Sunroof-power	175

Deduct:

Option	Value
No air cond	250
Manual trans	225

SONATA — FWD/2.0L-I4 (137hp)

Model	WS	Ret
Base 4dr Sdn	2300	3450
GL 4dr Sdn	2750	4150
GLS (6cyl) 4dr Sdn	3400	4875

Add:

Option	Value
3.0 Liter V6 (GL)	175
ABS brakes	150
Alloy wheels (std GLS)	50
CD player	75
Cruise ctrl (std GLS)	50
Leather seats	125
Sunroof-pwr	175

Deduct:

Option	Value
Manual trans	275

1995 — WS Ret

ACCENT — FWD/1.5L-I4 (92hp)

Model	WS	Ret
Base 4dr Sdn	1925	3025
Base 2dr Hbk	1725	2800
L (5sp) 2dr Hbk	1325	2250

Add:

Option	Value
ABS brakes	75
Cassette	25
Sunroof-manual	25
Wheels-alloy (std GT)	25

Deduct:

Option	Value
No air cond	225
Manual steering	25
Manual trans	200

ELANTRA — FWD/1.6L-I4 (113hp)

Model	WS	Ret
Base 4dr Sdn	1700	2775
GLS 4dr Sdn	2100	3225

Add:

Option	Value
ABS brakes	125
Alloy wheels	25
Cassette (std GLS)	25
CD player	50
Cruise ctrl	25
Premium sound	25
Sunroof-power	150

Deduct:

Option	Value
1.6 Litre	150
No air cond	225
Manual trans	200

SCOUPE — FWD/1.4L-I4 (92hp)

Model	WS	Ret
Base 2dr Cpe	1600	2650
LS 2dr Cpe	1950	3050
Turbo (5sp) 2dr Cpe	2000	3100

Add:

Option	Value
Alloy wheels (std Turbo)	25
Cassette (std Turbo,LS)	25
CD player	50
Cruise ctrl	25
Premium sound	25
Sunroof-manual	50

Deduct:
- No air cond 225
- Manual steering 25
- Manual trans 200

SONATA — FWD/2.0L-I4 (137hp)

Model	WS	Ret
Base 4dr Sdn	1900	3000
GL 4dr Sdn	2250	3375
GLS (6cyl) 4dr Sdn	2775	4175

Add:
- 3.0 Liter V6 150
- ABS brakes 125
- Alloy wheels (std GLS) 50
- CD player 50
- Cruise ctrl (std GLS) 25
- Leather seats 125
- Pwr dr locks (std GL,GLS) 25
- Pwr windows (std GL,GLS) 50
- Sunroof-pwr 150

Deduct:
- Manual trans 250

1994 — WS Ret

ELANTRA — FWD/1.6L-I4 (113hp)

Model	WS	Ret
Base 4dr Sdn	1175	2075
GLS 4dr Sdn	1500	2425

Add:
- ABS brakes 125
- Alloy wheels 25
- Cassette (std GLS) 25
- CD player 25
- Cruise ctrl 25
- Premium sound 25
- Sunroof-power 125

Deduct:
- No air cond 225
- Manual trans 200

EXCEL — FWD/1.5L-I4 (81hp)

Model	WS	Ret
Base 4dr Sdn	1025	1925
Base 2dr Hbk	875	1550
GL 4dr Sdn	1150	2050
GS 2dr Hbk	1000	1700

Add:
- Alloy wheels 25
- Cassette 25
- Sunroof-pwr 125

Deduct:
- No air cond 225
- Manual steering 25
- Manual trans 200

SCOUPE — FWD/1.5L-I4 (92hp)

Model	WS	Ret
Base 2dr Cpe	1275	2175
LS 2dr Cpe	1550	2475
Turbo (5sp) 2dr Cpe	1600	2650

Add:
- Alloy wheels (std Turbo) 25
- Cassette (std Turbo,LS) 25
- CD player 25
- Cruise ctrl 25
- Sunroof-manual 25

Deduct:
- No air cond 225
- Manual steering 25
- Manual trans 200

SONATA — FWD/2.0L-I4 (128hp)

Model	WS	Ret
Base 4dr Sdn	1475	2400
GLS 4dr Sdn	1775	2850

Add:
- 3.0 Liter V6 125
- ABS brakes 125
- Alloy wheels 25
- CD player 50
- Cruise ctrl (std GLS) 25
- Leather seats 100
- Pwr dr locks (std GLS) 25
- Pwr windows (std GLS) 25
- Sunroof-pwr 150

Deduct:
- Manual trans 225

1993 — WS Ret

ELANTRA — FWD/1.6L-I4 (113hp)

Model	WS	Ret
Base 4dr Sdn	1000	1700
GLS 4dr Sdn	1225	2125

Add:
- Alloy wheels 25
- Cassette (std GLS) 25
- Cruise ctrl 25
- Sunroof-power 125

Deduct:
- 1.6 Liter 4cyl 75
- No air cond 175
- Manual trans 175

EXCEL — FWD/1.5L-I4 (81hp)

Model	WS	Ret
Base (4sp) 4dr Sdn	725	1250
Base (4sp) 2dr Hbk	625	1125
GL 4dr Sdn	925	1625
GS 2dr Hbk	800	1475

Add:
- Alloy wheels 25
- Cassette 25
- Sunroof-pwr 100

Deduct:
- No air cond 175
- Manual steering 25
- Manual trans 175

SCOUPE — FWD/1.5L-I4 (92hp)

Model	WS	Ret
Base 2dr Cpe	1075	1975
LS 2dr Cpe	1275	2175
Turbo (5sp) 2dr Cpe	1325	2250

Add:
- Alloy wheels (std Turbo) 25
- Cassette (std Turbo) 25
- CD player 25
- Cruise ctrl 25
- Sunroof-manual 25

Deduct:
- No air cond 175
- Manual steering 25
- Manual trans 175

SONATA — FWD/2.0L-I4 (128hp)

Model	WS	Ret
Base 4dr Sdn	1225	2125
GLS 4dr Sdn	1500	2425

Add:
- 3.0 Liter V6 125
- ABS brakes 100
- Alloy wheels 25
- CD player 50
- Cruise ctrl (std GLS) 25
- Leather seats 75
- Pwr dr locks (std GLS) 25
- Pwr windows (std GLS) 25
- Sunroof-pwr 125

Deduct:
- Manual trans 200

1992 — WS Ret

ELANTRA — FWD/1.6L-I4 (113hp)

Model	WS	Ret
Base 4dr Sdn	800	1475
GLS 4dr Sdn	975	1675

Add:
- Alloy wheels 25
- Cruise ctrl 25
- Sunroof-power 75

Deduct:
- No air cond 175
- Manual trans 150

EXCEL — FWD/1.5L-I4 (81hp)

Model	WS	Ret
Base (4sp) 4dr Sdn	525	1000
Base (4sp) 2dr Hbk	475	950
GL 4dr Sdn	700	1225
GS 2dr Hbk	600	1100

Add:
- Alloy wheels 25
- Sunroof-pwr 75

Deduct:
- No air cond 175
- Manual trans 150

SCOUPE — FWD/1.5L-I4 (81hp)

Model	WS	Ret
Base 2dr Cpe	875	1550
LS 2dr Cpe	1075	1975

Add:
- Alloy wheels 25
- CD player 25
- Cruise control 25
- Sunroof-manual 25

Deduct:
- No air cond 175
- Manual trans 150

SONATA — FWD/2.0L-I4 (128hp)

Model	WS	Ret
Base 4dr Sdn	1025	1925
GLS 4dr Sdn	1250	2150

Add:
- 3.0 Liter V6 125
- ABS brakes 75
- Alloy wheels (std GLS) 25
- CD player 25
- Cruise ctrl 25
- Leather seats 50
- Pwr dr locks (std GLS) 25
- Pwr windows (std GLS) 25
- Sunroof-pwr 100

Deduct:
- No air cond 200
- Manual trans 200

1991 — WS Ret

EXCEL — FWD/1.5L-I4 (81hp)

Model	WS	Ret
Base (4sp) 4dr Sdn	375	825
Base (4sp) 2dr Hbk	325	775
GL 4dr Sdn	525	1000
GLS 4dr Sdn	575	1075
GS 2dr Hbk	450	925

Add:
- Alloy wheels 25
- Sunroof-pwr 50

Deduct:
- No air cond 150
- Manual trans 125

SCOUPE — FWD/1.5L-I4 (81hp)

Model	WS	Ret
Base 2dr Cpe	625	1125
LS 2dr Cpe	800	1475

Add:
- Alloy wheels 25
- Sunroof-manual 25

Deduct:
- No air cond 150
- Manual trans 125

SONATA — FWD/2.4L-I4 (116hp)

Model	WS	Ret
Base 4dr Sdn	775	1300
GLS 4dr Sdn	950	1650

Add:
- 3.0 liter V6 100
- Alloy wheels 25
- CD player 25
- Cruise ctrl 25
- Leather seats 50
- Pwr dr locks 25
- Pwr windows 25
- Sunroof-pwr 100

Deduct:
No air cond 175
Manual trans 175

1990 WS Ret

EXCEL FWD/1.5L-I4 (81hp)

	WS	Ret
Base (4sp) 4dr Sdn	125	525
Base (4sp) 2dr Hbk	75	475
GL 4dr Hbk	250	675
GL 4dr Sdn	250	675
GLS 4dr Sdn	325	775
GS 2dr Hbk	250	675

Add:
Sunroof-pwr 25

Deduct:
No air cond 125
Manual trans 125

SONATA FWD/2.4L-I4 (116hp)

	WS	Ret
Base 4dr Sdn	575	1075
GLS 4dr Sdn	725	1250

Add:
3.0 Liter V6 75
Alloy wheels 25
Leather seats 25
Pwr windows (std GLS) 25
Sunroof-pwr 75

Deduct:
No air cond 150
Manual trans 150

1989 WS Ret

EXCEL FWD/1.5L-I4 (68hp)

	WS	Ret
GL 4dr Hbk	200	625
GL 4dr Sdn	200	625
GL 2dr Hbk	175	600
GLS 4dr Hbk	200	625
GLS 4dr Sdn	200	625
GS 2dr Hbk	175	600
L (4sp) 4dr Sdn	100	500
L (4sp) 2dr Hbk	50	450

Add:
Sunroof-pwr 25

Deduct:
No air cond 75
Man trans (not Base Hbk) 75

SONATA FWD/2.4L-I4 (110hp)

	WS	Ret
Base 4dr Sdn	450	925
GLS 4dr Sdn	500	975

Add:
Sunroof-pwr 50

Deduct:
No air cond 125
Manual trans 125

1988 WS Ret

EXCEL FWD/1.5L-I4 (68hp)

	WS	Ret
GL 4dr Hbk	150	575
GL 4dr Sdn	150	575
GL 2dr Hbk	150	575
GLS 4dr Hbk	175	600
GLS 4dr Sdn	175	600
GS 2dr Hbk	150	575
L (4sp) 4dr Sdn	75	475
L (4sp) 2dr Hbk	50	450

Add:
Sunroof-pwr 25

Deduct:
No air cond 50
Man trans (not L) 50

INFINITI

2001 WS Ret

G20 FWD/2.0L-I4 (145hp)

	WS	Ret
Luxury 4dr Sdn	15775	18125
Touring 4dr Sdn	16375	18750

Add:
Moonroof-pwr (std Touring) . . . 525
Leather seats (std Touring) . . . 425
CD changer 325

I30 FWD/3.0L-V6 (227hp)

	WS	Ret
Luxury 4dr Sdn	21325	24725
Touring 4dr Sdn	23200	26750

Add:
CD changer 325
Traction cntrl 225
Navigation System 1025

Deduct:
No moonroof 675

Q45 RWD/4.1L-V8 (266hp)

	WS	Ret
Sedan 4dr Sdn		
Touring 4dr Sdn		

2000 WS Ret

G20 FWD/2.0L-I4 (145hp)

	WS	Ret
Luxury 4dr Sdn	14175	16425
Touring 4dr Sdn	14775	17050

Add:
Moonroof-pwr 400
Leather seats 325
CD changer 250

I30 FWD/3.0L-V6 (227hp)

	WS	Ret
Luxury 4dr Sdn	19300	22500
Touring 4dr Sdn	21100	24475

Add:
CD changer 250
Traction cntrl 175

Deduct:
No moonroof 525

Q45 RWD/4.1L-V8 (266hp)

	WS	Ret
Sedan 4dr Sdn	27725	30775
Touring 4dr Sdn	28375	31450

Add:
Anniv. Edit. 425
CD changer 300

1999 WS Ret

G20 FWD/2.0L-I4 (145hp)

	WS	Ret
Base 4dr Sdn	13575	15775
Touring 4dr Sdn	14100	16350

Add:
Moonroof-pwr 325
Pwr seat 100
Leather seats 275
CD changer 225

I30 FWD/3.0L-V6 (190hp)

	WS	Ret
Base 4dr Sdn	15875	18775
Limited 4dr Sdn	18275	21375
Touring 4dr Sdn	17575	20625

Add:
Moonroof-pwr (base) 325
Traction cntrl (base) 175
Leather seats (base) 275
CD changer (base) 225

Deduct:
Manual trans 550

Q45 RWD/4.1L-V8 (266hp)

	WS	Ret
Sedan 4dr Sdn	24025	26850
Touring 4dr Sdn	24600	27450

Add:
Touring pkg 725
CD changer 250

1998 WS Ret

I30 FWD/3.0L-V6 (190hp)

	WS	Ret
Sedan 4dr Sdn	13550	16225
Touring 4dr Sdn	15000	17800

Add:
Moonroof-pwr (std Trng) 275
Traction cntrl (std Trng) 150
Leather seats 225

Deduct:
Manual trans 450

Q45 RWD/4.1L-V8 (266hp)

	WS	Ret
Sedan 4dr Sdn	19850	22425

Add:
Touring pkg 600
CD changer 200

1997 WS Ret

I30 FWD/3.0L-V6 (190hp)

	WS	Ret
Sedan 4dr Sdn	11250	13575
Touring 4dr Sdn	12550	15000

Add:
Moonroof-pwr (std Trng) 225
Traction control 100
Leather seats 175

Deduct:
Manual trans 375

J30 RWD/3.0L-V6 (210hp)

	WS	Ret
Sedan 4dr Sdn	11950	14050

Add:
Touring pkg 500

Q45 RWD/4.1L-V8 (266hp)

	WS	Ret
Sedan 4dr Sdn	16775	19175

Add:
Touring pkg 500

1996 WS Ret

G20 FWD/2.0L-I4 (140hp)

	WS	Ret
Sedan 4dr Sdn	6150	7925

Add:
Leather seats 150
Moonroof-pwr 200
Touring pkg 150

Deduct:
Manual trans 275

I30 FWD/3.0L-V6 (190hp)

	WS	Ret
Sedan 4dr Sdn	8625	10550
Touring 4dr Sdn	9800	11775

Add:
Moonroof-pwr (std Trng) 200
Traction control 75
Leather seats 150

Deduct:
Manual trans 325

J30 RWD/3.0L-V6 (210hp)

	WS	Ret
Sedan 4dr Sdn	8950	10875

Add:
Touring pkg 425

Q45 RWD/4.5L-V8 (278hp)

	WS	Ret
Sedan 4dr Sdn	12450	14600

Add:
Touring pkg 425

Traction ctrl 250

1995 WS Ret

G20 FWD/2.0L-I4 (140hp)

	WS	Ret
Sedan 4dr Sdn	4850	6525

Add:
Leather seats 125
Moonroof-pwr 200
Touring pkg 125

Deduct:
Manual trans 250

J30 RWD/3.0L-V6 (210hp)

	WS	Ret
Sedan 4dr Sdn	7225	9050

Add:
Touring pkg 375

Q45 RWD/4.5L-V8 (278hp)

	WS	Ret
Sedan 4dr Sdn	9875	11875

Add:
Active suspension 975
Touring pkg 375
Traction ctrl (std susp) 225

1994 WS Ret

G20 FWD/2.0L-I4 (140hp)

	WS	Ret
Sedan 4dr Sdn	4200	5825

Add:
Leather seats 125
Sunroof-pwr 175
Touring pkg 100

Deduct:
Manual trans 225

J30 RWD/3.0L-V6 (210hp)

	WS	Ret
Sedan 4dr Sdn	6225	8000

Add:
Touring pkg 350

Q45 RWD/4.5L-V8 (278hp)

	WS	Ret
Sedan 4dr Sdn	7850	9725

Add:
Active suspension 875
Touring pkg 325
Traction ctrl (std susp) 200

1993 WS Ret

G20 FWD/2.0L-I4 (140hp)

	WS	Ret
Sedan 4dr Sdn	3625	5100

Add:
Leather seats 100
Sunroof-pwr 150

Deduct:
Manual trans 225

J30 RWD/3.0L-V6 (210hp)

	WS	Ret
Sedan 4dr Sdn	4975	6675

Add:
Touring pkg 300

Q45 RWD/4.5L-V8 (278hp)

	WS	Ret
Sedan 4dr Sdn	6225	8000

Add:
Active suspension 800
Touring pkg 300
Traction ctrl (std susp) 175

1992 WS Ret

G20 FWD/2.0L-I4 (140hp)

	WS	Ret
Sedan 4dr Sdn	2600	3975

Add:
Leather seats 75
Sunroof-pwr 150

Deduct:
Manual trans 200

M30 RWD/3.0L-V6 (162hp)

	WS	Ret
Convertible 2dr Cnv	5350	7075
Coupe 2dr Cpe	3625	5100

Q45 RWD/4.5L-V8 (278hp)

	WS	Ret
Sedan 4dr Sdn	5075	6775

Add:
Active suspension 775
Touring pkg 275
Traction ctrl (std susp) 175

1991 WS Ret

G20 FWD/2.0L-I4 (140hp)

	WS	Ret
Sedan 4dr Sdn	2225	3350

Add:
Leather seats 50
Sunroof-pwr 125

Deduct:
Manual trans 175

M30 RWD/3.0L-V6 (162hp)

	WS	Ret
Convertible 2dr Cnv	4600	6250
Coupe 2dr Cpe	3050	4500

Add:
CD player 25

Q45 RWD/4.5L-V8 (278hp)

	WS	Ret
Sedan 4dr Sdn	4175	5800

Add:
Active suspension 575
CD player 25
Touring pkg 250
Traction ctrl (std susp) 100

1990 WS Ret

M30 RWD/3.0L-V6 (162hp)

	WS	Ret
Coupe 2dr Cpe	2550	3925

Add:
CD player 25

Q45 RWD/4.5L-V8 (278hp)

	WS	Ret
Sedan 4dr Sdn	3525	5000

Add:
Touring pkg 300

ISUZU

1993 WS Ret

STYLUS FWD/1.6L-I4 (90hp)

	WS	Ret
S 4dr Sdn	1175	2075

Add:
Alloy wheels 25
Cassette 25
Pwr dr locks 25
Pwr windows 25

Deduct:
No air cond 175
Manual steering 25
Manual trans 175

1992 WS Ret

IMPULSE FWD/1.8L-I4 (140hp)

	WS	Ret
RS (5sp,Turbo) 2dr Hbk	1675	2725
XS 2+2 2dr Hbk	1300	2200
XS 2dr Hbk	1300	2200

Add:
ABS brakes 75
Alloy wheels (XS only) 25
Cruise ctrl 25
Pwr dr locks 25
Pwr windows 25
Sunroof-pwr 100

Deduct:
No air cond 175
Manual trans 150

STYLUS FWD/1.6L-I4 (95hp)

	WS	Ret
RS (5sp) 4dr Sdn	1150	2050
S 4dr Sdn	975	1675

Add:
Alloy wheels (std RS) 25
Cruise ctrl 25
Pwr dr locks 25
Pwr windows 25
Sunroof-pwr 75

Deduct:
No air cond 175
Man trans (not RS) 150

1991 WS Ret

IMPULSE FWD/1.6L-I4 (130hp)

	WS	Ret
RS (5sp,AWD) 2dr Hbk	1525	2450
XS 2dr Hbk	1125	2025

Add:
ABS brakes 50
Alloy wheels (XS) 25
Pwr windows 25
Sunroof-pwr 125

Deduct:
No air cond 175
Manual trans 150

STYLUS FWD/1.6L-I4 (95hp)

	WS	Ret
S 4dr Sdn	925	1625
XS (5sp) 4dr Sdn	1100	2000

Add:
Alloy wheels 25
Pwr windows 25
Sunroof-pwr 50

Deduct:
No air cond 150
Manual trans 125

1990 WS Ret

IMPULSE FWD/2.3L-I4 (110hp)

	WS	Ret
XS 2dr Hbk	1025	1925

Add:
Alloy wheels 25

Deduct:
Manual trans 125

1989 WS Ret

I-MARK FWD/1.5L-I4 (70hp)

	WS	Ret
LS (5sp,Turbo) 4dr Sdn	450	925
RS (5sp,Turbo) 4dr Sdn	400	850
RS (5sp,Turbo) 2dr Hbk	350	800
S 4dr Sdn	325	775
S 2dr Hbk	300	750
XS 4dr Sdn	375	825
XS 2dr Hbk	350	800

Add:

Deduct:
No air cond 75
Man trans(S,XS)) 75

IMPULSE FWD/2.3L-I4 (110hp)

	WS	Ret
Sport 2dr Hbk	775	1300

Deduct:
Manual trans 100

1988 WS Ret

I-MARK FWD/1.5L-I4 (110hp)

	WS	Ret
LS (5sp,Turbo) 4dr Sdn	325	775

Model	WS	Ret
RS (5sp,Turbo) 2dr Hbk	275	725
S 4dr Sdn	250	675
S 2dr Hbk	225	650
Turbo (5sp) 4dr Sdn	300	750
Turbo (5sp) 2dr Hbk	250	675
XS 4dr Sdn	275	725
XS 2dr Hbk	250	675

Add:

Deduct:
- No air cond . . . 50
- Man trans (S,XS) . . . 50

IMPULSE — FWD/2.3L-I4 (110hp)

Model	WS	Ret
Sport 2dr Hbk	800	1475

Deduct:
- No air cond . . . 75
- Manual trans . . . 50

JAGUAR

2001 — WS Ret

S-TYPE — RWD/3.0L-V6 (240hp)

Model	WS	Ret
3.0L 4dr Sdn		
4.0L (V8/281hp) 4dr Sdn		

XJ-8 — RWD/4.0L-V8 (290hp)

Model	WS	Ret
Base 4dr Sdn		
L 4dr Sdn		
Vanden Plas 4dr Sdn		
VDP Supercharged 4dr Sdn		

XJ-R — RWD/4.0L-V8 (370hp)

Model	WS	Ret
Supercharged 4dr Sdn		

XK8 — RWD/4.0L-V8 (290hp)

Model	WS	Ret
2dr Cnv		
2dr Cpe		

XKR — RWD/4.0L-V8 (370hp)

Model	WS	Ret
Supercharged 2dr Cnv		
Supercharged 2dr Cpe		

2000 — WS Ret

S-TYPE — RWD/3.0L-V6 (240hp)

Model	WS	Ret
3.0L 4dr Sdn	28325	32025
4.0L (V8/281hp) 4dr Sdn	31450	35200

Add:
- Premium sound . . . 300
- 6-disc CD changer . . . 300
- Navigation sys . . . 600
- Sport pkg w/17" wheels . . . 525

Deduct:
- No CD . . . 250
- No moonroof . . . 525

XJ-8 — RWD/4.0L-V8 (290hp)

Model	WS	Ret
Base 4dr Sdn	33600	37425
L 4dr Sdn	36900	40975
Vanden Plas 4dr Sdn	39725	43975
VDP Supercharged 4dr Sdn		

Add:
- Premium sound . . . 300
- Navigation sys . . . 600

Deduct:
- No CD . . . 325

XJ-R — RWD/4.0L-V8 (370hp)

Model	WS	Ret
Supercharged 4dr Sdn		

XK8 — RWD/4.0L-V8 (290hp)

Model	WS	Ret
2dr Cnv	48025	52675
2dr Cpe	43625	48150

Add:
- Navigation sys . . . 600
- Wheels-18" alloy (std XKR) . . . 575

Deduct:
- No CD . . . 325

XKR — RWD/4.0L-V8 (370hp)

Model	WS	Ret
Supercharged 2dr Cnv		
Supercharged 2dr Cpe	51550	56425

1999 — WS Ret

XJ-8 — RWD/4.0L-V8 (290hp)

Model	WS	Ret
Base 4dr Sdn	30675	34350
L 4dr Sdn	33700	37550
Vanden Plas 4dr Sdn	36300	40325

Add:
- Harmon Kardon sound . . . 500
- Traction ctrl . . . 300

Deduct:
- No CD . . . 275

XJ-R — RWD/4.0L-V8 (370hp)

Model	WS	Ret
Supercharged 4dr Sdn	37475	41600

XK8 — RWD/4.0L-V8 (290hp)

Model	WS	Ret
2dr Cnv	43025	47500
2dr Cpe	39175	43425

Add:
- Harmon Kardon Sound . . . 500
- Chrome wheels . . . 475
- Traction ctrl . . . 300

Deduct:
- No CD . . . 275

1998 — WS Ret

XJ-8 — RWD/4.0L-V8 (290hp)

Model	WS	Ret
Base 4dr Sdn	25600	29100
L 4dr Sdn	28200	31900
Vanden Plas 4dr Sdn	30425	34100

Add:
- Harmon Kardon sound . . . 425

Deduct:
- No CD . . . 225

XJ-R — RWD/4.0L-V8 (290hp)

Model	WS	Ret
Supercharged 4dr Sdn	33275	37075

XK8 — RWD/4.0L-V8 (290hp)

Model	WS	Ret
2dr Cnv	37625	41750
2dr Cpe	33375	37200

Add:
- Harmon Kardon Sound . . . 425
- Chrome wheels . . . 400

Deduct:
- No CD . . . 225

1997 — WS Ret

XJ-6 — RWD/4.0L-I6 (245hp)

Model	WS	Ret
Base 4dr Sdn	19800	22825
L 4dr Sdn	22125	25325
Vanden Plas 4dr Sdn	25425	28900

Add:
- Traction control . . . 250

Deduct:
- No CD . . . 175

XJ-R — RWD/4.0L-I6 (322hp)

Model	WS	Ret
Supercharged 4dr Sdn	25425	28900

XK8 — RWD/4.0L-V8 (290hp)

Model	WS	Ret
2dr Cnv	31525	35275
2dr Cpe	28000	31675

1996 — WS Ret

XJ-12 — RWD/6.0L-V12 (313hp)

Model	WS	Ret
Luxury 4dr Sdn	20725	23825

XJ-6 — RWD/4.0L-I6 (245hp)

Model	WS	Ret
Base 4dr Sdn	15825	18525
Vanden Plas 4dr Sdn	18775	21725

Add:
- Traction control . . . 200

Deduct:
- No CD . . . 150

XJ-R — RWD/4.0L-I6 (322hp)

Model	WS	Ret
Supercharged 4dr Sdn	20250	23300

XJS — RWD/4.0L-I6 (237hp)

Model	WS	Ret
Convertible 2dr Cnv	21050	24175

1995 — WS Ret

XJ-12 — RWD/6.0L-V12 (313hp)

Model	WS	Ret
Luxury 4dr Sdn	16375	19125

Add:
- CD changer . . . 150

XJ-6 — RWD/4.0L-I6 (245hp)

Model	WS	Ret
Base 4dr Sdn	12925	15400
Vanden Plas 4dr Sdn	15125	17775

Add:
- CD changer . . . 150
- Sunroof-power (Base) . . . 225

XJ-R — RWD/4.0L-I6 (322hp)

Model	WS	Ret
Supercharged 4dr Sdn	17775	20625

XJS — RWD/4.0L-I6 (237hp)

Model	WS	Ret
Convertible 2dr Cnv	16675	19450
Coupe 2dr Cpe	13725	16250

Add:
- 6.0 Liter V12 . . . 2600
- 5-spd manual trans . . . 1050
- 16" alloys (6cyl w/at) . . . 175
- CD changer . . . 150

1994 — WS Ret

XJ-12 — RWD/6.0L-V12 (301hp)

Model	WS	Ret
4dr Sdn	11750	14000

Add:
- CD changer . . . 125

XJ-6 — RWD/4.0L-I6 (223hp)

Model	WS	Ret
Base 4dr Sdn	8650	10675
Vanden Plas 4dr Sdn	10025	12150

Add:
- CD changer . . . 125
- Sunroof-power (Base) . . . 200

XJS — RWD/4.0L-I6 (234hp)

Model	WS	Ret
Convertible 2dr Cnv	13575	15950
Coupe 2dr Cpe	11000	13175

Add:
- 6.0 Liter V12 . . . 2325
- 5-spd manual trans . . . 950
- 16" alloys (6cyl w/at) . . . 150
- CD changer . . . 125

1993 — WS Ret

XJ-6 — RWD/4.0L-I6 (223hp)

Model	WS	Ret
Base 4dr Sdn	6925	8825
Vanden Plas 4dr Sdn	8025	10000

Add:
- CD changer . . . 100
- Sunroof-power (Base) . . . 175

XJS RWD/4.0L-I6 (234hp)

	WS	Ret
Convertible 2dr Cnv	11650	13875
Coupe 2dr Cpe	9225	11275
Add:		
CD changer	100	

1992 — WS Ret

XJ-6 RWD/4.0L-I6 (223hp)

	WS	Ret
Base 4dr Sdn	5300	7025
Majestic 4dr Sdn	6450	8225
Sovereign 4dr Sdn	5650	7400
Vanden Plas 4dr Sdn	6150	7925

XJS RWD/5.3L-V12 (263hp)

	WS	Ret
Convertible 2dr Cnv	10550	12575
Coupe 2dr Cpe	7875	9750

1991 — WS Ret

XJ-6 RWD/4.0L-I6 (223hp)

	WS	Ret
Base 4dr Sdn	4500	6150
Sovereign 4dr Sdn	4600	6250
Vanden Plas 4dr Sdn	5125	6825

XJS RWD/5.3L-V12 (263hp)

	WS	Ret
Convertible 2dr Cnv	9125	11075
Coupe 2dr Cpe	6450	8225

1990 — WS Ret

XJ-6 RWD/4.0L-I6 (223hp)

	WS	Ret
Base 4dr Sdn	4100	5725
Majestic 4dr Sdn	4425	6075
Sovereign 4dr Sdn	4400	6050
Vanden Plas 4dr Sdn	4725	6375

XJS RWD/5.3L-V12 (262hp)

	WS	Ret
Convertible 2dr Cnv	8525	10425
Coupe 2dr Cpe	5675	7425

1989 — WS Ret

XJ-6 RWD/3.6L-I6 (181hp)

	WS	Ret
Base 4dr Sdn	3600	5075
Vanden Plas 4dr Sdn	3675	5175

XJS RWD/5.3L-V12 (262hp)

	WS	Ret
Convertible 2dr Cnv	6925	8750
Coupe 2dr Cpe	4325	5950

1988 — WS Ret

XJ-6 RWD/3.6L-I6 (181hp)

	WS	Ret
Base 4dr Sdn	3025	4450
Vanden Plas 4dr Sdn	2900	4325

XJS RWD/5.3L-V12 (262hp)

	WS	Ret
Coupe 2dr Cpe	3475	4950
SC 2dr Cnv	5750	7500

KIA

2001 — WS Ret

OPTIMA FWD/

	WS	Ret
LX 4dr Sdn		
SE 4dr Sdn		
Add:		
ABS brakes	275	
Leater seats	375	
CD player	200	
Wheels-alloy	200	
Deduct:		
No cruise	175	

RIO FWD/

	WS	Ret
Base 4dr Sdn		
Add:		
ABS brakes	300	
Alloy Wheels (Base 2WD)	200	
Cassette	150	
CD Player	200	
Deduct:		
No air conditioning	750	

SEPHIA (5sp) FWD/1.8L-I4 (125hp)

	WS	Ret
Base 4dr Sdn		
LS 4dr Sdn		
Add:		
Alloy wheels	175	
Automatic trans	675	
CD changer	325	
CD player	200	
Cruise ctrl	175	
Deduct:		
No air conditioning	750	

SPECTRA FWD/

	WS	Ret
GS 4dr Hbk		
GSX 4dr Hbk		

2000 — WS Ret

SEPHIA (5sp) FWD/1.8L-I4 (125hp)

	WS	Ret
Base 4dr Sdn	5225	6950
LS 4dr Sdn	5750	7500
Add:		
Alloy wheels	150	
Automatic trans	525	
Cassette (std LS)	150	
CD player	175	
ABS brakes	225	
Deduct:		
No air conditioning	575	
Manual steering	150	

SPECTRA FWD/

	WS	Ret
GS 4dr Hbk	5850	7600
GSX 4dr Hbk	6400	8175

1999 — WS Ret

SEPHIA (5sp) FWD/1.8L-I4 (125hp)

	WS	Ret
Base 4dr Sdn	4375	6000
LS 4dr Sdn	4825	6500
Add:		
Alloy wheels	100	
Automatic trans	425	
Cassette	125	
CD player	125	
ABS brakes	175	
Deduct:		
No air conditioning	475	
Manual steering	125	

1998 — WS Ret

SEPHIA (5sp) FWD/1.8L-I4 (125hp)

	WS	Ret
LS 4dr Sdn	3750	5350
RS 4dr Sdn	3275	4750
Add:		
Alloy wheels	75	
Automatic trans	350	
Cassette	75	
CD player	100	
Premium sound	25	
ABS brakes	150	
Deduct:		
No air conditioning	400	
Manual steering	75	

1997 — WS Ret

SEPHIA (5sp) FWD/1.8L-I4 (122hp)

	WS	Ret
GS 4dr Sdn	3125	4575
LS 4dr Sdn	2600	3975
RS 4dr Sdn	2150	3275
Add:		
Alloy wheels	50	
Automatic trans	300	
Cassette (std GS)	50	
Premium sound	25	
ABS brakes	125	
Deduct:		
No air conditioning	325	
Manual steering	50	

1996 — WS Ret

SEPHIA (5sp) FWD/1.8L-I4 (105hp)

	WS	Ret
GS 4dr Sdn	2525	3900
LS 4dr Sdn	2025	3125
RS 4dr Sdn	1650	2700
Add:		
Alloy wheels	50	
Automatic trans	250	
Cassette (std GS)	25	
Cruise ctrl	25	
Premium sound	25	
ABS brakes	125	
Deduct:		
No air conditioning	275	
Manual steering	50	

1995 — WS Ret

SEPHIA (5sp) FWD/1.6L-I4 (88hp)

	WS	Ret
GS 4dr Sdn	2000	3100
LS 4dr Sdn	1600	2650
RS 4dr Sdn	1350	2275
Add:		
Alloy wheels	25	
Automatic trans	225	
Cassette (std GS)	25	
Cruise ctrl	25	
Premium sound	25	
Deduct:		
No air conditioning	250	
Manual steering	25	

1994 — WS Ret

SEPHIA (5sp) FWD/1.6L-V4 (88hp)

	WS	Ret
GS 4dr Sdn	1625	2675
LS 4dr Sdn	1300	2200
RS 4dr Sdn	1125	2025
Add:		
Alloy wheels	25	
Automatic trans	200	
Cassette (std GS)	25	
Cruise ctrl	25	
Deduct:		
No air conditioning	225	
Manual steering	25	

LEXUS

2001 — WS Ret

ES300 FWD/3.0L-V6 (210hp)

	WS	Ret
Luxury 4dr Sdn	25350	28825
Add:		
Nakamichi (incls CD chngr)	675	
Moonroof-power (std Coach)	650	
Chrome wheels	325	
Deduct:		
Cloth seats	550	

GS300 RWD/3.0L-I6 (220hp)

Luxury 4dr Sdn ....
5

GS430 RWD/4.3L-V8 (300hp)

Luxury 4dr Sdn ....

IS300 FWD/

Sport 4dr Sdn. 23100 26400

LS430 RWD/4.3L-V8 (300hp)

Luxury 4dr Sdn ....

2000 WS Ret

ES300 FWD/3.0L-V6 (210hp)

Luxury 4dr Sdn 22825 26100

Add:
- Nakamichi (incls CD chngr) . . . 525
- Coach trim 575
- Moonroof-power 525
- Chrome wheels 250
- Platinum trim 675

Deduct:
- Cloth seats 425

GS300 RWD/3.0L-I6 (220hp)

Luxury 4dr Sdn 27450 31100

Add:
- Nakamichi (incls CD chngr) . . . 550
- Navigation system 650
- Moonroof-power 525
- Chrome wheels 250

Deduct:
- Cloth seats 525

GS400 RWD/4.0L-V8 (300hp)

Luxury 4dr Sdn 32375 36125

Add:
- Nakamichi (incls CD chngr) . . . 650
- Navigation system 650
- Moonroof-power 525
- Chrome wheels 250

LS400 RWD/4.0L-V8 (290hp)

Luxury 4dr Sdn 36300 40325

Add:
- Air suspension 550
- Nakamichi (incls CD chngr) . . . 650
- Moonroof-pwr 525
- Navigation system 775
- Chrome wheels 250
- Platinum series 950

Deduct:
- No CD changer 325

SC RWD/3.0L-V6 (225hp)

SC300 2dr Cpe 29950 33575
SC400 (4.0L 8cyl) 2dr Cpe 34200 38075

Add:
- Nakamichi audio 650
- Chrome wheels 250
- Traction control 475
- Sunroof-pwr 450

Deduct:
- Manual trans 625
- Cloth seats 425

1999 WS Ret

ES300 FWD/3.0L-V6 (210hp)

Luxury 4dr Sdn 19750 22775

Add:
- CD changer 275
- Coach trim 475
- Nakamichi audio 225
- Moonroof-power 425
- Chrome wheels 225

Deduct:
- Cloth seats 350

GS300 RWD/3.0L-I6 (225hp)

Luxury 4dr Sdn 25300 28775

Add:
- Nakamichi (incls CD chngr) . . . 550
- Navigation system 525
- Moonroof-power 425
- Chrome wheels 225

Deduct:
- Cloth seats 425

GS400 RWD/4.0L-V8 (300hp)

Luxury 4dr Sdn 29350 32925

Add:
- Nakamichi (incls CD chngr) . . . 550
- Navigation system 525
- Moonroof-power 425
- Chrome wheels 225

LS400 RWD/4.0L-V8 (290hp)

Luxury 4dr Sdn 29575 33175

Add:
- Air suspension 450
- Nakamichi (incls CD chngr) . . . 550
- Moonroof-pwr 425
- Navigation system 650
- Chrome wheels 225

Deduct:
- No CD changer 275

SC RWD/3.0L-V6 (225hp)

SC300 2dr Cpe 25050 28500
SC400 (4.0L 8cyl) 2dr Cpe 28975 32750

Add:
- Nakamichi audio 550
- Chrome wheels 225
- Traction control 400
- Sunroof-pwr 375

Deduct:
- Manual trans 525
- Cloth seats 350

1998 WS Ret

ES300 FWD/3.0L-V6 (200hp)

Sedan 4dr Sdn 17275 20100

Add:
- CD changer 225
- Nakamichi audio 200
- Moonroof-power 350
- Chrome wheels 175

Deduct:
- Cloth seats 300

GS300 RWD/3.0L-I6 (225hp)

Sedan 4dr Sdn 22825 26100

Add:
- Nakamichi (incls CD chngr) . . . 450
- Navigation system 575
- Moonroof-power 350
- Traction control 325
- Chrome wheels 175

Deduct:
- Cloth seats 350

GS400 RWD/4.0L-V8 (300hp)

Sedan 4dr Sdn 25700 29200

Add:
- Nakamichi (incls CD chngr) . . . 450
- Navigation system 575
- Moonroof-power 350
- Traction control 325
- Chrome wheels 175

LS400 RWD/4.0L-V8 (290hp)

Sedan 4dr Sdn 26200 29750

Add:
- Air suspension 375
- Nakamichi (incls CD chngr) . . . 450
- Moonroof-pwr 350
- Chrome wheels 175

Deduct:
- No CD changer 225

SC RWD/3.0L-I6 (225hp)

SC300 2dr Cpe. 22300 25525
SC400 (4.0L 8cyl) 2dr Cpe 25650 29150

Add:
- Nakamichi (incls CD chngr) . . . 450
- Chrome wheels 175
- Traction control 325
- Sunroof-pwr 300

Deduct:
- Manual trans 425
- Cloth seats 300

1997 WS Ret

ES300 FWD/3.0L-V6 (200hp)

Sedan 4dr Sdn 15200 17850

Add:
- CD changer 175
- Moonroof-power 300
- Chrome wheels 100

Deduct:
- Cloth seats 225

GS300 RWD/3.0L-I6 (220hp)

Sedan 4dr Sdn 18550 21475

Add:
- Nakamichi (incls CD chngr) . . . 375
- Moonroof-power 300
- Traction control 275
- Chrome wheels 100

Deduct:
- Cloth seats 250

LS400 RWD/4.0L-V8 (260hp)

Sedan 4dr Sdn 22050 25250

Add:
- Air suspension 300
- Nakamichi (incls CD chngr) . . . 375
- Sunroof-pwr 250
- Traction control 275
- Chrome wheels 150

Deduct:
- No CD changer 175

SC RWD/3.0L-I6 (225hp)

SC300 2dr Cpe. 18450 21375
SC400 (4.0L 8cyl) 2dr Cpe 21450 24600

Add:
- Nakamichi (incls CD chngr) . . . 375
- Chrome wheels 150
- Traction control 275
- Sunroof-pwr 250

Deduct:
- Manual trans 350
- Cloth seats 250

1996 WS Ret

ES300 FWD/3.0L-V6 (188hp)

Sedan 4dr Sdn 11825 14200

Add:
- CD changer 150
- Leather seats 175
- Sunroof-power 250
- Chrome wheels 75
- Coach trim (incls Enkei whls) . . 350

Deduct:
- Manual trans 325

GS300 RWD/3.0L-I6 (220hp)

Sedan 4dr Sdn 16175 18900

Add:
- Nakamichi (incls CD chngr) . . . 300
- Sunroof-power . . . 250
- Traction control . . . 225
- Chrome wheels . . . 75

Deduct:
- Cloth seats . . . 200

LS400 — RWD/4.0L-V8 (260hp)

	WS	Ret
Sedan 4dr Sdn	18150	21050

Add:
- Air suspension . . . 250
- Nakamichi (incls CD chngr) . . . 300
- Sunroof-pwr . . . 200
- Traction control . . . 225
- Chrome wheels . . . 125

Deduct:
- No CD . . . 150

SC — RWD/3.0L-V6 (225hp)

	WS	Ret
SC300 2dr Cpe	16125	18850
SC400 (4.0L 8cyl) 2dr Cpe	18850	21800

Add:
- Nakamichi (incls CD chngr) . . . 300
- Chrome wheels . . . 125
- Traction control . . . 225
- Sunroof-pwr . . . 200

Deduct:
- Manual trans . . . 300
- Cloth seats . . . 200

1995 — WS Ret

ES300 — FWD/3.0L-V6 (188hp)

	WS	Ret
Sedan 4dr Sdn	10000	12225

Add:
- Leather seats . . . 150
- CD changer . . . 150
- Sunroof-power . . . 225
- Chrome wheels . . . 75

GS300 — RWD/3.0L-I6 (220hp)

	WS	Ret
Sedan 4dr Sdn	13175	15675

Add:
- Leather seats . . . 150
- Nakamichi (incls CD chngr) . . . 275
- Sunroof-power . . . 225
- Traction control . . . 200

LS400 — RWD/4.0L-V8 (260hp)

	WS	Ret
Sedan 4dr Sdn	15875	18575

Add:
- Air suspension . . . 225
- Nakamichi (incls CD chngr) . . . 275
- Sunroof-power . . . 225
- Traction control . . . 200
- Chrome wheels . . . 100

SC — RWD/3.0L-I6 (225hp)

	WS	Ret
SC300 2dr Cpe	12950	15425
SC400 (4.0L 8cyl) 2dr Cpe	15375	18050

Add:
- Leather seats (300) . . . 150
- Nakamichi (incls CD chngr) . . . 275
- Sunroof-power . . . 225
- Traction control . . . 200

Deduct:
- Manual trans . . . 275

1994 — WS Ret

ES300 — FWD/3.0L-V6 (188hp)

	WS	Ret
Sedan 4dr Sdn	8675	10800

Add:
- Leather seats . . . 125
- CD changer . . . 125
- Sunroof-power . . . 200

GS300 — RWD/3.0L-I6 (220hp)

	WS	Ret
Sedan 4dr Sdn	11450	13800

Add:
- Leather seats . . . 125
- Nakamichi (incls CD chngr) . . . 250
- Sunroof-power . . . 200
- Traction control . . . 175

LS400 — RWD/4.0L-V8 (250hp)

	WS	Ret
Sedan 4dr Sdn	12800	15250

Add:
- Air supension . . . 200
- Nakamichi (incls CD chngr) . . . 250
- Sunroof-power . . . 200
- Traction control . . . 175

SC — RWD/3.0L-I6 (225hp)

	WS	Ret
SC300 2dr Cpe	11275	13625
SC400 (4.0L 8cyl) 2dr Cpe	13425	15925

Add:
- Leather seats (300) . . . 125
- Nakamichi (incls CD chngr) . . . 250
- Sunroof-power . . . 200
- Traction control . . . 175

Deduct:
- Manual trans . . . 250

1993 — WS Ret

ES300 — FWD/3.0L-V6 (185hp)

	WS	Ret
Sedan 4dr Sdn	7300	9325

Add:
- Leather seats . . . 100
- Nakamichi (incls CD chngr) . . . 225
- Sunroof-power . . . 175
- Traction control . . . 175

GS300 — RWD/3.0L-I6 (220hp)

	WS	Ret
Sedan 4dr Sdn	10250	12500

Add:
- Leather seats . . . 100
- Nakamichi (incls CD chngr) . . . 225
- Sunroof-power . . . 175
- Traction control . . . 175

LS400 — RWD/4.0L-V8 (250hp)

	WS	Ret
Sedan 4dr Sdn	10725	13025

Add:
- Air suspension . . . 175
- Nakamichi (incls CD chngr) . . . 225
- Sunroof-power . . . 175
- Traction control . . . 175

SC — RWD/3.0L-I6 (225hp)

	WS	Ret
SC300 2dr Cpe	9950	12175
SC400 (4.0L 8cyl) 2dr Cpe	11500	13850

Add:
- Leather seats (300) . . . 125
- Nakamichi (incls CD chngr) . . . 225
- Sunroof-power . . . 175
- Traction control . . . 175

Deduct:
- Manual trans . . . 225

1992 — WS Ret

ES300 — FWD/3.0L-V6 (185hp)

	WS	Ret
Sedan 4dr Sdn	5950	7850

Add:
- Leather seats . . . 100
- CD player . . . 50
- Sunroof-power . . . 150

Deduct:
- Manual trans . . . 200
- No sunroof . . . 100

LS400 — RWD/4.0L-V8 (250hp)

	WS	Ret
Sedan 4dr Sdn	8650	10775

Add:
- Air supension . . . 175
- Nakamichi (incls CD chngr) . . . 225
- Traction control . . . 150

Deduct:
- No Sunroof . . . 150

SC — RWD/3.0L-I6 (225hp)

	WS	Ret
SC300 2dr Cpe	8850	11000
SC400 (4.0L 8cyl) 2dr Cpe	10250	12500

Add:
- Leather seats (300) . . . 100
- Nakamichi (incl CD chngr) . . . 225
- Traction control . . . 150

Deduct:
- Manual trans . . . 200
- No sunroof . . . 150

1991 — WS Ret

ES250 — FWD/2.5L-V6 (156hp)

	WS	Ret
Sedan 4dr Sdn	3875	5600

Add:
- CD player . . . 25
- Leather seats . . . 75
- Pwr seat . . . 25
- Sunroof-pwr . . . 125

Deduct:
- Manual trans . . . 175
- No Sunroof . . . 50

LS400 — RWD/4.0L-V8 (250hp)

	WS	Ret
Sedan 4dr Sdn	7825	9875

Add:
- Air suspension . . . 100
- Nakamichi (incls CD chngr) . . . 175
- Traction control . . . 125

Deduct:
- Cloth seats . . . 100
- No Sunroof . . . 125

1990 — WS Ret

ES250 — FWD/2.5L-V6 (156hp)

	WS	Ret
Sedan 4dr Sdn	3025	4550

Add:
- CD player . . . 25
- Leather seats . . . 50
- Sunroof-pwr . . . 100

Deduct:
- Manual trans . . . 150
- No sunroof . . . 50

LS400 — RWD/4.0L-V8 (250hp)

	WS	Ret
Sedan 4dr Sdn	6625	8600

Add:
- Air suspension . . . 100
- Nakamichi (incls CD chngr) . . . 175
- Traction control . . . 75

Deduct:
- Cloth seats . . . 50
- No sunroof . . . 100

LINCOLN

2001 — WS Ret

CONTINENTAL — FWD/4.6L-V8 (275hp)

	WS	Ret
Luxury 4dr Sdn	22625	25375

Add:
- Alpine audio . . . 775
- CD changer . . . 425
- Wheels-chrome . . . 300
- Moonroof-pwr . . . 575

LS — RWD/3.0L-V6 (210hp)

	WS	Ret
3.0 4dr Sdn	22400	25125
4.0 V8/252hp 4dr Sdn	25425	28325

Add:
- CD changer 400
- Alpine audio 300
- Sport pkg (std w/man.trans) . . . 525
- Moonroof-pwr 575
- Traction ctrl 275
- Wheels-polished alum 300

Deduct:
- Manual trans 725

TOWN CAR RWD/4.6L-V8 (220hp)

Model	WS	Ret
Cartier 4dr Sdn	22875	25625
Cartier LWB 4dr Sdn		
Executive 4dr Sdn	19900	22475
Executive LWB 4dr Sdn.		
Signature 4dr Sdn	21150	23800

Add:
- CD changer 400
- Touring pkg (incl 235hp V8) . . . 675
- Chrome wheels 325
- Moonroof-pwr 575

2000 WS Ret

CONTINENTAL FWD/4.6L-V8 (275hp)

Model	WS	Ret
Luxury 4dr Sdn	19600	22175

Add:
- Alpine audio 600
- CD changer 325
- Wheels-chrome 225
- Moonroof-pwr 450

LS RWD/3.0L-V6 (205hp)

Model	WS	Ret
3.0 4dr Sdn	18700	21200
4.0 V8/252hp 4dr Sdn	21675	24375

Add:
- CD changer 300
- Alpine audio 225
- Sport pkg (std w/man.trans) . . . 400
- Moonroof-pwr 450
- Traction ctrl 225
- Wheels-polished alum 225

Deduct:
- Manual trans 550

TOWN CAR RWD/4.6L-V8 (220hp)

Model	WS	Ret
Cartier 4dr Sdn	21325	24000
Executive 4dr Sdn	18400	20900
Signature 4dr Sdn	19675	22250

Add:
- CD changer 300
- Touring pkg (incl 215hp V8) . . . 525
- Chrome wheels 250
- Moonroof-pwr 450

1999 WS Ret

CONTINENTAL FWD/4.6L-V8 (275hp)

Model	WS	Ret
Luxury 4dr Sdn	15725	18050

Add:
- Alpine audio 500
- CD changer 275
- Integrated v/a phone 175
- Wheels-chrome 200
- Moonroof-pwr 375

TOWN CAR RWD/4.6L-V8 (220hp)

Model	WS	Ret
Cartier 4dr Sdn	18750	21275
Executive 4dr Sdn	16000	18350
Signature 4dr Sdn	17175	19600

Add:
- CD changer 275
- Integrated phone 175
- JBL audio (std Cartier) 275
- Chrome wheels 225
- Moonroof-pwr 375
- Traction control (std Cartier) . . 275

Deduct:
- Cloth seats 350

1998 WS Ret

CONTINENTAL FWD/4.6L-V8 (260hp)

Model	WS	Ret
Luxury 4dr Sdn	12850	15025

Add:
- JBL audio (incls CD chngr) . . . 425
- Chrome wheels 150
- Integrated phone 150
- Moonroof-pwr 300

MARK VIII RWD/4.6L-V8 (280hp)

Model	WS	Ret
Coupe 2dr Cpe	14650	16925
LSC 2dr Cpe	15400	17725

Add:
- CD changer 250
- Moonroof-pwr 300
- Chrome wheels 150
- Integrated phone 150

TOWN CAR RWD/4.6L-V8 (220hp)

Model	WS	Ret
Cartier 4dr Sdn	16125	18475
Executive 4dr Sdn	13775	16000
Signature 4dr Sdn	14800	17075

Add:
- CD changer 250
- Integrated phone 150
- JBL audio (std Cartier) 225
- Chrome wheels 175
- Moonroof-pwr 300
- Traction control (std Cartier) . . . 225

Deduct:
- Cloth seats 300

1997 WS Ret

CONTINENTAL FWD/4.6L-V8 (260hp)

Model	WS	Ret
Luxury 4dr Sdn	9900	11900

Add:
- Traction control 100
- Chrome wheels 125
- Integrated phone 125
- JBL audio (incls CD chngr) . . . 350
- Moonroof-pwr 250

MARK VIII RWD/4.6L-V8 (280hp)

Model	WS	Ret
Coupe 2dr Cpe	11825	13925
LSC 2dr Cpe	12525	14675

Add:
- CD changer 200
- JBL audio 175
- Moonroof-pwr 250
- Chrome wheels 125
- Integrated phone 125

TOWN CAR RWD/4.6L-V8 (210hp)

Model	WS	Ret
Cartier 4dr Sdn	13500	15700
Executive 4dr Sdn	11375	13450
Signature 4dr Sdn	12300	14425

Add:
- CD changer 200
- Integrated phone 125
- JBL audio (std Cartier) 175
- Lthr seats (std Cartier) 200
- Moonroof-pwr 250
- Traction control (std Cartier) . . . 175

1996 WS Ret

CONTINENTAL FWD/4.6L-V8 (260hp)

Model	WS	Ret
Luxury 4dr Sdn	7725	9575

Add:
- Traction control 75
- Chrome wheels 100
- Integrated phone 100
- JBL audio (incls CD chngr) . . . 275
- Sunroof-pwr 200

MARK VIII RWD/4.6L-V8 (280hp)

Model	WS	Ret
Coupe 2dr Cpe	8750	10675

Add:
- CD changer 175
- LSC pkg 250
- Diamond Anniv. 75
- JBL audio 150
- Sunroof-pwr 200
- Traction control 75
- Chrome wheels 100
- Integrated phone 100

TOWN CAR RWD/4.6L-V8 (210hp)

Model	WS	Ret
Cartier 4dr Sdn	10550	12575
Executive 4dr Sdn	8675	10600
Signature 4dr Sdn	9475	11450

Add:
- CD changer 175
- Integrated phone 100
- JBL audio (std Cartier) 150
- Lthr seats (std Cartier) 175
- Sunroof-pwr 200
- Traction control (std Cartier) . . 150

1995 WS Ret

CONTINENTAL FWD/4.6L-V8 (260hp)

Model	WS	Ret
Luxury 4dr Sdn	6175	7950

Add:
- CD changer 150
- Integrated phone 75
- JBL audio 150
- Moonroof-pwr 200

MARK VIII RWD/4.6L-V8 (280hp)

Model	WS	Ret
Coupe 2dr Cpe	6950	8775

Add:
- CD changer 150
- Integrated phone 75
- JBL audio 150
- Moonroof-pwr 200
- Traction control 50
- Chrome wheels 75

TOWN CAR RWD/4.6L-V8 (210hp)

Model	WS	Ret
Cartier 4dr Sdn	8250	10150
Executive 4dr Sdn	6700	8500
Signature 4dr Sdn	7350	9200

Add:
- CD changer 150
- Integrated phone 75
- JBL audio (std Cartier) 150
- Lthr seats (std Cartier) 150
- Sunroof-pwr 200
- Traction control (std Cartier) . . 150

1994 WS Ret

CONTINENTAL FWD/3.8L-V6 (160hp)

Model	WS	Ret
Executive 4dr Sdn	3925	5525
Signature Series 4dr Sdn	4475	6125

Add:
- CD player 50
- Integrated phone 75
- JBL audio (std Signature) 125
- Sunroof-pwr 175

MARK VIII RWD/4.6L-V8 (280hp)

Model	WS	Ret
Coupe 2dr Cpe	5475	7200

Add:
- CD player 50
- CD changer 125
- Integrated phone 75
- JBL audio 125
- Sunroof-pwr 175
- Traction control 50

TOWN CAR RWD/4.6L-V8 (210hp)

Model	WS	Ret
Cartier 4dr Sdn	6500	8300
Executive 4dr Sdn	5275	7000
Signature Series 4dr Sdn	5800	7550

Add:

CD player	50
Integrated phone	75
JBL audio (std Cartier)	125
Lthr seats (std Cartier)	125
Sunroof-pwr	175
Traction control	125

1993 — WS / Ret

CONTINENTAL — FWD/3.8L-V6 (160hp)

	WS	Ret
Executive 4dr Sdn	3125	4575
Signature Series 4dr Sdn	3550	5025

Add:

Alloy wheels (Exec only)	25
CD player	50
Integrated phone	50
JBL audio	100
Sunroof-pwr	150

MARK VIII — RWD/4.6L-V8 (280hp)

	WS	Ret
Coupe 2dr Cpe	4375	6000

Add:

CD player	50
Integrated phone	50
JBL audio	100
Sunroof-pwr	150
Traction control	50

TOWN CAR — RWD/4.6L-V8 (190hp)

	WS	Ret
Cartier 4dr Sdn	5125	6825
Executive 4dr Sdn	4200	5825
Signature Series 4dr Sdn	4575	6225

Add:

4.6L V8 w/dual exh.	75
CD player	50
Integrated phone	50
JBL audio (std Cartier)	100
Lthr seats (std Cartier)	125
Special wheels (Exec only)	50
Sunroof-pwr	150

1992 — WS / Ret

CONTINENTAL — FWD/3.8L-V6 (160hp)

	WS	Ret
Executive 4dr Sdn	2650	4050
Signature Series 4dr Sdn	2925	4350

Add:

CD player	25
Integrated phone	25
JBL audio	75
Special wheels (Exec only)	25
Sunroof-pwr	150

MARK VII — RWD/5.0L-V8 (225hp)

	WS	Ret
Bill Blass 2dr Cpe	3725	5325
LSC 2dr Cpe	3800	5400

Add:

CD player	25
Integrated phone	25
JBL audio	75
Sunroof-power	150

TOWN CAR — RWD/4.6L-V8 (190hp)

	WS	Ret
Cartier 4dr Sdn	3975	5600
Executive 4dr Sdn	3400	4875
Signature Series 4dr Sdn	3700	5200

Add:

4.6L V8 w/dual exh.	50
CD player	25
Integrated phone	25
JBL audio (std Cartier)	75
Lthr seats (std Cartier)	100
Special wheels (Exec only)	25
Sunroof-power	150

1991 — WS / Ret

CONTINENTAL — FWD/3.8L-V6 (155hp)

	WS	Ret
Executive 4dr Sdn	2025	3125
Signature Series 4dr Sdn	2325	3675

Add:

CD player	25
JBL audio	50
Special wheels (Base)	25
Sunroof-pwr	125

MARK VII — RWD/5.0L-V8 (225hp)

	WS	Ret
Bill Blass 2dr Cpe	2875	4275
LSC 2dr Cpe	2950	4375

Add:

CD player	25
JBL audio	50
Sunroof-pwr	125

TOWN CAR — RWD/4.6L-V8 (190hp)

	WS	Ret
Cartier 4dr Sdn	3275	4750
Executive 4dr Sdn	2775	4175
Signature Series 4dr Sdn	3000	4425

Add:

CD player	25
JBL audio	50
Lthr seats (std Cartier)	75
Spcl wheels (Base only)	25
Sunroof-pwr	125

1990 — WS / Ret

CONTINENTAL — FWD/3.8L-V6 (140hp)

	WS	Ret
Base 4dr Sdn	1600	2650
Signature Series 4dr Sdn	1775	2850

Add:

CD player	25
JBL audio	50
Spcl wheels (Base only)	25
Sunroof-pwr	100

MARK VII — RWD/5.0L-V8 (225hp)

	WS	Ret
Bill Blass 2dr Cpe	2225	3350
LSC 2dr Cpe	2300	3450

Add:

CD player	25
JBL audio	50
Sunroof-pwr	100

TOWN CAR — RWD/5.0L-V8 (150hp)

	WS	Ret
Base 4dr Sdn	2200	3325
Cartier Series 4dr Sdn	2600	3975
Signature Series 4dr Sdn	2375	3725

Add:

ABS brakes	25
CD player	25
JBL audio	50
Lthr seats (std Cartier)	50
Special wheels (Base only)	25
Sunroof-pwr	100

1989 — WS / Ret

CONTINENTAL — FWD/3.8L-V6 (140hp)

	WS	Ret
Base 4dr Sdn	1400	2325
Signature Series 4dr Sdn	1500	2425

Add:

CD player	25
JBL audio	25
Special wheels (Base)	25
Sunroof-pwr	75

MARK VII — RWD/5.0L-V8 (225hp)

	WS	Ret
Bill Blass 2dr Cpe	1850	2925
LSC 2dr Cpe	1825	2900

Add:

JBL audio	25
Sunroof-pwr	75

TOWN CAR — RWD/5.0L-V8 (150hp)

	WS	Ret
Base 4dr Sdn	1625	2675
Cartier Series 4dr Sdn	1900	3000
Signature Series 4dr Sdn	1800	2875

Add:

Carriage roof	25
CD player	25
Custom wheels (Base)	25
JBL audio	25
Lthr seats (std Cartier)	25
Sunroof-pwr	75

1988 — WS / Ret

CONTINENTAL — FWD/3.8L-V6 (140hp)

	WS	Ret
Base 4dr Sdn	1150	2050
Signature Series 4dr Sdn	1225	2125

Add:

JBL audio	25
Sunroof-pwr	50

MARK VII — RWD/5.0L-V8 (225hp)

	WS	Ret
Bill Blass 2dr Cpe	1525	2450
LSC 2dr Cpe	1550	2475

Add:

JBL audio	25
Sunroof-pwr	50

TOWN CAR — RWD/5.0L-V8 (150hp)

	WS	Ret
Base 4dr Sdn	1275	2175
Cartier 4dr Sdn	1450	2375
Signature Series 4dr Sdn	1375	2300

Add:

Carriage roof	25
JBL audio	25
Lthr seats (std Cartier)	25
Special wheels (Base)	25
Sunroof-pwr	50

MAZDA

2001 — WS / Ret

626 — FWD/2.0L-I4 (125hp)

	WS	Ret
ES 4dr Sdn	14100	16350
LX 4dr Sdn	11625	13725

Add:

2.5L-V6 (170hp)	500
ABS brakes	375
Cassette	200
6-disc CD chngr	350
Pwr seat	200
Moonroof-pwr	525
Wheels-15in alloy (std ES)	200

Deduct:

Manual trans	750

MIATA (5sp/auto) — RWD/1.8L-I4 (140hp)

	WS	Ret
LS 2dr Cnv		
MX-5 2dr Cnv		
SE (6sp) 2dr Cnv		

MILLENIA — FWD/2.5L-V6 (170hp)

	WS	Ret
P 4dr Sdn		
S 4dr Sdn		

PROTEGE — FWD/1.6L-I4 (103hp)

	WS	Ret
DX 4dr Sdn	9200	11150
ES (1.8L/122hp) 4dr Sdn	10850	12900
LX 4dr Sdn	9775	11750
MP3 (140hp) 4dr Sdn		

Add:

ABS brakes	275
Cassette	150
CD player (DX)	200
Moonroof-pwr	425

Deduct:

No air cond	725
Manual trans	650

2000 — WS Ret

626 FWD/2.0L-I4 (130hp)

	WS	Ret
ES 4dr Sdn	12375	14500
LX 4dr Sdn	10000	12000

Add:
- 2.5L-V6 (170hp) 400
- ABS brakes 275
- Cassette 150
- 6-disc CD chngr 275
- Pwr seat 150
- Moonroof-pwr 400
- Wheels-15in alloy (LX) 175

Deduct:
- Manual trans 575

MIATA (5sp/auto) RWD/1.8L-I4 (140hp)

	WS	Ret
LS 2dr Cnv	14125	16525
MX-5 2dr Cnv	12700	15000
Special Edit. (6sp) 2dr Cnv		

Add:
- ABS brakes 275
- Cruise ctrl (base) 150
- Pwr dr locks (base) 125
- Sports pkg 325
- Removable Htop 650

Deduct:
- No air cond 600

MILLENIA FWD/2.5L-V6 (170hp)

	WS	Ret
Base 4dr Sdn	15550	17875
Millennium Edition 4dr Sdn	19200	21750
S 4dr Sdn	18025	20500

Add:
- CD changer (std Millenium) 350
- Bose audio (Base) 300
- Lthr seats (Base) 350
- Moonroof-pwr (std Millenium) 425
- Traction ctrl (Base) 250
- Wheels-chrome (std Millenium) 200

PROTEGE FWD/1.6L-I4 (105hp)

	WS	Ret
DX 4dr Sdn	7575	9425
ES (1.8L/122hp) 4dr Sdn	9175	11125
LX 4dr Sdn	8250	10150

Add:
- ABS brakes 225
- Cassette 75
- CD player (Base) 175
- Sunroof-pwr 325

Deduct:
- No air cond 550
- Manual trans 500

1999 — WS Ret

626 FWD/2.0L-I4 (125hp)

	WS	Ret
ES 4dr Sdn	10625	12650
LX 4dr Sdn	8375	10275

Add:
- 2.5L-V6 (170hp) 325
- ABS brakes 225
- Cassette 125
- Bose sound 200
- Pwr seat 125
- Moonroof-pwr (std ES) 325
- Wheels-15in alloy 125

Deduct:
- No air cond 525
- Manual trans 475

MIATA (5sp/auto) RWD/1.8L-I4 (140hp)

	WS	Ret
10th Anniv 2dr Cnv	15050	17525
MX-5 2dr Cnv	11875	14125

Add:
- ABS brakes 225
- Alloy wheels (base) 125
- Bose sound (base) 150
- Cruise ctrl (base) 125
- Leather seats (base) 250
- Pwr windows (base) 100
- Pwr dr locks (base) 100
- Sports pkg (base) 275
- Removable Htop 550

Deduct:
- No air cond 500

MILLENIA FWD/2.5L-V6 (170hp)

	WS	Ret
Base 4dr Sdn	13275	15475
S 4dr Sdn	15525	17850

Add:
- CD changer 300
- Bose audio (std S) 250
- Lthr seats (Base) 300
- Moonroof-pwr (Base) 350
- Traction ctrl (Base) 200
- Pwr seat (Base) 125
- Wheels-chrome 150

PROTEGE FWD/1.6L-I4 (105hp)

	WS	Ret
DX 4dr Sdn	6250	8025
ES 4dr Sdn	7700	9550
LX 4dr Sdn	6850	8650

Add:
- ABS brakes 175
- Cassette 50
- CD player (Base) 125
- Sunroof-pwr 275
- Wheels-alloy (std ES) 125

Deduct:
- No air cond 450
- Manual trans 425

1998 — WS Ret

626 FWD/2.0L-I4 (125hp)

	WS	Ret
DX 4dr Sdn	7200	9025
ES (6cyl) 4dr Sdn	9800	11775
LX 4dr Sdn	7900	9775

Add:
- 2.5 Liter V6 (LX only) 275
- ABS brakes (std ES) 200
- Alloy wheels (std ES) 100
- Cassette 75
- CD player (std LX,ES) 125
- Bose sound 150
- Lthr seats (LX) 200
- Pwr seat (LX) 75
- Moonroof-pwr (std ES) 275

Deduct:
- No air cond 450
- Manual trans 400

MILLENIA FWD/2.5L-V6 (170hp)

	WS	Ret
Base 4dr Sdn	11400	13475
S 4dr Sdn	13350	15550

Add:
- CD changer 250
- Bose audio (std S) 200
- Lthr seats (Base) 250
- Moonroof-pwr (Base) 300
- Traction ctrl (Base) 150
- Polished whls 125

PROTEGE FWD/1.5L-I4 (92hp)

	WS	Ret
DX 4dr Sdn	5050	6750
ES 4dr Sdn	6300	8075
LX 4dr Sdn	5550	7275

Add:
- Alloy wheels 75
- ABS brakes (std ES) 150
- Cassette 50
- CD player 100
- Sunroof-pwr 225
- Wheels-alloy 100

Deduct:
- No air cond 375
- Manual trans 350

1997 — WS Ret

626 FWD/2.0L-I4 (114hp)

	WS	Ret
DX 4dr Sdn	4900	6575
ES (6cyl) 4dr Sdn	7325	9175
LX 4dr Sdn	5550	7275

Add:
- 2.5 Liter V6 (LX only) 225
- ABS brakes (std ES) 150
- Alloy wheels (std ES) 75
- Cassette (std LX,ES) 50
- CD player 100
- Pwr seat (LX) 50
- Moonroof-pwr (std ES) 225

Deduct:
- No air cond 375
- Manual trans 325

MIATA (5sp/auto) RWD/1.8L-I4 (133hp)

	WS	Ret
MX-5 2dr Cnv	7900	9775

Add:
- ABS brakes 175
- Alloy wheels 75
- CD player 100
- Cruise ctrl 50
- Leather seats 175
- Pwr windows 50
- R pkg 325
- Removable Htop 375

Deduct:
- No air cond 350

MILLENIA FWD/2.5L-V6 (170hp)

	WS	Ret
Base 4dr Sdn	9400	11350
L 4dr Sdn	10025	12025
S 4dr Sdn	11100	13150

Add:
- CD changer 200
- Bose audio (std S) 175
- Leather seats (Base) 200

MX-6 FWD/2.0L-I4 (114hp)

	WS	Ret
Base 2dr Cpe	7025	8850
LS (6cyl) 2dr Cpe	8825	10750

Add:
- ABS brakes 175
- CD player 100
- Leather seats (std M) 175
- Sunroof-pwr (Base) 175
- Pwr Seat 50

Deduct:
- No air cond 350
- Manual trans 300

PROTEGE FWD/1.5L-I4 (92hp)

	WS	Ret
DX 4dr Sdn	4025	5650
ES 4dr Sdn	5150	6850
LX 4dr Sdn	4475	6125

Add:
- Alloy wheels 50
- Cassette (DX) 25
- ABS brakes (std ES) 125
- Sunroof-pwr 175

Deduct:
- No air cond 325
- Manual trans 275

1996 — WS Ret

626 FWD/2.0L-I4 (114hp)

	WS	Ret
DX 4dr Sdn	3925	5525
ES (6cyl) 4dr Sdn	6050	7800
LX 4dr Sdn	4475	6125

Add:
- 2.5 Liter V6 (LX only) 175
- ABS brakes (std ES) 150
- Alloy wheels (std ES) 50
- Cassette (std LX,ES) 25

CD player 75
Pwr seat (LX) 25
Sunroof-pwr (std ES) 200

Deduct:
No air cond 300
Manual trans 275

MIATA (5sp/auto) RWD/1.8L-I4 (133hp)

M Edition 2dr Cnv	8350	10250
MX-5 2dr Cnv	6350	8125

Add:
ABS brakes (Base) 150
Alloy wheels (Base) 50
CD player (Base) 75
Cruise ctrl (Base) 25
Leather seats (Base) 150
Pwr windows (Base) 50
R pkg 250
Removable Htop 300

Deduct:
No air cond 275

MILLENIA FWD/2.5L-V6 (170hp)

Base 4dr Sdn	7550	9400
L 4dr Sdn	8075	9950
S 4dr Sdn	9075	11025

Add:
CD changer 175
Bose audio 150
Leather seats (Base) 175
Sunroof-pwr (Base) 200

MX-6 FWD/2.0L-I4 (114hp)

Base 2dr Cpe	5575	7300
LS (6cyl) 2dr Cpe	7175	9000
M-Edition (6cyl) 2dr Cpe	1	1

Add:
ABS brakes (std M) 150
CD player (std M) 75
Leather seats (std M) 150
Sunroof-pwr (Base) 150
Pwr Seat 25

Deduct:
No air cond 275
Manual trans 250

PROTEGE FWD/1.5L-I4 (92hp)

DX 4dr Sdn	3100	4550
ES 4dr Sdn	4175	5800
LX 4dr Sdn	3550	5025

Add:
Alloy wheels 50
Cassette (DX) 25
ABS brakes (std ES) 125
Sunroof-pwr 150

Deduct:
No air cond 250
Manual trans 225

1995 WS Ret

626 FWD/2.0L-I4 (118hp)

DX 4dr Sdn	3150	4600
ES (6cyl) 4dr Sdn	4600	6250
LX 4dr Sdn	3550	5025

Add:
2.5 Liter V6 (LX only) 175
ABS brakes (std ES) 125
Alloy wheels (std ES) 50
Cassette (std LX,ES) 25
CD player 50
Cruise ctrl (std LX,ES) 25
Pwr seat (LX) 25
Sunroof-pwr (std ES) 175

Deduct:
No air cond 275
Manual trans 250

929 RWD/3.0L-V6 (193hp)

Sedan 4dr Sdn	5925	7675

Add:
CD changer 150
CD player 75
Leather seats 150
Wood trim 100

MIATA (5sp/auto) RWD/1.8L-I4 (128hp)

M Edition 2dr Cnv	7075	8900
MX-5 2dr Cnv	5400	7125

Add:
ABS brakes (Base) 125
Alloy wheels (Base) 50
CD player 50
Cruise ctrl (Base) 25
Leather seats (Base) 125
Pwr windows (Base) 25
R pkg 250
Removable Htop 275

Deduct:
No air cond 250

MILLENIA FWD/2.5L-V6 (170hp)

Base 4dr Sdn	5775	7525
S 4dr Sdn	6725	8525

Add:
CD changer 150
Bose audio 125
Leather seats (Base) 150
Sunroof-pwr (Base) 175

MX-3 FWD/1.6L-I4 (105hp)

Base 2dr Hbk	3050	4500

Add:
ABS brakes 125
Alloy wheels 25
CD player 50
Cruise ctrl 25
Pwr dr locks 25
Pwr windows 25
Sunroof-pwr 150

Deduct:
No air cond 225
Manual trans 225

MX-6 FWD/2.0L-I4 (118hp)

Base 2dr Cpe	3850	5450
LS (6cyl) 2dr Cpe	5125	6825

Add:
ABS brakes 125
CD player 50
Leather seats 125
Sunroof-pwr 150

Deduct:
No air cond 250
Manual trans 225

PROTEGE FWD/1.5L-I4 (92hp)

DX 4dr Sdn	2450	3825
ES 4dr Sdn	3300	4775
LX 4dr Sdn	2775	4175

Add:
Alloy wheels 25
Cassette (std DX) 25
ABS brakes (std ES) 100
Sunroof-pwr 150

Deduct:
No air cond 225
Manual trans 200

RX-7 (5sp/auto) RWD/1.3L-R (255hp)

Turbo 2dr Cpe	13125	15925

Add:
Bose audio w/CD 175
Leather seats 150
Sunroof-pwr 175
R-2 pkg 325

1994 WS Ret

323 FWD/1.6L-I4 (82hp)

Base 2dr Hbk	1875	2975

Add:
Cassette 25
Cloth seats 50

Deduct:
No air cond 225
Manual steering 25
Manual trans 200

626 FWD/2.0L-I4 (118hp)

DX 4dr Sdn	2700	4100
ES (6cyl) 4dr Sdn	4025	5650
LX 4dr Sdn	3125	4575

Add:
2.5 Liter V6 (LX only) 150
ABS brakes 125
Alloy wheels (std ES) 25
Cassette (std LX,ES) 25
CD player 50
Cruise ctrl (std LX,ES) 25
Pwr seat (LX) 25
Sunroof-pwr 175

Deduct:
No air cond 250
Manual trans 225

929 RWD/3.0L-V6 (193hp)

Sedan 4dr Sdn	5025	6725

Add:
CD changer 150
CD player 50
Leather seats 125
Wood trim 75

MIATA (5sp/auto) RWD/1.8L-I4 (128hp)

M Edition 2dr Cnv	5800	7550
MX-5 2dr Cnv	4700	6350

Add:
ABS brakes 125
Alloy wheels (Base) 25
CD player 50
Cruise ctrl (Base) 25
Leather seats (Base) 125
Pwr windows (Base) 25
R pkg 225
Removable Htop 250

Deduct:
No air cond 225

MX-3 FWD/1.6L-I4 (105hp)

Base 2dr Hbk	2675	4075
GS (6cyl) 2dr Hbk	3475	4950

Add:
ABS brakes 100
Alloy wheels (std GS) 25
CD player 50
Cruise ctrl 25
Pwr dr locks 25
Pwr windows 25
Sunroof-pwr 125

Deduct:
No air cond 225
Manual trans 200

MX-6 FWD/2.0L-I4 (118hp)

Base 2dr Cpe	3350	4825
LS (6cyl) 2dr Cpe	4475	6125

Add:
ABS brakes 125
CD player 50
Leather seats 125
Sunroof-pwr 150

Deduct:
No air cond 225
Manual trans 200

PROTEGE — FWD/1.8L-I4 (103hp)

Model	WS	Ret
Base 4dr Sdn	2100	3225
DX 4dr Sdn	2475	3850
LX 4dr Sdn	2850	4250

Add:
- Alloy wheels . . . 25
- Cassette (std LX) . . . 25
- Pwr dr locks (std LX) . . . 25
- Pwr windows (std LX) . . . 25
- Sunroof-pwr . . . 125

Deduct:
- No air cond . . . 225
- Manual trans . . . 200

RX-7 (5sp/auto) — RWD/1.3L-R (255hp)

Model	WS	Ret
Turbo 2dr Cpe	11225	13825

Add:
- Bose audio w/CD . . . 150
- Leather seats . . . 125
- Sunroof-pwr . . . 175
- R-2 pkg . . . 300

1993 — WS Ret

323 — FWD/1.6L-I4 (82hp)

Model	WS	Ret
Base 2dr Hbk	925	1625
SE 2dr Hbk	1175	2075

Add:
- Cassette . . . 25

Deduct:
- No air cond . . . 175
- Manual steering . . . 25
- Manual trans . . . 175

626 — FWD/2.0L-I4 (118hp)

Model	WS	Ret
DX 4dr Sdn	1975	3075
ES (6cyl) 4dr Sdn	2900	4325
LX 4dr Sdn	2375	3725

Add:
- ABS brakes . . . 100
- Alloy wheels (std ES) . . . 25
- Cassette (std LX,ES) . . . 25
- CD player . . . 50
- Cruise ctrl (std LX,DX) . . . 25
- Leather seats . . . 100
- Sunroof-pwr . . . 150

Deduct:
- No air cond . . . 225
- Manual trans . . . 200

929 — RWD/3.0L-V6 (195hp)

Model	WS	Ret
Sedan 4dr Sdn	4175	5800

Add:
- CD changer . . . 125
- CD player . . . 50
- Leather seats . . . 100

MIATA (5sp/auto) — RWD/1.6L-I4 (116hp)

Model	WS	Ret
MX-5 2dr Cnv	4125	5750
Special Edition 2dr Cnv	4725	6375

Add:
- ABS brakes . . . 100
- Alloy wheels (Base only) . . . 25
- CD player . . . 50
- Cruise ctrl . . . 25
- Leather seats (Base only) . . . 100
- Pwr windows . . . 25
- Removable Htop . . . 225

Deduct:
- No air cond . . . 200

MX-3 — FWD/1.6L-I4 (88hp)

Model	WS	Ret
Base 2dr Hbk	2025	3125
GS (6cyl) 2dr Hbk	2725	4125

Add:
- ABS brakes . . . 75
- Alloy wheels (std GS) . . . 25
- CD player . . . 50
- Cruise ctrl . . . 25
- Pwr dr locks . . . 25
- Pwr windows . . . 25
- Sunroof-pwr . . . 100

Deduct:
- No air cond . . . 175
- Manual trans . . . 175

MX-6 — FWD/2.0L-I4 (118hp)

Model	WS	Ret
Base 2dr Cpe	2800	4200
LS (6cyl) 2dr Cpe	3650	5150

Add:
- ABS brakes . . . 125
- Alloy wheels (std LS) . . . 25
- CD player . . . 50
- Sunroof-pwr . . . 125

Deduct:
- No air cond . . . 200
- Manual trans . . . 200

PROTEGE — FWD/1.8L-I4 (103hp)

Model	WS	Ret
DX 4dr Sdn	1350	2275
LX 4dr Sdn	1700	2775

Add:
- Alloy wheels . . . 25
- Cassette (std LX) . . . 25
- Sunroof-pwr . . . 100

Deduct:
- No air cond . . . 175
- Manual trans . . . 175

RX-7 (5sp/auto) — RWD/1.3L-R (255hp)

Model	WS	Ret
Turbo 2dr Cpe	8700	11050

Add:
- Bose audio w/CD . . . 150
- Leather seats . . . 125
- Sunroof-pwr . . . 175
- R-2 pkg . . . 300

1992 — WS Ret

323 — FWD/1.6L-I4 (82hp)

Model	WS	Ret
Base 2dr Hbk	775	1300
SE 2dr Hbk	1000	1700

Add:

Deduct:
- No air cond . . . 175
- Manual trans . . . 150

626 — FWD/2.2L-I4 (110hp)

Model	WS	Ret
DX 4dr Sdn	1675	2725
LX 4dr Sdn	2000	3100

Add:
- ABS brakes . . . 75
- Alloy wheels . . . 25
- Cassette (std LX) . . . 25
- Cruise ctrl . . . 25
- Sunroof-pwr . . . 100

Deduct:
- No air cond . . . 200
- Manual trans . . . 200

929 — RWD/3.0L-V6 (195hp)

Model	WS	Ret
4dr Sdn	3575	5050

Add:
- CD changer . . . 100
- CD player . . . 25
- Leather seats . . . 75
- Sunroof-pwr . . . 150

MIATA (5sp/auto) — RWD/1.6L-I4 (116hp)

Model	WS	Ret
MX-5 2dr Cnv	3725	5325
Spcl Ed (Blk/Tan) 2dr Cnv	4175	5800

Add:
- ABS brakes . . . 75
- Alloy wheels (Base only) . . . 25
- Cassette . . . 25
- CD player . . . 25
- Cruise ctrl . . . 25
- Lthr seats (Base only) . . . 50
- Pwr windows . . . 25
- Removable Htop . . . 200

Deduct:
- No air cond . . . 175

MX-3 — FWD/1.6L-I4 (88hp)

Model	WS	Ret
Base 2dr Hbk	1750	2825
GS (6cyl) 2dr Hbk	2375	3725

Add:
- ABS brakes . . . 50
- Alloy wheels (std GS) . . . 25
- CD player . . . 25
- Cruise ctrl . . . 25
- Pwr dr locks . . . 25
- Pwr windows . . . 25
- Sunroof-pwr . . . 75

Deduct:
- No air cond . . . 175
- Manual trans . . . 150

MX-6 — FWD/2.2L-I4 (110hp)

Model	WS	Ret
DX 2dr Cpe	2250	3375
GT 2dr Cpe	2850	4250
LX 2dr Cpe	2525	3900

Add:
- ABS brakes . . . 75
- Alloy wheels (std GT) . . . 25
- CD player . . . 25
- Cruise ctrl (DX only) . . . 25
- Sunroof-pwr . . . 100

Deduct:
- No air cond . . . 175
- Manual trans . . . 175

PROTEGE — FWD/1.8L-I4 (103hp)

Model	WS	Ret
DX 4dr Sdn	1175	2075
LX 4dr Sdn	1525	2450

Add:
- Alloy wheels . . . 25
- Sunroof-pwr . . . 75

Deduct:
- No air cond . . . 175
- Manual trans . . . 150

1991 — WS Ret

323 — FWD/1.6L-I4 (82hp)

Model	WS	Ret
Base 2dr Hbk	700	1225
SE 2dr Hbk	825	1500

Add:

Deduct:
- No air cond . . . 150
- Manual trans . . . 125

626 — FWD/2.2L-I4 (110hp)

Model	WS	Ret
DX 4dr Sdn	1525	2450
GT (Turbo) 4dr Hbk	1950	3050
LX Touring 4dr Hbk	1775	2850
LX 4dr Sdn	1700	2775

Add:
- ABS brakes . . . 50
- Alloy wheels (DX,LX) . . . 25
- Cassette (DX only) . . . 25
- Cruise ctrl (DX only) . . . 25
- Sunroof-pwr (std LE) . . . 100

Deduct:
- No air cond . . . 175
- Manual trans . . . 175

929 — RWD/3.0L-V6 (158hp)

Model	WS	Ret
Base 4dr Sdn	2650	4050
S 4dr Sdn	2825	4225

Add:
- Lthr seats (Base only) . . . 75
- CD player . . . 25

Deduct:
- Manual trans . . . 175

MIATA RWD/1.6L-I4 (116hp)

Model	WS	Ret
MX-5 (5sp/AT) 2dr Cnv	3325	4800
Spcl Edit (5sp/AT) 2dr Cnv	3625	5100

Add:
- ABS brakes . . . 50
- Alloy wheels (std SE) . . . 25
- Cassette (std SE) . . . 25
- CD player (std SE) . . . 25
- Pwr windows (std SE) . . . 25
- Removable htp . . . 175

Deduct:
- No air cond . . . 175

MX-6 FWD/2.2L-I4 (110hp)

Model	WS	Ret
DX 2dr Cpe	1675	2725
GT 2dr Cpe	2100	3225
LE 2dr Cpe	1950	3050
LX 2dr Cpe	1850	2925

Add:
- ABS brakes . . . 50
- Alloy wheels (DX,LX) . . . 25
- Cassette (DX) . . . 25
- CD player . . . 25
- Sunroof-pwr . . . 100

Deduct:
- No air cond . . . 175
- Manual trans . . . 150

PROTEGE FWD/1.8L-I4 (103hp)

Model	WS	Ret
AWD 4dr Sdn	1475	2400
DX 4dr Sdn	1200	2100
LX 4dr Sdn	1400	2325

Add:
- Alloy wheels . . . 25
- Sunroof-pwr . . . 50

Deduct:
- No air cond . . . 150
- Manual trans . . . 125

RX-7 RWD/1.3L-R (160hp)

Model	WS	Ret
Base 2dr Cnv	5425	7150
Base 2dr Hbk	3275	4750
Turbo (5sp) 2dr Hbk	4225	5850

Add:
- CD player . . . 25
- Leather seats . . . 25

Deduct:
- Man trans (not Turbo) . . . 150

1990 WS Ret

323 FWD/1.6L-I4 (82hp)

Model	WS	Ret
Base 2dr Hbk	550	1050
SE 2dr Hbk	675	1200

Add:

Deduct:
- No air cond . . . 125
- Manual trans . . . 125

626 FWD/2.2L-I4 (110hp)

Model	WS	Ret
DX 4dr Sdn	1250	2150
GT 4dr Hbk	1600	2650
LX Touring 4dr Hbk	1475	2400
LX 4dr Sdn	1425	2350

Add:
- ABS brakes . . . 25
- Alloy wheels (DX,LX) . . . 25
- CD player . . . 25
- Sunroof-pwr . . . 75

Deduct:
- No air cond . . . 150
- Manual trans . . . 150

929 RWD/3.0L-V6 (158hp)

Model	WS	Ret
Base 4dr Sdn	2100	3225
S 4dr Sdn	2300	3450

Add:
- ABS brakes . . . 25
- CD player . . . 25
- Leather seats . . . 50

Deduct:
- Manual trans . . . 150

MIATA RWD/1.6L-I4 (116hp)

Model	WS	Ret
MX-5 (5sp) 2dr Cnv	2875	4275

Add:
- Alloy wheels . . . 25
- CD player . . . 25
- Hardtop-lift off . . . 125

Deduct:
- No air cond . . . 150

MX-6 FWD/2.2L-I4 (110hp)

Model	WS	Ret
DX 2dr Cpe	1450	2375
GT 2dr Cpe	1750	2825
LX 2dr Cpe	1625	2675

Add:
- ABS brakes . . . 25
- Alloy wheels (DX,LX) . . . 25
- CD player . . . 25
- Sunroof-pwr . . . 75

Deduct:
- No air cond . . . 150
- Manual trans . . . 150

PROTEGE FWD/1.8L-I4 (103hp)

Model	WS	Ret
AWD 4dr Sdn	1225	2125
LX 4dr Sdn	1175	2075
SE 4dr Sdn	1000	1700

Add:
- Sunroof-pwr . . . 25

Deduct:
- No air cond . . . 125
- Manual trans . . . 125

RX-7 RWD/1.3L-R (160hp)

Model	WS	Ret
Base 2dr Cnv	4350	5975
GTU 2dr Hbk	2450	3825
GXL 2dr Hbk	2650	4050
Turbo (5sp) 2dr Hbk	3375	4850

Add:
- 2+2 seating . . . 25
- CD player . . . 25
- Leather seats . . . 25
- Sunroof-pwr . . . 75

Deduct:
- No air cond . . . 150
- Manual trans (not Turbo) . . . 125

1989 WS Ret

323 FWD/1.6L-I4 (82hp)

Model	WS	Ret
Base 4dr Sdn	450	925
Base 2dr Hbk	450	925
GTX (5sp-AWD) 2dr Hbk	675	1200
LX 4dr Sdn	600	1100
SE 4dr Sdn	525	1000
SE 2dr Hbk	500	975

Add:

Deduct:
- No air cond . . . 75
- Man trans (not GTX) . . . 75

626 FWD/2.2L-I4 (110hp)

Model	WS	Ret
DX 4dr Sdn	950	1650
LX Touring 4dr Hbk	1075	1975
LX 4dr Sdn	1050	1950
Touring (Turbo) 4dr Hbk	1150	2050

Add:
- ABS brakes . . . 25
- Sunroof-pwr . . . 50

Deduct:
- No air cond . . . 125
- Manual trans . . . 125

929 RWD/3.0L-V6 (158hp)

Model	WS	Ret
Base 4dr Sdn	1625	2675

Add:
- ABS brakes . . . 25
- Leather seats . . . 25

Deduct:
- Manual trans . . . 125

MX-6 FWD/2.2L-I4 (110hp)

Model	WS	Ret
DX 2dr Cpe	950	1650
GT 2dr Cpe	1150	2050
LX 2dr Cpe	1050	1950

Add:
- ABS brakes . . . 25
- Sunroof-pwr . . . 50

Deduct:
- No air cond . . . 125

RX-7 RWD/1.3L-R (146hp)

Model	WS	Ret
Base 2dr Cnv	3575	5050
GTU 2dr Hbk	1975	3075
GXL 2dr Hbk	2075	3200
Turbo (5sp) 2dr Hbk	2200	3325

Add:
- 2+2 seating . . . 25
- Lthr seats (std Cnv) . . . 25
- Sunroof-pwr (GTU) . . . 50

Deduct:
- Manual trans (not Turbo) . . . 75

1988 WS Ret

323 FWD/1.6L-I4 (82hp)

Model	WS	Ret
Base 4dr Sdn	375	825
Base 4dr Wgn	350	800
Base 2dr Hbk	350	800
GT (5sp) 4dr Sdn	525	1000
GTX (5sp-AWD) 2dr Hbk	525	1000
LX 4dr Sdn	475	950
SE 4dr Sdn	450	925
SE 2dr Hbk	400	850

Add:

Deduct:
- No air cond . . . 50
- Man trans (not GTX) . . . 50

626 FWD/2.2L-I4 (110hp)

Model	WS	Ret
DX 4dr Sdn	750	1275
LX 4dr Hbk	850	1525
LX 4dr Sdn	825	1500
Turbo Touring 4dr Hbk	950	1650
Turbo 4dr Sdn	900	1600

Add:
- ABS brakes . . . 25
- Sunroof-pwr . . . 50

Deduct:
- No air cond . . . 100
- Manual trans . . . 75

929 RWD/3.0L-V6 (158hp)

Model	WS	Ret
Sedan 4dr Sdn	1350	2275

Add:
- Leather seats . . . 25
- Sunroof-pwr . . . 50

Deduct:
- Manual trans . . . 75

MX-6 FWD/2.2L-I4 (110hp)

Model	WS	Ret
DX 2dr Cpe	750	1275
GT 2dr Cpe	900	1600
LX 2dr Cpe	800	1475

Add:
- ABS brakes . . . 25
- Sunroof-pwr . . . 50

Deduct:
- No air cond 100
- Manual trans 50

RX-7 — RWD/1.3L-R (146hp)

Model	WS	Ret
Base (5sp) 2dr Cnv	3100	4550
GTU (5sp) 2dr Hbk	1575	2625
GXL 2dr Hbk	1650	2700
SE 2dr Hbk	1550	2475
Turbo (5sp) 2dr Hbk	1725	2800

Add:
- 2+2 seating 25
- ABS brakes 25
- Sunroof-pwr (SE,GTU) 50

Deduct:
- No air cond 100
- Man trans (SE,GXL) 50

MERCEDES

2001 — WS Ret

C-CLASS — RWD/2.6L-V6 (168hp)

Model	WS	Ret
240 4dr Sdn		
320 (6cyl/215hp) 4dr Sdn		

CL-CLASS — RWD/5.0L-V8 (302hp)

Model	WS	Ret
500 2dr Htp		
55 AMG (5.5L/349hp) 2dr Htp		
600 (12cyl/362hp) 2dr Htp		

CLK — RWD/3.2L-V6 (215hp)

Model	WS	Ret
320 2dr Cnv		
320 2dr Htp		
430 (4.3L-V8/275hp) 2dr Cnv		
430 (4.3L-V8/275hp) 2dr Htp		

E-CLASS — AWD/3.2L-V6 (221hp)

Model	WS	Ret
320 AWD 4dr Sdn	39800	44050
320 4dr Sdn	36950	41025
320 AWD 4dr Wgn	43550	48075
320 4dr Wgn	38850	43075
430 AWD (4.3L-V8/27 4sd	41200	45550
430 (4.3L-V8/275hp) 4sd.	43775	48300
E55 (5.5L-V8/349hp) 4dr Sdn		

Add:
- Bose Audio (std 430) 425
- Navigation System 800
- Sport pkg 1975
- Moonroof-pwr 650
- Silver/Espresso 2000

Deduct:
- No CD 400

S-CLASS — RWD/4.3L-V8 (268hp)

Model	WS	Ret
430 4dr Sdn	56750	62000
500 (5.0L/302hp) 4dr Sdn		
600 4dr Sdn		
S55 (5.5L/349hp) 4dr Sdn		

Add:
- Sport pkg w/18" AMG wheels . 1875
- Silver/Espresso 3325
- Active suspension 1025

Deduct:
- No CD 400

SL-CLASS — RWD/5.0L-V8 (302hp)

Model	WS	Ret
500 2dr Cnv		
600 (12cyl) 2dr Cnv		

SLK — RWD/2.3L-I4 (190hp)

Model	WS	Ret
230 2dr Cnv	32950	36750
320 (3.2L-V6/215hp) 2dr Cnv		

Add:
- Sport pkg (incls 17" alloys) . . . 1950
- CD changer 425
- Copper/Goldenrod 2100

Deduct:
- No CD 425

2000 — WS Ret

C-CLASS — RWD/2.3L-I4 (185hp)

Model	WS	Ret
230 4dr Sdn	22200	25425
280 (6cyl/194hp) 4dr Sdn	25250	28725
C43 (8cyl/302hp) 4dr Sdn		

Add:
- Bose audio (230) 300
- Mooroof-pwr (std C43) 425
- Sport pkg (incls 16" whls) 375
- CD Changer 325

CL-CLASS — RWD/5.0L-V8 (302hp)

Model	WS	Ret
500 2dr Htp		

CLK — RWD/3.2L-V6 (215hp)

Model	WS	Ret
320 2dr Cnv	42900	47375
320 2dr Htp	34725	38650
430 (4.3L-V8/275hp) Cnv	47025	51700
430 (4.3L-V8/275hp) 2dr ht	39475	43750

Add:
- CD Changer 275
- Moonroof-pwr 450
- Navigation sys 650
- Espresso/Slate Blue 1725

Deduct:
- No CD 300

E-CLASS — AWD/3.2L-V6 (221hp)

Model	WS	Ret
320 AWD 4dr Sdn	38950	43175
320 4dr Sdn	35425	39400
320 AWD 4dr Wgn	42675	47125
320 4dr Wgn	37300	41400
430 AWD (4.3L-V8) 4d Sdn	45900	50500
430 (4.3L-V8) 4d Sdn	42175	46600
E55 (5.5L-V8) 4dr Sdn	56750	62000

Add:
- Bose Audio (std 430) 325
- CD changer (MB) 325
- Sport pkg (E430 only) 1525
- Moonroof-pwr 500
- Silver/Espresso 1550

Deduct:
- No CD 300

S-CLASS — RWD/4.3L-V8 (268hp)

Model	WS	Ret
430 4dr Sdn	51850	56750
500 (5.0L/302hp) 4dr Sdn		

Add:
- Sport pkg w/18" AMG wheels . 1450
- Silver/Espresso 2575
- 4-place pwr seating 950

Deduct:
- No CD 300

SL-CLASS — RWD/5.0L-V8 (302hp)

Model	WS	Ret
500 2dr Cnv	55875	61050
600 (12cyl) 2dr Cnv		

Add:
- Glass roof 1900
- Adaptive damping (std 600) . . 1300
- Sport pkg 2050
- Black Diamond/Slate Blue . . . 1725

Deduct:
- No CD 325

SLK — RWD/2.3L-I4 (185hp)

Model	WS	Ret
Cpe/Rds 2dr Cnv	29350	32925

Add:
- Sport pkg (incls 17" alloys) . . . 1525
- CD changer 325
- Copper/Elec. Green 1625

Deduct:
- No CD 325

1999 — WS Ret

C-CLASS — RWD/2.3L-I4 (185hp)

Model	WS	Ret
230 4dr Sdn	20375	23450
280 (6cyl/194hp) 4dr Sdn.	23150	26450
C43 (8cyl/302hp) 4dr Sdn	35700	39700

Add:
- Bose audio (230) 250
- ESP susp. 350
- Mooroof-pwr (std C43) 350
- Stability control (230) 350
- Sport pkg (incls 16" whls) 300
- CD Changer 275

Deduct:
- Non adj. steering whl 150
- Vinyl seats 375

CL-CLASS — RWD/5.0L-V8 (315hp)

Model	WS	Ret
500 2dr Htp	55025	60150
600 (12cyl) 2dr Htp	1	1

Add:
- ESP susp (std 600) 350
- Adaptive damping (std 600) . . . 700

CLK — RWD/3.2L-V6 (215hp)

Model	WS	Ret
320 2dr Cnv	34875	38800
320 2dr Htp	30025	33650
430 2dr Htp	36325	40350

Add:
- CD Changer 225
- Moonroof-pwr 375
- ESP susp 350
- Seats-dual power contour 400

E-CLASS — RWD/3.2L-V6 (221hp)

Model	WS	Ret
300 TD 4dr Sdn	28375	32100
320 AWD 4dr Sdn	32500	36250
320 4dr Sdn	30475	34150
320 AWD 4dr Wgn	35925	39925
320 4dr Wgn	32225	35950
430 (8cyl) 4dr Sdn	36700	40775
E55 4dr Sdn	49000	53700

Add:
- Bose Audio (std 430) 275
- CD changer (MB) 275
- Sport pkg (incls 17" wheels) . . 1275
- Moonroof-pwr 400
- ESP susp. 400

Deduct:
- Cloth seats 350
- No CD 275

S-CLASS — RWD/4.2L-V8 (275hp)

Model	WS	Ret
320 (6cyl) 4dr Sdn	39325	43575
320 LWB (6cyl) 4dr Sdn.	40225	44500
420 4dr Sdn	43750	48275
500 4dr Sdn	52000	56925
600 (12cyl) 4dr Sdn	64625	70400

Add:
- Adaptive damping (std 600) . . . 775
- ESP suspension (std 600) . . . 400
- 4-place pwr seating 775

SL-CLASS — RWD/5.0L-V8 (302hp)

Model	WS	Ret
500 2dr Cnv	52500	57450
600 (12cyl) 2dr Cnv	72300	78600

Add:
- Glass roof 1575
- Sport pkg 1675

Deduct:
- No CD 275

SLK RWD/2.3L-I4 (185hp)

Model	WS	Ret
Cpe/Rds 2dr Cnv	27125	30750

Add:
- Sport pkg (incls 17" alloys) . . . 1250
- CD changer . . . 275

Deduct:
- No CD . . . 275

1998 — WS Ret

C-CLASS RWD/2.3L-I4 (148hp)

Model	WS	Ret
230 4dr Sdn	18050	20925
280 (6cyl/194hp) 4dr Sdn	20375	23450

Add:
- Bose audio (230) . . . 200
- ESP susp. . . . 300
- Mooroof-pwr . . . 300
- Traction control (230) . . . 300
- Sport pkg (C280) . . . 250
- CD Changer . . . 225

Deduct:
- Non adj. steering whl . . . 125
- Vinyl seats . . . 300

CL-CLASS RWD/5.0L-V8 (315hp)

Model	WS	Ret
500 2dr Htp	48800	53500
600 (12cyl) 2dr Htp	66725	72650

CLK RWD/3.2L-V6 (215hp)

Model	WS	Ret
320 2dr Htp	27475	31125

E-CLASS RWD/3.2L-V6 (221hp)

Model	WS	Ret
300 TD 4dr Sdn	25325	28800
320 AWD 4dr Sdn	29075	32650
320 4dr Sdn	27100	30725
320 AWD 4dr Wgn	32000	35775
320 4dr Wgn	28575	32300
430 (8cyl) 4dr Sdn	32400	36150

Add:
- Bose Audio (std 430) . . . 225
- CD changer (MB) . . . 225
- Sport pkg . . . 1050
- Moonroof-pwr . . . 350
- ESP susp. . . . 325

Deduct:
- Cloth seats . . . 300
- No CD . . . 225

S-CLASS RWD/4.2L-V8 (275hp)

Model	WS	Ret
320 (6cyl) 4dr Sdn	33100	36900
320 LWB (6cyl) 4dr Sdn	33900	37750
420 4dr Sdn	36900	40975
500 4dr Sdn	44100	48650
600 (12cyl) 4dr Sdn	54700	59800

Add:
- Adaptive damping (std 600) . . . 650
- Traction cntrl (320) . . . 625
- 4-place pwr seating . . . 650

SL-CLASS RWD/5.0L-V8 (215hp)

Model	WS	Ret
500 (8cyl) 2dr Cnv	46675	51325
600 (12cyl) 2dr Cnv	63200	68875

Add:
- Adaptive damping (std 600) . . . 725
- Sport pkg . . . 1400

Deduct:
- No CD . . . 225

SLK RWD/2.3L-I4 (185hp)

Model	WS	Ret
Cpe/Rds 2dr Cnv	24050	27425

Deduct:
- No CD . . . 225

1997 — WS Ret

C-CLASS RWD/2.3L-I4 (148hp)

Model	WS	Ret
230 4dr Sdn	15375	18050
280 (6cyl/194hp) 4dr Sdn	17550	20400
C36 (6cyl/276hp) 4dr Sdn	26400	29950

Add:
- Bose audio (220) . . . 175
- Leather seats (std C36) . . . 200
- Mooroof-pwr (std C36) . . . 225
- Traction control . . . 325
- Sport pkg (C280) . . . 225
- CD Changer . . . 175

Deduct:
- Non adj. steering whl . . . 100

E-CLASS RWD/3.2L-V6 (217hp)

Model	WS	Ret
300D 4dr Sdn	22575	25825
320 4dr Sdn	24200	27575
420 (8cyl) 4dr Sdn	29375	32950

Add:
- Bose Audio (std 420) . . . 175
- CD changer (MB) . . . 175
- Sport pkg . . . 875

Deduct:
- Cloth seats . . . 250
- No Moonroof . . . 300
- No CD . . . 175

S-CLASS RWD/4.2L-V8 (275hp)

Model	WS	Ret
320 (6cyl) 4dr Sdn	28850	32600
320 LWB (6cyl) 4dr Sdn	29550	33150
420 4dr Sdn	32275	36025
500 4dr Sdn	38850	43075
500 2dr Cpe	41925	45425
600 (12cyl) 4dr Sdn	55050	59000
600 (12cyl) 2dr Cpe	58075	62175

Add:
- Adaptive damping (std 600) . . . 525
- Traction cntrl (320) . . . 525
- 4-place pwr seating . . . 525

SL-CLASS RWD/3.2L-I6 (228hp)

Model	WS	Ret
320 2dr Cnv	34650	38575
500 (8cyl) 2dr Cnv	41050	44500
600 (12cyl) 2dr Cnv	56150	60150

Add:
- Adaptive damping (std 600) . . . 600
- Sport pkg . . . 1150

Deduct:
- No CD . . . 175

1996 — WS Ret

C-CLASS RWD/2.2L-I4 (147hp)

Model	WS	Ret
220 4dr Sdn	13400	15900
280 (6cyl/194hp) 4dr Sdn	15300	17975
C36 (6cyl/276hp) 4dr Sdn	23375	26700

Add:
- Bose audio (220) . . . 150
- Leather seats (std C36) . . . 175
- Moonroof-pwr (std C36) . . . 200
- Traction control . . . 275
- Sport pkg (C280) . . . 175
- CD Changer . . . 150

Deduct:
- Non adj. steering whl . . . 75

E-CLASS RWD/3.2L-I6 (217hp)

Model	WS	Ret
300D 4dr Sdn	18400	21325
320 4dr Sdn	19825	22850
420 (8cyl) 4dr Sdn	24350	27750

Add:
- Bose Audio (300D,320 Sdn) . . . 150
- Sport pkg . . . 725

Deduct:
- Cloth seats . . . 200
- No Sunroof . . . 250

S-CLASS RWD/4.2L-V8 (275hp)

Model	WS	Ret
320 (6cyl) 4dr Sdn	25375	28850
320 LWB (6cyl) 4dr Sdn	26025	29550
420 4dr Sdn	28400	32125
500 4dr Sdn	34225	37350
500 2dr Cpe	38625	42000
600 (12cyl) 4dr Sdn	48650	52300
600 (12cyl) 2dr Cpe	51525	55300

Add:
- Adaptive damping (std 600) . . . 475
- Traction cntrl (320) . . . 425
- 4-place pwr seating . . . 450

SL-CLASS RWD/3.2L-I6 (228hp)

Model	WS	Ret
320 2dr Cnv	30075	33725
500 (8cyl) 2dr Cnv	36400	39650
600 (12cyl) 2dr Cnv	51300	55075

Add:
- Adaptive damping (std 600) . . . 475
- Sport pkg . . . 950

1995 — WS Ret

C-CLASS RWD/2.2L-I4 (148hp)

Model	WS	Ret
220 4dr Sdn	12075	14475
280 (6cyl/194hp) 4dr Sdn	13675	16200
C36 (6cyl/276hp) 4dr Sdn	21450	24700

Add:
- Bose audio . . . 150
- Leather seats . . . 150
- Traction control . . . 275

Deduct:
- Non adj. steering whl . . . 50

E-CLASS RWD/3.2L-I6 (228hp)

Model	WS	Ret
300D 4dr Sdn	13600	16125
320 4dr Sdn	14800	17425
320 4dr Wgn	16825	19600
320 2dr Cnv	32000	35775
320 2dr Cpe	19475	22475
420 (8cyl) 4dr Sdn	18250	21150

Add:
- Prem sound (300D,320 Sdn) . . . 150
- Sportline pkg . . . 225
- Traction control . . . 375

Deduct:
- Cloth seats . . . 175

S-CLASS RWD/4.2L-V8 (275hp)

Model	WS	Ret
320 (6cyl) 4dr Sdn	21400	24550
320 LWB (6cyl) 4dr Sdn	22000	25200
350D (6cyl) 4dr Sdn	20000	23050
420 4dr Sdn	24250	27625
500 4dr Sdn	28775	32525
500 2dr Cpe	32600	36350
600 (12cyl) 4dr Sdn	40125	44400
600 (12cyl) 2dr Cpe	44525	49125

Add:
- Adaptive damping (std 600) . . . 425
- Trctn cntrl (std 500,600) . . . 450

SL-CLASS RWD/3.2L-I6 (228hp)

Model	WS	Ret
320 2dr Cnv	27350	30975
500 (8cyl) 2dr Cnv	33150	36950
600 (12cyl) 2dr Cnv	44500	49100

Add:
- Adaptive damping (std 600) . . . 400
- Traction control (320) . . . 400

1994 — WS Ret

C-CLASS RWD/2.2L-I4 (148hp)

Model	WS	Ret
220 4dr Sdn	9525	11725
280 (6cyl/194hp) 4dr Sdn	10875	13175

Add:
- Bose audio . . . 125
- Leather seats . . . 125
- Sunroof-pwr . . . 175
- Traction control . . . 250

Deduct:

Non adj steering whl	50

E-CLASS — RWD/3.2L-I6 (217hp)

Model	WS	Ret
320 4dr Sdn	13100	15575
320 4dr Wgn	14800	17425
320 2dr Cnv	28225	31925
320 2dr Cpe	17225	20050
420 (8cyl) 4dr Sdn	15575	18250
500 (8cyl) 4dr Sdn	25950	29475

Add:

Premium sound (320)	125
Sportline pkg	200
Traction control (std 500)	325

Deduct:

MB-tex (vinyl)	175

S-CLASS — RWD/4.2L-V8 (275hp)

Model	WS	Ret
320 (6cyl) 4dr Sdn	19225	22200
350D (6cyl) 4dr Sdn	39575	43800
420 4dr Sdn	21650	24825
500 4dr Sdn	25650	29150
500 2dr Cpe	26050	29575
600 (12cyl) 4dr Sdn	34200	38075
600 (12cyl) 2dr Cpe	37175	41275

Add:

Adaptive damping (std 600)	375
Trctn cntrl (std 500,600)	400

SL-CLASS — RWD/3.2L-I6 (229hp)

Model	WS	Ret
320 2dr Cnv	25300	28775
500 (8cyl) 2dr Cnv	29775	33400
600 (12cyl) 2dr Cnv	37700	41825

Add:

Adaptive damping (std 600)	375
Traction control (320)	375

1993 — WS Ret

190 — RWD/2.3L-I4 (130hp)

Model	WS	Ret
190E 2.3 4dr Sdn	6400	8350
190E 2.6 (6cyl) 4dr Sdn	7400	9425

Add:

Sportline Pack (2.6 only)	300
Sunroof-pwr (std 2.6)	175

Deduct:

Manual trans	275

300 — RWD/3.2L-I6 (217hp)

Model	WS	Ret
300D (5cyl) 4dr Sdn	10250	12500
300E 3.2 4dr Sdn	11150	13475
300E 2.8 4dr Sdn	10075	12325
300E 4Matic (AWD) 4dr Sdn	12375	14800
300SD (6cyl) 4dr Sdn	16725	19500
300SE (6cyl) 4dr Sdn	17150	19950
300TE 4dr Wgn	12750	15200
300TE 4Matic (AWD) 4dr Wgn	14050	16775
300CE 2dr Cnv	25625	29125
300SL 2dr Cnv	23250	26550
300CE 2dr Cpe	14825	17450

Add:

Traction control	325

400 — RWD/4.2L-V8 (275hp)

Model	WS	Ret
400E 4dr Sdn	12725	15175
400SEL 4dr Sdn	19475	22475

Add:

Traction control	375

500 — RWD/5.0L-V8 (315hp)

Model	WS	Ret
500E 4dr Sdn	19800	22825
500SEL 4dr Sdn	22475	25725
500SL (8cyl) 2dr Cnv	25400	28875
500SEC 2dr Cpe	24675	28100

600 — RWD/6.0L-V12 (389hp)

Model	WS	Ret
600SEL (12cyl) 4dr Sdn	28900	32650
600SL (12cyl) 2dr Cnv	30750	34450
600SEC (12cyl) 2dr Cpe	31775	35550

1992 — WS Ret

190 — RWD/2.3L-I4 (130hp)

Model	WS	Ret
190E 2.3 4dr Sdn	5575	7450
190E 2.6 (6cyl) 4dr Sdn	6450	8400

Add:

Sportline Pack (2.6 only)	250
Sunroof-pwr (std 2.6)	150

Deduct:

Manual trans	250
Vinyl seats (MB-tex)	125

300 — RWD/2.6L-I6 (158hp)

Model	WS	Ret
300D (5cyl) 4dr Sdn	8925	11075
300E 2.6 4dr Sdn	8825	10975
300E 3.0 4dr Sdn	9800	12025
300E 4Matic (AWD) 4dr Sdn	11800	14175
300SE (6cyl) 4dr Sdn	15175	17825
300SD (6cyl) 4dr Sdn	14825	17450
300TE 4Matic (AWD) 4dr Wgn	12450	14875
300TE 4dr Wgn	11000	13325
300SL 2dr Cnv	21050	24175
300CE 2dr Cpe	12850	15325

Add:

Air bag-passenger	50

Deduct:

Manual trans	250
No sunroof	150
Vinyl seats (MB-tex)	175

400 — RWD/4.2L-V8 (268hp)

Model	WS	Ret
400E 4dr Sdn	10975	13300
400SE 4dr Sdn	16525	19275

Deduct:

No sunroof	150

500 — RWD/5.0L-V8 (322hp)

Model	WS	Ret
500E 4dr Sdn	17925	20800
500SEL 4dr Sdn	19525	22525
500SL (8cyl) 2dr Cnv	22825	26100

Deduct:

No sunroof	150

600 — RWD/6.0L-V12 (402hp)

Model	WS	Ret
600SEL (12cyl) 4dr Sdn	23650	26975

1991 — WS Ret

190 — RWD/2.3L-I4 (130hp)

Model	WS	Ret
190E 2.3 4dr Sdn	5125	6975
190E 2.6 (6cyl) 4dr Sdn	5800	7700

Add:

Sunroof-pwr	125

Deduct:

Manual trans	225
Vinyl seats (MB-tex)	100

300 — RWD/2.6L-I6 (158hp)

Model	WS	Ret
300D (5cyl) 4dr Sdn	7650	9700
300E 2.6 4dr Sdn	7775	9825
300E 3.0 4dr Sdn	8225	10325
300E 4Matic (AWD) 4dr Sdn	9075	11225
300SE 4dr Sdn	11000	13325
300SEL 4dr Sdn	11400	13750
300TE 4dr Wgn	9875	12100
300TE 4Matic (AWD) 4dr Wgn	11025	13350
300SL 2dr Cnv	20125	23175
300CE 2dr Cpe	12300	14725

Add:

Sunroof-pwr	125

Deduct:

Manual trans (SL)	225
No sunroof (not SL)	125
Vinyl seats (MB-tex)	125

350 — RWD/3.5L-V6 (134hp)

Model	WS	Ret
350SD 4dr Sdn	10925	13225
350SDL 4dr Sdn	11250	13575

Deduct:

No sunroof	125

420 — RWD/4.2L-V8 (201hp)

Model	WS	Ret
420SEL 4dr Sdn	12050	14450

Deduct:

No sunroof	125

500 — RWD/5.0L-V8 (322hp)

Model	WS	Ret
500SL 2dr Cnv	21625	24800

560 — RWD/5.6L-V8 (238hp)

Model	WS	Ret
560SEL 4dr Sdn	13000	15475
560SEC 2dr Cpe	16275	19025

1990 — WS Ret

190 — RWD/2.6L-I6 (158hp)

Model	WS	Ret
190E 4dr Sdn	4975	6800

Add:

Sunroof-pwr	100

Deduct:

Manual trans	225
No sunroof	75
Vinyl seats (MB-tex)	75

300 — RWD/2.6L-I6 (158hp)

Model	WS	Ret
300D (5cyl) 4dr Sdn	6525	8475
300E 2.6 4dr Sdn	6700	8675
300E 3.0 4dr Sdn	7075	9075
300E 4Matic (AWD) 4dr Sdn	7800	9850
300SE 4dr Sdn	9450	11650
300SEL 4dr Sdn	9600	11800
300TE 4dr Wgn	8250	10350
300SL 2dr Cnv	17600	20450
300CE 2dr Cpe	11025	13350

Add:

Air bag-passenger	25

Deduct:

Vinyl seats (MB-tex)	100

350 — RWD/2.6L-I6 (158hp)

Model	WS	Ret
350SD 4dr Sdn	9500	11700
350SDL 4dr Sdn	10075	12325

Add:

Air bag-passenger	25

420 — RWD/4.2L-V8 (201hp)

Model	WS	Ret
420SEL 4dr Sdn	10875	13175

500 — RWD/5.6L-V8 (322hp)

Model	WS	Ret
500SL 2dr Cnv	19500	22500

560 — RWD/5.6L-V8 (238hp)

Model	WS	Ret
560SEL 4dr Sdn	11775	14150
560SEC 2dr Cpe	14450	17050

1989 — WS Ret

190 — RWD/2.6L-I6 (158hp)

Model	WS	Ret
190D 4dr Sdn	2900	4400
190E 2.6 (6cyl) 4dr Sdn	4500	6275

Add:

Power seat	25
Sunroof-power	100

Deduct:

Manual trans	175
Vinyl seats (MB-tex)	25

260 — RWD/2.6L-I6 (158hp)

Model	WS	Ret
260E 4dr Sdn	5600	7475

Add:

Power seat	25

Deduct:
- No sunroof 50
- Vinyl seats (MB-tex) 25

300 RWD/3.0L-I6 (177hp)

Model	WS	Ret
300E 4dr Sdn	6075	8000
300SE 4dr Sdn	7825	9875
300SEL 4dr Sdn	8025	10100
300TE 4dr Wgn	7450	9475
300CE 2dr Cpe	9650	11850

Add:
- Air bag-passenger 25

Deduct:
- No sunroof 50
- Vinyl seats (MB-tex) 25

420 RWD/4.2L-V8 (201hp)

Model	WS	Ret
420SEL 4dr Sdn	8450	10550

Deduct:
- No sunroof 125

560 RWD/5.6L-V8 (227hp)

Model	WS	Ret
560SEL 4dr Sdn	9000	11150
560SL 2dr Cnv	17675	20525
560SEC 2dr Cpe	13225	15725

1988 WS Ret

190 RWD/2.3L-I4 (130hp)

Model	WS	Ret
190D 4dr Sdn	2600	4075
190E 2.3 (4cyl) 4dr Sdn	3625	5225
190E 2.6 (6cyl) 4dr Sdn	4025	5750

Add:
- ABS brakes 25
- Leather seats 25
- Sunroof-pwr 50

Deduct:
- Manual trans 150

260 RWD/2.6L-I6 (158hp)

Model	WS	Ret
260E 4dr Sdn	5050	6900

Add:
- Leather seats 25
- Sunroof-pwr 50

Deduct:
- Manual trans 150

300 RWD/3.0L-I6 (177hp)

Model	WS	Ret
300E 4dr Sdn	5525	7400
300SE 4dr Sdn	7125	9125
300SEL 4dr Sdn	7375	9400
300TE 4dr Wgn	6700	8675
300CE 2dr Cpe	8450	10550

Add:
- Leather seats (E,TE) 25
- Sunroof-pwr 50

Deduct:
- Manual trans 150

420 RWD/4.2L-V8 (201hp)

Model	WS	Ret
420SEL 4dr Sdn	7725	9775

Deduct:
- No sunroof 100

560 RWD/5.6L-V8 (227hp)

Model	WS	Ret
560SEL 4dr Sdn	8150	10250
560SL 2dr Cnv	15150	17800
560SEC 2dr Cpe	12050	14450

MERCURY

2001 WS Ret

COUGAR RWD/

Model	WS	Ret
Base 2dr Hbk		
S 2dr Hbk		

GRAND MARQUIS RWD/4.6L-V8 (220hp)

Model	WS	Ret
GS 4dr Sdn	14375	16625
LS 4dr Sdn	15900	18250

Add:
- ABS brakes 350
- CD player 200
- CD changer 425
- Premium sound 200
- Leather seats 450
- Handling pkg (w/16" whls/235hp) 475
- Traction ctrl 250
- Wheels-alum (std LS) 200

SABLE FWD/3.0L-V6 (155hp)

Model	WS	Ret
GS 4dr Sdn	11175	13250
GS 4dr Wgn	12975	15150
LS 4dr Sdn	11625	13725
LS Premium (200hp) Wgn.	13175	15350

Add:
- 3.0L-V6 (200hp) 475
- ABS brakes (GS sdn) 375
- CD player 250
- MACH audio 400
- Leather seats 425
- Pwr seat (GS sdn) 200
- Sunroof-pwr 500
- Wheels-alum (GS sdn) 200
- Wheels-chrome 250
- Third seat (Wgn) 175

2000 WS Ret

COUGAR RWD/

Model	WS	Ret
2dr Hbk	10475	12500

Add:
- 2.5L-V6 (170hp) 425
- ABS brakes 250
- CD Player 200
- CD Changer 300
- Leather seats 275
- Pwr seat 150
- Cruise ctrl 150
- Sport grp (incls 16" alloys & 4WDB 275
- Sunroof-pwr 375
- Traction ctrl 200
- Wheels-alum 225

GRAND MARQUIS RWD/4.6L-V8 (200hp)

Model	WS	Ret
GS 4dr Sdn	12250	14375
LS 4dr Sdn	13750	15975

Add:
- ABS brakes 275
- CD player 175
- CD changer 325
- Premium sound 150
- Leather seats 350
- Handling pkg (incl 215hp V8) . . 375
- Traction ctrl 200
- Wheels-alum 175

MYSTIQUE FWD/2.0L-I4 (125hp)

Model	WS	Ret
GS 4dr Sdn	7950	9825
LS (2.5l-V6/170hp) 4dr Sdn	8950	10875

Add:
- ABS brakes 250
- Premium sound w/CD player . . 200
- Leather seats 250
- Sunroof-pwr 375
- Pwr seat 125
- Wheels-alloy (GS) 175
- Traction ctrl 200

Deduct:
- Manual trans 575

SABLE FWD/3.0L-V6 (155hp)

Model	WS	Ret
GS 4dr Sdn	9225	11175
GS 4dr Wgn	11925	14025
LS 4dr Sdn	10600	12625
LS (200hp V6) 4dr Wgn	12775	14925

Add:
- 3.0L-V6 (200hp) 375
- ABS brakes 275
- CD player 175
- MACH audio 300
- Leather seats 325
- Pwr seat (std LS) 150
- Sunroof-pwr 400
- Wheels-alum (std LS) 175
- Wheels-chrome 200
- Third seat (Wgn) 150

1999 WS Ret

COUGAR RWD/

Model	WS	Ret
2dr Hbk	9025	10975

Add:
- 2.5L-V6 (170hp) 350
- ABS brakes 225
- CD Player 150
- CD Changer 250
- Leather seats 225
- Pwr seat 100
- Cruise ctrl 100
- Sport grp (incls 16" alloys & 4WDB 225
- Sunroof-pwr 300
- Traction ctrl 150
- Wheels-polished alum 175

GRAND MARQUIS RWD/4.6L-V8 (200hp)

Model	WS	Ret
GS 4dr Sdn	10450	12475
LS 4dr Sdn	11800	13900

Add:
- 4.6L V8 w/dual exhaust 225
- ABS brakes 250
- CD player 125
- CD changer 275
- Premium sound 125
- Leather seats 300
- Handling pkg 300
- Traction ctrl 150
- Wheels-alum 125

MYSTIQUE FWD/2.0L-I4 (125hp)

Model	WS	Ret
GS 4dr Sdn	6425	8200
LS (2.5l-V6/170hp) 4dr Sdn	7525	9375

Add:
- ABS brakes 225
- Premium sound 50
- CD player 150
- Leather seats 225
- Sunroof-pwr 325
- Pwr seat 100
- Wheels-alloy (GS) 150
- Traction ctrl 150

Deduct:
- Manual trans 475
- No air cond 550

SABLE FWD/3.0L-V6 (145hp)

Model	WS	Ret
GS 4dr Sdn	7625	9475
LS (200hp V6) 4dr Sdn	8900	10825
LS (200hp V6) 4dr Wgn	10625	12650

Add:
- 3.0L-V6 (200hp) 300
- ABS brakes 225
- CD player 150
- MACH audio 250
- Leather seats 275
- Pwr seat (std LS) 125
- Sunroof-pwr 325
- Wheels-alum (std LS) 125
- Wheels-chrome 150
- Third seat (Wgn) 100

TRACER FWD/2.0L-I4 (110hp)

Model	WS	Ret
GS 4dr Sdn	5300	7025
LS 4dr Sdn	6025	7775
LS 4dr Wgn	6375	8150

Add:
- Cassette (GS) . . . 50
- Cruise ctrl . . . 125
- Luggage rack (Wgn) . . . 50
- Pwr dr locks (std wgn) . . . 125
- Pwr windows (std wgn) . . . 100
- Sunroof-pwr . . . 275
- Tilt wheel . . . 50
- ABS brakes . . . 175
- CD player . . . 125
- Lthr seats . . . 225
- Wheels-15" alum . . . 100
- Trio Pkg . . . 50

Deduct:
- No air cond . . . 450
- Manual trans . . . 425

1998

GRAND MARQUIS — RWD/4.6L-V8 (200hp)

Model	WS	Ret
GS 4dr Sdn	9025	10975
LS 4dr Sdn	10225	12225

Add:
- 4.6L V8 w/dual exhaust . . . 175
- ABS brakes . . . 200
- CD player . . . 100
- CD changer . . . 225
- Premium sound . . . 100
- Leather seats . . . 250
- Handling pkg . . . 250
- Alum wheels . . . 100

MYSTIQUE — FWD/2.0L-I4 (125hp)

Model	WS	Ret
GS 4dr Sdn	5325	7050
LS (6cyl) 4dr Sdn	6050	7800

Add:
- ABS brakes . . . 175
- Premium sound . . . 25
- CD player . . . 125
- Sunroof-pwr . . . 250
- Wheels-cast alum (GS) . . . 125
- Pwr seat . . . 75

Deduct:
- Manual trans . . . 400
- No air cond . . . 450

SABLE — FWD/3.0L-V6 (145hp)

Model	WS	Ret
GS 4dr Sdn	6425	8200
LS 4dr Sdn	7175	9000
LS 4dr Wgn	8600	10525

Add:
- 3.0L 200hp V6 . . . 250
- ABS brakes (std LS) . . . 200
- CD player . . . 125
- MACH audio . . . 200
- Leather seats . . . 225
- Pwr seat (std LS) . . . 75
- Sunroof-pwr . . . 275
- Wheels-alum (std LS) . . . 100
- Wheels-chrome . . . 125
- Third seat (Wgn) . . . 75

TRACER — FWD/2.0L-I4 (110hp)

Model	WS	Ret
GS 4dr Sdn	4475	6125
LS 4dr Sdn	5025	6725
LS 4dr Wgn	5350	7075

Add:
- Cassette . . . 50
- Cruise ctrl . . . 75
- Luggage rack (Wgn) . . . 25
- Pwr dr locks . . . 75
- Pwr windows . . . 75
- Sunroof-pwr . . . 225
- Tilt wheel . . . 25
- ABS brakes . . . 150
- CD player . . . 100
- Lthr seats . . . 200
- Alum wheels . . . 75
- Trio Pkg . . . 50

Deduct:
- No air cond . . . 375
- Manual trans . . . 350

1997

COUGAR — RWD/3.8L-V6 (145hp)

Model	WS	Ret
XR-7 2dr Cpe	6625	8425

Add:
- 4.6 Liter V8 . . . 300
- ABS brakes . . . 175
- Alloy wheels . . . 75
- CD player . . . 100
- Cruise ctrl . . . 50
- Leather seats . . . 150
- Pwr dr locks . . . 50
- Pwr seat . . . 50
- Sunroof-pwr . . . 200

GRAND MARQUIS — RWD/4.6L-V8 (190hp)

Model	WS	Ret
GS 4dr Sdn	6950	8775
LS 4dr Sdn	7900	9775

Add:
- 4.6L V8 w/dual exhaust . . . 150
- ABS brakes . . . 175
- Cruise ctrl (Base) . . . 50
- Premium sound . . . 75
- Leather seats . . . 200
- Alum wheels (Base) . . . 75
- Vinyl roof . . . 150

MYSTIQUE — FWD/2.0L-I4 (125hp)

Model	WS	Ret
Base 4dr Sdn	3975	5600
GS 4dr Sdn	4150	5775
LS 4dr Sdn	4550	6200

Add:
- 2.5L DOHC V6 . . . 250
- ABS brakes . . . 150
- Cassette (std LS) . . . 25
- Cruise ctrl . . . 50
- Premium sound . . . 25
- Pwr dr locks . . . 50
- CD player . . . 75
- Pwr windows . . . 75
- Sunroof-pwr . . . 225
- Wheels-cast alum (GS) . . . 75
- Pwr seat (std LS) . . . 50

Deduct:
- Manual trans . . . 325
- No air cond . . . 375

SABLE — FWD/3.0L-V6 (145hp)

Model	WS	Ret
G 4dr Sdn	4500	6150
GS 4dr Sdn	4875	6550
GS 4dr Wgn	5550	7275
LS 4dr Sdn	6275	8050
LS 4dr Wgn	6900	8725

Add:
- ABS brakes (std LS) . . . 175
- Cassette (std LS) . . . 50
- CD player . . . 100
- Cruise ctrl . . . 50
- MACH audio . . . 175
- Leather seats . . . 175
- Pwr dr locks (std LS) . . . 50
- Pwr seat (std LS) . . . 50
- Sunroof-pwr . . . 225
- Wheels-alum (std LS) . . . 75
- Third seat (Wgn) . . . 50

TRACER — FWD/2.0L-I4 (110hp)

Model	WS	Ret
GS 4dr Sdn	3400	4875
LS 4dr Sdn	3950	5550
LS 4dr Wgn	4275	5900

Add:
- Cassette . . . 25
- Cruise ctrl . . . 50
- Luggage rack (Wgn) . . . 25
- Pwr dr locks . . . 50
- Pwr windows . . . 50
- Sunroof-pwr . . . 175
- Tilt wheel . . . 25
- ABS brakes . . . 125
- CD player . . . 75
- Alum wheels . . . 50
- Trio Pkg . . . 25

Deduct:
- No air cond . . . 325
- Manual trans . . . 275

1996

COUGAR — RWD/3.8L-V6 (145hp)

Model	WS	Ret
XR-7 2dr Cpe	5000	6700

Add:
- 4.6 Liter V8 . . . 250
- ABS brakes . . . 150
- Alloy wheels . . . 50
- CD player . . . 75
- Cruise ctrl . . . 50
- Leather seats . . . 125
- Pwr dr locks . . . 25
- Pwr seat . . . 25
- Sunroof-pwr . . . 175

GRAND MARQUIS — RWD/4.6L-V8 (190hp)

Model	WS	Ret
GS 4dr Sdn	5425	7150
LS 4dr Sdn	6325	8100

Add:
- 4.6L V8 w/dual exhaust . . . 125
- ABS brakes . . . 150
- Cruise ctrl (Base) . . . 25
- Premium sound . . . 50
- Leather seats . . . 175
- Wheel upgrade (Base) . . . 50
- Vinyl roof . . . 125

MYSTIQUE — FWD/2.0L-I4 (125hp)

Model	WS	Ret
GS 4dr Sdn	3450	4925
LS 4dr Sdn	3850	5450

Add:
- 2.5L DOHC V6 . . . 225
- ABS brakes . . . 125
- Cassette (std LS) . . . 25
- Cruise ctrl . . . 25
- Premium sound . . . 25
- Pwr dr locks . . . 25
- CD player . . . 50
- Pwr windows . . . 50
- Sunroof-pwr . . . 175
- Tilt wheel . . . 25
- Wheels-cast alum (GS) . . . 50
- Pwr seat (std LS) . . . 25

Deduct:
- Manual trans . . . 275
- No air cond . . . 300

SABLE — FWD/3.0L-V6 (145hp)

Model	WS	Ret
G 4dr Sdn	3625	5100
GS 4dr Sdn	3925	5525
GS 4dr Wgn	4500	6150
LS 4dr Sdn	5125	6825
LS 4dr Wgn	5675	7425

Add:
- ABS brakes (std LS) . . . 150
- Cassette (std LS) . . . 25
- CD player . . . 75
- Cruise ctrl . . . 50
- JBL audio . . . 150
- Leather seats . . . 150
- Pwr dr locks (std LS) . . . 50
- Pwr seat (std LS) . . . 25
- Sunroof-pwr . . . 175
- Wheels-alum (std LS) . . . 50
- Third seat (Wgn) . . . 50

TRACER — FWD/1.9L-I4 (88hp)

Model	WS	Ret
Base 4dr Sdn	3025	4450
Base 4dr Wgn	3300	4775
LTS 4dr Sdn	3550	5025

Add:
- Cassette (std LTS) . . . 25
- Cruise ctrl (std LTS) . . . 25
- Luggage rack (Wgn) . . . 25

Pwr dr locks		25
Pwr windows		50
Sunroof-pwr		150
Tilt wheel (std LTS)		25
ABS brakes		125
CD player		50
Integrated child seat		25
Alum wheels (std LTS)		25
Deduct:		
No air cond		250
Manual trans		225

1995 — WS Ret

COUGAR RWD/3.8L-V6 (140hp)

	WS	Ret
XR-7 2dr Cpe	3975	5600
Add:		
4.6 Liter V8		225
ABS brakes		125
Alloy wheels		50
CD player		50
Cruise ctrl		25
Leather seats		125
JBL audio		150
Pwr dr locks		25
Power seat		25
Moonroof-pwr		150

GRAND MARQUIS RWD/4.6L-V8 (190hp)

	WS	Ret
GS 4dr Sdn	4375	6000
LS 4dr Sdn	5025	6725
Add:		
4.6L V8 w/dual exhaust		100
ABS brakes		125
Cruise ctrl		25
Integrated phone		75
JBL audio		150
Leather seats		150
Special wheels		50
Vinyl roof		100

MYSTIQUE FWD/2.0L-I4 (125hp)

	WS	Ret
GS 4dr Sdn	2650	4050
LS 4dr Sdn	3025	4450
Add:		
2.5L DOHC V6		200
ABS brakes		125
Cassette (std LS)		25
Cruise ctrl		25
Premium sound		25
Pwr dr locks		25
CD player		50
Pwr windows		25
Moonroof-pwr		175
Deduct:		
Manual trans		250
No air cond		275

SABLE FWD/3.0L-V6 (140hp)

	WS	Ret
GS 4dr Sdn	2825	4225
GS 4dr Wgn	3450	4925
LS 4dr Sdn	3700	5200
LS 4dr Wgn	4275	5900
Add:		
ABS brakes (std LS)		150
Cassette (std LS)		25
CD player		50
Cruise ctrl		25
JBL audio		150
Leather seats		125
Pwr dr locks		25
Pwr seat (std LS)		25
Pwr windows (std LS)		50
Special wheels (std LS)		50
Moonroof-pwr		175
Third seat (Wgn)		25

TRACER FWD/1.9L-I4 (88hp)

	WS	Ret
Base 4dr Sdn	2200	3325
Base 4dr Wgn	2475	3850
LTS 4dr Sdn	2625	4000
Add:		
Cassette (std LTS)		25
Cruise ctrl (std LTS)		25
Luggage rack (Wgn)		25
Pwr dr locks		25
Pwr windows		25
Sunroof-pwr		150
Tilt wheel (std LTS)		25
ABS brakes		100
CD player		50
Deduct:		
No air cond		225
Manual trans		200
Manual steering		25

1994 — WS Ret

COUGAR RWD/3.8L-V6 (140hp)

	WS	Ret
XR-7 2dr Cpe	3350	4825
Add:		
4.6 Liter V8		200
ABS brakes		125
Alloy wheels		25
Cassette		25
CD player		50
Cruise ctrl		25
Leather seats		100
JBL audio		125
Pwr dr locks		25
Power seat		25
Sunroof-pwr		150

GRAND MARQUIS RWD/4.6L-V8 (190hp)

	WS	Ret
GS 4dr Sdn	3725	5325
LS 4dr Sdn	4350	5975
Add:		
4.6L V8 w/dual exhaust		75
ABS brakes		125
Cruise ctrl		25
Integrated phone		75
JBL audio		125
Leather seats		125
Pwr seat		25
Special wheels		25
Vinyl roof		75

SABLE FWD/3.0L-V6 (140hp)

	WS	Ret
GS 4dr Sdn	2325	3675
GS 4dr Wgn	2800	4200
LS 4dr Sdn	3025	4450
LS 4dr Wgn	3500	4975
Add:		
3.8L 6-cyl (std LX wgn)		75
ABS brakes		125
Cassette		25
CD player		50
Cruise ctrl		25
JBL audio		125
Leather seats		125
Pwr dr locks		25
Pwr seat		25
Pwr windows (std LS)		25
Special wheels		25
Sunroof-pwr		150
Third seat (Wgn)		25

TOPAZ FWD/2.3L-I4 (96hp)

	WS	Ret
GS 4dr Sdn	1575	2625
GS 2dr Cpe	1525	2450
Add:		
3.0 Liter V6		175
Air bag-driver		75
Cassette		25
Cruise ctrl		25
Pwr dr locks		25
Pwr seat		25
Pwr windows		25
Deduct:		
No air cond		225
Manual trans		200

TRACER FWD/1.9L-I4 (88hp)

	WS	Ret
Base 4dr Sdn	1900	3000
Base 4dr Wgn	2100	3225
LTS 4dr Sdn	2275	3425
Add:		
Cassette (std LTS)		25
Cruise ctrl (std LTS)		25
Pwr dr locks		25
Pwr windows		25
Sunroof-pwr		125
Deduct:		
No air cond		225
Manual trans		200
Manual steering		25

1993 — WS Ret

CAPRI (5sp/AT) FWD/1.6L-I4 (100hp)

	WS	Ret
Base 2dr Cnv	2225	3350
XR2 2dr Cnv	2650	4050
Add:		
Cassette (std XR2)		25
Cruise ctrl (std XR2)		25
Leather seats		75
Removable hardtop		200
Special wheels (std XR2)		25
Deduct:		
No air cond		200

COUGAR RWD/3.8L-V6 (140hp)

	WS	Ret
XR-7 2dr Cpe	2600	3975
Add:		
5.0 Liter V8		175
ABS brakes		125
Alloy wheels		25
Cassette		25
CD player		50
Cruise ctrl		25
Leather seats		75
JBL audio		100
Pwr dr locks		25
Power seat		25
Sunroof-pwr		125

GRAND MARQUIS RWD/4.6L-V8 (190hp)

	WS	Ret
GS 4dr Sdn	2900	4325
LS 4dr Sdn	3325	4800
Add:		
4.6L V8 w/dual exhaust		75
ABS brakes		100
Cruise ctrl		25
Integrated phone		50
JBL audio		100
Leather seats		125
Pwr seat		25
Special wheels		25
Vinyl roof		75

SABLE FWD/3.0L-V6 (140hp)

	WS	Ret
GS 4dr Sdn	1825	2900
GS 4dr Wgn	2225	3350
LS 4dr Sdn	2375	3725
LS 4dr Wgn	2700	4100
Add:		
ABS brakes		125
Air bag-passenger		50
Cassette		25
CD player		50
Cruise ctrl		25
JBL audio		100
Leather seats		100
Pwr dr locks		25
Pwr seat		25
Pwr windows (std LS)		25
Special wheels		25
Sunroof-pwr		150
Third seat (Wgn)		25
3.8L 6-cylinder		75

TOPAZ FWD/2.3L-I4 (96hp)

Model	WS	Ret
GS 4dr Sdn	1250	2150
GS 2dr Cpe	1175	2075

Add:
- 3.0 Liter V6 . . . 150
- Air bag-driver . . . 75
- Cassette . . . 25
- Cruise ctrl . . . 25
- Pwr dr locks . . . 25
- Pwr seat . . . 25
- Pwr windows . . . 25

Deduct:
- No air cond . . . 200
- Manual trans . . . 175

TRACER FWD/1.9L-I4 (88hp)

Model	WS	Ret
Base 4dr Sdn	1375	2300
Base 4dr Wgn	1525	2450
LTS 4dr Sdn	1650	2700

Add:
- Cassette (std LTS) . . . 25
- Cruise ctrl (std LTS) . . . 25
- Pwr dr locks . . . 25
- Pwr windows . . . 25
- Sunroof-pwr . . . 100

Deduct:
- No air cond . . . 175
- Manual trans . . . 175
- Manual steering . . . 25

1992 — WS Ret

CAPRI (5sp/AT) FWD/1.6L-I4 (100hp)

Model	WS	Ret
Base 2dr Cnv	1900	3000
XR2 2dr Cnv	2200	3325

Add:
- Cassette (std XR2) . . . 25
- Cruise ctrl (std XR2) . . . 25
- Leather seats . . . 50
- Removable hardtop . . . 200
- Special wheels (std XR2) . . . 25

Deduct:
- No air cond . . . 175

COUGAR RWD/3.8L-V6 (140hp)

Model	WS	Ret
LS 2dr Cpe	2250	3375
XR-7 (8cyl) 2dr Cpe	2500	3875

Add:
- 5.0 Liter V8 (std XR-7) . . . 150
- ABS brakes (std XR-7) . . . 75
- Cassette . . . 25
- CD player . . . 25
- Cruise ctrl . . . 25
- Leather seats . . . 50
- JBL audio . . . 75
- Pwr dr locks . . . 25
- Pwr seat . . . 25
- Special wheels (std XR7) . . . 25
- Sunroof-pwr . . . 100

GRAND MARQUIS RWD/4.6L-V8 (190hp)

Model	WS	Ret
GS 4dr Sdn	2350	3700
LS 4dr Sdn	2650	4050

Add:
- 4.6L V8 w/dual exhaust . . . 50
- ABS brakes . . . 75
- Air bag-passenger . . . 25
- Cassette . . . 25
- Cruise ctrl . . . 25
- Integrated phone . . . 50
- JBL audio . . . 75
- Leather seats . . . 75
- Pwr seat . . . 25
- Special wheels . . . 25
- Vinyl roof . . . 50

SABLE FWD/3.0L-V6 (140hp)

Model	WS	Ret
GS 4dr Sdn	1475	2400
GS 4dr Wgn	1825	2900
LS 4dr Sdn	1950	3050
LS 4dr Wgn	2250	3375

Add:
- ABS brakes . . . 75
- Air bag-passenger . . . 25
- Cassette . . . 25
- CD player . . . 25
- Cruise ctrl . . . 25
- JBL audio . . . 75
- Leather seats . . . 75
- Pwr dr locks . . . 25
- Pwr seat . . . 25
- Pwr windows (std LS) . . . 25
- Special wheels . . . 25
- Sunroof-pwr . . . 100
- Third seat (Wgn) . . . 25

TOPAZ FWD/2.3L-I4 (96hp)

Model	WS	Ret
GS 4dr Sdn	1050	1950
GS 2dr Cpe	975	1675
LS 4dr Sdn	1200	2100
LTS (6cyl) 4dr Sdn	1200	2100
XR5 (6cyl) 2dr Cpe	1150	2050

Add:
- 3.0L V6 (std LTS,XR5) . . . 100
- Air bag-driver (GS) . . . 50
- Cruise ctrl (std LS,LTS) . . . 25
- Pwr dr locks(std LS,LTS) . . . 25
- Pwr windows (std LS,LTS) . . . 25

Deduct:
- No air cond . . . 175
- Manual trans . . . 175

TRACER FWD/1.9L-I4 (88hp)

Model	WS	Ret
Base 4dr Sdn	1150	2050
Base 4dr Wgn	1300	2200
LTS 4dr Sdn	1425	2350

Add:
- Cruise ctrl (std LTS) . . . 25
- Pwr dr locks . . . 25
- Pwr windows . . . 25
- Sunroof-pwr . . . 75

Deduct:
- No air cond . . . 175
- Manual trans . . . 150
- Manual steering . . . 25

1991 — WS Ret

CAPRI (5sp/AT) FWD/1.6L-I4 (100hp)

Model	WS	Ret
Base 2dr Cnv	1650	2700
XR2 2dr Cnv	1875	2975

Add:
- Cassette (std XR2) . . . 25
- Removable hardtop . . . 175
- Special wheels (std XR2) . . . 25

Deduct:
- No air cond . . . 175

COUGAR RWD/3.8L-V6 (140hp)

Model	WS	Ret
LS 2dr Cpe	2000	3100
XR-7 (8cyl) 2dr Cpe	2300	3450

Add:
- 5.0 Liter V8 (std XR7) . . . 125
- ABS brakes (std XR7) . . . 50
- Cassette . . . 25
- CD player . . . 25
- Cruise ctrl . . . 25
- JBL audio . . . 50
- Leather seats . . . 50
- Pwr dr locks . . . 25
- Special wheels (std XR7) . . . 25
- Sunroof-pwr . . . 100

Deduct:
- No air cond . . . 175

GRAND MARQUIS RWD/5.0L-V8 (150hp)

Model	WS	Ret
Colony Park GS 4dr Wgn	2125	3250
Colony Park LS 4dr Wgn	2350	3700
GS 4dr Sdn	2150	3275
LS 4dr Sdn	2250	3375

Add:
- Carriage roof . . . 25
- Cassette . . . 25
- Coach roof . . . 25
- Integrated phone . . . 25
- Leather seats . . . 50
- Pwr dr locks . . . 25
- Special wheels . . . 25
- Third seat (Wgn) . . . 25

SABLE FWD/3.0L-V6 (140hp)

Model	WS	Ret
GS 4dr Sdn	1175	2075
GS 4dr Wgn	1450	2375
LS 4dr Sdn	1400	2325
LS 4dr Wgn	1650	2700

Add:
- 3.8 Liter V6 . . . 50
- ABS brakes . . . 50
- Cassette . . . 25
- CD player . . . 25
- Cruise ctrl . . . 25
- JBL audio . . . 50
- Leather seats . . . 50
- Pwr dr locks . . . 25
- Pwr windows (std LS) . . . 25
- Special wheels . . . 25
- Sunroof-pwr . . . 100
- Third seat (Wgn) . . . 25

TOPAZ FWD/2.3L-I4 (96hp)

Model	WS	Ret
GS 4dr Sdn	900	1600
GS 2dr Cpe	850	1525
LS 4dr Sdn	1050	1950
LTS 4dr Sdn	1025	1925
XR5 2dr Cpe	975	1675

Add:
- 4-wheel drive . . . 175
- Air bag-driver . . . 25
- Pwr windows (GS only) . . . 25

Deduct:
- No air cond . . . 175
- Manual trans . . . 150

TRACER FWD/1.9L-I4 (88hp)

Model	WS	Ret
Base 4dr Sdn	825	1500
Base 4dr Wgn	900	1600
LTS 4dr Sdn	950	1650

Add:
- Pwr windows . . . 25
- Sunroof-pwr . . . 50

Deduct:
- No air cond . . . 150
- Manual trans . . . 125
- Manual steering . . . 25

1990 — WS Ret

COUGAR RWD/3.8L-V6 (140hp)

Model	WS	Ret
LS 2dr Cpe	1675	2725
XR-7 2dr Cpe	2125	3250

Add:
- ABS brakes (std XR7) . . . 25
- CD player . . . 25
- JBL audio . . . 50
- Leather seats . . . 25
- Special wheels (std XR7) . . . 25
- Sunroof-pwr . . . 75

Deduct:
- Manual trans (XR-7) . . . 125

GRAND MARQUIS RWD/5.0L-V8 (150hp)

Model	WS	Ret
Colony Park GS 4dr Wgn	1700	2775
Colony Park LS 4dr Wgn	1775	2850
GS 4dr Sdn	1625	2675
LS 4dr Sdn	1750	2825

Add:
- Coach roof . . . 25

Leather seats . . . 25
Special wheels . . . 25

SABLE FWD/3.0L-V6 (140hp)

	WS	Ret
GS 4dr Sdn	950	1650
GS 4dr Wgn	1125	2025
LS 4dr Sdn	1150	2050
LS 4dr Wgn	1350	2275

Add:
3.8L V6 . . . 25
ABS brakes . . . 25
CD player . . . 25
JBL audio . . . 50
Leather seats . . . 25
Pwr windows (std LS) . . . 25
Special wheels . . . 25
Sunroof-pwr . . . 75

TOPAZ FWD/2.3L-I4 (98hp)

	WS	Ret
GS 4dr Sdn	750	1275
GS 2dr Cpe	750	1275
LS 4dr Sdn	875	1550
LTS 4dr Sdn	850	1525
XR5 2dr Cpe	825	1500

Add:
4-wheel drive . . . 150

Deduct:
No air cond . . . 150
Manual trans . . . 125

1989 WS Ret

COUGAR RWD/3.8L-V6 (140hp)

	WS	Ret
LS 2dr Cpe	1350	2275
XR-7 2dr Cpe	1700	2775

Add:
CD player . . . 25
JBL audio . . . 25
Leather seats . . . 25
Sunroof-pwr . . . 50

Deduct:
Manual trans (XR-7) . . . 100

GRAND MARQUIS RWD/5.0L-V8 (150hp)

	WS	Ret
Colony Park GS 4dr Wgn	1375	2300
Colony Park LS 4dr Wgn	1525	2450
GS 4dr Sdn	1275	2175
LS 4dr Sdn	1425	2350

Add:
Leather seats . . . 25

SABLE FWD/3.0L-V6 (140hp)

	WS	Ret
GS 4dr Sdn	750	1275
GS 4dr Wgn	925	1625
LS 4dr Sdn	925	1625
LS 4dr Wgn	1075	1975

Add:
3.8 Liter V6 . . . 25
JBL audio . . . 25
Leather seats . . . 25
Sunroof-pwr . . . 50

Deduct:
No air cond . . . 125

TOPAZ FWD/2.3L-I4 (98hp)

	WS	Ret
GS 4dr Sdn	550	1050
GS 2dr Cpe	550	1050
LS 4dr Sdn	675	1200
LTS 4dr Sdn	625	1125
XR5 2dr Cpe	600	1100

Add:
4-wheel drive . . . 100

Deduct:
No air cond . . . 100
Manual trans . . . 100

TRACER FWD/1.6L-I4 (82hp)

	WS	Ret
Base 4dr Hbk	625	1125
Base 4dr Wgn	675	1200
Base 2dr Hbk	575	1075

Add:

Deduct:
No air cond . . . 75
Manual trans . . . 75

1988 WS Ret

COUGAR RWD/3.8L-V6 (140hp)

	WS	Ret
LS 2dr Cpe	1000	1700
XR-7 (8cyl) 2dr Cpe	1125	2025

Add:
5.0 Liter V8 (std XR7) . . . 50
Leather seats . . . 25
Sunroof-pwr . . . 50

Deduct:
No air cond . . . 100

GRAND MARQUIS RWD/5.0L-V8 (150hp)

	WS	Ret
Colony Park GS 4dr Wgn	1075	1975
Colony Park LS 4dr Wgn	1175	2075
GS 4dr Sdn	1025	1925
LS 4dr Sdn	1125	2025

Add:
Leather seats . . . 25

SABLE FWD/3.0L-V6 (140hp)

	WS	Ret
GS 4dr Sdn	550	1050
GS 4dr Wgn	625	1125
LS 4dr Sdn	675	1200
LS 4dr Wgn	725	1250

Add:
3.8 Liter V6 . . . 25
Leather seats . . . 25
Sunroof-pwr . . . 50

Deduct:
No air cond . . . 100

TOPAZ FWD/2.3L-I4 (98hp)

	WS	Ret
GS 4dr Sdn	475	950
GS 2dr Cpe	450	925
LS 4dr Sdn	500	975
LTS 4dr Sdn	475	950
XR5 2dr Cpe	450	925

Add:
4-wheel drive . . . 50

Deduct:
No air cond . . . 75
Manual trans . . . 75

TRACER FWD/1.6L-I4 (82hp)

	WS	Ret
Base 4dr Hbk	475	950
Base 4dr Wgn	525	1000
Base 2dr Hbk	475	950

Add:

Deduct:
No air cond . . . 50
Manual trans . . . 50

MERKUR

1989 WS Ret

SCORPIO RWD/2.9L-V6 (144hp)

	WS	Ret
Sedan 4dr Sdn	1175	2075

Add:
Leather seats . . . 25
Sunroof-pwr . . . 50

XR4Ti RWD/2.3L-I4 (175hp)

	WS	Ret
Hatchback 2dr Hbk	1475	2400

1988 WS Ret

SCORPIO RWD/2.9L-V6 (144hp)

	WS	Ret
Sedan 4dr Sdn	875	1550

Add:
Leather seats . . . 25
Sunroof-pwr . . . 50

XR4Ti RWD/2.3L-I4 (175hp)

	WS	Ret
Hatchback 2dr Hbk	1125	2025

Add:
Leather seats . . . 25
Sunroof-pwr . . . 50

MITSUBISHI

2001 WS Ret

DIAMANTE FWD/3.5L-V6 (210hp)

	WS	Ret
ES 4dr Sdn		
LS 4dr Sdn		

ECLIPSE FWD/2.4L-I4 (154hp)

	WS	Ret
GS 2dr Cnv		
GS 2dr Hbk	12600	14750
GT (200hp V6) 2dr Cnv		
GT (200hp V6) 2dr Hbk	14075	16325
RS 2dr Hbk	11675	13775

Add:
ABS brakes . . . 375
CD changer . . . 400
Pwr seat . . . 200
Lthr seats . . . 325
Sunroof-power (std GS) . . . 400
Infinity audio (std cnv) . . . 225
Manual trans . . . 675

GALANT FWD/2.4L-I4 (145hp)

	WS	Ret
DE 4dr Sdn	9925	11925
ES 4dr Sdn	10875	12925
GTZ (V6/195hp) 4dr Sdn	13925	16475
LS (V6/195hp) 4dr Sdn	13400	15600

Add:
ABS brakes (ES 4cyl) . . . 325
Infinity Audio . . . 225
Moonroof-pwr (ES) . . . 475
Wheels-alloy (std LS,GTZ) . . . 200

MIRAGE FWD/1.8L-I4 (113hp)

	WS	Ret
DE (1.5L/92hp) 2dr Sdn		
ES 4dr Sdn	7775	9650
LS 4dr Sdn	8775	10700
LS 2dr Sdn		

Add:
Cruise control (std LS) . . . 175
Moonroof-pwr . . . 550
CD player (DE cpe) . . . 225
Pwr door locks (std LS) . . . 175
Power windows (std LS) . . . 175
Sport pkg (incl alloy whls) . . . 225

Deduct:
No air cond . . . 725
Manual trans . . . 650

2000 WS Ret

DIAMANTE FWD/3.5L-V6 (210hp)

	WS	Ret
ES 4dr Sdn	14475	16725
LS 4dr Sdn	16250	18625

Add:
Weather pkg (incls trac ctrl) . . . 375

ECLIPSE FWD/2.4L-I4 (154hp)

	WS	Ret
GS 2dr Hbk	11275	13350
GT (V6) 2dr Hbk	12700	14850
RS 2dr Hbk	10325	12350

Add:

- ABS brakes 275
- CD changer 300
- Pwr seat 150
- Lthr seats 250
- Sunroof-power (std GS) 300
- Infinity audio (RS,GS) 175
- Manual trans 525

GALANT FWD/2.4L-I4 (145hp)

Model	WS	Ret
DE 4dr Sdn	9650	11625
ES 4dr Sdn	10600	12625
GTZ (V6/195hp) 4dr Sdn	13600	15800
LS (V6/195hp) 4dr Sdn	13100	15275

Add:

- ABS brakes (ES 4cyl) 250
- CD player (ES) 175
- Moonroof-pwr (ES) 375
- Wheels-alloy (std LS,GTZ) . . . 150

MIRAGE FWD/1.8L-I4 (113hp)

Model	WS	Ret
DE 4dr Sdn	7000	8825
DE 2dr Sdn	6050	7800
LS 4dr Sdn	8000	9875
LS 2dr Sdn	7075	8900

Add:

- Cruise control (std LS sdn) . . . 150
- CD player (DE cpe) 175
- Power windows (DE cpe) 150

Deduct:

- No air cond 550
- Manual trans 500

1999 WS Ret

3000GT FWD/3.0L-V6 (161hp)

Model	WS	Ret
Base 2dr Hbk	16725	19125
SL 2dr Hbk	19700	22275
VR-4 (Turbo-AWD) Hbk	23825	26650

Add:

- CD changer 275
- CD player (Base) 125
- Infinity audio (Base) 150
- Leather seats (Base) 250

Deduct:

- Man trans (Base,SL) 425

DIAMANTE FWD/3.5L-V6 (210hp)

Model	WS	Ret
Base 4dr Sdn	13750	15975

Add:

- Leather seats 250
- CD changer 275
- Moonroof-pwr 325
- Wheels-16" alum 125
- Wheels-chrome 150

Deduct:

- Wheel covers 175
- Manual seat 100
- No CD player 125

ECLIPSE FWD/2.0L-I4 (140hp)

Model	WS	Ret
GS Spyder 2dr Cnv	12050	14175
GS 2dr Hbk	10775	12825
GS-T Spyder (Turbo) Cnv	14075	16325
GS-T (Turbo) 2dr Hbk	12725	14875
GSX (AWD-Turbo) 2dr Hbk	14575	16850
RS 2dr Hbk	9900	11900

Add:

- ABS brakes 225
- Alloys (RS,GS) 125
- CD changer 250
- CD player (RS,GS) 150
- Cruise (std RS,GS) 125
- Lthr seats(std GSX,GS-T Spy) . 225
- Pwr dr locks (std Spy,GSX) . . . 125
- Pwr windows(std Spy,GS-T,GSX) 100
- Sunroof-power (std GSX) 250
- Infinity audio (RS,GS) 125
- Wheels-alum (RS,GS) 125

Deduct:

- No air cond 500
- Manual trans 425
- No cassette 125

GALANT FWD/2.4L-I4 (145hp)

Model	WS	Ret
DE 4dr Sdn	8550	10450
ES 4dr Sdn	9425	11375
GTZ (V6/195hp) 4dr Sdn	12175	14300
LS (V6/195hp) 4dr Sdn	11725	13825

Add:

- ABS brakes 225
- CD player 150
- CD changer 275
- Moonroof-pwr (std LS,GTZ) . . . 300
- Wheels-alloy (std LS,GTZ) 125

MIRAGE FWD/1.5L-I4 (92hp)

Model	WS	Ret
DE 4dr Sdn	5725	7475
DE 2dr Sdn	4850	6525
LS 4dr Sdn	6650	8450
LS 2dr Sdn	5800	7550

Add:

- ABS brakes 175
- Cruise control (std LS sdn) . . . 125
- Cassette 50
- CD player (std LS cpe) 150
- Power windows (std LS sdn) . . . 125

Deduct:

- No air cond 450
- Manual trans 425

1998 WS Ret

3000GT FWD/3.0L-V6 (161hp)

Model	WS	Ret
Base 2dr Hbk	14175	16425
SL 2dr Hbk	16725	19125
VR-4 (Turbo-AWD) Hbk	20150	22750

Add:

- CD changer 225
- CD player (Base) 100
- Infinity audio (Base) 125
- Leather seats (Base) 200

Deduct:

- Man trans (Base,SL) 350

DIAMANTE FWD/3.5L-V6 (210hp)

Model	WS	Ret
ES 4dr Sdn	11350	13425
LS 4dr Sdn	13025	15200

Add:

- CD player (ES) 100
- Leather seats (ES) 200
- CD changer 225
- Moonroof-pwr (ES) 275
- Wheels-16" alum (ES) 100
- Wheels-chrome 125

Deduct:

- Wheel covers 150
- Manual seat 75

ECLIPSE FWD/2.0L-I4 (140hp)

Model	WS	Ret
GS Spyder 2dr Cnv	10950	13000
GS 2dr Hbk	9475	11450
GS-T Spyder (Turbo) Cnv.	12925	15100
GS-T (Turbo) 2dr Hbk	11200	13275
GSX (AWD-Turbo) 2dr Hbk	12725	14875
RS 2dr Hbk	8750	10675

Add:

- ABS brakes 200
- Alloys (RS,GS) 100
- CD changer 200
- CD player (RS,GS) 125
- Cruise (std RS,GS) 75
- Lthr seats(std GSX,GS-T Spy) . . 175
- Pwr dr locks (std Spy,GSX) . . . 75
- Pwr windows(std Spy,GS-T,GSX) 75
- Sunroof-power (std GSX) 200
- Infinity audio (RS,GS) 75
- Wheels-alum (RS,GS) 100

Deduct:

- No air cond 425
- Manual trans 350
- No cassette 75

GALANT FWD/2.4L-I4 (141hp)

Model	WS	Ret
DE 4dr Sdn	6825	8625
ES 4dr Sdn	7925	9800
LS 4dr Sdn	8850	10775

Add:

- ABS brakes (std LS) 200
- Cassette (DE) 75
- CD player 125
- CD changer 225
- Moonroof-pwr (std LS) 250
- Wheels-alloy (std LS) 100

Deduct:

- No air cond 450
- Manual trans 375

MIRAGE FWD/1.5L-I4 (92hp)

Model	WS	Ret
DE 4dr Sdn	4975	6675
DE 2dr Sdn	4275	5900
LS 4dr Sdn	5775	7525
LS 2dr Sdn	5050	6750

Add:

- ABS brakes 150
- Cruise control 75
- Cassette 50
- CD player (std LS) 100
- Power windows 75

Deduct:

- No air cond 375
- Manual steering 75
- Manual trans 350

1997 WS Ret

3000GT FWD/3.0L-V6 (161hp)

Model	WS	Ret
Base 2dr Hbk	12400	14550
SL 2dr Hbk	14725	17000
VR-4 (Turbo-AWD) 2dr Hbk	18325	20825

Add:

- CD changer 175
- CD player (Base) 75
- Infinity audio (Base) 100
- Leather seats (Base) 175
- Sunroof-pwr 225

Deduct:

- Man trans (Base,SL) 300

DIAMANTE FWD/3.5L-V6 (210hp)

Model	WS	Ret
ES 4dr Sdn	10050	12050
LS 4dr Sdn	11525	13600

Add:

- ABS brakes 150
- CD player 75
- CD changer 175
- Moonroof-pwr 225
- Wheels-16" alum (ES) 75
- Leather seats (ES) 175

Deduct:

- Wheel covers 125
- Manual seat 50

ECLIPSE FWD/2.0L-I4 (140hp)

Model	WS	Ret
Base 2dr Hbk	6575	8375
GS Spyder 2dr Cnv	9975	11975
GS 2dr Hbk	7900	9775
GS-T Spyder 2dr Cnv	11650	13750
GS-T 2dr Hbk	9425	11375
GSX (AWD) 2dr Hbk	10875	12925
RS 2dr Hbk	7250	9075

Add:

- ABS brakes 150
- Alloys (std Turbo,GSX) 75
- CD changer 175
- CD player 100
- Cruise (std Turbo,GSX) 50

- Lthr seats(std GSX,GS-T Spy) . . 150
- Pwr dr locks(std Turbo,GSX) . . . 50
- Pwr windows(std Turbo,GSX) . . 50
- Sunroof-power 175
- Infinity audio (RS,GS) 75
- Wheels-alum (GS) 75

Deduct:

- No air cond 350
- Manual trans 300
- No cassette 50

GALANT — FWD/2.4L-I4 (141hp)

	WS	Ret
DE 4dr Sdn	5525	7250
ES 4dr Sdn	6550	8350
LS 4dr Sdn	7175	9000

Add:

- ABS brakes 150
- Cassette (DE) 50
- CD player 100
- CD changer 175
- Moonroof-pwr 200
- Wheels-alloy (std LS) 75

Deduct:

- No air cond 375
- Manual trans 325

MIRAGE — FWD/1.4L-I4 (92hp)

	WS	Ret
DE 4dr Sdn	3925	5525
DE 2dr Sdn	3225	4675
LS 4dr Sdn	4600	6250
LS 2dr Sdn	3975	5600

Add:

- ABS brakes 125
- Cruise control 50
- Cassette (std LS cpe) 25
- CD player 75
- Power windows 50

Deduct:

- No air cond 325
- Manual steering 50
- Manual trans 275

1996 — WS Ret

3000GT — FWD/3.0L-V6 (218hp)

	WS	Ret
Base 2dr Hbk	9750	11725
SL Spyder 2dr Cnv.	19025	21550
SL 2dr Hbk	11725	13825
VR-4 Spyder (Turbo-AWD)	23275	26050
VR-4 (Turbo-AWD) 2dr Hbk	15300	17600

Add:

- CD changer (std Cnv) 150
- Sunroof-pwr 175
- Wheels-chrome (SL Cpe) 75

Deduct:

- Man trans (Base,SL) 250

DIAMANTE — FWD/3.0L-V6 (202hp)

	WS	Ret
ES 4dr Sdn	6325	8100

Add:

- CD changer 150
- Sunroof-pwr 175

ECLIPSE — FWD/2.0L-I4 (140hp)

	WS	Ret
GS Spyder 2dr Cnv	7850	9725
GS Turbo 2dr Hbk	7500	9350
GS 2dr Hbk	6125	7900
GS-T Spyder 2dr Cnv	9125	11075
GSX (AWD) 2dr Hbk	8725	10650
RS 2dr Hbk	5525	7250

Add:

- ABS brakes 150
- Alloys (std Turbo,GSX) 50
- CD changer 150
- CD player 75
- Cruise (std Turbo,GSX) 25
- Leather seats (std GSX) 125
- Pwr dr locks(std Turbo,GSX) . . . 25
- Pwr windows(std Turbo,GSX) . . 50
- Sunroof-power 150
- Infinity audio (RS,GS) 25
- Wheels-alum (GS) 50

Deduct:

- No air cond 275
- Manual trans 250
- No cassette 25

GALANT — FWD/2.4L-I4 (141hp)

	WS	Ret
ES 4dr Sdn	5000	6700
LS 4dr Sdn	5475	7200
S 4dr Sdn	4125	5750

Add:

- ABS brakes 150
- Cassette (S) 25
- CD player 75
- CD changer 150
- Cruise ctrl (S) 25
- Infinity audio 50
- Sunroof-pwr 175
- Pwr dr locks (S) 25
- Pwr windows (S) 50
- Wheels-alloy (std LS) 50

Deduct:

- No air cond 300
- Manual trans 275

MIRAGE — FWD/1.5L-I4 (92hp)

	WS	Ret
LS 2dr Sdn	2600	3975
S 4dr Sdn	2500	3875
S 2dr Sdn	1900	3000

- Cassette (std LS) 25
- CD player 75

Deduct:

- No air cond 250
- Manual steering 25
- Manual trans 225

1995 — WS Ret

3000GT — FWD/3.0L-V6 (222hp)

	WS	Ret
Base 2dr Hbk	8650	10575
SL Spyder 2dr Cnv	16900	19300
SL 2dr Hbk	10450	12475
VR-4 Spyder (Turbo-AWD)	20425	23050
VR-4 (Turbo-AWD) 2dr Hbk	13450	15650

Add:

- CD changer (std Cnv) 150
- Sunroof-man 50
- Sunroof-pwr 175
- Wheels-chrome (SL Cpe) 75

Deduct:

- No air cond 275
- Man trans (not VR-4) 225

DIAMANTE — FWD/3.0L-V6 (175hp)

	WS	Ret
4dr Wgn	3725	5325
ES 4dr Sdn	3650	5150
LS 4dr Sdn	5475	7200

Add:

- ABS brakes (std LS) 125
- CD changer 150
- CD player 75
- Leather seats (std LS) 150
- Sunroof-pwr 175
- Traction control 75

Deduct:

- Manual seat 25

ECLIPSE — FWD/2.0L-I4 (140hp)

	WS	Ret
GS Turbo 2dr Hbk	5750	7500
GS 2dr Hbk	4725	6375
GSX (AWD) 2dr Hbk	6725	8525
RS 2dr Hbk	4300	5925

Add:

- ABS brakes 125
- Alloys (std Turbo,GSX) 50
- CD changer 125
- CD player 50
- Cruise (std Turbo,GSX) 25
- Leather seats (std GSX) 100
- Pwr dr locks(std Turbo,GSX) . . . 25
- Pwr windows(std Turbo,GSX) . . 25
- Sunroof-power 125
- Infinity audio (RS,GS) 25

Deduct:

- No air cond 250
- Manual steering 25
- Manual trans 225
- No cassette 25

EXPO — FWD/2.4L-I4 (136hp)

	WS	Ret
Wagon 4dr Wgn	3525	5000

Add:

- ABS brakes 125
- All-wheel drive 400
- Cassette 25
- Cruise ctrl 25
- Luggage rack 25
- Pwr dr locks 25

Deduct:

- No air cond 275

GALANT — FWD/2.4L-I4 (141hp)

	WS	Ret
ES 4dr Sdn	4425	6075
LS 4dr Sdn	4825	6500
S 4dr Sdn	3675	5175

Add:

- ABS brakes 125
- Cassette (S) 25
- CD player 50
- CD changer 150
- Infinity audio 50
- Leather seats 125
- Pwr seat 50

Deduct:

- No air cond 275
- Manual trans 250

MIRAGE — FWD/1.5L-I4 (92hp)

	WS	Ret
ES 4dr Sdn	2275	3425
ES 2dr Sdn	1800	2875
LS 4dr Sdn	2475	3850
LS 2dr Sdn	2150	3275
S 4dr Sdn	2100	3225
S 2dr Sdn	1650	2700

Add:

- ABS brakes 125
- Alloy wheels (std LS Cpe) 25
- Cassette (std LS) 25
- CD player 50
- Cruise ctrl (std LS sdn) 25
- Power dr locks (std LS sdn) . . . 25
- Power windows (std LS sdn) . . . 25
- Tilt wheel (std LS) 25

Deduct:

- No air cond 225
- Manual steering 25
- Manual trans 200

1994 — WS Ret

3000GT — FWD/3.0L-V6 (222hp)

	WS	Ret
Base 2dr Hbk	5675	7425
SL 2dr Hbk	7100	8925
VR-4 (Turbo-AWD) 2dr Hbk	9100	11050

Add:

- CD changer 125
- Leather seats (std VR4) 125
- Sunroof-man 50
- Wheels-chrome 50

Deduct:

- No air cond 250
- Manual trans 200

DIAMANTE — FWD/3.0L-V6 (175hp)

	WS	Ret
ES 4dr Sdn	3475	4950
ES 4dr Wgn	3575	5050

LS 4dr Sdn.............. 4725 6375

Add:
ABS brakes (std LS) 125
CD changer 125
CD player 50
Euro handling pkg 150
Leather seats (std LS) 125
Sunroof-pwr 150
Traction control 75

ECLIPSE FWD/1.8L-I4 (92hp)

Base 2dr Hbk............ 2175 3300
GS DOHC 2dr Hbk 3100 4550
GS Turbo 2dr Hbk........ 3550 5025
GS 2dr Hbk 2600 3975
GSX (AWD) 2dr Hbk 4325 5950

Add:
ABS brakes (std GSX) 125
Alloys (std Turbo,GSX) 25
Cassette (Base) 25
CD player 50
Cruise (std Turbo,GSX) 25
Leather seats 75
Pwr dr locks (std Turbo,GSX) ... 25
Pwr windws (std Turbo,GSX) ... 25
Sunroof-manual 50

Deduct:
No air cond 225
Manual steering 25
Manual trans 200

EXPO FWD/2.4L-I4 (136hp)

LRV 3dr Wgn............ 2325 3675
LRV Sport 3dr Wgn....... 3000 4425
Wagon 4dr Wgn.......... 3050 4500

Add:
ABS brakes 125
All-wheel drive 350
Alloy wheels (Base) 25
Cassette (std Sport) 25
CD player 50
Cruise ctrl (std Sport) 25
Pwr dr locks (std Sport) 25
Pwr windows (std Sport) 25
Sunroof-pwr 150

Deduct:
No air cond 250
Manual trans 225

GALANT FWD/2.4L-I4 (141hp)

ES 4dr Sdn 2650 4050
GS 4dr Sdn 3425 4900
LS 4dr Sdn............. 2825 4225
S 4dr Sdn.............. 2050 3150

Add:
ABS brakes 125
Cassette (S) 25
CD player (std GS) 50

Deduct:
No air cond 250
Manual trans 225

MIRAGE FWD/1.5L-I4 (92hp)

ES 4dr Sdn 1625 2675
ES 2dr Sdn 1125 2025
LS 4dr Sdn............. 1950 3050
LS 2dr Sdn............. 1450 2375
S 4dr Sdn.............. 1450 2375
S (5sp) 2dr Sdn 725 1250

Add:
ABS brakes 100
Alloy wheels (std LS Cpe) 25
Cassette (std LS) 25
CD player 50
Cruise ctrl (std LS sdn) 25
Power dr locks (std LS sdn) 25
Power windows (std LS sdn) ... 25

Deduct:
No air cond 225
Manual steering 25
Manual trans 200

1993 WS Ret

3000GT FWD/3.0L-V6 (300hp)

Base 2dr Hbk 4825 6500
SL 2dr Hbk 6025 7775
VR-4 (Turbo-AWD) 2dr Hbk 7475 9325

Add:
CD changer 100
Leather seats (std VR4) 100
Sunroof-man 50

Deduct:
No air cond 200
Manual trans 175

DIAMANTE FWD/3.0L-V6 (175hp)

ES 4dr Sdn 3025 4450
ES 4dr Wgn............ 3100 4550
LS 4dr Sdn 4125 5750

Add:
ABS brakes (std LS) 100
Alloy wheels (std LS) 25
CD player 50
Euro handling pkg 150
Leather seats (std LS) 100

ECLIPSE FWD/1.8L-I4 (92hp)

Base 2dr Hbk 1875 2975
GS DOHC 2dr Hbk 2650 4050
GS Turbo 2dr Hbk........ 3025 4450
GS 2dr Hbk 2250 3375
GSX (AWD) 2dr Hbk...... 3725 5325

Add:
ABS brakes (std GSX) 100
Alloys (std Turbo,GSX) 25
Cassette (Base) 25
CD player 50
Cruise (std Turbo,GSX) 25
Leather seats 75
Pwr dr locks (std Turbo,GSX) .. 25
Pwr windws (std Turbo,GSX) .. 25
Sunroof-manual 50

Deduct:
No air cond 200
Manual steering 25
Manual trans 175

EXPO FWD/2.4L-I4 (136hp)

Base 4dr Wgn........... 2525 3900
LRV 3dr Wgn 1975 3075
LRV Sport 3dr Wgn....... 2575 3950
SP 4dr Wgn............ 2625 4000

Add:
ABS brakes 100
Cassette (std Sport) 25
Cruise ctrl (std Sport) 25
Pwr dr locks (std Sport) 25
Pwr windows (std Sport) 25
Sunroof-pwr 125
All-wheel drive 325

Deduct:
No air cond 225
Manual trans 200

GALANT FWD/2.0L-I4 (121hp)

ES 4dr Sdn 2125 3250
LS 4dr Sdn 2275 3425
S 4dr Sdn 1625 2675

Add:
Alloy wheels (std LS) 25
Cassette 25
CD player 50
Pwr dr locks (std ES,LS) 25
Pwr windows (std ES,LS) 25
Sunroof-power 125

Deduct:
No air cond 225
Manual trans 200

MIRAGE FWD/1.5L-I4 (92hp)

ES 4dr Sdn............. 1400 2325
ES 2dr Sdn............. 975 1675
LS 4dr Sdn 1625 2675
LS 2dr Sdn 1225 2125
S 4dr Sdn 1175 2075
S (5sp) 2dr Sdn 575 1075

Add:
ABS brakes 75
Alloy wheels (std LS Cpe) 25
Cassette (std ES,LS) 25
CD player 50
Cruise ctrl (std LS) 25
Power dr locks (std LS) 25
Power windows (std LS) 25

Deduct:
No air cond 175
Manual steering 25
Manual trans 175

PRECIS FWD/1.5L-I4 (81hp)

Base 2dr Hbk 475 950

Add:
Cassette 25

Deduct:
No air cond 175
Manual steering 25
Manual trans 175

1992 WS Ret

3000GT FWD/3.0L-V6 (222hp)

Base 2dr Hbk 4150 5775
SL 2dr Hbk............ 4975 6675
VR-4 (Turbo-AWD) 2dr Hbk. 6075 7850

Add:
ABS brakes (Base only) 75
CD player 25
Cruise ctrl 25
Leather seats 75
Pwr dr locks (Base only) 25
Pwr windows (Base only) 25
Sunroof-manual 25

Deduct:
No air cond 200
Manual trans 175

DIAMANTE FWD/3.0L-V6 (175hp)

Base 4dr Sdn 2450 3825
LS 4dr Sdn 3175 4625

Add:
ABS brakes (Std LS) 75
Alloy wheels (std LS) 25
CD player 25
Cruise ctrl (std LS) 25
Euro handling pkg 100
Leather seats 75

ECLIPSE FWD/1.8L-I4 (92hp)

Base 2dr Hbk 1600 2650
GS 2dr Hbk............. 1800 2875
GS DOHC 2dr Hbk........ 2075 3200
GS Turbo 2dr Hbk 2425 3800
GSX Turbo (AWD) 2dr Hbk . 2675 4075

Add:
ABS brakes 75
Alloys (std Turbo,GSX) 25
Cassette (Base) 25
CD player 25
Cruise (std Turbo,GSX) 25
Leather seats 50
Pwr dr locks 25
Pwr windows 25
Sunroof-manual 25

Deduct:
No air cond 175
Manual steering 25

Manual trans	175

EXPO FWD/1.8L-I4 113hp)

Model	WS	Ret
Base 4dr Wgn	2250	3375
Base 3dr Wgn	1925	3025
LRV 3dr Wgn	1650	2700
SP 4dr Wgn	2325	3675

Add:

ABS brakes	75
Alloy wheels	25
Cassette	25
Cruise Ctrl (std SP)	25
Pwr dr locks	25
Pwr windows	25
Sunroof-pwr	100
All-wheel drive	300

Deduct:

No air cond	200
Manual trans	175

GALANT FWD/2.0L-I4 (102hp)

Model	WS	Ret
Base 4dr Sdn	1275	2175
GS 4dr Sdn	1800	2875
GSR (5sp) 4dr Sdn	2250	3375
GSX (AWD) 4dr Sdn	2050	3150
LS 4dr Sdn	1550	2475
VR-4 (5sp,AWD) 4dr Sdn	2825	4225

Add:

ABS brakes (std VR-4)	75
Alloy wheels (std GSR,VR4)	25
Cassette (Base)	25
CD player	25
Cruise control (Base)	25
Power dr locks (Base)	25
Power windows (Base)	25
Sunroof-power	100

Deduct:

No air cond	200
Manual trans (not GSR,VR-4)	175

MIRAGE FWD/1.5L-I4 (92hp)

Model	WS	Ret
Base 4dr Sdn	750	1275
Base 2dr Hbk	650	1150
GS 4dr Sdn	1075	1975
LS 4dr Sdn	875	1550
VL 2dr Hbk	625	1125

Add:

Alloy wheels	25
Cruise ctrl	25

Deduct:

No air cond	175
Manual trans	150

PRECIS FWD/1.5L-I4 (81hp)

Model	WS	Ret
Base 2dr Hbk	600	1100

Add:

Deduct:

No air cond	150
Manual trans	150

1991 — WS — Ret

3000GT FWD/3.0L-V6 (122hp)

Model	WS	Ret
Base 2dr Hbk	3450	4925
SL 2dr Hbk	4200	5825
VR-4 (Turbo-AWD) 2dr Hbk.	5100	6800

Add:

ABS brakes (Base only)	50
CD player	25
Cruise ctrl	25
Leather seats	50
Pwr dr locks (Base only)	25
Pwr windows (Base only)	25

Deduct:

No air cond	175
Manual trans	150

ECLIPSE FWD/1.8L-I4 (92hp)

Model	WS	Ret
Base 2dr Hbk	1325	2250
GS 2dr Hbk	1550	2475
GS DOHC 2dr Hbk	1750	2825
GS Turbo 2dr Hbk	2025	3125
GSX AWD Turbo 2dr Hbk	2275	3425

Add:

ABS brakes	50
Alloy wheels (std GS-T,GSX)	25
Cassette (Base)	25
CD player	25
Pwr windows	25
Sunroof-pwr	100

Deduct:

No air cond	175
Manual trans	150

GALANT FWD/2.0L-I4 (102hp)

Model	WS	Ret
Base 4dr Sdn.	1100	2000
GS 4dr Sdn	1500	2425
GSR (5sp) 4dr Sdn	1850	2925
GSX (AWD) 4dr Sdn	1700	2775
LS 4dr Sdn	1300	2200
VR-4 (5sp,AWD) 4dr Sdn	2350	3700

Add:

ABS brakes	50
Alloy wheels	25
Cassette	25
CD player	25
Pwr dr locks	25
Pwr windows	25
Sunroof-pwr	100

Deduct:

No air cond	175
Manual trans (not GSR,VR-4)	175

MIRAGE FWD/1.5L-I4 (92hp)

Model	WS	Ret
Base 4dr Sdn.	575	1075
Base 2dr Hbk.	550	1050
GS 4dr Sdn	900	1600
LS 4dr Sdn	725	1250
VL 2dr Hbk	525	1000

Add:

Alloy wheels	25
Pwr windows	25

Deduct:

No air cond	150
Manual trans	125

PRECIS FWD/1.5L-I4 (81hp)

Model	WS	Ret
Base 2dr Hbk.	425	900
RS 2dr Hbk	500	975

Add:

Sunroof-pwr	50

Deduct:

No air cond	125
Manual trans	100

1990 — WS — Ret

ECLIPSE FWD/2.0L-I4 (135hp)

Model	WS	Ret
Base 2dr Hbk.	1200	2100
GS 2dr Hbk	1325	2250
GS DOHC 2dr Hbk	1450	2375
GS Turbo (5sp) 2dr Hbk	1575	2625
GSX Turbo (AWD) 2dr Hbk.	1675	2725

Add:

Alloy wheels (Base,GS)	25
CD player	25
Sunroof-manual	25

Deduct:

No air cond	150
Manual trans	125

GALANT FWD/2.0L-I4 (102hp)

Model	WS	Ret
Base 4dr Sdn.	1050	1950
GS 4dr Sdn	1300	2200
GSX (5sp,AWD) 4dr Sdn	1425	2350
LS 4dr Sdn	1175	2075

Add:

ABS brakes	25
Eurotech pkg	50
Pwr windows (Base)	25
Sunroof-pwr	75

Deduct:

No air cond	150
Manual trans (not GSX)	150

MIRAGE FWD/1.5L-I4 (81hp)

Model	WS	Ret
Base 4dr Sdn	500	975
Base 2dr Hbk	450	925
RS 4dr Sdn	675	1200
RS (5sp) 2dr Hbk	500	975
VL (4sp) 2dr Hbk.	325	775

Add:

Deduct:

No air cond	125
Manual trans (not VL,RS)	125

PRECIS FWD/1.5L-I4 (81hp)

Model	WS	Ret
L 2dr Hbk	300	750
RS 2dr Hbk	325	775

Add:

Sunroof-pwr	25

Deduct:

No air cond	100
Manual trans	50

SIGMA FWD/3.0L-V6 (142hp)

Model	WS	Ret
Luxury sdn 4dr Sdn	1625	2675

Add:

ABS brakes	25
Eurotech pkg	75
Leather seats	25
Sunroof-pwr	75

1989 — WS — Ret

GALANT FWD/2.0L-I4 (102hp)

Model	WS	Ret
Base 4dr Sdn	850	1525
GS (5sp) 4dr Sdn	1025	1925
LS 4dr Sdn	975	1675

Add:

ABS brakes	25
Sunroof-pwr	50

Deduct:

No air cond	150
Man trans (not GS)	125

MIRAGE FWD/1.5L-I4 (81hp)

Model	WS	Ret
Base 4dr Sdn	400	850
Base 2dr Hbk	350	800
LS 4dr Sdn	425	900
Turbo (5sp) 2dr Hbk	400	850
VL 4dr Sdn	300	750
VL 2dr Hbk	275	725

Add:

Deduct:

No air cond	75
Manual trans (not Turbo)	75

PRECIS FWD/1.5L-I4 (68hp)

Model	WS	Ret
L (4sp) 2dr Hbk	250	675
LS 4dr Hbk	275	725
LS 2dr Hbk	250	675
RS (5sp) 2dr Hbk	250	675

Add:

Sunroof-pwr	25

Deduct:

No air cond	75
Man trans (LS only)	75

SIGMA FWD/3.0L-V6 (142hp)

Model	WS	Ret
Sedan 4dr Sdn	1325	2250

Add:

ABS brakes	25

Eurotech pkg	25	
Leather seats	25	
Sunroof-pwr	50	

STARION RWD/2.6L-I4 (188hp)

	WS	Ret
ESI-R 2dr Hbk	1250	2150

Add:
- Leather seats . . . 25
- Sport Handling pkg . . . 25
- Sunroof-pwr . . . 50

Deduct:
- Manual trans . . . 100

1988 WS Ret

CORDIA FWD/2.0L-I4 (88hp)

	WS	Ret
L 2dr Hbk	400	850
Turbo (5sp) 2dr Hbk	400	850

Add:

Deduct:
- No air cond . . . 75
- Manual trans (not Turbo) . . . 75

GALANT SIGMA FWD/3.0L-V6 (142hp)

	WS	Ret
Luxury 4dr Sdn	825	1500

Add:
- ABS brakes . . . 25
- Leather seats . . . 25
- Sunroof-pwr . . . 25

Deduct:
- Manual trans . . . 75

MIRAGE FWD/1.5L-I4 (68hp)

	WS	Ret
Base 4dr Sdn	300	750
Turbo 2dr Hbk	325	775

Add:
- Sunroof-pwr . . . 25

Deduct:
- No air cond . . . 50
- Manual trans . . . 50

PRECIS FWD/1.5L-I4 (68hp)

	WS	Ret
Base (4sp) 2dr Hbk	225	650
LS 4dr Hbk	250	675
LS 2dr Hbk	225	650
RS (5sp) 2dr Hbk	225	650

Add:
- Sunroof-pwr . . . 25

Deduct:
- No air cond . . . 25
- Man trans (LS only) . . . 50

STARION RWD/2.6L-I4 (188hp)

	WS	Ret
ESI 2dr Hbk	1100	2000
ESI-R 2dr Hbk	1125	2025

Add:
- Sunroof-pwr . . . 50

Deduct:
- Manual trans . . . 50

TREDIA FWD/2.0L-I4 (88hp)

	WS	Ret
L 4dr Sdn	325	775
LS 4dr Sdn	350	800

Deduct:
- No air cond . . . 75
- Manual trans . . . 75

NISSAN

2001 WS Ret

ALTIMA FWD/2.4L-I4 (155hp)

	WS	Ret
GLE 4dr Sdn	12875	15050
GXE 4dr Sdn	10775	12825
SE 4dr Sdn	12100	14225
XE 4dr Sdn	10050	12050

Add:
- ABS brakes . . . 350
- Cassette (GXE) . . . 175
- CD player (GXE) . . . 200
- Cruise ctrl (GXE) . . . 200
- Leather seats (std GLE) . . . 425
- Moonroof-pwr . . . 475
- Pwr seat (std GLE) . . . 200
- Wheels-alloy (std SE,GLE) . . . 275
- CD changer . . . 275

Deduct:
- No air cond . . . 800
- Manual trans . . . 700

MAXIMA FWD/3.0L-V6 (222hp)

	WS	Ret
GLE 4dr Sdn	18075	20550
GXE 4dr Sdn	15425	17750
SE 4dr Sdn	16500	18875

Add:
- Traction ctrl . . . 200
- Bose audio (std GLE) . . . 350
- CD player (GXE) . . . 250
- CD changer . . . 375
- Leather seats (std GLE) . . . 425
- Pwr seat (std GLE) . . . 175
- Moonroof-pwr . . . 525
- Wheels alum (GXE) . . . 200

Deduct:
- Manual trans . . . 750

SENTRA FWD/1.8L-I4 (126hp)

	WS	Ret
CA 4dr Sdn		
GXE 4dr Sdn	10175	12050
SE 4dr Sdn	10375	12275
XE 4dr Sdn	9150	11100

Add:
- ABS brakes . . . 300
- CD changer . . . 275
- CD player (XE) . . . 200
- Luxury pkg (w/alloy whls) (GXE) . 300
- Moonroof-pwr . . . 425
- Performance pkg (w/16" alloys) . 300

Deduct:
- No air cond . . . 750
- Manual trans . . . 650

2000 WS Ret

ALTIMA FWD/2.4L-I4 (155hp)

	WS	Ret
GLE 4dr Sdn	11825	13925
GXE 4dr Sdn	9800	11775
SE 4dr Sdn	11125	13200
XE 4dr Sdn	9050	11000

Add:
- ABS brakes . . . 275
- Cassette (GXE) . . . 150
- CD player (GXE) . . . 175
- Cruise ctrl (GXE) . . . 150
- Leather seats (std GLE) . . . 325
- Moonroof-pwr . . . 375
- Pwr seat (std GLE) . . . 150
- Wheels-alloy . . . 200

Deduct:
- No air cond . . . 625
- Manual trans . . . 550

MAXIMA FWD/3.0L-V6 (222hp)

	WS	Ret
GLE 4dr Sdn	16800	19200
GXE 4dr Sdn	14225	16475
SE 4dr Sdn	15275	17575

Add:
- Traction ctrl . . . 150
- Bose audio (std GLE) . . . 275
- CD player (GXE) . . . 175
- CD changer . . . 275
- Leather seats (std GLE) . . . 325
- Pwr seat (std GLE) . . . 150
- Moonroof-pwr . . . 400
- Wheels alum (GXE) . . . 175

Deduct:
- Manual trans . . . 575

SENTRA FWD/1.8L-I4 (126hp)

	WS	Ret
GXE 4dr Sdn	9500	11350
SE 4dr Sdn	9725	11600
XE 4dr Sdn	8500	10400

Add:
- ABS brakes . . . 225
- Cassette (XE) . . . 75
- CD player (XE) . . . 175
- Luxury pkg (w/alloy whls) (GXE) 225
- Moonroof-pwr . . . 325
- Performance pkg (w/16" alloys) . 225

Deduct:
- No air cond . . . 575
- Manual trans . . . 500

1999 WS Ret

ALTIMA FWD/2.4L-I4 (150hp)

	WS	Ret
GLE 4dr Sdn	10650	12675
GXE 4dr Sdn	8725	10650
SE 4dr Sdn	9950	11950
XE 4dr Sdn	8025	9900

Add:
- ABS brakes . . . 225
- Cassette (XE) . . . 125
- CD player (XE) . . . 150
- Cruise ctrl (XE) . . . 125
- Leather seats (std GLE) . . . 275
- Moonroof-pwr . . . 300
- Wheels-polished alloy . . . 175

Deduct:
- No air cond . . . 525
- Manual trans . . . 450

MAXIMA FWD/3.0L-V6 (190hp)

	WS	Ret
GLE 4dr Sdn	14850	17125
GXE 4dr Sdn	12475	14625
SE 4dr Sdn	13450	15650

Add:
- ABS brakes . . . 225
- Bose audio (std GLE) . . . 225
- CD player (GXE) . . . 150
- CD changer . . . 225
- Leather seats (std GLE) . . . 275
- Pwr seat (std GLE) . . . 100
- Moonroof-pwr . . . 325
- Wheels alum (GXE) . . . 125

Deduct:
- Manual trans . . . 475

SENTRA FWD/1.6L-I4 (115hp)

	WS	Ret
GXE 4dr Sdn	7775	9550
SE 4dr Sdn	7925	9700
XE 4dr Sdn	6850	8650

Add:
- ABS brakes (incl 4WDB) . . . 225
- Cassette (Base) . . . 50
- CD player (std SE Ltd) . . . 150
- Cruise cntrl (XE) . . . 125
- Moonroof-pwr . . . 275

Deduct:
- No air cond . . . 475
- Manual trans . . . 425

1998 WS Ret

200SX FWD/1.6L-I4 (115hp)

	WS	Ret
Base 2dr Cpe	5725	7475
SE 2dr Cpe	6475	8275
SE-R 2dr Cpe	7375	9225

Add:
- ABS brakes . . . 200
- Cassette . . . 50
- CD player (Base) . . . 100
- Moonroof-pwr . . . 250

Deduct:
- No air cond 425
- Manual trans (not R) 350
- No Cassette 50

240SX FWD/2.4L-I4 (155hp)

Model	WS	Ret
Base 2dr Cpe	10075	12075
LE 2dr Cpe	12950	15125
SE 2dr Cpe	11450	13525

Add:
- ABS brakes 200
- Alloy wheels (Base) 100
- Leather seats (std LE) 200
- Cruise ctrl (Base) 75
- Pwr dr locks (Base) 75
- Moonroof-pwr (std LE) 250
- Tilt wheel (Base) 25
- CD player (std LE) 125
- CD changer 200

Deduct:
- No air cond 425
- Manual trans 350
- No Cassette 75

ALTIMA FWD/2.4L-I4 (150hp)

Model	WS	Ret
GLE 4dr Sdn	9400	11350
GXE 4dr Sdn	7750	9625
SE 4dr Sdn	8775	10700
XE 4dr Sdn	7175	9000

Add:
- ABS brakes 175
- Cassette (std SE,GLE) 75
- CD player (XE) 125
- Cruise ctrl (std SE,GLE) 75
- Leather seats (std GLE) 225
- Moonroof-pwr 250

Deduct:
- No air cond 425
- Manual trans 375

MAXIMA FWD/3.0L-V6 (190hp)

Model	WS	Ret
GLE 4dr Sdn	13075	15250
GXE 4dr Sdn	11075	13125
SE 4dr Sdn	11825	13925

Add:
- ABS brakes 200
- Bose audio (std GLE) 200
- CD player (GXE) 125
- CD changer 200
- Leather seats (std GLE) 225
- Pwr seat (std GLE) 75
- Moonroof-pwr 275
- Wheels alum (GXE) 100

Deduct:
- Manual trans 400

SENTRA FWD/1.6L-I4 (115hp)

Model	WS	Ret
Base (5sp) 4dr Sdn	5075	6575
GLE 4dr Sdn	6900	8625
GXE 4dr Sdn	6575	8275
SE 4dr Sdn	6750	8475
XE 4dr Sdn	5800	7550

Add:
- ABS brakes 175
- Cassette (Base) 50
- CD player 125
- Cruise cntrl (std GXE,GLE) 75
- Moonroof-pwr 225

Deduct:
- No air cond 400
- Manual trans 350

1997 WS Ret

200SX FWD/1.6L-I4 (115hp)

Model	WS	Ret
Base 2dr Cpe	5150	6850
SE 2dr Cpe	5800	7550
SE-R 2dr Cpe	6600	8400

Add:
- ABS brakes 150
- Cassette (Base) 25
- Moonroof-pwr 200

Deduct:
- No air cond 350
- Manual trans (not R) 300
- No Cassette 25

240SX FWD/2.4L-I4 (155hp)

Model	WS	Ret
Base 2dr Cpe	7550	9400
LE 2dr Cpe	10175	12175
SE 2dr Cpe	8825	10750

Add:
- ABS brakes 150
- Alloy wheels (Base) 75
- Leather seats (std LE) 150
- Cruise ctrl (Base) 50
- Pwr dr locks (Base) 50
- Moonroof-pwr (std LE) 200
- Tilt wheel (Base) 25
- CD player (std LE) 75
- CD changer 150

Deduct:
- No air cond 350
- Manual trans 300
- No Cassette 50

ALTIMA FWD/2.4L-I4 (150hp)

Model	WS	Ret
GLE 4dr Sdn	7725	9575
GXE 4dr Sdn	6225	8000
SE 4dr Sdn	7175	9000
XE 4dr Sdn	5675	7425

Add:
- ABS brakes 150
- Cassette (std SE,GLE) 50
- CD player 75
- Cruise ctrl (std SE,GLE) 50
- Leather seats 175
- Moonroof-pwr (std GLE) 225

Deduct:
- No air cond 350
- Manual trans 300

MAXIMA FWD/3.0L-V6 (190hp)

Model	WS	Ret
GLE 4dr Sdn	11250	13325
GXE 4dr Sdn	9375	11325
SE 4dr Sdn	10150	12150

Add:
- ABS brakes 150
- Bose audio (std GLE) 150
- CD player (Base) 100
- CD changer 150
- Leather seats (std GLE) 175
- Pwr seat (std GLE) 50
- Moonroof-pwr 225
- Wheels alum (Base) 75

Deduct:
- Manual trans 325

SENTRA FWD/1.6L-I4 (115hp)

Model	WS	Ret
Base (5sp) 4dr Sdn	3950	5400
GLE 4dr Sdn	5600	7250
GXE 4dr Sdn	5300	6950
XE 4dr Sdn	4600	6250

Add:
- ABS brakes 150
- Cassette (Base) 25
- CD player 75
- Cruise cntrl (std GXE,GLE) 50
- Moonroof-pwr 175

Deduct:
- No air cond 325
- Manual trans 275

1996 WS Ret

200SX FWD/1.6L-I4 (115hp)

Model	WS	Ret
Base 2dr Cpe	3925	5525
SE 2dr Cpe	4500	6150
SE-R 2dr Cpe	5175	6875

Add:
- ABS brakes 150
- Sunroof-pwr 175

Deduct:
- No air cond 275
- Manual trans (not R) 250
- No Cassette 25

240SX RWD/2.4L-I4 (155hp)

Model	WS	Ret
Base 2dr Cpe	5600	7325
SE 2dr Cpe	6750	8550

Add:
- ABS brakes 150
- Alloy wheels (std SE) 50
- Leather seats 125
- Cruise ctrl (std SE) 25
- Pwr dr locks (std SE) 25
- Sunroof-pwr 175

Deduct:
- No air cond 275
- Manual trans 250
- No Cassette 25

300ZX (5sp/auto) RWD/3.0L-V6 (222hp)

Model	WS	Ret
2+2 2dr Hbk	13675	16200
Base 2dr Cnv	16575	19350
Base 2dr Hbk	13425	15925
Turbo 2dr Hbk	16025	18750

Add:
- Leather seats (std Cnv) 150
- T-roof 375

ALTIMA FWD/2.4L-I4 (150hp)

Model	WS	Ret
GLE 4dr Sdn	6300	8075
GXE 4dr Sdn	4925	6625
SE 4dr Sdn	5775	7525
XE 4dr Sdn	4525	6175

Add:
- ABS brakes 150
- CD player 75
- Cruise ctrl (std SE,GLE) 25
- Leather seats 150
- Sunroof-pwr (std SE,GLE) 175

Deduct:
- No air cond 300
- Manual trans 250

MAXIMA FWD/3.0L-V6 (190hp)

Model	WS	Ret
GLE 4dr Sdn	8550	10450
GXE 4dr Sdn	6900	8725
SE 4dr Sdn	7575	9425

Add:
- ABS brakes 150
- Bose audio (std GLE) 125
- CD player (std GLE) 75
- Leather seats (std GLE) 150
- Pwr seat (std GLE) 50
- Sunroof-pwr 200

Deduct:
- Manual trans 275

SENTRA FWD/1.6L-I4 (115hp)

Model	WS	Ret
Base (5sp) 4dr Sdn	2675	4075
GLE 4dr Sdn	4250	5875
GXE 4dr Sdn	3975	5600
XE 4dr Sdn	3350	4825

Add:
- ABS brakes 150
- Cassette (Base) 25
- Cruise cntrl (std GXE,GLE) 25
- Sunroof-pwr (std GLE) 150

Deduct:
- No air cond 275
- Manual trans 225

1995 — WS / Ret

200SX — FWD/1.6L-I4 (115hp)

Model	WS	Ret
Base 2dr Cpe	3000	4425
SE 2dr Cpe	3475	4950
SE-R (5sp) 2dr Cpe	4025	5650

Add:
- ABS brakes 125
- Sunroof-pwr 150

Deduct:
- No air cond 250
- Manual trans (not R) 225

240SX — RWD/2.4L-I4 (155hp)

Model	WS	Ret
Base 2dr Cpe	3800	5400
SE 2dr Cpe	4450	6100

Add:
- ABS brakes 125
- Alloy wheels (std SE) 50
- Leather seats 125
- Sunroof-power (SE Cpe) 150

Deduct:
- No air cond 250
- Manual trans 225

300ZX (5sp/auto) — RWD/3.0L-V6 (222hp)

Model	WS	Ret
2+2 2dr Hbk	11175	13375
Base 2dr Cnv	13150	15475
Base 2dr Hbk	10675	12850
Turbo 2dr Hbk	12750	15050

Add:
- Leather seats (std Cnv) 150
- T-roof 350

ALTIMA — FWD/2.4L-I4 (150hp)

Model	WS	Ret
GLE 4dr Sdn	4950	6650
GXE 4dr Sdn	3950	5550
SE 4dr Sdn	4475	6125
XE 4dr Sdn	3675	5175

Add:
- ABS brakes 125
- Cassette (std SE,GLE) 25
- CD player 50
- Cruise ctrl (std SE,GLE) 25
- Leather seats 150
- Sunroof-pwr (std SE,GLE) 175

Deduct:
- No air cond 275
- Manual trans 225

MAXIMA — FWD/3.0L-V6 (190hp)

Model	WS	Ret
GLE 4dr Sdn	6700	8500
GXE 4dr Sdn	5400	7125
SE 4dr Sdn	5975	7725

Add:
- ABS brakes 125
- Bose audio (std GLE) 125
- CD player (std GLE) 50
- Leather seats (std GLE) 150
- Pwr seat (std GLE) 25
- Sunroof-pwr 175

Deduct:
- Manual trans 250

SENTRA — FWD/1.6L-I4 (116hp)

Model	WS	Ret
E (5sp) 4dr Sdn	2100	3225
GLE 4dr Sdn	3400	4875
GXE 4dr Sdn	3125	4575
XE 4dr Sdn	2625	4000

Add:
- ABS brakes 125
- Cassette (Base) 25
- Cruise control (std GXE,GLE) 25
- Sunroof-pwr (std GLE) 150

Deduct:
- No air cond 250
- Manual trans 200

1994 — WS / Ret

240SX — RWD/2.4L-I4 (155hp)

Model	WS	Ret
SE 2dr Cnv	4875	6550

Add:
- ABS brakes 125
- Alloy wheels (std SE) 25
- Leather seats 100
- Sunroof-power (SE Cpe) 150

Deduct:
- No air cond 225
- Manual trans 200

300ZX (5sp/auto) — RWD/3.0L-V6 (222hp)

Model	WS	Ret
2+2 2dr Hbk	10025	12025
Base 2dr Cnv	11425	13500
Base 2dr Hbk	9550	11525
Turbo 2dr Hbk	11450	13525

Add:
- Leather seats 125
- T-roof 300

ALTIMA — FWD/2.4L-I4 (150hp)

Model	WS	Ret
GLE 4dr Sdn	4400	6050
GXE 4dr Sdn	3450	4925
SE 4dr Sdn	3950	5550
XE 4dr Sdn	3200	4650

Add:
- ABS brakes 100
- Cassette (std SE,GLE) 25
- CD player 50
- Cruise ctrl (std SE,GLE) 25
- Leather seats 125
- Sunroof-pwr (std SE) 150

Deduct:
- No air cond 250
- Manual trans 200

MAXIMA — FWD/3.0L-V6 (160hp)

Model	WS	Ret
GXE 4dr Sdn	4850	6525
SE 4dr Sdn	5350	7075

Add:
- ABS brakes 125
- Bose audio (std SE) 100
- CD player 50
- Leather seats 125
- Pwr seat 25
- Sunroof-pwr 175

Deduct:
- Manual trans 225

SENTRA — FWD/1.6L-I4 (110hp)

Model	WS	Ret
E 4dr Sdn	2075	3200
E 2dr Sdn	2000	3100
GXE 4dr Sdn	2700	4100
SE 2dr Sdn	2375	3725
SE-R (5sp) 2dr Sdn	2625	4000
XE 4dr Sdn	2325	3675
XE 2dr Sdn	2250	3375

Add:
- ABS brakes 100
- Air Bag-driver 75
- Cassette (std GXE,XE) 25
- Cruise control (std GXE,XE) 25
- Sunroof-pwr 125

Deduct:
- No air cond 225
- Manual steering 25
- Man trans (not SE-R) 200

1993 — WS / Ret

240SX — RWD/2.4L-I4 (155hp)

Model	WS	Ret
Base 2dr Cpe	2550	3925
Base 2dr Hbk	2675	4075
SE 2dr Cnv	4125	5750
SE 2dr Cpe	3000	4425
SE 2dr Hbk	3150	4600

Add:
- ABS brakes 100
- Handling pkg 50
- Leather seats 75
- Sunroof-manual (SE Hbk) 50
- Sunroof-power (SE Cpe) 125

Deduct:
- No air cond 200
- Manual trans 175

300ZX (5sp/auto) — RWD/3.0L-V6 (222hp)

Model	WS	Ret
2dr Cnv	9725	11700
2+2 2dr Hbk	8100	9975
Base 2dr Hbk	7725	9575
Turbo 2dr Hbk	8775	10700

Add:
- Bose audio 100
- Leather seats 100
- T-roof 275

ALTIMA — FWD/2.4L-I4 (150hp)

Model	WS	Ret
GLE 4dr Sdn	3375	4850
GXE 4dr Sdn	2700	4100
SE 4dr Sdn	3075	4525
XE 4dr Sdn	2550	3925

Add:
- ABS brakes 100
- Cassette 25
- CD player 50
- Cruise ctrl (std SE,GLE) 25
- Leather seats 100
- Sunroof-pwr 150

Deduct:
- No air cond 200
- Manual trans 200

MAXIMA — FWD/3.0L-V6 (160hp)

Model	WS	Ret
GXE 4dr Sdn	3800	5400
SE 4dr Sdn	4450	6100

Add:
- ABS brakes (std SE) 100
- Bose audio (std SE) 75
- Leather seats 100
- Pwr seat 25
- Sunroof-pwr 150

Deduct:
- Manual trans 200

NX — FWD/1.6L-I4 (110hp)

Model	WS	Ret
1600 2dr Cpe	2025	3125
2000 2dr Cpe	2625	4000

Add:
- ABS brakes 75
- Cassette (std 2000) 25
- Cruise ctrl 25
- Pwr dr locks 25
- Pwr windows 25
- T-roof 250

Deduct:
- No air cond 175
- Manual trans 175

SENTRA — FWD/1.6L-I4 (110hp)

Model	WS	Ret
E 4dr Sdn	1550	2475
E 2dr Sdn	1500	2425
GXE 4dr Sdn	2175	3300
SE 2dr Sdn	1825	2900
SE-R (5sp) 2dr Sdn	2300	3450
XE 4dr Sdn	1700	2775
XE 2dr Sdn	1650	2700

Add:
- ABS brakes 75
- Air Bag-driver 75
- Cassette (std GXE) 25
- Cruise control (std GXE) 25
- Sunroof-pwr 100

Deduct:
- No air cond 200

Manual steering 25
Man trans (not SE-R) 175

1992 WS Ret

240SX RWD/2.4L-I4 (155hp)

Model	WS	Ret
Base 2dr Cpe	2200	3325
Base 2dr Hbk	2275	3425
LE 2dr Hbk	2825	4225
SE 2dr Cnv	3600	5075
SE 2dr Cpe	2500	3875
SE 2dr Hbk	2575	3950

Add:
ABS brakes 75
Handling pkg 50
Sunroof-manual (SE Hbk) 25
Sunroof-power (SE Cpe) 100

Deduct:
No air cond 175
Manual trans 175

300ZX (5sp/auto) RWD/3.0L-V6 (222hp)

Model	WS	Ret
2+2 2dr Hbk	6550	8350
Base 2dr Hbk	6225	8000
Turbo 2dr Hbk	7100	8925

Add:
Bose audio 75
Leather seats 75
T-roof 250

MAXIMA FWD/3.0L-V6 (160hp)

Model	WS	Ret
GXE 4dr Sdn	3275	4750
SE 4dr Sdn	3650	5150

Add:
ABS brakes 75
Air Bag-driver 50
Bose audio (std SE) 50
Leather seats 75
Pwr seat 25
Sunroof-pwr 125

Deduct:
Manual trans 200

NX FWD/1.6L-I4 (110hp)

Model	WS	Ret
1600 2dr Cpe	1575	2625
2000 2dr Cpe	2000	3100

Add:
ABS brakes 50
Cruise ctrl 25
Pwr dr locks 25
Pwr windows 25
T-roof 250

Deduct:
No air cond 175
Manual trans 150

SENTRA FWD/1.6L-I4 (110hp)

Model	WS	Ret
E 4dr Sdn	1200	2100
E 2dr Sdn	1200	2100
GXE 4dr Sdn	1625	2675
SE 2dr Sdn	1375	2300
SE-R (5sp) 2dr Sdn	1525	2450
XE 4dr Sdn	1325	2250
XE 2dr Sdn	1275	2175

Add:
ABS brakes 50
Cruise ctrl 25
Sunroof-pwr 75

Deduct:
No air cond 175
Man trans (not SE-R) 150

STANZA FWD/2.4L-I4 (138hp)

Model	WS	Ret
GXE 4dr Sdn	2050	3150
SE 4dr Sdn	2200	3325
XE 4dr Sdn	1775	2850

Add:
ABS brakes 50
Cruise ctrl 25
Pwr dr locks 25
Pwr windows 25
Sunroof-pwr 100

Deduct:
No air cond 200
Manual trans 175

1991 WS Ret

240SX RWD/2.4L-I4 (155hp)

Model	WS	Ret
Base 2dr Cpe	1825	2900
Base 2dr Hbk	1900	3000
LE 2dr Hbk	2400	3775
SE 2dr Cpe	2100	3225
SE 2dr Hbk	2175	3300

Add:
ABS brakes 50
Handling pkg 25
Sunroof-manual 25
Sunroof-pwr 100

Deduct:
No air cond 175
Manual trans 150

300ZX (5sp/auto) RWD/3.0L-V6 (222hp)

Model	WS	Ret
2+2 2dr Hbk	5625	7350
Base 2dr Hbk	5350	7075
Turbo 2dr Hbk	6100	7875

Add:
Air bag-driver 25
Bose audio 50
Leather pkg 75
T-roof 175

MAXIMA FWD/3.0L-V6 (160hp)

Model	WS	Ret
GXE 4dr Sdn	2800	4200
SE 4dr Sdn	3100	4550

Add:
Bose audio 50
Leather seats 50
Sport pkg (incls. ABS) 150
Sunroof-pwr (std SE) 125

Deduct:
Manual trans 175

NX FWD/1.6L-I4 (110hp)

Model	WS	Ret
1600 2dr Cpe	1300	2200
2000 2dr Cpe	1675	2725

Add:
ABS brakes 50
T-roof 175

Deduct:
No air cond 150
Manual trans 125

SENTRA FWD/1.6L-I4 (110hp)

Model	WS	Ret
E 4dr Sdn	1025	1925
E 2dr Sdn	975	1675
GXE 4dr Sdn	1350	2275
SE 2dr Sdn	1125	2025
SE-R (5sp) 2dr Sdn	1225	2125
XE 4dr Sdn	1125	2025
XE 2dr Sdn	1075	1975

Add:
ABS brakes 50
Sunroof-pwr 50

Deduct:
No air cond 150
Man trans (not SE-R) 125

STANZA FWD/2.4L-I4 (138hp)

Model	WS	Ret
GXE 4dr Sdn	1575	2625
XE 4dr Sdn	1425	2350

Add:
ABS brakes 50
Pwr dr locks 25
Pwr windows 25
Sunroof-pwr 100

Deduct:
No air cond 175
Manual trans 150

1990 WS Ret

240SX RWD/2.4L-I4 (140hp)

Model	WS	Ret
SE 2dr Hbk	1800	2875
XE 2dr Cpe	1625	2675

Add:
ABS brakes 25
Sunroof-manual 25
Sunroof-pwr 75

Deduct:
No air cond 150
Manual trans 125

300ZX (5sp/auto) RWD/3.0L-V6 (222hp)

Model	WS	Ret
GS 2dr Hbk	4775	6425
GS 2+2 2dr Hbk	5000	6700
Turbo 2dr Hbk	5525	7250

Add:
Bose audio 50
Leather seats 25

AXXESS FWD/2.4L-I4 (138hp)

Model	WS	Ret
SE Mini Van	1525	2450
XE Mini Van	1350	2275

Add:
Pwr windows 25
Sunroof-pwr 75
Third seat 25

Deduct:
No air cond 150
Manual trans 150

MAXIMA FWD/3.0L-V6 (160hp)

Model	WS	Ret
GXE 4dr Sdn	2325	3675
SE 4dr Sdn	2575	3950

Add:
ABS brakes 25
Leather seats 25
Sunroof-pwr 75

Deduct:
Manual trans 150

PULSAR NX FWD/1.6L-I4 (90hp)

Model	WS	Ret
XE 2dr Hbk	1150	2050

Deduct:
No air cond 125
Manual trans 125

SENTRA FWD/1.6L-I4 (90hp)

Model	WS	Ret
Base (4sp) 2dr Sdn	800	1475
SE 2dr Hbk	1100	2000
XE 4dr Sdn	950	1650
XE 4dr Wgn	1025	1925
XE Sport 2dr Hbk	1050	1950
XE 2dr Sdn	925	1625

Add:

Deduct:
No air cond 125
Man trans (not Base) 125

STANZA FWD/2.4L-I4 (138hp)

Model	WS	Ret
GXE 4dr Sdn	1525	2450
XE 4dr Sdn	1325	2250

Add:
ABS brakes 25
Sunroof-pwr 50

Deduct:
No air cond 150
Manual trans 125

1989 WS Ret

240SX RWD/2.4L-I4 (140hp)

Model	WS	Ret
SE 2dr Hbk	1500	2425
XE 2dr Cpe	1350	2275
Add:		
ABS brakes	25	
Sunroof-manual	25	
Sunroof-pwr	50	
Deduct:		
No air cond	125	
Manual trans	100	

300ZX RWD/3.0L-V6 (165hp)

Model	WS	Ret
GS 2dr Hbk	3500	4975
GS 2+2 2dr Hbk	3675	5175
Turbo 2dr Hbk	4050	5675
Add:		
Leather seats	25	
Deduct:		
Manual trans	125	

MAXIMA FWD/3.0L-V6 (160hp)

Model	WS	Ret
GXE 4dr Sdn	1850	2925
SE 4dr Sdn	2050	3150
Add:		
ABS brakes	25	
Bose audio (std SE)	25	
Leather seats	25	
Sunroof-pwr (std SE)	50	
Deduct:		
Manual trans	125	

PULSAR NX FWD/1.6L-I4 (90hp)

Model	WS	Ret
SE 2dr Hbk	925	1625
XE 2dr Hbk	800	1475
Deduct:		
No air cond	75	
Manual trans	75	

SENTRA FWD/1.6L-I4 (90hp)

Model	WS	Ret
Base (4sp) 2dr Sdn	550	1050
E 4dr Sdn	750	1275
E 4dr Wgn	775	1300
E 2dr Sdn	725	1250
SE 2dr Hbk	900	1600
XE 4dr Sdn	775	1300
XE 4dr Wgn	825	1500
XE 2dr Hbk	825	1500
XE 2dr Sdn	750	1275
Add:		
Deduct:		
No air cond	75	
Man trans (not Base)	75	

STANZA FWD/2.0L-I4 (94hp)

Model	WS	Ret
E 4dr Sdn	1075	1975
GXE 4dr Sdn	1175	2075
Add:		
Sunroof-pwr	50	
Deduct:		
No air cond	125	
Manual trans	125	

1988 WS Ret

200SX RWD/2.0L-I4 (99hp)

Model	WS	Ret
SE (6cyl) 2dr Hbk	900	1600
XE 2dr Hbk	825	1500
XE 2dr Sdn	800	1475
Add:		
Sunroof-pwr	25	
Deduct:		
No air cond	100	
Manual trans	75	

300ZX RWD/3.0L-V6 (165hp)

Model	WS	Ret
GS 2dr Hbk	2125	3250
GS 2+2 2dr Hbk	2125	3250
Turbo 2dr Hbk	2250	3375
Add:		
Leather seats	25	
Deduct:		
Manual trans	75	

MAXIMA FWD/3.0L-V6 (157hp)

Model	WS	Ret
GXE 4dr Sdn	1175	2075
GXE 4dr Wgn	1250	2150
SE 4dr Sdn	1300	2200
Add:		
Leather seats	25	
Sunroof-pwr	50	
Deduct:		
Manual trans	75	

PULSAR NX FWD/1.6L-I4 (70hp)

Model	WS	Ret
SE 2dr Hbk	675	1200
XE 2dr Hbk	600	1100
Deduct:		
No air cond	50	
Manual trans	50	

SENTRA FWD/1.6L-I4 (70hp)

Model	WS	Ret
Base (4sp) 2dr Sdn	400	850
E 4dr Sdn	475	950
E 4dr Wgn	500	975
E 2dr Hbk	450	925
E 2dr Sdn	450	925
GXE 4dr Sdn	600	1100
SE 2dr Hbk	625	1125
XE 4dr Sdn	550	1050
XE 4dr Wgn	600	1100
XE 2dr Hbk	575	1075
XE 2dr Sdn	525	1000
Add:		
4-wheel drive (5sp only)	75	
Sunroof-pwr	25	
Deduct:		
No air cond	50	
Man trans (not Base)	50	

STANZA FWD/2.0L-I4 (94hp)

Model	WS	Ret
E 4dr Sdn	750	1275
GXE 4dr Sdn	825	1500
XE 4dr Wgn	800	1475
Add:		
Sunroof-pwr	25	
Deduct:		
No air cond	75	
Manual trans	75	

OLDSMOBILE

2001 WS Ret

ALERO FWD/3.4L-V6 (170hp)

Model	WS	Ret
GL 4dr Sdn	10725	12775
GL 2dr Cpe	10550	12575
GLS 4dr Sdn	12050	14175
GLS 2dr Cpe	11875	13975
GX (4cyl) 4dr Sdn	9925	11925
GX (4cyl) 2dr Cpe	9750	11725
Add:		
Premium sound	175	
Pwr seat (std GLS)	200	
Lthr seats (std GLS)	400	
Moonroof-pwr	475	
Wheels-alloy (std GLS)	200	
Deduct:		
2.4L-I4 (150hp)	525	
No Cassette	200	

INTRIGUE FWD/3.5L-V6 (215hp)

Model	WS	Ret
GL 4dr Sdn	12400	14550
GLS 4dr Sdn	14550	16825
GX 4dr Sdn	11750	13850
Add:		
CD player (std GLS)	200	
Bose Sound	25	
Lthr seats (std GLS)	400	
Pwr seat (GX)	200	
Moonroof-power	475	
Wheels-chrome	250	

2000 WS Ret

ALERO FWD/3.4L-V6 (170hp)

Model	WS	Ret
GL 4dr Sdn	9125	11075
GL 2dr Cpe	8950	10875
GLS 4dr Sdn	10425	12450
GLS 2dr Cpe	10250	12250
GX (4cyl) 4dr Sdn	8325	10225
GX (4cyl) 2dr Cpe	8150	10025
Add:		
Cruise ctrl (GX)	150	
Premium sound	100	
Pwr seat (std GLS)	150	
Lthr seats (std GLS)	300	
Moonroof-pwr	375	
Wheels-alloy (std GLS)	175	
Deduct:		
2.4L-I4 (150hp)	400	
No Cassette	150	

INTRIGUE FWD/3.5L-V6 (215hp)

Model	WS	Ret
GL 4dr Sdn	10400	12425
GLS 4dr Sdn	12450	14600
GX 4dr Sdn	9750	11725
Add:		
Sterling edit. (GLS)	350	
Bose Sound	25	
CD player (std GLS)	175	
CD changer	300	
Lthr seats (std GLS)	300	
Pwr seat (GX)	150	
Moonroof-power	375	
Wheels-chrome	200	

1999 WS Ret

88 ROYALE FWD/3.8L-V6 (205hp)

Model	WS	Ret
50th Anniv 4dr Sdn	1	1
Base 4dr Sdn	7925	9800
LS 4dr Sdn	9625	11600
LSS 4dr Sdn	10775	12825
Add:		
CD player (std Anniv)	125	
Lthr seats (std Anniv)	250	
Moonroof-pwr	300	
Wheels-alum (Base)	125	
Wheels-chrome	150	

ALERO FWD/3.4L-V6 (170hp)

Model	WS	Ret
GL 4dr Sdn	8325	10225
GL 2dr Cpe	8175	10075
GLS 4dr Sdn	9550	11525
GLS 2dr Cpe	9425	11375
GX (4cyl) 4dr Sdn	7600	9450
GX (4cyl) 2dr Cpe	7500	9350
Add:		
Cruise ctrl (GX)	100	
Premium sound	50	
Pwr seat (std GLS)	125	
Lthr seats	250	
Moonroof-pwr	300	
Wheels-alloy (std GLS)	125	
Deduct:		
2.4L-I4 (150hp)	325	
No Cassette	125	

AURORA FWD/4.0L-V8 (250hp)

	WS	Ret
Sport 4dr Sdn	14150	16400
Add:		
Bose audio w/CD	225	
CD changer	275	
Moonroof-pwr	375	
Wheels-chrome	225	

CUTLASS FWD/3.1L-V6 (150hp)

GL 4dr Sdn	7800	9675
GLS 4dr Sdn	8950	10875
CD player	150	
Lthr seats (std GLS)	250	
Pwr seat (std GLS)	125	
Moonroof-power	300	
Wheels-alum (std GLS)	125	

INTRIGUE FWD/3.8L-V6 (195hp)

GL 4dr Sdn	9375	11325
GLS 4dr Sdn	11275	13350
GX 4dr Sdn	8775	10700
Add:		
3.5L-V6 (215hp)	150	
CD player (std GLS)	125	
CD changer	250	
Lthr seats (std GLS)	250	
Pwr seat (GX)	125	
Moonroof-power	300	
Wheels-chrome	150	

1998 WS Ret

88 ROYALE FWD/3.8L-V6 (205hp)

Base 4dr Sdn	6900	8725
LS 4dr Sdn	8325	10225
LSS 4dr Sdn	9225	11175
Add:		
3.8L-240hp SC-V6	400	
CD player (std LSS)	100	
Lthr seats (std LSS)	200	
Moonroof-pwr	250	
Wheels-alum (Base)	100	
Wheels-chrome	125	

ACHIEVA FWD/2.4L-I4 (150hp)

SL 4dr Sdn	4825	6500
Deduct:		
Manual trans	375	

AURORA FWD/4.0L-V8 (250hp)

Sport 4dr Sdn	11725	13825
Add:		
Bose audio	200	
CD changer	225	
Moonroof-pwr	300	
Wheels-chrome	175	

CUTLASS FWD/3.1L-V6 (155hp)

GL 4dr Sdn	6725	8525
GLS 4dr Sdn	7675	9525
Add:		
CD player	125	
Lthr seats (std GLS)	200	
Pwr seat (std GLS)	75	
Moonroof-power	250	
Wheels-alum (std GLS)	100	

INTRIGUE FWD/3.8L-V6 (195hp)

Base 4dr Sdn	7675	9525
GL 4dr Sdn	9150	11100
GLS 4dr Sdn	9950	11950
Add:		
Bose sound	125	
CD player	100	
CD changer	200	
Lthr seats	200	
Pwr seat (std GL)	75	
Moonroof-power	250	
Wheels-chrome	125	

REGENCY FWD/3.8L-V6 (205hp)

4dr Sdn	10575	12600
Add:		
Moonroof-pwr	250	

1997 WS Ret

88 ROYALE FWD/3.8L-V6 (205hp)

Base 4dr Sdn	5550	7275
LS 4dr Sdn	6850	8650
LSS 4dr Sdn	7650	9500
Add:		
CD player	100	
Leather seats (std LSS)	175	
Moonroof-pwr	225	
Premium sound	25	
Pwr seat (std LSS)	50	
Wheels-alum (Base)	75	
Wheels-chrome	75	

ACHIEVA FWD/2.4L-I4 (150hp)

SC 2dr Cpe	3925	5525
SL 4dr Sdn	4125	5750
Add:		
3.1 Liter V6	225	
Cassette (std Ser. II)	25	
CD player	75	
Cruise ctrl (SL I)	50	
Moonroof-pwr	200	
Pwr seat	25	
Pwr windows (std Ser. II)	50	
Deduct:		
Manual trans	300	

AURORA FWD/4.0L-V8 (250hp)

Sport 4dr Sdn	9800	11775
Add:		
Bose audio (incls CD player)	200	
CD changer	175	
Moonroof-pwr	250	
Wheels-chrome	125	

CUTLASS FWD/3.1L-V6 (160hp)

Base 4dr Sdn	5750	7500
GLS 4dr Sdn	6625	8425
Add:		
CD player	100	
Lthr seats (std GLS)	175	
Pwr seat (std GLS)	75	
Moonroof-power	225	
Wheels-alum (std GLS)	100	

CUTLASS SUPREME FWD/3.IL-V6 (160hp)

SL 4dr Sdn	5900	7650
SL 2dr Cpe	5800	7550
Add:		
CD player	100	
Leather seats	175	
Pwr seat (SLI)	50	
Moonroof-power	225	

REGENCY FWD/3.8L-V6 (205hp)

4dr Sdn	8475	10375
Add:		
Moonroof-pwr	225	

1996 WS Ret

88 ROYALE FWD/3.8L-V6 (205hp)

Base 4dr Sdn	4750	6400
LS 4dr Sdn	5900	7650
LSS 4dr Sdn	6625	8425
Add:		
Cassette (std LS)	25	
CD player	75	
Cruise ctrl (std LS)	50	
Leather seats (std LSS)	150	
Premium sound	25	
Pwr seat (std LSS)	25	
Special wheels (Base)	50	
Wheels-chrome	50	
3.8L Superchared V6	225	

98 REGENCY FWD/3.8L-V6 (205hp)

Elite 4dr Sdn	6900	8725
Add:		
CD player	75	
Sunroof-pwr	200	

ACHIEVA FWD/2.4L-I4 (150hp)

SC 2dr Cpe	3150	4600
SL 4dr Sdn	3325	4800
Add:		
3.1 Liter V6	175	
Cassette	25	
CD player	50	
Cruise ctrl	25	
Pwr seat	25	
Pwr windows	50	
Wheel upgrade	50	
Sunroof-pwr	175	
Deduct:		
No air cond	300	
Manual trans	250	

AURORA FWD/4.0L-V8 (250hp)

Sport 4dr Sdn	7775	9650
Add:		
Bose audio (incls CD chngr)	175	
Sunroof-pwr	200	
Wheels-chrome	100	

CIERA FWD/3.1L-V6 (160hp)

SL 4dr Sdn	3850	5450
SL Cruiser 4dr Wgn	4250	5875
Add:		
Leather seats	150	
Cruise ctrl (std wgn)	25	
Luggage rack (wgn)	25	
Premium sound	25	
Pwr windows (std wgn)	50	
Special wheels	50	
Third seat (Wgn only)	50	
Deduct:		
4cyl	175	

CUTLASS SUPREME FWD/3.1L-V6 (160hp)

SL 4dr Sdn	5075	6775
SL 2dr Cpe	4975	6675
Add:		
3.4L DOHC V6	225	
CD player	75	
Leather seats	150	
Pwr seat	25	
Sunroof-power	200	
Wheel upgrade	50	

1995 WS Ret

88 ROYALE FWD/3.8L-V6 (205hp)

Base 4dr Sdn	3700	5200
LS 4dr Sdn	4600	6250
Add:		
Cassette (std LS)	25	
CD player	50	
Cruise ctrl (std LS)	25	
Leather seats (std LSS)	125	
LSS pkg (over LS)	400	
Premium sound	25	
Pwr seat (std LSS)	25	
Special wheels (std LSS)	50	
3.8L Superchared V6	225	

98 REGENCY FWD/3.8L-V6 (205hp)

Elite 4dr Sdn	5700	7450
Add:		
3.8L Supercharged V6	175	
CD player	50	
Leather seats	150	

- Sunroof-pwr 200

ACHIEVA FWD/2.3L-I4 (150hp)

Model	WS	Ret
S 4dr Sdn	2500	3875
S 2dr Cpe	2425	3800

Add:
- 3.1 Liter V6 150
- Cassette 25
- CD player 50
- Cruise ctrl 25
- Premium sound 25
- Pwr seat 25
- Pwr windows 25
- Special wheels 25
- Sunroof-pwr 150

Deduct:
- No air cond 275
- Manual trans 225

AURORA FWD/4.0L-V8 (250hp)

Model	WS	Ret
Sport 4dr Sdn	5975	7725

Add:
- Delco/Bose audio 175
- Sunroof-pwr 200

Deduct:
- Cloth seats 125

CIERA FWD/3.1L-V6 (160hp)

Model	WS	Ret
SL 4dr Sdn	2875	4275
SL Cruiser 4dr Wgn	3275	4750

Add:
- Leather seats 125
- Luggage rack (Wgn) 25
- Premium sound 25
- Pwr seat 25
- Pwr windows 25
- Special wheels 50
- Third seat (Wgn only) 25

Deduct:
- 4cyl 175

CUTLASS SUPREME FWD/3.1L-V6 (160hp)

Model	WS	Ret
Convertible 2dr Cnv	6200	8375
S 4dr Sdn	4025	5650
S 2dr Cpe	3925	5525

Add:
- 3.4L DOHC V6 200
- Cassette (std Cnv) 25
- CD player 50
- Cruise ctrl (std Cnv) 25
- Leather seats (std Cnv) 125
- Premium sound 25
- Pwr seat (std Cnv) 25
- SL trim 150
- Special wheels (std Cnv) 50
- Sunroof-power 175

1994 — WS / Ret

88 ROYALE FWD/3.8L-V6 (170hp)

Model	WS	Ret
Base 4dr Sdn	3125	4575
LS 4dr Sdn	3925	5525

Add:
- Cassette (std LS) 25
- CD player 50
- Cruise ctrl (std LS) 25
- Leather seats (std LSS) 125
- LSS pkg (over LS) 350
- Pwr dr locks (std LS,LSS) 25
- Pwr seat (std LSS) 25
- Special wheels (std LSS) 25

98 REGENCY FWD/3.8L-V6 (170hp)

Model	WS	Ret
Base 4dr Sdn	4475	6125
Elite 4dr Sdn	4950	6650

Add:
- 3.8L Supercharged V6 175
- CD player 50
- Leather seats 125
- Premium sound 25
- Sunroof-pwr 175

ACHIEVA FWD/2.3L-I4 (115hp)

Model	WS	Ret
S 4dr Sdn	1950	3050
S 2dr Cpe	1925	3025
SC 2dr Cpe	2450	3825
SL 4dr Sdn	2525	3900

Add:
- 2.3L Quad4 HO (std SC) 50
- 3.1 Liter V6 125
- Cassette (S) 25
- CD player 25
- Cruise ctrl (S) 25
- Pwr seat 25
- Pwr windows 25
- Special wheels 25
- Sunroof-pwr 150

Deduct:
- No air cond 250
- Manual trans 200

CUTLASS CIERA FWD/3.1L-V6 (160hp)

Model	WS	Ret
S 4dr Sdn	2375	3725
S Cruiser 4dr Wgn	2725	4125

Add:
- Cassette 25
- Cruise ctrl 25
- Leather seats 125
- Luggage rack (Wgn) 25
- Pwr seat 25
- Pwr windows 25
- Special wheels 25
- Third seat (Wgn only) 25

Deduct:
- 4cyl 150

CUTLASS SUPREME FWD/3.1L-V6 (160hp)

Model	WS	Ret
Convertible 2dr Cnv	5175	7100
S 4dr Sdn	3375	4850
S 2dr Cpe	3300	4775

Add:
- 3.4L DOHC V6 (std Int'l) 175
- Cassette (std Cnv) 25
- CD player 50
- Cruise ctrl (std Cnv) 25
- Leather seats 125
- Pwr seat (std Cnv) 25
- Pwr windows (std Cnv) 25
- Special wheels (std Cnv) 25
- Sunroof-power 175
- Tilt wheel 25
- SL trim 100

1993 — WS / Ret

88 ROYALE FWD/3.8L-V6 (170hp)

Model	WS	Ret
Base 4dr Sdn	2825	4225
LS 4dr Sdn	3200	4650

Add:
- Cassette (std LS) 25
- CD player 50
- Cruise ctrl (std LS) 25
- Leather seats 100
- LSS pkg (over LS) 225
- Pwr dr locks (std LS) 25
- Pwr seat 25
- Special wheels (std LSS) 25

98 REGENCY FWD/3.8L-V6 (170hp)

Model	WS	Ret
Base 4dr Sdn	3725	5325
Elite 4dr Sdn	4075	5700
Touring 4dr Sdn	4800	6450

Add:
- CD player 50
- Leather seats (std Touring) 100
- Special wheels (Base) 25
- Sunroof-pwr 150

ACHIEVA FWD/2.3L-I4 (115hp)

Model	WS	Ret
S 4dr Sdn	1625	2675
S 2dr Cpe	1600	2650
SL 4dr Sdn	2000	3100
SL 2dr Cpe	1950	3050

Add:
- 2.3L Quad4 HO 50
- 3.3 Liter V6 125
- Cassette (std SL) 25
- CD player 25
- Cruise ctrl 25
- Pwr dr locks 25
- Pwr seat 25
- Pwr windows 25
- SC pkg 325
- SCX pkg 250
- Sport performance pkg 175
- Special wheels 25

Deduct:
- No air cond 200
- Manual trans 200

CUTLASS CIERA FWD/3.3L-V6 (160hp)

Model	WS	Ret
S 4dr Sdn	2025	3125
S Cruiser 4dr Wgn	2275	3425
SL 4dr Sdn	2275	3425
SL Cruiser 4dr Wgn	2525	3900

Add:
- Air Bag-driver (std SL) 75
- Cassette (SL) 25
- Cruise ctrl 25
- Leather seats 100
- Luggage rack (Wgn) 25
- Pwr seat 25
- Pwr windows 25
- Special wheels 25
- Third seat (S Wgn only) 25
- Tilt wheel (std SL) 25

Deduct:
- 4cyl 125

CUTLASS SUPREME FWD/3.1L-V6 (140hp)

Model	WS	Ret
Convertible 2dr Cnv	4400	6100
International 4dr Sdn	3550	5025
International 2dr Cpe	3500	4975
S 4dr Sdn	2650	4050
S 2dr Cpe	2625	4000

Add:
- 3.4L DOHC V6 (std Int'l) 175
- ABS brakes (std Int'l) 100
- Cassette (S only) 25
- CD player 50
- Cruise ctrl (std Int'l) 25
- Leather seats 100
- Pwr seat 25
- Pwr windows (std Cnv) 25
- Special wheels (std Int'l) 25
- Sunroof-power 150
- Tilt wheel 25

1992 — WS / Ret

88 ROYALE FWD/3.8L-V6 (170hp)

Model	WS	Ret
Base 4dr Sdn	2400	3775
LS 4dr Sdn	2825	4225

Add:
- ABS brakes (std LS) 75
- Cassette (std LS) 25
- CD player 25
- Cruise ctrl (std LS) 25
- Leather seats 75
- LSS pkg (over LS) 175
- Pwr dr locks (std LS) 25
- Pwr seat 25
- Pwr windows 25
- Special wheels (std LSS) 25

98 REGENCY FWD/3.8L-V6 (170hp)

Model	WS	Ret
Base 4dr Sdn	3075	4525
Elite 4dr Sdn	3425	4900
Touring 4dr Sdn	4000	5625

Add:

CD player	25
Lthr seats (std Touring)	75
Special wheels (Base)	25
Sunroof-pwr	150

ACHIEVA FWD/2.3L-I4 (120hp)

S 4dr Sdn	1375	2300
S 2dr Cpe	1325	2250
SL 4dr Sdn	1625	2675
SL 2dr Cpe	1625	2675

Add:

2.3 Liter 16V Quad4 (Base)	50
3.3 Liter V6	125
CD player	25
Cruise control	25
Pwr windows	25
SC pkg	300
SCX pkg	225
Sport performance pkg	175
Special wheels	25

Deduct:

No air cond	175
Manual trans	175

CUSTOM CRUISER RWD/5.0L-V8 (170hp)

Wagon 4dr Wgn	2975	4400

Add:

Cassette	25
CD player	25
Cruise ctrl	25
Integrated phone	25
Leather seats	75
Pwr dr locks	25
Pwr seat	25
Pwr windows	25
Special wheels	25

CUTLASS CIERA FWD/3.3L-V6 (160hp)

S 4dr Sdn	1600	2650
S Cruiser 4dr Wgn	1825	2900
SL 4dr Sdn	1875	2975
SL Cruiser 4dr Wgn	2100	3225

Add:

Cassette (std SL)	25
Cruise ctrl	25
Leather seats	75
Pwr dr locks	25
Pwr seat	25
Pwr windows	25
Special wheels	25
Third seat (S Wgn only)	25

Deduct:

4cyl	125

CUTLASS SUPREME FWD/3.4L-V6 (200hp)

Convertible 2dr Cnv	3750	5350
International 4dr Sdn	2850	4250
International 2dr Cpe	2825	4225
S 4dr Sdn	2300	3450
S 2dr Cpe	2250	3375
SL 4dr Sdn	2400	3775
SL 2dr Cpe	2350	3700

Add:

3.4L DOHC V6 (std Int'l)	150
ABS brakes (std Int'l)	75
Cassette (S only)	25
CD player	25
Cruise ctrl (std Int'l)	25
Leather seats	75
Pwr dr locks (std Int'l)	25
Pwr seat	25
Pwr windows (std Cnv)	25
Spcl wheels (std Int'l)	25
Sunroof-pwr	100

TORONADO FWD/3.8L-V6 (170hp)

Base 2dr Cpe	3975	5600
Trofeo 2dr Cpe	4375	6000

Add:

CD player	25
Integrated phone	50
Lthr seats (std Trofeo)	75
Sunroof-pwr	150

1991 — WS Ret

88 ROYALE FWD/3.8L-V6 (165hp)

Base 4dr Sdn	1875	2975
Base 2dr Cpe	1800	2875
Brougham 4dr Sdn	2125	3250
Brougham 2dr Cpe	2050	3150

Add:

ABS brakes	50
Air bag-driver	25
Cassette (std Brhgm)	25
CD player	25
Cruise ctrl	25
Leather seats	50
Pwr dr locks	25
Pwr windows	25
Special wheels	25

98 REGENCY FWD/3.8L-V6 (170hp)

Elite 4dr Sdn	2725	4125
Touring 4dr Sdn	3175	4625

Add:

CD player	25
Lthr seats (std Touring)	50
Sunroof-pwr	125

CUSTOM CRUISER RWD/5.0L-V8 (170hp)

Wagon 4dr Wgn	2575	3950

Add:

CD player	25
Integrated phone	25
Leather seats	50
Special wheels	25

CUTLASS CALAIS FWD/2.5L-I4 (110hp)

Base 4dr Sdn	1325	2250
Base 2dr Cpe	1325	2250
International 4dr Sdn	1775	2850
International 2dr Cpe	1775	2850
S 4dr Sdn	1400	2325
S 2dr Cpe	1400	2325
SL 4dr Sdn	1500	2425
SL 2dr Cpe	1525	2450

Add:

2.3L Quad4 4cyl (Base,S)	25
442 pkg (S-incl HO Quad4)	225
Pwr windows	25
Special wheels	25
Sunroof-pwr	75

Deduct:

No air cond	175
Man trans (not 442)	150

CUTLASS CIERA FWD/3.3L-V6 (160hp)

Base 4dr Sdn	1575	2625
S 4dr Sdn	1625	2675
S 2dr Cpe	1575	2625
S Cruiser 4dr Wgn	1700	2775
SL 4dr Sdn	1800	2875
SL Cruiser 4dr Wgn	1900	3000

Add:

Cassette (std SL)	25
Cruise ctrl	25
Leather seats	50
Pwr dr locks	25
Pwr windows	25
Special wheels	25
Third seat (Wgn)	25

Deduct:

4cyl	100
No air cond	175

CUTLASS SUPREME FWD/3.1L-V6 (140hp)

Base 4dr Sdn	1925	3025
Base 2dr Cpe	1900	3000
Convertible 2dr Cnv	3425	4900
International 4dr Sdn	2250	3375
International 2dr Cpe	2225	3350
SL 4dr Sdn	2100	3225
SL 2dr Cpe	2075	3200

Add:

3.4L DOHC V6 (std Int'l)	125
ABS brakes	50
Cassette (Base only)	25
Cruise ctrl (std Int'l)	25
Leather seats	50
Pwr dr locks (std Int'l)	25
Pwr windows (std Cnv)	25
Special wheels (Base)	25
Sunroof-pwr	100

TORONADO FWD/3.8L-V6 (170hp)

Base 2dr Cpe	2675	4075
Trofeo 2dr Cpe	3000	4425

Add:

CD player	25
Integrated phone	25
Lthr seats (std Trofeo)	50
Sunroof-pwr	125

1990 — WS Ret

88 ROYALE FWD/3.8L-V6 (165hp)

Base 4dr Sdn	1525	2450
Base 2dr Cpe	1475	2400
Brougham 4dr Sdn	1650	2700
Brougham 2dr Cpe	1600	2650

Add:

ABS brakes	25
CD player	25
Leather seats	25
Pwr windows	25
Special wheels	25
Sunroof-pwr	75

98 REGENCY FWD/3.8L-V6 (165hp)

Base 4dr Sdn	1850	2925
Brougham 4dr Sdn	1975	3075
Touring 4dr Sdn	2225	3350

Add:

ABS brakes (std Touring)	25
CD player	25
Delco/Bose audio	50
Lthr seats (std Touring)	25
Sunroof-pwr	100

CUSTOM CRUISER RWD/5.0L-V8 (140hp)

Wagon 4dr Wgn	1750	2825

Add:

Pwr windows	25
Special wheels	25

CUTLASS CALAIS FWD/2.5L-I4 (110hp)

Base 4dr Sdn	1125	2025
Base 2dr Cpe	1125	2025
International 4dr Sdn	1400	2325
International 2dr Cpe	1400	2325
S 4dr Sdn	1200	2100
S 2dr Cpe	1200	2100
SL 4dr Sdn	1250	2150
SL 2dr Cpe	1275	2175

Add:

2.3L DOHC Quad4 (S)	25
Leather seats	25
Sunroof-manual	25

Deduct:

No air cond	150
Man trans (not 442)	125

CUTLASS CIERA FWD/3.3L-V6 (160hp)

Model	WS	Ret
Base 4dr Sdn	1275	2175
International 4dr Sdn	1550	2475
International 2dr Cpe	1525	2450
S 4dr Sdn	1350	2275
S 2dr Cpe	1325	2250
S Cruiser 4dr Wgn	1450	2375
SL 4dr Sdn	1450	2375
SL Cruiser 4dr Wgn	1550	2475

Add:
- Leather seats ... 25
- Pwr windows ... 25
- Spcl wheels (std Int'l) ... 25
- Sunroof-pwr ... 75

Deduct:
- 4cyl ... 100
- No air cond ... 150

CUTLASS SUPREME FWD/3.1L-V6 (135hp)

Model	WS	Ret
Base 4dr Sdn	1475	2400
Base 2dr Cpe	1450	2375
International 4dr Sdn	1725	2800
International 2dr Cpe	1725	2800
SL 4dr Sdn	1600	2650
SL 2dr Cpe	1575	2625

Add:
- ABS brakes ... 25
- Leather seats ... 25
- Pwr windows ... 25
- Special wheels (Base) ... 25
- Sunroof-pwr ... 75
- Pwr dr locks (std Int'l) ... 25

TORONADO FWD/3.8L-V6 (165hp)

Model	WS	Ret
Base 2dr Cpe	2100	3225
Trofeo 2dr Cpe	2250	3375

Add:
- ABS brakes (std Trofeo) ... 25
- CD player ... 25
- Delco/Bose audio ... 50
- Lthr seats (std Touring) ... 25
- Sunroof-pwr ... 100

1989 WS Ret

88 ROYALE FWD/3.8L-V6 (165hp)

Model	WS	Ret
Base 4dr Sdn	1200	2100
Base 2dr Cpe	1200	2100
Brougham 4dr Sdn	1325	2250
Brougham 2dr Cpe	1275	2175

Add:
- CD player ... 25
- Leather seats ... 25

98 ROYALE FWD/3.8L-V6 (165hp)

Model	WS	Ret
Base 4dr Sdn	1425	2350
Brougham 4dr Sdn	1550	2475
Touring 4dr Sdn	1750	2825

Add:
- CD player ... 25
- Delco/Bose audio ... 25
- Lthr seats (std Touring) ... 25
- Sunroof-pwr ... 75

CUSTOM CRUISER RWD/5.0L-V8 (140hp)

Model	WS	Ret
Wagon 4dr Wgn	1375	2300

Add:

CUTLASS CALAIS FWD/2.5L-I4 (112hp)

Model	WS	Ret
Base 4dr Sdn	900	1600
Base 2dr Cpe	900	1600
International 4dr Sdn	1125	2025
International 2dr Cpe	1125	2025
S 4dr Sdn	950	1650
S 2dr Cpe	950	1650
SL 4dr Sdn	1000	1700
SL 2dr Cpe	1000	1700

Add:
- 2.3L HO 4cyl (std Int'l) ... 25
- 3.3 Liter V6 ... 50
- CD player ... 25
- Leather seats ... 25
- Quad4 appearance pkg (S) ... 50

Deduct:
- No air cond ... 100
- Manual trans ... 100

CUTLASS CIERA FWD/2.5L-V6 (98hp)

Model	WS	Ret
Base 4dr Sdn	1075	1975
Base 2dr Cpe	1075	1975
Cruiser 4dr Wgn	1200	2100
International 4dr Sdn	1275	2175
International 2dr Cpe	1250	2150
SL 4dr Sdn	1175	2075
SL Cruiser 4dr Wgn	1225	2125
SL 2dr Cpe	1125	2025

Add:
- Leather seats ... 25
- Sunroof-pwr ... 50

Deduct:
- 4cyl ... 50
- No air cond ... 125

CUTLASS SUPREME FWD/2.8L-V6 (130hp)

Model	WS	Ret
Base 2dr Cpe	1175	2075
International 2dr Cpe	1400	2325
SL 2dr Cpe	1250	2150

Add:
- CD player ... 25
- Leather seats ... 25
- Sunroof-pwr ... 50

Deduct:
- No air cond ... 125

TORONADO FWD/3.8L-V6 (165hp)

Model	WS	Ret
Base 2dr Cpe	1600	2650
Trofeo 2dr Cpe	1725	2800

Add:
- CD player ... 25
- Delco/Bose audio ... 25
- Lthr seats (std Trofeo) ... 25
- Sunroof-pwr ... 75

1988 WS Ret

88 ROYALE FWD/3.8L-V6 (150hp)

Model	WS	Ret
Base 4dr Sdn	875	1550
Base 2dr Cpe	850	1525
Brougham 4dr Sdn	925	1625
Brougham 2dr Cpe	900	1600

Add:
- Leather seats ... 25

98 REGENCY FWD/3.8L-V6 (165hp)

Model	WS	Ret
Base 4dr Sdn	975	1675
Brougham 4dr Sdn	1000	1700
Touring 4dr Sdn	1125	2025

Add:
- Delco/Bose audio ... 25
- Leather seats ... 25
- Sunroof-pwr ... 50

CUSTOM CRUISER RWD/5.0L-V8 (140hp)

Model	WS	Ret
Wagon 4dr Wgn	975	1675

Add:

CUTLASS CALAIS FWD/2.5L-I4 (98hp)

Model	WS	Ret
Base 4dr Sdn	675	1200
Base 2dr Cpe	675	1200
International 4dr Sdn	800	1475
International 2dr Cpe	800	1475
SL 4dr Sdn	725	1250
SL 2dr Cpe	725	1250

Add:
- 3.0 Liter 6cyl ... 50
- 2.3L HO 4cyl (std Int'l) ... 25

Deduct:
- No air cond ... 75
- Manual trans ... 75

CUTLASS CIERA FWD/2.8L-V6 (125hp)

Model	WS	Ret
Base 4dr Sdn	700	1225
Base 2dr Cpe	675	1200
Brougham 4dr Sdn	750	1275
Brougham Cruiser 4dr Wgn	800	1475
Cruiser 4dr Wgn	750	1275
International 4dr Sdn	800	1475
International 2dr Cpe	800	1475
SL 2dr Cpe	700	1225

Add:
- Leather seats ... 25

Deduct:
- 4cyl ... 50
- No air cond ... 100

CUTLASS SUPREME FWD/2.8L-V6 (125hp)

Model	WS	Ret
Base 2dr Cpe	925	1625
Classic (V8-RWD) 2dr Cpe	1075	2000
Classic Brgm (V8-RW 2dr Cpe	1150	2100
International 2dr Cpe	1025	1925
SL 2dr Cpe	950	1650

Add:
- Sunroof-pwr ... 50
- T-tops (Classic) ... 75

Deduct:
- 6cyl ... 50
- No air cond ... 100

FIRENZA FWD/2.0L-I4 (90hp)

Model	WS	Ret
Base 4dr Sdn	500	975
Base 2dr Cpe	500	975
Cruiser 4dr Wgn	525	1000

Add:

Deduct:
- No air cond ... 75
- Manual trans ... 75

TORONADO FWD/3.8L-V6 (165hp)

Model	WS	Ret
Base 2dr Cpe	1250	2150
Trofeo 2dr Cpe	1325	2250

Add:
- Delco/Bose audio ... 25
- Leather seats ... 25
- Sunroof-pwr ... 50

PLYMOUTH

2000 WS Ret

BREEZE FWD/2.0L-I4 (132hp)

Model	WS	Ret
Base 4dr Sdn	8025	9900

Add:
- ABS Brakes ... 275
- Cassette ... 150
- CD player ... 175
- CD changer ... 275
- Pwr seat ... 125
- Pwr dr locks ... 150
- Pwr windows ... 175

Deduct:
- Manual Trans ... 575

NEON FWD/2.0L-I4 (132hp)

Model	WS	Ret
(See Dodge Neon)	1	1

PROWLER RWD/

Model	WS	Ret
2dr Cnv	37000	41225

1999 WS Ret

BREEZE FWD/2.0L-I4 (132hp)

Model	WS	Ret
Base 4dr Sdn	6800	8600

Add:
- ABS Brakes . . . 225
- Cassette . . . 125
- CD player . . . 125
- CD changer . . . 225
- Pwr dr locks . . . 100
- Pwr windows . . . 125

Deduct:
- Manual Trans . . . 475

NEON FWD/2.0L-I4 (132hp)

(See Dodge Neon) . . . 1 1

PROWLER RWD/

2dr Cnv. . . . 34675 38700

1998 WS Ret

BREEZE FWD/2.0L-I4 (132hp)

Base 4dr Sdn . . . 5225 6950

Add:
- ABS Brakes . . . 175
- Cassette . . . 75
- CD player . . . 100
- CD changer . . . 200
- Pwr dr locks . . . 75
- Pwr windows . . . 100

Deduct:
- Manual Trans . . . 400

NEON FWD/2.0L-I4 (132hp)

(See Dodge Neon) . . . 1 1

1997 WS Ret

BREEZE FWD/2.0L-I4 (132hp)

Base 4dr Sdn . . . 4150 5775

Add:
- ABS Brakes . . . 150
- Cassette . . . 50
- CD player . . . 75
- CD changer . . . 150
- Pwr dr locks . . . 50
- Pwr windows . . . 75

Deduct:
- Manual Trans . . . 325

NEON FWD/2.0L-I4 (132hp)

(See Dodge Neon) . . .

PROWLER RWD/

2dr Cnv. . . .

1996 WS Ret

BREEZE FWD/2.0L-I4 (132hp)

Base 4dr Sdn . . . 3175 4625

Add:
- ABS Brakes . . . 150
- Cassette . . . 25
- CD player . . . 50
- Integrated child seat . . . 25
- Pwr dr locks . . . 50
- Pwr windows . . . 50
- Sunroof-pwr . . . 175
- Wheels-alloy . . . 50

Deduct:
- Manual Trans . . . 275

NEON FWD/2.0L-I4 (132hp)

(See Dodge Neon) . . . 1 1

1995 WS Ret

ACCLAIM FWD/2.5L-I4 (100hp)

Base 4dr Sdn . . . 2150 3275

Add:
- 3.0 Liter V6 . . . 175
- Pwr dr locks . . . 25
- Pwr seat . . . 25
- Pwr windows . . . 50
- Wheels-alloy . . . 25

NEON FWD/2.0L-I4 (132hp)

(See Dodge Neon) . . . 1 1

1994 WS Ret

ACCLAIM FWD/2.5L-I4 (100hp)

Base 4dr Sdn. . . . 1550 2475

Add:
- 3.0 Liter V6 . . . 175
- ABS brakes . . . 125
- Cassette . . . 25
- Cruise ctrl . . . 25
- Pwr dr locks . . . 25
- Pwr seat . . . 25
- Pwr windows . . . 25
- Tilt wheel . . . 25
- Wheels-alloy . . . 25

Deduct:
- No air cond . . . 250
- Manual trans . . . 225

COLT FWD/1.5L-I4 (92hp)

(See Dodge, GL=ES) . . . 1 1

LASER FWD/1.8L-I4 (92hp)

Base 2dr Hbk. . . . 2150 3275
RS Turbo 2dr Hbk . . . 3375 4850
RS AWD Turbo 2dr Hbk . . . 4050 5675
RS 2dr Hbk . . . 2550 3925

Add:
- ABS brakes . . . 125
- Alloy wheels (std 4WD) . . . 25
- Casette (std RS) . . . 25
- CD player . . . 50
- Cruise ctrl . . . 25
- Pwr dr locks . . . 25
- Pwr windows . . . 25
- Sunroof-manual . . . 50

Deduct:
- No air cond . . . 225
- Manual steering . . . 25
- Manual trans . . . 200

SUNDANCE FWD/2.2L-I4 (93hp)

Base 4dr Hbk. . . . 1325 2250
Base 2dr Hbk. . . . 1250 2150
Duster (6cyl) 4dr Hbk . . . 1875 2975
Duster (6cyl) 2dr Hbk . . . 1825 2900

Add:
- ABS brakes . . . 100
- Alloy wheels . . . 25
- Cassette . . . 25
- CD player . . . 25
- Cruise ctrl . . . 25
- Pwr dr locks . . . 25
- Pwr windows . . . 25
- Sunroof-manual . . . 25

Deduct:
- 4cyl (Duster only) . . . 150
- No air cond . . . 225
- Manual trans . . . 200

VISTA FWD/1.8L-I4 (113hp)

Base 4 dr Wgn. . . . 2350 3700
SE 4 dr Wgn . . . 2675 4075

Add:
- ABS brakes . . . 125
- All-wheel drive . . . 325
- Cassette . . . 25
- Cruise control . . . 25
- Luggage rack . . . 25

Deduct:
- No air conditiong . . . 225
- Manual trans . . . 175
- Manual steering . . . 25

1993 WS Ret

ACCLAIM FWD/2.5L-I4 (100hp)

Base 4dr Sdn . . . 1250 2150

Add:
- 3.0 Liter V6 . . . 150
- ABS brakes . . . 100
- Cassette . . . 25
- Cruise ctrl . . . 25
- Pwr dr locks . . . 25
- Pwr seat . . . 25
- Pwr windows . . . 25
- Tilt wheel . . . 25

Deduct:
- No air cond . . . 225
- Manual trans . . . 200

COLT FWD/1.8L-I4 (113hp)

(See Dodge Colt) . . . 1 1

LASER FWD/2.0L-I4 (135hp)

Base 2dr Hbk . . . 1800 2875
RS Turbo 2dr Hbk. . . . 2850 4250
RS AWD Turbo 2dr Hbk . . . 3550 5025
RS 2dr Hbk. . . . 2150 3275

Add:
- ABS brakes . . . 100
- Alloy wheels (std 4WD) . . . 25
- Casette (std RS) . . . 25
- CD player . . . 50
- Cruise ctrl . . . 25
- Pwr dr locks . . . 25
- Pwr windows . . . 25
- Sunroof-manual . . . 50

Deduct:
- No air cond . . . 200
- Manual steering . . . 25
- Manual trans . . . 175

SUNDANCE FWD/2.5L-I4 (100hp)

Duster (6cyl) 4dr Hbk . . . 1550 2475
Duster (6cyl) 2dr Hbk . . . 1550 2475
Highline 4dr Hbk. . . . 1150 2050
Highline 2dr Hbk. . . . 1075 1975

Add:
- Alloy wheels . . . 25
- Cassette . . . 25
- CD player . . . 25
- Cruise ctrl . . . 25
- Pwr dr locks . . . 25
- Pwr windows . . . 25
- Sunroof-manual . . . 25

Deduct:
- 4cyl (Duster only) . . . 125
- No air cond . . . 175
- Manual trans . . . 175

VISTA FWD/2.4L-I4 (145hp)

Base 4 dr Wgn . . . 1975 3075
SE 4 dr Wgn . . . 2250 3375

Add:
- ABS brakes . . . 75
- All-wheel drive . . . 300
- Cassette . . . 25
- Cruise control . . . 25
- Luggage rack . . . 25

Deduct:
- No air conditiong . . . 225
- Manual trans . . . 175
- Manual steering . . . 25

1992 WS Ret

ACCLAIM FWD/2.5L-I4 (100hp)

Base 4dr Sdn . . . 1125 2025

Add:
- 3.0 Liter V6 . . . 125
- ABS brakes . . . 75
- Cassette . . . 25

Cruise ctrl	25
Pwr dr locks	25
Pwr seat	25
Pwr windows	25
Deduct:	
No air cond	200
Manual trans	200

COLT — FWD/1.8L-I4 (113hp)

(See Dodge Colt)	1	1

LASER — FWD/1.8L-I4 (92hp)

Base 2dr Hbk	1550	2475
RS 2dr Hbk	1800	2875
RS Turbo 2dr Hbk	2250	3375
RS 4WD Turbo 2dr Hbk	2525	3900
Add:		
ABS brakes	75	
Casette (std RS)	25	
CD player	25	
Cruise ctrl	25	
Pwr dr locks	25	
Pwr windows	25	
Special wheels	25	
Sunroof-manual	25	
Deduct:		
No air cond	175	
Manual trans	150	

SUNDANCE — FWD/2.2L-I4 (93hp)

America 4dr Hbk	750	1275
America 2dr Hbk	700	1225
Duster (6cyl) 4dr Hbk	1225	2125
Duster (6cyl) 2dr Hbk	1175	2075
Highline 4dr Hbk	975	1675
Highline 2dr Hbk	925	1625
Add:		
CD player	25	
Cruise ctrl	25	
Pwr dr locks	25	
Pwr windows	25	
Special wheels	25	
Sunroof-manual	25	
Deduct:		
No air cond	175	
Manual trans	150	

VISTA — FWD/1.8L-I4 (113hp)

Base 4 dr Wgn	1600	2650
SE 4 dr Wgn	1850	2925
Add:		
ABS brakes	75	
All-wheel drive	300	
Cassette	25	
Cruise control	25	
Deduct:		
No air conditiong	200	
Manual trans	150	
Manual steering	25	

1991 — WS / Ret

ACCLAIM — FWD/2.5L-I4 (100hp)

	WS	Ret
Base 4dr Sdn	925	1625
LE 4dr Sdn	1050	1950
LX (6cyl) 4dr Sdn	1175	2075
Add:		
3.0 Liter V6 (std LX)	100	
ABS brakes	50	
Cassette (std LX)	25	
Cruise ctrl (std LE, LX)	25	
Pwr dr locks	25	
Pwr windows	25	
Special wheels (std LX)	25	
Sunroof-manual	25	
Deduct:		
No air cond	175	
Manual trans	175	

COLT — FWD/1.5L-I4 (92hp)

(See Dodge Colt)	1	1

LASER — FWD/1.8L-I4 (92hp)

Base 2dr Hbk	1325	2250
RS 2dr Hbk	1550	2475
RS Turbo 2dr Hbk	1900	3000
Add:		
ABS brakes	50	
Cassette (std RS)	25	
CD player	25	
Pwr windows	25	
Special wheels	25	
Sunroof-manual	25	
Deduct:		
No air cond	175	
Manual trans	150	

SUNDANCE — FWD/2.2L-I4 (93hp)

America 4dr Hbk	600	1100
America 2dr Hbk	550	1050
Highline 4dr Hbk	800	1475
Highline 2dr Hbk	775	1300
RS 4dr Hbk	975	1675
RS 2dr Hbk	925	1625
Add:		
2.5 Liter 4cyl Turbo	50	
Pwr windows	25	
Special wheels	25	
Sunroof-manual	25	
Deduct:		
No air cond	150	
Manual trans	125	

VISTA — FWD/2.0L-I4 (96hp)

Base 4 dr Wgn	1175	2075
Add:		
All-wheel drive	175	
Pwr windows	25	
Deduct:		
No air cond	150	
Man trans (not AWD)	125	

1990 — WS / Ret

ACCLAIM — FWD/2.5L-I4 (100hp)

	WS	Ret
Base 4dr Sdn	775	1300
LE 4dr Sdn	850	1525
LX 4dr Sdn	950	1650
Add:		
2.5 Liter 4cyl Turbo	50	
3.0 Liter V6 (std LX)	75	
Infinity audio	25	
Pwr windows	25	
Special wheels (std LX)	25	
Sunroof-pwr	75	
Deduct:		
No air cond	150	
Manual trans	150	

COLT — FWD/1.5L-I4 (75hp)

(See Dodge Colt)	1	1

HORIZON — FWD/2.2L-I4 (93hp)

Base 4dr Hbk	500	975
Add:		
Deduct:		
No air cond	125	
Manual trans	125	

LASER — FWD/1.8L-I4 (92hp)

Base 2dr Hbk	1175	2075
RS 2dr Hbk	1325	2250
RS Turbo 2dr Hbk	1475	2400
Add:		
2.0L DOHC 4cyl (RS)	50	
Special wheels	25	
Sunroof-manual	25	
Deduct:		
No air cond	150	
Manual trans	125	

SUNDANCE — FWD/2.2L-I4 (93hp)

Base 4dr Hbk	500	975
Base 2dr Hbk	475	950
Add:		
2.5 Liter 4cyl Turbo	50	
RS trim	75	
Sunroof-pwr	50	
Deduct:		
No air cond	125	
Manual trans	125	

VISTA — FWD/2.0L-I4 (96hp)

Base 4 dr Wgn	975	1675
Add:		
4-wheel drive	150	
Deduct:		
No air cond	125	
Man trans (not 4WD)	125	

1989 — WS / Ret

ACCLAIM — FWD/2.5L-I4 (100hp)

	WS	Ret
Base 4dr Sdn	700	1225
LE 4dr Sdn	725	1250
LX 4dr Sdn	800	1475
Add:		
2.5 Liter 4cyl Turbo	50	
Sunroof-manual	25	
Deduct:		
No air cond	125	
Manual trans	125	

COLT — FWD/1.5L-I4 (81hp)

(See Dodge Colt)	1	1

GRAN FURY — RWD/5.2L-V8 (140hp)

Salon 4dr Sdn	500	975
Deduct:		
No air cond	125	

HORIZON — FWD/2.2L-I4 (93hp)

America 4dr Hbk	400	850
Add:		
Deduct:		
No air cond	75	
Manual trans	75	

RELIANT — FWD/2.2L-I4 (93hp)

America 4dr Sdn	600	1100
America 2dr Cpe	575	1075
Add:		
Deduct:		
No air cond	100	
Manual trans	100	

SUNDANCE — FWD/2.2L-I4 (93hp)

Hatchback 4dr Hbk	425	900
Hatchback 2dr Hbk	400	850
Add:		
2.5 Liter 4cyl Turbo	50	
RS pkg	50	
Deduct:		
No air cond	75	
Manual trans	75	

VISTA — FWD/2.0L-I4 (96hp)

Base 4 dr Wgn	825	1500
Add:		
4-wheel drive	100	
Deduct:		
No air cond	75	
Man trans (not 4WD)	75	

1988 — WS / Ret

CARAVELLE — FWD/2.2L-I4 (97hp)

Model	WS	Ret
Base 4dr Sdn	425	900
SE 4dr Sdn	450	925

Add:
2.2 Liter 4cyl Turbo 25

Deduct:
No air cond 100

COLT — FWD/1.5L-I4 (68hp)

Model	WS	Ret
(See Dodge Colt)	1	1

GRAN FURY — RWD/5.2L-V8 (140hp)

Model	WS	Ret
Base 4dr Sdn	425	900
Salon 4dr Sdn	400	850

Deduct:
No air cond 100

HORIZON — FWD/2.2L-I4 (97hp)

Model	WS	Ret
America 4dr Hbk	350	800

Add:

Deduct:
No air cond 50
Manual trans 50

RELIANT — FWD/2.2L-I4 (97hp)

Model	WS	Ret
America 4dr Sdn	475	950
America 4dr Wgn	500	975
America 2dr Cpe	475	950

Add:

Deduct:
No air cond 75
Manual trans 75

SUNDANCE — FWD/2.2L-I4 (97hp)

Model	WS	Ret
Hatchback 4dr Hbk	350	800
Hatchback 2dr Hbk	350	800

Add:
2.2 Liter 4cyl Turbo 25
RS trim 50

Deduct:
No air cond 50
Manual trans 50

VISTA — FWD/2.0L-I4 (96hp)

Model	WS	Ret
Base 4 dr Wgn	725	1250

Add:
4-wheel drive 50

Deduct:
No air cond 50
Man trans (not 4WD) 50

PONTIAC

2001 — WS / Ret

BONNEVILLE — FWD/3.8L-V6 (205hp)

Model	WS	Ret
SE 4dr Sdn	13600	15800
SLE 4dr Sdn	16600	19000
SSEi (SC V6) 4dr Sdn	17525	19975

Add:
CD player (std SSEi) 225
12-disc CD chngr 400
Leather seats (std SSEi) 400
Power seat (SSEi) 200
Moonroof-pwr 500
Wheels-chrome 300

FIREBIRD — RWD/3.8L-V6 (200hp)

Model	WS	Ret
Base 2dr Cnv		
Base 2dr Cpe		
Formula (8cyl) 2dr Cpe		

GRAND AM — FWD/2.4L-I4 (150hp)

Model	WS	Ret
GT (V6/170hp) 4dr Sdn	10925	12975
GT (V6/170hp) 2dr Cpe	10975	13025
SE 4dr Sdn	9500	11475

Add:
3.4L-V6 (170hp)(SE) 500
Leather seats 325
CD player 200
Cruise ctrl 200
Pwr seat 200
Pwr windows (std GT) 175
Moonroof-pwr 475
Wheels-alum (std GT) 200

Deduct:
Manual trans 675

GRAND PRIX — FWD/3.8L-V6 (200hp)

Model	WS	Ret
GT 4dr Sdn	13000	15175
GT 2dr Cpe	12900	15075
GTP (SC 240hp V6) 4dr Sdn	14975	17275
GTP (SC 240hp V6) 2dr Cpe	14875	17150
SE 4dr Sdn	10975	13025

Add:
CD player (std GTP) 225
Bose Audio 225
Cruise ctrl (SE) 175
Leather seats 400
Power seat (std GTP) 200
Moonroof-pwr 500
Wheels-alum (SE) 200

Deduct:
3.1L V6 (160hp) 425

SUNFIRE — FWD/2.2L-I4 (115hp)

Model	WS	Ret
GT 2dr Cpe	10000	12000
SE 4dr Sdn	8425	10325
SE 2dr Cpe	8325	10225

Add:
2.4L-I4 (150hp) (SE) 150
CD player (SE) 200
Cruise ctrl 200
Pwr dr locks 200
Pwr windows 175
Moonroof-pwr 425
Tilt wheel (SE) 100
Wheels-alum (SE) 175

Deduct:
Manual trans 650

TRANS AM — RWD/5.7L-V8 (310hp)

Model	WS	Ret
2dr Cnv		
2dr Cpe		

Pwr seat (std Cnv) 150
Pwr windows (base Cpe) 150
T-tops 600
Traction ctrl 200
WS6 Ram Air pkg 1625
Wheels-chrome 225

Deduct:
Manual trans 500

2000 — WS / Ret

BONNEVILLE — FWD/3.8L-V6 (205hp)

Model	WS	Ret
SE 4dr Sdn	12875	15050
SLE 4dr Sdn	15950	18300
SSEi (SC V6) 4dr Sdn	16750	19150

Add:
Alloy wheels (SE) 175
CD player (std SSEi) 175
12-disc CD chngr 300
Leather seats (std SSEi) 300
Power seat (SE) 150
Moonroof-pwr 400
Wheels-chrome 250

FIREBIRD — RWD/3.8L-V6 (200hp)

Model	WS	Ret
Base 2dr Cnv	14700	16975
Base 2dr Cpe	12850	15025
Formula (8cyl) 2dr Cpe	14875	17150

Add:
CD changer 275
Monsoon audio (base Cpe) 200
Lthr seats 250
Pwr dr locks (base Cpe) 150

GRAND AM — FWD/2.4L-I4 (150hp)

Model	WS	Ret
GT (V6/175hp) 4dr Sdn	10200	12200
GT (V6/175hp) 2dr Cpe	10250	12250
SE 4dr Sdn	8800	10725
SE 2dr Cpe	8800	10725

Add:
3.4L-V6 (170hp)(SE) 375
Leather seats 250
CD player 175
Cruise ctrl 150
Pwr seat 150
Pwr windows (std GT) 150
Tilt wheel (std GT) 75
Moonroof-pwr 350
Wheels-alum (std GT) 175

Deduct:
Manual trans 525

GRAND PRIX — FWD/3.8L-V6 (200hp)

Model	WS	Ret
GT 4dr Sdn	12275	14400
GT 2dr Cpe	12175	14300
GTP (SC 240hp V6) 4dr Sdn	14225	16475
GTP (SC 240hp V6) 2dr Cpe	14125	16375
SE 4dr Sdn	10300	12325

Add:
CD player (std GTP) 175
CD changer w/Bose 275
Cruise ctrl (SE) 150
Leather seats 300
Power seat (std GTP) 150
Moonroof-pwr 400
Wheels-alum (SE) 175

Deduct:
3.1L V6 (160hp) 325

SUNFIRE — FWD/2.2L-I4 (115hp)

Model	WS	Ret
GT 2dr Cnv		
GT 2dr Cpe	9150	11100
SE 4dr Sdn	7650	9500
SE 2dr Cpe	7575	9425

Add:
2.4L-I4 (150hp) (SE) 75
Cassette 75
CD player (SE) 175
Cruise ctrl (std cnv) 150
Pwr dr locks (std cnv) 150
Pwr windows (std cnv) 150
Moonroof-pwr 325
Tilt wheel (SE) 75
Wheels-alum (SE) 150

Deduct:
Manual trans 500

TRANS AM — RWD/5.7L-V8 (305hp)

Model	WS	Ret
2dr Cnv		
2dr Cpe		

Add:
CD changer 250
T-tops 600
Traction ctrl 200
WS6 Ram Air pkg 1525
Wheels-chrome 225

Deduct:
Manual trans 500

1999 — WS / Ret

BONNEVILLE — FWD/3.8L-V6 (205hp)

Model	WS	Ret
SE 4dr Sdn	9775	11750
SSE 4dr Sdn	12450	14600

SSEi (SC V6) 4dr Sdn	13300	15500

Add:
- Cassette (SE) . . . 100
- SLE trim (SE) . . . 350
- CD player . . . 150
- Leather seats (SE) . . . 250
- Premium sound (SE) . . . 50
- Power seat (SE) . . . 125
- Moonroof-pwr . . . 325
- Wheels-alum (SE) . . . 150
- Wheels-chrome . . . 200

FIREBIRD RWD/3.8L-V6 (200hp)

Base 2dr Cnv	13675	15900
Base 2dr Cpe	12000	14125
Formula (8cyl) 2dr Cpe	13875	16100

Add:
- CD changer . . . 225
- Monsoon audio (base Cpe) . . . 150
- Lthr seats . . . 225
- Pwr dr locks (base Cpe) . . . 125
- Pwr seat (std Cnv) . . . 125
- Pwr windows (base Cpe) . . . 125
- T-tops . . . 500
- Traction ctrl . . . 150
- WS6 Ram Air pkg . . . 1325
- Wheels-chrome . . . 175

Deduct:
- Manual trans . . . 425

GRAND AM FWD/2.4L-I4 (150hp)

GT (V6/175hp) 4dr Sdn	9000	10925
GT (V6/175hp) 2dr Cpe	9050	11000
SE 4dr Sdn	7750	9625
SE 2dr Cpe	7750	9625

Add:
- 3.4L-V6 (170hp) (SE) . . . 325
- Leather seats . . . 225
- CD player . . . 125
- Cruise ctrl . . . 125
- Pwr seat . . . 125
- Pwr windows (std GT) . . . 100
- Tilt wheel (std GT) . . . 50
- Moonroof-pwr . . . 300
- Wheels-alum (std GT) . . . 125

Deduct:
- Manual trans . . . 425
- No Cassette . . . 125

GRAND PRIX FWD/3.8L-V6 (200hp)

GT 4dr Sdn	9800	11775
GT 2dr Cpe	9700	11675
GTP (SC 240hp V6) 4dr Sdn	11525	13600
GTP (SC 240hp V6) 2dr Cpe	11425	13500
SE 4dr Sdn	7950	9825

Add:
- Cassette (std GT sdn) . . . 125
- CD player (std GTP) . . . 150
- CD changer w/Bose . . . 225
- Cruise ctrl (SE) . . . 100
- Leather seats . . . 250
- Power seat (std GTP) . . . 125
- Moonroof-pwr . . . 325
- Wheels-alum (SE) . . . 125

Deduct:
- 3.1L V6 (160hp) . . . 275

SUNFIRE FWD/2.2L-I4 (115hp)

GT 2dr Cnv	9575	11550
GT 2dr Cpe	7900	9775
SE 4dr Sdn	6500	8300
SE 2dr Cpe	6400	8175

Add:
- 2.4L-I4 (150hp) (SE) . . . 50
- Cassette . . . 50
- CD player (SE) . . . 125
- Cruise ctrl (std cnv) . . . 125
- Pwr dr locks (std cnv) . . . 100
- Pwr windows (std cnv) . . . 100
- Moonroof-pwr . . . 275
- Tilt wheel (SE) . . . 50
- Wheels-alum (SE) . . . 100

Deduct:
- No air cond . . . 450
- Manual trans . . . 425

TRANS AM RWD/5.7L-V8 (305hp)

2dr Cnv	17800	20450
2dr Cpe	16000	18525

Add:
- CD changer . . . 225
- T-tops . . . 500
- Traction ctrl . . . 175
- WS6 Ram Air pkg . . . 1250
- 30th Anniv. pkg . . . 625
- Wheels-chrome . . . 175

Deduct:
- Manual trans . . . 425

1998 — WS — Ret

BONNEVILLE FWD/3.8L-V6 (205hp)

	WS	Ret
SE 4dr Sdn	8200	10100
SSE 4dr Sdn	10525	12550
SSEi (SC V6) 4dr Sdn	11200	13275

Add:
- Alloy wheels (SE) . . . 100
- SLE trim (SE) . . . 300
- Cassette (SE) . . . 75
- CD player . . . 125
- Leather seats . . . 200
- Premium sound (SE) . . . 25
- Power seat (SE) . . . 75
- Moonroof-pwr . . . 275
- Wheels-alum (SE) . . . 125
- Wheels-chrome . . . 150

FIREBIRD RWD/3.8L-V6 (200hp)

Base 2dr Cnv	12075	14200
Base 2dr Cpe	10275	12300
Formula (8cyl) 2dr Cpe	12025	14150

Add:
- CD changer . . . 200
- Leather seats . . . 175
- Premium sound . . . 25
- Pwr dr locks (std Cnv) . . . 75
- Pwr windows (std Cnv) . . . 75
- T-tops . . . 425
- Traction ctrl . . . 125
- WS6 Ram Air pkg . . . 1100
- Wheels-chrome . . . 150

Deduct:
- Manual trans . . . 350

GRAND AM FWD/2.4L-I4 (150hp)

GT 4dr Sdn	7125	8950
GT 2dr Cpe	7175	9000
SE 4dr Sdn	6025	7775
SE 2dr Cpe	6025	7775

Add:
- 3.1L-155hp V6 . . . 275
- Leather seats . . . 175
- Cassette . . . 50
- CD player . . . 100
- Cruise ctrl . . . 75
- Pwr seat . . . 75
- Pwr windows . . . 75
- Tilt wheel (std GT) . . . 25
- Moonroof-pwr . . . 250
- Wheels-alum (std GT) . . . 100

Deduct:
- Manual trans . . . 350

GRAND PRIX FWD/3.8L-V6 (200hp)

GT 4dr Sdn	9675	11650
GT 2dr Cpe	9600	11575
SE 4dr Sdn	8075	9950

Add:
- Cassette (std GT sdn) . . . 75
- CD player . . . 125
- CD changer . . . 200
- Cruise ctrl (std GT) . . . 75
- Leather seats . . . 200
- GTP pkg (incls SC eng) . . . 675
- Power seat . . . 75
- Moonroof-pwr . . . 275
- Wheels-alloy (std GT) . . . 100

Deduct:
- 3.1L V6 (160hp) . . . 225

SUNFIRE FWD/2.4L-I4 (150hp)

GT 2dr Cpe	6700	8500
SE 4dr Sdn	5475	7200
SE 2dr Cnv	7350	9200
SE 2dr Cpe	5425	7150

Add:
- Cassette . . . 50
- CD player (std cnv,GT) . . . 100
- Cruise ctrl (std SE cnv) . . . 75
- Pwr dr locks . . . 75
- Pwr windows . . . 75
- Moonroof-pwr . . . 225
- Tilt wheel (std Cnv,GT) . . . 25
- Wheels-alum (std GT) . . . 75

Deduct:
- No air cond . . . 375
- Manual trans . . . 350

TRANS AM RWD/5.7L-V8 (305hp)

2dr Cnv	15875	18400
2dr Cpe	14050	16450

Add:
- CD player (std conv) . . . 125
- T-tops . . . 425
- Traction ctrl . . . 150
- WS6 Ram Air pkg . . . 1050

Deduct:
- Manual trans . . . 350

1997 — WS — Ret

BONNEVILLE FWD/3.8L-V6 (205hp)

	WS	Ret
SE 4dr Sdn	6650	8450
SSE 4dr Sdn	8750	10675
SSEi 4dr Sdn	9400	11350

Add:
- 3.8L-V6/SC (240hp) (std SSEi) . 300
- Alloy wheels (SE) . . . 75
- Cassette (SE) . . . 50
- CD player . . . 100
- SLE trim (SE) . . . 225
- Leather seats . . . 175
- Premium sound (SE) . . . 25
- Power seat (SE) . . . 50
- Moonroof-pwr . . . 225
- Wheels-alum (SE) . . . 75
- Wheels-chrome . . . 125

FIREBIRD RWD/3.8L-V6 (200hp)

Base 2dr Cnv	10075	12075
Base 2dr Cpe	8175	10075
Formula (8cyl) 2dr Cnv	11225	13300
Formula (8cyl) 2dr Cpe	9625	11600

Add:
- CD player . . . 100
- Cruise (std Cnv) . . . 50
- Leather seats . . . 150
- Premium sound . . . 25
- Pwr dr locks (std Cnv) . . . 50
- Pwr windows (std Cnv) . . . 50
- T-tops . . . 350
- Traction ctrl . . . 100
- WS6 Ram Air pkg . . . 900

Deduct:
- Manual trans . . . 300

GRAND AM FWD/2.4L-I4 (150hp)

GT 4dr Sdn	5875	7625
GT 2dr Cpe	5900	7650
SE 4dr Sdn	4875	6550

Model	WS	Ret
SE 2dr Cpe	4875	6550

Add:

Option	
3.1L 6cyl (FI-155hp)	225
Leather seats	150
Cassette	25
CD player	75
Cruise ctrl	50
Pwr seat	50
Pwr windows	50
Tilt wheel (std GT)	25
Moonroof-pwr	200
Wheels-alum (std GT)	75

Deduct:

Option	
Manual trans	300

GRAND PRIX FWD/3.8L-V6 (195hp)

Model	WS	Ret
GT 4dr Sdn	8425	10325
GT 2dr Cpe	8375	10275
SE 4dr Sdn	7000	8825

Add:

Option	
3.8L SC/V6 (FI-240hp)	325
Cassette (std GT sdn)	50
CD player	75
CD changer	150
Cruise ctrl (std SE sdn)	50
Leather seats	175
GTP pkg (incls SC eng)	425
Power seat	50
Moonroof-pwr	225
Wheels-alloy (std GT)	75

Deduct:

SUNFIRE FWD/2.2L-I4 (120hp)

Model	WS	Ret
GT 2dr Cpe	5650	7400
SE 4dr Sdn	4550	6200
SE 2dr Cnv	6150	7925
SE 2dr Cpe	4475	6125

Add:

Option	
Cassette	25
CD player	75
Cruise ctrl (std SE cnv)	50
Pwr dr locks	50
Pwr windows	50
Moonroof-pwr	175
Tilt wheel (std Cnv,GT)	25
Wheels-alum (std GT)	50

Deduct:

Option	
No air cond	325
Manual trans	275

TRANS AM RWD/5.7L-V8 (285hp)

Model	WS	Ret
2dr Cnv	13000	15175
2dr Cpe	10950	13000

Add:

Option	
CD player	100
Leather seats	150
T-tops	350
Traction ctrl	100
WS6 Ram Air pkg	850

Deduct:

Option	
Manual trans	300

1996 WS Ret

BONNEVILLE FWD/3.8L-V6 (205hp)

Model	WS	Ret
SE 4dr Sdn	5500	7225
SSE 4dr Sdn	7400	9250
SSEi 4dr Sdn	7925	9800

Add:

Option	
3.8L-V6/SC (240hp) (std SSEi)	250
Cassette (SE)	25
CD player	75
Leather seats	150
Premium sound	25
Power seat (SE)	25
Sport Luxury(SLE) pkg (SE)	525
Sunroof-pwr	175
Wheels-alum (SE)	50

FIREBIRD RWD/3.8L-V6 (200hp)

Model	WS	Ret
Base 2dr Cnv	7825	9700
Base 2dr Cpe	6250	8025
Formula (8cyl) 2dr Cnv	8975	10900
Formula (8cyl) 2dr Cpe	7725	9575

Add:

Option	
CD player	75
Cruise (std Cnv)	25
Leather seats	125
Premium sound	25
Pwr dr locks (std Cnv)	25
Pwr windows (std Cnv)	50
T-tops	275
Traction ctrl	75

Deduct:

Option	
No air cond	300
Manual trans	250

GRAND AM FWD/2.4L-I4 (150hp)

Model	WS	Ret
GT 4dr Sdn	4700	6350
GT 2dr Cpe	4725	6375
SE 4dr Sdn	3875	5475
SE 2dr Cpe	3875	5475

Add:

Option	
3.1 Liter V6	175
Leather seats	125
Cassette	25
CD player	50
Cruise ctrl	25
Pwr seat	25
Pwr windows	50
Tilt wheel (std GT)	25
Sunroof-pwr	175
Wheels-alum (std GT)	50

Deduct:

Option	
No air cond	275
Manual trans	250

GRAND PRIX FWD/3.1L-V6 (160hp)

Model	WS	Ret
SE 4dr Sdn	4675	6325
SE 2dr Cpe	4550	6200

Add:

Option	
3.4 Liter DOHC V6	225
ABS brakes	150
Cassette (std Cpe)	25
CD player	75
Cruise ctrl (std SE Cpe)	50
Leather seats	150
GTP pkg	275
GT pkg	400
Pwr seat	25
Wheels-alloy (std Cpe)	50

SUNFIRE FWD/2.2L-I4 (120hp)

Model	WS	Ret
GT 2dr Cpe	4500	6150
SE 4dr Sdn	3600	5075
SE 2dr Cnv	4875	6550
SE 2dr Cpe	3525	5000

Add:

Option	
Alloy wheels (std GT)	50
Cassette	25
CD player	50
Cruise ctrl	25
Pwr dr locks	25
Pwr windows	50
Sunroof-pwr	150
Tilt wheel (std Cnv,GT)	25
Wheels-alum (std GT)	25

Deduct:

Option	
No air cond	250
Manual trans	225

TRANS AM RWD/5.7L-V8 (285hp)

Model	WS	Ret
2dr Cnv	10275	12300
2dr Cpe	8525	10425

Add:

Option	
CD player	75
Leather seats	125
T-tops	275
Traction ctrl	75

Deduct:

Option	
No air cond	300
Manual trans	250

1995 WS Ret

BONNEVILLE FWD/3.8L-V6 (200hp)

Model	WS	Ret
SE 4dr Sdn	4300	5925
SSE 4dr Sdn	5775	7525
SSEi 4dr Sdn	6300	8075

Add:

Option	
3.8L-V6 (240hp) (std SSEi)	225
Cassette (SE)	25
CD player	50
Leather seats	125
Premium sound	25
Power seat (SE)	25
Sport Luxury pkg (SE)	450
Sunroof-pwr	175
Wheels-alum (SE)	50

FIREBIRD RWD/3.4L-V6 (160hp)

Model	WS	Ret
Base 2dr Cnv	6500	8300
Base 2dr Cpe	4900	6575
Formula (8cyl) 2dr Cnv	7875	9750
Formula (8cyl) 2dr Cpe	6275	8050

Add:

Option	
CD player	50
Cruise (Formula Cnv)	25
Leather seats	100
Premium sound	25
Pwr dr locks (Base Cpe)	25
Pwr win (std Formula Cnv)	25
T-tops	275
Traction ctrl	75

Deduct:

Option	
No air cond	275
Manual trans	225

GRAND AM FWD/2.3L-I4 (150hp)

Model	WS	Ret
GT 4dr Sdn	3675	5175
GT 2dr Cpe	3700	5200
SE 4dr Sdn	2950	4375
SE 2dr Cpe	2950	4375

Add:

Option	
3.1 Liter V6	175
Leather seats	100
Alloy wheels (std GT)	25
Cassette	25
CD player	50
Cruise ctrl	25
Pwr seat	25
Pwr windows	25
Tilt wheel (std GT)	25
Sunroof-pwr	150

Deduct:

Option	
No air cond	250
Manual trans	225

GRAND PRIX FWD/3.1L-V6 (160hp)

Model	WS	Ret
SE 4dr Sdn	3775	5375
SE 2dr Cpe	3675	5175

Add:

Option	
3.4 Liter DOHC V6	200
ABS brakes	125
Cassette (std Cpe)	25
CD player	50
Cruise ctrl (std SE Cpe)	25
Leather seats	125
GTP trim	275
GT pkg	375
Pwr seat	25
Wheels-alloy (std Cpe)	50

SUNFIRE FWD/2.2L-I4 (120hp)

Model	WS	Ret
GT 2dr Cpe	3600	5075
SE 4dr Sdn	3025	4450
SE 2dr Cnv	4500	6150
SE 2dr Cpe	2975	4400

Add:

Alloy wheels (std GT)	25
Cassette	25
CD player	50
Cruise ctrl	25
Pwr windows (std Cnv)	25
Sunroof-manual	50
Tilt wheel (std Cnv,GT)	25

Deduct:

No air cond	225
Manual trans	200

TRANS AM RWD/5.7L-V8 (275hp)

2dr Cnv	8325	10225
2dr Cpe	6775	8575

Add:

CD player	50
Leather seats	100
T-tops	275
Traction ctrl	75

Deduct:

No air cond	275
Manual trans	225

1994 WS Ret

BONNEVILLE FWD/3.8L-V6 (170hp)

SE 4dr Sdn	3850	5450
SSE 4dr Sdn	5150	6850
SSEi 4dr Sdn	5575	7300

Add:

Alloy wheels (SE)	25
Cassette (SE only)	25
CD player	50
Cruise ctrl (SE only)	25
Leather seats	125
Power seat (SE only)	25
Sport Luxury pkg	400
Sunroof-pwr	150

FIREBIRD RWD/3.4L-V6 (160hp)

Base 2dr Cnv	5800	7575
Base 2dr Cpe	4350	5975
Formula (8cyl) 2dr Cnv	7225	8975
Formula (8cyl) 2dr Cpe	5575	7300

Add:

CD player	50
Cruise ctrl	25
Leather seats	75
Pwr dr locks	25
Pwr windows	25
Lift-off roof	250

Deduct:

No air cond	250
Manual trans	200

GRAND AM FWD/2.3L-I4 (115hp)

GT 4dr Sdn	3175	4625
GT 2dr Cpe	3200	4650
SE 4dr Sdn	2575	3950
SE 2dr Cpe	2575	3950

Add:

2.3L 4cyl DOHC (SE only)	100
3.1 Liter V6 (SE)	150
3.1 Liter V6 (GT)	50
Alloy wheels (std GT)	25
Cassette	25
CD player	25
Cruise ctrl	25
Pwr seat	25
Pwr windows	25

Deduct:

No air cond	225
Manual trans	200

GRAND PRIX FWD/3.1L-V6 (160hp)

SE 4dr Sdn	3150	4600
SE 2dr Cpe	3075	4525

Add:

3.4 Liter DOHC V6	175
ABS brakes	125
Cassette (std Cpe)	25
CD player	50
Cruise ctrl (std SE Cpe)	25
Leather seats	125
GTP trim	250
GT pkg	300
Pwr seat	25
Wheels-alloy (std Cpe)	25

SUNBIRD FWD/2.0L-I4 (110hp)

LE 4dr Sdn	2100	3225
LE 2dr Cnv	3400	4875
LE 2dr Cpe	2075	3200
SE (6cyl) 2dr Cpe	2975	4400

Add:

3.1 Liter V6	175
Alloy wheels	25
Cassette	25
CD player	25
Cruise ctrl	25
Pwr windows (std Cnv)	25
Sunroof-manual	25

Deduct:

No air cond	225
Manual trans	200

TRANS AM RWD/5.7L-V8 (275hp)

GT 2dr Cnv	7250	9075
GT 2dr Cpe	6300	8075
Trans Am 2dr Cpe	5950	7700

Add:

CD player	50
Lift-off roof	250
Leather seats	75

Deduct:

No air cond	250
Manual trans	200

1993 WS Ret

BONNEVILLE FWD/3.8L-V6 (170hp)

SE 4dr Sdn	3000	4425
SSE 4dr Sdn	3950	5550
SSEi 4dr Sdn	4500	6150

Add:

Air Bag-psngr (std SSEi)	50
Alloy wheels (SE)	25
Cassette (SE only)	25
CD player	50
Cruise ctrl (SE only)	25
Leather seats	100
Power seat (SE only)	25
Sunroof-pwr	150

FIREBIRD RWD/3.4L-V6 (160hp)

Base 2dr Cpe	3350	4825
Formula (8cyl) 2dr Cpe	4125	5750

Add:

CD player	50
Cruise ctrl	25
Leather seats	75
Pwr dr locks	25
Pwr windows	25
T-tops	225

Deduct:

No air cond	225
Manual trans	200

GRAND AM FWD/2.3L-I4 (115hp)

GT 4dr Sdn	2450	3825
GT 2dr Cpe	2450	3825
SE 4dr Sdn	1875	2975
SE 2dr Cpe	1875	2975

Add:

2.3L 4cyl DOHC (SE only)	75
3.3 Liter V6 (SE)	150
3.3 Liter V6 (GT)	50
Alloy wheels	25
Cassette	25
CD player	25
Cruise ctrl	25
Pwr seat	25
Pwr windows	25

Deduct:

No air cond	200
Manual trans	175

GRAND PRIX FWD/3.lL-V6 (140hp)

GT 2dr Cpe	3050	4500
LE 4dr Sdn	2350	3700
SE 4dr Sdn	2550	3925
SE 2dr Cpe	2500	3875
STE 4dr Sdn	3200	4650

Add:

3.4 Liter DOHC V6	175
ABS brakes (std STE,GT)	100
Cassette (std STE,GT)	25
CD player	50
Cruise ctrl (std STE,GT)	25
Leather seats	100
GTP trim (GT)	200
Pwr seat (std STE,GT)	25
Pwr windows (std STE,GT)	25
Alloy wheels (SE only)	25
Tilt wheel (std STE,GT)	25

LEMANS FWD/1.6L-I4 (74hp)

Base (4sp) 2dr Cpe	525	1000
SE 4dr Sdn	1025	1925
SE 2dr Cpe	850	1525

Add:

Cassette	25
Sunroof-manual	25

Deduct:

No air cond	175
Manual trans	175
Manual steering (not VL)	25

SUNBIRD FWD/2.0L-I4 (110hp)

GT (6cyl) 2dr Cpe	2425	3800
LE 4dr Sdn	1575	2625
LE 2dr Cpe	1550	2475
SE 4dr Sdn	1750	2825
SE 2dr Cnv	2600	3975
SE 2dr Cpe	1725	2800

Add:

3.1 Liter V6 (std GT)	150
Alloy wheels (std GT)	25
Cassette	25
CD player	25
Cruise ctrl	25
Pwr windows (std Cnv)	25
Sunroof-manual	25

Deduct:

No air cond	175
Manual trans	175

TRANS AM RWD/5.7L-V8 (275hp)

Trans Am 2dr Cpe	4725	6375

Add:

CD player	50
T-tops	225
Leather seats	75

Deduct:

No air cond	225
Manual trans	200

1992 WS Ret

BONNEVILLE FWD/3.8L-V6 (170hp)

SE 4dr Sdn	2550	3925
SSE 4dr Sdn	3375	4850
SSEi 4dr Sdn	3900	5500

Add:

ABS brakes (SE only)	75
Air bag-psgr (std SSEi)	25

Cassette (SE only) 25
CD player 25
Cruise ctrl (std SSEi) 25
Leather seats 75
Pwr seat (SE) 25
Special wheels (SE) 25
Sunroof-pwr 100

FIREBIRD RWD/5.0L-V8 (170hp)

Base 2dr Cnv	3875	5475
Base 2dr Cpe	2775	4175
Formula 2dr Cpe	3300	4775

Add:
5.0L TBI V8 75
5.7 Liter V8 225
CD player 25
Cruise ctrl 25
Leather seats 50
Pwr dr locks 25
Pwr windows 25
Special wheels 25
T-tops 200

Deduct:
6cyl 125
No air cond 200
Manual trans 175

GRAND AM FWD/2.3L-I4 (120hp)

GT 4dr Sdn	2025	3125
GT 2dr Cpe	2025	3125
SE 4dr Sdn	1575	2625
SE 2dr Cpe	1575	2625

Add:
2.3L 4cyl DOHC (SE only) 50
3.3 Liter V6 (SE) 125
3.3 Liter V6 (GT) 25
CD player 25
Cruise ctrl 25
Pwr seat 25
Pwr windows 25
Special wheels 25

Deduct:
No air cond 175
Manual trans 175

GRAND PRIX FWD/3.1L-V6 (140hp)

GT 2dr Cpe	2600	3975
GTP 2dr Cpe	3100	4550
LE 4dr Sdn	2025	3125
SE 4dr Sdn	2225	3350
SE 2dr Cpe	2175	3300
STE 4dr Sdn	2750	4150

Add:
3.4 Liter DOHC V6 150
ABS brakes (LE,SE) 75
Cassette (std STE,GT) 25
CD player 25
Cruise ctrl 25
Leather seats 75
Pwr dr locks (std GT, STE) 25
Pwr seat (std STE,GT) 25
Pwr windows (std GT) 25
Special wheels (LE)) 25
GTP trim (GT) 150

LEMANS FWD/1.6L-I4 (74hp)

SE 4dr Sdn	800	1475
SE 2dr Cpe	650	1150
VL (4sp) 2dr Cpe	400	850

Add:
Sunroof-manual 25

Deduct:
No air cond 175
Manual trans 150
Manual steering 25

SUNBIRD FWD/2.0L-I4 (111hp)

GT (6cyl) 2dr Cpe	2075	3200
LE 4dr Sdn	1375	2300
LE 2dr Cpe	1350	2275
SE 4dr Sdn	1500	2425
SE 2dr Cnv	2300	3450
SE 2dr Cpe	1525	2450

Add:
3.1 Liter V6 (std GT) 125
CD player 25
Cruise ctrl 25
Pwr windows (std Cnv) 25
Special wheels (std GT) 25
Sunroof-manual 25

Deduct:
No air cond 175
Manual trans 150

TRANS AM RWD/5.0L-V8 (205hp)

GTA 2dr Cpe	4225	5850
Trans Am 2dr Cnv	4725	6375
Trans Am 2dr Cpe	3650	5150

Add:
5.7 Liter V8 175
CD player 25
Cruise ctrl (std GTA) 25
Leather seats 50
Pwr dr locks (std GTA) 25
Pwr windows (std GTA) 25
T-tops 200

Deduct:
No air cond 200
Manual trans 175

1991 WS Ret

6000 FWD/3.1L-V6 (140hp)

LE 4dr Sdn	1400	2325
LE 4dr Wgn	1525	2450
SE 4dr Sdn	1575	2625

Add:
Cassette (std SE) 25
CD player 25
Cruise ctrl (std SE) 25
Pwr dr locks (std SE) 25
Pwr windows (std SE) 25
Special wheels 25

Deduct:
4cyl 100
No air cond 175

BONNEVILLE FWD/3.8L-V6 (165hp)

LE 4dr Sdn	1775	2850
SE 4dr Sdn	2025	3125
SSE 4dr Sdn	2600	3975

Add:
ABS brakes (std SSE) 50
Cassette (LE only) 25
CD player 25
Cruise ctrl (LE only) 25
Integrated phone 25
Leather seats 50
Pwr dr locks (LE only) 25
Pwr windows (LE only) 25
Special wheels (std SSE) 25
Sunroof-pwr 100

FIREBIRD RWD/5.0L-V8 (170hp)

Base 2dr Cnv	3650	5150
Base 2dr Cpe	2600	3975
Formula 2dr Cpe	2950	4375

Add:
5.0L HO V8 50
5.7 Liter V8 175
CD player 25
Leather seats 25
Pwr windows 25
Special wheels (Base only) 25
T-tops 175

Deduct:
6cyl 100
No air cond 175
Manual trans 150

GRAND AM FWD/2.3L-I4 (160hp)

Base 4dr Sdn	975	1675
Base 2dr Cpe	975	1675
LE 4dr Sdn	1100	2000
LE 2dr Cpe	1100	2000
SE 4dr Sdn	1400	2325
SE 2dr Cpe	1400	2325

Add:
2.3L Quad4 4cyl (std SE) 25
CD player 25
Cruise ctrl (std SE) 25
Pwr windows (std SE) 25
Special wheels (std SE) 25
Sunroof-manual 25

Deduct:
No air cond 175
Manual trans 150

GRAND PRIX FWD/3.1L-V6 (140hp)

GT 2dr Cpe	2025	3125
LE 4dr Sdn	1700	2775
SE 4dr Sdn	1875	2975
SE 2dr Cpe	1875	2975
STE 4dr Sdn	2250	3375

Add:
ABS brakes 50
Cassette (std STE) 25
CD player 25
Cruise ctrl (std GT,STE) 25
Leather seats 50
Pwr dr locks(std GT,STE) 25
Pwr windows (std GT,STE) . . . 25
Special wheels (std GT) 25

LEMANS FWD/1.6L-I4 (74hp)

LE 4dr Sdn	575	1075
LE 2dr Cpe	525	1000
VL (4sp) 2dr Cpe	325	775

Add:
Sunroof-manual 25

Deduct:
No air cond 150
Manual trans 125
Manual steering 25

SUNBIRD FWD/2.0L-I4 (96hp)

Base 4dr Sdn	825	1500
Base 2dr Cpe	800	1475
GT 2dr Cpe	1500	2425
LE 4dr Sdn	975	1675
LE 2dr Cnv	1650	2700
LE 2dr Cpe	950	1650
SE 2dr Cpe	1125	2025

Add:
3.1 Liter V6 (std GT) 100
CD player 25
Pwr windows (std Cnv) 25
Special wheels (std GT) 50
Sunroof-manual 25
Sunroof-pwr 50

Deduct:
No air cond 150
Manual trans 125

TRANS AM RWD/5.0L-V8 (205hp)

2dr Cnv	4400	6050
2dr Cpe	3025	4450
GTA 2dr Cpe	3475	4950

Add:
5.0L HO V8 50
5.7 Liter V8 (std GTA) 175
CD player 25
Leather seats 25
Pwr windows (std GTA) 25
T-tops 175

Deduct:
No air cond 175
Manual trans 150

1990 — WS Ret

6000 — FWD/3.1L-V6 (140hp)

Model	WS	Ret
LE 4dr Sdn	1175	2075
LE 4dr Wgn	1225	2125
SE 4dr Sdn	1250	2150
SE 4dr Wgn	1325	2250

Add:
- 4-wheel drive . . . 175
- CD player . . . 25
- Pwr windows (std SE) . . . 25
- Special wheels (std SE) . . . 25

Deduct:
- 4cyl . . . 75
- No air cond . . . 150

BONNEVILLE — FWD/3.8L-V6 (165hp)

Model	WS	Ret
LE 4dr Sdn	1425	2350
SE 4dr Sdn	1625	2675
SSE 4dr Sdn	2150	3275

Add:
- ABS brakes (std SSE) . . . 25
- CD player . . . 25
- Leather seats . . . 25
- Special wheels (LE only) . . . 25
- Sunroof-pwr . . . 100

FIREBIRD — RWD/5.0L-V8 (170hp)

Model	WS	Ret
Base 2dr Cpe	2125	3250
Formula 2dr Cpe	2450	3825

Add:
- 5.0L HO V8 . . . 50
- 5.7 Liter V8 . . . 175
- CD player . . . 25
- Leather seats . . . 25
- T-tops . . . 150

Deduct:
- 6cyl . . . 75
- No air cond . . . 150
- Manual trans . . . 125

GRAND AM — FWD/2.5L-I4 (110hp)

Model	WS	Ret
LE 4dr Sdn	925	1625
LE 2dr Cpe	925	1625
SE 4dr Sdn	1175	2075
SE 2dr Cpe	1175	2075

Add:
- 2.3L 4cyl Quad4 (LE) . . . 50
- Sunroof-manual . . . 25

Deduct:
- No air cond . . . 150
- Manual trans . . . 125

GRAND PRIX — FWD/3.1L-V6 (140hp)

Model	WS	Ret
LE 4dr Sdn	1450	2375
LE 2dr Cpe	1425	2350
SE 2dr Cpe	1650	2700
STE 4dr Sdn	1800	2875
Turbo STE 4dr Sdn	4025	5650
Turbo SE 2dr Cpe	4150	5775

Add:
- CD player . . . 25
- Leather seats . . . 25
- Pwr windows (std SE,STE) . . . 25
- Spcl wheels (std SE,STE) . . . 25
- Sunroof-pwr . . . 75

LEMANS — FWD/1.6L-I4 (74hp)

Model	WS	Ret
GSE 2dr Cpe	475	950
LE 4dr Sdn	500	975
VL (4sp) 2dr Cpe	250	675

Add:
- Sunroof-manual . . . 25

Deduct:
- No air cond . . . 125
- Manual trans . . . 125

SUNBIRD — FWD/2.0L-I4 (96hp)

Model	WS	Ret
GT Turbo 2dr Cpe	1150	2050
LE 4dr Sdn	775	1300
LE 2dr Cnv	1375	2300
LE 2dr Cpe	775	1300
SE 2dr Cpe	875	1550

Add:
- 2.0L 4cyl Turbo (std GT) . . . 50
- Sunroof-manual . . . 25

Deduct:
- No air cond . . . 125
- Manual trans . . . 125

TRANS AM — RWD/5.0L-V8 (225hp)

Model	WS	Ret
2dr Cpe	2475	3850
GTA 2dr Cpe	2875	4275

Add:
- 5.0L HO V8 . . . 50
- 5.7 Liter V8 (std GTA) . . . 175
- CD player . . . 25
- Leather seats . . . 25
- Pwr windows (std GTA) . . . 25
- T-tops . . . 175

Deduct:
- No air cond . . . 150
- Manual trans . . . 125

1989 — WS Ret

6000 — FWD/2.8L-V6 (125hp)

Model	WS	Ret
LE 4dr Sdn	875	1550
LE 4dr Wgn	975	1675
SE 4dr Sdn	950	1650
SE 4dr Wgn	1025	1925
STE (AWD) 4dr Sdn	1475	2400

Add:
- CD Player . . . 25

Deduct:
- 4cyl . . . 50
- No air cond . . . 125

BONNEVILLE — FWD/3.8L-V6 (165hp)

Model	WS	Ret
LE 4dr Sdn	850	1525
SE 4dr Sdn	1025	1925
SSE 4dr Sdn	1400	2325

Add:
- CD player . . . 25
- Leather seats . . . 25
- Sunroof-pwr . . . 50

FIREBIRD — RWD/5.0L-V8 (170hp)

Model	WS	Ret
Base 2dr Cpe	1850	2925
Formula 2dr Cpe	2025	3125

Add:
- 5.0L EFI V8 . . . 50
- 5.7 Liter V8 . . . 150
- Cd player . . . 25
- Leather seats . . . 25
- T-tops . . . 100

Deduct:
- 6cyl . . . 75
- No air cond . . . 125
- Manual trans . . . 100

GRAND AM — FWD/2.3L-I4 (110hp)

Model	WS	Ret
LE 4dr Sdn	750	1275
LE 2dr Cpe	750	1275
SE 4dr Sdn	850	1525
SE 2dr Cpe	850	1525

Add:
- 2.3L Quad4 4cyl(LE only) . . . 25

Deduct:
- No air cond . . . 100
- Manual trans . . . 100

GRAND PRIX — FWD/2.8L-V6 (130hp)

Model	WS	Ret
Base 2dr Cpe	975	1675
LE 2dr Cpe	1025	1925
SE 2dr Cpe	1125	2025

Add:
- Leather seats . . . 25
- Sunroof-pwr . . . 50

LEMANS — FWD/1.6L-I4 (74hp)

Model	WS	Ret
GSE 2dr Cpe	325	775
LE 4dr Sdn	300	750
LE 2dr Cpe	275	725
SE 4dr Sdn	325	775
VL (4sp) 2dr Cpe	175	600

Add:

Deduct:
- No air cond . . . 75
- Manual trans . . . 75

SAFARI — RWD/5.0L-V8 (140hp)

Model	WS	Ret
Wagon 4dr Wgn	925	1625

Add:
- Sunroof-pwr . . . 50

SUNBIRD — FWD/2.0L-I4 (96hp)

Model	WS	Ret
GT Turbo 2dr Cnv	900	1600
GT Turbo 2dr Cpe	825	1500
LE 4dr Sdn	625	1125
LE 2dr Cpe	600	1100
SE 2dr Cpe	675	1200

Add:
- 2.0L 4cyl Turbo (std GT) . . . 50

Deduct:
- No air cond . . . 75
- Manual trans . . . 75

TRANS AM — RWD/5.7L-V8 (225hp)

Model	WS	Ret
Anniv Turbo (6cyl) 2dr Cpe	7650	9600
GTA 2dr Cpe	2525	3900
T/A 2dr Cpe	2275	3425

Deduct:
- No air cond . . . 125
- Manual trans . . . 100

1988 — WS Ret

6000 — FWD/2.8L-V6 (125hp)

Model	WS	Ret
Base 4dr Sdn	725	1250
Base 4dr Wgn	775	1300
LE 4dr Sdn	725	1250
LE 4dr Wgn	750	1275
SE 4dr Sdn	725	1250
SE 4dr Wgn	800	1475
STE 4dr Sdn	900	1600

Add:
- Sunroof-pwr . . . 50

Deduct:
- 4cyl . . . 50
- No air cond . . . 100

BONNEVILLE — FWD/3.8L-V6 (150hp)

Model	WS	Ret
LE 4dr Sdn	700	1225
SE 4dr Sdn	800	1475
SSE 4dr Sdn	1100	2000

Add:
- Leather seats . . . 25
- Sunroof-pwr . . . 50

FIERO — RWD/2.5L-I4 (98hp)

Model	WS	Ret
Base 2dr Cpe	1125	2025
Formula (V6) 2dr Cpe	1250	2150
GT (V6) 2dr Cpe	2300	3500

Add:

Deduct:
- No air cond . . . 100
- Manual trans (except GT) . . . 50

FIREBIRD — RWD/5.0L-V8 (160hp)

Model	WS	Ret
Base 2dr Cpe	1475	2400

Formula 2dr Cpe 1625 2675

Add:
5.0L 205hp V8 50
5.7 Liter V8 125
T-tops 75

Deduct:
6cyl 50
No air cond 100
Manual trans 75

GRAND AM FWD/2.3L-I4 (98hp)

	WS	Ret
Base 4dr Sdn	550	1050
Base 2dr Cpe	550	1050
LE 4dr Sdn	575	1075
LE 2dr Cpe	575	1075
SE 4dr Sdn	700	1225
SE 2dr Cpe	700	1225

Add:
2.0L 4cyl Turbo (SE) 25
2.3L Quad 4cyl (std SE) 25

Deduct:
No air cond 75
Manual trans 75

GRAND PRIX FWD/2.8L-V6 (125hp)

	WS	Ret
Base 2dr Cpe	775	1300
LE 2dr Cpe	825	1500
SE 2dr Cpe	875	1550

Add:

Deduct:
No air cond 100

LEMANS FWD/1.6L-I4 (74hp)

	WS	Ret
Base 4dr Sdn	200	625
Base 2dr Cpe	175	600
SE 4dr Sdn	200	625
VL (4sp) 2dr Cpe	125	525

Add:

Deduct:
No air cond 50
Manual trans 50

SAFARI RWD/5.0L-V8 (140hp)

	WS	Ret
Wagon 4dr Wgn	675	1200

Add:

SUNBIRD FWD/2.0L-I4 (96hp)

	WS	Ret
Base 4dr Sdn	400	850
GT Turbo 2dr Cnv	600	1100
GT Turbo 2dr Cpe	550	1050
SE 4dr Sdn	450	925
SE 4dr Wgn	475	950
SE 2dr Cpe	475	950

Add:
2.0L 4cyl Turbo (std GT) 25

Deduct:
No air cond 50
Manual trans 50

TRANS AM RWD/5.0L-V8 (205hp)

	WS	Ret
GTA 2dr Cpe	2000	3100
T/A 2dr Cpe	1800	2875

Deduct:
No air cond 100
Manual trans 75

PORSCHE

2001 — WS / Ret

911 (6sp) AWD/3.4L-H6 (300hp)

Carrera 4 Cabrio 2dr Cnv ......
Carrera Cabrio 2dr Cnv ....
Carrera 4 2dr Cpe ....
Carrera 2dr Cpe ....
Turbo (3.6L/415hp) 2dr Cpe ....

BOXSTER RWD/2.5L-H6 (201hp)

	WS	Ret
Base (5sp) 2dr Cnv	38550	42750
S (6sp/3.2L-250hp)) Cnv	44950	49575

Add:
Full lthr int 1100
Sport pkg (incls 17/18" whls) . 1825
Sport Tour (incls 17/18" whls) . 3550
Technic pkg (incls 17/18" whls) . 725
Hardtop 1475
Tiptronic 1100
Wheels-17" (Base) 375
CD changer (std Spt Trng) ... 375
Carbon pkg 1950
Wood pkg 975
GPS Nav sys 775

Deduct:
No CD 325

2000 — WS / Ret

911 (6sp) AWD/3.4L-H6 (300hp)

	WS	Ret
Carrera 4 Cabrio 2dr Cnv		
Carrera Cabrio 2dr Cnv	64575	69650
Carrera 4 2dr Cpe	61050	65925
Carrera 2dr Cpe	57075	61725

Add:
CD changer 375
HiFi sound 425
Full lthr interior 2800
Tiptronic 900
Carbon pkg 1500
Wood pkg 750
Chrome&alum pkg 675
Navigation sys 600

Deduct:
No CD 250

BOXSTER RWD/2.5L-H6 (201hp)

	WS	Ret
Base (5sp) 2dr Cnv	35975	39975
S (6sp/3.2L-250hp)) Cnv	41575	45500

Add:
Full lthr int 850
Sport pkg (incls 17/18" whls) . 1425
Sport Tour (incls 17/18" whls) . 2750
Technic pkg (incls 17/18" whls) . 575
Hardtop 1150
Tiptronic 850
Wheels-17" (Base) 275
CD changer (std Spt Trng) ... 275
Carbon pkg 1525
Wood pkg 750
GPS Nav sys 600

Deduct:
No CD 250

1999 — WS / Ret

911 (6sp) AWD/3.4L-H6 (296hp)

	WS	Ret
Carrera 4 Cabrio 2dr Cnv	63225	68225
Carrera Cabrio 2dr Cnv	58350	63075
Carrera 4 2dr Cpe	56000	60600
Carrera 2dr Cpe	52100	56475

Add:
CD changer 300
HiFi sound 350
Full lthr interior 2325
Tiptronic 725
Carbon pkg 1250
Wood pkg 625
Chrome&alum pkg 550

Deduct:
No CD 225

BOXSTER (5sp) RWD/2.5L-H6 (201hp)

	WS	Ret
2dr Cnv	32000	35775

Add:
Full lthr int 700
Sport pkg (incls 17/18" whls) . 1175
Sport Tour (incls 17/18" whls) . 2275
Technic pkg (incls 17/18" whls) 475
Hardtop 950
Tiptronic 700
Wheels-17" 225
CD changer (std Spt Trng) ... 225
Carbon pkg 1250
Wood pkg 625
GPS Nav sys 500

Deduct:
No CD 225

1998 — WS / Ret

911 (6sp) AWD/3.4L-H6 (296hp)

	WS	Ret
Carrera 4 Cabrio 2dr Cnv	54550	59050
Carrera Cabrio 2dr Cnv	51150	55450
Carrera 4 2dr Cpe	51675	56025
Carrera S 2dr Cpe	46225	50350
Carrera Targa 2dr Cpe	50350	54625

Add:
CD changer 250
Full leather interior 1900
Tiptronic 600
Carbon pkg 1025
Wood pkg 500

Deduct:
No CD 175

BOXSTER (5sp) RWD/2.5L-F6 (201hp)

	WS	Ret
2dr Cnv	29625	33225

Add:
Full lthr int 575
Sport pkg (incls 17" whls) ... 975
Sport Tour (incls 17" whls) ... 1875
Technic pkg (incls 17" whls) .. 400
Hardtop 775
Tiptronic 575
Wheels-17" 200
CD changer (std Spt Trng) ... 200

Deduct:
No CD 175

1997 — WS / Ret

911 (6sp) AWD/3.6L-F6 (282hp)

	WS	Ret
C-4 Cabriolet 2dr Cnv	50275	54525
C-4S 2dr Cpe	47650	51850
Carrera Cabrio 2dr Cnv	46900	51050
Carrera 2dr Cpe	41750	45700
Carrera Targa 2dr Cpe	45000	49150
Turbo 2dr Cpe	73675	80075

Add:
CD changer 200
Full leather interior 1525
Tiptronic 500
Carbon pkg 750
Wood pkg 375

Deduct:
No CD 150

BOXSTER (5sp) RWD/2.5L-F6 (201hp)

	WS	Ret
2dr Cnv	25575	29075

Add:
Sport pkg (incls 17" whls) ... 800
Sport Tour (incls 17" whls) ... 1550
Technic pkg (incls 17" whls) .. 325
Hardtop 650
Tiptronic 475
Wheels-17" 150
CD changer (std Spt Trng) ... 150

Deduct:
No CD 150

1996 — WS / Ret

911 (6sp) AWD/3.6L-F6 (282hp)

	WS	Ret
C-4 Cabriolet 2dr Cnv	45425	49500
C-4 2dr Cpe	39075	42900

Model	WS	Ret
C-4S 2dr Cpe	41075	44975
Carrera Cabrio 2dr Cnv	41575	45500
Carrera 2dr Cpe	36575	40225
Carrera Targa 2dr Cpe	39450	43275
Turbo 2dr Cpe	66675	71875

Add:

CD changer	175
CD player	125
Full leather interior	1275
Tiptronic	425
Carbon pkg	525
Wood pkg	300

1995 — WS — Ret

911 (6sp) — AWD/3.6L-F6 (270hp)

Model	WS	Ret
C-4 Cabriolet 2dr Cnv	40475	44325
C-4 2dr Cpe	34350	37875
Carrera Cabrio 2dr Cnv	36125	39750
Carrera 2dr Cpe	32175	35550

Add:

CD changer	150
CD player	100
Full leather interior	1175
Tiptronic	375
Wood pkg	275

928 — RWD/5.4L-I4 (345hp)

Model	WS	Ret
928GTS 2dr Cpe	32325	35725

Add:

Full leather interior	1175

968 (6sp) — RWD/3.0L-I4 (236hp)

Model	WS	Ret
Cabriolet 2dr Cnv	21300	24200
Coupe 2dr Cpe	16000	18525

Add:

CD changer	150
Full leather interior	725
Integrated phone	125
Leather seats	150
Wood pkg	150

1994 — WS — Ret

911 (5sp) — RWD/3.6L-F6 (270hp)

Model	WS	Ret
C-2 Cabriolet 2dr Cnv	34525	38050
C-2 2dr Cpe	30525	33875
C-4 2dr Cpe	32125	35500
C-4 (wide body) 2dr Cpe	33900	37375
RS America 2dr Cpe	30150	33800
Speedster 2dr Cnv	34450	37975
Turbo 2dr Cpe	42775	46775
Turbo Slantnose 2dr Cpe	1	1

Add:

CD changer	150
CD player	75
Full leather interior	1050
Sunroof-pwr (RS America)	200
Tiptronic	350
Wood pkg	175

928 — RWD/5.4L-V8 (345hp)

Model	WS	Ret
GTS 2dr Cpe	28575	32300

Add:

Full leather interior	1050

968 (6sp) — RWD/3.0L-I4 (236hp)

Model	WS	Ret
Cabriolet 2dr Cnv	19050	22025
Coupe 2dr Cpe	14250	16825

Add:

CD changer	150
Full leather interior	650
Integrated phone	100
Leather seats	125
Wood pkg	150

1993 — WS — Ret

911 (5sp) — RWD/3.6L-F6 (247hp)

Model	WS	Ret
C-2 Cabriolet 2dr Cnv	30350	33675
C-2 2dr Cpe	27500	30850
C-2 Targa 2dr Cpe	27800	31150
C-2 Turbo 2dr Cpe	35900	39525
C-4 Cabriolet 2dr Cnv	29550	32825
C-4 2dr Cpe	28525	31925
C-4 Targa 2dr Cpe	28825	32250
RS America 2dr Cpe	25875	29100
Speedster 2dr Cnv	31325	34725

Add:

CD changer	125
CD player	75
Full leather interior	875
Sunroof-pwr (RS America)	175
Tiptronic	300

928 — RWD/5.4L-V8 (247hp)

Model	WS	Ret
GTS 2dr Cpe	24850	28000

Add:

CD player	75
Full leather interior	875

968 (6sp) — RWD/3.0L-I4 (236hp)

Model	WS	Ret
Cabriolet 2dr Cnv	16550	19125
Coupe 2dr Cpe	12375	14650

Add:

CD changer	125
Full leather interior	525
Leather seats	125

1992 — WS — Ret

911 (5sp) — RWD/3.6L-F6 (247hp)

Model	WS	Ret
C-2 Cabriolet 2dr Cnv	27600	30950
C-2 2dr Cpe	24150	27250
C-2 Targa 2dr Cpe	24350	27475
C-2 Turbo 2dr Cpe	33500	36950
C-4 Cabriolet 2dr Cnv	29075	32325
C-4 2dr Cpe	25525	28725
C-4 Targa 2dr Cpe	25750	28975

Add:

CD changer	100
CD player	50
Full leather interior	875

968 (6sp) — RWD/3.0L-I4 (236hp)

Model	WS	Ret
Cabriolet 2dr Cnv	14675	17300
Coupe 2dr Cpe	10500	12775

Add:

CD changer	100
Full leather interior	500
Leather seats	100

1991 — WS — Ret

911 (5sp) — RWD/3.6L-F6 (247hp)

Model	WS	Ret
C-2 Cabriolet 2dr Cnv	25400	28875
C-2 2dr Cpe	22200	25425
C-2 Targa 2dr Cpe	22375	25600
C-2 Turbo 2dr Cpe	31150	34875
C-4 Cabriolet 2dr Cnv	26725	30300
C-4 2dr Cpe	23475	26800
C-4 Targa 2dr Cpe	23650	26975

Add:

CD player	25
Full leather interior	675

928 — RWD/5.0L-V8 (316hp)

Model	WS	Ret
S4 2dr Cpe	18700	21625

Add:

CD player	25
Full leather interior	675

944 (5sp) — RWD/3.0L-I4 (208hp)

Model	WS	Ret
S2 Cabriolet 2dr Cnv	11225	13550
S2 2dr Cpe	8050	10125

Add:

CD player	25
Leather interior	125
Leather seats	50

1990 — WS — Ret

911 (5sp) — RWD/3.6L-F6 (247hp)

Model	WS	Ret
C-2 Cabriolet 2dr Cnv	22050	25250
C-2 2dr Cpe	19350	22350
C-2 Targa 2dr Cpe	19500	22500
C-4 Cabriolet 2dr Cnv	23525	26850
C-4 2dr Cpe	20425	23500
C-4 Targa 2dr Cpe	20575	23675

Add:

CD player	25
Full leather interior	575
Leather seats	50

928 — RWD/5.0L-V8 (316hp)

Model	WS	Ret
928S 2dr Cpe	16250	19000

Add:

CD player	25
Full leather interior	575

944 S2 (5sp) — RWD/3.0L-I4 (208hp)

Model	WS	Ret
Cabriolet 2dr Cnv	9575	11775
Coupe 2dr Cpe	6750	8725

Add:

CD player	25
Leather interior	100
Leather seats	50

1989 — WS — Ret

911 (5sp) — RWD/3.2L-F6 (214hp)

Model	WS	Ret
Cabriolet 2dr Cnv	20450	23525
Coupe 2dr Cpe	18300	21200
Speedster 2dr Cnv	36750	40825
Targa 2dr Cpe	18375	21275
Turbo Cabriolet 2dr Cnv	32100	35900
Turbo 2dr Cpe	25600	29100
Turbo Targa 2dr Cpe	25600	29100

Add:

CD player	25
Leather seats	50
Full leather interior	450
930S Slant nose (Turbo)	3100
Turbo look	2275

928 — RWD/5.0L-V8 (316hp)

Model	WS	Ret
928S 2dr Cpe	13825	16375

Add:

CD player	25
Full leather interior	450

944 (5sp) — RWD/2.7L-I4 (162hp)

Model	WS	Ret
944S 2dr Cpe	6775	8750
944 2dr Cpe	6400	8350
Turbo 2dr Cpe	8250	10350

Add:

CD player	25
Leather interior	75
Leather seats	25

1988 — WS — Ret

911 (5sp) — RWD/3.2L-F6 (214hp)

Model	WS	Ret
Cabriolet 2dr Cnv	18600	21525
Coupe 2dr Cpe	16600	19375
Targa 2dr Cpe	16650	19425
Turbo Cabriolet 2dr Cnv	26050	29575
Turbo 2dr Cpe	22500	25750
Turbo Targa 2dr Cpe	22500	25750

Add:

Option	Value
Sunroof-pwr (Base)	75
930S Slant nose (Turbo)	3100
Turbo look (Base)	1950

924 (5sp) RWD/2.5L-I4 (158hp)

Model	WS	Ret
924S 2dr Cpe	4750	6525

Add:

Option	Value
Leather seats	25
Sunroof-pwr	50

928 RWD/5.0L-V8 (316hp)

Model	WS	Ret
928S 2dr Cpe	11700	14075

944 (5sp) RWD/2.5L-I4 (158hp)

Model	WS	Ret
944 2dr Cpe	5375	7250
944S 2dr Cpe	5675	7575
Turbo 2dr Cpe	7325	9350

Add:

Option	Value
ABS brakes	25
Leather seats	25

SAAB

2001 — WS / Ret

9-3 FWD/2.0L-I4T (185hp)

Model	WS	Ret
Base 4dr Hbk		
Base 2dr Cnv		
Base 2dr Hbk		
SE (205hp) 4dr Hbk		
SE (205hp) 2dr Cnv		
Viggen (2.3L/230hp) 4dr Hbk		
Viggen (2.3L/230hp) 2dr Cnv		
Viggen (2.3L/230hp) 2dr Hbk		

9-5 FWD/

Model	WS	Ret
Aero (230hp) 4dr Hbk		
Aero (230hp) 4dr Wgn		
Base 4dr Hbk	24350	27475
Base 4dr Wgn	25400	28600
SE V6t (200hp) 4dr Hbk		
SE V6t (200hp) 4dr Wgn		

Add:

Option	Value
Harmon Kardon audio (2.3t)	350
Lthr seats (2.3t)	475
Wheels-17" alloy (std Aero)	500
Moonroof-pwr (2.3t)	475
Wheels-BBS (Aero only)	350

2000 — WS / Ret

9-3 FWD/2.0L-I4T (185hp)

Model	WS	Ret
Base 4dr Hbk	15575	18075
Base 2dr Cnv	22350	25125
Base 2dr Hbk	15275	17750
SE (205hp) 4dr Hbk	18575	21300
SE (205hp) 2dr Cnv	25500	28700
Viggen (2.3L/230hp) 2dr Cnv		
Viggen (2.3L/230hp) 2dr Hbk		

Add:

Option	Value
Lthr seats (Base hbk)	350
Moonroof-power (std Base)	425

9-5 FWD/

Model	WS	Ret
Aero (230hp) 4dr Hbk	1	1
Aero (230hp) 4dr Wgn	1	1
Base 4dr Hbk	21900	24850
Base 4dr Wgn	22950	25975
SE V6t (200hp) 4dr Hbk	25200	28375
SE V6t (200hp) 4dr Wgn	26075	29325

Add:

Option	Value
3.0L-V6 (200hp)	650
Lthr seats (2.3t)	375
Wheels-17" alloy (std Aero)	375
Moonroof-pwr (2.3t)	375

Option	Value
Gary Fisher (2.3t)	1375

1999 — WS / Ret

9-3 FWD/2.0L-I4T (185hp)

Model	WS	Ret
S 4dr Hbk	13275	15625
S 2dr Cnv	19650	22450
S 2dr Hbk	12975	15300
SE 4dr Hbk	16000	18525
SE 2dr Cnv	22450	25425
Viggen (2.3L/230hp) 2dr Hbk	23150	26175

Add:

Option	Value
Lthr seats (Base)	275
Aero kit	550
Moonroof-power (std SE)	350

9-5 FWD/

Model	WS	Ret
Base 4dr Hbk	17125	19750
Base 4dr Wgn	18600	21325
SE 4dr Hbk	19000	21750
SE 4dr Wgn	20450	23300

Add:

Option	Value
3.0L-V6 (200hp)	525
Lthr seats (Base)	300
Styling pkg (w/17" whls)	400
Moonroof-pwr (Base)	300

1998 — WS / Ret

900 FWD/2.0L-I4 (185hp)

Model	WS	Ret
S 4dr Hbk	10100	12225
S 2dr Cnv	14475	16900
S (Turbo) 2dr Hbk	9875	11975
SE Turbo 4dr Hbk	12725	15025
SE Turbo 2dr Cnv	17825	20500
SE Turbo 2dr Hbk	12575	14875

Add:

Option	Value
Leather seats (std SE,conv)	225
Moonroof-power (std SE)	300

Deduct:

Option	Value
Manual trans	375

9000 FWD/2.3L-I4 (225hp)

Model	WS	Ret
CSE 4dr Hbk	14400	16825

Deduct:

Option	Value
Manual trans	400

1997 — WS / Ret

900 FWD/2.3L-I4 (150hp)

Model	WS	Ret
S 4dr Hbk	8725	10750
S 2dr Cnv	12525	14825
S 2dr Hbk	8500	10500
SE (6cyl) 4dr Hbk	11300	13500
SE Turbo 4dr Hbk	11125	13325
SE Turbo 2dr Cnv	15550	18050
SE (6cyl) 2dr Cnv	15250	17725
SE Turbo 2dr Hbk	10950	13125

Add:

Option	Value
Leather seats (S Cpe,Hbk)	200
Moonroof-power (S)	250

Deduct:

Option	Value
Manual trans	325

9000 FWD/2.3L-I4 (170hp)

Model	WS	Ret
Aero 4dr Hbk	15225	17700
CS 4dr Hbk	10750	12925
CSE (6cyl) 4dr Hbk	14100	16500
CSE 4dr Hbk	13900	16300

Add:

Option	Value
3.0L 24V V6 (CSE)	375
Leather seats (std CSE,Aero)	175
Moonroof-pwr (std CSE,Aero)	250

Deduct:

Option	Value
Manual trans	325

1996 — WS / Ret

900 FWD/2.3L-I4 (150hp)

Model	WS	Ret
S 4dr Hbk	6875	8775
S 2dr Cnv	10075	12200
S 2dr Hbk	6700	8575
SE (6cyl) 4dr Hbk	9150	11200
SE Turbo 2dr Cnv	12725	15025
SE (6cyl) 2dr Cnv	12425	14700
SE Turbo 2dr Hbk	8875	10925

Add:

Option	Value
Dual child seats	25
Alloy wheels (S)	75
Leather seats (S Cpe,Hbk)	150
Sunroof-power (S)	200

Deduct:

Option	Value
Manual trans	275

9000 FWD/2.3L-I4 (170hp)

Model	WS	Ret
Aero 4dr Hbk	12600	14900
CS 4dr Hbk	8650	10675
CSE (6cyl) 4dr Hbk	11600	13825
CSE 4dr Hbk	11400	13625

Add:

Option	Value
2.3L HO Turbo	175
3.0L 24V V6	300
Leather seats (CD,CS)	150
Sunroof-power (CD,CS)	200

Deduct:

Option	Value
Manual trans	275

1995 — WS / Ret

900 FWD/2.3L-I4 (150hp)

Model	WS	Ret
S 4dr Hbk	6175	8025
S 2dr Cnv	8600	10625
S 2dr Hbk	6025	7875
SE (6cyl) 4dr Hbk	8025	10000
SE Turbo 2dr Hbk	8150	10125
Turbo 2dr Cnv	10650	12800

Add:

Option	Value
2.5L 24V V6 (S Cnv)	200
Alloy wheels (S)	75
Leather seats (S Hbk)	150
Sunroof-power (S)	175

Deduct:

Option	Value
Manual trans	250

9000 FWD/2.3L-I4 (170hp)

Model	WS	Ret
Aero 4dr Hbk	10575	12725
CDE (6cyl) 4dr Sdn	9525	11600
CS 4dr Hbk	7275	9200
CSE (6cyl) 4dr Hbk	9675	11775
CSE 4dr Hbk	9575	11650

Add:

Option	Value
2.3L HO Turbo	150
3.0L 24V V6	300
Leather seats (CD,CS)	150
Sunroof-power (CD,CS)	200

Deduct:

Option	Value
Manual trans	250

1994 — WS / Ret

900 FWD/2.0L-I4 (150hp)

Model	WS	Ret
S 4dr Hbk	4700	6425
S 2dr Cnv	6800	8700
S 2dr Hbk	4525	6225
SE (6cyl) 4dr Hbk	6200	8050
SE Turbo 2dr Hbk	6150	8000
Turbo 2dr Cnv	8175	10175

Add:

Option	Value
2.5L 24V V6 (S Hbk)	125
Leather seats (S Hbk)	125
Sunroof-power (S)	175

Deduct:
Manual trans 225

9000 FWD/2.3L-I4 (146hp)

Model	WS	Ret
Aero Turbo 4dr Hbk	9300	11375
CDE Turbo 4dr Sdn	8025	10000
CS 4dr Hbk	6075	7925
CS Turbo 4dr Hbk	7400	9325
CSE 4dr Hbk	7025	8925
CSE Turbo 4dr Hbk	8150	10125

Add:
Leather seats (CD,CS) 125
Sunroof-power (CD,CS) 175

Deduct:
Manual trans 225

1993 WS Ret

900 FWD/2.1L-I4 (140hp)

Model	WS	Ret
S 4dr Sdn	3900	5500
S 2dr Cnv	5525	7250
S 2dr Hbk	3825	5425
Turbo 2dr Cnv	6550	8350
Turbo 2dr Hbk	5275	7000

Add:
Alloy wheels (S Hbk,Sdn) 25
Cruise ctrl (S Hbk,Sdn) 25
Leather seats 100
Sunroof-power (std Turbo) . . . 150

Deduct:
Manual trans 200

9000 FWD/2.3L-I4 (150hp)

Model	WS	Ret
Aero 4dr Hbk	6475	8275
CD Turbo 4dr Sdn	5200	6900
CD 4dr Sdn	4575	6225
CDE Turbo 4dr Sdn	5100	6800
CDE 4dr Sdn	4550	6200
CS 4dr Hbk	4725	6375
CS Turbo 4dr Hbk	5475	7200
CSE 4dr Hbk	5475	7200
CSE Turbo 4dr Hbk	6225	8000

Add:
Leather seats (CD,CS) 100
Sunroof-power (CD,CS) 150

Deduct:
Manual trans 200

1992 WS Ret

900 FWD/2.1L-I4 (140hp)

Model	WS	Ret
Base 4dr Sdn	3075	4525
Base 2dr Hbk	3000	4425
S 4dr Sdn	3475	4950
S 2dr Cnv	4875	6550
S 2dr Hbk	3375	4850
Turbo 2dr Cnv	5825	7575
Turbo 2dr Hbk	4650	6300

Deduct:
Manual trans 175

9000 FWD/2.3L-I4 (150hp)

Model	WS	Ret
Base 4dr Hbk	3875	5475
CD 4dr Sdn	4150	5775
S 4dr Hbk	4300	5925
Turbo 4dr Hbk	4875	6550
Turbo CD 4dr Sdn	4600	6250

Deduct:
Manual trans 200

1991 WS Ret

900 FWD/2.1L-I4 (140hp)

Model	WS	Ret
Base 4dr Sdn	2625	4000
Base 2dr Hbk	2575	3950
S 4dr Sdn	2900	4325
S 2dr Hbk	2825	4225
SPG (5sp) 2dr Hbk	3675	5175
Turbo 2dr Cnv	5400	7125
Turbo 2dr Hbk	3525	5000

Deduct:
Manual trans 150

9000 FWD/2.3L-I4 (150hp)

Model	WS	Ret
Base 4dr Hbk	3425	4900
CD 4dr Sdn	3675	5175
S 4dr Hbk	3725	5325
Turbo 4dr Hbk	4475	6125
Turbo CD 4dr Sdn	4425	6075

Deduct:
Manual trans 175

1990 WS Ret

900 FWD/2.0L-I4 (128hp)

Model	WS	Ret
Base 4dr Sdn	2150	3275
Base 2dr Hbk	2125	3250
S 4dr Sdn	2450	3825
S 2dr Hbk	2400	3775
SPG (5sp) 2dr Hbk	3025	4450
Turbo 4dr Sdn	2950	4375
Turbo 2dr Cnv	4750	6400
Turbo 2dr Hbk	2950	4375

Deduct:
Manual trans 125

9000 FWD/2.0L-I4 (130hp)

Model	WS	Ret
S 4dr Hbk	3150	4600
S 4dr Sdn	3100	4550
Turbo 4dr Hbk	3775	5375
Turbo CD 4dr Sdn	3725	5325

Add:
Lthr seats (std Turbo) 50
Sunroof-pwr (std Turbo) 100

Deduct:
Manual trans 150

1989 WS Ret

900 FWD/2.0L-I4 (128hp)

Model	WS	Ret
Base 4dr Sdn	1550	2500
Base 2dr Hbk	1550	2500
S 4dr Sdn	1750	2850
S 2dr Hbk	1750	2850
SPG (5sp) 2dr Hbk	2375	3775
Turbo 4dr Sdn	2325	3725
Turbo 2dr Cnv	3800	5450
Turbo 2dr Hbk	2325	3725

Add:
Leather seats 25

Deduct:
Manual trans 100

9000 FWD/2.0L-I4 (130hp)

Model	WS	Ret
S 4dr Hbk	2250	3425
Turbo 4dr Hbk	2650	4075
Turbo CD 4dr Sdn	2675	4100

Add:
Leather seats (S only) 25

Deduct:
Manual trans 125

1988 WS Ret

900 FWD/2.0L-I4 (110hp)

Model	WS	Ret
Base 4dr Sdn	1050	1950
Base 2dr Hbk	1000	1700
S 4dr Sdn	1200	2100
S 2dr Hbk	1175	2075
Turbo 2dr Cnv	2875	4275
Turbo 2dr Hbk	1675	2725

Add:
Leather seats 25
SPG pkg 150

Deduct:
Manual trans 75

9000 FWD/2.0L-I4 (125hp)

Model	WS	Ret
S 4dr Hbk	1200	2100
Turbo 4dr Hbk	1375	2300

Add:
Leather seats (S only) 25

Deduct:
Manual trans 75

SATURN

2001 WS Ret

L-SERIES FWD/

Model	WS	Ret
LS 4dr Sdn		
LS1 4dr Sdn		
LS2 4dr Sdn		
LW1 4dr Wgn		
LW2 4dr wgn		

SC1 FWD/1.9L-I4 (100hp)

Model	WS	Ret
Coupe 3dr Cpe	8000	9875

SC2 FWD/1.9L-I4 (124hp)

Model	WS	Ret
Coupe 3dr Cpe	9250	11200

Add:
ABS brakes 300
Alloy wheels 200
Cruise ctrl 200
Leather seats 325
Premium sound 100
Pwr dr locks 200
Pwr windows 175
Moonroof-pwr 450

Deduct:
No air cond 725
Manual trans 625
No cassette 200

SL FWD/1.9L-I4 (100hp)

Model	WS	Ret
Sedan (5sp) 4dr Sdn	6275	8050

SL1 FWD/1.9L-I4 (100hp)

Model	WS	Ret
Sedan 4dr Sdn	7175	9100

SL2 FWD/1.9L-I4 (124hp)

Model	WS	Ret
Touring 4dr Sdn	8525	10550

SW2 FWD/1.9L-I4 (124hp)

Model	WS	Ret
Wagon 4dr Wgn		

Add:
ABS brakes 300
Alloy wheels 175
Cassette (std SWP) 200
CD player 200
Cruise ctrl 200
Leather seats 325
Premium sound 100
Pwr dr locks 200
Pwr windows 175
Sunroof-pwr 450

Deduct:
No air cond 725
Manual trans 625

2000 WS Ret

L-SERIES FWD/

Model	WS	Ret
LS 4dr Sdn	8175	10075
LS1 4dr Sdn	9025	10975
LS2 4dr Sdn	10425	12450

LW1 4dr Wgn 9700 11675
LW2 4dr wgn 11100 13150

Add:
ABS brakes 250
Pwr seat 150
Cassette 150
CD player 175
Lthr seats 300
Moonroof-pwr 325
Premium sound 75

SC1 FWD/1.9L-I4 (100hp)

Coupe 3dr Cpe 6950 8775

SC2 FWD/1.9L-I4 (124hp)

Coupe 3dr Cpe 8150 10025

Add:
ABS brakes 250
Alloy wheels 175
CD player 175
Cruise ctrl 150
Leather seats 250
Premium sound 75
Pwr dr locks 150
Pwr windows 150
Moonroof-pwr 350

Deduct:
No air cond 550
Manual trans 475
No cassette 150

SL FWD/1.9L-I4 (100hp)

Sedan (5sp) 4dr Sdn 5225 6950

SL1 FWD/1.9L-I4 (100hp)

Sedan 4dr Sdn 6100 7950

SL2 FWD/1.9L-I4 (124hp)

Touring 4dr Sdn 7475 9425

SW1 FWD/1.9L-I4 (100hp)

Wagon 4dr Wgn 6825 8725

SW2 FWD/1.9L-I4 (124hp)

Wagon 4dr Wgn 8000 9975

Add:
ABS brakes 250
Alloy wheels 150
Cassette (std SWP) 150
CD player 175
Cruise ctrl 150
Leather seats 250
Premium sound 75
Pwr dr locks 150
Pwr windows 150
Sunroof-pwr 350

Deduct:
No air cond 550
Manual trans 475

1999 WS Ret

SC1 FWD/1.9L-I4 (100hp)

Coupe 3dr Cpe 7050 8875
Coupe 2dr Cpe 6775 8575

SC2 FWD/1.9L-I4 (124hp)

Coupe 3dr Cpe 8350 10250
Coupe 2dr Cpe 8100 9975

Add:
ABS brakes 200
Alloy wheels 125
CD player 125
Cruise ctrl 125
Leather seats 225
Premium sound 50
Pwr dr locks 125
Pwr windows 100
Moonroof-pwr 275

Deduct:
No air cond 450
Manual trans 400
No cassette 125

SL FWD/1.9L-I4 (100hp)

Sedan (5sp) 4dr Sdn 5125 6825

SL1 FWD/1.9L-I4 (100hp)

Sedan 4dr Sdn 5950 7700

SL2 FWD/1.9L-I4 (124hp)

Touring 4dr Sdn 7200 9025

SW1 FWD/1.9L-I4 (100hp)

Wagon 4dr Wgn 6600 8400

SW2 FWD/1.9L-I4 (124hp)

Wagon 4dr Wgn 7700 9550

Add:
ABS brakes 200
Alloy wheels 100
Cassette (std SWP) 125
CD player 125
Cruise ctrl 125
Leather seats 225
Premium sound 50
Pwr dr locks 125
Pwr windows 100
Sunroof-pwr 300

Deduct:
No air cond 450
Manual trans 400

1998 WS Ret

SC1 FWD/1.9L-I4 (100hp)

Coupe 2dr Cpe 5950 7700

SC2 FWD/1.9L-I4 (124hp)

Coupe 2dr Cpe 7100 8925

SL FWD/1.9L-I4 (100hp)

Sedan (5sp) 4dr Sdn 4675 6325

SL1 FWD/1.9L-I4 (100hp)

Sedan 4dr Sdn 5375 7100

SL2 FWD/1.9L-I4 (124hp)

SW1 FWD/1.9L-I4 (100hp)

Wagon 4dr Wgn 5900 7650

SW2 FWD/1.9L-I4 (124hp)

Wagon 4dr Wgn 6875 8675

Add:
ABS brakes 150
Alloy wheels 75
Cassette 75
CD player 100
Cruise ctrl 75
Leather seats 175
Premium sound 25
Pwr dr locks 75
Pwr windows 75
Sunroof-pwr 250

Deduct:
No air cond 375
Manual trans 325

1997 WS Ret

SC1 FWD/1.9L-I4 (100hp)

Coupe 2dr Cpe 4950 6650

SC2 FWD/1.9L-I4 (124hp)

Coupe 2dr Cpe 6000 7750

Add:
ABS brakes 125
CD player 75
Cruise ctrl 50
Leather seats 150
Premium sound 25
Pwr dr locks 50
Pwr windows 50
Moonroof-pwr 200

Deduct:
No air cond 325
Manual trans 275
No cassette 50

SL FWD/1.9L-I4 (100hp)

Sedan (5sp) 4dr Sdn 3950 5550

SL1 FWD/1.9L-I4 (100hp)

Sedan 4dr Sdn 4525 6175

SL2 FWD/1.9L-I4 (124hp)

Touring 4dr Sdn 5525 7250

SW1 FWD/1.9L-I4 (100hp)

Wagon 4dr Wgn 5075 6775

SW2 FWD/1.9L-I4 (124hp)

Wagon 4dr Wgn 5925 7675

Add:
ABS brakes 125
Cassette 50
CD player 75
Cruise ctrl 50
Leather seats 150
Premium sound 25
Pwr dr locks 50
Pwr windows 50
Sunroof-pwr 200

Deduct:
No air cond 325
Manual trans 275

1996 WS Ret

SC1 FWD/1.9L-I4 (100hp)

Coupe 2dr Cpe 3850 5450

SC2 FWD/1.9L-I4 (124hp)

Coupe 2dr Cpe 4725 6375

Add:
ABS brakes 125
CD player 50
Cruise ctrl 25
Leather seats 125
Premium sound 25
Pwr dr locks 25
Pwr windows 50
Sunroof-pwr 175

Deduct:
No air cond 250
Manual trans 225
No cassette 25

SL FWD/1.9L-I4 (100hp)

Sedan (5sp) 4dr Sdn 2925 4350

SL1 FWD/1.9L-I4 (100hp)

Sedan 4dr Sdn 3475 4950

SL2 FWD/1.9L-I4 (124hp)

Touring 4dr Sdn 4350 5975

SW1 FWD/1.9L-I4 (100hp)

Wagon 4dr Wgn 3950 5550

SW2 FWD/1.9L-I4 (124hp)

Wagon 4dr Wgn 4650 6300

Add:
ABS brakes 125
Cassette 25
CD player 50
Cruise ctrl 25
Leather seats 125
Premium sound 25
Pwr dr locks 25
Pwr windows 50

Sunroof-pwr 175

Deduct:
No air cond 250
Manual trans 225

1995 WS Ret

SC1 FWD/1.9L-I4 (100hp)
Coupe 2dr Cpe 3300 4775

SC2 FWD/1.9L-I4 (124hp)
Coupe 2dr Cpe 4150 5775

Add:
ABS brakes 125
Cassette 25
CD player 50
Cruise ctrl 25
Leather seats 100
Premium sound 25
Pwr dr locks 25
Pwr windows 25
Sunroof-pwr 150

Deduct:
No air cond 225
Manual trans 200

SL FWD/1.9L-I4 (100hp)
Sedan (5sp) 4dr Sdn 2525 3900

SL1 FWD/1.9L-I4 (100hp)
Sedan 4dr Sdn 3025 4450

SL2 FWD/1.9L-I4 (124hp)
Touring 4dr Sdn 3800 5400

SW1 FWD/1.9L-I4 (100hp)
Wagon 4dr Wgn 3400 4875

SW2 FWD/1.9L-I4 (124hp)
Wagon 4dr Wgn 4100 5725

Add:
ABS brakes 125
Cassette 25
CD player 50
Cruise ctrl 25
Leather seats 100
Premium sound 25
Pwr dr locks 25
Pwr windows 25
Sunroof-pwr 150

Deduct:
No air cond 225
Manual trans 200

1994 WS Ret

SC1 FWD/1.9L-I4 (85hp)
Coupe 2dr Cpe 2850 4250

SC2 FWD/1.9L-I4 (124hp)
Coupe 2dr Cpe 3575 5050

Add:
ABS brakes 100
Cassette 25
CD player 25
Cruise ctrl 25
Leather seats 75
Pwr dr locks 25
Pwr windows 25
Sunroof-pwr 125

Deduct:
No air cond 225
Manual trans 175

SL FWD/1.9L-I4 (85hp)
Sedan (5sp) 4dr Sdn 2200 3325

SL1 FWD/1.9L-I4 (85hp)
Sedan 4dr Sdn 2600 3975

SL2 FWD/1.9L-I4 (124hp)
Touring 4dr Sdn 3275 4750

SW1 FWD/1.9L-I4 (85hp)
Wagon 4dr Wgn 2975 4400

SW2 FWD/1.9L-I4 (124hp)
Wagon 4dr Wgn 3550 5025

Add:
ABS brakes 100
Cassette 25
CD player 25
Cruise ctrl 25
Leather seats 75
Pwr dr locks 25
Pwr windows 25
Sunroof-pwr 125

Deduct:
No air cond 225
Manual trans 175

1993 WS Ret

SC1 FWD/1.9L-I4 (85hp)
Coupe 2dr Cpe 2350 3700

SC2 FWD/1.9L-I4 (124hp)
Coupe 2dr Cpe 2925 4350

Add:
ABS brakes 75
Cassette 25
CD player 25
Cruise ctrl 25
Leather seats 75
Pwr dr locks 25
Pwr windows 25
Sunroof-pwr 125

Deduct:
No air cond 175
Manual trans 175

SL FWD/1.9L-I4 (85hp)
Sedan (5sp) 4dr Sdn 1775 2850

SL1 FWD/1.9L-I4 (85hp)
Sedan 4dr Sdn 2100 3225

SL2 FWD/1.9L-I4 (124hp)
Touring 4dr Sdn 2650 4050

SW1 FWD/1.9L-I4 (85hp)
Wagon 4dr Wgn 2425 3800

SW2 FWD/1.9L-I4 (124hp)
Wagon 4dr Wgn 2875 4275

Add:
ABS brakes 75
Cassette 25
CD player 25
Cruise ctrl 25
Leather seats 75
Pwr dr locks 25
Pwr windows 25
Sunroof-pwr 125

Deduct:
No air cond 175
Manual trans 175

1992 WS Ret

SC FWD/1.9L-I4 (85hp)
Coupe 2dr Cpe 2075 3200

Add:
ABS brakes 50
Air bag-driver 50
CD player 25
Cruise ctrl 25
Leather seats 50
Pwr dr locks 25
Pwr windows 25
Sunroof-pwr 100

Deduct:
No air cond 175
Manual trans 150

SL FWD/1.9L-I4 (85hp)
Sedan (5sp) 4dr Sdn 1275 2175

SL1 FWD/1.9L-I4 (85hp)
Sedan 4dr Sdn 1550 2475

SL2 FWD/1.9L-I4 (124hp)
Touring 4dr Sdn 1875 2975

Add:
ABS brakes 50
Air bag-driver 50
CD player 25
Cruise ctrl 25
Leather seats 50
Pwr dr locks 25
Pwr windows 25
Sunroof-pwr 100

Deduct:
No air cond 175
Manual trans 150

1991 WS Ret

SC FWD/1.9L-I4 (85hp)
Coupe 2dr Cpe 1775 2850

Add:
ABS brakes 50
CD player 25
Pwr windows 25
Sunroof-pwr 75

Deduct:
No air cond 150
Manual trans 125

SL FWD/1.9L-I4 (85hp)
Sedan (5sp) 4dr Sdn 1100 2000

SL1 FWD/1.9L-I4 (85hp)
Sedan 4dr Sdn 1300 2200

SL2 FWD/1.9L-I4 (123hp)
Touring 4dr Sdn 1600 2650

Add:
ABS brakes 50
CD player 25
Pwr windows 25
Sunroof-pwr 75

Deduct:
No air cond 150
Manual trans 125

STERLING

1991 WS Ret

827 FWD/2.7L-V6 (160hp)
Si 4dr Sdn 2525 3900
SL 4dr Sdn 2700 4100
SLi 4dr Sdn 2800 4200

Deduct:
Manual trans 175

1990 WS Ret

827 FWD/2.7L-V6 (160hp)
S 4dr Sdn 2100 3225
Si 4dr Sdn 2325 3675
SL 4dr Sdn 2425 3800
SLi 4dr Sdn 2550 3925

Add:
ABS brakes (S only) 25

	WS	Ret
Leather seats (S only)	50	
Deduct:		
Manual trans	150	

1989 — WS Ret

827 FWD/2.7L-V6 (161hp)

	WS	Ret
S 4dr Sdn	1575	2625
SL 4dr Sdn	1675	2725
SLi 4dr Sdn	1750	2825
Add:		
ABS brakes (S only)	25	
Leather seats (S only)	25	
Deduct:		
Manual trans	125	

1988 — WS Ret

825 FWD/2.5L-V6 (151hp)

	WS	Ret
S 4dr Sdn	1200	2100
SL 4dr Sdn	1275	2175
Add:		
ABS brakes (std SL)	25	
Leather seats (std SL)	25	
Deduct:		
Manual trans	75	

SUBARU

2001 — WS Ret

FORRESTER AWD/2.5L-H4 (165hp)

	WS	Ret
L 4dr Wgn		
S 4dr Wgn		

IMPREZA AWD/2.2L-H4 (142hp)

	WS	Ret
2.5 RS 2dr Cpe		
L 4dr Sdn		
L 4dr Wgn		
L 2dr Cpe		
Outback 4dr Wgn		

LEGACY AWD/2.5L-H4 (165hp)

	WS	Ret
GT 4dr Sdn		
GT Ltd 4dr Sdn		
GT 4dr Wgn		
L 4dr Sdn		
L 4dr Wgn		

OUTBACK AWD/2.5L-H4 (165hp)

	WS	Ret
Base 4dr Wgn		
LL bean (3.0L-H6/21 4dr Wgn		
Outback Ltd 4dr Sdn		
Outback Ltd 4dr Wgn		
VDC (3.0L H6/212hp) 4dr Sdn		

2000 — WS Ret

FORRESTER AWD/2.5L-H4 (165hp)

	WS	Ret
L 4dr Wgn	13700	15925
S 4dr Wgn	15075	17375
Add:		
Outdoor pkg (incls brush guard)	325	
Alloy wheels (std S)	175	
CD player	175	
CD changer	300	
Premium sound	125	

IMPREZA AWD/2.2L-H4 (142hp)

	WS	Ret
2.5 RS 2dr Cpe		
L 4dr Sdn	10575	12600
L 4dr Wgn	11375	13450
L 2dr Cpe	10375	12400
Outback 4dr Wgn	12700	14850
Add:		
ABS brakes (L)	250	
CD player	175	
CD changer	275	
Premium sound	125	
Cruise ctrl (L)	150	
Luggage rack (L)	125	
Wheels-alloy (std RS)	175	
Deduct:		
Manual trans	525	

LEGACY AWD/2.5L-H4 (165hp)

	WS	Ret
Brighton 4dr Wgn	11925	14025
GT 4dr Sdn	13750	15975
GT Ltd 4dr Sdn	14700	16975
GT 4dr Wgn	15050	17350
L 4dr Sdn	12075	14200
L 4dr Wgn	13025	15200
Alloy wheels (Brighton,L)	175	
Premium audio (std GT Ltd)	125	
CD player (std Gt Ltd)	175	
CD changer	300	
Cruise ctrl (Brighton)	150	
Moonroof-pwr (std GT)	375	
Moonroof-dual	525	
Lthr seats (std GT Ltd)	350	
Deduct:		
Manual trans	575	

OUTBACK AWD/2.5L-H4 (165hp)

	WS	Ret
Outback Ltd 4dr Sdn	16400	18775
Outback 4dr Wgn	15350	17675
Outback Ltd 4dr Wgn	17450	19900
Add:		
CD player	175	
Premium sound	125	
Deduct:		
Manual trans	575	

1999 — WS Ret

FORRESTER AWD/2.5L-H4 (165hp)

	WS	Ret
Base (5sp) 4dr Wgn	11725	13825
L 4dr Wgn	13100	15275
S 4dr Wgn	14075	16325
Add:		
ABS brakes (Base)	225	
Alloy wheels (std S)	125	
CD player	125	
CD changer	250	
Cruise ctrl (std S)	125	

IMPREZA AWD/2.2L-H4 (142hp)

	WS	Ret
2.5 RS 2dr Cpe	1	1
L 4dr Sdn	9225	11175
L 4dr Wgn	9925	11925
L 2dr Cpe	9050	11000
Outback 4dr Wgn	11200	13275
Add:		
ABS brakes (L)	225	
CD player	125	
CD changer	225	
Premium audio	100	
Cruise ctrl	125	
Luggage rack (L)	100	
Wheels-alloy (std RS)	150	
Deduct:		
No air cond	500	
Manual trans	450	

LEGACY AWD/2.5L-H4 (165hp)

	WS	Ret
Brighton (2.2L/142h 4dr Wgn	11600	13700
GT 4dr Sdn	13250	15450
GT Ltd 4dr Sdn	14125	16375
GT 4dr Wgn	14450	16700
L (2.2L/142hp) 4dr Sdn	11725	13825
L (2.2L/142hp) 4dr Wgn	12600	14750
Outback 4dr Wgn	15100	17400
Outback Ltd 4dr Wgn	16050	18400
Sport Util 4dr Sdn	14100	16350
Sport Util Ltd 4dr Sdn	15000	17300
Add:		
ABS brakes (Brighton)	225	
Alloy wheels (Brighton,L)	125	
Premium audio	100	
CD player (std Ltd)	125	
CD changer	250	
Cruise ctrl (Brighton)	125	
Moonroof-pwr (L)	300	
Moonroof-dual (Outbk Ltd)	425	
Lthr seats	300	
Deduct:		
No air cond	525	
Manual trans	475	

1998 — WS Ret

FORRESTER AWD/2.5L-F4 (165hp)

	WS	Ret
Base (5sp) 4dr Wgn	10350	12375
L 4dr Wgn	11050	13100
S 4dr Wgn	12425	14575
Add:		
ABS brakes (Base)	175	
Alloy wheels (std S)	100	
CD player	100	
CD changer	200	
Cruise ctrl (std S)	75	

IMPREZA AWD/2.4L-F4 (165hp)

	WS	Ret
L 4dr Sdn	7450	9300
L 4dr Wgn	8025	9900
L 2dr Cpe	7300	9125
Outback 4dr Wgn	9125	11075
RS 2dr Cpe	9550	11525
Add:		
ABS brakes (std Outback,RS)	175	
CD player	100	
CD changer	200	
Cruise ctrl	75	
Wheels-alloy (std RS)	100	
Deduct:		
No air cond	425	
Manual trans	375	

LEGACY AWD/2.5L-F4 (165hp)

	WS	Ret
Brighton (2.2L/142h 4dr Wgn	9125	11075
GT 4dr Sdn	10575	12600
GT Ltd 4dr Sdn	11275	13350
GT 4dr Wgn	11550	13650
L (2.2L/142hp) 4dr Sdn	9250	11200
L (2.2L/142hp) 4dr Wgn	10025	12025
Outback Ltd 4dr Wgn	12825	15000
Outback 4dr Wgn	12075	14200
Add:		
ABS brakes (Brighton)	175	
Alloy wheels (Brighton,L)	100	
CD player (std Ltd)	100	
CD changer	200	
Cruise ctrl (Brighton)	75	
Moonroof-dual (Outback Ltd)	350	
Deduct:		
No air cond	450	
Manual trans	375	

1997 — WS Ret

IMPREZA AWD/1.8L-F4 (115hp)

	WS	Ret
Brighton (5sp) 2dr Cpe	4875	6550
L 4dr Sdn	6350	8125
L 4dr Wgn	6875	8675
L 2dr Cpe	6200	7975
Outback 4dr Wgn	7875	9750
Add:		
ABS brakes (std Outback)	150	
CD player	75	
CD changer	150	
Cruise ctrl	50	

- Pwr dr locks (Brighton) . . . 25
- Pwr windows (Brighton) . . . 50
- Wheels-alloy . . . 75

Deduct:
- No air cond . . . 350
- Manual trans . . . 300

LEGACY — AWD/2.5L-F4 (165hp)

Model	WS	Ret
Brighton (2.2L/137h 4dr Wgn	7525	9375
GT 4dr Sdn	8850	10775
GT 4dr Wgn	9750	11725
L (2.2L/137hp) 4dr Sdn	7675	9525
L (2.2L/137hp) 4dr Wgn	8275	10175
LSi 4dr Sdn	9725	11700
LSi 4dr Wgn	10325	12350
Outback 4dr Wgn	9975	11975
Outback Ltd 4dr Wgn	10400	12425

Add:
- ABS brakes (Brighton) . . . 150
- Alloy wheels (Brighton,L) . . . 75
- CD player . . . 75
- CD changer . . . 175
- Cruise ctrl (Brighton) . . . 50

Deduct:
- No air cond . . . 375
- Manual trans . . . 325

SVX — AWD/3.3L-F6 (230hp)

Model	WS	Ret
L 2dr Cpe	10475	12500
LSi 2dr Cpe	14000	16225

Add:
- CD changer (std LSi) . . . 175

1996 — WS Ret

IMPREZA — AWD/2.2L-F4 (135hp)

Model	WS	Ret
Brighton (5sp) 2dr Cpe	3500	4975
L 4dr Sdn	4750	6400
L 4dr Wgn	5250	6975
L 2dr Cpe	4625	6275
LX 4dr Sdn	5400	7125
LX 4dr Wgn	5900	7650
LX 2dr Cpe	5275	7000
Outback 4dr Wgn	6100	7875

Add:
- ABS brakes (L) . . . 125
- CD player . . . 50
- CD changer . . . 125
- Cruise ctrl . . . 25
- Pwr dr locks (Brighton) . . . 25
- Pwr windows (std LX) . . . 25
- Wheels-alloy (std LX cpe) . . . 50

Deduct:
- No air cond . . . 300
- Man trans (not Base) . . . 250

LEGACY — AWD/2.2L-F4 (135hp)

Model	WS	Ret
Brighton 4dr Wgn	5775	7525
L 4dr Sdn	5900	7650
L 4dr Wgn	6450	8225
LS 4dr Sdn	7050	8875
LS 4dr Wgn	7625	9475
LSi 4dr Sdn	7850	9725
LSi 4dr Wgn	8400	10300
Outback 4dr Wgn	8175	10075

Add:
- ABS brakes (L) . . . 150
- Alloy wheels . . . 50
- CD player . . . 50
- CD changer . . . 150
- Cruise ctrl (Brighton,L) . . . 25

Deduct:
- No air cond . . . 300
- Manual trans . . . 275
- Front-wheel drive (L) . . . 425

SVX — AWD/3.3L-F6 (230hp)

Model	WS	Ret
L 2dr Cpe	7500	9350
LSi 2dr Cpe	10625	12650

Add:
- CD changer (std LSi) . . . 150

1995 — WS Ret

IMPREZA — FWD/1.8L-F4 (110hp)

Model	WS	Ret
Base (5sp) 4dr Sdn	2300	3450
Base (5sp) 2dr Cpe	2200	3325
L 4dr Sdn	3275	4750
L 2dr Cpe	3150	4600
L (AWD) 4dr Wgn	3975	5600
LX (AWD) 4dr Sdn	4600	6250
LX (AWD) 4dr Wgn	4900	6575
LX (AWD) 2dr Sdn	4500	6150
Outback (AWD) 4dr Wgn	4775	6425

Add:
- ABS brakes (L) . . . 125
- All-wheel drive (L) . . . 325
- Cassette (std LX) . . . 25
- Pwr dr locks (std LX) . . . 25
- Pwr windows (std LX) . . . 25
- Sunroof-pwr (std LX) . . . 150

Deduct:
- No air cond . . . 250
- Man trans (not Base) . . . 225

LEGACY — AWD/2.2L-F4 (135hp)

Model	WS	Ret
Base (FWD-5sp) 4dr Sdn	3975	5600
Brighton 4dr Wgn	5400	7125
L 4dr Sdn	4625	6275
L 4dr Wgn	5150	6850
LS 4dr Sdn	5900	7650
LS 4dr Wgn	6475	8275
LSi 4dr Sdn	6050	7800
LSi 4dr Wgn	6600	8400
Outback 4dr Wgn	6375	8150

Add:
- ABS brakes (L) . . . 125
- Alloy wheels . . . 50
- Cassette (Base) . . . 25
- CD player . . . 50
- Cruise ctrl (Base,L) . . . 25
- CD Changer . . . 125

Deduct:
- No air cond . . . 275
- Manual trans . . . 250
- FWD (L) . . . 350

SVX — FWD/3.3L-F6 (230hp)

Model	WS	Ret
L 2dr Cpe	5150	6850
L (AWD) 2dr Cpe	5875	7625
LSi (AWD) 2dr Cpe	7950	9825

Add:
- CD player (std LSi) . . . 75

1994 — WS Ret

IMPREZA — FWD/1.8L-F4 (110hp)

Model	WS	Ret
Base (5spd) 4dr Sdn	1925	3025
L 4dr Sdn	2625	4000
L 4dr Wgn	2775	4175
LS (AWD) 4dr Sdn	3925	5525
LS (AWD) 4dr Wgn	4200	5825

Add:
- Air bag-psngr (std LS) . . . 50
- ABS brakes (L) . . . 100
- All-wheel drive (L) . . . 300
- Cassette . . . 25
- Pwr dr locks (std LS) . . . 25
- Pwr windows (std LS) . . . 25
- Sunroof-pwr (std LS) . . . 125

Deduct:
- No air cond . . . 250
- Man trans (not Base) . . . 200

JUSTY — FWD/1.2L-I3 (73hp)

Model	WS	Ret
DL (5sp) 2dr Hbk	1000	1700
GL (AWD-5sp) 4dr Hbk	1625	2675

Add:
- Cassette . . . 25

Deduct:
- No air cond . . . 200

LEGACY — FWD/2.2L-F4 (130hp)

Model	WS	Ret
L 4dr Sdn	3600	5075
L 4dr Wgn	3975	5600
LS 4dr Sdn	4700	6350
LS 4dr Wgn	5150	6850
LSi (AWD) 4dr Sdn	4975	6675
LSi (AWD) 4dr Wgn	5400	7125
Spt Turbo (AWD) 4dr Sdn	5075	6775
Touring (AWD) 4dr Wgn	5550	7275

Add:
- 4-wheel drive (L,LS) . . . 275
- ABS brakes (L) . . . 125
- Alloy wheels . . . 25
- Cassette (L) . . . 25
- CD player . . . 25
- Cruise ctrl . . . 25
- Premium sound . . . 25

Deduct:
- No air cond . . . 250
- Manual trans . . . 225

LOYALE — AWD/1.8L-F4 (90hp)

Model	WS	Ret
Wagon 4dr Wgn	3100	4550

Add:
- Cassette . . . 25
- Cruise ctrl . . . 25

Deduct:
- Manual trans . . . 200

SVX — FWD/3.3L-F6 (230hp)

Model	WS	Ret
L 2dr Cpe	4350	5975
LS 2dr Cpe	5125	6825
LSi (AWD) 2dr Cpe	6950	8775

Add:
- CD player (std LSi) . . . 50

1993 — WS Ret

JUSTY — FWD/1.2L-I3 (73hp)

Model	WS	Ret
Base (5sp) 2dr Hbk	650	1150
GL (Auto,AWD) 4dr Hbk	1200	2100
GL (Auto) 2dr Hbk	950	1650

Add:
- 4-wheel drive (2dr) . . . 150
- Automatic trans (Base only) . . . 175
- Cassette . . . 25

Deduct:
- No air cond . . . 175

LEGACY — FWD/2.2L-F4 (130hp)

Model	WS	Ret
L 4dr Sdn	1850	2925
L 4dr Wgn	2175	3300
LS 4dr Sdn	2700	4100
LS 4dr Wgn	3050	4500
LSi 4dr Sdn	3175	4625
LSi 4dr Wgn	3525	5000
Spt Turbo AWD 4dr Sdn	3375	4850

Add:
- 4-wheel drive (std Sport) . . . 225
- ABS brakes (L only) . . . 100

Deduct:
- No air cond . . . 225
- Manual trans . . . 200

LOYALE — FWD/1.8L-F4 (90hp)

Model	WS	Ret
Sedan 4dr Sdn	1600	2650
Wagon 4dr Wgn	1800	2875

Add:
- 4-wheel drive . . . 225

Deduct:
- Manual trans . . . 175

SVX
AWD/3.3L-F6 (230hp)

	WS	Ret
Coupe 2dr Cpe	5350	7075
Add:		
Touring (incls lthr,CD,sunrf)	300	

1992 WS Ret

JUSTY (5sp)
FWD/1.2L-I3 (66hp)

	WS	Ret
DL 2dr Hbk	525	1000
GL (AWD) 4dr Hbk	975	1675
GL 2dr Hbk	750	1275
Add:		
4-wheel drive (2dr)	150	
Automatic trans	150	
Deduct:		
No air cond	150	

LEGACY
FWD/2.2L-F4 (130hp)

	WS	Ret
L 4dr Sdn	1600	2650
L 4dr Wgn	1800	2875
LE Turbo AWD 4dr Wgn	2675	4075
LS 4dr Sdn	2325	3675
LS 4dr Wgn	2625	4000
LSi 4dr Sdn	2700	4100
Spt Turbo AWD 4dr Sdn	2850	4250
Add:		
4-wheel drive (std Sport)	225	
ABS brakes (L only)	50	
Air bag-driver	50	
Cassette (L only)	25	
Pwr dr locks (L only)	25	
Pwr windows (L only)	25	
Deduct:		
No air cond	200	
Manual trans	175	

LOYALE
FWD/1.8L-F4 (90hp)

	WS	Ret
Base 4dr Sdn	1325	2250
Base 4dr Wgn	1500	2425
Add:		
4-wheel drive	225	
Deduct:		
Manual trans	175	

SVX
AWD/3.3L-F6 (230hp)

	WS	Ret
Coupe 2dr Cpe	4325	5950
Add:		
Touring pkg	300	

1991 WS Ret

JUSTY (5sp)
FWD/1.2L-I3 (66hp)

	WS	Ret
DL 2dr Hbk	475	950
GL (AWD) 4dr Hbk	700	1225
GL 2dr Hbk	525	1000
Add:		
4-wheel drive (2dr)	100	
Automatic trans	125	
Deduct:		
No air cond	125	

LEGACY
FWD/2.2L-F4 (130hp)

	WS	Ret
L 4dr Sdn	1500	2425
L 4dr Wgn	1675	2725
LS 4dr Sdn	1925	3025
LS 4dr Wgn	2150	3275
LSi 4dr Sdn	2050	3150
Spt Turbo AWD 4dr Sdn	2425	3800
Add:		
4-wheel drive(std Sport)	175	
ABS brakes (L only)	50	
Cassette (L only)	25	
Cruise ctrl (L only)	25	
Pwr dr locks (L only)	25	
Pwr windows (L only)	25	
Deduct:		
No air cond	175	
Manual trans	175	

LOYALE
FWD/1.8L-F4 (90hp)

	WS	Ret
Base 4dr Sdn	1225	2125
Base 4dr Wgn	1425	2350
Add:		
4-wheel drive	175	
Deduct:		
Manual trans	175	

XT
FWD/1.8L-F4 (97hp)

	WS	Ret
GL 2dr Cpe	1500	2425
XT-6 (6cyl) 2dr Cpe	1900	3000
Add:		
4-wheel drive	175	
Deduct:		
No air cond	175	
Manual trans	150	

1990 WS Ret

JUSTY (5sp)
FWD/1.2L-I3 (66hp)

	WS	Ret
DL 2dr Hbk	375	825
GL (AWD) 4dr Hbk	525	1000
GL 2dr Hbk	425	900
Add:		
4-wheel drive	50	
Automatic trans	75	
Deduct:		
No air cond	100	

LEGACY
FWD/2.2L-F4 (130hp)

	WS	Ret
Base 4dr Sdn	1000	1700
Base 4dr Wgn	1150	2050
L 4dr Sdn	1225	2125
L 4dr Wgn	1425	2350
LS 4dr Sdn	1625	2675
LS 4dr Wgn	1725	2800
Add:		
4-wheel drive	150	
ABS brakes	25	
Deduct:		
No air cond	150	
Manual trans	150	

LOYALE
FWD/1.8L-F4 (115hp)

	WS	Ret
Hatchback 2dr Hbk	950	1650
RS 2dr Hbk	1175	2075
Sedan 4dr Sdn	1000	1700
Wagon 4dr Wgn	1175	2075
Add:		
4-wheel drive	150	
Deduct:		
No air cond	150	
Manual trans	125	

1989 WS Ret

DL
FWD/1.8L-F4 (90hp)

	WS	Ret
Coupe 2dr Cpe	750	1275
Sedan 4dr Sdn	775	1300
Wagon 4dr Wgn	875	1550
Add:		
4-wheel drive	100	
Deduct:		
No air cond	100	
Manual trans	100	

GL
FWD/1.8L-F4 (73hp)

	WS	Ret
Coupe 2dr Cpe	825	1500
Hatchback 2dr Hbk	575	1075
RX Turbo (AWD) 2dr Cpe	3050	4500
Sedan 4dr Sdn	875	1550
Wagon 4dr Wgn	950	1650
Add:		
1.8 Liter turbo	50	
4-wheel drive	100	
Deduct:		
Manual trans	100	

GL-10
FWD/1.8L-F4 (115hp)

	WS	Ret
Sedan 4dr Sdn	900	1600
Wagon 4dr Wgn	975	1675
Add:		
4-wheel drive	100	
Deduct:		
Manual trans	100	

JUSTY (5sp)
FWD/1.2L-I3 (166hp)

	WS	Ret
DL 2dr Hbk	325	775
GL 2dr Hbk	375	825
RS (AWD) 2dr Hbk	425	900
Add:		
4-wheel drive	50	
Automatic trans	25	
Deduct:		
No air cond	75	

XT
FWD/1.8L-F4 (96hp)

	WS	Ret
GL 2dr Cpe	1150	2050
XT-6 (6cyl) 2dr Cpe	1275	2175
Add:		
4-wheel drive	100	
Deduct:		
No air cond	100	
Manual trans	100	

1988 WS Ret

DL
FWD/1.8L-F4 (90hp)

	WS	Ret
Coupe 2dr Cpe	550	1050
Sedan 4dr Sdn	575	1075
Wagon 4dr Wgn	650	1150
Add:		
4-wheel drive	50	
Deduct:		
No air cond	75	
Manual trans	75	

GL
FWD/1.8L-F4 (84hp)

	WS	Ret
Coupe 2dr Cpe	625	1125
Hatchback 2dr Hbk	475	950
RX (5sp) 4dr Sdn	2475	3850
RX (5sp) 2dr Cpe	2450	3825
Sedan 4dr Sdn	700	1225
Wagon 4dr Wgn	750	1275
Add:		
4cyl turbo (std RX)	25	
4-wheel drive (std RX)	50	
Deduct:		
No air cond	75	
Man trans (not RX)	75	

GL-10
FWD/1.8L-F4 (90hp)

	WS	Ret
Sedan 4dr Sdn	700	1225
Wagon 4dr Wgn	750	1275
Add:		
4cyl turbo	25	
4-wheel drive	50	
Deduct:		
Manual trans	75	

JUSTY (5sp)
FWD/1.2L-I3 (66hp)

	WS	Ret
Base 2dr Hbk	250	675
GL 2dr Hbk	300	750
RS 2dr Hbk	325	775
Add:		
4-wheel drive (std RS)	25	
Automatic trans	25	
Deduct:		
No air cond	25	

XT
FWD/1.8L-F4 (96hp)

	WS	Ret
DL (5sp) 2dr Cpe	875	1550

GL 2dr Cpe	950	1650
XT-6 (6cyl) 2dr Cpe	1050	1950

Deduct:
No air cond 100
Manual trans (not DL) 50

SUZUKI

2001 WS Ret

ESTEEM (5sp) FWD/1.8L-I4 (122hp)

	WS	Ret
GL 4dr Sdn	1	1
GL 4dr Wgn	1	1
GLX 4dr Sdn	1	1
GLX 4dr Wgn	1	1

Add:
Auto trans 550

Deduct:
No air cond 650

SWIFT (5sp) FWD/1.3L-I4 (79hp)

	WS	Ret
GA 2dr Hbk	1	1
GL 2dr Hbk	1	1

Add:
Automatic trans 550

Deduct:
No air cond 650

2000 WS Ret

ESTEEM (5sp) FWD/1.8L-I4 (122hp)

	WS	Ret
GL 4dr Sdn	5575	7300
GL Sport 4dr Sdn	5925	7675
GL 4dr Wgn	5750	7500
GLX 4dr Sdn	6350	8125
GLX 4dr Wgn	6525	8325

Add:
Auto trans 425

Deduct:
No air cond 500

SWIFT (5sp) FWD/1.3L-I4 (79hp)

	WS	Ret
GA 2dr Hbk	4425	6075
GL 2dr Hbk	4875	6550

Add:
Automatic trans 425

Deduct:
No air cond 500

1999 WS Ret

ESTEEM (5sp) FWD/1.6L-I4 (95hp)

	WS	Ret
GL 4dr Sdn	4825	6500
GL 4dr Wgn	4975	6675
GLX 4dr Sdn	5525	7250
GLX 4dr Wgn	5675	7425

Add:
Auto trans 350

Deduct:
No air cond 425

SWIFT (5sp) FWD/1.3L-I4 (79hp)

	WS	Ret
Base 2dr Hbk	3400	4875

Add:
Automatic trans 350
Cassette 125
ABS brakes 225

Deduct:
No air cond 425

1998 WS Ret

ESTEEM (5sp) FWD/1.6L-I4 (95hp)

	WS	Ret
GL 4dr Sdn	3675	5175
GL 4dr Wgn	3800	5400
GLX 4dr Sdn	4250	5875
GLX 4dr Wgn	4400	6050

Add:
Auto trans 300

Deduct:
No air cond 350

SWIFT (5sp) FWD/1.3L-I4 (79hp)

	WS	Ret
Base 2dr Hbk	2650	4050

Add:
Automatic trans 300
Cassette 75
ABS brakes 200

Deduct:
No air cond 350

1997 WS Ret

ESTEEM (5sp) FWD/1.6L-I4 (98hp)

	WS	Ret
GL 4dr Sdn	2525	3900
GLX 4dr Sdn	3050	4500

Add:
ABS brakes 125
Auto trans 250
Cruise ctrl 50

Deduct:
No air cond 300

SWIFT (5sp) FWD/

	WS	Ret
Base 2dr Hbk	1675	2725

Add:
Automatic trans 250
Cassette 50
ABS brakes 150

Deduct:
No air cond 300

1996 WS Ret

ESTEEM (5sp) FWD/1.6L-I4 (98hp)

	WS	Ret
GL 4dr Sdn	1850	2925
GLX 4dr Sdn	2300	3450

Add:
Auto trans 200
Cassette 25
ABS brakes 125
Cruise ctrl 25

Deduct:
No air cond 250

SWIFT (5sp) FWD/1.3L-I4 (70hp)

	WS	Ret
Base 2dr Hbk	1425	2350

Add:
Automatic trans 200
Cassette 25
ABS brakes 125

Deduct:
No air cond 250

1995 WS Ret

ESTEEM (5sp) FWD/1.6L-I4 (98hp)

	WS	Ret
GL 4dr Sdn	1525	2450
GLX 4dr Sdn	1900	3000

SWIFT (5sp) FWD/1.3L-I4 (70hp)

	WS	Ret
Base 2dr Hbk	1150	2050

Add:
Automatic trans 200
Cassette 25
ABS brakes 100

Deduct:
No air cond 225

1994 WS Ret

SWIFT (5sp) FWD/1.3L-I4 (70hp)

	WS	Ret
GA 4dr Sdn	775	1300
GA 2dr Hbk	675	1200
GS 4dr Sdn	1075	1975
GT 2dr Hbk	1125	2025

Add:
Automatic trans 175
Cassette (GA) 25

Deduct:
No air cond 200

1993 WS Ret

SWIFT (5sp) FWD/1.3L-I4 (70hp)

	WS	Ret
GA 4dr Sdn	500	975
GA 2dr Hbk	450	925
GS 4dr Sdn	750	1275
GT 2dr Hbk	775	1300

Add:
Automatic trans 175

Deduct:
No air cond 175

1992 WS Ret

SWIFT (5sp) FWD/1.3L-I4 (70hp)

	WS	Ret
GA 4dr Sdn	375	825
GA 2dr Hbk	325	775
GS 4dr Sdn	525	1000
GT 2dr Hbk	550	1050

Add:
Automatic trans 150

Deduct:
No air cond 150

1991 WS Ret

SWIFT (5sp) FWD/1.3L-I4 (70hp)

	WS	Ret
GA 4dr Sdn	300	750
GA 2dr Hbk	250	675
GS 4dr Sdn	425	900
GT 2dr Hbk	450	925

Add:
Automatic trans 125

Deduct:
No air cond 125

1990 WS Ret

SWIFT (5sp) FWD/1.3L-I4 (70hp)

	WS	Ret
GA 4dr Sdn	225	650
GA 2dr Hbk	200	625
GS 4dr Sdn	325	775
GT 2dr Hbk	350	800

Add:
Automatic trans 75

Deduct:
No air cond 100

1989 WS Ret

SWIFT (5sp) FWD/1.3L-I4 (100hp)

	WS	Ret
GLX (Auto trans) 4dr Hbk	175	600
GTi 2dr Hbk	225	650

Add:

Deduct:
No air cond 75

TOYOTA

2001 WS Ret

AVALON FWD/3.0L-V6 (210hp)

	WS	Ret
XL 4dr Sdn	19875	22900
XLS 4dr Sdn	22600	25850

Add:
- Pwr buckets (XL) 200
- 6-disc CD changer 400
- Leather seats 400
- Moonroof-pwr 500
- Wheels-alloy (std XLS) 225

CAMRY FWD/2.2L-I4 (136hp)

CE 4dr Sdn	12200	14625
LE 4dr Sdn	13450	15975
XLE 4dr Sdn	16150	19075

Add:
- 3.0L-V6 (194hp) 700
- Pwr seat (std XLE) 200
- Traction control 200
- JBL audio w/CD (std XLE) 250
- CD changer 400
- Cruise ctrl (CE) 175
- Leather seats 400
- Moonroof-pwr 500
- Pwr dr locks (CE) 175
- Pwr windows (CE) 200
- Wood dash accent 175
- Wheels-chrome 325
- Wheels-alloy (std XLE) 200

Deduct:
- No air cond 825
- Manual trans 725
- No ABS brakes 425

CELICA FWD/2.2L-I4 (140hp)

GT 2dr Cnv		
GT-S (180hp) 2dr Hbk		

COROLLA FWD/1.8L-I4 (125hp)

CE 4dr Sdn	9600	11800
LE 4dr Sdn	10325	12600
S 4dr Sdn		

Add:
- ABS brakes 325
- Alloy wheels 175
- Cassette (std LE) 150
- CD player 200
- CD changer 400
- Cruise ctrl 200
- Pwr dr locks 200
- Pwr windows 175
- Sunroof-pwr 425

Deduct:
- No air cond 775
- Manual trans 675

ECHO FWD/1.5L-I4 (108hp)

Base 4dr Sdn	9475	11675
Base 2dr Sdn	9025	11175
Roxy 4dr Sdn		

Add:
- ABS brakes 300
- Cassette (std Roxy) 175
- CD player (std Roxy) 200
- 6-disc CD chngr 400
- Wheels-alloy (std Roxy) 200

Deduct:
- No air cond. 725
- Manual trans 775
- Manual steering 225

MR2 RWD/1.8L-I4 (138hp)

Spyder 2dr Cnv		

SOLARA RWD/3.0L-V6 (200hp)

SE 2dr Cnv		
SE 2dr Cpe	15600	18275
SLE 2dr Cnv		
SLE 2dr Cpe	17600	20450

Add:
- ABS brakes (SE 4cyl) 325
- Pwr seat (SE 4cyl) 175
- Lthr seats (std SLE) 450
- Wheels-16" alloy (std SLE) 250
- Moonroof-pwr 475
- JBL audio (std SLE) 200

Deduct:
- Manual trans 725
- No CD player 200
- 2.2L-I4/135hp 550

2000 — WS Ret

AVALON FWD/3.0L-V6 (210hp)

	WS	Ret
XL 4dr Sdn	17900	20775
XLS 4dr Sdn	20800	23900

Add:
- Pwr buckets (XL) 175
- 6-disc CD changer 300
- Leather seats 300
- Moonroof-pwr 400
- Wheels-alloy (std XLS) 175

CAMRY FWD/2.2L-I4 (136hp)

	WS	Ret
CE 4dr Sdn	10775	13075
LE 4dr Sdn	11950	14350
XLE 4dr Sdn	14650	17425

Add:
- 3.0L-V6 (194hp) 550
- JBL audio (std XLE) 175
- Traction control 150
- CD player (std XLE) 175
- CD changer 300
- Cruise ctrl (CE) 150
- Leather seats 300
- Moonroof-pwr 400
- Pwr dr locks (CE) 150
- Pwr windows (CE) 175
- Elite pkg (w/wood dash) 175
- Wheels-alloy (std XLE) 175

Deduct:
- No air cond 650
- Manual trans 575
- No ABS brakes 325

CELICA FWD/2.2L-I4 (140hp)

	WS	Ret
GT 2dr Cnv	13200	15700
GT-S (180hp) 2dr Hbk	15675	18375

Add:
- ABS brakes 275
- 6-disc CD changer 300
- Leather seats 250
- Premium sound (std GT-S) 75
- Moonroof-pwr 375

Deduct:
- Manual trans (not GT-S) 525

COROLLA FWD/1.8L-I4 (125hp)

	WS	Ret
CE 4dr Sdn	8825	10975
LE 4dr Sdn	9550	11750
VE 4dr Sdn	7825	9875

Add:
- ABS brakes 250
- Alloy wheels 150
- Cassette (VE) 75
- CD player 175
- CD changer 300
- Cruise ctrl 150
- Pwr dr locks (std LE) 150
- Pwr windows (std LE) 150
- Sunroof-pwr 325

Deduct:
- No air cond 600
- Manual steering 125
- Manual trans 525

ECHO FWD/1.5L-I4 (108hp)

	WS	Ret
Base 4dr Sdn	8100	10175
Base 2dr Sdn	7675	9725

Add:
- ABS brakes 225
- Cassette 125
- CD player 175
- 6-disc CD chngr 300
- Wheels-alloy 175

Deduct:
- No air cond. 550
- Manual trans 600
- Manual steering 175

MR2 RWD/1.8L-I4 (138hp)

	WS	Ret
Spyder 2dr Cnv	17850	20725

SOLARA RWD/3.0L-V6 (200hp)

	WS	Ret
SE 2dr Cnv	19400	22400
SE 2dr Cpe	13400	15900
SLE 2dr Cnv	21425	24575
SLE 2dr Cpe	15375	18050

Add:
- ABS brakes (4cyl) 250
- Pwr seat 150
- Lthr seats (std SLE) 350
- Wheels-16" alloy (std SLE) 200
- Moonroof-pwr 375
- JBL audio (std SLE) 175

Deduct:
- Manual trans 575
- No CD player 175
- 2.2L-I4/135hp 425

1999 — WS Ret

AVALON FWD/3.0L-V6 (200hp)

	WS	Ret
XL 4dr Sdn	13950	16500
XLS 4dr Sdn	16475	19225

Add:
- CD player (XL) 150
- Pwr buckets (XL) 125
- CD changer 250
- Dash-Burlwood 100
- Leather seats 250
- Moonroof-pwr 325
- Wheels-alloy (std XLS) 150

CAMRY FWD/2.2L-I4 (133hp)

	WS	Ret
CE 4dr Sdn	9800	12025
LE 4dr Sdn	10925	13225
XLE 4dr Sdn	13325	15975

Add:
- 3.0L-V6 (194hp) 450
- Traction control 125
- CD player (std XLE) 150
- CD changer 250
- Cruise ctrl (CE) 100
- Leather seats 250
- Moonroof-pwr 325
- Pwr dr locks (CE) 100
- Pwr windows (CE) 125
- Elite pkg 150
- Wheels-alloy (std XLE) 150

Deduct:
- No air cond 525
- Manual trans 475
- No ABS brakes 275

CELICA FWD/2.2L-I4 (135hp)

	WS	Ret
GT 2dr Cnv	16250	19000
GT 2dr Hbk	13375	15875

Add:
- ABS brakes 225
- CD changer 250
- Leather seats 225
- Premium sound 50
- Moonroof-pwr 300

Deduct:
- No air cond 500
- Manual trans 425
- No cassette 25
- Wheel covers 150

COROLLA FWD/1.8L-I4 (120hp)

	WS	Ret
CE 4dr Sdn	7850	9925
LE 4dr Sdn	8450	10550
VE 4dr Sdn	6875	8850

Add:
- ABS brakes . . . 225
- Alloy wheels . . . 100
- Cassette (VE) . . . 50
- CD player . . . 125
- 6-disc CD changer . . . 250
- Cruise ctrl . . . 125
- Pwr dr locks (std LE) . . . 125
- Pwr windows (std LE) . . . 100
- Sunroof-pwr . . . 275

Deduct:
- No air cond . . . 500
- Manual steering . . . 100
- Manual trans . . . 425

SOLARA — RWD/3.0L-V6 (200hp)

Model	WS	Ret
SE 2dr Cpe	12875	15350
SLE (3.0L-V6/200hp) 2dr Cpe	14700	17325

Add:
- ABS brakes (4cyl) . . . 225
- Pwr seat . . . 100
- Lther seats . . . 300
- Wheels-15" alloy (std SLE) . . . 150
- Wheels-16" alloy . . . 150
- Moonroof-pwr . . . 300
- JBL audio (std SLE) . . . 125

Deduct:
- Manual trans . . . 475
- No CD player . . . 125
- 2.2L-I4/135hp . . . 400

1998 — WS Ret

AVALON — FWD/3.0L-V6 (200hp)

Model	WS	Ret
XL 4dr Sdn	12300	14725
XLS 4dr Sdn	14450	17050

Add:
- CD player (XL) . . . 125
- CD changer . . . 200
- Dash-Burlwood . . . 75
- Leather seats . . . 200
- Moonroof-pwr . . . 275
- Wheels-alloy (std XLS) . . . 125

CAMRY — FWD/2.2L-I4 (133hp)

Model	WS	Ret
CE 4dr Sdn	8600	10725
LE 4dr Sdn	9575	11775
XLE 4dr Sdn	11650	14025

Add:
- 3.0 Liter V6 . . . 375
- CD player (std XLE) . . . 125
- CD changer . . . 200
- Cruise ctrl (CE) . . . 75
- Leather seats . . . 200
- Moonroof-pwr . . . 275
- Pwr dr locks (CE) . . . 75
- Pwr windows (CE) . . . 100
- Elite pkg . . . 125
- Wheels-alloy (std XLE) . . . 125

Deduct:
- No air cond . . . 450
- Manual trans . . . 375
- No ABS brakes . . . 225

CELICA — FWD/2.2L-I4 (135hp)

Model	WS	Ret
GT 2dr Cnv	14475	17075
GT 2dr Cpe	11775	14150
GT 2dr Hbk	11425	13775

Add:
- ABS brakes . . . 175
- CD player (std Cnv) . . . 125
- CD changer . . . 200
- Cruise ctrl . . . 75
- Leather seats . . . 175
- Premium sound . . . 25
- Moonroof-pwr . . . 250

Deduct:
- No air cond . . . 425
- Manual trans . . . 350
- No cassette . . . 25
- Wheel covers . . . 125

COROLLA — FWD/1.8L-I4 (120hp)

Model	WS	Ret
CE 4dr Sdn	7125	9125
LE 4dr Sdn	7700	9750
VE 4dr Sdn	6325	8275

Add:
- ABS brakes . . . 175
- Alloy wheels . . . 75
- Cassette (VE) . . . 50
- CD player . . . 100
- CD changer . . . 200
- Cruise ctrl . . . 75
- Pwr dr locks (std LE) . . . 75
- Pwr windows (std LE) . . . 75
- Sunroof-pwr . . . 225

Deduct:
- No air cond . . . 425
- Manual steering . . . 75
- Manual trans . . . 350

SUPRA — RWD/3.0L-V6 (220hp)

Model	WS	Ret
Base 2dr Cpe	18700	21625
Turbo 2dr Cpe	22150	25375

Add:
- CD changer . . . 225
- Leather seats . . . 250
- Sport roof . . . 525

Deduct:
- Manual trans . . . 375

TERCEL — FWD/1.5L-I4 (93hp)

Model	WS	Ret
CE 2dr Sdn	6175	8100

Add:
- ABS brakes . . . 150
- CD player . . . 100
- CD changer . . . 200
- Pwr dr locks . . . 50
- Pwr windows . . . 75

Deduct:
- No air cond . . . 375
- Manual steering . . . 75
- Manual trans . . . 350

1997 — WS Ret

AVALON — FWD/3.0L-V6 (200hp)

Model	WS	Ret
XL 4dr Sdn	10150	12400
XLS 4dr Sdn	12050	14450

Add:
- CD player . . . 75
- CD changer . . . 175
- Leather seats . . . 175
- Moonroof-pwr . . . 225
- Wheels-alloy (std XLS) . . . 75

CAMRY — FWD/2.2L-I4 (133hp)

Model	WS	Ret
CE 4dr Sdn	7525	9550
LE 4dr Sdn	8375	10475
XLE 4dr Sdn	10275	12525

Add:
- 3.0 Liter V6 . . . 300
- Cassette (CE) . . . 50
- CD player . . . 75
- CD changer . . . 175
- Cruise ctrl (CE) . . . 50
- Leather seats . . . 175
- Moonroof-pwr . . . 225
- Pwr dr locks (CE) . . . 50
- Pwr windows (CE) . . . 75
- Elite pkg . . . 75
- Wheels-alloy (std XLE) . . . 75

Deduct:
- No air cond . . . 375
- Manual trans . . . 325
- No ABS brakes . . . 175

CELICA — FWD/1.8L-I4 (105hp)

Model	WS	Ret
GT 2dr Cnv	12800	15250
GT 2dr Hbk	10775	13075
ST 2dr Cpe	9050	11200
ST 2dr Hbk	9400	11600

Add:
- ABS brakes . . . 150
- CD player . . . 100
- CD changer . . . 175
- Cruise ctrl . . . 50
- Leather seats . . . 150
- Premium sound . . . 25
- Pwr dr lks (std GT) . . . 50
- Pwr windows (std GT) . . . 50
- Moonroof-pwr . . . 200

Deduct:
- No air cond . . . 350
- Manual trans . . . 300
- Wheel covers . . . 100

COROLLA — FWD/1.6L-I4 (100hp)

Model	WS	Ret
Base 4dr Sdn	4950	6775
CE 4dr Sdn	5600	7475
DX 4dr Sdn	6200	8125

Add:
- ABS brakes . . . 150
- Alloy wheels . . . 50
- Cassette . . . 25
- CD player . . . 75
- CD changer . . . 175
- Cruise ctrl . . . 50
- Pwr dr locks . . . 50
- Pwr windows . . . 50
- Sunroof-man . . . 75
- Tilt wheel . . . 25

Deduct:
- No air cond . . . 350
- Manual steering . . . 50
- Manual trans . . . 300

PASEO — FWD/1.5L-I4 (93hp)

Model	WS	Ret
2dr Cnv	7675	9725
2dr Cpe	6450	8400

Add:
- ABS brakes . . . 125
- Alloy wheels . . . 50
- Cassette . . . 25
- CD player . . . 75
- CD changer . . . 175
- Criuse ctrl . . . 50
- Pwr dr locks . . . 25
- Pwr windows . . . 75
- Sunroof-manual . . . 100

Deduct:
- No air cond . . . 325
- Manual trans . . . 275

SUPRA — RWD/3.0L-V6 (220hp)

Model	WS	Ret
Base 2dr Cpe	16575	19350
Turbo 2dr Cpe	19775	22800

Add:
- CD player . . . 125
- CD changer . . . 175
- Leather seats . . . 200
- Sport roof . . . 425

Deduct:
- Manual trans . . . 325

TERCEL — FWD/1.5L-I4 (93hp)

Model	WS	Ret
CE 4dr Sdn	5125	6975
CE 2dr Sdn	4950	6775

Add:
- ABS brakes . . . 125
- Cassette . . . 25
- CD player . . . 75
- CD changer . . . 175
- Pwr dr locks . . . 25
- Pwr windows . . . 75
- Sunroof-manual . . . 75

Deduct:
- No air cond . . . 325
- Manual steering . . . 50
- Manual trans . . . 275

1996 — WS Ret

AVALON FWD/3.0L-V6 (192hp)

	WS	Ret
XL 4dr Sdn	7725	9775
XLS 4dr Sdn	9400	11600
Add:		
ABS brakes (std XLS)	150	
CD player	50	
CD changer	150	
Leather seats	150	
Moonroof-pwr	175	
Wheels-alloy (std XLS)	50	

CAMRY FWD/2.2L-I4 (125hp)

	WS	Ret
LE 4dr Sdn	6625	8600
LE 4dr Wgn	7200	9200
LE 2dr Cpe	6400	8350
SE (6cyl) 4dr Sdn	8125	10200
SE (6cyl) 2dr Cpe	7950	10025
XLE 4dr Sdn	8250	10350
Add:		
3.0 Liter V6 (std SE)	250	
ABS brakes (std XLE)	150	
Cassette (DX only)	25	
CD player	50	
CD changer	150	
Cruise ctrl (DX)	50	
Leather seats	150	
Sunroof-pwr	175	
Pwr dr locks (DX)	50	
Pwr windows (DX)	50	
Elite pkg	50	
Third seat-wgn	50	
Wheels-alloy (std SE,XLE)	50	
Deduct:		
No air cond	300	
Manual trans	275	

CELICA FWD/1.8L-I4 (110hp)

	WS	Ret
GT 2dr Cnv	10400	12675
GT 2dr Cpe	8100	10175
GT 2dr Hbk	8400	10500
ST 2dr Cpe	6925	8925
ST 2dr Hbk	7225	9250
Add:		
ABS brakes	150	
Alloy wheels	50	
CD player	75	
CD changer	150	
Cruise ctrl	25	
Leather seats	125	
Premium sound	25	
Pwr dr lks (std GT)	25	
Pwr windows (std GT)	50	
Sunroof-pwr	175	
Tilt wheel (std GT)	25	
Deduct:		
No air cond	275	
Manual trans	250	

COROLLA FWD/1.6L-I4 (100hp)

	WS	Ret
Base 4dr Sdn	4300	6050
DX 4dr Sdn	4850	6650
DX 4dr Wgn	5550	7425
Add:		
ABS brakes	125	
Alloy wheels	50	
Cassette	25	
CD player	50	
CD changer	150	
Cruise ctrl	25	
Pwr dr locks	25	
Pwr windows	50	
Sunroof-man	50	
Tilt wheel	25	
Deduct:		
No air cond	275	
Manual steering	25	
Manual trans	250	

PASEO FWD/1.5L-I4 (93hp)

	WS	Ret
Coupe 2dr Cpe	4950	6775
Add:		
ABS brakes	125	
Alloy wheels	50	
Cassette	25	
CD player	50	
CD changer	150	
Criuse ctrl	25	
Pwr dr locks	25	
Pwr windows	25	
Sunroof-manual	75	
Deduct:		
No air cond	250	
Manual trans	225	

SUPRA RWD/3.0L-V6 (220hp)

	WS	Ret
Base 2dr Cpe	13400	15900
Turbo 2dr Cpe	16200	18925
Add:		
CD player	75	
CD changer	150	
Leather seats	175	
Sport roof	350	
Deduct:		
Manual trans	275	

TERCEL FWD/1.5L-I4 (93hp)

	WS	Ret
Base 2dr Sdn	3625	5225
DX 4dr Sdn	4150	5900
DX 2dr Sdn	3950	5675
Add:		
ABS brakes	125	
Cassette	25	
CD player	50	
CD changer	150	
Pwr dr locks	25	
Pwr windows	50	
Sunroof-manual	50	
Deduct:		
No air cond	250	
Manual steering	25	
Manual trans	225	

1995 — WS Ret

AVALON FWD/3.0L-V6 (192hp)

	WS	Ret
XL 4dr Sdn	6825	8800
XLS 4dr Sdn	8350	10450
Add:		
ABS brakes (std XLS)	125	
Alloy wheels (std XLS)	50	
CD player	50	
CD changer	125	
Leather seats	125	
Moonroof-pwr	175	

CAMRY FWD/2.2L-I4 (125hp)

	WS	Ret
DX 4dr Sdn	4875	6675
DX 2dr Cpe	4700	6475
LE 4dr Sdn	5500	7375
LE 4dr Wgn	5950	7850
LE 2dr Cpe	5350	7200
SE (6cyl) 4dr Sdn	6850	8825
SE (6cyl) 2dr Cpe	6750	8725
XLE 4dr Sdn	6950	8950
Add:		
3.0 Liter V6 (std SE)	250	
ABS brakes (std XLE)	125	
Alloy wheels (std XLE,SE)	50	
Cassette (DX only)	25	
CD player	50	
CD changer	125	
Cruise ctrl (DX)	25	
Leather seats	125	
Sunroof-pwr	175	
Pwr dr locks (DX)	25	
Pwr windows (DX)	50	
Elite pkg	50	
Third seat-wgn	50	
Deduct:		
No air cond	275	
Manual trans	250	

CELICA FWD/1.8L-I4 (110hp)

	WS	Ret
GT 2dr Cpe	8075	10150
GT 2dr Hbk	8325	10425
ST 2dr Cpe	6950	8950
ST 2dr Hbk	7225	9250
Add:		
ABS brakes	125	
Alloy wheels	50	
CD player	50	
CD changer	125	
Cruise ctrl	25	
Leather seats	100	
Premium sound	25	
Pwr dr lks (std GT)	25	
Pwr windows (std GT)	25	
Sunroof-pwr	150	
Tilt wheel (std GT)	25	
Deduct:		
No air cond	250	
Manual trans	225	

COROLLA FWD/1.6L-I4 (100hp)

	WS	Ret
Base 4dr Sdn	3500	5075
DX 4dr Sdn	3950	5675
DX 4dr Wgn	4475	6250
LE 4dr Sdn	4525	6300
Add:		
ABS brakes	125	
Alloy wheels	25	
Cassette	25	
CD player	50	
CD changer	125	
Cruise ctrl (std LE)	25	
Pwr dr locks (std LE)	25	
Pwr windows (std LE)	25	
Sunroof-pwr	150	
Tilt wheel (std LE)	25	
Deduct:		
No air cond	250	
Manual steering	25	
Manual trans	225	

MR2 RWD/2.2L-I4 (135hp)

	WS	Ret
Base 2dr Cpe	7875	9950
Turbo (5sp) 2dr Cpe	9425	11625
Add:		
ABS brakes	125	
CD player	50	
CD changer	125	
Cruise ctrl (std Turbo)	25	
Leather seats	100	
Premium sound (std Turbo)	25	
Pwr dr locks (std Turbo)	25	
Pwr windows (std Turbo)	25	
Sunroof-manual	75	
T-roof (std Turbo)	325	
Deduct:		
No air cond	250	
Manual steering	25	

PASEO FWD/1.5L-I4 (100hp)

	WS	Ret
Coupe 2dr Cpe	3900	5625
Add:		
ABS brakes	125	
Alloy wheels	25	
Cassette	25	
CD player	50	
CD changer	125	
Criuse ctrl	25	
Sunroof-manual	50	
Deduct:		
No air cond	225	
Manual trans	200	

SUPRA RWD/3.0L-V6 (220hp)

Model	WS	Ret
Base 2dr Cpe	12175	14575
Turbo 2dr Cpe	14475	17075

Add:

CD player	75
CD changer	150
Leather seats	150
Sport roof	325

Deduct:

Manual trans	250

TERCEL FWD/1.5L-I4 (93hp)

Model	WS	Ret
Base 2dr Sdn	2775	4250
DX 4dr Sdn	3250	4800
DX 2dr Sdn	3025	4550

Add:

ABS brakes	100
Cassette	25
CD player	50
CD changer	125
Pwr dr locks	25
Pwr windows	50

Deduct:

No air cond	225
Manual steering (not Base)	25
Manual trans	225

1994 WS Ret

CAMRY FWD/2.2L-I4 (125hp)

Model	WS	Ret
DX 4dr Sdn	4325	6075
DX 4dr Wgn	4625	6400
DX 2dr Cpe	3925	5650
LE 4dr Sdn	4525	6300
LE 4dr Wgn	4875	6675
LE 2dr Cpe	4425	6175
SE (6cyl) 4dr Sdn	5650	7525
SE (6cyl) 2dr Cpe	5575	7450
XLE 4dr Sdn	5725	7625

Add:

3.0 Liter V6 (std SE)	225
ABS brakes	125
Alloy wheels (std XLE,SE)	25
Cassette (DX only)	25
CD player	50
CD changer	125
Cruise ctrl (DX)	25
Leather seats	125
Sunroof-pwr (std XLE)	150
Pwr dr locks (DX)	25
Pwr windows (DX)	25
Third seat-wgn	50

Deduct:

No air cond	250
Manual trans	225

CELICA FWD/1.8L-I4 (110hp)

Model	WS	Ret
GT 2dr Cpe	6825	8800
GT 2dr Hbk	7000	9000
ST 2dr Cpe	5875	7775
ST 2dr Hbk	6075	8000

Add:

ABS brakes	125
Alloy wheels	25
Cassette (ST only)	25
CD player	50
CD changer	125
Cruise ctrl	25
Leather seats	75
Pwr dr lks	25
Pwr windows	25
Sunroof-pwr	150
Tilt wheel (std GT)	25

Deduct:

No air cond	225
Manual trans	200

COROLLA FWD/1.6L-I4 (105hp)

Model	WS	Ret
Base 4dr Sdn	2925	4425
DX 4dr Sdn	3325	4900
DX 4dr Wgn	3775	5475
LE 4dr Sdn	3875	5600

Add:

ABS brakes	100
Alloy wheels	25
Cassette	25
CD player	25
CD changer	125
Cruise ctrl	25
Pwr dr locks (std LE)	25
Pwr windows (std LE)	25
Sunroof-pwr	125

Deduct:

No air cond	225
Manual steering	25
Manual trans	200

MR2 RWD/2.2L-I4 (130hp)

Model	WS	Ret
Base 2dr Cpe	6700	8675
Turbo (5sp) 2dr Cpe	8000	10075

Add:

ABS brakes	125
CD player	50
CD changer	125
Cruise ctrl (std Turbo)	25
Leather seats	75
Pwr dr locks (std Turbo)	25
Pwr windows (std Turbo)	25
Sunroof-manual	75
T-roof (std Turbo)	275

Deduct:

No air cond	225
Manual steering	25

PASEO FWD/1.5L-I4 (100hp)

Model	WS	Ret
Coupe 2dr Cpe	3225	4775

Add:

ABS brakes	75
Alloy wheels	25
Cassette	25
CD player	25
CD changer	125
Criuse ctrl	25
Sunroof-manual	50

Deduct:

No air cond	225
Manual trans	200

SUPRA RWD/3.0L-V6 (220hp)

Model	WS	Ret
Base 2dr Cpe	10500	12775
Turbo 2dr Cpe	12400	14825

Add:

CD player	50
CD changer	125
Leather seats	125
Sport roof	300

TERCEL FWD/1.5L-I4 (82hp)

Model	WS	Ret
Base (4sp) 2dr Sdn	2300	3500
DX 4dr Sdn	2825	4325
DX 2dr Sdn	2675	4150

Add:

ABS brakes	75
Cassette	25
CD player	25
CD changer	125

Deduct:

No air cond	225
Manual steering (not Base)	25
Man trans (not Base)	200

1993 WS Ret

CAMRY FWD/2.2L-I4 (130hp)

Model	WS	Ret
DX 4dr Sdn	3550	5125
DX 4dr Wgn	3700	5300
LE 4dr Sdn	4025	5750
LE 4dr Wgn	4325	6075
SE (6cyl) 4dr Sdn	4700	6475
XLE 4dr Sdn	4800	6600

Add:

3.0 Liter V6	200
ABS brakes	100
Alloy wheels (std XLE,SE)	25
Cassette (DX only)	25
CD player	50
Cruise ctrl (DX,SE)	25
Leather seats	100
Sunroof-pwr (std XLE)	150
Pwr dr locks (std LE,XLE)	25
Pwr windows (std LE,XLE)	25
Third seat-wgn	25

Deduct:

No air cond	225
Manual trans	200

CELICA FWD/1.6L-I4 (103hp)

Model	WS	Ret
All-Trac (5sp-AWD) 2dr Hbk	6575	8525
GT 2dr Cnv	6675	8650
GT 2dr Cpe	4325	6075
GT 2dr Hbk	4450	6225
GT-S 2dr Hbk	4950	6775
ST 2dr Cpe	3775	5475

Add:

ABS brakes (std All-Trac)	100
Alloy whls (ST,GT only)	25
Cassette (ST only)	25
CD player	50
Cruise (std All-Trac)	25
Leather seats	75
Pwr dr lks (std All-Trac)	25
Pwr windows (std All-Trac)	25
Sunroof-pwr	125

Deduct:

No air cond	200
Manual trans (not All-Trac)	175

COROLLA FWD/1.8L-I4 (115hp)

Model	WS	Ret
Base 4dr Sdn	2425	3875
Dlx 4dr Sdn	2725	4200
Dlx 4dr Wgn	3075	4625
LE 4dr Sdn	3150	4700

Add:

ABS brakes	75
Alloy wheels	25
Cassette	25
Cruise ctrl (std LE)	25
Pwr dr locks (std LE)	25
Pwr windows (std LE)	25
Sunroof-pwr	100

Deduct:

No air cond	200
Manual steering	25
Manual trans	175

MR2 RWD/2.2L-I4 (135hp)

Model	WS	Ret
Base 2dr Cpe	4925	6750
Turbo (5sp) 2dr Cpe	5900	7800

Add:

ABS brakes	100
CD player	50
Cruise ctrl (std Turbo)	25
Leather seats	75
Pwr dr locks (std Turbo)	25
Pwr windows (std Turbo)	25
Sunroof-manual	50
T-roof	250

Deduct:

No air cond	200
Manual steering	25

PASEO FWD/1.5L-I4 (100hp)

Model	WS	Ret
Coupe 2dr Cpe	2425	3875

Add:

ABS brakes	75
Alloy wheels	25

Cassette 25
Criuse ctrl 25
Sunroof-manual 50

Deduct:
No air cond 175
Manual trans 175

SUPRA RWD/3.0L-V6 (220hp)

Base 2dr Cpe	9625	11825
Turbo 2dr Cpe	11525	13875

Add:
CD player 50
CD changer 100
Leather seats 100
Sport roof 250

TERCEL FWD/1.5L-I4 (82hp)

Base (4sp) 2dr Sdn	1525	2500
Dlx 4dr Sdn	1825	2975
Dlx 2dr Sdn	1700	2825
LE 4dr Sdn	2075	3250

Add:
ABS brakes 75
Cassette 25

Deduct:
No air cond 175
Manual steering (not Base) 25
Man trans (not Base) 175

1992 WS Ret

CAMRY FWD/2.2L-I4 (125hp)

DX 4dr Sdn	3025	4550
DX 4dr Wgn	3150	4700
LE 4dr Sdn	3400	4975
LE 4dr Wgn	3700	5300
SE (6cyl) 4dr Sdn	4050	5775
XLE 4dr Sdn	4150	5900

Add:
3.0 Liter V6 125
ABS brakes 75
Alloy wheels (LE only) 25
Cassette (std LE,XLE) 25
CD player 25
Cruise ctrl (DX) 25
Leather seats 75
Sunroof-pwr (std XLE) 100
Third seat-wgn 25

Deduct:
No air cond 200
Manual trans 175

CELICA FWD/1.6L-I4 (103hp)

All-Trac (5sp-AWD) 2dr Hbk	5375	7250
GT 2dr Cnv	5725	7625
GT 2dr Cpe	3725	5425
GT 2dr Hbk	3825	5525
GT-S 2dr Hbk	4325	6075
ST 2dr Cpe	3275	4825

Add:
ABS brakes 75
Alloy whls (ST,GT only) 25
Cassette (ST,GT only) 25
CD player 25
Cruise (std All-Trac) 25
Leather seats 50
Pwr dr lks (std ATrac) 25
Pwr windows (std All-Trac) 25
Sunroof-pwr 100

Deduct:
No air cond 175
Manual trans (not All-Trac) . . . 175

COROLLA FWD/1.6L-I4 (102hp)

All-Trac (AWD) 4dr Wgn	2700	4175
Base 4dr Sdn	2025	3200
Dlx 4dr Sdn	2250	3450
Dlx 4dr Wgn	2450	3900
LE 4dr Sdn	2525	3975

Add:
Alloy wheels 25
Cruise ctrl 25
Pwr dr locks 25
Pwr windows 25
Sunroof-pwr 75

Deduct:
No air cond 175
Manual trans 175

CRESSIDA RWD/3.0L-V6 (190hp)

Sedan 4dr Sdn	4600	6375

Add:
ABS brakes 75
CD player 25
Leather seats 75
Pwr seat 25
Sunroof-pwr 125

MR2 RWD/2.2L-I4 (130hp)

Base 2dr Cpe	4200	5950
Turbo (5sp) 2dr Cpe	4825	6625

Add:
ABS brakes 75
Alloy wheels (Base) 25
Cassette 25
CD player 25
Cruise ctrl 25
Leather seats 50
Pwr dr locks 25
Pwr windows 25
Sunroof-pwr 100
T-roof 250

Deduct:
No air cond 175
Manual steering 25

PASEO FWD/1.5L-I4 (100hp)

Coupe 2dr Cpe	2075	3250

Add:
Alloy wheels 25
Criuse ctrl 25
Sunroof-manual 75

Deduct:
No air cond 175
Manual trans 150

SUPRA RWD/3.0L-V6 (200hp)

Base 2dr Hbk	5325	7175
Turbo 2dr Hbk	5950	7850

Add:
ABS brakes 75
CD player 25
Leather seats 75
Sports pkg 50
Sunroof-pwr 150
Targa roof (lift off) 200

Deduct:
Manual trans 175

TERCEL FWD/1.5L-I4 (82hp)

Base (4sp) 2dr Sdn	1250	2200
Dlx 4dr Sdn	1550	2525
Dlx 2dr Sdn	1425	2400
LE 4dr Sdn	1725	2850

Add:

Deduct:
No air cond 175
Man trans (not Base) 150

1991 WS Ret

CAMRY FWD/2.0L-I4 (115hp)

Base 4dr Sdn	1900	3050
Dlx 4dr Sdn	2175	3375
Dlx 4dr Wgn	2300	3500
LE 4dr Sdn	2475	3925
LE (6cyl) 4dr Wgn	2675	4150

Add:
3.0 Liter V6 100
ABS brakes 50
Alloy wheels 25
Cassette 25
Cruise ctrl. 25
Leather seats 50
Pwr dr locks 25
Pwr seat 25
Pwr windows 25
Sunroof-pwr 100

Deduct:
No air cond 175
Manual trans 175

CELICA FWD/1.6-I4 (103hp)

All-Trac (5sp-AWD) 2dr Hbk	4550	6325
GT 2dr Cnv	4675	6450
GT 2dr Cpe	3050	4600
GT 2dr Hbk	3125	4675
GT-S 2dr Hbk	3500	5075
ST 2dr Cpe	2725	4200

Add:
ABS brakes 50
Alloy wheels (GT) 25
Cassette (ST,GT) 25
CD player 25
Leather seats 25
Pwr windows (GT,GT-S) 25
Sunroof-pwr 100

Deduct:
No air cond 175
Manual trans (not All-Trac) . . . 150

COROLLA FWD/1.6L-I4 (102hp)

Base 4dr Sdn	1750	2875
Dlx 4dr Sdn	1900	3050
Dlx 4dr Wgn	2025	3200
Dlx All-Trac (AWD) 4dr Wgn	2275	3475
GT-S Sport (5sp) 2dr Cpe	2450	3900
LE 4dr Sdn	2075	3250
SR5 Sport 2dr Cpe	2150	3350

Add:
Alloy wheels (std GTS) 25
Pwr windows 25

Deduct:
No air cond 175
Man trans (not GT-S) 150

CRESSIDA RWD/3.0L-V6 (190hp)

Sedan 4dr Sdn	4050	5775

Add:
ABS brakes 50
CD player 25
Leather seats 50
Sunroof-pwr 125

MR2 RWD/2.2L-I4 (130hp)

Base 2dr Cpe	3850	5575
Turbo (5sp) 2dr Cpe	4225	5975

Add:
ABS brakes 50
Cassette (std Turbo) 25
CD player 25
Leather seats 25
Pwr windows 25
Sunroof-manual 25
T-roof 175

Deduct:
No air cond 175

SUPRA RWD/3.0L-V6 (200hp)

Base 2dr Hbk	4175	5925
Turbo 2dr Hbk	4525	6300

Add:
ABS brakes (std Turbo) 50
CD player 25
Leather seats 50
Sunroof-pwr 125

Targa roof (lift off)	200	

Deduct:

Manual trans	150	

TERCEL FWD/1.5L-I4 (82hp)

Model	WS	Ret
Base (4sp) 2dr Sdn	1050	1975
Dlx 4dr Sdn	1300	2250
Dlx 2dr Sdn	1225	2175
LE 4dr Sdn	1450	2425

Add:

Deduct:

No air cond	150
Man trans (not Base)	125

1990 WS Ret

CAMRY FWD/2.0L-I4 (115hp)

Model	WS	Ret
Base 4dr Sdn	1625	2725
Dlx 4dr Sdn	1875	3025
Dlx 4dr Wgn	1950	3100
LE 4dr Sdn	2100	3275
LE (6cyl) 4dr Wgn	2300	3500

Add:

3.0 Liter V6	75
ABS brakes	25
Alloy wheels	25
Leather seats	25
Pwr windows	25
Sunroof-pwr	75

Deduct:

No air cond	150
Manual trans	150

CELICA FWD/2.2L-I4 (130hp)

Model	WS	Ret
All-Trac (5sp-AWD) 2dr Hbk	3750	5450
GT 2dr Cpe	2500	3950
GT 2dr Hbk	2575	4025
GT-S 2dr Hbk	2850	4350
ST 2dr Cpe	2275	3475

Add:

ABS brakes	25
Leather seats	25
Sunroof-pwr	75

Deduct:

No air cond	150
Manual trans (not All-Trac)	150

COROLLA FWD/1.6L-I4 (102hp)

Model	WS	Ret
Base 4dr Sdn	1500	2475
Dlx 4dr Sdn	1625	2725
Dlx 4dr Wgn	1700	2825
Dlx All-Trac (AWD) 4dr Wgn	1900	3050
GT-S (5sp) 2dr Cpe	2100	3275
LE 4dr Sdn	1775	2900
SR5 All-Trac (5sp-A 4dr Wgn	2075	3250
SR5 2dr Cpe	1850	3000

Add:

Sunroof-pwr	50

Deduct:

No air cond	150
Man trans (not GT-S)	125

CRESSIDA RWD/3.0L-V6 (190hp)

Model	WS	Ret
Sedan 4dr Sdn	3450	5025

Add:

ABS brakes	25
CD player	25
Leather seats	25
Sunroof-pwr	100

SUPRA RWD/3.0L-V6 (200hp)

Model	WS	Ret
Base 2dr Hbk	3325	4900
Turbo 2dr Hbk	3625	5225

Add:

ABS brakes	25
CD player	25
Leather seats	25
Sports pkg	25

Targa roof (lift off)	100

Deduct:

Manual trans	125

TERCEL FWD/1.5L-I4 (78hp)

Model	WS	Ret
Base 2dr Cpe	975	1700
Base 2dr Hbk	1025	1950
Dlx 2dr Cpe	1125	2075
EZ (4sp) 2dr Hbk	900	1625

Add:

Deduct:

No air cond	125
Man trans (not EZ)	125

1989 WS Ret

CAMRY FWD/2.0L-I4 (115hp)

Model	WS	Ret
Base 4dr Sdn	1325	2275
Dlx 4dr Sdn	1500	2475
Dlx 4dr Wgn	1550	2525
LE 4dr Sdn	1600	2700
LE 4dr Wgn	1675	2800

Add:

3.0 Liter V6	50
ABS brakes	25
Leather seats	25
Sunroof-pwr	50

Deduct:

No air cond	125
Manual trans	125

CELICA FWD/2.0L-I4 (115hp)

Model	WS	Ret
All-Trac (5sp-AWD) 2dr Hbk	2700	4175
GT 2dr Cnv	2425	3875
GT 2dr Cpe	1450	2425
GT 2dr Hbk	1450	2425
GT-S 2dr Cpe	1625	2725
GT-S 2dr Hbk	1675	2800
ST 2dr Cpe	1275	2225

Add:

ABS brakes	25
Leather seats	25
Sunroof-pwr	50

Deduct:

No air cond	125
Manual trans (not All-Trac)	100

COROLLA FWD/1.6L-I4 (90hp)

Model	WS	Ret
Dlx 4dr Sdn	1100	2025
Dlx 4dr Wgn	1150	2100
GT-S (5sp) 2dr Cpe	1450	2425
LE 4dr Sdn	1225	2175
SR5 (5sp-AWD) 4dr Wgn	1550	2525
SR5 2dr Cpe	1275	2225

Add:

Sunroof-pwr	50
AWD (std SR5 wgn)	175

Deduct:

No air cond	100
Man trans(not GTS,AWD)	100

CRESSIDA RWD/3.0L-V6 (190hp)

Model	WS	Ret
Sedan 4dr Sdn	2500	3950

Add:

ABS brakes	25
Leather seats	25
Sunroof-pwr	75

MR2 RWD/1.6L-I4 (115hp)

Model	WS	Ret
Base 2dr Cpe	1900	3050
SC 2dr Cpe	2050	3225

Add:

Leather seats	25
Sunroof-pwr	50
T-roof (Base)	125

Deduct:

No air cond	125

SUPRA RWD/3.0L-V6 (200hp)

Model	WS	Ret
Base 2dr Hbk	2775	4250
Turbo 2dr Hbk	2925	4425

Add:

ABS brakes	25
Leather seats	25
Sports pkg	25

Deduct:

Manual trans	100

TERCEL FWD/1.5L-I4 (78hp)

Model	WS	Ret
Base 2dr Cpe	700	1250
Base 2dr Hbk	725	1275
Dlx 4dr Hbk	875	1600
Dlx 2dr Cpe	800	1525
Dlx 2dr Hbk	825	1550
EZ (5sp) 2dr Hbk	575	1100

Add:

Deduct:

No air cond	75
Man trans (not EZ)	75

1988 WS Ret

CAMRY FWD/2.0L-I4 (115hp)

Model	WS	Ret
Base 4dr Sdn	1075	2000
Dlx 4dr Sdn	1225	2175
Dlx 4dr Wgn	1275	2225
LE 4dr Sdn	1350	2300
LE 4dr Wgn	1375	2350

Add:

3.0 liter V6	50
ABS brakes	25
Leather seats	25
Sunroof-pwr	50

Deduct:

No air cond	100
Manual trans	75

CELICA FWD/2.0L-I4 (115hp)

Model	WS	Ret
All-Trac (5sp-AWD) 2dr Hbk	2100	3275
GT 2dr Cnv	1925	3075
GT 2dr Cpe	975	1700
GT 2dr Hbk	1025	1950
GT-S (5sp) 2dr Cpe	1150	2100
GT-S (5sp) 2dr Hbk	1200	2150
ST 2dr Cpe	925	1650

Add:

ABS brakes	25
Sunroof-pwr	50

Deduct:

No air cond	75
Man trans (not GTS,All-Trac)	75

COROLLA FWD/1.6L-I4 (90hp)

Model	WS	Ret
Dlx 4dr Sdn	875	1600
Dlx 4dr Wgn	925	1650
FX 2dr Hbk	1675	2800
FX-16 2dr Hbk	2000	3175
FX-16 GTS 2dr Hbk	2225	3425
GT-S (5sp) 2dr Cpe	1250	2200
LE 4dr Sdn	1000	1725
SR5 (5sp) 4dr Wgn	1250	2200
SR5 2dr Cpe	1025	1950

Add:

Sunroof-pwr	25

Deduct:

No air cond	75
Man trans(not GTS,AWD)	75

CRESSIDA RWD/2.8L-V6 (156hp)

Model	WS	Ret
Sedan 4dr Sdn	1975	3125

Add:

Leather seats	25
Sunroof-pwr	50

Deduct:
Manual trans 75

MR2 RWD/1.6L-I4 (112hp)

Base 2dr Cpe. 1450 2425
SC 2dr Cpe 1550 2525

Add:
Sunroof-pwr 50
T-roof 50

Deduct:
No air cond 100

SUPRA RWD/3.0L-V6 (200hp)

Base 2dr Hbk 2200 3400
Turbo 2dr Hbk 2350 3775

Add:
ABS brakes 25
Leather seats 25
Sports pkg 25
Targa roof (lift off) 75

Deduct:
Manual trans 50

TERCEL FWD/1.5L-I4 (78hp)

Base 2dr Cpe. 500 1000
Base 2dr Hbk 500 1000
Dlx 4dr Hbk 575 1100
Dlx (AWD) 4dr Wgn 1050 1975
Dlx 2dr Cpe 575 1100
Dlx 2dr Hbk 600 1125
EZ (4sp) 2dr Hbk 450 950
SR5 (5sp-AWD) 4dr Wgn . . 1125 2075

Add:
Sunroof-pwr 25

Deduct:
No air cond 50
Man trns(not EZ,SR5 wgn) 50

VOLKSWAGEN

2001 WS Ret

BEETLE FWD/2.0L-I4 (115hp)

GL 2dr Cpe 13150 15325
GLS 2dr Cpe 13700 15925
GLS TDI (1.9L TD) 2dr Cpe. . . . .
GLS Turbo (150hp) 2dr Cpe . . . .
GLX Turbo (150hp) 2dr Cpe . . . .

Add:
CD Changer 400
Lthr seats (std GLX) 450
Moonroof-pwr (std GLX) 475
Wheels-17in. alloy (Turbo) . . . 200

Deduct:
Manual trans 550

CABRIO FWD/2.0L-I4 (115hp)

GL 2dr Cnv. . . . .
GLS 2dr Cnv . . . .
GLX 2dr Cnv . . . .

GOLF FWD/2.0L-I4 (115hp)

GL 2dr Hbk. 12500 14650
GL TDI 2dr Hbk . . . .
GLS 4dr Hbk 13500 15700
GLS TDI 4dr Hbk. . . . .
GLS 1.8 Turbo 4dr Hbk . . . .

Add:
Alloy wheels 175
Monsoon audio 225

Deduct:
No air cond 675
Man trans (GL) 625

GTI FWD/2.0L-I4 (115hp)

GLS Turbo (150hp) 2dr Hbk . . . .
GLX (V6/174hp) 2dr Hbk. . . . . . .

JETTA FWD/2.0L-I4 (115hp)

GL 4dr Sdn 13600 15800
GL TDI 4dr Sdn. . . . .
GLS 4dr Sdn 14775 17050
GLS TDI 4dr Sdn. . . . .
GLS 1.8 Turbo 4dr Sdn. . . . .
GLX (6cyl) 4dr Sdn 16600 19000
Wolfsburg 4dr Sdn . . . .

Add:
2.8L-V6 (174hp) (GLS) 675
CD changer 400
Leather seats (std GLX) 400
Moonroof-pwr (std GLX) 450
Pwr windows (GL) 200
Monsoon sound (std GLX) . . . 175
Wheels-alloy (std GLX) 225

Deduct:
No air cond 675
Man trans (not TDI) 625

PASSAT FWD/1.8L-I4T (150hp)

GLS 4dr Sdn 16600 19000
GLS 4dr Wgn. 17750 20200
GLX (6cyl) 4dr Sdn 19125 21675
GLX (6cyl) 4dr Wgn. 20300 22900

Add:
2.8L-V6(190hp) (std GLX) 925
Leather seats (std GLX) 450
Moonroof-power (std GLX) . . . 500
CD Changer 400
4motion AWD 1775
Monsoon audio 225
Wheels-16" alloy (std GLX) . . . 225

Deduct:
Manual transmission 800

2000 WS Ret

BEETLE FWD/2.0L-I4 (115hp)

GL 2dr Cpe 11925 14025
GLS 2dr Cpe 12800 14975
GLS TDI (1.9L TD) 2dr Cpe 13275 15475
GLS Turbo (150hp) 2dr Cpe13600 15800
GLX Turbo (150hp) 2dr Cpe14475 16725

Add:
CD Changer 300
Lthr seats (std GLX) 350
Moonroof-pwr (std GLX) 375
Wheels-alloy (std GLX) 175

Deduct:
Manual trans 425

CABRIO FWD/2.0L-I4 (115hp)

GL 2dr Cnv 13350 15550
GLS 2dr Cnv 14800 17075

Add:
Alloy wheels (GL) 175
CD Changer 325
Power windows (GL) 150
Cruise ctrl (GL) 150

Deduct:
No air cond 550
Manual trans 475

GOLF FWD/2.0L-I4 (115hp)

GL 2dr Hbk 10875 12925
GL TDI 2dr Hbk. 11275 13350
GLS 4dr Hbk 12025 14150
GLS TDI 4dr Hbk. 12475 14625
GLS 1.8 Turbo 4dr Hbk. . . 13450 15650

Add:
ABS brakes 250
Alloy wheels 150
CD player 175

Deduct:
No air cond 525
Man trans (GL) 475

GTI FWD/2.0L-I4 (115hp)

GLS Turbo (150hp) 2dr Hbk14075 16325
GLX (V6/174hp) 2dr Hbk . 15450 17775

Add:
CD Changer 300
Leather seats 300

JETTA FWD/2.0L-I4 (115hp)

GL 4dr Sdn 12400 14550
GL TDI 4dr Sdn. 12975 15150
GLS 4dr Sdn. 13700 15925
GLS TDI 4dr Sdn 14250 16500
GLS 1.8 Turbo 4dr Sdn . . 14925 17225
GLX (6cyl) 4dr Sdn. 15400 17725

Add:
2.8L-V6 (174hp) (GLS) 525
CD changer 300
Leather seats (std GLX) 300
Moonroof-pwr (std GLX) 350
Pwr windows (GL) 175
Monsoon sound 150
Wheels-alloy (std GLX) 175

Deduct:
No air cond 525
Man trans (not TDI) 475

PASSAT FWD/1.8L-I4T (150hp)

GLS 4dr Sdn. 14975 17275
GLS 4dr Wgn 16125 18475
GLX (6cyl) 4dr Sdn. 17475 19925
GLX (6cyl) 4dr Wgn 18650 21150

Add:
2.8L-V6(174hp) (std GLX) . . . 700
Leather seats (std GLX) 350
Moonroof-power (std GLX) . . . 400
CD Changer 300
4motion AWD 1375
Wheels-16" alloy (std GLX) . . . 200

Deduct:
Manual transmission 625

1999 WS Ret

BEETLE FWD/2.0L-I4 (115hp)

GL 2dr Cpe. 11150 13225
GLS 2dr Cpe. 11575 13675
GLS Turbo (150hp) 2dr Cpe12375 14500
GLX Turbo (150hp) 2dr Cpe13400 15600
TDI (1.9L TD) 2dr Cpe . . . 12675 14825

Add:
CD Changer 250
Lthr seats (std GLX) 300
Moonroof-pwr (std GLX) 300
Wheels-alloy (std GLX) 150

Deduct:
Manual trans 350

CABRIO FWD/2.0L-I4 (115hp)

GL 2dr Cnv 13050 15225
GL (New A4) 2dr Cnv. . . . 12550 14700
GLS 2dr Cnv. 14375 16625
GLS (New A4) 2dr Cnv. . . 13850 16075

Add:
Alloy wheels (GL) 150
CD Changer 275
Power windows (GL) 100
Cruise ctrl (GL) 100

Deduct:
No air cond 450
Manual trans 400

GOLF FWD/2.0L-I4 (115hp)

GL 4dr Hbk. 8650 10575
GL (New A4) 2dr Hbk. 9600 11575
GL TDI (New A4) 2dr Hbk 1 1
GLS (New A4) 4dr Hbk. . . 10300 12325

GLS TDI (New A4) 4dr Hbk 1 1
GTI (New A4) 2dr Hbk 11475 13550
Wolfsburg 4dr Hbk 9050 11000

Add:
ABS brakes (std GTI) 225
Alloy wheels (std GTI) 100
CD player 150

Deduct:
No air cond 450
Man trans (GL) 400

GTI VR6 (5sp) FWD/2.8L-V6 (174hp)

2dr Hbk 12325 14450

Add:
CD Changer 250
Leather seats 250

JETTA FWD/2.0L-I4 (115hp)

GL 4dr Sdn 10475 12500
GL (New A4) 4dr Sdn 10975 13025
GL TDI (New A4) 4dr Sdn
GLS (New A4) 4dr Sdn 11925 14025
GLS TDI (New A4) 4dr Sdn
GLX (6cyl) 4dr Sdn 14200 16450
GLX (New A4) (6cyl) 4dr Sdn 14525 16800
TDI (5sp) 4dr Sdn 11575 13675
Wolfsburg 4dr Sdn 11475 13550

Add:
ABS brakes (std GLX) 225
Cassette (GL,GT) 125
CD changer 250
Cruise ctrl (std GLS,GLX) 125
Leather seats 250
Moonroof-pwr (std GLX) 275
Pwr windows (std GLX) 125
Bose sound 100
Wheels-alloy (std GLX) 150

Deduct:
No air cond 450
Man trans (not TDI) 400

PASSAT FWD/1.8L-I4T (150hp)

GLS TDI (5sp) 4dr Sdn
GLS 4dr Sdn 14950 17250
GLS 4dr Wgn 16000 18350
GLX (6cyl) 4dr Sdn 17250 19675

Add:
2.8L-V6(174hp) (std GLX) 600
Leather seats (std GLX) 300
Moonroof-power (std GLX) 325
CD Changer 250
Wheels-16" alloy (std GLX) 150

Deduct:
Manual transmission 475

1998 WS Ret

BEETLE FWD/2.0L-I4 (115hp)

2dr Cpe 10100 12100
TDI (1.9L TD) 2dr Cpe 10600 12625

Add:
ABS brakes 175
Alloy wheels 125
CD Changer 225
Cruise ctrl 75
Power windows 75
Moonroof-pwr 250

Deduct:
Manual trans 300

CABRIO FWD/2.0L-I4 (115hp)

GL 2dr Cnv 10650 12675
GLS 2dr Cnv 11750 13850

Add:
Alloy wheels (GL) 125
CD Changer 225
Power windows (GL) 75
Cruise ctrl (GL) 75

Deduct:
No air cond 375
Manual trans 325

GOLF FWD/2.0L-I4 (115hp)

GL 4dr Hbk 7625 9475
GTI 2dr Hbk 8825 10750
K2 4dr Hbk 7725 9575

Add:
ABS brakes (std GTI) 175
Alloy wheels (std GTI) 75
Cassette (std GTI,K2) 75
CD player 125

Deduct:
No air cond 375
Man trans (GL) 325

GTI VR6 (5sp) FWD/2.8L-V6 (172hp)

2dr Hbk 10975 13025

Add:
CD Changer 200
Leather seats 200

JETTA FWD/2.0L-I4 (115hp)

GL 4dr Sdn 8100 9975
GLS 4dr Sdn 8975 10900
GLX (6cyl) 4dr Sdn 11350 13425
GT 4dr Sdn 8500 10400
TDI (5sp) 4dr Sdn 9175 11125

Add:
ABS brakes (std GLX) 175
Cassette (GL,GT) 75
CD changer 200
Cruise ctrl (std GLS,GLX) 75
Leather seats 200
Moonroof-pwr (std GLX) 225
Pwr windows (std GLX) 100
Bose sound 75
Wheels-alloy (GL,K2) 125

Deduct:
No air cond 375
Man trans (not TDI) 325

PASSAT FWD/1.8L-I4 (150hp)

GLS TDI (5sp) 4dr Sdn
GLS 4dr Sdn 12250 14375
GLX (6cyl) 4dr Sdn 14675 16950

Add:
2.8L-V6 (174hp) (GLS) 475
Leather seats 200
Moonroof-power 275
CD Changer 200

Deduct:
Manual transmission 400

1997 WS Ret

CABRIO FWD/2.0L-I4 (115hp)

Base 2dr Cnv 8950 10875
Highline 2dr Cnv 10025 12025

Add:
Alloy wheels (Base) 75
CD Changer 200
Power windows (Base) 50

Deduct:
No air cond 325
Manual trans 275

GOLF FWD/2.0L-I4 (115hp)

GL 4dr Hbk 6300 8075
GL 2dr Hbk 6075 7850
GTI 2dr Hbk 7200 9025
K2 4dr Hbk 6700 8500
K2 2dr Hbk 6500 8300
TDI (5sp) 4dr Hbk

Add:
ABS brakes (std GTI) 150
Alloy wheels (std GTI) 50
Cassette (std GTI,K2) 50
CD player 100

Deduct:
No air cond 300
Man trans (GL) 275

GTI VR6 (5sp) FWD/2.8L-V6 (172hp)

2dr Hbk 8800 10725

Add:
CD Changer 175
Leather seats 175

JETTA FWD/2.0L-I4 (115hp)

GL 4dr Sdn 7250 9075
GLS 4dr Sdn 8025 9900
GLX (6cyl) 4dr Sdn 10200 12200
GT 4dr Sdn 7625 9475
TDI (5sp) 4dr Sdn

Add:
ABS brakes (std GLX) 150
Cassette (std GLS,GLX) 50
CD changer 175
Cruise ctrl (std GLS,GLX) 50
Leather seats 175
Moonroof-pwr (std GLX) 200
Wheels-alloy (std GLS,GLX) 75

Deduct:
No air cond 300
Man trans (not TDI) 275

PASSAT FWD/2.8L-V6 (172hp)

GLX (6cyl) 4dr Sdn 9625 11600
GLX (6cyl) 4dr Wgn 9925 11925
TDI (5sp) 4dr Sdn 9000 10925
TDI (5sp) 4dr Wgn

Add:
Leather seats 175
Moonroof-power 225
CD Changer 175
ABS brakes (std GLX) 150

Deduct:
Manual transmission 325

1996 WS Ret

CABRIO FWD/2.0L-I4 (115hp)

2dr Cnv 7725 9575

Add:
Alloy wheels 50
CD Changer 150
Leather seats 125

Deduct:
No air cond 250
Manual trans 225

GOLF FWD/2.0L-I4 (115hp)

GL 4dr Hbk 4925 6625
GL 2dr Hbk 4725 6375
GTI 2dr Hbk 6075 7850
TDI (5sp) 4dr Hbk

Add:
ABS brakes (std GTI) 150
Alloy wheels (std GTI) 50
Cassette (std GTI) 25
CD player 75

Deduct:
No air cond 250
Manual trans (GL) 225

GTI VR6 (5sp) FWD/2.8L-V6 (172hp)

2dr Hbk 7700 9550

Add:
CD Changer 150
Leather seats 150

Deduct:
No air cond 250

JETTA FWD/2.0L-I4 (115hp)

GL 4dr Sdn 5650 7400

	WS	Ret
GLS 4dr Sdn	6375	8150
GLX (6cyl) 4dr Sdn	8300	10200
TDI (5sp) 4dr Sdn		
Trek 4dr Sdn	5775	7525
Wolfsburg (5sp) 4dr Sdn	5800	7550

Add:
- ABS brakes (std GLX) ... 150
- Cassette ... 25
- CD changer ... 150
- Cruise ctrl (GL,Trek) ... 25
- Leather seats ... 150
- Moonroof-pwr (std GLX,WB) ... 150
- Wheels-alloy ... 50

Deduct:
- No air cond ... 250
- Man trans (not TDI,WB) ... 225

PASSAT — FWD/2.0L-I4 (115hp)

	WS	Ret
GLS 4dr Sdn	5825	7575
GLX (6cyl) 4dr Sdn	6125	7900
GLX (6cyl) 4dr Wgn	6400	8175
TDI (5sp) 4dr Sdn		
TDI (5sp) 4dr Wgn		

Add:
- Leather seats ... 150
- Sunroof-power ... 175
- CD Changer ... 150
- ABS brakes (std GLX) ... 150

Deduct:
- Manual trans ... 275

1995 — WS Ret

CABRIOLET — FWD/2.0L-I4 (115hp)

	WS	Ret
2dr Cnv	6575	8375

Add:
- Alloy wheels ... 50
- CD Changer ... 150
- Leather seats ... 125

Deduct:
- No air cond ... 225
- Manual trans ... 200

GOLF — FWD/2.0L-I4 (115hp)

	WS	Ret
Base (5sp) 4dr Hbk	5125	6825
GL 4dr Hbk	4075	5700
GL 2dr Hbk	3950	5550
Sport 2dr Hbk	4400	6050

Add:
- ABS brakes ... 125
- Alloy wheels (std Sport) ... 25
- Cassette ... 25
- CD player ... 50

Deduct:
- No air cond ... 225
- Manual trans ... 200

GTI VR6 (5sp) — FWD/2.8L-V6 (172hp)

	WS	Ret
2dr Hbk	5150	6850

Add:
- CD Changer ... 125

Deduct:
- No air cond ... 225

JETTA — FWD/2.0L-I4 (115hp)

	WS	Ret
Base (5sp) 4dr Sdn	3950	5550
GL 4dr Sdn	4625	6275
GLS 4dr Sdn	5275	7000
GLX (6cyl) 4dr Sdn	6350	8125

Add:
- ABS brakes (std GLX) ... 125
- Cassette ... 25
- CD changer ... 125
- Cruise ctrl (GL) ... 25
- Leather seats ... 125

Deduct:
- No air cond ... 225
- Manual trans ... 200

PASSAT — FWD/2.8L-V6 (115hp)

	WS	Ret
GLS 4dr Sdn	5125	6825
GLX 4dr Sdn	6025	7775
GLX 4dr Wgn	6225	8000

Add:
- Leather seats ... 125
- Sunroof-power (std GLX) ... 175
- CD Changer ... 125

Deduct:
- Manual trans ... 250

1994 — WS Ret

CORRADO — FWD/2.8L-V6 (178hp)

	WS	Ret
SLC (5sp/auto) 2dr Cpe	6675	8475

Add:
- Leather seats ... 75
- Sunroof-pwr ... 150

GOLF — FWD/2.0L-I4 (115hp)

	WS	Ret
GL 4dr Hbk	3500	4975
GL 2dr Hbk	3400	4875
LTD Edition 2dr Hbk	3500	4975

Add:
- ABS brakes ... 125
- Alloy wheels ... 25
- Cassette ... 25
- CD player ... 50

Deduct:
- No air cond ... 200
- Manual trans ... 175

JETTA — FWD/2.0L-I4 (115hp)

	WS	Ret
GL 4dr Sdn	3950	5550
GLS 4dr Sdn	4550	6200
GLX (6cyl) 4dr Sdn	5425	7150
LTD Edition 4dr Sdn	5575	7300

Add:
- ABS brakes (std GLX) ... 100
- Cassette (GL) ... 25
- CD changer ... 125
- Cruise ctrl (GL) ... 25
- Leather seats ... 125
- Sunroof-pwr (std Ltd Ed) ... 125

Deduct:
- No air cond ... 200
- Manual trans ... 175

PASSAT — FWD/2.8L-V6 (172hp)

	WS	Ret
GLX 4dr Sdn	4800	6450
GLX 4dr Wgn	4975	6675

Add:
- Leather seats ... 125
- Sunroof-power (std GLX) ... 150

Deduct:
- Manual trans ... 225

1993 — WS Ret

CABRIOLET — FWD/1.8L-I4 (94hp)

	WS	Ret
Base 2dr Cnv	3900	5500

Add:
- Pwr roof ... 125

Deduct:
- No air cond ... 175
- Manual trans ... 175

CORRADO — FWD/2.8L-V6 (174hp)

	WS	Ret
SLC (5sp/auto) 2dr Cpe	5350	7075

Add:
- Leather seats ... 75
- Sunroof-pwr ... 150

FOX — FWD/1.8L-I4 (81hp)

	WS	Ret
Base (5sp) 2dr Sdn	800	1475
GL (5sp) 4dr Sdn	1125	2025

Add:
- Cassette ... 25

Deduct:
- No air cond ... 175

GOLF III — FWD/2.0L-I4 (115hp)

	WS	Ret
GL 4dr Hbk	2775	4175

Add:
- Cassette ... 25

Deduct:
- No air cond ... 175
- Manual trans ... 150

JETTA III — FWD/2.0L-I4 (115hp)

	WS	Ret
GL 4dr Sdn	3150	4600

Add:
- Cassette ... 25

Deduct:
- No air cond ... 175
- Manual trans ... 150

PASSAT — FWD/2.0L-I4 (134hp)

	WS	Ret
GL 4dr Sdn	3200	4650
GLX (6cyl) 4dr Sdn	3950	5550
GLX (6cyl) 4dr Wgn	4150	5775

Add:
- Leather seats ... 100
- Sunroof-power (std GLX) ... 150

Deduct:
- Manual trans ... 200

1992 — WS Ret

CABRIOLET — FWD/1.8L-I4 (94hp)

	WS	Ret
Base 2dr Cnv	3250	4725
Carat 2dr Cnv	3775	5375

Add:
- Power roof ... 100

Deduct:
- No air cond ... 175
- Manual trans ... 150

CORRADO (5sp/AT) — FWD/1.8L-I4 (158hp)

	WS	Ret
Base 2dr Cpe	3400	4875
SLC 2dr Cpe	4025	5650

Add:
- ABS brakes ... 75
- Leather seats ... 50
- Sunroof-pwr ... 125

FOX — FWD/1.8L-I4 (81hp)

	WS	Ret
Base (4sp) 2dr Sdn	725	1250
GL (5sp) 4dr Sdn	1000	1700

Add:

Deduct:
- No air cond ... 150

GOLF — FWD/1.8L-I4 (100hp)

	WS	Ret
GL 4dr Hbk	1800	2875
GL 2dr Hbk	1725	2800
GTI (5sp) 2dr Hbk	2075	3200
GTI 16V (5sp) 2dr Hbk	2550	3925

Add:
- Sunroof-manual ... 25

Deduct:
- No air cond ... 175
- Man trans (not GTI) ... 150

JETTA — FWD/1.6L-I4 (100hp)

	WS	Ret
Carat 4dr Sdn	2250	3375
GL 4dr Sdn	2025	3125
GLI (5sp) 4dr Sdn	2750	4150

Add:
- ABS brakes ... 50
- Cruise ctrl ... 25
- Pwr windows ... 25
- Sunroof-manual ... 25

Deduct:
- 4cyl Diesel engine . . . 125
- No air cond . . . 175
- Man trans (not GLI) . . . 175

PASSAT FWD/2.0L-I4 (134hp)

Model	WS	Ret
CL 4dr Sdn	2500	3875
GL 4dr Sdn	2675	4075
GL 4dr Wgn	2775	4175

Add:
- ABS brakes . . . 75
- Alloy wheels . . . 25
- Cassette (std GL) . . . 25
- Leather seats . . . 75
- Sunroof-pwr . . . 100

Deduct:
- No air cond . . . 200
- Manual trans . . . 175

1991 WS Ret

CABRIOLET FWD/1.8L-I4 (94hp)

Model	WS	Ret
Base 2dr Cnv	2800	4200
Carat 2dr Cnv	3250	4725

Deduct:
- No air cond . . . 150
- Manual trans . . . 125

CORRADO FWD/1.8L-I4 (158hp)

Model	WS	Ret
Coupe (5sp/auto) 2dr Cpe	2975	4400

Add:
- ABS brakes . . . 50
- Leather seats . . . 25
- Sunroof-pwr . . . 100

FOX FWD/1.8L-I4 (81hp)

Model	WS	Ret
Base (4sp) 2dr Sdn	575	1075
GL (5sp) 4dr Sdn	875	1550

Add:

Deduct:
- No air cond . . . 125

GOLF FWD/1.8L-I4 (100hp)

Model	WS	Ret
GL 4dr Hbk	1500	2425
GL 2dr Hbk	1450	2375
GTI (5sp) 2dr Hbk	1750	2825
GTI-16V (5sp) 2dr Hbk	2150	3275

Add:
- Sunroof-manual . . . 25

Deduct:
- No air cond . . . 150
- Man trans (not GTI) . . . 125

JETTA FWD/1.8L-I4 (100hp)

Model	WS	Ret
Carat 4dr Sdn	1900	3000
GL 4dr Sdn	1700	2775
GL 2dr Sdn	1600	2650
GLI (5sp) 4dr Sdn	2350	3700

Add:
- ABS brakes . . . 50
- Sunroof-manual . . . 25

Deduct:
- 4cyl diesel . . . 125
- No air cond . . . 175
- Man trans (not GLI) . . . 150

PASSAT FWD/2.0L-I4 (134hp)

Model	WS	Ret
GL 4dr Sdn	2225	3350
GL 4dr Wgn	2375	3725

Add:
- ABS brakes . . . 50
- Alloy wheels . . . 25
- Cassette . . . 25
- Cruise ctrl . . . 25
- Leather seats . . . 50
- Pwr dr locks . . . 25
- Pwr windows . . . 25

Deduct:
- Manual trans . . . 175

1990 WS Ret

CABRIOLET FWD/1.8L-I4 (94hp)

Model	WS	Ret
Base 2dr Cnv	2475	3850
Boutique 2dr Cnv	2600	3975

Add:
- Alloy wheels (std Btque) . . . 25

Deduct:
- No air cond . . . 125
- Manual trans . . . 125

CORRADO FWD/1.8L-I4 (158hp)

Model	WS	Ret
Coupe (5sp) 2dr Cpe	2600	3975

Add:
- ABS brakes . . . 25
- Leather seats . . . 25
- Sunroof-pwr . . . 75

FOX (4sp) FWD/1.8L-I4 (81hp)

Model	WS	Ret
Base 2dr Sdn	425	900
GL 4dr Sdn	500	975
GL Sport (5sp) 2dr Sdn	525	1000
GL 2dr Wgn	525	1000

Add:
- Sunroof-manual . . . 25

Deduct:
- No air cond . . . 100

GOLF FWD/1.8L-I4 (100hp)

Model	WS	Ret
GL 4dr Hbk	1225	2125
GL 2dr Hbk	1225	2125
GTI (16V-5sp) 2dr Hbk	1500	2425

Add:
- Sunroof-manual . . . 25

Deduct:
- No air cond . . . 125
- Man trans (not GTI) . . . 125

JETTA FWD/1.8L-I4 (100hp)

Model	WS	Ret
Carat 4dr Sdn	1625	2675
GL 4dr Sdn	1425	2350
GL 2dr Sdn	1375	2300
GLI (5sp) 4dr Sdn	1900	3000

Add:
- ABS brakes . . . 25
- Sunroof-manual . . . 25

Deduct:
- 4cyl diesel . . . 100
- No air cond . . . 150
- Man trans (not GLI) . . . 125

PASSAT FWD/2.0L-I4 (134hp)

Model	WS	Ret
GL 4dr Sdn	1850	2925
GL 4dr Wgn	1950	3050

Add:
- ABS brakes . . . 25
- Alloy wheels . . . 25
- Leather seats . . . 25
- Pwr windows . . . 25
- Sunroof-pwr . . . 75

Deduct:
- Manual trans . . . 150

1989 WS Ret

CABRIOLET FWD/1.8L-I4 (90hp)

Model	WS	Ret
Base 2dr Cnv	1975	3075
Boutique 2dr Cnv	2050	3150

Add:

Deduct:
- No air cond . . . 75
- Manual trans . . . 75

FOX FWD/1.8L-I4 (81hp)

Model	WS	Ret
Base (4sp) 2dr Sdn	325	775
GL (4sp) 4dr Sdn	400	850
GL Sport (5sp) 4dr Sdn	475	950
GL (4sp) 2dr Sdn	325	775
GL Sport (5sp) 2dr Sdn	450	925
GL (4sp) 2dr Wgn	425	900

Add:

Deduct:
- No air cond . . . 75

GOLF FWD/1.8L-I4 (100hp)

Model	WS	Ret
Base 2dr Hbk	875	1550
GL 4dr Hbk	1000	1700
GL 2dr Hbk	1000	1700
GTI (5sp) 2dr Hbk	1275	2175

Add:

Deduct:
- No air cond . . . 75
- Man trans (not GTI) . . . 75

JETTA FWD/1.8L-I4 (100hp)

Model	WS	Ret
Base 4dr Sdn	1175	2075
Base 2dr Sdn	1150	2050
Carat 4dr Sdn	1325	2250
GL 4dr Sdn	1200	2100
GLI (5sp) 4dr Sdn	1525	2450

Add:
- ABS brakes . . . 25

Deduct:
- No air cond . . . 100
- Man trans (not GLI) . . . 100

1988 WS Ret

CABRIOLET FWD/1.8L-I4 (90hp)

Model	WS	Ret
Base 2dr Cnv	1600	2650
Boutique 2dr Cnv	1675	2725

Add:

Deduct:
- No air cond . . . 50
- Manual trans . . . 50

FOX (4sp) FWD/1.8L-I4 (81hp)

Model	WS	Ret
Base 2dr Sdn	300	750
GL 4dr Sdn	375	825
GL 2dr Wgn	375	825

Add:

Deduct:
- No air cond . . . 25

GOLF FWD/1.8L-I4 (100hp)

Model	WS	Ret
Base 2dr Hbk	750	1275
GL 4dr Hbk	825	1500
GL 2dr Hbk	800	1475
GT 4dr Hbk	875	1550
GT 2dr Hbk	875	1550
GTI (5sp) 2dr Hbk	975	1675

Add:

Deduct:
- No air cond . . . 50
- Man trans (not GTI) . . . 50

JETTA FWD/1.8L-I4 (100hp)

Model	WS	Ret
Base 4dr Sdn	950	1650
Base 2dr Sdn	925	1625
Carat 4dr Sdn	1025	1925
GL 4dr Sdn	1000	1700
GLI (5sp) 4dr Sdn	1175	2075

Add:

Deduct:
- No air cond . . . 75
- Man trans (not GLI) . . . 50

QUANTUM FWD/2.2L-I5 (110hp)

Model	WS	Ret
GL 4dr Sdn	1125	2025
GL 4dr Wgn	1125	2025
GL Syncro (AWD) 4dr Wgn	1275	2175

Deduct:
Manual trans 75

SCIROCCO FWD/1.8L-I4 (123hp)

Coupe (5sp) 2dr Cpe 1075 1975
Add:
Deduct:
No air cond 75

VOLVO

2001 WS Ret

40 SERIES FWD/1.9L-I4 (160hp)

S40 4dr Sdn
S40 Sport 4dr Sdn
V40 4dr Wgn

60 SERIES FWD/

S60 2.4 4dr Sdn 22400 25125
S60 2.4t (197hp) 4dr Sdn 23850 26675
S60 T-5 (2.3L/247hp 4dr Sdn
Add:
CD changer 400
Lthr seats 450
Moonroof-pwr 500
Deduct:
Manual transmission 800
No CD 200

70 SERIES FWD/2.4L-I5 (168hp)

C70 LT (190hp) 2dr Cnv
C70 HT (2.3L/236hp) 2dr Cnv
C70 HT (2.3L/236hp) Cpe
V70 2.4 4dr Wgn 23725 26525
V70 T-5 4dr Wgn
Add:
CD changer 400
Lthr seats (std cnv) 450
Pwr seat (Base) 175
Wood Trim (C70) 225
Moonroof-pwr (Base 2.4) 500
CD player (std T5,Cpe) 200
Deduct:
Manual transmission 800

70 SERIES AWD AWD/2.4L-I5 (190hp)

V70XC 4dr Wgn

80 SERIES RWD/2.9L-I6 (201hp)

S80 4dr Sdn
S80 T-6 (2.8L/268hp 4dr Sdn

2000 WS Ret

40 SERIES FWD/1.9L-I4 (160hp)

S40 4dr Sdn 15550 17875
V40 4dr Wgn 16600 19000
Add:
CD player 175
Moonroof-pwr 400
Lthr seats 325
Pwr seat 150

70 SERIES FWD/2.4L-I5 (168hp)

C70 LT (190hp) 2dr Cnv 27025 30025
C70 HT (2.3L/236hp) 2dr Cnv
C70 LT (190hp) 2dr Cpe 21425 24100
C70 HT (2.3L/236hp) Cpe
S70 4dr Sdn 18525 21025
S70 SE 4dr Sdn 19400 21950
S70 GLT (190hp) 4dr Sdn 19950 22525
S70 GLT SE (190hp) 4sd 20825 23475
S70 T-5 (2.3L/236hp 4sd 21825 24525
V70 4dr Wgn 19825 22400
V70 SE 4dr Wgn 20650 23275
V70 GLT (190hp) 4dr Wgn 21075 23725
Add:
CD changer 300
Lthr seats (Base) 350
Pwr seat (Base) 150
Wood Trim (C70) 175
Moonroof-pwr (Base sdn) 400
CD player (std T5,Cpe) 175
Deduct:
Manual transmission 625

70 SERIES AWD AWD/2.4L-I5 (190hp)

S70 4dr Sdn 21550 24225
V70XC 4dr Wgn 24575 27425
V70XC SE 4dr Wgn 25050 27950
V70R (2.3L/261hp) 4dr Wgn
Add:
CD changer 300
Lthr seats (Base) 350
Moonroof-pwr (Base) 400

80 SERIES RWD/2.9L-I6 (201hp)

S80 4dr Sdn 23100 25875
S80 T-6 (2.8L/268hp) 4sd 26850 29850
Add:
Navigation sys 600
Moonroof-pwr 400
Wheels-17" alloy 225
Traction ctrl 375
CD changer 300
Deduct:
Cloth seats 375

1999 WS Ret

70 SERIES FWD/2.4L-I5 (162hp)

C70 2dr Cnv 26925 29925
C70 LT 2dr Cpe 21300 23975
C70 HT (2.3L/236hp) Cpe 23900 26725
S70 4dr Sdn 15725 18050
S70 GLT (190hp) 4dr Sdn 17025 19450
S70 T-5 (2.3L/236hp 4sd 20500 23125
V70 4dr Wgn 16925 19325
V70 GLT (190hp) 4dr Wgn 18100 20575
V70 T-5 (2.3L/236hp) Wgn 21550 24225
Add:
Alloy wheels (Base) 150
Lthr seats 300
Pwr seat (Base) 100
Wood Trim (std R) 150
Moonroof-pwr (Base sdn) 325
CD player (std T5,Cpe) 125
Deduct:
Manual transmission 550

70 SERIES AWD AWD/2.4L-I5 (190hp)

S70 4dr Sdn 20675 23300
V70 4dr Wgn 21975 24675
V70XC 4dr Wgn 23375 26175
V70R (2.3L/247hp) Wgn 23100 25875
Add:
Alloy wheels (Base) 150
Lthr seats (std R) 300
Wood Trim (std R) 150
Moonroof-pwr (std R) 325

80 SERIES RWD/2.9L-I6 (201hp)

S80 4dr Sdn 21625 24300
S80 T-6 (2.8L/268hp 4dr Sdn 25075 27975

1998 WS Ret

70 SERIES FWD/2.5L-I5 (168hp)

C70 2dr Cpe 19075 21600
S70 4dr Sdn 12675 14825
S70 GLT (190hp) 4dr Sdn 13775 16000
S70 T-5 (2.3L/236hp 4sd 16875 19275
V70 4dr Wgn 13675 15900
V70 GLT (190hp) 4dr Wgn 14700 16975
V70 T-5 (2.3L/236hp Wgn 17800 20250
Add:
Alloy wheels (Base) 125
Lthr seats 250
Pwr seat (Base) 75
Wood Trim (std R) 125
Moonroof-pwr (Base) 275
Deduct:
Manual transmission 425

70 SERIES AWD AWD/2.3L-I5 (236hp)

V70 4dr Wgn 18575 21075
V70XC 4dr Wgn 19775 22350
V70R (2.3L/236hp) Wgn 20525 23150
Add:
Alloy wheels (Base) 125
Lthr seats (Base) 250
Wood Trim (std R) 125
Moonroof-pwr 275

90 SERIES RWD/3.0L-I6 (181hp)

S90 4dr Sdn 15350 17675
V90 4dr Wgn 16350 18725
Add:
CD player 125

1997 WS Ret

850 FWD/2.4L-I5 (168hp)

Base 4dr Sdn 10550 12575
Base 4dr Wgn 11450 13525
GLT (190hp) 4dr Sdn 11550 13650
GLT (190hp) 4dr Wgn 12375 14500
R (2.3L/240hp) 4dr Sdn 15475 17800
R (2.3L/240hp) 4dr Wgn 15725 18050
T-5 (2.3L/222hp) 4dr Sdn 13925 16150
T-5 (2.3L/222hp) 4dr Wgn 14800 17075
Add:
Alloy wheels (Base) 100
Air Bag-side impact 50
Lthr seats (std R) 200
Pwr seat (Base,GLT) 50
Traction control (std R) 175
Wood Trim (std R) 75
Moonroof-pwr (Base) 225
Deduct:
Manual transmission 350

960 RWD/2.9L-V6 (181hp)

960 4dr Sdn 12650 14800
960 4dr Wgn 13500 15700
Add:
CD player 75

1996 WS Ret

850 FWD/2.4L-I5 (168hp)

Base 4dr Sdn 9400 11350
Base 4dr Wgn 10250 12250
GLT (190hp) 4dr Sdn 10300 12325
GLT (190hp) 4dr Wgn 11050 13100
Platinum 4dr Sdn 13500 15700
Platinum 4dr Wgn 14250 16500
R 4dr Sdn 14075 16325
R 4dr Wgn 14300 16550
Turbo 4dr Sdn 10775 12825
Turbo 4dr Wgn 11450 13525
Add:
Alloy wheels (Base) 75
Air Bag-side impact 175
Lthr seats (std Plat,R) 175
Pseat (Base,GLT,Turbo Sdn) 50
Traction control (std Plat,R) 175
Wood Trim (std Plat,R) 50
Deduct:
Manual transmission 275

960 — RWD/2.9L-V6 (181hp)

	WS	Ret
960 4dr Sdn	10700	12750
960 4dr Wgn	11475	13550

Add:
CD Changer . . . 175

1995 — WS Ret

850 — FWD/2.4L-I5 (168hp)

	WS	Ret
Base 4dr Sdn	8350	10250
Base 4dr Wgn	9000	10925
GLT (190hp) 4dr Sdn	9000	10925
GLT (190hp) 4dr Wgn	9600	11575
Turbo 4dr Sdn	9800	11775
Turbo 4dr Wgn	10275	12300

Add:
Alloy wheels (Base) . . . 50
Air Bag-side impact . . . 175
Lthr seats . . . 150
Pwr seat . . . 25
Traction control . . . 150
Wood trim . . . 50

Deduct:
Manual transmission . . . 250

940 — RWD/2.3L-I4 (114hp)

	WS	Ret
Base 4dr Sdn	7200	9025
Base 4dr Wgn	7875	9750
Turbo 4dr Sdn	8275	10175
Turbo 4dr Wgn	8875	10800

Add:
Alloy wheels . . . 50
Leather seats (Base) . . . 75
Pwr seat (Base) . . . 50
Sunroof-pwr . . . 175

960 — RWD/2.9L-V6 (181hp)

	WS	Ret
960 4dr Sdn	8800	10725
960 4dr Wgn	9625	11600

Add:
CD Changer . . . 175

1994 — WS Ret

850 — FWD/2.4L-I5 (168hp)

	WS	Ret
Base 4dr Sdn	7350	9200
Base 4dr Wgn	7900	9775
Turbo 4dr Sdn	8575	10475
Turbo 4dr Wgn	9000	10925

Add:
Alloy wheels-15" (Base) . . . 50
Alloy wheels-16" (Turbo) . . . 50
Lthr seats (std Turbo) . . . 125
Pwr seat . . . 25
Traction control . . . 125
Sunroof-pwr (std Turbo) . . . 150
Wood trim . . . 50

Deduct:
Manual transmission . . . 225

940 — RWD/2.3L-I4 (114hp)

	WS	Ret
Base 4dr Sdn	6250	8025
Base 4dr Wgn	6850	8650
Turbo 4dr Sdn	7200	9025
Turbo 4dr Wgn	7725	9575

Add:
Alloy wheels-16" (Turbo) . . . 25
Alloy wheels-15" (Base) . . . 25

960 — RWD/2.9L-V6 (201hp)

	WS	Ret
960 4dr Sdn	7650	9500
960 4dr Wgn	8350	10250

Add:
Alloy wheels . . . 50

1993 — WS Ret

240 — RWD/2.3L-I4 (114hp)

	WS	Ret
Base 4dr Sdn	4550	6200
Base 4dr Wgn	5000	6700

Add:
Alloy wheels . . . 25

Deduct:
Manual transmission . . . 200

850 — FWD/2.4L-I5 (168hp)

	WS	Ret
GLT 4dr Sdn	6325	8100

Add:
Lthr seats (std GLTS) . . . 125
Traction control . . . 50

Deduct:
Manual transmission . . . 225

940 — RWD/2.3L-I4 (114hp)

	WS	Ret
GL 4dr Sdn	5525	7250
GL 4dr Wgn	5925	7675
Turbo 4dr Sdn	6425	8200
Turbo 4dr Wgn	6750	8550

Add:
Alloy wheels (16-inch) . . . 25

960 — RWD/3.0L-V6 (201hp)

	WS	Ret
960 4dr Sdn	6275	8050
960 4dr Wgn	6825	8625

Add:
Sunroof-power . . . 175

1992 — WS Ret

240 — RWD/2.3L-I4 (114hp)

	WS	Ret
Base 4dr Sdn	4000	5625
Base 4dr Wgn	4425	6075
GL 4dr Sdn	4225	5850

Add:
ABS brakes . . . 75
Alloy wheels . . . 25
Leather seats . . . 75

Deduct:
Manual trans . . . 200

740 — RWD/2.3L-I4 (114hp)

	WS	Ret
Base 4dr Sdn	4575	6225
Base 4dr Wgn	4950	6650
GL 4dr Wgn	5175	6875
GL Turbo 4dr Wgn	5500	7225

Add:
Alloy wheels (Base,GL) . . . 25
Leather seats . . . 100
Sunroof-man (Base only) . . . 50

940 — RWD/2.3L-I4 (114hp)

	WS	Ret
GL 4dr Sdn	4875	6550
Turbo 4dr Sdn	5700	7450
Turbo 4dr Wgn	6000	7750

Add:
Alloy wheels (std Turbo) . . . 25
Lthr seats (std Turbo) . . . 100
Pwr seat . . . 25

960 — RWD/3.0L-V6 (201hp)

	WS	Ret
960 4dr Sdn	5450	7175
960 4dr Wgn	5950	7700

1991 — WS Ret

240 — RWD/2.3L-I4 (114hp)

	WS	Ret
Base 4dr Sdn	3700	5200
Base 4dr Wgn	4025	5650
SE 4dr Wgn	4200	5825

Add:
ABS brakes (std SE) . . . 50
Leather seats . . . 50

Deduct:
Manual trans . . . 175

740 — RWD/2.3L-I4 (114hp)

	WS	Ret
Base 4dr Sdn	3850	5450
Base 4dr Wgn	4175	5800
SE Turbo 4dr Sdn	4725	6375
SE Turbo 4dr Wgn	5050	6750
Turbo 4dr Sdn	4450	6100
Turbo 4dr Wgn	4750	6400

Add:
ABS brakes . . . 50
Leather seats . . . 75

Deduct:
Manual trans . . . 175

940 — RWD/2.3L-I4 (153hp)

	WS	Ret
GLE 4dr Sdn	4575	6225
GLE 4dr Wgn	4900	6575
SE Turbo 4dr Sdn	5325	7050
SE Turbo 4dr Wgn	5675	7425
Turbo 4dr Sdn	4975	6675
Turbo 4dr Wgn	5325	7050

Add:
Lthr seats (std Turbo) . . . 75

COUPE — RWD/2.3L-I4 (188hp)

	WS	Ret
Turbo 2dr Cpe	6200	7975

1990 — WS Ret

240 — RWD/2.3L-I4 (114hp)

	WS	Ret
Base 4dr Sdn	2950	4375
Base 4dr Wgn	3225	4675
DL 4dr Sdn	3050	4500
DL 4dr Wgn	3350	4825

Deduct:
Manual trans . . . 150

740 — RWD/2.3L-I4 (114hp)

	WS	Ret
Base 4dr Sdn	2825	4225
Base 4dr Wgn	3275	4750
GL 4dr Sdn	2950	4375
GL 4dr Wgn	3400	4875
GLE 4dr Sdn	3250	4725
GLE 4dr Wgn	3650	5150
Turbo 4dr Sdn	3575	5050
Turbo 4dr Wgn	4050	5675

Add:
ABS brakes . . . 25
Leather seats . . . 50

Deduct:
Manual trans . . . 150

760 — RWD/2.8L-V6 (144hp)

	WS	Ret
GLE 4dr Sdn	3325	4800
GLE Turbo 4dr Sdn	3700	5200
GLE Turbo 4dr Wgn	3925	5525

780 — RWD/2.8L-V6 (144hp)

	WS	Ret
GLE 2dr Cpe	4575	6225
Turbo (4cyl) 2dr Cpe	4775	6425

1989 — WS Ret

240 — RWD/2.3L-I4 (114hp)

	WS	Ret
DL 4dr Sdn	2450	3825
DL 4dr Wgn	2625	4000
GL 4dr Sdn	2600	3975
GL 4dr Wgn	2750	4150

Add:
Leather seats . . . 25

Deduct:
Manual trans . . . 125

740 RWD/2.3L-I4 (114hp)

Model	WS	Ret
GL 4dr Sdn	2550	3925
GL 4dr Wgn	2700	4100
GLE 4dr Sdn	2700	4100
GLE 4dr Wgn	2850	4250
Turbo 4dr Sdn	2825	4225
Turbo 4dr Wgn	2975	4400

Add:
ABS brakes (GL only) 25
Leather (std GLE Wgns) 25

Deduct:
Manual trans 125

760 RWD/2.8L-V6 (145hp)

Model	WS	Ret
GLE 4dr Sdn	3225	4675
GLE Turbo 4dr Sdn	3425	4900
GLE Turbo 4dr Wgn	3550	5025

780 RWD/2.8L-V6 (145hp)

Model	WS	Ret
GLE 2dr Cpe	4000	5625
Turbo (4cyl) 2dr Cpe	4175	5800

1988 WS Ret

240 RWD/2.3L-I4 (114hp)

Model	WS	Ret
DL 4dr Sdn	1975	3075
DL 4dr Wgn	2150	3275
GL 4dr Sdn	2125	3250
GL 4dr Wgn	2275	3425

Add:
Lthr seats(std GL wgn) 25

Deduct:
Manual trans 75

740 RWD/2.3L-I4 (114hp)

Model	WS	Ret
GLE 4dr Sdn	2075	3200
GLE Turbo 4dr Sdn	2300	3450
GLE 4dr Wgn	2175	3300
GLE Turbo 4dr Wgn	2375	3725

Add:
ABS brakes (std Turbo) 25
Air bag-drvr (std Turbo) 25
Lthr seats (std Wgns) 25

Deduct:
Manual trans 75

760 RWD/2.3L-I4 (140hp)

Model	WS	Ret
GLE Turbo 4dr Sdn	2850	4250
GLE Turbo 4dr Wgn	2950	4375

780 RWD/2.9L-V6 (174hp)

Model	WS	Ret
GLE 2dr Cpe	3200	4650

TRUCKS, VANS & SPORT UTILITIES

ACURA

2001 WS Ret

MDX AWD/

Model	WS	Ret
Luxury 4dr Utl		

Add:
Navigation System 800

1999 WS Ret

SLX 4WD/3.5l-V6 (215hp)

Model	WS	Ret
Luxury 4dr Utl	15375	18025

1998 WS Ret

SLX 4WD/3.5L-V6 (215hp)

Model	WS	Ret
Luxury 4dr Utl	13950	16350

1997 WS Ret

SLX 4WD/3.2L-V6 (190hp)

Model	WS	Ret
Luxury 4dr Utl	10225	12400

Add:
Premium pkg 475

1996 WS Ret

SLX 4WD/

Model	WS	Ret
Luxury 4dr Utl	8500	10900

Add:
Premium pkg 375

BMW

2001 WS Ret

X5 4WD/4.4L-V8 (282hp)

Model	WS	Ret
3.0i 4dr Utl		
4.4i (4.4L-V8/282hp 4dr Utl		

Deduct:
Leatherette (vinyl) seats 875

2000 WS Ret

X5 AWD/4.4L-V8 (282hp)

Model	WS	Ret
4.4i 4dr Utl		

CADILLAC

2000 WS Ret

ESCALADE 4WD/5.7L-V8 (255hp)

Model	WS	Ret
Luxury 4dr Utl	27625	30975

1999 WS Ret

ESCALADE 4WD/5.7L-V8 (255hp)

Model	WS	Ret
Luxury 4dr Utl	24000	27350

CHEVROLET

2001 WS Ret

ASTRO RWD/4.3L-V6 (190hp)

Model	WS	Ret
Cargo Mini Van	11350	13825
LS Mini Van	13100	15950

Add:
All wheel drive 2050
LS trim 975
LT trim 1625

BLAZER RWD/4.3L-V6 (190hp)

Model	WS	Ret
LS 4dr Utl	13100	15950
LS 2dr Utl	11850	14425

Add:
4-wheel drive 2300
LT trim 1825
ZR2 off-road pkg 725
Trailblazer trim 1000
Extreme pkg 1100

C1500 SILVERADO RWD/4.8L-V8 (270hp)

Model	WS	Ret
Ext.Cab Fltsde Sbed Pkp	14175	16700
Ext.Cab Sptsde Sbed Pkp.	14675	17275
Ext.Cab Fltsde Lbed Pkp	14575	17150
Fleetside Sbed Pkp	12325	15000
Fleetside Lbed Pkp	12500	15225
Sportside Sbed Pkp	12650	15475

C2500 SILVERADO RWD/5.3L-V8 (285hp)

Model	WS	Ret
Crew Cab Fltsde HD Sbed		
Crew Cab Fltsde HD Lbed		
Ext.Cab Fltsde HD Sbed	15175	17875
Ext.Cab Fltsde 4WD Sbed	14550	17125
Ext.Cab Fltsde HD Lbed	15450	18200
Ext.Cab Fltsde Lbed Pkp	15025	17700
Fleetside Lbed Pkp	12825	15625
Fltsde HD Lbed Pkp	13425	15800

Add:
4-wheel drive 2525
LS trim (std C1500) 1100
LT trim 1600

Deduct:
6cyl (not Work Truck) 525

G1500 VAN RWD/5.0L-V8 (220hp)

Model	WS	Ret
Express 135" WB Psgr	14450	17025
Express 135" WB Cargo	12200	14850

G2500 VAN RWD/5.7L-V8 (255hp)

Model	WS	Ret
Express 135" WB Psgr	14875	17525
Express 135" WB Cargo	12625	15375

Deduct:
6cyl 525

S10 PICKUP RWD/4.3L-V6 (180hp)

Model	WS	Ret
Crew Cab Fltsde Sbed Pkp		
Fleetside Sbed Pkp	8150	10500
Fleetside Lbed Pkp	8275	10675
Fleetside ExCab Pkp	9550	11625
Sportside Sbed Pkp	8425	10850
Sportside ExCab Pkp	9800	11925

Add:
4-wheel drive 2300
3rd door (Ext Cab) 225
LS trim 975
Low Ride Sport Susp. 325
Xtreme pkg (incls Sport Susp.) . 1550
ZR2 off-road pkg 1100

Deduct:
4cyl 475

SUBURBAN RWD/5.3L-V8 (285hp)

Model	WS	Ret
C1500 LS 4dr Utl	22925	26375
C2500 LS 4dr Utl	23825	27400

Add:
4-wheel drive 2525

LT trim 1850

TAHOE 4WD/4.8L-V8 (275hp)

Base 4dr Utl	20800	23925
LS 4dr Utl	23250	26750
LT 4dr Utl	24725	28450

Add:
- LT trim 2075
- Z-71 1250

Deduct:
- 2-wheel drive 2400

TRACKER (5sp) RWD/2.0L-I4 (127hp)

LT 4WD (AT/V6) 4dr Utl . . . .
SoftTop 2dr Utl . . . .
Wagon 4dr Utl . . . .
ZR2 4WD (AT/V6) 2dr Utl . . . . . .

VENTURE FWD/3.4L-V6 (185hp)

Extended Mini Van	14650	17250
SWB Mini Van	13200	15550

Add:
- LS trim 725
- LT trim 1425
- Traction ctrl 150
- Sliding door-pwr 250
- Warner Bros. trim (LT) 450
- Wheels-alloy (Base) 200

2000 WS Ret

ASTRO RWD/4.3L-V6 (190hp)

Cargo Mini Van	10525	12825
Window Mini Van	11775	14350

Add:
- All wheel drive 1600
- LS trim 750
- LT trim 1275

BLAZER RWD/4.3L-V6 (190hp)

LS 4dr Utl	11675	14225
LS 2dr Utl	10650	12975

Add:
- 4-wheel drive 1775
- LT trim 1425
- ZR2 pkg 550
- Trailblazer trim 775

C1500 SILVERADO RWD/4.8L-V8 (270hp)

Ext.Cab Fltsde Sbed Pkp	12825	15625
Ext.Cab Sptsde Sbed Pkp	13275	15625
Ext.Cab Fltsde Lbed Pkp	13175	15500
Fleetside Sbed Pkp	11150	13575
Fleetside Lbed Pkp	11325	13800
Sportside Sbed Pkp	11450	14025
Work Truck (6cyl) Sbed Pkp	9825	11975
Work Truck (6cyl) Lbed Pkp	9975	12150

C2500 4WD/5.3L-V8 (285hp)

Ext.Cab Fltsde HD 4WD Sbed	17825	20625
Ext.Cab Fltsde HD Lbed	15300	18025
*Fltsde HD Lbed Pkp	12800	15600

Add:
- 4-wheel drive 1975
- LS trim (std C1500) 850
- LT trim 1225

Deduct:
- 6cyl (not Work Truck) 425

** Old Style*

C2500 SILVERADO RWD/5.3L-V8 (285hp)

Ext.Cab Fltsde Sbed Pkp	13150	15475
Ext.Cab Fltsde Lbed Pkp	13600	16025
Fleetside Lbed Pkp	11600	14125

Add:
- 4-wheel drive 1975
- LS trim (std C1500) 850
- LT trim 1225

Deduct:
- 6cyl (not Work Truck) 425

G1500 VAN RWD/5.0L-V8 (220hp)

Express 135" WB Psgr Van	13225	15575
Express 135" WB Cargo Van	11250	13700

G2500 VAN RWD/5.7L-V8 (255hp)

Express 135" WB Psgr Van	13650	16075
Express 135" WB Cargo Van	11650	14200

Add:
- LS Trim 1050

Deduct:
- 6cyl 425

S10 PICKUP RWD/4.3L-V6 (180hp)

Fleetside Sbed Pkp	7625	9825
Fleetside Lbed Pkp	7700	9925
Fleetside ExCab Pkp	8925	11500
Sportside Sbed Pkp	7825	10075
Sportside ExCab Pkp	9125	11125

Add:
- 4-wheel drive 1775
- 3rd door (std 4WD) 175
- LS trim 750
- Low Ride suspension 250
- Xtreme pkg (incls LR susp.) . . 1200
- ZR2 pkg 850

Deduct:
- 4cyl 375

SUBURBAN RWD/5.3L-V8 (285hp)

C1500 4dr Utl	18925	21775
C2500 4dr Utl	19675	22625

Add:
- 4-wheel drive 1975
- LS trim 1075
- LT trim 1425

TAHOE 4WD/4.8L-V8 (275hp)

Limited (OS) 4dr Utl	18300	21275
Wagon 4dr Utl	20550	23650

Add:
- ZR2 trim (old style) 775
- LS trim 950

Deduct:
- 2-wheel drive 1875

TRACKER (5sp) RWD/1.6L-I4 (97hp)

SoftTop 2dr Utl	6825	8800
Wagon 4dr Utl	7300	9400

Add:
- 4-wheel drive 1400
- 2.0L-I4 (127hp) (std 4dr) 375
- Automatic trans 525
- ABS Brakes 250
- Hardtop (2dr) 250

VENTURE FWD/3.4L-V6 (185hp)

Cargo Mini Van	11675	14225
Extended Mini Van	13250	15600
SWB Mini Van	11825	14400

Add:
- LS trim 550
- LT trim 1125
- Traction ctrl 125
- Sliding door-pwr 200
- Warner Bros. trim (LT) 350
- Wheels-alloy (Base) 175

Deduct:
- Psngr slider only 325

1999 WS Ret

ASTRO RWD/4.3L-V6 (190hp)

Cargo Mini Van	9350	11400
Window Mini Van	10775	13125

Add:
- All wheel drive 1325
- LS trim 625
- LT trim 1050

BLAZER RWD/4.3L-V6 (190hp)

Sport Util 4dr Utl	10200	12425
Sport Util 2dr Utl	9275	11300

Add:
- 4-wheel drive 1475
- LS trim 625
- LT trim 1175
- ZR2 pkg 425
- Trailblazer trim 575

C1500 RWD/5.0L-V8 (230hp)

LS Ext.Cab Fltsde (Sbed Pkp	13550	15950

C1500 SILVERADO RWD/5.0L-V8 (230hp)

Ext.Cab Fltsde Sbed Pkp	12175	14825
Ext.Cab Sptsde Sbed Pkp	12675	15450
Ext.Cab Fltsde Lbed Pkp	12525	15250
Fleetside Sbed Pkp	10650	12975
Fleetside Lbed Pkp	10775	13125
Sportside Sbed Pkp	10900	13350
Work Truck (6cyl) Sbed Pkp	9350	11400
Work Truck (6cyl) Lbed Pkp	9525	11600

C2500 4WD/5.7L-V8 (255hp)

Ext.Cab Fltsde 4WD Sbed	16150	18675
*Ext.Cab Fltsde Lbed Pkp	14100	16600
*Fltsde Lbed Pkp	11550	14075

Add:
- 4-wheel drive 1625
- LS trim (std C1500) 700

Deduct:
- 6cyl (not Work Truck) 350

** Old Style*

C2500 SILVERADO RWD/5.7L-V8 (255hp)

Ext.Cab Fltsde Sbed Pkp	12500	15225
Ext.Cab Fltsde Lbed Pkp	12950	15775
Fleetside Lbed Pkp	11050	13450

Add:
- 4-wheel drive 1625
- LS trim (std C1500) 700

Deduct:
- 6cyl (not Work Truck) 350

G1500 VAN RWD/5.0L-V8 (220hp)

Express 135" wb Psgr Van	12100	14750
Express 135" wb Cargo Van	10425	12700

G2500 VAN RWD/5.7L-V8 (220hp)

Express 135" wb Psgr Van	12450	15175
Express 135" wb Cargo Van	10775	13125

Add:
- LS Trim 875

Deduct:
- 6cyl 350

S10 PICKUP RWD/4.3L-V6 (180hp)

Fleetside Sbed Pkp	6650	8575
Fleetside Lbed Pkp	6750	8700
Fleetside ExCab Pkp	7800	10050
Sportside Sbed Pkp	6850	8825
Sportside ExCab Pkp	7975	10275

Add:
- 4-wheel drive 1475
- 3rd door (std 4WD ext cab) . . . 150
- Xtreme pkg 850
- LS trim 625
- SS trim 300
- ZR2 pkg 700

Deduct:
- 4cyl 300

Check Truck Equipment Table on page 4

SUBURBAN RWD/5.7L-V8 (255hp)

C1500 4dr Utl	14575	17250
C2500 4dr Utl	15150	17925

Add:
- 4-wheel drive . . . 1625
- LS trim . . . 875
- LT trim . . . 1175

TAHOE 4WD/5.7L-V8 (255hp)

Sport Util 2dr Utl	14625	17300
Wagon 4dr Utl	16450	19125

Add:
- Sport pkg (2dr) . . . 175
- LS trim (2dr) . . . 775
- LT trim (4dr) . . . 600
- LT trim (2dr) . . . 1475

Deduct:
- 2-wheel drive . . . 1550

TRACKER (5sp) RWD/1.6L-I4 (97hp)

SoftTop 2dr Utl	6100	7875
Wagon 4dr Utl	6575	8475

Add:
- 4-wheel drive . . . 1150
- 2.0L-I4 (127hp) (std 4dr) . . . 300
- Automatic trans . . . 425
- ABS Brakes . . . 225
- Hardtop . . . 200

VENTURE FWD/3.4L-V6 (185hp)

Cargo Mini Van	10650	12975
Extended Mini Van	12050	14675
SWB Mini Van	10300	12550

Add:
- LT trim . . . 1025
- LS trim . . . 475
- Traction ctrl . . . 75
- Sliding door-pwr . . . 150
- Integrated child seat(s) . . . 50
- Wheels-alloy . . . 125

Deduct:
- Psngr slider only . . . 275

1998 — WS — Ret

ASTRO RWD/4.3L-V6 (190hp)

Cargo Mini Van	8100	10450
Window Mini Van	9350	11400

Add:
- 4-wheel drive . . . 1100
- LS trim . . . 500
- LT trim . . . 875

BLAZER RWD/4.3L-V6 (190hp)

Sport Util 4dr Utl	9025	11625
Sport Util 2dr Utl	8225	10600

Add:
- 4-wheel drive . . . 1225
- LS trim . . . 525
- LT trim . . . 975

C1500 PICKUP RWD/5.0L-V8 (230hp)

Ext.Cab Fltsde Sbed Pkp	10875	13250
Ext.Cab Sptsde Sbed Pkp	11225	13675
Ext.Cab Fltsde Lbed Pkp	11175	13600
Fleetside Sbed Pkp	9500	11575
Fleetside Lbed Pkp	9650	11750
Sportside Sbed Pkp	9750	11925
Work Truck (6cyl) Sbed Pkp	8350	10775
Work Truck (6cyl) Lbed Pkp	8500	10950

C2500 PICKUP RWD/5.0L-V8 (230hp)

Ext.Cab Fltsde Sbed Pkp	11150	13575
Ext.Cab Fltsde Lbed Pkp	11525	14025
Fleetside Lbed Pkp	9900	12050

Add:
- 4-wheel drive . . . 1350
- Third door (ext. cab) . . . 150
- Silverado trim . . . 725

Deduct:
- 6cyl (not Work Truck) . . . 275

G1500 VAN RWD/5.0L-V8 (220hp)

Chevyvan 135" wb Cargo	9175	11175
Express 135" wb Psgr	10800	13150

G2500 VAN RWD/5.7L-V8 (255hp)

Chevyvan 135" wb Cargo	9525	11600
Express 135" wb Psgr	11100	13525

Add:
- LS Trim . . . 725

Deduct:
- 6cyl . . . 275

S10 PICKUP RWD/4.3L-V6 (175hp)

Fleetside Sbed Pkp	5650	7275
Fleetside Lbed Pkp	5725	7375
Fleetside ExCab Pkp	6600	8500
Sportside Sbed Pkp	5825	7500
Sportside ExCab Pkp	6775	8725

Add:
- 4-wheel drive . . . 1225
- Third door (ext. cab) . . . 125
- LS trim . . . 525
- SS trim . . . 250
- ZR2 pkg . . . 475

Deduct:
- 4cyl . . . 250

SUBURBAN RWD/5.7L-V8 (255hp)

C1500 4dr Utl	12975	15875
C2500 4dr Utl	13475	15950

Add:
- 4-wheel drive . . . 1350
- LS trim . . . 725
- LT trim . . . 975

TAHOE 4WD/5.7L-V8 (255hp)

Sport Util 2dr Utl	13175	15600
Wagon 4dr Utl	14800	17500

Add:
- Sport pkg . . . 150
- LS trim (2dr) . . . 625
- LT trim (2dr) . . . 1125
- LT trim (4dr) . . . 500

Deduct:
- 2-wheel drive . . . 1275

TRACKER (5sp) RWD/1.6L-I4 (95hp)

SoftTop 2dr Utl	4100	5700
Wagon 4dr Utl	4625	6425

Add:
- 4-wheel drive . . . 950
- Automatic trans . . . 350
- ABS Brakes . . . 175
- Hardtop . . . 150

VENTURE FWD/3.4L-V6 (180hp)

Extended Mini Van	8500	10950
SWB Mini Van	8700	11225

Add:
- LS trim . . . 450
- Traction ctrl . . . 50
- Sliding door-pwr . . . 125
- Integrated child seat(s) . . . 50
- Wheels-alloy . . . 100

Deduct:
- Psngr slider only . . . 225

1997 — WS — Ret

ASTRO RWD/4.3L-V6 (190hp)

Cargo Mini Van	6750	8700
Window Mini Van	7750	10000

Add:
- 4-wheel drive . . . 900
- LS trim . . . 425
- LT trim . . . 725

BLAZER RWD/4.3L-V6 (190hp)

Sport Util 4dr Utl	7750	10000
Sport Util 2dr Utl	7050	9100

Add:
- 4-wheel drive . . . 1000
- LS trim . . . 425
- LT trim . . . 775

C1500 PICKUP RWD/5.0L-V8 (230hp)

Ext.Cab Fltsde Sbed Pkp	9625	11725
Ext.Cab Sptsde Sbed Pkp	9950	12125
Ext.Cab Fltsde Lbed Pkp	9875	12025
Fleetside Sbed Pkp	8400	10825
Fleetside Lbed Pkp	8525	11000
Sportside Sbed Pkp	8600	11150
Work Truck (6cyl) Sbed Pkp	7375	9500
Work Truck (6cyl) Lbed Pkp	7450	9600

C2500 PICKUP RWD/5.0L-V8 (230hp)

Ext.Cab Fltsde Sbed Pkp	9850	12000
Ext.Cab Fltsde Lbed Pkp	10175	12400
Fleetside Lbed Pkp	8725	11250

Add:
- 4-wheel drive . . . 1100
- Third door (ext. cab) . . . 125
- Silverado trim . . . 525

Deduct:
- 6cyl (not Work Truck) . . . 225

G1500 VAN RWD/4.3L-V8 (200hp)

Chevyvan 135" wb Cargo	8000	10300
Express 135" wb Psgr	9525	11600

G2500 VAN RWD/5.7L-V8 (245hp)

Chevyvan 135" wb Cargo	8300	10700
Express 135" wb Psgr	9800	11925

Add:
- LS Trim . . . 600

Deduct:
- 6cyl . . . 225

S10 PICKUP RWD/4.3L-V6 (180hp)

Fleetside Sbed Pkp	4850	6750
Fleetside Lbed Pkp	4925	6850
Fleetside ExCab Pkp	5650	7275
Sportside Sbed Pkp	5000	6950
Sportside ExCab Pkp	5825	7500

Add:
- 4-wheel drive . . . 1000
- Third door (ext. cab) . . . 75
- LS trim . . . 425
- SS trim . . . 200
- ZR2 pkg . . . 400

Deduct:
- 4cyl . . . 225

SUBURBAN RWD/5.7L-V8 (255hp)

C1500 4dr Utl	11500	14075
C2500 4dr Utl	11950	14625

Add:
- 4-wheel drive . . . 1100
- LS trim . . . 575
- LT trim . . . 750

TAHOE 4WD/5.7L-V8 (255hp)

Sport Util 2dr Utl	10725	13125
Wagon 4dr Utl	12050	14750

Add:
- Sport pkg . . . 100
- LS trim (2dr) . . . 500
- LT trim . . . 900

Deduct:
- 2-wheel drive . . . 1050

VENTURE FWD/3.4L-V6 (180hp)

Passenger Mini Van	7250	9350

Add:
LS trim . . . 350
Traction ctrl . . . 25
Sliding door-pwr . . . 100
Integrated child seat(s) . . . 25

Deduct:
Psngr slider only . . . 175

1996 — WS Ret

ASTRO — RWD/4.3L-V6 (190hp)

Model	WS	Ret
Cargo Mini Van	5450	7575
Window Mini Van	6275	8100

Add:
4-wheel drive . . . 750
LS trim . . . 350
LT trim . . . 600

BLAZER — RWD/4.3L-V6 (190hp)

Model	WS	Ret
Sport Util 4dr Utl	6350	8175
Sport Util 2dr Utl	5775	7450

Add:
4-wheel drive . . . 825
LS trim . . . 350
LT trim . . . 625

C1500 PICKUP — RWD/5.0L-V8 (220hp)

Model	WS	Ret
Ext.Cab Fltsde Sbed Pkp	8325	10725
Ext.Cab Sptsde Sbed Pkp	8625	11125
Ext.Cab Fltsde Lbed Pkp	8575	11050
Fleetside Sbed Pkp	7250	9350
Fleetside Lbed Pkp	7375	9500
Sportside Sbed Pkp	7450	9650
Work Truck (6cyl) Lbed Pkp	6475	8350

C2500 PICKUP — RWD/5.0L-V8 (230hp)

Model	WS	Ret
Ext.Cab Fltsde Sbed Pkp	8550	11025
Ext.Cab Fltsde Lbed Pkp	8850	11400
Fleetside Lbed Pkp	7550	9725

Add:
4-wheel drive . . . 925
Third door (ext. cab) . . . 75
Silverado trim . . . 400

Deduct:
6cyl (not Work Truck) . . . 200

G1500 VAN — RWD/4.3L-V8 (200hp)

Model	WS	Ret
Chevyvan 135" wb Cargo	7100	9150
Express 135" wb Psgr	8550	11025

G2500 VAN — RWD/4.3L-V8 (200hp)

Model	WS	Ret
Chevyvan 135" wb Cargo	7350	9475
Express 135" wb Psgr	8800	11350

Add:
LS Trim . . . 500

Deduct:
6cyl . . . 200

LUMINA APV — FWD/3.4L-V6 (180hp)

Model	WS	Ret
Cargo Mini Van	4075	5675
Passenger Mini Van	5250	7300

Sliding door-pwr . . . 75
Integrated child seat(s) . . . 25

S10 PICKUP — RWD/4.3L-V6 (180hp)

Model	WS	Ret
Fleetside Sbed Pkp	4000	5550
Fleetside Lbed Pkp	4075	5675
Fleetside ExCab Pkp	4775	6650
Sportside Sbed Pkp	4125	5725
Sportside ExCab Pkp	4875	6775

Add:
4.3L 195hp V6 . . . 75
4-wheel drive . . . 825
Third door (ext. cab) . . . 50
LS trim . . . 350
SS trim . . . 175
ZR2 pkg . . . 325

Deduct:
4cyl . . . 175

SUBURBAN — RWD/5.7L-V8 (250hp)

Model	WS	Ret
C1500 4dr Utl	10300	12600
C2500 4dr Utl	10700	13100

Add:
4-wheel drive . . . 925
LS trim . . . 475
LT trim . . . 625

TAHOE — 4WD/5.7L-V8 (250hp)

Model	WS	Ret
Sport Util 2dr Utl	9175	11225
Wagon 4dr Utl	10500	12850

Add:
Sport pkg . . . 75
LS trim (2dr) . . . 400
LT trim . . . 700

Deduct:
2-wheel drive . . . 875

1995 — WS Ret

ASTRO — RWD/4.3L-V6 (190hp)

Model	WS	Ret
Cargo Mini Van	4400	6125
CS Mini Van	5250	7300

Add:
4-wheel drive . . . 675
CL trim . . . 325
LT trim . . . 550

BLAZER — RWD/4.3L-V6 (200hp)

Model	WS	Ret
Sport Util 4dr Utl	5150	7150
Sport Util 2dr Utl	4700	6525

Add:
4-wheel drive . . . 775
LS trim . . . 325
LT trim . . . 550

C1500 PICKUP — RWD/5.0L-V8 (175hp)

Model	WS	Ret
Ext.Cab Fltsde Sbed Pkp	7125	9175
Ext.Cab Sptsde Sbed Pkp	7350	9475
Ext.Cab Fltsde Lbed Pkp	7325	9450
Fleetside Sbed Pkp	6225	8025
Fleetside Lbed Pkp	6300	8125
Sportside Sbed Pkp	6375	8250
Work Truck (6cyl) Lbed Pkp	5525	7125

C2500 PICKUP — RWD/5.0L-V8 (175hp)

Model	WS	Ret
Ext.Cab Fltsde Sbed Pkp	7300	9400
Ext.Cab Fltsde Lbed Pkp	7500	9675
Fleetside Lbed Pkp	6450	8325

Add:
4-wheel drive . . . 850
Silverado trim . . . 375

Deduct:
6cyl (not Work Truck) . . . 175

G10 VAN — RWD/4.3L-V8 (150hp)

Model	WS	Ret
Chevyvan Swb Van	5925	7650
Chevyvan Lwb Van	6050	7800

G20 VAN — RWD/4.3L-V8 (150hp)

Model	WS	Ret
Chevyvan Swb Van	6175	7950
Chevyvan Lwb Van	6250	8050
Sportvan Lwb Van	7175	9300

Add:
Beauville trim (Sportvan) . . . 525

Deduct:
6cyl . . . 175

LUMINA APV — FWD/3.1L-V6 (120hp)

Model	WS	Ret
Cargo Mini Van	2375	3700
Passenger Mini Van	3750	5450

Add:
3.8 Liter V6 . . . 125
LS trim . . . 350
Sliding door-pwr . . . 50
Integrated child seat . . . 25

S10 PICKUP — RWD/4.3L-V6 (195hp)

Model	WS	Ret
Pickup Sbed Pkp	3325	4825
Pickup Lbed Pkp	3400	4925
Pickup ExCab Pkp	4175	5800

Add:
4.3L 195hp V6 . . . 75
4-wheel drive . . . 775
4-wheel ABS (2WD) . . . 50
LS trim . . . 325
SS trim . . . 150

Deduct:
4cyl (not EL) . . . 175

SUBURBAN — RWD/5.7L-V8 (200hp)

Model	WS	Ret
C1500 4dr Utl	8700	11275
C2500 4dr Utl	9100	11150

Add:
4-wheel drive . . . 850
LS trim . . . 450
LT trim . . . 575

TAHOE — 4WD/5.7L-V8 (200hp)

Model	WS	Ret
Sport Util 2dr Utl	8900	11525
Wagon 4dr Utl	10250	12550

Add:
Sport pkg . . . 75
LS trim (2dr) . . . 375
LT trim (over LS) . . . 550

Deduct:
2-wheel drive . . . 800

1994 — WS Ret

ASTRO — RWD/4.3L-V6 (165hp)

Model	WS	Ret
Cargo Mini Van	3450	5000
Passenger Mini Van	4175	5800

Add:
4-wheel drive . . . 625
CL trim . . . 300
LT trim . . . 500
Extended van . . . 325

BLAZER — 4WD/5.7L-V8 (200hp)

Model	WS	Ret
Sport Util 2dr Utl	8525	11000

Add:
Sport pkg . . . 425
Silverado trim . . . 375

C1500 PICKUP — RWD/5.0L-V8 (175hp)

Model	WS	Ret
Ext.Cab Fltsde Sbed Pkp	6725	8675
Ext.Cab Sptsde Sbed Pkp	6825	8800
Ext.Cab Fltsde Lbed Pkp	6800	8775
Fleetside Sbed Pkp	5775	7450
Fleetside Lbed Pkp	5875	7575
Sportside Sbed Pkp	5925	7675
Work Truck (6cyl) Lbed Pkp	5075	7050

C2500 PICKUP — RWD/5.0L-V8 (175hp)

Model	WS	Ret
Ext.Cab Fltsde Sbed Pkp	6900	8900
Ext.Cab Fltsde Lbed Pkp	6975	9000
Fleetside Lbed Pkp	6025	7775

Add:
4-wheel drive . . . 775
Cheyenne trim . . . 175
Sport pkg . . . 350
Silverado trim . . . 325

Deduct:
6cyl (not Work Truck) . . . 150

G10 VAN — RWD/5.0L-V8 (170hp)

Model	WS	Ret
Chevyvan Swb Van	5275	7325
Chevyvan Lwb Van	5400	7500

G20 VAN — RWD/5.0L-V8 (170hp)

Model	WS	Ret
Chevyvan Swb Van	5450	7575
Chevyvan Lwb Van	5550	7150
Sportvan Lwb Van	6350	8175

Check Truck Equipment Table on page 4

Add:

Beauville trim (Sportvan)	475

Deduct:

6cyl	150

LUMINA APV FWD/3.1L-V6 (120hp)

Cargo Mini Van	2150	3350
Passenger Mini Van	3250	4725

Add:

3.8 Liter V6	100
LS trim	300
Sliding door-pwr	50

S10 BLAZER RWD/4.3L-V6 (165hp)

Sport Util 4dr Utl	3750	5450
Sport Util 2dr Utl	3100	4500

Add:

4-wheel drive	700
Tahoe trim (std 4dr)	300
Tahoe LT trim	525

S10 PICKUP RWD/4.3L-V6 (165hp)

Pickup Sbed Pkp	3000	4350
Pickup Lbed Pkp	3075	4475
Pickup ExCab Pkp	3675	5325

Add:

4-wheel drive	700
4-wheel ABS	50
LS trim	300
SS trim	150

Deduct:

4cyl (not EL)	150

SUBURBAN RWD/5.7L-V8 (200hp)

C1500 4dr Utl	8300	10750
C2500 4dr Utl	8625	11175

Add:

4-wheel drive	775
Silverado trim	450

1993 WS Ret

ASTRO RWD/4.3L-V6 (165hp)

Cargo Mini Van	2225	3450
Passenger Mini Van	2875	4300

Add:

4-wheel drive	550
Air Bag	75
CL trim	250
LT trim	450
Extended van	300

BLAZER 4WD/5.7L-V8 (210hp)

Sport Util 2dr Utl	7500	9675

Add:

Sport pkg	375
Silverado trim	325

C1500 PICKUP RWD/5.7L-V8 (210hp)

454SS Sbed Pkp	7900	10325
Ext.Cab Fltsde Sbed Pkp	5750	7400
Ext.Cab Sptsde Sbed Pkp	6000	7725
Ext.Cab Fltsde Lbed Pkp	5900	7600
Fleetside Sbed Pkp	4975	6925
Fleetside Lbed Pkp	5050	7025
Sportside Sbed Pkp	5150	7200
Work Truck (6cyl) Lbed Pkp	4300	5975

C2500 PICKUP RWD/5.7L-V8 (210hp)

Ext.Cab Fltsde Sbed Pkp	5900	7600
Ext.Cab Fltsde Lbed Pkp	6025	7775
Fleetside Lbed Pkp	5175	7200

Add:

4-wheel drive	700
Cheyenne trim	150
Sport pkg	325
Silverado trim	300

Deduct:

6cyl (not Work Truck)	150

G10 VAN RWD/5.0L-V8 (170hp)

Chevyvan Swb Van	4100	5700
Chevyvan Lwb Van	4200	5850
Sportvan Swb Van	4775	6650
Sportvan Lwb Van	4875	6775

G20 VAN RWD/5.0L-V8 (170hp)

Chevyvan Swb Van	4275	5950
Chevyvan Lwb Van	4400	6125
Sportvan Lwb Van	5050	7025

Add:

Beauville trim (Sportvan)	425

Deduct:

6cyl	150

LUMINA APV FWD/3.IL-V6 (120hp)

Cargo Mini Van	1875	3050
Passenger Mini Van	2700	4025

Add:

3.8 Liter V6	75
LS trim	275

S10 BLAZER RWD/4.3L-V6 (165hp)

Sport Util 4dr Utl	3175	4600
Sport Util 2dr Utl	2850	4250

Add:

4-wheel drive	625
Tahoe trim (std 4dr)	275
Tahoe LT trim	450

S10 PICKUP RWD/2.8L-V6 (125hp)

EL (4cyl-4sp) Sbed Pkp	2075	3225
Pickup Sbed Pkp	2425	3775
Pickup Lbed Pkp	2450	3800
Pickup ExCab Pkp	2925	4250

Add:

4.3L-V6 (160hp)	75
4-wheel drive	625
Tahoe trim	275

Deduct:

4cyl (not EL)	125

SUBURBAN RWD/5.7L-V8 (210hp)

C1500 4dr Utl	7525	9750
C2500 4dr Utl	7825	10125

Add:

4-wheel drive	700
Silverado trim	400

1992 WS Ret

ASTRO RWD/4.3L-V6 (150hp)

Cargo Mini Van	2000	3100
CS Passenger Mini Van	2475	3850

Add:

4-wheel drive	475
CL trim	250
LT trim	425
Extended van	300

BLAZER 4WD/5.7L-V8 (210hp)

Sport Util 2dr Utl	6100	7875

Add:

Sport pkg	300
Silverado trim	300

C1500 PICKUP RWD/5.0L-V8 (175hp)

454SS Sbed Pkp	6825	8925
Ext.Cab Sptsde Sbed Pkp	5100	7100
Ext.Cab Fltsde Sbed Pkp	4925	6850
Ext.Cab Fltsde Lbed Pkp	5025	7000
Fleetside Sbed Pkp	4200	5850
Fleetside Lbed Pkp	4250	5900
Sportside Sbed Pkp	4350	6075
Work Truck (6cyl) Lbed Pkp	3625	5250

C2500 PICKUP RWD/5.0L-V8 (175hp)

Ext.Cab Fltsde Sbed Pkp	5075	7050
Ext.Cab Fltsde Lbed Pkp	5150	7150
Fleetside Lbed Pkp	4400	6125

Add:

4-wheel drive	650
Scottsdale trim	150
Sport pkg	250
Silverado trim	250

Deduct:

6cyl (not Work Truck)	125

G10 VAN RWD/5.0L-V8 (170hp)

Chevyvan Swb Van	2900	4325
Chevyvan Lwb Van	2950	4275
Sportvan Swb Van	3475	5050
Sportvan Lwb Van	3575	5200

G20 VAN RWD/5.0L-V8 (170hp)

Chevyvan Swb Van	3025	4400
Chevyvan Lwb Van	3100	4500
Sportvan Lwb Van	3700	5375

Add:

Beauville trim (Sportvan)	425

Deduct:

6cyl	125

LUMINA APV FWD/3.1L-V6 (120hp)

Cargo Mini Van	1550	2525
Passenger Mini Van	2100	3250

Add:

3.8 Liter V6	50
CL trim	250

S10 BLAZER RWD/4.3L-V6 (160hp)

Sport Util 4dr Utl	2775	4150
Sport Util 2dr Utl	2500	3725

Add:

4-wheel drive	575
Tahoe trim (std 4dr)	225
Sport pkg	250
Tahoe LT trim	425

S10 PICKUP RWD/2.8L-V6 (125hp)

EL (4cyl-4sp) Sbed Pkp	1800	2925
Pickup Sbed Pkp	2025	3150
Pickup Lbed Pkp	2050	3175
Pickup ExCab Pkp	2400	3725

Add:

4.3L-V6	75
4-wheel drive	575
Tahoe trim	225

Deduct:

4cyl (not EL)	125

SUBURBAN RWD/5.7L-V8 (190hp)

C1500 4dr Utl	6850	8875
C2500 4dr Utl	7100	9200

Add:

4-wheel drive	650
Silverado trim	350

1991 WS Ret

ASTRO RWD/4.3L-V6 (150hp)

Cargo Mini Van	1825	2975
Passenger Mini Van	2100	3250

Add:

4-wheel drive	425
CL trim	225
LT trim	400
Extended van	275

BLAZER 4WD/5.7L-V8 (210hp)

Sport Util 2dr Utl	3950	5500

Add:

Silverado trim	275

C1500 PICKUP — RWD/4.3L-V8 (160hp)

Model	WS	Ret
454SS Sbed Pkp	5575	7300
Extended Cab Sbed Pkp	4000	5550
Extended Cab Lbed Pkp	4075	5675
Fleetside Sbed Pkp	3475	5050
Fleetside Lbed Pkp	3525	5125
Sportside Sbed Pkp	3600	5250
Work Truck (6cyl) Lbed Pkp	2875	4300

C2500 PICKUP — RWD/4.3L-V8 (160hp)

Model	WS	Ret
Extended Cab Sbed Pkp	4125	5725
Extended Cab Lbed Pkp	4225	5875
Fleetside Lbed Pkp	3650	5300

Add:
- 4-wheel drive . . . 575
- Scottsdale trim . . . 125
- Sport pkg . . . 250
- Silverado trim . . . 225
- Z-71 pkg . . . 25

Deduct:
- 6cyl (not Work Truck) . . . 100

G10 VAN — RWD/5.0L-V8 (170hp)

Model	WS	Ret
Chevyvan Swb Van	2275	3525
Chevyvan Lwb Van	2325	3600
Sportvan Swb Van	2750	4100
Sportvan Lwb Van	2825	4225

G20 VAN — RWD/5.0L-V8 (170hp)

Model	WS	Ret
Chevyvan Swb Van	2400	3725
Chevyvan Lwb Van	2475	3850
Sportvan Lwb Van	2925	4250

Add:
- Beauville (Sportvan) . . . 350

Deduct:
- 6cyl . . . 100

LUMINA APV — FWD/3.1L-V6 (120hp)

Model	WS	Ret
Cargo Mini Van	1275	2075
Passenger Mini Van	1600	2600

Add:
- CL trim . . . 225

S10 BLAZER — RWD/4.3L-V6 (160hp)

Model	WS	Ret
Sport Util 4dr Utl	2425	3775
Sport Util 2dr Utl	2025	3150

Add:
- 4-wheel drive . . . 525
- Tahoe trim (std 4dr) . . . 150
- Sport pkg . . . 250

S10 PICKUP — RWD/2.8L-V6 (125hp)

Model	WS	Ret
EL (4cyl-5sp) Sbed Pkp	1350	2200
Pickup Sbed Pkp	1575	2550
Pickup Lbed Pkp	1600	2600
Pickup ExCab Pkp	1850	3000

Add:
- 4.3L-V6 (160hp) . . . 50
- 4-wheel drive . . . 525
- Tahoe trim . . . 150
- Sport pkg . . . 250

Deduct:
- 4cyl (not EL) . . . 100

SUBURBAN — RWD/5.7L-V8 (210hp)

Model	WS	Ret
R1500 4dr Utl	4625	6425
R2500 4dr Utl	4850	6750

Add:
- 4-wheel drive . . . 600
- Silverado trim . . . 325

1990 — WS Ret

ASTRO — RWD/4.3L-V6 (150hp)

Model	WS	Ret
Cargo Mini Van	1425	2325
Passenger Mini Van	1675	2725

Add:
- 4-wheel drive . . . 375
- CL trim . . . 200
- LT trim . . . 400
- Extended van . . . 250

Deduct:
- 4cyl . . . 75

BLAZER — 4WD/5.7L-V8 (210hp)

Model	WS	Ret
Sport Util 2dr Utl	3450	5000

Add:
- Silverado trim . . . 250

C1500 PICKUP — RWD/5.0L-V8 (170hp)

Model	WS	Ret
454SS Sbed Pkp	4925	6950
Extended Cab Sbed Pkp	3600	5225
Extended Cab Lbed Pkp	3650	5300
Fleetside Sbed Pkp	3050	4425
Fleetside Lbed Pkp	3100	4500
Sportside Sbed Pkp	3175	4625
Work Truck (6cyl) Lbed Pkp	2550	3800

C2500 PICKUP — RWD/5.0L-V8 (170hp)

Model	WS	Ret
Extended Cab Sbed Pkp	3700	5375
Extended Cab Lbed Pkp	3775	5475
Fleetside Lbed Pkp	3225	4675

Add:
- 4-wheel drive . . . 550
- Scottsdale trim . . . 75
- Silverado trim . . . 200
- Z-71 pkg . . . 25

Deduct:
- 6cyl (not Work Truck) . . . 75

G10 VAN — RWD/5.0L-V8 (170hp)

Model	WS	Ret
Chevyvan Swb Van	1950	3025
Chevyvan Lwb Van	2025	3150
Sportvan Swb Van	2400	3725
Sportvan Lwb Van	2475	3850

G20 VAN — RWD/5.0L-V8 (170hp)

Model	WS	Ret
Chevyvan Swb Van	2075	3225
Chevyvan Lwb Van	2125	3300
Sportvan Lwb Van	2575	3850

Add:
- Beauville (Sportvan) . . . 325

Deduct:
- 6cyl . . . 75

LUMINA APV — FWD/3.1L-V6 (120hp)

Model	WS	Ret
Cargo Mini Van	1000	1750
Passenger Mini Van	1250	2025

Add:
- CL trim . . . 200

S10 BLAZER — RWD/4.3L-V6 (160hp)

Model	WS	Ret
Sport Util 4dr Utl	1925	3000
Sport Util 2dr Utl	1700	2750

Add:
- 4-wheel drive (2dr) . . . 500
- Tahoe trim . . . 150
- Sport pkg . . . 225

S10 PICKUP — RWD/2.8L-V6 (125hp)

Model	WS	Ret
EL (4cyl-5sp) Sbed Pkp	1200	2100
Pickup Sbed Pkp	1350	2200
Pickup Lbed Pkp	1375	2225
Pickup ExCab Pkp	1550	2525

Add:
- 4.3L-V6 (160hp) . . . 50
- 4-wheel drive . . . 500
- Durango trim . . . 50
- Tahoe trim . . . 125
- Sport pkg . . . 225

Deduct:
- 4cyl (not EL) . . . 75

SUBURBAN — RWD/5.7L-V8 (210hp)

Model	WS	Ret
R1500 4dr Utl	3750	5450
R2500 4dr Utl	3925	5450

Add:
- 4-wheel drive . . . 550
- Silverado . . . 300

1989 — WS Ret

ASTRO — RWD/4.3L-V6 (150hp)

Model	WS	Ret
Cargo Mini Van	1150	2000
Passenger Mini Van	1300	2100

Add:
- CL trim . . . 150
- LT trim . . . 350

Deduct:
- 4cyl . . . 50

BLAZER — 4WD/5.7L-V8 (210hp)

Model	WS	Ret
Sport Util 2dr Utl	2925	4250

Add:
- Silverado trim . . . 225

C1500 PICKUP — RWD/5.0L-V8 (175hp)

Model	WS	Ret
Extended Cab Sbed Pkp	3250	4725
Extended Cab Lbed Pkp	3300	4800
Fleetside Sbed Pkp	2725	4075
Fleetside Lbed Pkp	2825	4225
Sportside Sbed Pkp	2875	4300

C2500 PICKUP — RWD/5.0L-V8 (175hp)

Model	WS	Ret
Crew Cab 4dr Pkp	3650	5300
Extended Cab Sbed Pkp	3350	4850
Extended Cab Lbed Pkp	3475	5050
Fleetside Lbed Pkp	2925	4250

Add:
- 4-wheel drive . . . 500
- Scottsdale trim . . . 50
- Silverado trim . . . 175
- Z-71 trim . . . 25

Deduct:
- 6cyl . . . 75

G10 VAN — RWD/5.0L-V8 (170hp)

Model	WS	Ret
Chevyvan Swb Van	1525	2475
Chevyvan Lwb Van	1575	2550
Sportvan Swb Van	1850	3000
Sportvan Lwb Van	1925	3000

G20 VAN — RWD/5.0L-V8 (170hp)

Model	WS	Ret
Chevyvan Swb Van	1600	2600
Chevyvan Lwb Van	1650	2675
Sportvan Lwb Van	2025	3150

Add:
- Beauville (Sportvan) . . . 300

Deduct:
- 6cyl . . . 75

S10 BLAZER — RWD/2.8L-V6 (125hp)

Model	WS	Ret
Sport Util 2dr Utl	1300	2100

Add:
- 4-wheel drive . . . 450
- Tahoe trim . . . 125
- Sport pkg . . . 200

S10 PICKUP — RWD/2.8L-V6 (125hp)

Model	WS	Ret
EL (4cyl-5sp) Sbed Pkp	1050	1825
Pickup Sbed Pkp	1175	2050
Pickup Lbed Pkp	1200	2100
Pickup ExCab Pkp	1325	2150

Add:
- 4.3L-V6 (160hp) . . . 50
- 4-wheel drive . . . 450
- Durango trim . . . 25
- Tahoe trim . . . 50
- Sport pkg . . . 175

Check Truck Equipment Table on page 4

Deduct:
4cyl (not EL) 50

SUBURBAN RWD/5.7L-V8 (210hp)

R1500 4dr Utl 3150 4575
R2500 4dr Utl 3325 4825

Add:
4-wheel drive 500
Silverado trim 275

1988 WS Ret

ASTRO RWD/4.3L-V6 (150hp)

Cargo Mini Van 850 1650
Passenger Mini Van 1000 1750

Add:
CL trim 150
LT trim 325

Deduct:
4cyl 50

BLAZER 4WD/5.7L-V8 (210hp)

Sport Util 2dr Utl 2425 3775

Add:
Silverado trim 175

C1500 PICKUP RWD/5.0L-V8 (na)

Extended Cab Lbed Pkp . . . 3000 4350
Fleetside Sbed Pkp 2300 3575
Fleetside Lbed Pkp 2400 3725
Sportside Sbed Pkp 2475 3850

C2500 PICKUP RWD/5.0L-V8 (na)

Crew Cab Fltsde Pkp 3225 4675
Extended Cab Lbed Pkp . . . 3150 4575
Fleetside Lbed Pkp 2575 3850

Add:
4-wheel drive 425
Scottsdale trim 25
Silverado trim 150

Deduct:
6cyl 50

G10 VAN RWD/5.0L-V8 (170hp)

Chevyvan Swb Van 1175 2050
Chevyvan Lwb Van 1200 2100
Sportvan Swb Van 1425 2325
Sportvan Lwb Van 1475 2400

G20 VAN RWD/5.0L-V8 (170hp)

Chevyvan Swb Van 1225 2150
Chevyvan Lwb Van 1275 2075
Sportvan Lwb Van 1550 2525

Add:
Bonaventure (Sportvan) 200
Beauville (Sportvan) 250

Deduct:
6cyl 50

S10 BLAZER RWD/2.8L-V6 (125hp)

Sport Util 2dr Utl 1075 1875

Add:
4-wheel drive 375
Sport pkg 100
High Country pkg 175

Deduct:
4cyl 50

S10 PICKUP RWD/2.8L-V6 (125hp)

EL (4cyl-5sp) Sbed Pkp 875 1675
Pickup Sbed Pkp 975 1875
Pickup Lbed Pkp 1000 1750
Pickup Ext.Cab Pkp 1100 1925

Add:
4-wheel drive 375
Durango trim 25
Tahoe trim 75
Sport pkg 175

Deduct:
4cyl (not EL) 50

SUBURBAN RWD/5.7L-V8 (195hp)

R10 4dr Utl 2700 4025
R20 4dr Utl 2825 4225

Add:
4-wheel drive 425
Silverado trim 250

CHRYSLER

2001 WS Ret

TOWN & COUNTRY FWD/3.3L-V6 (180hp)

Limited Mini Van 21675 24825
LX Mini Van . . . .
LXi Mini Van 20275 23225

Add:
3.8L-V6/215hp (std AWD,EX,Ltd) 325
All-wheel drive 2175
Infinity Audio 225
Wheels-alum (LX) 200

Deduct:
Wheel covers 200

Voyager FWD/

Base Mini Van 13200 15550
LX Mini Van 14100 16600

Add:
ABS brakes (std LX) 350
Infinity audio 225
Wheels-alloy 225

Deduct:
2.4L-I4 (140/150hp) 800

2000 WS Ret

TOWN & COUNTRY FWD/3.3L-V6 (158hp)

Limited Mini Van 18125 20975
LX Mini Van 14900 17550
LXi Mini Van 16700 19325

Add:
3.8L-V6 (180hp) std AWD,LXi . . 250
All-wheel drive 1675
Wheels-alum (LX) 150

Deduct:
Wheel covers 175

Voyager FWD/

Base Mini Van 9550 11625
Grand Base Mini Van 10750 13100
Grand SE Mini Van 12200 14850
SE Mini Van 11025 13425

Add:
ABS brakes (STD se) 275
Infinity audio 175
Wheels-alloy 175

1999 WS Ret

TOWN & COUNTRY FWD/3.3L-V6 (158hp)

Limited Mini Van 15425 18150
LX Mini Van 13175 15500
LXi Mini Van 14100 16600
SX Mini Van 12500 15225

Add:
3.8L-V6 (180hp) std AWD,LXi . . 225
All-wheel drive 1400

Deduct:
Wheel covers 125

1998 WS Ret

TOWN & COUNTRY FWD/3.3L-V6 (158hp)

LX Mini Van 11450 13950
LXi Mini Van 12925 15750
SX Mini Van 10850 13225

Add:
3.8L-V6 (180hp) std AWD,LXi . 150
All-wheel drive 1150

1997 WS Ret

TOWN & COUNTRY FWD/3.3L-V6 (158hp)

LX Mini Van 9725 11850
LXi Mini Van 11000 13400
SX Mini Van 9175 11175

Add:
3.8L-V6 (166hp) std AWD,LXi . 125
All-wheel drive 950

1996 WS Ret

TOWN & COUNTRY FWD/3.3L-V6 (158hp)

Base Mini Van 7725 9950
LX Mini Van 8225 10600
LXi Mini Van 9350 11400

Add:
4-wheel drive 750

Deduct:
Psgr slider only 175

1995 WS Ret

TOWN & COUNTRY FWD/3.8L-V6 (162hp)

Luxury Mini Van 5425 7550

Add:
4-wheel drive 675

1994 WS Ret

TOWN & COUNTRY FWD/3.8L-V6 (162hp)

Luxury Mini Van 4775 6650

Add:
4-wheel drive 625

1993 WS Ret

TOWN & COUNTRY FWD/3.3L-V6 (150hp)

Luxury Mini Van 4100 5700

1992 WS Ret

TOWN & COUNTRY FWD/3.3L-V6 (150hp)

Luxury Mini Van 3775 5475

Add:
Leather seats 75

1991 WS Ret

TOWN & COUNTRY FWD/3.3L-V6 (150hp)

Luxury Mini Van 3400 4925

Add:
Air bag-driver 25

1990 WS Ret

TOWN & COUNTRY FWD/3.3L-V6 (150hp)

Luxury Mini Van 2925 4250

DAIHATSU

1992 WS Ret

ROCKY (5sp) 4WD/1.6L-I4 (94hp)

SE Cnv 2dr Utl 1750 2850
SX Htp 2dr Utl 1875 3050

Add:
Hardtop (SE) 25

1991 — WS / Ret

ROCKY (5sp) 4WD/1.6L-I4 (94hp)

Model	WS	Ret
SE Cnv 2dr Utl	1550	2525
SX Htp 2dr Utl	1625	2650

1990 — WS / Ret

ROCKY (5sp) 4WD/1.6L-I4 (94hp)

Model	WS	Ret
SE Cnv 2dr Utl	1325	2150
SX Cnv 2dr Utl	1350	2200

DODGE

2001 — WS / Ret

BR1500 PICKUP RWD/5.2L-V8 (230hp)

Model	WS	Ret
Club Cab Sbed Pkp	13550	15950
Quad Cab Sbed Pkp	14600	17275
Quad Cab Lbed Pkp	14850	17575
Sweptline Sbed Pkp	11325	13800
Sweptline Lbed Pkp	11525	14025
WS (6cyl) Sbed Pkp	9700	11825
WS (6cyl) Lbed Pkp	9900	12050

BR2500 PICKUP RWD/5.9L-V8 (245hp)

Model	WS	Ret
Quad Cab Sbed Pkp	14225	16750
Quad Cab Lbed Pkp	14400	16950
Sweptline Lbed Pkp	11975	14575

Add:
- 8.0L-V10 (300hp) . . . 1350
- 5.9L 6cyl turbo diesel . . . 2450
- 5.9L 6cyl HO turbo diesel . . . 2775
- 4-wheel drive . . . 2525
- Sport pkg . . . 650
- 4-wheel ABS . . . 225
- SLT trim . . . 1475

Deduct:
- 3.9L (6cyl-175hp) . . . 525

CARAVAN FWD/3.3L-V6 (180hp)

Model	WS	Ret
Grand SE Lwb Van	13900	16375
Grand EX Lwb Van	15725	18200
Grand Sport Lwb Van	14975	17625
Grand ES Lwb Van	18925	21675
SE Swb Van	12625	15375
Sport Swb Van	13725	16150

Add:
- 3.8L (V6-215hp) (std AWD,EX) . 375
- All-wheel drive . . . 2100
- ABS brakes (Base) . . . 300
- ES pkg (over LE) . . . 475
- Integrated child seat . . . 200
- Traction cntrl (FWD SE,Sport) . 175

Deduct:
- 2.4L (4cyl-150hp) . . . 500
- Psgr slider only . . . 425
- No ABS brakes . . . 425

DAKOTA PICKUP RWD/3.9L-V6 (175hp)

Model	WS	Ret
Club Cab ExCab Pkp	11400	13875
Quad Cab Sbed Pkp		
Sweptline Sbed Pkp	9750	11875

Add:
- 4-wheel drive . . . 2450
- 4-wheel ABS . . . 325
- 5.3L-230hp V8 . . . 675
- 5.9L-250hp V8 . . . 950
- Sport trim . . . 600
- SLT trim . . . 1350
- R/T pkg . . . 1575

Deduct:
- 2.5L (4cyl-120hp) . . . 500

DURANGO 4WD/5.2L-V8 (230hp)

Model	WS	Ret
R/T 4dr Utl	20200	23250
SLT 4dr Utl	19100	21875
Sport 4dr Utl	18125	20975

Add:
- 4-wheel ABS . . . 300
- SLT Plus (SLT) . . . 1325
- Infinity audio . . . 350
- Third Seat . . . 450
- R/T pkg . . . 1650

Deduct:
- 3.9L (6cyl-175hp) . . . 525
- 2-wheel drive . . . 2400

RAM VAN 1500 RWD/5.2L-V8 (230hp)

Model	WS	Ret
Cargo Swb Van	11625	14150
Cargo Lwb Van	11825	14400
Wagon Swb Van	13400	15775

RAM VAN 2500 RWD/5.2L-V8 (230hp)

Model	WS	Ret
Cargo Lwb Van	12100	14750
Maxivan Lwb Van	12675	15450
Maxiwagon Lwb Van	14600	17200
Wagon Lwb Van	14000	16475

Deduct:
- 3.9L (6cyl-175hp) . . . 525

2000 — WS / Ret

BR1500 PICKUP RWD/5.2L-V8 (230hp)

Model	WS	Ret
Club Cab Sbed Pkp	13025	15875
Quad Cab Sbed Pkp	13650	16150
Quad Cab Lbed Pkp	13875	16425
Sweptline Sbed Pkp	10800	13150
Sweptline Lbed Pkp	11025	13425
WS (6cyl) Sbed Pkp	9175	11175
WS (6cyl) Lbed Pkp	9375	11425

BR2500 PICKUP RWD/5.9L-V8 (245hp)

Model	WS	Ret
Quad Cab Sbed Pkp	13875	16325
Quad Cab Lbed Pkp	13975	16450
Sweptline Lbed Pkp	11450	13950

Add:
- 8.0L-V10 (300hp) . . . 1050
- 5.9L 6cyl turbo diesel . . . 1900
- 4-wheel drive . . . 1975
- Sport pkg . . . 500
- 4-wheel ABS . . . 175
- SLT trim . . . 1150
- Quad Cab (over Club) . . . 850

Deduct:
- 3.9L (6cyl-175hp) . . . 425

CARAVAN FWD/3.3L-V6 (158hp)

Model	WS	Ret
Base Swb Van	10350	12600
Grand Base Lwb Van	11575	14100
Grand LE Lwb Van	13425	15800
Grand SE Lwb Van	12625	15375
Grand Sport AWD Lwb Van		
SE Swb Van	11375	13850

Add:
- 3.8L (V6-180hp) (std AWD,ES) . 275
- All-wheel drive . . . 1625
- ABS brakes (Base) . . . 225
- ES pkg (over LE) . . . 375
- Integrated child seat . . . 150
- Traction cntrl (std ES) . . . 100

Deduct:
- 2.4L (4cyl-150hp) . . . 400
- Psgr slider only . . . 325
- No ABS brakes . . . 325

DAKOTA PICKUP RWD/3.9L-V6 (175hp)

Model	WS	Ret
Club Cab ExCab Pkp	10050	12250
Quad Cab Sport Sbed Pkp	13200	15550
Sweptline Sbed Pkp	8375	10800

Add:
- 4-wheel drive . . . 1900
- 4-wheel ABS . . . 250
- 5.3L-230hp V8 . . . 525
- 5.9L-250hp V8 . . . 725
- Sport trim . . . 450
- SLT trim . . . 1050
- R/T pkg . . . 1225

Deduct:
- 2.5L (4cyl-120hp) . . . 400

DURANGO 4WD/5.2L-V8 (230hp)

Model	WS	Ret
SLT 4dr Utl	17050	19725
Sport 4dr Utl	16375	18950

Add:
- 4-wheel ABS . . . 250
- SLT Plus trim . . . 1025
- Infinity audio . . . 275
- Third Seat . . . 350
- R/T pkg . . . 1300

Deduct:
- 3.9L (6cyl-175hp) . . . 400
- 2-wheel drive . . . 1875

RAM VAN 1500 RWD/5.2L-V8 (230hp)

Model	WS	Ret
Cargo Swb Van	10625	12950
Cargo Lwb Van	10825	13175
Wagon Swb Van	12400	15100

RAM VAN 2500 RWD/5.2L-V8 (230hp)

Model	WS	Ret
Cargo Lwb Van	11125	13550
Maxivan Lwb Van	11675	14225
Maxiwagon Lwb Van	13675	16100
Wagon Lwb Van	13050	15900

Add:
- 4-wheel ABS . . . 250
- Premium trim . . . 575

Deduct:
- 3.9L (6cyl-175hp) . . . 425

1999 — WS / Ret

BR1500 PICKUP RWD/5.2L-V8 (230hp)

Model	WS	Ret
Club Cab Sbed Pkp	12100	14750
Club Cab Lbed Pkp	12275	14950
Sweptline Sbed Pkp	10100	12300
Sweptline Lbed Pkp	10275	12525
WS (6cyl) Sbed Pkp	8575	11050
WS (6cyl) Lbed Pkp	8725	11250

BR2500 PICKUP RWD/5.9L-V8 (245hp)

Model	WS	Ret
Club Cab Sbed Pkp	12775	15550
Club Cab Lbed Pkp	12950	15775
HD Lbed Pkp	11225	13675
Sweptline Lbed Pkp	10850	13225

Add:
- 8.0L-V10 (300hp) . . . 850
- 5.9L 6cyl turbo diesel . . . 1575
- 4-wheel drive . . . 1625
- Sport pkg . . . 400
- SLT trim . . . 950
- Quad Cab (over Club) . . . 700

Deduct:
- 3.9L (6cyl-175hp) . . . 350

CARAVAN FWD/3.3L-V6 (158hp)

Model	WS	Ret
Base Swb Van	8375	10800
Grand Base Lwb Van	9500	11575
Grand LE Lwb Van	11175	13600
Grand SE Lwb Van	10450	12725
LE Swb Van	10050	12250
SE Swb Van	9325	11350

Add:
- 3.8L (V6-186hp) (std AWD,ES) . 225
- All-wheel drive . . . 1350
- Sport pkg (over SE) . . . 200
- ES pkg (over LE) . . . 300
- Integrated child seat . . . 125
- Traction cntrl (std ES) . . . 50

Deduct:
- 2.4L (4cyl-150hp) . . . 325
- Psgr slider only . . . 275

No ABS brakes 275

DAKOTA PICKUP RWD/3.9L-V6 (175hp)

Club Cab ExCab Pkp 9250 11275
Sweptline Sbed Pkp 7650 9850
Sweptline Lbed Pkp 7825 10075

Add:
4-wheel drive 1575
4-wheel ABS 225
5.3L-230hp V8 425
5.9L-250hp V8 600
Sport trim 375
SLT trim 850
R/T pkg 1025

Deduct:
2.5L (4cyl-120hp) 325

DURANGO 4WD/5.2L-V8 (230hp)

SLT 4dr Utl 15325 18050

Add:
4-wheel ABS 200
SLT Plus trim 850
Infinity audio 225
Third Seat 275

Deduct:
3.9L (6cyl-175hp) 325
2-wheel drive 1550

RAM VAN 1500 RWD/5.2L-V8 (230hp)

Cargo Swb Van 9150 11150
Cargo Lwb Van 9325 11350
Maxiwagon Lwb Van 11375 13850
Wagon Swb Van 10825 13175

RAM VAN 2500 RWD/5.2L-V8 (230hp)

Cargo Swb Van 9575 11650
Cargo Lwb Van 9850 12000
Maxivan Lwb Van 10375 12625
Maxiwagon Lwb Van 11900 14500
Wagon Lwb Van 11325 13800

Add:
4-wheel ABS 200
Premium trim 475

Deduct:
3.9L (6cyl-175hp) 350

1998 WS Ret

BR1500 PICKUP RWD/5.2L-V8 (230hp)

Club Cab Sbed Pkp 11025 13425
Club Cab Lbed Pkp 11200 13650
Sweptline Sbed Pkp 9300 11325
Sweptline Lbed Pkp 9475 11550
WS (6cyl) Sbed Pkp 7925 10225
WS (6cyl) Lbed Pkp 8100 10450

BR2500 PICKUP RWD/5.9L-V8 (245hp)

Club Cab Sbed Pkp 11575 14100
Club Cab Lbed Pkp 11775 14350
HD Lbed Pkp 10325 12575
Sweptline Lbed Pkp 9975 12150

Add:
8.0 Liter V10 775
5.9L 6cyl turbo diesel 1300
4-wheel drive 1350
Sport pkg 350
ST trim (Reg. cab) 225
Laramie SLT 775
Quad Cab (over Club) 575

Deduct:
3.9L (6cyl-175hp) 275

CARAVAN FWD/3.3L-V6 (158hp)

Base Swb Van 7800 10050
Grand Base Lwb Van 8825 11375
Grand LE Lwb Van 10325 12575
Grand SE Lwb Van 9675 11775
LE Swb Van 9325 11350
SE Swb Van 8675 11175

Add:
3.8L (V6-180hp) (std AWD,ES) 200
All-wheel drive 1125
Sport pkg (over SE) 150
ES pkg (over LE) 250
Integrated child seat 75

Deduct:
2.4L (4cyl-150hp) 275
Psgr slider only 225
No ABS brakes 225

DAKOTA PICKUP RWD/3.9L-V6 (175hp)

Club Cab ExCab Pkp 8225 10600
Sweptline Sbed Pkp 6825 8800
Sweptline Lbed Pkp 6975 9000

Add:
4-wheel drive 1300
4-wheel ABS 175
5.3L-230hp V8 400
Sport trim 325
SLT trim 725
R/T pkg 850

Deduct:
2.5L (4cyl-120hp) 275

DURANGO 4WD/5.2L-V8 (230hp)

SLT 4dr Utl 13675 16100

Add:
4-wheel ABS 150
SLT Plus trim 700
Infinity audio 200
Third Seat 275

Deduct:
3.9L (6cyl-175hp) 300
2-wheel drive 1400

RAM VAN 1500 RWD/5.2L-V8 (230hp)

Cargo Swb Van 8000 10300
Cargo Lwb Van 8200 10575
Maxiwagon Lwb Van 10100 12300
Window Swb Van 9675 11775

RAM VAN 2500 RWD/5.9L-V8 (245hp)

Cargo Swb Van 8450 10900
Cargo Lwb Van 9900 12050
Maxivan Lwb Van 10350 12600
Maxiwagon Lwb Van 10525 12825
Window Lwb Van 10100 12300

Add:
4-wheel ABS 150
Sport trim 350
SLT trim 800

Deduct:
3.9L (6cyl-175hp) 275

1997 WS Ret

BR1500 PICKUP RWD/5.2L-V8 (235hp)

Club Cab Sbed Pkp 10200 12425
Club Cab Lbed Pkp 10350 12600
Sweptline Sbed Pkp 8600 11075
Sweptline Lbed Pkp 8750 11275
WS (6cyl) Sbed Pkp 7400 9550
WS (6cyl) Lbed Pkp 7525 9700

BR2500 PICKUP RWD/5.9L-V8 (235hp)

Club Cab Sbed Pkp 10700 13025
Club Cab Lbed Pkp 10850 13225
HD Lbed Pkp 9525 11600
Sweptline Lbed Pkp 9225 11225

Add:
8.0 Liter V10 625
5.9L 6cyl turbo diesel 1075
4-wheel drive 1100
Sport pkg 275
ST trim (Reg. cab) 175
Laramie SLT 600

Deduct:
3.9L (6cyl-175hp) 225

CARAVAN FWD/3.3L-V6 (158hp)

Base Swb Van 6050 7800
Grand Base Lwb Van 6900 8900
Grand LE Lwb Van 8325 10725
Grand SE Lwb Van 7725 9950
LE Swb Van 7400 9550
SE Swb Van 6825 8800

Add:
4-wheel drive 900
Sport pkg (over SE) 125
ES pkg (over LE) 225
Integrated child seat 75

Deduct:
2.4L (4cyl-150hp) 225
Psgr slider only 175
No ABS brakes 175

DAKOTA PICKUP RWD/3.9L-V6 (175hp)

Club Cab ExCab Pkp 7375 9500
Sweptline Sbed Pkp 6175 7950
Sweptline Lbed Pkp 6300 8125

Add:
4-wheel drive 1075
4-wheel ABS 150
5.3L-230hp V8 325
Sport trim 250
SLT trim 525

Deduct:
2.5L (4cyl-120hp) 225

RAM VAN 1500 RWD/5.2L-V8 (235hp)

Cargo Swb Van 7125 9175
Cargo Lwb Van 7275 9375
Window Swb Van 8750 11275

RAM VAN 2500 RWD/5.9L-V8 (235hp)

Cargo Swb Van 7350 9475
Cargo Lwb Van 7475 9625
Maxivan Lwb Van 7900 10175
Maxiwagon Lwb Van 9550 11625
Window Lwb Van 9125 11125

Add:
4-wheel ABS 125
SLT trim 550

Deduct:
3.9L (6cyl-175hp) 225

1996 WS Ret

BR1500 PICKUP RWD/5.2L-V8 (220hp)

Club Cab Sbed Pkp 8875 11450
Club Cab Lbed Pkp 9000 11600
Sweptline Sbed Pkp 7425 9575
Sweptline Lbed Pkp 7550 9725
WS (6cyl) Sbed Pkp 6350 8175
WS (6cyl) Lbed Pkp 6475 8350

BR2500 PICKUP RWD/5.2L-V8 (220hp)

Club Cab Sbed Pkp 9275 11300
Club Cab Lbed Pkp 9425 11475
HD Lbed Pkp 8275 10675
Sweptline Lbed Pkp 8000 10300

Add:
8.0 Liter V10 525
5.9L 6cyl turbo diesel 975
4-wheel drive 925
Sport pkg 225
ST trim (Reg. cab) 175
Laramie SLT 425

Deduct:
6cyl 200

CARAVAN FWD/3.3L-V6 (158hp)

Base Swb Van 4475 6225
Grand Base Lwb Van 5250 7300

Model	WS	Ret
Grand LE Lwb Van	6450	8325
Grand SE Lwb Van	5950	7675
LE Swb Van	5675	7325
SE Swb Van	5150	7150

Add:

Option	Value
4-wheel drive	750
Sport pkg (over SE)	100
ES pkg (over LE)	175
Integrated child seat	25

Deduct:

Option	Value
4cyl	175
Psgr slider only	150
No ABS brakes	150

DAKOTA PICKUP — RWD/3.9L-V6 (175hp)

Model	WS	Ret
Club Cab ExCab Pkp	5125	7125
Club Cab Sport ExCab Pkp.	5225	7275
Sport Sbed Pkp	4075	5675
Sweptline Sbed Pkp	4025	5600
Sweptline Lbed Pkp.	4125	5725
WS Sbed Pkp	3875	5400
WS Lbed Pkp.	3975	5525

Add:

Option	Value
4-wheel drive	900
4-wheel ABS	125
5.3 Liter V8	275
SLT trim	425

Deduct:

Option	Value
4cyl	175

RAM VAN 1500 — RWD/5.2L-V8 (220hp)

Model	WS	Ret
Cargo Swb Van	6225	8025
Cargo Lwb Van	6350	8175
Window Swb Van	7750	10000

RAM VAN 2500 — RWD/5.2L-V8 (220hp)

Model	WS	Ret
Cargo Swb Van	6425	8275
Cargo Lwb Van	6550	8450
Maxivan Lwb Van	6900	8900
Maxiwagon Lwb Van	8500	10950
Window Lwb Van.	8100	10450

Add:

Option	Value
4-wheel ABS	100
SLT trim	475

Deduct:

Option	Value
6cyl	200

1995 — WS — Ret

BR1500 PICKUP — RWD/5.2L-V8 (220hp)

Model	WS	Ret
Club Cab Sbed Pkp.	7400	9550
Club Cab Lbed Pkp	7500	9675
S (6cyl) Sbed Pkp	5275	7325
S (6cyl) Lbed Pkp	5375	7475
Sweptline Sbed Pkp	6200	8000
Sweptline Lbed Pkp.	6300	8125

BR2500 PICKUP — RWD/5.2L-V8 (220hp)

Model	WS	Ret
Club Cab Sbed Pkp.	7775	10025
Club Cab Lbed Pkp	7875	10150
HD Lbed Pkp	6875	8850
Sweptline Lbed Pkp.	6650	8575

Add:

Option	Value
8.0 Liter V10	475
5.9L 6cyl turbo diesel	900
4-wheel drive	850
Laramie SLT	400
ST trim	175

Deduct:

Option	Value
6cyl	175

CARAVAN — FWD/3.3L-V6 (158hp)

Model	WS	Ret
Base Swb Van	2600	3825
Cargo Van Swb Van	1675	2675
Grand Base Lwb Van	3250	4650
Grand C/V Lwb Van.	2300	3525
Grand LE Lwb Van	4300	5900
Grand SE Lwb Van	3875	5300
LE Swb Van	3625	5175
SE Swb Van	3150	4500

Add:

Option	Value
4-wheel drive	675
4-wheel ABS (std LE)	150
Sport pkg (over SE)	75
ES pkg (over LE)	175
Integrated child seat	25

Deduct:

Option	Value
4cyl	175

DAKOTA PICKUP — RWD/3.9L-V6 (175hp)

Model	WS	Ret
Club Cab ExCab Pkp	4675	6500
Club Cab Sport ExCab Pkp	4750	6600
S (4cyl-5sp) Sbed Pkp	3075	4475
S (4cyl-5sp) Lbed Pkp.	3150	4575
Sport Sbed Pkp.	3775	5475
Sweptline Sbed Pkp	3725	5400
Sweptline Lbed Pkp	3775	5475

Add:

Option	Value
4-wheel drive	825
4-wheel ABS	125
5.3 Liter V8	250
SLT trim	400

Deduct:

Option	Value
4cyl (not S)	175

RAM VAN 1500 — RWD/5.2L-V8 (220hp)

Model	WS	Ret
Cargo Swb Van.	5075	7050
Cargo Lwb Van.	5150	7150
Window Swb Van	6475	8350

RAM VAN 2500 — RWD/5.2L-V8 (220hp)

Model	WS	Ret
Cargo Swb Van.	5225	7275
Cargo Lwb Van.	5325	7400
Maxivan Lwb Van	5650	7275
Maxiwagon Lwb Van.	7100	9150
Window Lwb Van	6800	8775

Add:

Option	Value
4-wheel ABS (Cargo)	75
SLT trim	450

Deduct:

Option	Value
6cyl	175

1994 — WS — Ret

B150 VAN — RWD/5.2L-V8 (235hp)

Model	WS	Ret
Cargo Swb Van.	4375	6075
Cargo Lwb Van.	4550	6325
Window Swb Van	5775	7450

B250 VAN — RWD/5.2L-V8 (235hp)

Model	WS	Ret
Cargo Swb Van.	4550	6325
Cargo Lwb Van.	4650	6475
Maxivan Lwb Van	4950	6875
Maxiwagon Lwb Van.	6250	8050
Window Lwb Van	6000	7725

Add:

Option	Value
4-wheel ABS	100
LE Decor trim	400

Deduct:

Option	Value
6cyl	150

BR1500 PICKUP — RWD/5.2L-V8 (215hp)

Model	WS	Ret
S (6cyl) Sbed Pkp	4800	6675
S (6cyl) Lbed Pkp	4900	6825
Sweptline Sbed Pkp	5600	7225
Sweptline Lbed Pkp	5675	7325

BR2500 PICKUP — RWD/5.2L-V8 (215hp)

Model	WS	Ret
HD Lbed Pkp.	6175	7950
Sweptline Lbed Pkp	6000	7725

Add:

Option	Value
8.0 Liter V10	425
5.9L 6cyl turbo diesel	800
4-wheel drive	775
Laramie SLT	375
ST trim	150

CARAVAN — FWD/3.3L-V6 (158hp)

Model	WS	Ret
Base Swb Van	2125	3300
Cargo Van Swb Van.	1100	1925
Grand Base Lwb Van	2725	4075
Grand C/V Lwb Van	1600	2600
Grand LE Lwb Van.	3575	5200
Grand SE Lwb Van.	3175	4600
LE Swb Van	3000	4350
SE Swb Van	2625	3925

Add:

Option	Value
4-wheel drive	625
4-wheel ABS	125
Sport pkg (over SE)	50
ES pkg (over LE)	150
Integrated child seat	25

Deduct:

Option	Value
4cyl	150

DAKOTA PICKUP — RWD/3.9L-V6 (180hp)

Model	WS	Ret
Club Cab ExCab Pkp	3975	5525
Club Cab Sport ExCab Pkp	4025	5600
S (4cyl-5sp) Sbed Pkp	2700	4025
S (4cyl-5sp) Lbed Pkp	2750	4100
Sport Sbed Pkp	3250	4725
Sweptline Sbed Pkp	3200	4650
Sweptline Lbed Pkp	3275	4750

Add:

Option	Value
4-wheel drive	750
4-wheel ABS	75
5.3 Liter V8	225
ST trim	375

Deduct:

Option	Value
4cyl (not S)	150

1993 — WS — Ret

B150 VAN — RWD/5.2L-V8 (230hp)

Model	WS	Ret
Cargo Swb Van	3300	4800
Cargo Lwb Van.	3475	5050
Window Swb Van	4300	5975
Window Lwb Van	4500	6250

B250 VAN — RWD/5.2L-V8 (230hp)

Model	WS	Ret
Cargo Swb Van	3500	5075
Cargo Lwb Van.	3625	5250
Maxivan Lwb Van.	3825	5325
Maxiwagon Lwb Van	4875	6775
Window Lwb Van	4625	6425

Add:

Option	Value
LE Decor trim	400

Deduct:

Option	Value
6cyl	150

CARAVAN — FWD/3.3L-V6 (150hp)

Model	WS	Ret
Base Swb Van	1575	2550
Cargo Van Swb Van.	925	1775
Grand Base Lwb Van	2000	3100
Grand C/V Lwb Van	1300	2100
Grand LE Lwb Van.	2700	4025
Grand SE Lwb Van.	2425	3775
LE Swb Van	2275	3525
SE Swb Van	1975	3075

Add:

Option	Value
4-wheel drive	550
ABS brakes	100
ES pkg (over LE)	150

Deduct:

Option	Value
4cyl	125

D150 PICKUP — RWD/5.2L-V8 (230hp)

Model	WS	Ret
Club Cab Sbed Pkp	4375	6075
Club Cab Lbed Pkp	4450	6200
Sweptline Sbed Pkp	3525	5125
Sweptline Lbed Pkp	3600	5225

Check Truck Equipment Table on page 4

D250 PICKUP — RWD/5.2L-V8 (230hp)

Model	WS	Ret
Club Cab Lbed Pkp	4700	6525
Sweptline Lbed Pkp	3825	5325

Add:
- 6cyl turbo diesel 675
- 4-wheel drive 700
- LE Decor trim 325

Deduct:
- 6cyl 150

DAKOTA PICKUP — RWD/3.9L-V6 (180hp)

Model	WS	Ret
Club Cab ExCab Pkp	3425	4975
S (4cyl-5sp) Sbed Pkp	2500	3725
Sport Sbed Pkp	2850	4250
Sweptline Sbed Pkp	2825	4225
Sweptline Lbed Pkp	2850	4250

Add:
- V8 engine 200
- 4-wheel drive 650
- LE trim 325

Deduct:
- 4cyl (not S) 125

RAM 50 PICKUP — RWD/2.4L-I4 (116hp)

Model	WS	Ret
Base Sbed Pkp	1925	3000
Base Lbed Pkp	1975	3075
SE Sbed Pkp	2125	3300

Add:
- 4-wheel drive 625

RAMCHARGER — RWD/5.9L-V8 (230hp)

Model	WS	Ret
150 2dr Utl	4625	6425
150S 2dr Utl	4200	5850

Add:
- 4-wheel drive 700
- LE trim 300
- Canyon Sport 300

1992 — WS Ret

B150 VAN — RWD/5.2L-V8 (230hp)

Model	WS	Ret
Cargo Swb Van	2550	3800
Cargo Lwb Van	2625	3925
Window Swb Van	3375	4900
Window Lwb Van	3525	5125

B250 VAN — RWD/5.2L-V8 (230hp)

Model	WS	Ret
Cargo Swb Van	2675	4000
Cargo Lwb Van	2725	4075
Maxivan Lwb Van	2900	4325
Maxiwagon Lwb Van	3800	5525
Window Lwb Van	3650	5300

Add:
- LE Decor trim 325

Deduct:
- 6cyl 125

CARAVAN — FWD/3.3L-V6 (150hp)

Model	WS	Ret
Base Swb Van	1400	2275
Cargo Van Swb Van	775	1500
Grand Base Lwb Van	1700	2750
Grand C/V Lwb Van	1050	1825
Grand LE Lwb Van	2250	3500
Grand SE Lwb Van	2025	3150
LE Swb Van	1925	3000
SE Swb Van	1700	2750

Add:
- 4-wheel drive 475
- ABS brakes 75
- ES trim (over LE) 100

Deduct:
- 4cyl 125

D150 PICKUP — RWD/5.2L-V8 (230hp)

Model	WS	Ret
Club Cab Sbed Pkp	3450	5000
Club Cab Lbed Pkp	3525	5125
Sweptline Sbed Pkp	2900	4325
Sweptline Lbed Pkp	2950	4275

D250 PICKUP — RWD/5.2L-V8 (230hp)

Model	WS	Ret
Club Cab Lbed Pkp	3700	5375
Sweptline Lbed Pkp	3150	4575

Add:
- 6cyl turbo diesel 575
- 4-wheel drive 650
- LE Decor trim 275

Deduct:
- 6cyl 125

DAKOTA PICKUP — RWD/3.9L-V6 (180hp)

Model	WS	Ret
Club Cab ExCab Pkp	2900	4325
S (4cyl-5sp) Sbed Pkp	2175	3375
Sport Sbed Pkp	2500	3725
Sweptline Sbed Pkp	2450	3800
Sweptline Lbed Pkp	2525	3775

Add:
- V8 engine 175
- 4-wheel drive 625
- LE trim 275

Deduct:
- 4cyl (not S) 125

RAM 50 PICKUP — RWD/2.4L-I4 (116hp)

Model	WS	Ret
Base Sbed Pkp	1675	2725
Base Lbed Pkp	1725	2800
SE Sbed Pkp	1850	3000

RAMCHARGER — RWD/5.2L-V8 (230hp)

Model	WS	Ret
150S 2dr Utl	3150	4575
150 2dr Utl	3525	5125

Add:
- 4-wheel drive 650
- LE trim 275
- Canyon Sport 300

1991 — WS Ret

B150 VAN — RWD/5.2L-V8 (170hp)

Model	WS	Ret
Cargo Swb Van	1825	2975
Cargo Lwb Van	1875	3050
Window Swb Van	2625	3925
Window Lwb Van	2650	3950

B250 VAN — RWD/5.2L-V8 (170hp)

Model	WS	Ret
Cargo Swb Van	1950	3025
Cargo Lwb Van	1975	3075
Maxivan Lwb Van	2125	3300
Maxiwagon Lwb Van	2900	4325
Window Lwb Van	2775	4150

Add:
- LE Decor trim 300

Deduct:
- 6cyl 100

CARAVAN — FWD/3.0L-V6 (142hp)

Model	WS	Ret
Base Swb Van	1200	2100
Cargo Van Swb Van	525	1100
Grand C/V Lwb Van	775	1500
Grand LE Lwb Van	1850	3000
Grand SE Lwb Van	1650	2675
LE Swb Van	1575	2550
SE Swb Van	1425	2325

Add:
- 4-wheel drive 400
- Air bag-driver 50
- ES pkg (over LE) 75

Deduct:
- 4cyl 100

D150 PICKUP — RWD/5.2L-V8 (170hp)

Model	WS	Ret
Club Cab Sbed Pkp	2750	4100
Club Cab Lbed Pkp	2775	4150
S Sbed Pkp	2275	3525
S Lbed Pkp	2275	3525
Sweptline Sbed Pkp	2375	3700
Sweptline Lbed Pkp	2400	3725

D250 PICKUP — RWD/5.2L-V8 (170hp)

Model	WS	Ret
Club Cab Lbed Pkp	2975	4325
Sweptline Lbed Pkp	2575	3850

Add:
- 6cyl turbo diesel 475
- 4-wheel drive 575
- SE Decor trim 150
- LE Decor trim 250

Deduct:
- 6cyl 100

DAKOTA PICKUP — RWD/3.9L-V6 (125hp)

Model	WS	Ret
Club Cab ExCab Pkp	2525	3775
S (4cyl-5sp) Sbed Pkp	1975	3075
Sport Sbed Pkp	2250	3500
Sport ExCab Pkp	2550	3800
Sweptline Sbed Pkp	2175	3375
Sweptline Lbed Pkp	2200	3425

Add:
- V8 engine 150
- 4-wheel drive 550
- SE trim 150
- LE trim 250

Deduct:
- 4cyl (not S) 100

RAM 50 PICKUP — RWD/2.4L-I4 (116hp)

Model	WS	Ret
Base Sbed Pkp	1475	2400
Base Lbed Pkp	1475	2400
Base ExCab Pkp	1700	2750
LE ExCab Pkp	1850	3000
SE Sbed Pkp	1600	2600
SE (4WD-6cyl) ExCab Pkp	2800	4175

Add:
- 6cyl (std SE 4WD) 125
- 4-wheel drive 525

RAMCHARGER — RWD/5.2L-V8 (170hp)

Model	WS	Ret
150S 2dr Utl	2325	3600
150 2dr Utl	2550	3800

Add:
- 4-wheel drive 575
- LE Decor trim 225

1990 — WS Ret

B150 VAN — RWD/5.9L-V8 (190hp)

Model	WS	Ret
Cargo Swb Van	1525	2475
Cargo Lwb Van	1550	2525
Window Swb Van	2225	3450
Window Lwb Van	2250	3500

B250 VAN — RWD/5.9L-V8 (190hp)

Model	WS	Ret
Cargo Swb Van	1625	2650
Cargo Lwb Van	1650	2675
Maxivan Lwb Van	1775	2875
Maxiwagon Lwb Van	2500	3725
Window Lwb Van	2375	3700

Add:
- LE Decor trim 300

Deduct:
- 6cyl 75

CARAVAN — FWD/3.0L-V6 (142hp)

Model	WS	Ret
Base Swb Van	825	1600
Cargo Van Swb Van	275	700
Grand C/V Lwb Van	475	1000
Grand LE Lwb Van	1300	2100
Grand SE Lwb Van	1200	2100
LE Swb Van	1125	1975
SE Swb Van	1025	1800

Add:
- ES pkg (over LE) 50

Deduct:

4cyl		100

D150 PICKUP RWD/5.2L-V8 (170hp)

Model	WS	Ret
Club Cab Sbed Pkp	2325	3600
Club Cab Lbed Pkp	2325	3600
S Sbed Pkp	1975	3075
S Lbed Pkp	2025	3150
Sweptline Sbed Pkp	2025	3150
Sweptline Lbed Pkp	2075	3225

D250 PICKUP RWD/5.2L-V8 (170hp)

Model	WS	Ret
Club Cab Lbed Pkp	2475	3850
Sweptline Lbed Pkp	2200	3425
Add:		
6cyl turbo diesel		400
4-wheel drive		550
SE Decor trim		150
LE Decor trim		200
Deduct:		
6cyl		75

DAKOTA PICKUP RWD/3.9L-V6 (125hp)

Model	WS	Ret
Club Cab ExCab Pkp	1925	3000
Convertible Sbed Pkp	2175	3375
S (4cyl-5sp) Sbed Pkp	1575	2550
Sport Sbed Pkp	1825	2975
Sport Cnv Sbed Pkp	2275	3525
Sport ExCab Pkp	2050	3175
Sweptline Sbed Pkp	1700	2750
Sweptline Lbed Pkp	1725	2800
Add:		
4-wheel drive		500
SE trim		150
LE trim		225
Deduct:		
4cyl (not S)		75

RAM 50 PICKUP RWD/2.0L-I4 (90hp)

Model	WS	Ret
Base Sbed Pkp	1250	2025
Base Lbed Pkp	1300	2100
Base ExCab Pkp	1425	2325
LE ExCab Pkp	1600	2600
SE Sbed Pkp	1350	2200
SE (4WD-6cyl) ExCab Pkp	1875	3050
Add:		
6cyl (std SE 4WD)		100
4-wheel drive		500

RAMCHARGER RWD/5.2L-V8 (170hp)

Model	WS	Ret
150S 2dr Utl	1750	2850
150 2dr Utl	1875	3050
Add:		
4-wheel drive		550
LE Decor trim		225

1989 WS Ret

B150 VAN RWD/5.2L-V8 (170hp)

Model	WS	Ret
Cargo Swb Van	1300	2100
Cargo Lwb Van	1325	2150
Window Swb Van	1925	3000
Window Lwb Van	1975	3075
Add:		
Prospector trim		125
LE Decor trim		250

B250 VAN RWD/5.2L-V8 (170hp)

Model	WS	Ret
Cargo Swb Van	1350	2200
Cargo Lwb Van	1400	2275
Maxivan Lwb Van	1475	2400
Maxiwagon Lwb Van	2075	3225
Window Lwb Van	2025	3150
Add:		
Prospector trim		125
LE Decor trim		250
Deduct:		
6cyl		50

CARAVAN FWD/3.0L-V6 (125hp)

Model	WS	Ret
Base Swb Van	525	1100
Cargo Van Swb Van	250	650
Grand C/V Lwb Van	375	950
Grand LE Lwb Van	950	1825
Grand SE Lwb Van	850	1650
LE Swb Van	800	1550
SE Swb Van	700	1475
Deduct:		
4cyl		75

D100 PICKUP RWD/5.2L-V8 (170hp)

Model	WS	Ret
Sweptline Sbed Pkp	1625	2650
Sweptline Lbed Pkp	1625	2650

D150 PICKUP RWD/5.2L-V8 (170hp)

Model	WS	Ret
Sweptline Sbed Pkp	1650	2675
Sweptline Lbed Pkp	1650	2675

D250 PICKUP RWD/5.2L-V8 (170hp)

Model	WS	Ret
Sweptline Lbed Pkp	1725	2800
Add:		
6cyl turbo diesel		375
4-wheel drive		500
Prospector trim		100
LE Decor trim		150
Deduct:		
6cyl		50

DAKOTA PICKUP RWD/3.9L-V6 (125hp)

Model	WS	Ret
S (4cyl-5sp) Sbed Pkp	1375	2225
Shelby (V8) Sbed Pkp	2325	3600
Sport Sbed Pkp	1525	2475
Sport Cnv Sbed Pkp	2075	3225
Sweptline Sbed Pkp	1475	2400
Sweptline Lbed Pkp	1450	2350
Add:		
4-wheel drive		475
Prospector trim		50
SE trim		125
LE trim		175
Deduct:		
4cyl (not S)		50

RAIDER 4WD/2.6L-I4 (109hp)

Model	WS	Ret
Sport Util 2dr Utl	1650	2675

RAM 50 PICKUP RWD/2.0L-I4 (90hp)

Model	WS	Ret
Base Sbed Pkp	1075	1875
Base Lbed Pkp	1100	1925
Base ExCab Pkp	1175	2050
Sport Lbed Pkp	1150	2000
Sport ExCab Pkp	1275	2075
Add:		
4-wheel drive		450

RAMCHARGER RWD/5.2L-V8 (170hp)

Model	WS	Ret
100 2dr Utl	1300	2100
150 2dr Utl	1400	2275
Add:		
4-wheel drive		500
LE Decor trim		175

1988 WS Ret

B150 VAN RWD/5.2L-V8 (na)

Model	WS	Ret
Cargo Swb Van	925	1775
Cargo Lwb Van	925	1775
Window Swb Van	1425	2325
Window Lwb Van	1450	2350

B250 VAN RWD/5.2L-V8 (na)

Model	WS	Ret
Cargo Swb Van	975	1875
Cargo Lwb Van	975	1875
Maxivan Lwb Van	1050	1825
Maxiwagon Lwb Van	1550	2525
Window Lwb Van	1475	2400
Add:		
Royal SE trim		150
Deduct:		
6cyl		50

CARAVAN FWD/2.6L-V6 (104hp)

Model	WS	Ret
Base Swb Van	475	1000
Cargo Van Swb Van	175	450
Grand C/V Lwb Van	275	700
Grand LE Lwb Van	800	1550
Grand SE Lwb Van	650	1375
LE Swb Van	725	1525
SE Swb Van	575	1225
Deduct:		
4cyl		50

D100 PICKUP RWD/5.2L-V8 (na)

Model	WS	Ret
Sweptline Sbed Pkp	1375	2225
Sweptline Lbed Pkp	1350	2200

D150 PICKUP RWD/5.2L-V8 (na)

Model	WS	Ret
Sweptline Sbed Pkp	1375	2225
Sweptline Lbed Pkp	1375	2225

D250 PICKUP RWD/5.2L-V8 (na)

Model	WS	Ret
Sweptline Lbed Pkp	1450	2350
Add:		
4-wheel drive		425
Prospector trim		75
LE Decor trim		100
Deduct:		
6cyl		50

DAKOTA PICKUP RWD/3.9L-V6 (125hp)

Model	WS	Ret
S (4cyl-5sp) Sbed Pkp	1125	1975
Sport Sbed Pkp	1225	2150
Sweptline Sbed Pkp	1175	2050
Sweptline Lbed Pkp	1200	2100
Add:		
4-wheel drive		400
Prospector trim		25
SE trim		100
LE trim		150
Deduct:		
4cyl (not S)		50

RAIDER 4WD/2.6L-I4 (109hp)

Model	WS	Ret
Sport Util 2dr Utl	1225	2150

RAM 50 PICKUP RWD/2.0L-I4 (90hp)

Model	WS	Ret
Base Sbed Pkp	875	1675
Base Lbed Pkp	900	1725
Base ExCab Pkp	975	1875
Custom Lbed Pkp	925	1775
Sport Lbed Pkp	975	1875
Sport ExCab Pkp	1050	1825
Add:		
4-wheel drive		375

RAMCHARGER RWD/5.2L-V8 (na)

Model	WS	Ret
100 2dr Utl	850	1650
150 2dr Utl	925	1775
Add:		
4-wheel drive		425
Prospector trim		75
LE Decor trim		150

FORD

2001 WS Ret

ECONOLINE RWD/4.6L-V8 (215hp)

Model	WS	Ret
E150 XL Psgr Van	14975	17625
E150 Cargo Van	12150	14800
E250 Cargo Van	12525	15250

Check Truck Equipment Table on page 4

Add:
4-wheel ABS 275
6.8L-V10 (305hp)(1-ton) 875
XLT trim 1350
Chateau trim 1725

Deduct:
4.2L 6cyl 525

ESCAPE 4WD/3.0L-V6 (200hp)

XLS 4dr Utl	15875	18650
XLT 4dr Utl	16775	19700

Add:
Mach Audio 325

Deduct:
2.0L-I4 (130hp) 675
2-wheel drive 1650

EXCURSION RWD/6.8L-V10 (310hp)

Limited 4dr Utl	23475	27275
XLT 4dr Utl	20725	24075

Add:
7.3L-V8 TD (235hp) 2225
4-wheel drive 2625
Entertainment center 800

Deduct:
No Third seat 775

EXPEDITION RWD/5.4L-V8 (260hp)

XLT 4dr Utl	18750	21775

Add:
5.4L-V8 (260hp) 525
4-wheel drive 2625
Eddie Bauer 2575
Sport trim 450
Entertainment center 800

Deduct:
4.6L-V8 (215hp) 675

EXPLORER RWD/4.0L-V6 (210hp)

Sport 2dr Utl	11675	14225
XLS 4dr Utl	13000	15825

Add:
4.0L-V6 (210hp) std EB,Ltd . . 425
5.0L-V8 (215hp) 525
4-wheel drive 2300
XLT trim 1125
Eddie Bauer 2350
Limited 3550
Mach audio (std Ltd) 350

F150 PICKUP RWD/4.6L-V8 (220hp)

Harley Crew Cab Sty Sbed Pkp		
Lightning (5.4L SC) Sbed	24475	28025
XL Flareside Sbed Pkp	11525	14375
XL Styleside Sbed Pkp		
XL Super Cab Stysde Sbed	13350	15725
XL Super Cab Flrsde Sbed	15325	18050
XL Styleside Lbed Pkp	11525	14025
XL Super Cab Stysde Lbed	13550	15950
XLT Supercrew Stysd Sbed	18125	20975

F250 PICKUP RWD/5.4L-V8 (260hp)

XL SD Supercrew Sbed	18575	21275
XL Styleside Lbed Pkp	12150	14800
XL Super Cab Lbed Pkp	14225	16750
XL SD Supercrew Lbed 18720475		

Add:
4-wheel drive 2525
4-wheel ABS (XL) 275
XLT trim 1175
Lariat trim 2325

Deduct:
6cyl (not S) 525

RANGER RWD/3.0L-V6 (145hp)

XL Flareside Sbed Pkp	8575	11050
XL Sbed Pkp	8300	10700
XL Super Cab Sbed Pkp	9850	12000
XL Super Cab Flares Sbed	9975	12150
XL Lbed Pkp	8525	11000

Add:
4.0 Liter V6 500
4-wheel drive 2300
4-wheel ABS 225
XLT trim 750
Trailhead pkg 1000

Deduct:
2.3L-I4 (119hp) 500
2.5L-I4 (135hp) 450

WINDSTAR FWD/3.8L-V6 (200hp)

Cargo Mini Van		
Limited Mini Van	18925	21675
LX Mini Van	13725	16150
SE Mini Van	14550	17125
SE Sport Mini Van	15250	17950
SEL Mini Van	16700	19325

Add:
Alloy wheels (std LX,Ltd) 300
Traction ctrl 175
Pwr sliding door 225
Entertainment center 800

Deduct:
Psgr slider only 450

2000 WS Ret

ECONOLINE RWD/4.6L-V8 (215hp)

E150 XL Psgr Van	13500	15900
E150 Cargo Van	11350	13825
E250 Cargo Van	11725	14275

Add:
4-wheel ABS 225
6.8L-V10 (305hp)(1-ton) 675
XL trim (cargo) 575
XLT trim 1050
Chateau trim 1350

Deduct:
4.2L 6cyl 425

EXCURSION RWD/6.8L-V10 (310hp)

Limited 4dr Utl	20900	24275
XLT 4dr Utl	18300	21500

Add:
7.3L-V8 TD (235hp) 1725
4-wheel drive 2050

EXPEDITION RWD/5.4L-V8 (260hp)

XLT 4dr Utl	16600	19500

Add:
5.4L-V8 (260hp) 400
4-wheel drive 2050
Eddie Bauer 2000
Sport trim 350

Deduct:
4.6L-V8 (215hp) 525

EXPLORER RWD/4.0L-V6 (160hp)

Sport 2dr Utl	10550	12850
XLS 4dr Utl	11800	14375

Add:
4.0L-V6 (210hp) std EB,Ltd . . 325
5.0L-V8 (215hp) 400
4-wheel drive 1775
XLT trim 875
Sport pkg 725
Eddie Bauer 1825
Limited 2750
Mach audio (std Ltd) 275

F150 PICKUP RWD/4.6L-V8 (220hp)

Harley Super Cab Fl Sbed	21550	24675
Lightning (5.4L SC) Sbed	20725	23725
Work Styleside (6cy Sbed	9550	11925
Work SCab Stysde (6 Sbed	11425	13925
Work Styleside (6cy Lbed	9750	11875
Work SCab Stysde (6 Lbed	11650	14200
XL Flareside Sbed Pkp	10400	12975
XL Styleside Sbed Pkp	10200	12425
XL Super Cab Stysde Sbed	12150	14800
XL Super Cab Flrsde Sbed	14175	16700
XL Styleside Lbed Pkp	10400	12675
XL Super Cab Stysde Lbed	12350	15050

F250 PICKUP RWD/5.4L-V8 (260hp)

Work Styleside (6cy Lbed	10375	12700
Work Super Cab (6cy Lbed	12350	15125
XL Styleside Lbed Pkp	11000	13400
XL Super Cab Lbed Pkp	13075	15925

Add:
4-wheel drive 1975
4-wheel ABS (Work,XL) 225
XLT trim 925
Lariat trim 1800

Deduct:
6cyl (not S) 425

RANGER RWD/3.0L-V6 (145hp)

XL Flareside Sbed Pkp	7650	9850
XL Sbed Pkp	7100	9150
XL Super Cab Sbed Pkp	8650	11150
XL Super Cab Flares Sbed	8900	11475
XL Lbed Pkp	7300	9400

Add:
4.0 Liter V6 375
4-wheel drive 1775
Extended cab w/4drs 675
4-wheel ABS 175
XLT trim 575
Trailhead pkg 775

Deduct:
2.5L-I4 (119hp) 400

WINDSTAR FWD/3.8L-V6 (200hp)

Base (3.0L V6/150hp) Van	11125	13550
Cargo Mini Van		
Limited Mini Van	17700	20475
LX Mini Van	12825	15625
SE Mini Van	13325	15700
SEL Mini Van	15475	18225

Add:
Alloy wheels (std LX,Ltd) 225
Traction ctrl 150
Pwr sliding door 175

Deduct:
Psgr slider only 350

1999 WS Ret

ECONOLINE RWD/4.6L-V8 (215hp)

E150 XL Psgr Van	12525	15250
E150 Cargo Van	10750	13100
E250 Cargo Van	11100	13525

Add:
4-wheel ABS 175
6.8L-V10 (305hp)(1-ton) 575
XL trim (cargo) 475
XLT trim 850
Chateau trim 1125

Deduct:
6cyl 350

EXPEDITION RWD/4.6L-V8 (240hp)

XLT 4dr Utl	15225	18200

Add:
5.4L-V8 (260hp) 325
4-wheel drive 1675
Eddie Bauer 1650

EXPLORER RWD/4.0L-V6 (160hp)

XL 4dr Utl	10675	13000
XL 2dr Utl	9450	11500

Add:
4.0L-V6 (210hp) std EB,Ltd . . 275
5.0L-V8 (215hp) 325

4-wheel drive 1475
XLT trim 725
Sport pkg 600
Eddie Bauer 1500
Limited 2275
JBL audio (std Ltd) 225

F150 PICKUP RWD/4.6L-V8 (220hp)

Model		
Work Styleside (6cyl) Sbed	9000	11875
Work SC Stysde (6) Sbed	10825	13175
Work Styleside (6cy Lbed	9175	11175
Work SC Stysde (6) Lbed	11000	13400
XL Flareside Sbed Pkp	9800	12225
XL Styleside Sbed Pkp	9625	11725
XL Super Cab Stysde Sbed	11450	13950
XL Super Cab Flrsde Sbed	13375	15750
XL Styleside Lbed Pkp	9800	11925
XL Super Cab Stysde Lbed	11625	14150

F250 PICKUP RWD/5.4L-V8 (260hp)

Model		
Work Super Cab (6) Sbed	11625	14225
Work Styleside (6cyl) Lbed	9775	11975
XL Super Cab Sbed Pkp	12250	14925
XL Styleside Lbed Pkp	10400	12675

Add:
4-wheel drive 1625
4-wheel ABS (std Lariat) 175
XLT trim 750
Lariat trim 1500

Deduct:
6cyl (not S) 350

RANGER RWD/3.0L-V6 (150hp)

Model		
XL Flareside Sbed Pkp	7000	9025
XL Sbed Pkp	6475	8350
XL Super Cab Sbed Pkp	7850	10125
XL Super Cab Flares Sbed	8125	10475
XL Lbed Pkp	6650	8575

Add:
4.0 Liter V6 325
4-wheel drive 1475
4-wheel ABS 150
Extended cab w/4drs 525
XLT trim 475
STX pkg 650

Deduct:
4cyl 325

WINDSTAR FWD/3.8L-V6 (200hp)

Model		
Base (3.0L V6/150hp Van	10075	12275
Cargo Mini Van		
LX Mini Van	11475	13975
SE Mini Van	13275	15625
SEL Mini Van	15300	18025

Add:
Alloy wheels (std LX,Ltd) 200
Traction ctrl 100

Deduct:
Psgr slider only 275

1998 WS Ret

ECONOLINE RWD/4.6L-V8 (215hp)

Model	WS	Ret
E150 XL Psgr Van	10975	13375
E150 Cargo Van	9175	11175
E250 Cargo Van	9500	11575

Add:
4-wheel ABS 150
XL trim (cargo) 375
XLT trim 700
Chateau trim 900

Deduct:
6cyl 275

EXPEDITION RWD/4.6L-V8 (215hp)

Model	WS	Ret
XLT 4dr Utl	13300	15900

Add:
5.4L-V8 (230hp) 275
Four-wheel drive 1400
Eddie Bauer 1350
Mach Sound 150

EXPLORER RWD/4.0L-V6 (160hp)

Model	WS	Ret
XL 4dr Utl	9700	11825
XL 2dr Utl	8600	11075

Add:
4.0L-V6 (210hp) std EB,Ltd 275
5.0L-V8 (215hp) 325
4-wheel drive 1225
XLT trim 600
Sport pkg 500
Eddie Bauer 1250
Limited 1875
JBL audio (std Ltd) 200

F150 PICKUP RWD/4.6L-V8 (220hp)

Model	WS	Ret
S Styleside (6cyl) Sbed Pkp	8050	10625
S Sup Cab Stysde (6) Sbed	9650	11750
S Styleside (6cyl) Lbed Pkp	8250	10625
S Sup Cab Stysde (6) Lbed	9800	11925
XL Flareside Sbed Pkp	8775	11600
XL Styleside Sbed Pkp	8625	11125
XL Super Cab Stysde Sbed	10225	12450
XL Super Cab Flrsde Sbed	11825	14400
XL Styleside Lbed Pkp	8775	11300
XL Super Cab Stysde Lbed	10400	12675

F250 PICKUP RWD/4.6L-V8 (220hp)

Model	WS	Ret
S Super Cab (6cyl) Sbed Pkp	10425	12750
S Styleside (6cyl) Lbed Pkp	8775	11375
XL Super Cab Sbed Pkp	10975	13375
XL Styleside Lbed Pkp	9325	11350

Add:
4-wheel drive 1350
4-wheel ABS (std Lariat) 150
XLT trim 625
Lariat trim 1225

Deduct:
6cyl (not S) 275

RANGER RWD/3.0L-V6 (145hp)

Model	WS	Ret
Splash Sbed Pkp	7000	9025
Splash Super Cab Sbed Pkp	8000	10300
XL Sbed Pkp	5500	7650
XL Super Cab Sbed Pkp	6775	8725
XL Lbed Pkp	5675	7325

Add:
4.0 Liter V6 275
4-wheel drive 1225
4-wheel ABS 125
Extended cab w/4drs 475
XLT trim 400
STX pkg 525

Deduct:
4cyl 275

WINDSTAR FWD/3.0L-V6 (150hp)

Model	WS	Ret
Base Mini Van	8025	10350
Cargo Mini Van	7550	9725
GL Mini Van	8575	11050
LX Mini Van	9900	12050

Add:
Alloy wheels (std LX,Ltd) 150
Traction ctrl 75

1997 WS Ret

AEROSTAR RWD/3.0L-V6 (140hp)

Model	WS	Ret
XLT Wagon Mini Van	5950	7675

Add:
4.0 Liter V6 (std 4WD) 150
4-wheel drive 950
Extended Wgn 425

ECONOLINE RWD/4.2L-V8 (215hp)

Model	WS	Ret
E150 XL Psgr Van	9675	11775
E150 Cargo Van	8050	10375
E250 Cargo Van	8350	10775

Add:
4-wheel ABS 125
XL trim 325

Deduct:
6cyl 225

EXPEDITION RWD/4.6L-V8 (215hp)

Model	WS	Ret
XLT 4dr Utl	11025	13625

Add:
5.4L-V8 (230hp) 275
4-wheel drive 1325
Eddie Bauer 1125
Mach Sound 125

EXPLORER RWD/4.0L-V6 (160hp)

Model	WS	Ret
XL 4dr Utl	8450	10900
XL 2dr Utl	7425	9575

Add:
4.0L-V6 (210hp) std EB,Ltd 225
5.0L-V8 (215hp) 275
4-wheel drive 1000
XLT trim 500
Sport pkg 400
Eddie Bauer 1025
Limited 1550
JBL audio (std Ltd) 150

F150 PICKUP RWD/4.6L-V8 (220hp)

Model	WS	Ret
S Styleside (6cyl) Sbed Pkp	7150	9450
S Sup Cab Stysde (6) Sbed	8600	11075
S Styleside (6cyl) Lbed Pkp	7300	9400
S Sup Cab Stysde (6) Lbed	8750	11275
XL Flareside Sbed Pkp	7800	10300
XL Styleside Sbed Pkp	7650	9850
XL Super Cab Stysde Sbed	9100	11075
XL Super Cab Flrsde Sbed	10550	12850
XL Styleside Lbed Pkp	7800	10050
XL Super Cab Stysde Lbed	9275	11300

F250 PICKUP RWD/4.6L-V8 (220hp)

Model	WS	Ret
S Super Cab (6cyl) Sbed	9250	11325
S Styleside (6cyl) Lbed Pkp	7750	10050
XL Super Cab Sbed Pkp	9725	11850
XL Styleside Lbed Pkp	8300	10700

Add:
4-wheel drive 1100
4-wheel ABS (std Lariat) 125
XLT trim 525
Lariat trim 1025

Deduct:
6cyl (not S) 225

RANGER RWD/3.0L-V6 (147hp)

Model	WS	Ret
Splash Sbed Pkp	6000	7725
Splash Super Cab Sbed Pkp	6875	8850
XL Sbed Pkp	4600	6400
XL Super Cab Sbed Pkp	5725	7375
XL Lbed Pkp	4775	6650

Add:
4.0 Liter V6 225
4-wheel drive 1000
4-wheel ABS 100
Psngr Air Bag 100
XLT trim 325
STX pkg 425

Deduct:
4cyl 225

WINDSTAR FWD/3.0L-V6 (150hp)

Model	WS	Ret
Base Mini Van	6625	8550
Cargo Mini Van	6225	8025
GL Mini Van	7125	9175
LX Mini Van	8300	10700

Add:
Alloy wheels (std LX) 125
Traction ctrl 50

Check Truck Equipment Table on page 4

1996 — WS / Ret

AEROSTAR — RWD/3.0L-V6 (140hp)

Model	WS	Ret
XLT Wagon Mini Van	5025	7000
Add:		
4.0 Liter V6 (std 4WD)	150	
4-wheel drive	750	
Extended Wgn	350	

BRONCO — 4WD/5.0L-V8 (199hp)

Model	WS	Ret
Bronco 2dr Utl	9400	11450
Add:		
XLT trim	525	
Eddie Bauer	850	
Deduct:		
6cyl	200	

ECONOLINE — RWD/5.0L-V8 (199hp)

Model	WS	Ret
E150 XL Psgr Van	8550	11025
E150 Cargo Van	6750	8700
E250 Cargo Van	7025	9050
Add:		
4-wheel ABS	75	
XL trim	250	
Deduct:		
6cyl	200	

EXPLORER — RWD/4.0L-V6 (160hp)

Model	WS	Ret
XL 4dr Utl	7050	9100
XL 2dr Utl	6175	7950
Add:		
5.0L-V8 (215hp)	275	
4-wheel drive	825	
XLT trim	400	
Sport pkg	325	
Eddie Bauer	850	
Limited	1325	
JBL audio (std Ltd)	125	

F150 PICKUP — RWD/5.0L-V8 (199hp)

Model	WS	Ret
S Styleside (6cyl) Sbed Pkp	4650	6475
S S.Cab Stysde (6cy Sbed	5925	7650
S Styleside (6cyl) Lbed Pkp.	4775	6650
S S.Cab Stysde (6cy Lbed	6050	7800
Styleside Sbed Pkp	5775	7450
Styleside Lbed Pkp	5900	7600
Super Cab Stysde Sbed Pkp	7050	9100
Super Cab Stysde Lbed Pkp	7200	9275

F250 PICKUP — RWD/5.0L-V8 (199hp)

Model	WS	Ret
Styleside Lbed Pkp	6325	8150
Super Cab Lbed Pkp	7625	9825
Add:		
4-wheel drive	925	
XLT trim	425	
Eddie Bauer trim	825	
Deduct:		
6cyl (not S)	200	

RANGER — RWD/3.0L-V6 (147hp)

Model	WS	Ret
Splash Sbed Pkp	5050	7025
Splash Super Cab Sbed Pkp	5850	7550
XL Sbed Pkp	3750	5450
XL Super Cab Sbed Pkp	4775	6650
XL Lbed Pkp	3875	5400
Add:		
4.0 Liter V6	175	
4-wheel drive	825	
4-wheel ABS	75	
Psngr Air Bag	75	
XLT trim	275	
STX pkg	350	
Deduct:		
4cyl	175	

WINDSTAR — FWD/3.0L-V6 (150hp)

Model	WS	Ret
Cargo Mini Van	4550	6325
GL Mini Van	5350	7450
LX Mini Van	6375	8225
Add:		
Alloy wheels (std LX)	100	

1995 — WS / Ret

AEROSTAR — RWD/3.0L-V6 (135hp)

Model	WS	Ret
Cargo Van Mini Van	2525	3775
Window Van Mini Van	2675	4000
XLT Wagon Mini Van	3875	5400
Add:		
4.0 Liter V6 (std 4WD)	150	
4-wheel drive (Extended)	675	
Eddie Bauer	750	
Extended van	350	

BRONCO — 4WD/5.0L-V8 (195hp)

Model	WS	Ret
Bronco 2dr Utl	7875	10150
Add:		
XLT trim	475	
Eddie Bauer	800	
Deduct:		
6cyl	175	

CLUB WAGON — RWD/5.8L-V8 (210hp)

Model	WS	Ret
XL Lwb Van	7050	9100
Add:		
XLT trim	475	
Chateau trim	725	
Deduct:		
6cyl	175	

ECONOLINE — RWD/5.8L-V8 (210hp)

Model	WS	Ret
E150 Cargo Lwb Van	5700	7350
E250 Cargo Lwb Van	5875	7575
Add:		
4-wheel ABS	125	
XL trim	250	
Deduct:		
6cyl	175	

EXPLORER — RWD/4.0L-V6 (160hp)

Model	WS	Ret
XL 4dr Utl	5600	7225
XL 2dr Utl	4850	6750
Add:		
4-wheel drive	775	
XLT trim	375	
Sport pkg	300	
Expedition	475	
Eddie Bauer	800	
Limited	1225	
JBL audio (std Ltd)	125	

F150 PICKUP — RWD/5.0L-V8 (205hp)

Model	WS	Ret
Lightning Sbed Pkp	7000	9150
S Styleside (6cyl) Sbed Pkp	3975	5525
S S.Cab Stysde (6cyl) Sbed	5100	7100
S Styleside (6cyl) Lbed Pkp	4050	5625
S S.Cab Stysde (6cyl) Lbed	5225	7275
Styleside Lbed Pkp	5075	7050
XL Flareside Sbed Pkp	5150	7150
XL Styleside Sbed Pkp	4975	6925
XL Super Cab Flrsde Sbed.	6225	8025
XL Super Cab Stysde Sbed	6100	7875
XL Super Cab Stysde Lbed	6225	8025

F250 PICKUP — RWD/5.8L-V8 (210hp)

Model	WS	Ret
XL Styleside Lbed Pkp	5450	7575
XL Super Cab Lbed Pkp	6575	8475
Add:		
4-wheel drive	850	
XLT trim	400	
Eddie Bauer trim	750	
Deduct:		
6cyl (not S)	175	

RANGER — RWD/3.0L-V6 (147hp)

Model	WS	Ret
Splash Sbed Pkp	4200	5850
XL Sbed Pkp.	3250	4725
XL Super Cab Sbed Pkp	4075	5675
XL Lbed Pkp	3350	4850
Add:		
4.0 Liter V6	175	
4-wheel drive	775	
4-wheel ABS	50	
XLT trim	250	
STX pkg	325	
Deduct:		
4cyl	175	

WINDSTAR — FWD/3.8L-V6 (155hp)

Model	WS	Ret
GL Mini Van	4125	5725
LX Mini Van	5100	7100

1994 — WS / Ret

AEROSTAR — RWD/3.0L-V6 (135hp)

Model	WS	Ret
Cargo Van Mini Van	1600	2600
Window Van Mini Van	1725	2800
XL Wagon Mini Van	2875	4300
Add:		
4.0L V6	100	
4-wheel drive	625	
XLT trim	425	
Eddie Bauer	675	
Extended van	325	

BRONCO — 4WD/5.0L-V8 (195hp)

Model	WS	Ret
Bronco 2dr Utl.	6800	8775
Add:		
XLT trim	425	
Eddie Bauer	700	
Deduct:		
6cyl	150	

CLUB WAGON — RWD/5.0L-V8 (195hp)

Model	WS	Ret
Wagon Lwb Van	6125	7900
Add:		
XLT trim	425	
Chateau trim	650	
Deduct:		
6cyl	150	

ECONOLINE — RWD/5.0L-V8 (195hp)

Model	WS	Ret
E150 Cargo Lwb Van	5025	7000
E250 Cargo Lwb Van	5200	7225
Add:		
4-wheel ABS	100	
XL trim	225	
Deduct:		
6cyl	150	

EXPLORER — RWD/4.0L-V6 (160hp)

Model	WS	Ret
XL 4dr Utl	3875	5400
XL 2dr Utl	3225	4675
Add:		
4-wheel drive	700	
XLT trim	350	
Eddie Bauer	700	
Limited	1100	
Sport	250	
JBL audio	100	

F150 PICKUP — RWD/5.0L-V8 (195hp)

Model	WS	Ret
Flareside Sbed Pkp	4825	6700
Lightning Sbed Pkp	6675	8725
S Styleside (6cyl) Sbed Pkp	3800	5525
S S.Cab Stysde (6cyl) Sbed	4775	6650
S Styleside (6cyl) Lbed Pkp	3875	5400
S S.Cab Stysde (6cyl) Lbed	4875	6775
Styleside Sbed Pkp	4675	6500
Styleside Lbed Pkp.	4775	6650
Super Cab Flrsde Sbed Pkp	5700	7350

Super Cab Stysde Sbed Pkp 5625 7250
Super Cab Stysde Lbed Pkp 5700 7350

F250 PICKUP RWD/5.0L-V8 (205hp)

Styleside Lbed Pkp 5075 7050
Super Cab Lbed Pkp 6025 7775

Add:
4-wheel drive 775
XLT trim 350

Deduct:
6cyl (not S) 150

RANGER RWD/3.0L-V6 (140hp)

Splash Sbed Pkp 3675 5325
XL Sbed Pkp 2800 4175
XL Super Cab Sbed Pkp . . . 3550 5150
XL Lbed Pkp 2900 4325

Add:
4.0 Liter V6 125
4-wheel drive 700
XLT trim 225
STX pkg 300

Deduct:
4cyl 150

1993 WS Ret

AEROSTAR RWD/3.0L-V6 (135hp)

Cargo Van Mini Van 1250 2025
Window Van Mini Van 1375 2225
XL Wagon Mini Van 2300 3575

Add:
4.0L V6 (std 4WD) 75
4-wheel drive 550
XLT trim 375
Eddie Bauer 600
Extended van 300

BRONCO 4WD/5.0L-V8 (185hp)

Bronco 2dr Utl 5900 7600

Add:
XLT trim 375
Eddie Bauer 600

Deduct:
6cyl 150

CLUB WAGON RWD/5.0L-V8 (185hp)

Wagon Lwb Van 4650 6475

Add:
XLT trim 375
Chateau trim 600

Deduct:
6cyl 150

ECONOLINE RWD/5.0L-V8 (185hp)

E150 Cargo Lwb Van 4000 5550
E250 Cargo Lwb Van 4150 5775

Add:
XL trim 200

Deduct:
6cyl 150

EXPLORER RWD/4.0L-V6 (155hp)

XL 4dr Utl 3275 4750
XL 2dr Utl 2700 4025

Add:
4-wheel drive 625
XLT trim 300
Eddie Bauer 625
Limited 975
Sport 250
JBL audio (std Limited) 75

F150 PICKUP RWD/5.0L-V8 (185hp)

Flareside Sbed Pkp 3925 5450
Lightning Sbed Pkp 5625 7350
S Styleside (6cyl) Sbed Pkp 3075 4475
S Styleside (6cyl) Lbed Pkp. 3125 4525
Styleside Sbed Pkp 3825 5325
Styleside Lbed Pkp 3925 5450
Super Cab Flrsde Sbed Pkp 4800 6675
Super Cab Stysde Sbed Pkp 4725 6575
Super Cab Stysde Lbed Pkp 4800 6675

Deduct:
6cyl (not S) 150

F250 PICKUP RWD/5.0L-V8 (185hp)

Styleside Lbed Pkp 4175 5800
Super Cab Lbed Pkp 5075 7050

Add:
4-wheel drive 700
XLT trim 325

Deduct:
6cyl (not S) 150

RANGER RWD/3.0L-V6 (145hp)

Splash Sbed Pkp 2825 4225
XL Sbed Pkp 2325 3600
XL Super Cab Sbed Pkp . . . 2975 4325
XL Lbed Pkp 2400 3725

Add:
4.0 Liter V6 100
4-wheel drive 625
XLT trim 200
STX pkg 275

Deduct:
4cyl 125

1992 WS Ret

AEROSTAR RWD/3.0L-V6 (145hp)

Cargo Van Mini Van 1050 1825
Window Van Mini Van 1175 2050
XL Wagon Mini Van 1950 3025

Add:
4.0L V6 (std 4WD) 50
4-wheel drive 475
XLT trim 300
Eddie Bauer 550
Extended van 275

BRONCO 4WD/4.9L-V8 (185hp)

Bronco 2dr Utl 4925 6850

Add:
XLT trim 300
Nite trim 375
Eddie Bauer 525

Deduct:
6cyl 125

CLUB WAGON RWD/5.0L-V8 (185hp)

Wagon Lwb Van 4050 5625

Add:
XLT trim 300
Chateau trim 450

Deduct:
6cyl 125

ECONOLINE RWD/5.0L-V8 (185hp)

E150 Cargo Lwb Van 3300 4800
E250 Cargo Lwb Van 3500 5075

Add:
XL trim 150

Deduct:
6cyl 125

EXPLORER RWD/4.0L-V6 (155hp)

XL 4dr Utl 2950 4275
XL 2dr Utl 2425 3775

Add:
4-wheel drive 575
Sport trim 225
XLT trim 275
Eddie Bauer 525

F150 PICKUP RWD/5.0L-V8 (185hp)

Flareside Sbed Pkp 3500 5075
S Styleside (6cyl) Sbed Pkp . 2675 4000
S S.Cab Stsde(6cyl) Sbed . . 3400 4925
S Styleside (6cyl) Lbed Pkp . 2750 4100
S S.Cab Stsde(6cyl) Lbed . . 3525 5125
Styleside Sbed Pkp 3325 4825
Styleside Lbed Pkp 3400 4925
Super Cab Stysde Sbed Pkp 4125 5725
Super Cab Flrsde Sbed Pkp 4175 5800
Super Cab Stysde Lbed Pkp 4175 5800

F250 PICKUP RWD/5.0L-V8 (185hp)

Styleside Lbed Pkp 3675 5325
Super Cab Lbed Pkp 4500 6250

Add:
4-wheel drive 650
XL trim 150
Sport pkg 250
Nite trim 375
Lariat trim 300

Deduct:
6cyl (not S) 125

RANGER RWD/2.9L-V6 (140hp)

Base Sbed Pkp 1825 2975
Base Lbed Pkp 1875 3050
S (4cyl-5sp) Sbed Pkp 1450 2350
Super Cab Sbed Pkp 2400 3725

Add:
4-wheel drive 575
XLT trim 175
Sport pkg 250
STX trim 225

Deduct:
4cyl 125

1991 WS Ret

AEROSTAR RWD/3.0L-V6 (145hp)

Cargo Van Mini Van 800 1550
Window Van Mini Van 925 1775
XL Wagon Mini Van 1650 2675

Add:
4.0L V6 (std 4WD) 50
4-wheel drive 400
XLT trim 275
Eddie Bauer 500
Extended van 275

BRONCO 4WD/5.0L-V8 (185hp)

Sport Util 2dr Utl 3750 5450

Add:
XLT trim 275
Nite trim 300
Eddie Bauer 500

Deduct:
6cyl 100

CLUB WAGON RWD/5.0L-V8 (185hp)

E150 Lwb Van 3375 4900
E250 Lwb Van 3525 5125

Add:
XLT trim 275

Deduct:
6cyl 100

ECONOLINE RWD/5.0L-V8 (185hp)

E150 Cargo Lwb Van 2575 3850
E250 Cargo Lwb Van 2675 4000

Add:
XL trim 125

Deduct:
6cyl 100

EXPLORER RWD/4.0L-V6 (155hp)

XL 4dr Utl 2525 3775

Check Truck Equipment Table on page 4

Model	WS	Ret
XL 2dr Utl	2050	3175

Add:
- 4-wheel drive 525
- Sport 225
- XLT trim 275
- Eddie Bauer 500

F150 PICKUP RWD/5.0L-V8 (185hp)

Model	WS	Ret
S Styleside (6cyl) Sbed Pkp	2225	3450
S Styleside (6cyl) Lbed Pkp.	2300	3575
Styleside Sbed Pkp	2800	4175
Styleside Lbed Pkp	2875	4300
Super Cab Sbed Pkp	3500	5075
Super Cab Lbed Pkp	3550	5150

F250 PICKUP RWD/5.0L-V8 (185hp)

Model	WS	Ret
Styleside Lbed Pkp	3075	4475
Super Cab Lbed Pkp	3775	5475

Add:
- 4-wheel drive 575
- XL trim 125
- Lariat trim 275
- Nite trim 300

Deduct:
- 6cyl (not S) 100

RANGER RWD/2.9L-V6 (140hp)

Model	WS	Ret
Base Sbed Pkp	1600	2600
Base Lbed Pkp.	1625	2650
S (4cyl-5sp) Sbed Pkp	1250	2025
Super Cab Sbed Pkp	2075	3225

Add:
- 4-wheel drive 525
- XLT trim 150
- STX trim 225

Deduct:
- 4cyl 100

1990 WS Ret

AEROSTAR RWD/3.0L-V6 (145hp)

Model	WS	Ret
Cargo Van Mini Van	575	1225
Window Van Mini Van	650	1375
XL Wagon Mini Van	1350	2200

Add:
- 4.0L V6 (std 4WD) 25
- 4-wheel drive 375
- XLT trim 225
- Eddie Bauer 500
- Extended van 250

BRONCO 4WD/5.0L-V8 (185hp)

Model	WS	Ret
Sport Util 2dr Utl.	3175	4600

Add:
- XL Sport trim 175
- XLT trim 225
- Eddie Bauer 475

Deduct:
- 6cyl 75

BRONCO II RWD/2.9L-V6 (140hp)

Model	WS	Ret
Sport Util 2dr Utl.	1200	2100

Add:
- 4-wheel drive 500
- XL Sport trim 175
- XLT trim 225
- Eddie Bauer 475

CLUB WAGON RWD/5.0L-V8 (185hp)

Model	WS	Ret
E150 Lwb Van	2725	4075
E250 Lwb Van	2800	4175

Add:
- XLT trim 225

Deduct:
- 6cyl 75

ECONOLINE RWD/5.0L-V8 (185hp)

Model	WS	Ret
E150 Cargo Swb Van	1975	3075
E150 Cargo Lwb Van	2000	3100
E250 Cargo Lwb Van	2125	3300

Add:
- XL trim 75

Deduct:
- 6cyl 75

F150 PICKUP RWD/5.0L-V8 (185hp)

Model	WS	Ret
S Styleside (6cyl) Sbed Pkp	1875	3050
S Styleside (6cyl) Lbed Pkp	1925	3000
Styleside Sbed Pkp	2375	3700
Styleside Lbed Pkp	2450	3800
Super Cab Sbed Pkp	2925	4250
Super Cab Lbed Pkp	3000	4350

F250 PICKUP RWD/5.0L-V8 (185hp)

Model	WS	Ret
Styleside Lbed Pkp	2625	3925
Super Cab Lbed Pkp	3150	4575

Add:
- 4-wheel drive 550
- XL trim 75
- XLT trim 225

Deduct:
- 6cyl (not S) 75

RANGER RWD/2.9L-V6 (140hp)

Model	WS	Ret
Base Sbed Pkp	1350	2200
Base Lbed Pkp	1425	2325
S (4cyl-5sp) Sbed Pkp.	1150	2000
Super Cab Sbed Pkp	1800	2925

Add:
- 4-wheel drive 500
- XLT trim 150
- STX trim 200

Deduct:
- 4cyl 75

1989 WS Ret

AEROSTAR RWD/3.0L-V6 (145hp)

Model	WS	Ret
Cargo Van Mini Van	350	900
Window Van Mini Van	425	1075
XL Wagon Mini Van	800	1550

Add:
- XLT trim 225
- Eddie Bauer 400
- Extended van 225

BRONCO 4WD/5.0L-V8 (185hp)

Model	WS	Ret
Sport Util 2dr Utl	2500	3725

Add:
- XL Sport trim 225
- Eddie Bauer 350

Deduct:
- 6cyl 75

BRONCO II RWD/2.9L-V6 (140hp)

Model	WS	Ret
Sport Util 2dr Utl	950	1825

Add:
- 4-wheel drive 450
- XL Sport trim 175
- XLT trim 200
- Eddie Bauer 350

CLUB WAGON RWD/5.0L-V8 (185hp)

Model	WS	Ret
E150 Lwb Van	2000	3100
E250 Lwb Van	2075	3225

Add:
- XLT trim 225

Deduct:
- 6cyl 75

ECONOLINE RWD/5.0L-V8 (185hp)

Model	WS	Ret
E150 Cargo Swb Van	1625	2650
E150 Cargo Lwb Van	1700	2750
E250 Cargo Lwb Van	1800	2925

Add:
- XL trim 50

Deduct:
- 6cyl 75

F150 PICKUP RWD/4.9L-V6 (150hp)

Model	WS	Ret
S Styleside (6cyl) Sbed Pkp	1525	2475
S Styleside (6cyl) Lbed Pkp	1575	2550
Styleside Sbed Pkp	1900	2950
Styleside Lbed Pkp	1975	3075
Super Cab Sbed Pkp	2400	3725
Super Cab Lbed Pkp	2475	3850

F250 PICKUP RWD/5.8L-V8 (210hp)

Model	WS	Ret
Styleside Lbed Pkp	2100	3250
Super Cab Lbed Pkp	2625	3925

Add:
- 4-wheel drive 500
- XL trim 50
- XLT trim 200

Deduct:
- 6cyl (not S) 75

RANGER RWD/2.9L-V6 (140hp)

Model	WS	Ret
Base Sbed Pkp	950	1825
Base Lbed Pkp	1025	1800
S (4cyl-5sp) Sbed Pkp	750	1450
S (4cyl-5sp) Lbed Pkp	800	1550
Super Cab Sbed Pkp	1350	2200

Add:
- 4-wheel drive 450
- XLT trim 100
- STX trim 175
- GT pkg 225

Deduct:
- 4cyl 50

1988 WS Ret

AEROSTAR RWD/3.0L-V6 (145hp)

Model	WS	Ret
Cargo Van Mini Van	225	575
Wagon Mini Van	625	1325
Window Van Mini Van	275	700

Add:
- XLT trim 150
- Eddie Bauer 300

Deduct:
- 4cyl 50

BRONCO 4WD/5.0L-V8 (na)

Model	WS	Ret
Sport Util 2dr Utl	2125	3300

Add:
- XL Sport trim 150
- XLT trim 150
- Eddie Bauer 300

Deduct:
- 6cyl 50

BRONCO II RWD/2.9L-V6 (140hp)

Model	WS	Ret
Sport Util 2dr Utl	675	1425

Add:
- 4-wheel drive 425
- XL Sport trim 150
- XLT trim 175
- Eddie Bauer 300

CLUB WAGON RWD/5.0L-V8 (na)

Model	WS	Ret
E150 Lwb Van	1600	2600
E250 Lwb Van	1700	2750

Add:
- XLT trim 150

Deduct:
- 6cyl 50

ECONOLINE RWD/5.0L-V8 (185hp)

Model	WS	Ret
E150 Cargo Swb Van	1350	2200
E150 Cargo Lwb Van	1400	2275
E250 Cargo Lwb Van	1475	2400

Add:
- XL trim 50

XLT trim	125	

Deduct:

6cyl	50	

F150 PICKUP RWD/5.0L-V8 (na)

S Styleside (6cyl) Sbed Pkp	1275	2075
S Styleside (6cyl) Lbed Pkp.	1325	2150
Styleside Sbed Pkp	1625	2650
Styleside Lbed Pkp	1675	2725
Super Cab Sbed Pkp	2000	3100
Super Cab Lbed Pkp	2050	3175

F250 PICKUP RWD/5.8L-V8 (na)

Styleside Lbed Pkp	1800	2925
Super Cab Lbed Pkp	2200	3425

Add:

4-wheel drive	425
XL trim	25
XLT trim	150

Deduct:

6cyl (not S)	50

RANGER RWD/2.9L-V6 (140hp)

Base Sbed Pkp	825	1600
Base Lbed Pkp	825	1600
S (4cyl-5sp) Sbed Pkp.	600	1275
Super Cab Sbed Pkp	1100	1925

Add:

4-wheel drive	375
XLT trim	50
STX trim	150
GT pkg	175

Deduct:

4cyl	50

GEO

1997

TRACKER (5sp) RWD/1.6L-I4 (95hp)

	WS	Ret
SoftTop 2dr Utl	3175	4600
Wagon 4dr Utl	3600	5225

Add:

4-wheel drive	800
Automatic trans	300
ABS Brakes	150
LSi trim	325
Hardtop	125

1996

TRACKER (5sp) RWD/1.6L-I4 (95hp)

	WS	Ret
SoftTop 2dr Utl	2350	3650
Wagon 4dr Utl	2725	4075

Add:

4-wheel drive	650
Automatic trans	250
LSi trim	250
Hardtop	75

1995

TRACKER (5sp) RWD/4.3L-I4 (195hp)

	WS	Ret
SoftTop 2dr Utl	1850	3000

Add:

4-wheel drive	600
Automatic trans	225
LSi trim	250
Hardtop	50

1994

TRACKER (5sp) RWD/1.6L-I4 (80hp)

	WS	Ret
SoftTop 2dr Utl	1575	2550

Add:

4-wheel drive	550
Automatic trans	200
LSi trim	225
Hardtop	50

1993

TRACKER (5sp) RWD/1.6L-I4 (80hp)

	WS	Ret
SoftTop 2dr Utl	1200	2100

Add:

4-wheel drive	475
Automatic trans	175
LSi trim	200
Hardtop	50

1992

TRACKER (5sp) RWD/1.6L-I4 (80hp)

	WS	Ret
SoftTop 2dr Utl	975	1875

Add:

4-wheel drive	400
Automatic trans	150
LSi trim	175
Hardtop	25

1991

TRACKER (5sp) RWD/1.6L-I4 (80hp)

	WS	Ret
SoftTop 2dr Utl	900	1725

Add:

4-wheel drive	325
Automatic trans	125
LSi trim	175
Hardtop	25

1990

TRACKER (5sp) 4WD/1.6L-I4 (80hp)

	WS	Ret
SoftTop 2dr Utl	1325	2150

Add:

Automatic trans	100
LSi trim	150
Hardtop	25

1989

TRACKER (5sp) 4WD/1.6L-I4 (80hp)

	WS	Ret
SoftTop 2dr Utl	1225	2150

Add:

Automatic trans	75
LSi trim	100
Hardtop	25

GMC

2001

DENALI 4WD/6.0L-V8 (320hp)

	WS	Ret
Luxury 4dr Utl		

ENVOY 4WD/4.3L-V6 (190hp)

	WS	Ret
Luxury 4dr Utl		

G1500 VAN RWD/5.0L-V8 (220hp)

	WS	Ret
Savana 135" wb Psngr Van	14450	17025
Savana 135" wb Cargo Van	12825	15625

G2500 VAN RWD/5.7L-V8 (255hp)

	WS	Ret
Savana 135" wb Psngr Van	14875	17525
Savana 135" wb Cargo Van	12625	15375

Add:

SLE trim	1350

Deduct:

4.3L-V6 (200hp)	525

JIMMY RWD/4.3L-V6 (190hp)

	WS	Ret
SLE 4dr Utl	13450	15825
SLS 2dr Utl	12175	14825

Add:

4-wheel drive	2300
SLT trim	2200
Diamond Edit. trim	2425
Bose Audio	200

SAFARI RWD/4.3L-V6 (190hp)

	WS	Ret
Cargo Mini Van	11425	13925
SLE Passenger Mini Van	13175	15500

Add:

All-wheel drive	2050
SLT trim	1750

SIERRA 1500 RWD/4.8L-V8 (270hp)

	WS	Ret
Ext.Cab Sptsde Sbed Pkp	14750	17450
Ext.Cab Wdsde Sbed Pkp	14250	16775
Ext.Cab Wdsde Lbed Pkp	14650	17250
HD CrewCab Sbed Pkp		
Sportside Sbed Pkp	12700	15550
Wideside Sbed Pkp	12400	15100
Wideside Lbed Pkp	12575	15325

SIERRA 2500 RWD/5.3L-V8 (285hp)

	WS	Ret
CrewCab Wdsde HD Sbed Pkp		
CrewCab Wdsde HD (6 Lbed Pkp		
Ext.Cab Wdsde 4WD Sbed	14600	17200
Ext.Cab Wdsde HD Lbed	15525	18275
Wideside HD Sbed	13475	15875
Wideside Lbed Pkp	12950	15775

Note: HD models come with 6.0L V8

Add:

4-wheel drive	2525
SLE trim	750
SLT trim	1675

Deduct:

4.3L-V6 (200hp)	525

SONOMA PICKUP RWD/4.3L-V6 (180hp)

	WS	Ret
SL Sbed Pkp	8175	10550
SL ExCab Wdsde Sbed Pkp	9575	11650
SL ExCab Sptsde Sbed Pkp	9825	11975
SL Lbed Pkp	8325	10725
SLS Sport Sptsde Sbed Pkp	8800	11350
SLS CrewCab 4WD Sbed Pkp		

Add:

4-wheel drive	2300
Third door (std 4WD ext cab)	250
SLS trim (std Club Cab)	550
SLE trim	975
ZR2 pkg	1000
Sport suspension	350

Deduct:

4cyl	475

YUKON 4WD/4.8L-V8 (270hp)

	WS	Ret
SLE 4dr Utl	23450	26975

Add:

SLT trim	975

Deduct:

2-wheel drive	2400

YUKON XL RWD/

	WS	Ret
SLE 1500 4dr Utl		
SLE 2500 4dr Utl		

2000

DENALI 4WD/5.7L-V8 (255hp)

	WS	Ret
Luxury 4dr Utl	24475	28150

ENVOY 4WD/4.3L-V6 (190hp)

	WS	Ret
Luxury 4dr Utl	16550	19250

G1500 VAN RWD/5.0L-V8 (220hp)

	WS	Ret
Savana 135" wb Psngr Van	13225	15575
Savana 135" wb Cargo Van	11250	13700

G2500 VAN RWD/5.7L-V8 (255hp)

	WS	Ret
Savana 135" wb Psngr Van	13650	16075
Savana 135" wb Cargo Van	11650	14200

Check Truck Equipment Table on page 4

Add:
SLE trim 1050

Deduct:
6cyl 425

JIMMY RWD/4.3L-V6 (190hp)

	WS	Ret
SLE 4dr Utl.	12025	14650
SLS 2dr Utl.	10975	13375

Add:
4-wheel drive 1775
SLE trim (4dr) 1375
SLT trim 1700
Diamond Edit. tirm 1900

SAFARI RWD/4.3L-V6 (190hp)

	WS	Ret
Cargo Mini Van	10350	12600
SL Passenger Mini Van	11850	14425

Add:
All-wheel drive 1600
SLE trim 750
SLT trim 1350

SIERRA 1500 RWD/4.8L-V8 (270hp)

	WS	Ret
Ext.Cab Sptsde Sbed Pkp	13350	15800
Ext.Cab Wdsde Sbed Pkp	12900	15700
Ext.Cab Wdsde Lbed Pkp	13250	15600
Special (6cyl) Sbed Pkp	9875	12025
Special (6cyl) Lbed Pkp	10050	12250
Sportside Sbed Pkp	11475	14050
Wideside Sbed Pkp	11225	13675
Wideside Lbed Pkp	11400	13875

SIERRA 2500 RWD/5.3L-V8 (285hp)

	WS	Ret
Ext.Cab Wdsde HD 4WD Sbed Pkp	17900	20700
Ext.Cab Wdsde Sbed Pkp	13200	15550
*Ext.Cab Wdsde HD Lbed	15350	18075
Ext.Cab Wdsde Lbed Pkp	13650	16075
*Wideside HD Sbed Pkp	12875	15675
Wideside Lbed Pkp	11650	14200

** Old Style*

Add:
4-wheel drive 1975
Fourth door (ext. cab) 225
SLE trim 600
SLT trim 1300

Deduct:
6cyl (not Special) 425

SONOMA PICKUP RWD/4.3L-V6 (180hp)

	WS	Ret
SL Sbed Pkp	7650	9850
SL ExCab Wdsde Sbed Pkp	8950	11525
SL ExCab Sptsde Sbed Pkp	9125	11125
SL Lbed Pkp	7750	10000
SLS Sport Sptsde Sbed Pkp	8325	10725

Add:
4-wheel drive 1775
Third door (std 4WD ext cab) . . 200
SLS trim (std Club Cab) 425
SLE trim 750
ZR2 pkg 725

Deduct:
4cyl 375

YUKON 4WD/4.8L-V8 (270hp)

	WS	Ret
SLE 4dr Utl.	20750	23875

Add:
SLT trim 750

Deduct:
2-wheel drive 1875

YUKON XL RWD/

	WS	Ret
SLE 1500 4dr Utl	19125	22000
SLE 2500 4dr Utl	19900	22900

1999 WS Ret

DENALI 4WD/5.7L-V8 (255hp)

	WS	Ret
Luxury 4dr Utl	25500	28875

ENVOY 4WD/4.3L-V6 (190hp)

	WS	Ret
Luxury 4dr Utl	18600	21400

G1500 VAN RWD/5.0L-V8 (220hp)

	WS	Ret
Savana 135" wb Psngr Van	12100	14750
Savana 135" wb Cargo Van	10425	12700

G2500 VAN RWD/5.7L-V8 (255hp)

	WS	Ret
Savana 135" wb Psngr Van	12450	15175
Savana 135" wb Cargo Van	10775	13125

Add:
SLE trim 875

Deduct:
6cyl 350

JIMMY RWD/4.3L-V6 (190hp)

	WS	Ret
Base 4dr Utl.	10525	12825
Base 2dr Utl.	9575	11650

Add:
4-wheel drive 1475
SLS trim 375
SLE trim (4dr) 1125
SLT trim 1400

SAFARI RWD/4.3L-V6 (190hp)

	WS	Ret
Cargo Mini Van	9425	11475
SLX Passenger Mini Van	10825	13175

Add:
All-wheel drive 1325
SLE trim 625
SLT trim 1125

SIERRA 1500 RWD/4.8L-V8 (255hp)

	WS	Ret
*Ext.Cab Wdsde Sbed Pkp	13650	16075
Ext.Cab Sptsde Sbed Pkp.	12800	15675
Ext.Cab Wdsde Sbed Pkp.	12325	15000
Ext.Cab Wdsde Lbed Pkp.	12700	15475
Special (6cyl) Sbed Pkp	9500	11575
Special (6cyl) Lbed Pkp	9650	11750
Sportside Sbed Pkp	11025	13500
Wideside Sbed Pkp.	10775	13125
Wideside Lbed Pkp	10950	13325

SIERRA 2500 RWD/5.3L-V8 (270hp)

	WS	Ret
*Ext.Cab Wdsde 4WD Sbed	16275	18825
Ext.Cab Wdsde Sbed Pkp.	12700	15475
*Ext.Cab WdsdeLbed Pkp	14200	16725
Ext.Cab Wdsde Lbed Pkp.	13100	15950
*Wideside Sbed Pkp	11650	14200
Wideside Lbed Pkp	11175	13600

** Old Style*

Add:
4-wheel drive 1625
Fourth door (ext. cab) 175
SLE trim 475
SLT trim 1075

Deduct:
6cyl (not Special) 350

SONOMA PICKUP RWD/4.3L-V6 (175hp)

	WS	Ret
Ext.Cab Wdsde Sbed Pkp.	7825	10075
Ext.Cab Sptsde Sbed Pkp.	8000	10300
SL Sbed Pkp	6675	8600
SL Lbed Pkp	6800	8775
SLS Sport Sptsde Sbed Pkp.		

Add:
4-wheel drive 1475
Third door (std 4WD ext cab) . . 150
SLS trim (std Club Cab) 350
SLE trim 625
ZR2 pkg 600

Deduct:
4cyl 300

SUBURBAN RWD/5.7L-V8 (255hp)

	WS	Ret
C1500 4dr Utl	14750	17450
C2500 4dr Utl	15350	18150

Add:
4-wheel drive 1625
SLE trim 1100
SLT trim 1500

YUKON 4WD/5.7L-V8 (255hp)

	WS	Ret
SL 4dr Utl	16650	19350
SL 2dr Utl	14825	17550

Add:
SLT trim 625

Deduct:
2-wheel drive 1550

1998 WS Ret

ENVOY 4WD/

	WS	Ret
Luxury 4dr Utl	16875	19625

G1500 VAN RWD/5.0L-V8 (220hp)

	WS	Ret
Savana 135" wb Psngr Van	10800	13150
Van 135" wb Cargo Van	9175	11175

G2500 VAN RWD/5.7L-V8 (250hp)

	WS	Ret
Savana 135" wb Psngr Van	11100	13525
Van 135" wb Cargo Van	9525	11600

Add:
SLE trim 725

Deduct:
6cyl 275

JIMMY RWD/4.3L-V6 (190hp)

	WS	Ret
Base 4dr Utl	9325	11350
Base 2dr Utl	8500	10950

Add:
4-wheel drive 1225
SLS trim 325
SLE trim (4dr) 950
SLT trim 1175

SAFARI RWD/4.3L-V6 (190hp)

	WS	Ret
Cargo Mini Van	8100	10450
SLX Passenger Mini Van	9375	11425

Add:
All-wheel drive 1100
SLE trim 525
SLT trim 925

SIERRA 1500 RWD/5.0L-V8 (230hp)

	WS	Ret
Ext.Cab Sptsde Sbed Pkp	11350	13900
Ext.Cab Wdsde Sbed Pkp	11000	13400
Ext.Cab Wdsde Lbed Pkp	11325	13800
Special (6cyl) Sbed Pkp	8475	10925
Special (6cyl) Lbed Pkp	8600	11075
Sportside Sbed Pkp	9850	12050
Wideside Sbed Pkp	9600	11700
Wideside Lbed Pkp.	9775	11900

SIERRA 2500 RWD/5.0L-V8 (230hp)

	WS	Ret
Ext.Cab Wdsde Sbed Pkp	11225	13675
Ext.Cab Wdsde Lbed Pkp	11625	14150
Wideside Lbed Pkp.	10050	12250

Add:
4-wheel drive 1350
Third door (ext. cab) 125
SLE trim 400
SLT trim 750

Deduct:
6cyl (not Special) 275

SONOMA PICKUP RWD/4.3L-V6 (175hp)

	WS	Ret
Ext.Cab Wdsde Sbed Pkp	6625	8550
Ext.Cab Sptsde Sbed Pkp	6800	8775

	WS	Ret
SL Sbed Pkp	5675	7325
SL Lbed Pkp	5775	7450
SLS Sport Sptsde Sbed Pkp	6275	8100

Add:
4-wheel drive 1225
Third door (ext. cab) 125
SLS trim (std Club Cab) 300
SLE trim 525
ZR2 pkg 500

Deduct:
4cyl 250

SUBURBAN RWD/5.7L-V8 (255hp)

	WS	Ret
C1500 4dr Utl	13150	15550
C2500 4dr Utl	13675	16175

Add:
4-wheel drive 1350
SLE trim 775
SLT trim 1025

YUKON 4WD/

	WS	Ret
SL 4dr Utl	15000	17750
SL 2dr Utl	13375	15825

Add:
SL trim (2dr) 400
SLS trim 625
SLT trim 1050

Deduct:
2-wheel drive 1275

1997 WS Ret

G1500 VAN RWD/5.0L-V8 (220hp)

	WS	Ret
Savana 135" wb Psngr Van.	9525	11600
Van 135" wb Cargo Van	8000	10300

G2500 VAN RWD/5.7L-V8 (220hp)

	WS	Ret
Savana 135" wb Psngr Van.	9800	11925
Van 135" wb Cargo Van	8300	10700

Add:
SLE trim 600

Deduct:
6cyl 225

JIMMY RWD/4.3L-V6 (190hp)

	WS	Ret
Base 4dr Utl	7975	10275
Base 2dr Utl	7275	9375

Add:
4-wheel drive 1000
SLS trim 250
SLE trim 775
SLT trim 875

SAFARI RWD/4.3L-V6 (190hp)

	WS	Ret
Cargo Mini Van	6750	8700
SLX Passenger Mini Van	7800	10050

Add:
4-wheel drive 900
SLE trim 425
SLT trim 725

SIERRA 1500 RWD/5.0L-V8 (220hp)

	WS	Ret
Ext.Cab Sptsde Sbed Pkp.	10050	12300
Ext.Cab Wdsde Sbed Pkp.	9750	11875
Ext.Cab Wdsde Lbed Pkp	9975	12150
Special (6cyl) Sbed Pkp	7375	9500
Special (6cyl) Lbed Pkp.	7575	9775
Sportside Sbed Pkp	8525	11050
Wideside Sbed Pkp	8650	11150
Wideside Lbed Pkp	8650	11150

SIERRA 2500 RWD/5.7L-V8 (250hp)

	WS	Ret
Ext.Cab Wdsde Sbed Pkp.	9950	12125
Ext.Cab Wdsde Lbed Pkp.	10300	12550
Wideside Lbed Pkp	8150	10500

Add:
4-wheel drive 1100
Third door (ext. cab) 100
SLE trim 300
SLT trim 550

Deduct:
6cyl (not Special) 225

SONOMA PICKUP RWD/4.3L-V6 (175hp)

	WS	Ret
Ext.Cab Wdsde Sbed Pkp	5700	7350
Ext.Cab Sptsde Sbed Pkp	5850	7550
SL Sbed Pkp	4900	6825
SL Lbed Pkp	4975	6925
SLS Sport Sptsde Sbed Pkp	5475	7625

Add:
4-wheel drive 1000
Third door (ext. cab) 75
SLS trim 225
SLE trim 450
ZR2 pkg 400

Deduct:
4cyl 225

SUBURBAN RWD/5.7L-V8 (255hp)

	WS	Ret
C1500 4dr Utl	11650	14250
C2500 4dr Utl	12100	14800

Add:
4-wheel drive 1100
SLE trim 625
SLT trim 825

YUKON 4WD/5.7L-V8 (255hp)

	WS	Ret
SL 4dr Utl	12175	14900
SL 2dr Utl	10825	13250

Add:
SL trim (2dr) 325
SLS trim 500
SLT trim 850

Deduct:
2-wheel drive 1050

1996 WS Ret

G1500 VAN RWD/5.0L-V8 (220hp)

	WS	Ret
Savana 135" wb Psngr Van	8550	11025
Van 135" wb Cargo Van	7100	9150

G2500 VAN RWD/5.7L-V8 (250hp)

	WS	Ret
Savana 135" wb Psngr Van	8800	11350
Van 135" wb Cargo Van	7350	9475

Add:
SLE trim 500

Deduct:
6cyl 200

JIMMY RWD/4.3L-V6 (190hp)

	WS	Ret
Sport Util 4dr Utl	6550	8450
Sport Util 2dr Utl	5975	7700

Add:
4-wheel drive 825
SLE trim (2dr) 225
SLT trim (2dr) 825
SLT trim (4dr) 600

SAFARI RWD/4.3L-V6 (190hp)

	WS	Ret
Cargo Mini Van	5450	7575
SLX Passenger Mini Van	6300	8125

Add:
4-wheel drive 750
SLE trim 350
SLT trim 600

SIERRA 1500 RWD/5.0L-V8 (230hp)

	WS	Ret
Ext.Cab Sptsde Sbed Pkp	8725	11300
Ext.Cab Wdsde Sbed Pkp	8425	10850
Ext.Cab Wdsde Lbed Pkp.	8700	11225
Special (6cyl) Sbed Pkp	6375	8225
Special (6cyl) Lbed Pkp	6575	8475
Sportside Sbed Pkp	7550	9775
Wideside Sbed Pkp.	7375	9500
Wideside Lbed Pkp.	7475	9625

SIERRA 2500 RWD/5.7L-V8 (255hp)

	WS	Ret
Ext.Cab Wdsde Sbed Pkp	8675	11175
Ext.Cab Wdsde Lbed Pkp	8950	11525
Wideside Lbed Pkp	7700	9925

Add:
4-wheel drive 925
Third door 75
SLE trim 250
SLT trim 400

Deduct:
6cyl (not Special) 200

SONOMA PICKUP RWD/4.3L-V6 (180hp)

	WS	Ret
Ext.Cab Wdsde Sbed Pkp	4800	6675
Ext.Cab Sptsde Sbed Pkp	4900	6825
SL Sbed Pkp	4000	5550
SL Lbed Pkp	4075	5675

Add:
4-wheel drive 825
Third door (ext. cab) 50
SLS trim 175
SLE trim 375
ZR2 pkg 325

Deduct:
4cyl 175

SUBURBAN RWD/5.7L-V8 (255hp)

	WS	Ret
C1500 4dr Utl	10450	12800
C2500 4dr Utl	10850	13275

Add:
4-wheel drive 925
SLE trim 525
SLT trim 675

YUKON 4WD/5.7L-V8 (200hp)

	WS	Ret
SL 4dr Utl	10625	13000
SL 2dr Utl	9275	11350

Add:
SL trim (2dr) 275
SLS trim 425
SLT trim 700

Deduct:
2-wheel drive 875

1995 WS Ret

G1500 VAN RWD/5.0L-V8 (175hp)

	WS	Ret
Vandura Swb Van	5925	7650
Vandura Lwb Van.	6050	7800

G2500 VAN RWD/5.0L-V8 (175hp)

	WS	Ret
Rally Wagon Lwb Van	7175	9250
Vandura Lwb Van.	6250	8050

Add:
STX trim 600

Deduct:
6cyl 175

JIMMY RWD/4.3L-V8 (195hp)

	WS	Ret
Sport Util 4dr Utl	5300	7375
Sport Util 2dr Utl	4800	6675

Add:
4-wheel drive 775
SLE trim 200
SLS trim 350
SLT trim 750

SAFARI RWD/4.3L-V6 (190hp)

	WS	Ret
Cargo Mini Van.	4400	6125
Passenger Mini Van	5250	7300

Add:
4-wheel drive 675
SLE trim 325
SLT trim 550

SIERRA 1500 RWD/5.7L-V8 (200hp)

	WS	Ret
Ext.Cab Sptsde Sbed Pkp	7450	9650
Ext.Cab Wdsde Sbed Pkp	7200	9275

Check Truck Equipment Table on page 4

Ext.Cab Wdsde Lbed Pkp 7400 9550
Special (6cyl) Lbed Pkp 5600 7225
Sportside Sbed Pkp 6450 8350
Wideside Sbed Pkp 6300 8125
Wideside Lbed Pkp 6400 8250

SIERRA 2500 RWD/5.7L-V8 (200hp)

Ext.Cab Wdsde Sbed Pkp 7375 9500
Ext.Cab Wdsde Lbed Pkp 7575 9775
Wideside Lbed Pkp 6600 8500

Add:
4-wheel drive 850
SL trim 225
SLE trim 375

Deduct:
6cyl (not Special) 175

SONOMA PICKUP RWD/4.3L-V6 (155hp)

SL Sbed Pkp 3325 4825
SL Ext.Cab Sbed Pkp 4200 5850
SL Lbed Pkp 3400 4925

Add:
4-wheel drive 775
4-wheel ABS (2WD) 50
SLS trim 175
SLE trim 350

Deduct:
4cyl 175

SUBURBAN RWD/5.7L-V8 (200hp)

C1500 4dr Utl 8825 11425
C2500 4dr Utl 9225 11300

Add:
4-wheel drive 850
SLE trim 475
SLT trim 625

YUKON 4WD/5.7L-V8 (200hp)

Sport Util 2dr Utl 9000 11650
Wagon 4dr Utl 10350 12675

Add:
SL trim (2dr) 250
SLS trim 400
SLT trim 650

Deduct:
2-wheel drive 800

1994 WS Ret

C1500 PICKUP RWD/5.0L-V8 (175hp)

Ext.Cab Sptsde Sbed Pkp 6925 8975
Ext.Cab Wdsde Sbed Pkp 6800 8775
Ext.Cab Wdsde Lbed Pkp 6900 8900
Special (6cyl) Lbed Pkp 5200 7225
Sportside Sbed Pkp 6025 7800
Wideside Sbed Pkp 5875 7575
Wideside Lbed Pkp 5950 7675

C2500 PICKUP RWD/5.0L-V8 (175hp)

Ext.Cab Wdsde Sbed Pkp 6975 9000
Ext.Cab Wdsde Lbed Pkp 7075 9125
Wideside Lbed Pkp 6100 7875

Add:
4-wheel drive 775
SLX trim 200
SLE trim 325

Deduct:
6cyl 150

G1500 VAN RWD/5.0L-V8 (170hp)

Vandura Swb Van 5275 7325
Vandura Lwb Van 5400 7500

G2500 VAN RWD/5.0L-V8 (170hp)

Rally Wagon Lwb Van 6350 8175
Vandura Lwb Van 5550 7150

Add:
STX trim 525

Deduct:
6cyl 150

S15 JIMMY RWD/4.3L-V6 (165hp)

Sport Util 4dr Utl 3750 5450
Sport Util 2dr Utl 3100 4500

Add:
4-wheel drive 700
SLE trim (2dr) 225
SLS trim 300
SLT trim 500

Deduct:
4cyl 150

SAFARI RWD/4.3L-V6 (165hp)

Cargo Mini Van 3450 5000
Passenger Mini Van 4175 5800

Add:
4-wheel drive 625
SLE trim 300
SLT trim 500
Extended van 325

SONOMA PICKUP RWD/4.3L-V6 (165hp)

SL Sbed Pkp 3000 4350
SL Ext.Cab Sbed Pkp 3675 5325
SL Lbed Pkp 3075 4475

Add:
4-wheel drive 700
SLS trim 150
SLE trim 325

Deduct:
4cyl 150

SUBURBAN RWD/5.7L-V8 (200hp)

C1500 4dr Utl 8400 10875
C2500 4dr Utl 8725 11300

Add:
4-wheel drive 775
SLE trim 425

TYPHOON * AWD/4.3L-V6 (280hp)

Turbo 2dr Utl 11325 14000

YUKON 4WD/5.7L-V8 (210hp)

Sport Util 2dr Utl 8525 11000

Add:
Sport trim 475
SLE trim 425

1993 WS Ret

C1500 PICKUP RWD/5.7L-V8 (190hp)

Ext.Cab Sptsd Sbed Pkp 6050 7825
Ext.Cab Wdsde Sbed Pkp 5850 7550
Ext.Cab Wdsde Lbed Pkp 5900 7600
Special (6cyl) Lbed Pkp 4450 6200
Sportside Sbed Pkp 5225 7300
Wideside Sbed Pkp 5050 7025
Wideside Lbed Pkp 5150 7150

C2500 PICKUP RWD/5.7L-V8 (190hp)

Ext.Cab Wdsde Sbed Pkp 6025 7775
Ext.Cab Wdsde Lbed Pkp 6125 7900
Wideside Lbed Pkp 5275 7325

Add:
4-wheel drive 700
SLX trim 200
Sport pkg 325
SLE trim 300

Deduct:
6cyl 150

G1500 VAN RWD/5.7L-V8 (195hp)

Rally Wagon Swb Van 4775 6650
Rally Wagon Lwb Van 4875 6775
Vandura Swb Van 4100 5700
Vandura Lwb Van 4200 5850

G2500 VAN RWD/5.7L-V8 (190hp)

Rally Wagon Lwb Van 5100 7100
Vandura Lwb Van 4475 6225

Add:
STX trim 475

Deduct:
6cyl 150

S15 JIMMY RWD/4.3L-V6 (160hp)

Sport Util 4dr Utl 3175 4600
Sport Util 2dr Utl 2850 4250

Add:
4-wheel drive 625
SLE trim (2dr) 200
SLS trim 275
SLT trim 450

Deduct:
4cyl 125

SAFARI RWD/4.3L-V6 (165hp)

Cargo Mini Van 2225 3450
Passenger Mini Van 2875 4300

Add:
GT pkg 225
SLE trim 250
SLT trim 450
Extended van 300

SONOMA PICKUP RWD/4.3L-V6 (160hp)

Base Sbed Pkp 2425 3775
Base Lbed Pkp 2450 3800
Extended cab Sbed Pkp 2925 4250
Special Sbed Pkp 2200 3425

Add:
4-wheel drive 625
SLS trim 150
SLE trim 275

Deduct:
4cyl 125

SUBURBAN RWD/5.7L-V8 (210hp)

C1500 4dr Utl 7625 9875
C2500 4dr Utl 7925 10275

Add:
4-wheel drive 700
SLE trim 400

TYPHOON 4WD * AWD/4.3L-V6 (385hp)

Turbo 2dr Utl 10175 12575

YUKON 4WD/5.7L-V8 (210hp)

Sport Util 2dr Utl 7500 9675

Add:
Sport pkg 400
SLE trim 350

1992 WS Ret

C1500 PICKUP RWD/5.0L-V8 (170hp)

Ext.Cab Sptsde Sbed Pkp 5175 7225
Ext.Cab Wdsde Sbed Pkp 5000 6950
Ext.Cab Wdsde Lbed Pkp 5075 7050
Special (6cyl) Lbed Pkp 3700 5375
Sportside Sbed Pkp 4500 6300
Wideside Sbed Pkp 4275 5950
Wideside Lbed Pkp 4350 6050

C2500 PICKUP RWD/5.0L-V8 (175hp)

Ext.Cab Wdsde Sbed Pkp 5175 7200
Ext.Cab Wdsde Lbed Pkp 5225 7275
Wideside Lbed Pkp 4525 6300

Add:
4-wheel drive 650
SLX trim 150
Sport pkg 250
SLE trim 250

Deduct:

6cyl	125	

G1500 VAN — RWD/5.0L-V8 (170hp)

Rally Wagon Swb Van	3500	5075
Rally Wagon Lwb Van	3600	5225
Vandura Swb Van	2900	4325
Vandura Lwb Van	2950	4275

G2500 VAN — RWD/5.0L-V8 (170hp)

Rally Wagon Lwb Van	3725	5400
Vandura Lwb Van	3100	4500
Add:		
STX trim	425	
Deduct:		
6cyl	125	

S15 JIMMY — RWD/4.3L-V6 (160hp)

Sport Util 4dr Utl	2775	4150
Sport Util 2dr Utl	2500	3725
Add:		
4-wheel drive	575	
SLE trim (2dr)	200	
SLS trim	250	
SLT trim	425	
Deduct:		
4cyl	125	

SAFARI — RWD/4.3L-V6 (150hp)

Cargo Mini Van	2000	3100
Passenger Mini Van	2475	3850
Add:		
4-wheel drive	475	
GT pkg	225	
SLE trim	250	
SLT trim	425	
Extended van	300	

SONOMA PICKUP — RWD/2.8L-V6 (125hp)

Base Sbed Pkp	2025	3150
Base Lbed Pkp	2050	3175
Extended cab Sbed Pkp	2400	3725
Special Sbed Pkp	1850	3000
Add:		
4-wheel drive (not Syclone)	575	
SLE trim	225	
Deduct:		
4cyl	125	

SUBURBAN — RWD/5.7L-V8 (210hp)

C1500 4dr Utl	6975	9025
C2500 4dr Utl	7200	9325
Add:		
4-wheel drive	650	
SLE trim	350	

SYCLONE * — AWD/4.3L-V6 (280hp)

Sport Sbed Pkp	9275	11475

TYPHOON 4WD * — AWD/4.3L-V6 (280hp)

Turbo 2dr Utl	8375	10950

YUKON 4WD — 4WD/5.7L-V8 (210hp)

Sport Util 2dr Utl	6175	7950
Add:		
Sport pkg	300	
SLE trim	275	

1991 — WS Ret

C1500 PICKUP — RWD/5.0L-V8 (170hp)

Extended Cab Sbed Pkp	4075	5675
Extended Cab Lbed Pkp	4175	5800
Special (6cyl) Lbed Pkp	2950	4275
Sportside Sbed Pkp	3675	5350
Wideside Sbed Pkp	3550	5150
Wideside Lbed Pkp	3625	5250

C2500 PICKUP — RWD/5.0L-V8 (170hp)

Extended Cab Sbed Pkp	4225	5875
Extended Cab Lbed Pkp	4300	5975
Wideside Lbed Pkp	3750	5450
Add:		
4-wheel drive	575	
SLX trim	125	
SLE trim	225	
Sport pkg	250	
Z-71 pkg	25	
Deduct:		
6cyl	100	

G1500 VAN — RWD/5.0L-V8 (170hp)

Rally Wagon Swb Van	2750	4100
Rally Wagon Lwb Van	2825	4225
Vandura Swb Van	2275	3525
Vandura Lwb Van	2325	3600

G2500 VAN — RWD/5.0L-V8 (400hp)

Rally Wagon Lwb Van	2975	4325
Vandura Swb Van	2400	3725
Vandura Lwb Van	2475	3850
Add:		
STX trim	350	
Deduct:		
6cyl	100	

JIMMY — 4WD/5.7L-V8 (210hp)

Sport Util 2dr Utl	4025	5600
Add:		
SLE trim	275	

S15 JIMMY — RWD/4.3L-V6 (160hp)

Sport Util 4dr Utl	2425	3775
Sport Util 2dr Utl	2025	3150
Add:		
4-wheel drive	525	
SLE trim (2dr)	150	
SLS trim	250	
Deduct:		
4cyl	100	

SAFARI — RWD/4.3L-V6 (150hp)

Cargo Mini Van	1825	2975
Passenger Mini Van	2125	3300
Add:		
4-wheel drive	400	
SLE trim	225	
SLT trim	400	
Extended van	275	

SONOMA PICKUP — RWD/4.3L-V6 (280hp)

Base Sbed Pkp	1575	2550
Base Lbed Pkp	1600	2600
Extended cab Sbed Pkp	1850	3000
Special Sbed Pkp	1400	2275
Add:		
4-wheel drive (not Syclone)	525	
SLE trim	175	
Deduct:		
4cyl	100	

SUBURBAN — RWD/5.7L-V8 (210hp)

R1500 4dr Utl	4725	6575
R2500 4dr Utl	4950	6875
Add:		
4-wheel drive	575	
SLE trim	300	

SYCLONE * — AWD/4.3L-V6 (280hp)

Sport Sbed Pkp	7600	9950
Add:		
4-wheel drive (not Syclone)	525	
SLE trim	175	
Deduct:		
4cyl	100	

1990 — WS Ret

C1500 PICKUP — RWD/5.0L-V8 (170hp)

Extended Cab Sbed Pkp	3650	5300
Extended Cab Lbed Pkp	3725	5400
Special (6cyl) Lbed Pkp	2625	3925
Sportside Sbed Pkp	3225	4700
Wideside Sbed Pkp	3100	4500
Wideside Lbed Pkp	3175	4600

C2500 PICKUP — RWD/5.0L-V8 (170hp)

Extended Cab Sbed Pkp	3775	5475
Extended Cab Lbed Pkp	3825	5325
Wideside Lbed Pkp	3275	4750
Add:		
4-wheel drive	550	
Sierra SLX trim	75	
Sierra SLE trim	200	
Z-71 pkg	25	
Deduct:		
6cyl	75	

G1500 VAN — RWD/5.0L-V8 (170hp)

Rally Wagon Swb Van	2400	3725
Rally Wagon Lwb Van	2475	3850
Vandura Swb Van	1950	3025
Vandura Lwb Van	2025	3150

G2500 VAN — RWD/5.0L-V8 (170hp)

Rally Wagon Lwb Van	2575	3850
Vandura Swb Van	2075	3225
Vandura Lwb Van	2125	3300
Add:		
STX trim	325	
Deduct:		
6cyl	75	

JIMMY — 4WD/5.7L-V8 (210hp)

Sport Util 2dr Utl	3475	5050
Add:		
SLE trim	250	

S15 JIMMY — RWD/4.3L-V6 (160hp)

4wd 4dr Utl	1925	3000
Sport Util 2dr Utl	1700	2750
Add:		
4-wheel drive (2dr)	500	
Sierra Classic trim	150	
Gypsy trim	225	
Deduct:		
4cyl	75	

S15 PICKUP — RWD/4.3L-V6 (160hp)

Base Sbed Pkp	1400	2275
Base Lbed Pkp	1425	2325
Extended cab Sbed Pkp	1600	2600
Special (4cyl-5sp) Sbed Pkp	1250	2025
Add:		
4-wheel drive	500	
High Sierra trim	50	
Sierra Classic trim	150	
Deduct:		
4cyl	75	

SAFARI — RWD/4.3L-V6 (150hp)

Cargo Mini Van	1425	2325
Passenger Mini Van	1725	2800
Add:		
4-wheel drive	375	
SLE trim	200	
SLT trim	200	
Extended van	250	
Deduct:		
4cyl	75	

SUBURBAN — RWD/5.7L-V8 (210hp)

R1500 4dr Utl	3825	5325

Check Truck Equipment Table on page 4

	WS	Ret
R2500 4dr Utl	4025	5600
Add:		
4-wheel drive	550	
SLE trim	275	

1989	WS	Ret
C1500 PICKUP RWD/4.3L-V8 (160hp)		
Extended Cab Sbed Pkp	3275	4750
Extended Cab Lbed Pkp	3375	4900
Sportside Sbed Pkp	2950	4300
Wideside Sbed Pkp	2800	4175
Wideside Lbed Pkp	2875	4300
C2500 PICKUP RWD/4.3L-V8 (160hp)		
Crew Cab Wdsde Pkp	3750	5450
Extended Cab Sbed Pkp	3400	4925
Extended Cab Lbed Pkp	3525	5125
Wideside Lbed Pkp	2975	4325
Add:		
4-wheel drive	500	
SLX trim	50	
SLE trim	175	
Deduct:		
6cyl	75	
G1500 VAN RWD/5.0L-V8 (170hp)		
Rally Wagon Swb Van	1850	3000
Rally Wagon Lwb Van	1925	3000
Vandura Swb Van	1525	2475
Vandura Lwb Van	1575	2550
G2500 VAN RWD/5.0L-V8 (170hp)		
Rally Wagon Lwb Van	2025	3150
Vandura Swb Van	1600	2600
Vandura Lwb Van	1650	2675
Add:		
STX trim	300	
Deduct:		
6cyl	75	
JIMMY 4WD/5.7L-V8 (210hp)		
Sport Util 2dr Utl	2925	4250
Add:		
SLE trim	225	
S15 JIMMY RWD/4.3L-V6 (160hp)		
Sport Util 2dr Utl	1300	2100
Add:		
4-wheel drive	450	
Sierra Classic trim	125	
Gypsy trim	175	
Deduct:		
4cyl	50	
S15 PICKUP RWD/4.3L-V6 (160hp)		
Base Sbed Pkp	1175	2050
Base Lbed Pkp	1200	2100
Extended cab Sbed Pkp	1325	2150
Special (4cyl-5sp) Sbed Pkp	1050	1825
Add:		
4-wheel drive	450	
High Sierra trim	50	
Sierra Classic trim	125	
Deduct:		
4cyl	50	
SAFARI RWD/4.3L-V6 (150hp)		
Cargo Mini Van	1150	2000
Passenger Mini Van	1325	2150
Add:		
SLE trim	150	
SLT trim	350	
Deduct:		
4cyl	50	
SUBURBAN RWD/5.7L-V8 (210hp)		
R1500 4dr Utl	3150	4575
R2500 4dr Utl	3325	4825
Add:		
4-wheel drive	500	
SLE trim	275	

1988	WS	Ret
C1500 PICKUP RWD/5.0L-V8 (175hp)		
Extended Cab Lbed Pkp	3050	4425
Sportside Sbed Pkp	2550	3825
Wideside Sbed Pkp	2375	3700
Wideside Lbed Pkp	2500	3725
C2500 PICKUP RWD/5.0L-V8 (175hp)		
Crew Cab Wdsde Pkp	3275	4750
Extended Cab Lbed Pkp	3200	4650
Wideside Lbed Pkp	2625	3925
Add:		
4-wheel drive	425	
High Sierra trim	25	
Sierra SLX trim	25	
Sierra SLE trim	175	
Deduct:		
6cyl	50	
G1500 VAN RWD/5.0L-V8 (170hp)		
Rally Wagon Swb Van	1425	2325
Rally Wagon Lwb Van	1475	2400
Vandura Swb Van	1175	2050
Vandura Lwb Van	1200	2100
G2500 VAN RWD/5.0L-V8 (170hp)		
Rally Wagon Lwb Van	1550	2525
Vandura Swb Van	1225	2150
Vandura Lwb Van	1275	2075
Add:		
STX trim	250	
Deduct:		
6cyl	50	
JIMMY 4WD/5.7L-V8 (210hp)		
Sport Util 2dr Utl	2500	3725
Add:		
Sierra Classic trim	175	
S15 JIMMY RWD/2.8L-V6 (125hp)		
Sport Util 2dr Utl	1075	1875
Add:		
4-wheel drive	375	
Sierra Classic trim	100	
Gypsy trim	175	
Deduct:		
4cyl	50	
S15 PICKUP RWD/4.3L-V6 (160hp)		
Base Sbed Pkp	975	1875
Base Lbed Pkp	1000	1750
Extended cab Sbed Pkp	1100	1925
Special (4cyl-5sp) Sbed Pkp	875	1675
Add:		
4-wheel drive	375	
High Sierra trim	25	
Sierra Classic trim	100	
Deduct:		
4cyl	50	
SAFARI RWD/4.3L-V6 (150hp)		
Cargo Mini Van	850	1650
Passenger Mini Van	1025	1800
Add:		
SLE trim	150	
SLT trim	325	
Deduct:		
4cyl	50	
SUBURBAN RWD/5.7L-V8 (195hp)		
R1500 4dr Utl	2775	4150
R2500 4dr Utl	2900	4325
Add:		
4-wheel drive	425	
Sierra Classic trim	225	

HONDA

2001	WS	Ret
CR-V 4WD/2.0L-I4 (146hp)		
EX 4dr Utl		
LX 4dr Utl		
SE 4dr Utl		
ODYSSEY FWD/3.5L-V6 (210hp)		
EX Mini Van	23100	26050
LX Mini Van	21050	23750
PASSPORT RWD/3.2L-V6 (205hp)		
EX 4dr Utl		
LX 4dr Utl		

2000	WS	Ret
CR-V 4WD/2.0L-I4 (146hp)		
EX 4dr Utl	14550	16875
LX 4dr Utl	13500	15650
SE 4dr Utl		
Deduct:		
2-wheel drive	1425	
ODYSSEY FWD/3.5L-V6 (210hp)		
EX Mini Van	20450	23075
LX Mini Van	18525	20900
PASSPORT RWD/3.2L-V6 (205hp)		
EX 4dr Utl	16425	19100
LX 4dr Utl	13450	15925
Add:		
4-wheel drive	1725	

1999	WS	Ret
CR-V 4WD/2.0L-I4 (146hp)		
EX 4dr Utl	13550	15725
LX 4dr Utl	12550	15050
Deduct:		
2-wheel drive	1175	
ODYSSEY FWD/3.5L-V6 (210hp)		
EX Mini Van	18750	21150
LX Mini Van	16900	19275
PASSPORT RWD/3.2L-V6 (205hp)		
EX 4dr Utl	14900	17625
LX 4dr Utl	12100	14800
Add:		
4-wheel drive	1425	
Alloy wheels (std EX)	200	

1998	WS	Ret
CR-V 4WD/2.0L-I4 (126hp)		
EX 4dr Utl	12050	14450
LX 4dr Utl	11175	13400
Deduct:		
2-wheel drive	975	
ODYSSEY FWD/2.2L-I4 (140hp)		
EX Mini Van	13925	16150
LX Mini Van	12900	15475
PASSPORT RWD/3.2L-V6 (205hp)		
EX 4dr Utl	12875	15750
LX 4dr Utl	10375	12700
Add:		
4-wheel drive	1175	

Alloy wheels (std EX)	150	

1997	WS	Ret
CR-V 4WD/2.0L-I4 (126hp)		
4dr Utl	10150	12175
ODYSSEY FWD/2.2L-I4 (140hp)		
EX Mini Van	11650	13975
LX Mini Van	10600	12725
PASSPORT RWD/3.2L-V6 (190hp)		
EX 4dr Utl	10475	12825
LX 4dr Utl	8325	10775
Add:		
4-wheel drive	975	
16" alloy wheels (std EX)	125	

1996	WS	Ret
ODYSSEY FWD/2.2L-I4 (140hp)		
EX Mini Van	10125	12150
LX Mini Van	9150	10975
PASSPORT RWD/3.2L-V6 (190hp)		
DX (4cyl-5sp) 4dr Utl	5525	7125
EX 4dr Utl	9225	11300
LX 4dr Utl	7250	9400
Add:		
4-wheel drive	800	
16" alloy wheels (std EX)	100	

1995	WS	Ret
ODYSSEY FWD/2.2L-I4 (140hp)		
EX Mini Van	8725	11250
LX Mini Van	7900	10175
PASSPORT RWD/3.2L-V6 (175hp)		
DX (4cyl-5sp) 4dr Utl	4000	5600
EX (4WD) 4dr Utl	7525	9750
LX 4dr Utl	5525	7150
Add:		
4-wheel drive	750	
16" alloy wheels (std EX)	75	

1994	WS	Ret
PASSPORT RWD/3.2L-V6 (175hp)		
DX (4cyl-5sp) 4dr Utl	3500	5100
EX (4WD) 4dr Utl	6775	8775
LX 4dr Utl		
Add:		
4-wheel drive	675	
16" alloy wheels (LX)	75	

HYUNDAI

2001	WS	Ret
SANTA FE 4WD/		
GL 4dr Utl	14350	16975
GLS 4dr Utl	14650	17325
LX 4dr Utl	15075	17825
Deduct:		
2-wheel drive	1800	
2.4L-I4 (149hp)	600	

INFINITI

1999	WS	Ret
QX4 4WD/3.3L-V6 (168hp)		
Luxury 4dr Utl	18150	20700

1998	WS	Ret
QX4 4WD/3.3L-V6 (168hp)		
Luxury 4dr Utl	16350	18650

1997	WS	Ret
QX4 4WD/3.3L-V6 (168hp)		
Luxury 4dr Utl	14775	17150

ISUZU

2001	WS	Ret
HOMBRE (5sp) RWD/2.2L-I4 (120hp)		
S Sbed Pkp		
XS Sbed Pkp		
XS ExCab Pkp		
RODEO RWD/3.2L-V6 (205hp)		
LS 4dr Utl	13200	15300
LSE 4dr Utl	15250	17700
S 4dr Utl	10175	12200
Add:		
4-wheel drive	2525	
Wheels-alloy (S,LS 2WD)	275	
Ironman	450	
Anniv. pkg (LS)	1025	
SE pkg (LS)	1075	
Deduct:		
2.2L (4cyl-120hp)	550	
TROOPER 4WD/3.5L-V6 (215hp)		
Limited 4dr Utl	17850	20350
LS 4dr Utl	16350	18650
S 4dr Utl	15175	17600
Add:		
Anniv. Edition	1250	

2000	WS	Ret
HOMBRE (5sp) RWD/2.2L-I4 (120hp)		
S Sbed Pkp	6225	7900
XS Sbed Pkp	6825	8675
XS ExCab Pkp	8750	11125
Add:		
4.3L-V6 (175hp)	400	
4-wheel drive	1700	
Automatic trans	500	
RODEO RWD/3.2L-V6 (205hp)		
LS 4dr Utl	11700	14050
LSE 4dr Utl	13450	15600
S 4dr Utl	8725	11075
Add:		
4-wheel drive	1950	
Ironman	350	
Wheels-alloy (S,LS 2WD)	225	
Deduct:		
2.2L (4cyl-120hp)	425	
TROOPER 4WD/3.5L-V6 (215hp)		
Limited 4dr Utl	16225	18500
LS 4dr Utl	15100	17525
S 4dr Utl	14050	16300

1999	WS	Ret
AMIGO RWD/2.2L-I4 (130hp)		
2dr Utl	8450	10725
Add:		
4-wheel drive	1175	
Automatic trans	425	
Wheels-16in alloy	150	
HOMBRE (5sp) RWD/2.2L-I4 (120hp)		
S Sbed Pkp	5100	6975
XS Sbed Pkp	5650	7175
XS ExCab Pkp	7375	9375
Add:		
4.3L-V6 (175hp)	325	
4-wheel drive	1400	
Automatic trans	400	
OASIS FWD/2.3L-I4 (150hp)		
S Mini Van	13025	15625
RODEO RWD/3.2L-V6 (205hp)		
LS 4dr Utl	11000	13200
S 4dr Utl	8250	10475
Add:		
4-wheel drive	1625	
Sport pkg (S)	200	
Wheels-alloy (S)	200	
Deduct:		
2.2L (4cyl-120hp)	350	
TROOPER 4WD/3.5L-V6 (215hp)		
S 4dr Utl	12950	15550
Add:		
Performance pkg	300	
Luxury trim	875	

1998	WS	Ret
AMIGO RWD/2.2L-I4 (130hp)		
2dr Utl	6875	8725
Add:		
4-wheel drive	975	
Automatic trans	350	
HOMBRE (5sp) RWD/2.2L-I4 (220hp)		
S Sbed Pkp	4275	5850
XS Sbed Pkp	4825	6600
XS ExCab Pkp	6100	7750
Add:		
4.3L 6cyl-175hp	300	
4-wheel drive	1125	
OASIS FWD/2.2L-I4 (150hp)		
LS Mini Van	13125	15225
S Mini Van	11875	14250
RODEO RWD/3.2L-V6 (205hp)		
LS 4dr Utl	9925	11900
S 4dr Utl	7475	9500
Add:		
4-wheel drive	1350	
Sport pkg (S)	150	
16in alloys (std LS)	150	
Deduct:		
2.2L (4cyl-120hp)	300	
TROOPER 4WD/3.5L-V6 (215hp)		
S 4dr Utl	11300	13550
Add:		
Performance pkg w/upgraded 4wd575		

1997	WS	Ret
HOMBRE (5sp) RWD/2.2L-I4 (118hp)		
S Sbed Pkp	3875	5400
XS Sbed Pkp	4275	5950
XS ExCab Pkp	5325	7375
Add:		
4.3L 6cyl-175hp	250	
OASIS FWD/2.2L-I4 (140hp)		
LS Mini Van	10225	12400
S Mini Van	9150	11100
RODEO RWD/3.2L-V6 (190hp)		
LS 4dr Utl	7750	10000

Check Truck Equipment Table on page 4

	WS	Ret
S 4dr Utl	5575	7175

Add:
- 4-wheel drive 1100
- 4-wheel ABS 150
- 16in alloys (std LS) 125

Deduct:
- 2.6L (4cyl-120hp) 250

TROOPER 4WD/3.2L-V6 (190hp)

	WS	Ret
Limited 4dr Utl	14425	16975
LS 4dr Utl	11775	14350
S 4dr Utl	9875	12025

1996 WS Ret

HOMBRE (5sp) RWD/2.2L-I4 (118hp)

	WS	Ret
S Sbed Pkp	3325	4825
XS Sbed Pkp	3750	5450

OASIS FWD/2.2L-I4 (140hp)

	WS	Ret
LS Mini Van	8875	11375
S Mini Van	7850	10075

RODEO RWD/3.2L-V6 (190hp)

	WS	Ret
LS 4dr Utl	7150	9225
S 4dr Utl	5200	7225

Add:
- 4-wheel drive 925
- 4-wheel ABS 150
- 16in alloys (std LS) 100

Deduct:
- 4cyl 175

TROOPER 4WD/3.2L-V6 (190hp)

	WS	Ret
Limited 4dr Utl	12250	14925
LS 4dr Utl	9975	12150
S 4dr Utl	8250	10625

Add:
- 4-wheel ABS (std Ltd) 150

1995 WS Ret

PICKUP (5sp) RWD/2.3L-I4 (100hp)

	WS	Ret
S Sbed Pkp	2575	3850
S Lbed Pkp	2675	4000

Add:
- Automatic trans 225

RODEO RWD/3.2L-V6 (175hp)

	WS	Ret
LS 4dr Utl	5675	7325
S 4dr Utl	4025	5600

Add:
- 4-wheel drive 850
- 16in alloys (std LS) 75

Deduct:
- 4cyl 175

TROOPER 4WD/3.2L-V6 (175hp)

	WS	Ret
Limited 4dr Utl	10375	12625
LS 4dr Utl	8375	10800
RS 2dr Utl	7750	10000
S 4dr Utl	6850	8825

Add:
- 4-wheel ABS (std Ltd) 125

1994 WS Ret

AMIGO (5sp) RWD/2.6L-I4 (120hp)

	WS	Ret
S 2dr Utl	3175	4600
XS 2dr Utl	3600	5225

Add:
- 4-wheel drive 625
- Automatic trans 200

PICKUP (5sp) RWD/2.3L-I4 (96hp)

	WS	Ret
S Sbed Pkp	2300	3575
S Lbed Pkp	2375	3700
S ExCab Pkp	2850	4250

Add:
- 6cyl engine 175
- Automatic trans 200

RODEO RWD/3.2L-V6 (175hp)

	WS	Ret
LS 4dr Utl	4825	6700
S 4dr Utl	3575	5200

Add:
- 4-wheel drive 750
- 16in alloys (std LS) 75

Deduct:
- 4cyl 150

TROOPER 4WD/3.2L-V6 (175hp)

	WS	Ret
LS 4dr Utl	6775	8725
RS 2dr Utl	6250	8050
S 4dr Utl	5475	7625

Add:
- 4-wheel ABS (S,RS) 125

1993 WS Ret

AMIGO (5sp) RWD/2.3L-I4 (96hp)

	WS	Ret
S 2dr Utl	2750	4100
XS 2dr Utl	3025	4400

Add:
- 4-wheel drive 575
- Automatic trans 175

PICKUP (5sp) RWD/2.3L-I4 (96hp)

	WS	Ret
S Sbed Pkp	1975	3075
S Lbed Pkp	2025	3150
S ExCab Pkp	2850	4250

Add:
- 6cyl engine 150
- 4-wheel drive 625
- Automatic trans 175

RODEO RWD/3.1L-V6 (175hp)

	WS	Ret
LS 4dr Utl	4025	5600
S 4dr Utl	2150	3350

Add:
- 4-wheel drive 625

Deduct:
- 4cyl 125

TROOPER 4WD/3.2L-V6 (175hp)

	WS	Ret
LS 4dr Utl	7225	9325
RS 2dr Utl	6275	8100
S 4dr Utl	4825	6700

1992 WS Ret

AMIGO (5sp) RWD/2.3L-I4 (96hp)

	WS	Ret
S 2dr Utl	2550	3800
XS 2dr Utl	2800	4175

Add:
- 4-wheel drive 500
- Automatic trans 150

PICKUP (5sp) RWD/2.3L-I4 (96hp)

	WS	Ret
LS ExCab Pkp	2200	3425
S Sbed Pkp	1700	2750
S Lbed Pkp	1750	2850
S ExCab Pkp	1975	3075

Add:
- 6cyl engine 125
- 4-wheel drive 575
- Automatic trans 175

RODEO RWD/3.1L-V6 (120hp)

	WS	Ret
LS 4dr Utl	3700	5375
S 4dr Utl	3075	4475
XS 4dr Utl	3375	4900

Add:
- 4-wheel drive 575

Deduct:
- 4cyl 125

TROOPER 4WD/3.2L-V6 (175hp)

	WS	Ret
LS 4dr Utl	4950	6875
S 4dr Utl	4175	5800

Deduct:
- 4cyl 125

1991 WS Ret

AMIGO (5sp) RWD/2.3L-I4 (96hp)

	WS	Ret
S 2dr Utl	2200	3425
XS 2dr Utl	2425	3775

Add:
- 4-wheel drive 450
- Automatic trans 150

PICKUP (5sp) RWD/2.3L-I4 (96hp)

	WS	Ret
LS ExCab Pkp	1775	2875
S Sbed Pkp	1375	2225
S Lbed Pkp	1425	2325
S ExCab Pkp	1575	2550

Add:
- 6cyl engine 150
- 4-wheel drive 525
- Automatic trans 150
- LS trim (4WD) 325

RODEO RWD/3.1L-V6 (120hp)

	WS	Ret
LS 4dr Utl	3125	4525
S (5sp) 4dr Utl	2650	3950
XS 4dr Utl	2900	4325

Add:
- 4-wheel drive 525

Deduct:
- 4cyl 100

TROOPER 4WD/2.8L-V6 (120hp)

	WS	Ret
LS 4dr Utl	3600	5225
S (4cyl) 4dr Utl	2800	4175
SE 4dr Utl	3325	4825
XS 4dr Utl	3025	4400

1990 WS Ret

AMIGO (5sp) RWD/2.3L-I4 (96hp)

	WS	Ret
S 2dr Utl	1975	3075
XS 2dr Utl	2150	3350

Add:
- 4-wheel drive 375
- Automatic trans 125

PICKUP (5sp) RWD/2.3L-I4 (96hp)

	WS	Ret
LS Sbed Pkp	1250	2025
LS ExCab Pkp	1425	2325
S Sbed Pkp	1100	1925
S Lbed Pkp	1125	1975
S ExCab Pkp	1275	2075
XS Sbed Pkp	1150	2000
XS ExCab Pkp	1350	2200

Add:
- 4-wheel drive 500
- Automatic trans 125

TROOPER 4WD/2.8L-V6 (120hp)

	WS	Ret
LS 4dr Utl	2625	3925
RS 2dr Utl	2225	3450
S 4dr Utl	2250	3500
XS 4dr Utl	2350	3650

1989 WS Ret

AMIGO (5sp) RWD/2.3L-I4 (96hp)

	WS	Ret
S 2dr Utl	1675	2725
XS 2dr Utl	1750	2850

Add:
- Automatic trans 100

PICKUP (5sp) RWD/2.3L-I4 (96hp)

LS Sbed Pkp	1050	1825
LS ExCab Pkp	1150	2000
S Sbed Pkp	950	1825
S Lbed Pkp	975	1875
S ExCab Pkp	1075	1875
XS Sbed Pkp	1000	1750
XS ExCab Pkp	1100	1925

Add:
- 4-wheel drive . . . 450
- Automatic trans . . . 100

TROOPER 4WD/2.8L-V6 (120hp)

LS 4dr Utl	2125	3300
RS 2dr Utl	2000	3100
S 4dr Utl	1950	3025
XS 4dr Utl	2000	3100

1988 — WS Ret

PICKUP (5sp) RWD/2.3L-I4 (96hp)

LS Sbed Pkp	900	1725
LS ExCab Pkp	975	1875
S Sbed Pkp	850	1650
S Lbed Pkp	875	1675
S 1-Ton Lbed Pkp	875	1675

Add:
- 4-wheel drive . . . 375
- Automatic trans . . . 50

TROOPER 4WD/2.6L-I4 (120hp)

LS 4dr Utl	1500	2425
Ltd 4dr Utl	1550	2525
S 4dr Utl	1350	2200
S 2dr Utl	1275	2075
XS 4dr Utl	1375	2225
XS 2dr Utl	1350	2200

JEEP

2001 — WS Ret

CHEROKEE RWD/4.0L-I6 (190hp)

Limited 4dr Utl	12275	15025
Sport 4dr Utl	11250	13775
Sport 2dr Utl	10375	12700

Add:
- 4-wheel drive . . . 2300
- 4-wheel ABS . . . 375

Deduct:
- 2.5L (4cyl-125hp) . . . 550

GRAND CHEROKEE 4WD/4.0L-I6 (195hp)

Laredo 4dr Utl	17400	20225
Limited 4dr Utl	20450	23525

Add:
- 4.7L-V8 (235hp) . . . 825
- Infinity audio (std Ltd) . . . 275

Deduct:
- 2-wheel drive . . . 2025

WRANGLER (5M/AT) 4WD/4.0L-I6 (181hp)

Sahara 2dr Utl	15850	18600
SE (4cyl) 2dr Utl	10625	13125
Sport 2dr Utl	14800	17675

Add:
- ABS brakes . . . 325
- Sound bar (SE) . . . 200
- Alloy wheels (std Sahara) . . . 225
- Hardtop . . . 825

2000 — WS Ret

CHEROKEE RWD/4.0L-I6 (190hp)

Classic 4dr Utl	11225	13750
Limited 4dr Utl	12150	14875
SE 4dr Utl	9475	11600
SE 2dr Utl	8500	11000
Sport 4dr Utl	10275	12575
Sport 2dr Utl	9375	11475

Add:
- 4-wheel drive . . . 1775
- 4-wheel ABS . . . 275

Deduct:
- 2.5L (4cyl-125hp) . . . 425

GRAND CHEROKEE 4WD/4.0L-I6 (195hp)

Laredo 4dr Utl	16075	18700
Limited 4dr Utl	19100	21975

Add:
- 4.7L-V8 (235hp) . . . 650
- Infinity audio (std Ltd) . . . 225

Deduct:
- 2-wheel drive . . . 1575

WRANGLER (5M/AT) 4WD/4.0L-I6 (181hp)

Sahara 2dr Utl	15125	18075
SE (4cyl) 2dr Utl	11750	14525
Sport 2dr Utl	14100	16850

Add:
- ABS brakes . . . 250
- Sound bar (std Sahara) . . . 150
- Alloy wheels (std Sahara) . . . 175
- Hardtop . . . 650

1999 — WS Ret

CHEROKEE RWD/4.0L-I6 (190hp)

Classic 4dr Utl	9875	12075
Limited 4dr Utl	10750	13150
SE 4dr Utl	8275	10725
SE 2dr Utl	7325	9500
Sport 4dr Utl	9000	11650
Sport 2dr Utl	8150	10550

Add:
- 4-wheel drive . . . 1475
- 4-wheel ABS . . . 225

Deduct:
- 2.5L (4cyl-125hp) . . . 350

GRAND CHEROKEE 4WD/4.0L-I6 (195hp)

Laredo 4dr Utl	14850	17575
Limited 4dr Utl	17725	20600

Add:
- 4.7L-V8 (235hp) . . . 525
- Infinity audio (std Ltd) . . . 175

Deduct:
- 2-wheel drive . . . 1300

WRANGLER (5M/AT) 4WD/4.0L-I6 (181hp)

Sahara 2dr Utl	13650	16300
SE (4cyl) 2dr Utl	11750	14525
Sport 2dr Utl	12625	15600

Add:
- ABS brakes . . . 225
- Sound bar (std Sahara) . . . 125
- Alloy wheels (std Sahara) . . . 150
- Hardtop . . . 525

1998 — WS Ret

CHEROKEE RWD/4.0L-I6 (190hp)

Classic 4dr Utl	8700	11275
Classic 2dr Utl	7950	10300
Limited 4dr Utl	9425	11525
SE 4dr Utl	7250	9400
SE 2dr Utl	6450	8350
Sport 4dr Utl	7900	10225
Sport 2dr Utl	7175	9300

Add:
- 4-wheel drive . . . 1225
- 4-wheel ABS . . . 200

Deduct:
- 2.5L (4cyl-125hp) . . . 300

GRAND CHEROKEE 4WD/4.0L-I6 (185hp)

Laredo 4dr Utl	11575	14175
Limited 4dr Utl	13925	16475
TSi 4dr Utl	12125	14850

Add:
- 5.2L-220hp V8 . . . 325
- 5.9L-245hp V8 (5.9 Ltd) . . . 850
- Orvis Pkg (Ltd) . . . 150
- SE Z-pkg (Laredo) . . . 250

Deduct:
- 2-wheel drive . . . 1075

WRANGLER (5M/AT) 4WD/4.0L-I6 (181hp)

Sahara 2dr Utl	12025	14875
SE (4cyl) 2dr Utl	10425	12875
Sport 2dr Utl	11200	13850

Add:
- ABS brakes . . . 200
- Sound bar (std Sahara) . . . 100
- Wheels-alloy (std Sahara) . . . 125
- Hardtop . . . 450

1997 — WS Ret

CHEROKEE RWD/4.0L-I6 (190hp)

Country 4dr Utl	7250	9400
Country 2dr Utl	6575	8525
SE 4dr Utl	5975	7750
SE 2dr Utl	5275	7375
Sport 4dr Utl	6575	8525
Sport 2dr Utl	5925	7675

Add:
- 4-wheel drive . . . 1000
- 4-wheel ABS . . . 175

Deduct:
- 2.5L (4cyl-125hp) . . . 250

GRAND CHEROKEE 4WD/4.0L-I6 (185hp)

Laredo 4dr Utl	9875	12075
Limited 4dr Utl	11900	14575
TSi 4dr Utl	10300	12600

Add:
- 5.2L-220hp V8 . . . 275
- Orvis Pkg (Ltd) . . . 125

Deduct:
- 2-wheel drive . . . 875

WRANGLER (5M/AT) 4WD/4.0L-I6 (181hp)

Sahara 2dr Utl	10050	12425
SE (4cyl) 2dr Utl	8600	11250
Sport 2dr Utl	9300	11500

Add:
- ABS brakes . . . 150
- Sound bar (std Sahara) . . . 75
- Wheels-alloy (std Sahara) . . . 100
- Hardtop . . . 425

1996 — WS Ret

CHEROKEE RWD/4.0L-I6 (190hp)

Country 4dr Utl	5875	7600
Country 2dr Utl	5300	7400
SE 4dr Utl	4725	6600
SE 2dr Utl	4025	5625
Sport 4dr Utl	5250	7325
Sport 2dr Utl	4675	6525

Add:
- 4-wheel drive . . . 825
- 4-wheel ABS . . . 150

Deduct:
- 4cyl . . . 200

GRAND CHEROKEE 4WD/4.0L-I6 (185hp)

Laredo 4dr Utl	8275	10725

Check Truck Equipment Table on page 4

	WS	Ret
Limited 4dr Utl	10050	12300
SE 4dr Utl.	7650	9900

Add:

5.2 Liter V8	225

Deduct:

2-wheel drive	725

1995 — WS Ret

CHEROKEE — RWD/4.0L-I6 (190hp)

	WS	Ret
Country 4dr Utl.	4600	6425
Country 2dr Utl.	4025	5625
SE 4dr Utl.	3575	5225
SE 2dr Utl.	3000	4375
Sport 4dr Utl.	4025	5625
Sport 2dr Utl.	3525	5150

Add:

4-wheel drive	775

Deduct:

4cyl	175

GRAND CHEROKEE — 4WD/4.0L-I6 (190hp)

	WS	Ret
Laredo 4dr Utl	6875	8900
Limited 4dr Utl	8450	10950
SE 4dr Utl.	6350	8225

Add:

5.2 Liter V8	200

Deduct:

2-wheel drive	675

WRANGLER (5M/AT) — 4WD/4.0L-I6 (180hp)

	WS	Ret
S (4cyl) 2dr Utl	5450	7700
SE 2dr Utl.	6225	8150

Add:

ABS brakes	125
Sahara trim	425
Renegade trim	550
Hardtop	400
Sound bar	75
Wheels-alloy	100

1994 — WS Ret

CHEROKEE — RWD/4.0L-I6 (190hp)

	WS	Ret
Country 4dr Utl.	4025	5625
Country 2dr Utl.	3600	5250
SE 4dr Utl.	3175	4625
SE 2dr Utl.	2700	4050
Sport 4dr Utl.	3575	5225
Sport 2dr Utl.	3125	4550

Add:

4-wheel drive	700

Deduct:

4cyl	175

GRAND CHEROKEE — 4WD/4.0L-I6 (190hp)

	WS	Ret
Laredo 4dr Utl	5800	7525
Limited 4dr Utl	7125	9225
SE 4dr Utl.	5400	7550

Add:

5.2 Liter V8	175

Deduct:

2-wheel drive	600

WRANGLER (5M/AT) — 4WD/4.0L-I6 (180hp)

	WS	Ret
S (4cyl) 2dr Utl	5000	7050
SE 2dr Utl.	5750	7525

Add:

ABS brakes	100
Sahara trim	375
Renegade trim	500
Hardtop	375
Sound bar	50
Wheels-alloy	75

1993 — WS Ret

CHEROKEE — RWD/4.0L-I6 (190hp)

	WS	Ret
Base 4dr Utl.	2725	4075
Base 2dr Utl.	2275	3550
Country 4dr Utl	3450	5025
Country 2dr Utl	3025	4400
Sport 4dr Utl	3050	4450
Sport 2dr Utl	2625	3925

Add:

4-wheel drive	625
ABS brakes	125

Deduct:

4cyl	150

GRAND CHEROKEE — 4WD/4.0L-I6 (190hp)

	WS	Ret
Base 4dr Utl.	4625	6475
Laredo 4dr Utl	4975	6950
Limited 4dr Utl	6225	8075

Add:

5.2 Liter V8	175

Deduct:

2-wheel drive	550

WRANGLER (5M/AT) — 4WD/4.0L-I6 (180hp)

	WS	Ret
S (4cyl) 2dr Utl.	4350	6150
Utility 2dr Utl	5075	7150

Add:

ABS brakes	100
Sahara trim	325
Renegade trim	450
Hardtop	350
Sound bar	50
Wheels-alloy	50

Deduct:

4cyl (not S)	125

1992 — WS Ret

CHEROKEE — RWD/4.0L-I6 (190hp)

	WS	Ret
Base 4dr Utl.	2325	3625
Base 2dr Utl.	1950	3050
Briarwood (4WD) 4dr Utl.	3725	5425
Limited (4WD) 4dr Utl	3800	5550

Add:

4-wheel drive	575
Laredo trim	475

Deduct:

4cyl	125

COMANCHE — RWD/4.0L-I6 (190hp)

	WS	Ret
Pickup Sbed Pkp	2425	3775
Pickup Lbed Pkp	2475	3850

Add:

4-wheel drive	575
Sport pkg	100
Pioneer trim	150
Eliminator pkg	275

Deduct:

4cyl	125

WRANGLER (5M/AT) — 4WD/4.0L-I6 (160hp)

	WS	Ret
S (4cyl) 2dr Utl.	3825	5400
Utility 2dr Utl	4400	6200

Add:

Islander trim	150
Sahara trim	300
Renegade trim	425
Hardtop	325
Sound bar	25
Wheels-alloy	50

Deduct:

4cyl (not S)	125

1991 — WS Ret

CHEROKEE — RWD/4.0L-I6 (190hp)

	WS	Ret
Base 4dr Utl	1950	3050
Base 2dr Utl	1600	2600
Briarwood (4WD) 4dr Utl	3175	4625
Limited (4WD) 4dr Utl.	3250	4750

Add:

4-wheel drive	525
Sport pkg	100
Laredo trim	425

Deduct:

4cyl	100

COMANCHE — RWD/4.0L-I6 (190hp)

	WS	Ret
Pickup Sbed Pkp	2000	3125
Pickup Lbed Pkp.	2050	3200

Add:

4-wheel drive	525
Pioneer trim	125
Eliminator pkg	250

Deduct:

4cyl	100

GRAND WAGONEER — 4WD/5.9L-V8 (144hp)

	WS	Ret
Wagon 4dr Utl.	4850	6775

WRANGLER (5M/AT) — 4WD/4.0L-I6 (180hp)

	WS	Ret
S (4cyl) 2dr Utl	3500	5150
Utility 2dr Utl.	4000	5650

Add:

Islander trim	150
Sahara trim	275
Hardtop	300
Sound bar	25
Wheels-alloy	25

Deduct:

4cyl (not S)	100

1990 — WS Ret

CHEROKEE — RWD/4.0L-I6 (173hp)

	WS	Ret
Base 4dr Utl	1575	2575
Base 2dr Utl	1275	2075
Limited (4WD) 4dr Utl.	2700	4050
Limited (4WD) 2dr Utl.	2400	3750

Add:

4-wheel drive	500
Laredo trim (Base)	375

Deduct:

4cyl	75

COMANCHE — RWD/4.0L-I6 (173hp)

	WS	Ret
Pickup Sbed Pkp	1725	2825
Pickup Lbed Pkp.	1725	2825

Add:

4-wheel drive	500
Pioneer trim	100
Eliminator pkg	225

Deduct:

4cyl	75

GRAND WAGONEER — 4WD/5.9L-V8 (144hp)

	WS	Ret
Wagon 4dr Utl.	4050	5650

WAGONEER — 4WD/4.0L-I6 (173hp)

	WS	Ret
Limited 4dr Utl.	2550	3825

WRANGLER (5M/AT) — 4WD/4.2L-I6 (112hp)

	WS	Ret
S (4cyl) 2dr Utl	3175	4675
Utility 2dr Utl	3625	5350

Add:

Islander trim	100
Sahara trim	250
Laredo trim	300
Hardtop	300
Wheels-alloy	25

Deduct:
- 4cyl (not S) 75

1989 WS Ret

CHEROKEE RWD/4.0L-I6 (177hp)

	WS	Ret
Base 4dr Utl	1250	2050
Base 2dr Utl	1025	1800
Limited (4WD) 4dr Utl	2175	3400
Limited (4WD) 2dr Utl	1950	3050

Add:
- 4-wheel drive 450
- Sport trim (Base) 50
- Pioneer trim (Base) 100
- Laredo trim (Base) 300

Deduct:
- 4cyl 50

COMANCHE RWD/4.0L-I6 (177hp)

	WS	Ret
Pickup Sbed Pkp	1350	2200
Pickup Lbed Pkp	1375	2250

Add:
- 4-wheel drive 450
- Pioneer trim 75
- Eliminator pkg 200

Deduct:
- 4cyl 50

GRAND WAGONEER 4WD/5.9L-V8 (hp)

	WS	Ret
Wagon 4dr Utl	3150	4600

WAGONEER 4WD/4.0L-I6 (173hp)

	WS	Ret
Limited 4dr Utl	2050	3200

WRANGLER (5M/AT) 4WD/4.2L-I6 (112hp)

	WS	Ret
S (4cyl) 2dr Utl	2825	4275
Util 2dr Utl	3150	4650

Add:
- Islander trim 75
- Sahara trim 225
- Laredo trim 250
- Hardtop 275

Deduct:
- 4cyl (not S) 50

1988 WS Ret

CHEROKEE RWD/4.0L-I6 (177hp)

	WS	Ret
Base 4dr Utl	1125	1975
Base 2dr Utl	925	1800
Limited (4WD) 4dr Utl	1900	2975
Limited (4WD) 2dr Utl	1700	2775

Add:
- 4-wheel drive 375
- Pioneer trim (Base) 50
- Chief trim (Base) 125
- Laredo trim (Base) 225

Deduct:
- 4cyl 50

COMANCHE RWD/4.0L-I6 (177hp)

	WS	Ret
Pickup Sbed Pkp	1150	2025
Pickup Lbed Pkp	1175	2050

Add:
- 4-wheel drive 375
- Pioneer trim 50
- Chief trim 75
- Laredo trim 125

Deduct:
- 4cyl 50

GRAND WAGONEER 4WD/5.9L-V8 (na)

	WS	Ret
Wagon 4dr Utl	2650	3975

WAGONEER 4WD/4.0L-I6 (177hp)

	WS	Ret
Limited 4dr Utl	1800	2950

WRANGLER (5M/AT) 4WD/4.2L-I6 (112hp)

	WS	Ret
S (4cyl) 2dr Utl	2500	3750
Util 2dr Utl	2800	4200

Add:
- Sahara trim 175
- Laredo trim 225
- Hardtop 250

Deduct:
- 4cyl (not S) 50

KIA

2001 WS Ret

SPORTAGE 4WD/2.0L-I4 (130hp)

	WS	Ret
Base 4dr Utl	10600	12900
EX 4dr Utl	11175	13600
Limited 4dr Utl	11425	13925
Soft top 2dr Utl		

Add:
- ABS brakes 300
- Alloy Wheels (Base 2WD) 200

Deduct:
- 2-wheel drive 1950

2000 WS Ret

SPORTAGE 4WD/2.0L-I4 (130hp)

	WS	Ret
Base 4dr Utl	9075	11050
EX 4dr Utl	9650	11750
Soft top 2dr Utl	7375	9500

Add:
- ABS brakes 225
- Alloy Wheels (Base 2WD) 175

Deduct:
- 2-wheel drive 1525

1999 WS Ret

SPORTAGE 4WD/2.0L-I4 (130hp)

	WS	Ret
Base 4dr Utl	7750	10000
EX 4dr Utl	8850	11400
Soft top (5sp) 2dr Utl	6325	8150

Add:
- Alloy Wheels (Base 2WD) 125

Deduct:
- 2-wheel drive 1250

1998 WS Ret

SPORTAGE 4WD/2.0L-I4 (130hp)

	WS	Ret
Base 4dr Utl	6575	8475
EX 4dr Utl	7775	10025

Add:
- Alloy Wheels (Base 2WD) 100

Deduct:
- 2-wheel drive 1050

1997 WS Ret

SPORTAGE 4WD/2.0L-I4 (130hp)

	WS	Ret
Base 4dr Utl	5575	7175
EX 4dr Utl	6650	8575

Add:
- Alloy Wheels (Base 2WD) 75

Deduct:
- 2-wheel drive 850

1996 WS Ret

SPORTAGE 4WD/2.0L-I4 (130hp)

	WS	Ret
Base 4dr Utl	4375	6075
EX 4dr Utl	5400	7500

Deduct:
- 2-wheel drive 675

1995 WS Ret

SPORTAGE 4WD/2.0L-I4 (94hp)

	WS	Ret
Base 4dr Utl	3325	4825
EX 4dr Utl	4200	5850

Add:
- 2.0L DOHC 4cyl 200

Deduct:
- 2-wheel drive 625

LAND ROVER

2001 WS Ret

DISCOVERY 4WD/4.0L-V8 (188hp)

	WS	Ret
Series II SD 4dr Utl		
Series II LE 4dr Utl		
Series II SE 4dr Utl		

RANGE ROVER 4WD/4.6L-V8 (222hp)

	WS	Ret
4.6 SE 4dr Utl		
4.6 HSE 4dr Utl		

2000 WS Ret

DISCOVERY 4WD/4.0L-V8 (188hp)

	WS	Ret
Series II 4dr Utl	22000	25200

Add:
- Rear jump seats 500
- 6-disc CD changer 300
- Active suspension 675
- Dual sunroofs 475

RANGE ROVER 4WD/4.0L-V8 (188hp)

	WS	Ret
4.0 SE 4dr Utl	32900	36525
4.6 HSE 4dr Utl	38075	42275

Add:
- Navigation system 950

1999 WS Ret

DISCOVERY 4WD/4.0L-V8 (188hp)

	WS	Ret
SD 4dr Utl	19000	21750
Series II (188hp) 4dr Utl	21750	24900

Add:
- Rear jump seats 400
- Dual sunroofs 325

RANGE ROVER 4WD/4.0L-V8 (188hp)

	WS	Ret
4.0 SE 4dr Utl	30000	33300
4.6 HSE 4dr Utl	35700	39650

Add:
- Navigation system 775

1998 WS Ret

DISCOVERY 4WD/4.0L-V8 (182hp)

	WS	Ret
LE 4dr Utl	17325	20050
LSE 4dr Utl	19400	22200

Add:
- Rear jump seats 325
- Dual sunroofs 300

RANGE ROVER 4WD/4.0L-V8 (190hp)

	WS	Ret
4.0 SE 4dr Utl	24475	28025
4.6 HSE 4dr Utl	28850	32500

1997 WS Ret

DEFENDER 90 4WD/4.0L-V8 (182hp)

	WS	Ret
Utility 2dr Utl	31075	34500

Add:
- Safari cage 400

Check Truck Equipment Table on page 4

	WS	Ret
DISCOVERY 4WD/4.0L-V8 (182hp)		
SD 4dr Utl	13975	16450
SE 4dr Utl	14900	17550
SE7 4dr Utl	15475	18225
XD 4dr Utl	16100	18725
Add:		
Leather seats (SD)	225	
Rear jump seats (std SE7)	275	
Dual sunroofs	275	
RANGE ROVER 4WD/4.0L-V8 (190hp)		
4.0 SE 4dr Utl	21175	24250
4.6 HSE 4dr Utl	25825	29100
Add:		
Kensington Pkg.	450	

1996

	WS	Ret
DISCOVERY 4WD/4.0L-V8 (182hp)		
SD 4dr Utl	11500	14000
SE 4dr Utl	12600	15350
Add:		
Leather seats (SD)	175	
Rear jump seats (std SE7)	225	
Dual sunroofs	225	
RANGE ROVER 4WD/4.0L-V8 (212hp)		
4.0 SE 4dr Utl	18575	21275
4.6 HSE 4dr Utl	21900	25075

1995

	WS	Ret
DEFENDER 90 4WD/3.9L-V8 (182hp)		
Utility 2dr Utl	27425	30900
Add:		
Alloy wheels	125	
Side door glass	200	
Aluminum wheels	75	
Safari cage	300	
DISCOVERY 4WD/3.9L-V8 (182hp)		
Wagon 4dr Utl	9825	11975
Add:		
Dual air conditioning	175	
Rear jump seats	200	
Sunroof-dual pwr	225	
Leather seats	175	
RANGE ROVER 4WD/4.2L-V8 (182hp)		
4.0 SE 4dr Utl	14175	16700
County Classic 4dr Utl	12175	14825
County LWB 4dr Utl	13850	16300

1994

	WS	Ret
DEFENDER 90 4WD/3.9L-V8 (182hp)		
Utility 2dr Utl	25450	28825
Add:		
Alloy wheels	100	
Side door glass	175	
DISCOVERY 4WD/3.9L-V8 (182hp)		
Wagon 4dr Utl	8900	11475
Add:		
Dual air conditioning	175	
Rear jump seats	200	
Sunroof-dual pwr	300	
Leather seats	150	
RANGE ROVER 4WD/3.9L-V8 (182hp)		
County 4dr Utl	11275	13725
County LWB 4dr Utl	12575	15325

1993

	WS	Ret
RANGE ROVER 4WD/3.9L-V8 (182hp)		
County 4dr Utl	9900	12050
County LWB 4dr Utl	11025	13425

1992

	WS	Ret
RANGE ROVER 4WD/3.9L-V8 (180hp)		
County SE 4dr Utl	9450	11500
Wagon 4dr Utl	8625	11125

1991

	WS	Ret
RANGE ROVER 4WD/3.9L-V8 (178hp)		
County SE 4dr Utl	8150	10500
Wagon 4dr Utl	7375	9500

1990

	WS	Ret
RANGE ROVER 4WD/3.9L-V8 (178hp)		
County 4dr Utl	7150	9225
Wagon 4dr Utl	6525	8400

1989

	WS	Ret
RANGE ROVER 4WD/3.9L-V8 (178hp)		
County 4dr Utl	6000	7725
Wagon 4dr Utl	5525	7125

1988

	WS	Ret
RANGE ROVER 4WD/3.5L-V8 (150hp)		
Wagon 4dr Utl	4575	6350

LEXUS

2001

	WS	Ret
LX 470 4WD/4.7L-V8 (230hp)		
Luxury SUV 4dr Utl		
RX 300 4WD/		
Luxury SUV 4dr Utl		

2000

	WS	Ret
LX 470 4WD/4.7L-V8 (230hp)		
Luxury SUV 4dr Utl	39350	44350
Add:		
Nakamichi (incl CD chngr)	525	
RX 300 4WD/		
Luxury SUV 4dr Utl	26100	29550
Add:		
CD chngr	275	
Premium audio sys	300	
Chrome wheels	250	
Traction cntrl (2WD)	200	
Deduct:		
2-wheel drive	1675	

1999

	WS	Ret
LX 470 4WD/4.7L-V8 (230hp)		
Luxury SUV 4dr Utl	35675	40200
RX 300 4WD/		
Luxury SUV 4dr Utl	23200	26700
Add:		
CD chngr	275	
Premium audio sys	300	
Chrome wheels	225	
Traction cntrl (2WD)	150	
Deduct:		
2-wheel drive	1400	

1998

	WS	Ret
LX 470 4WD/4.5L-V6 (212hp)		
Luxury SUV 4dr Utl	32700	36850

1997

	WS	Ret
LX 450 4WD/4.5L-I6 (212hp)		
Luxury SUV 4dr Utl	23150	26900

1996

	WS	Ret
LX 450 4WD/4.5L-V6 (212hp)		
Luxury SUV 4dr Utl	19675	22850

LINCOLN

2001

	WS	Ret
Navigator 4WD/5.4L-V8 (300hp)		
Luxury SUV 4dr Utl	28300	32050
Add:		
Navigation sys	775	
Alpine audio	300	
Entertainment System	800	
Wheels-chrome	300	
Deduct:		
2-wheel drive	2250	

2000

	WS	Ret
Navigator 4WD/5.4L-V8 (300hp)		
Luxury SUV 4dr Utl	26825	30375
Add:		
Navigation sys	600	
Alpine audio	225	
Wheels-chrome	225	
Deduct:		
2-wheel drive	1750	

1999

	WS	Ret
Navigator 4WD/5.4L-V8 (260hp)		
Luxury SUV 4dr Utl	23150	26625
Add:		
Alpine audio	200	
Wheels-chrome	200	
Deduct:		
2-wheel drive	1475	

1998

	WS	Ret
Navigator 4WD/5.4L-V8 (230hp)		
Luxury SUV 4dr Utl	20075	23100
Deduct:		
2-wheel drive	1250	

MAZDA

2001

	WS	Ret
B2500 RWD/2.5L-I4 (119hp)		
SE Sbed Pkp		
SE 3000 (V6) ExCab Pkp		
SX Sbed Pkp		
MPV RWD/		
DX Mini Van	14150	16750
ES Mini Van	16975	19750
LX Mini Van	15075	17750
Add:		
Entertainment Sys	775	
Touring pkg	500	
GFX pkg	350	
Deduct:		
No ABS	325	
TRIBUTE 4WD/		
DX 4dr Utl		

ES 4dr Utl . . . .
LX 4dr Utl. . . . .

2000 WS Ret

B2500 RWD/2.5L-I4 (119hp)

	WS	Ret
SE Sbed Pkp	6500	8375
SE ExCab Pkp	7900	10175
SX Sbed Pkp	5875	7575
Add:		
3.0L-V6 (143hp) (B3000)	350	
4.0L-V6 (160hp) (B4000)	800	
4-wheel drive	1750	
Automatic trans	500	
Troy Lee edit.	675	

MPV RWD/

	WS	Ret
DX Mini Van	12450	15250
ES Mini Van	15275	18075
LX Mini Van	13425	15800
Add:		
Entertainment Sys	600	
Touring pkg	375	
Deduct:		
No ABS	250	

1999 WS Ret

B2500 RWD/2.5L-I4 (119hp)

	WS	Ret
SE Sbed Pkp	6100	7875
SE ExCab Pkp	7375	9500
SX Sbed Pkp	5375	7475
Add:		
3.0L-V6 (143hp) (B3000)	300	
4.0L-V6 (160hp) (B4000)	675	
4-wheel drive	1450	
Automatic trans	425	
Troy Lee pkg	550	

1998 WS Ret

B2500 RWD/2.5L-I4 (119hp)

	WS	Ret
SE Sbed Pkp	5400	7500
SE ExCab Pkp	7100	9150
SX Sbed Pkp	4775	6650
SX ExCab Pkp	5950	7675
Add:		
3.0L 6cyl (B3000)	250	
4.0L 6cyl (B4000)	550	
4-wheel drive	1200	
Automatic trans	350	
SE trim (4WD)	250	
SE trim (2WD)	200	

MPV RWD/3.0L-V6 (155hp)

	WS	Ret
ES Mini Van	11475	13975
LX Mini Van	10050	12250
Add:		
4-wheel drive	1100	
All-Sport pkg	250	

1997 WS Ret

B2300 RWD/2.3L-I4 (112hp)

	WS	Ret
Base Sbed Pkp	4075	5675
Base ExCab Pkp	5125	7125
SE ExCab Pkp	6200	8000
Add:		
4.0L 6cyl (B4000)	450	
4-wheel drive	1000	
Automatic trans	300	
SE trim (4WD)	200	
SE trim (2WD)	175	

MPV RWD/3.0L-V6 (155hp)

	WS	Ret
ES Mini Van	9800	11925
LX Mini Van	8625	11125
Add:		
4-wheel drive	900	
All-Sport pkg	225	

1996 WS Ret

B2300 RWD/2.3L-I4 (112hp)

	WS	Ret
Base Sbed Pkp	3275	4750
Base Lbed Pkp	3350	4850
Base ExCab Pkp	4300	5975
Add:		
3.0L 6cyl (B3000)	175	
4.0L 6cyl (B4000)	400	
4-wheel drive	825	
SE trim (std 4.0 Liter)	150	
LE trim	275	

MPV RWD/3.0L-V6 (155hp)

	WS	Ret
DX Mini Van	6475	8350
ES Mini Van	7525	9700
LX Mini Van	6950	8950
Add:		
4-wheel drive	750	

1995 WS Ret

B2300 RWD/2.3L-I4 (112hp)

	WS	Ret
Base Sbed Pkp	3050	4425
Base Lbed Pkp	3100	4500
Base ExCab Pkp	3925	5450
Add:		
3.0L 6cyl (B3000)	175	
4.0L 6cyl (B4000)	375	
4-wheel drive	775	
SE trim (std 4.0 Liter)	125	
LX trim	250	

MPV RWD/3.0L-V6 (155hp)

	WS	Ret
L Mini Van	4650	6475
LX Mini Van	5100	7100
LXE Mini Van	5575	7175
Add:		
4-wheel drive	675	

1994 WS Ret

B2300 RWD/2.3L-I4 (98hp)

	WS	Ret
Base Sbed Pkp	2725	4075
Base ExCab Pkp	3350	4850
SE (B3000) Lbed Pkp	3075	4475
Add:		
3.0L 6cyl (B3000)	150	
4.0L 6cyl (B4000)	350	
4-wheel drive	700	
SE trim (std 4.0 Liter)	125	
LX trim	225	

MPV RWD/2.6L-I4 (121hp)

	WS	Ret
Passenger Mini Van	3375	4900
Add:		
3.0 Liter V6	150	
4-wheel drive	625	

NAVAJO RWD/4.0L-V6 (160hp)

	WS	Ret
DX (5sp) 2dr Utl	2850	4250
LX 2dr Utl	3625	5250
Add:		
4-wheel drive	700	

1993 WS Ret

B-SERIES (5sp) RWD/2.6L-I4 (121hp)

	WS	Ret
Base Sbed Pkp	2350	3650
Base Lbed Pkp	2425	3775
Base ExCab Pkp	2975	4325
Add:		
2.6 Liter 4cyl	50	
4-wheel drive	625	
Automatic trans	175	
SE-5 trim	125	
LE-5 trim	200	

MPV RWD/2.6L-I4 (121hp)

	WS	Ret
Passenger Mini Van	2875	4300
Add:		
3.0 Liter V6	150	
4-wheel drive	550	

NAVAJO RWD/4.0L-V6 (160hp)

	WS	Ret
DX (5sp) 2dr Utl	2325	3600
LX 2dr Utl	2950	4275
Add:		
4-wheel drive	625	

1992 WS Ret

B-SERIES (5sp) RWD/2.2L-I4 (85hp)

	WS	Ret
Base Sbed Pkp	2100	3250
Base Lbed Pkp	2125	3300
Base ExCab Pkp	2600	3875
Add:		
2.6 Liter 4cyl	25	
4-wheel drive	575	
Automatic trans	175	
SE-5 trim	75	
LE-5 trim	175	

MPV RWD/2.6L-I4 (121hp)

	WS	Ret
Cargo Mini Van	1925	3000
Passenger Mini Van	2725	4075
Add:		
3.0 Liter 6cyl	125	
4-wheel drive	475	

NAVAJO RWD/4.0L-V6 (155hp)

	WS	Ret
DX (5sp) 2dr Utl	2125	3300
LX 2dr Utl	2650	3950
Add:		
4-wheel drive	575	

1991 WS Ret

B-SERIES (5sp) RWD/2.2L-I4 (91hp)

	WS	Ret
Base Sbed Pkp	1825	2975
Base Lbed Pkp	1850	3000
Base ExCab Pkp	2225	3450
Add:		
2.6 Liter 4cyl	25	
4-wheel drive	525	
Automatic trans	150	
SE-5 trim	50	
LE-5 trim	150	

MPV RWD/2.6L-I4 (121hp)

	WS	Ret
Cargo Mini Van	1800	2925
Passenger Mini Van	2500	3725
Add:		
3.0 Liter V6	125	
4-wheel drive	400	

NAVAJO 4WD/4.0L-V6 (155hp)

	WS	Ret
LX 2dr Utl	2250	3500

1990 WS Ret

B-SERIES (5sp) RWD/2.2L-I4 (85hp)

	WS	Ret
Base Sbed Pkp	1675	2725
Base Lbed Pkp	1725	2800
Base ExCab Pkp	2025	3150
Add:		
2.6 Liter 4cyl	25	
4-wheel drive	500	
Automatic trans	125	
SE-5 trim	50	
LE-5 trim	125	

 Check Truck Equipment Table on page 4

MPV RWD/2.6L-I4 (121hp)

	WS	Ret
Cargo Mini Van	1625	2650
Passenger Mini Van	2175	3375
Add:		
3.0 Liter V6	125	
4-wheel drive	375	

1989 — WS Ret

B-SERIES (5sp) RWD/2.2L-I4 (85hp)

	WS	Ret
Base Sbed Pkp	1350	2200
Base Lbed Pkp	1400	2275
LX ExCab Pkp	1675	2725
Add:		
4-wheel drive	450	
Automatic trans	100	
SE-5 trim	50	
LE trim	125	

MPV RWD/2.6L-I4 (121hp)

	WS	Ret
Cargo Mini Van	1475	2400
Passenger Mini Van	1900	2950
Add:		
3.0 Liter V6	100	
4-wheel drive	325	

1988 — WS Ret

B-SERIES (5sp) RWD/2.2L-I4 (85hp)

	WS	Ret
Base Sbed Pkp	1225	2150
Base Lbed Pkp	1225	2150
Base ExCab Pkp	1450	2350
Add:		
4-wheel drive	375	
Automatic trans	50	
SE-5 trim	25	
LX trim	200	

MERCEDES

2001 — WS Ret

M-Class 4WD/3.2L-V6 (215hp)

	WS	Ret
ML320 4dr Utl		
ML430 (4.3L-V8/268hp) 4dr Utl		
ML55 (5.5L-V8/342hp) 4dr Utl		
Add:		
Bose audio (std ML55)	250	
Running boards	550	
Skyview roof-pwr	1225	
Third seat	675	
Offroad pkg (w/brush guard)	775	
Cognac/Mystic Green	1250	

2000 — WS Ret

M-Class 4WD/3.2L-V6 (215hp)

	WS	Ret
ML320 4dr Utl	27125	31325
ML430 (4.3L-V8) 4dr Utl	31400	35725
ML55 (5.5L-V8) 4dr Utl	45250	50975
Add:		
Bose audio (std ML55)	200	
Running boards	425	
Skyview roof-pwr	950	
Third seat	525	
Offroad pkg (w/brush guard)	600	

1999 — WS Ret

M-Class 4WD/3.2L-V6 (215hp)

	WS	Ret
ML320 4dr Utl	23150	27150
ML430 (4.3L-V8) 4dr Utl	27575	31825
Add:		
Bose audio	150	
Running boards	350	
Skyview roof-pwr	775	

1998 — WS Ret

M-Class 4WD/3.2L-V6 (215hp)

	WS	Ret
ML320 4dr Utl	20425	23950
Add:		
Bose audio	125	
Running boards	300	

MERCURY

2001 — WS Ret

MOUNTAINEER AWD/5.0L-V8 (215hp)

	WS	Ret
SUV 4dr Utl	18025	20950
Add:		
Monterey trim	325	
Premium trim	450	
Wheels-chrome	275	
Mach Audio	275	
Deduct:		
2-wheel drive	2000	
4.0L-V6 (200hp)	450	

VILLAGER AWD/3.3L-V6 (170hp)

	WS	Ret
Base Mini Van	14275	16550
Estate Mini Van	16400	18700
Sport Mini Van	16050	18300
Add:		
ABS Brakes	375	
Entertainment Center w/VCR	775	

2000 — WS Ret

MOUNTAINEER AWD/5.0L-V8 (215hp)

	WS	Ret
SUV 4dr Utl	16550	19250
Add:		
Monterey trim	250	
Premium trim	350	
Wheels-chrome	225	
Deduct:		
2-wheel drive	1550	
4.0L-V6 (200hp)	350	

VILLAGER AWD/3.3L-V6 (170hp)

	WS	Ret
Base Mini Van	12375	14850
Estate Mini Van	14550	16875
Sport Mini Van	14200	16475
Add:		
ABS Brakes	275	
Entertainment Center w/VCR	600	

1999 — WS Ret

MOUNTAINEER AWD/5.0L-V8 (215hp)

	WS	Ret
4dr Utl	13375	15825
Deduct:		
2-wheel drive	1300	
4.0L-V6 (200hp)	325	

VILLAGER AWD/3.3L-V6 (170hp)

	WS	Ret
Base Mini Van	11450	14025
Estate Mini Van	13500	15975
Sport Mini Van	13175	15600
Add:		
ABS Brakes (GS)	225	

1998 — WS Ret

MOUNTAINEER AWD/5.0L-V8 (215hp)

	WS	Ret
4dr Utl	12125	14850
Deduct:		
2-wheel drive	1075	
4.0L-V6 (200hp)	275	

VILLAGER AWD/3.0L-V6 (151hp)

	WS	Ret
GS Mini Van	8825	11200
LS Mini Van	10050	12050
Nautica Mini Van	10450	12550
Add:		
ABS Brakes (GS)	200	

1997 — WS Ret

MOUNTAINEER AWD/5.0L-V8 (211hp)

	WS	Ret
4dr Utl	9925	12150

VILLAGER AWD/3.0L-V6 (151hp)

	WS	Ret
GS Mini Van	7450	9450
LS Mini Van	8600	10925
Nautica Mini Van	8950	11375
Add:		
ABS Brakes (GS)	150	

1996 — WS Ret

VILLAGER FWD/3.0L-V6 (151hp)

	WS	Ret
GS Mini Van	5575	7175
LS Mini Van	6500	8375
Nautica Mini Van	6825	8800

1995 — WS Ret

VILLAGER FWD/3.0L-V6 (151hp)

	WS	Ret
GS Mini Van	4450	6200
LS Mini Van	5250	7300
Nautica Mini Van	5550	7150

1994 — WS Ret

VILLAGER FWD/3.0L-V6 (151hp)

	WS	Ret
GS Mini Van	4175	5800
LS Mini Van	4750	6600
Nautica Mini Van	4975	6925

1993 — WS Ret

VILLAGER FWD/3.0L-V6 (151hp)

	WS	Ret
GS Mini Van	3350	4850
LS Mini Van	3850	5350

MITSUBISHI

2001 — WS Ret

MONTERO 4WD/3.5L-V6 (200hp)

	WS	Ret
Base 4dr Utl		
Endevour 4dr Utl		

MONTERO SPORT RWD/3.0L-V6 (173hp)

	WS	Ret
ES (3.0L-V6/173hp) 4dr Utl	12200	14850
LS (3.0L-V6/173hp) 4dr Utl	14975	17625
LTD (3.5L-V6/200hp) 4d Utl	18325	21200
XLS (3.0L-V6/173hp 4d Utl	16500	19100
XS (3.5L-V6/200hp) 4d Utl	17425	20150
Add:		
Four-wheel drive	2100	
Infinit audio	250	

2000 — WS Ret

MONTERO 4WD/3.5L-V6 (200hp)

	WS	Ret
Base 4dr Utl	16150	18675
Endevour 4dr Utl	17500	20250
Add:		
CD changer	325	
Infinity audio	275	

MONTERO SPORT RWD/3.0L-V6 (173hp)

	WS	Ret
ES (3.0L-V6/173hp) 4dr Utl	10675	13000
LS (3.0L-V6/173hp) 4dr Utl	13450	15825
LTD (3.5L-V6/200hp) 4d Utl	16500	19100

	WS	Ret
XLS (3.0L-V6/173hp 4dr Utl	14975	17625

Add:
- Four-wheel drive 1625
- Infinit audio 200

1999 WS Ret

MONTERO 4WD/3.5L-V6 (200hp)

	WS	Ret
Base 4dr Utl	14600	17200

Add:
- CD changer 275
- Infinity audio 225
- Chrome wheels 225

MONTERO SPORT RWD/3.0L-V6 (173hp)

	WS	Ret
ES (4cyl-5sp) 4dr Utl	8625	11125
LS (3.0L-V6/173hp) 4dr Utl	11150	13575
LTD (3.5L-V6/200hp) 4d Utl	14075	16575
XLS (3.0L-V6/173hp) 4d Utl	12575	15325

Add:
- Four-wheel drive 1350
- Wheels-alloy (std XLS) 150

1998 WS Ret

MONTERO 4WD/3.5L-V6 (200hp)

	WS	Ret
LS 4dr Utl	12925	15750

Add:
- CD changer 225
- Infinity audio 200
- Chrome wheels 175

MONTERO SPORT RWD/3.0L-V6 (173hp)

	WS	Ret
ES (4cyl-5sp) 4dr Utl	7275	9375
LS 4dr Utl	9525	11600
XLS 4dr Utl	10775	13125

Add:
- Four-wheel drive 1200
- Wheels-alloy (std XLS) 125

1997 WS Ret

MONTERO 4WD/3.5L-V6 (200hp)

	WS	Ret
LS 4dr Utl	10975	13375
SR 4dr Utl	13600	16025

Add:
- ABS brakes (std SR) 200
- Leather & Wood pkg 200
- Chrome wheels 100

MONTERO SPORT RWD/3.0L-V6 (173hp)

	WS	Ret
ES (4cyl-5sp) 4dr Utl	6700	8625
LS 4dr Utl	8625	11125
XLS (4WD) 4dr Utl	11725	14275

Add:
- Four-wheel drive 1125
- ABS brakes 200
- Wheels-alloy (std XLS) 100

1996 WS Ret

MONTERO 4WD/3.0L-V6 (177hp)

	WS	Ret
LS 4dr Utl	9825	11975
SR 4dr Utl	12100	14750

Add:
- ABS brakes (std SR) 150
- Leather & Wood pkg 175
- Chrome wheels 75

1995 WS Ret

MIGHTY MAX (5sp) RWD/2.4L-I4 (116hp)

	WS	Ret
Base Sbed Pkp	2775	4150

Add:
- Automatic trans 225

MONTERO 4WD/3.0L-V6 (177hp)

	WS	Ret
LS 4dr Utl	7950	10250
SR 4dr Utl	9975	12150

Add:
- ABS brakes (std SR) 150
- Leather & Wood pkg 150
- Chrome wheels 75

1994 WS Ret

MIGHTY MAX (5sp) RWD/2.4L-I4 (116hp)

	WS	Ret
Base Sbed Pkp	2450	3800
Base ExCab Pkp	3075	4475

Add:
- 6cyl 175
- 4-wheel drive 700
- Automatic trans 200
- Sport trim 100

MONTERO 4WD/3.0L-V6 (183hp)

	WS	Ret
LS 4dr Utl	7100	9150
SR 4dr Utl	8825	11375

Add:
- ABS brakes (std SR) 125
- Leather & Wood pkg 125

1993 WS Ret

MIGHTY MAX (5sp) RWD/2.4L-I4 (116hp)

	WS	Ret
Base Sbed Pkp	2050	3175
Base ExCab Pkp	2650	3950

Add:
- 6cyl 150
- 4-wheel drive 625
- Automatic trans 175
- Sport trim 75

MONTERO 4WD/3.0L-V6 (151hp)

	WS	Ret
Base 4dr Utl	5300	7375
LS 4dr Utl	6400	8250
RS 4dr Utl	5650	7275
SR 4dr Utl	8025	10350

Add:
- ABS brakes (std LS,SR) 125
- Leather & Wood pkg 100

1992 WS Ret

MIGHTY MAX (5sp) RWD/2.4L-I4 (116hp)

	WS	Ret
Base Sbed Pkp	1700	2750
Base ExCab Pkp	2050	3175

Add:
- 6cyl 150
- 4-wheel drive 575
- Automatic trans 175
- SE trim 25

MONTERO 4WD/3.0L-V6 (151hp)

	WS	Ret
Base 4dr Utl	4475	6225
LS 4dr Utl	5500	7650
RS 4dr Utl	4775	6650
SR 4dr Utl	6925	8925

1991 WS Ret

MIGHTY MAX (5sp) RWD/2.4L-I4 (116hp)

	WS	Ret
Base Sbed Pkp	1550	2525
Base ExCab Pkp	1825	2975

Add:
- 6cyl engine 100
- 4-wheel drive 525
- Automatic trans 150
- SE trim 25

MONTERO 4WD/3.0L-V6 (143hp)

	WS	Ret
Base (5sp) 4dr Utl	2650	3950
LS 4dr Utl	3900	5425
RS 4dr Utl	3250	4725

1990 WS Ret

MIGHTY MAX (5sp) RWD/2.4L-I4 (116hp)

	WS	Ret
Base Sbed Pkp	1325	2150
Base ExCab Pkp	1575	2550

Add:
- 6cyl engine 100
- 4-wheel drive 500
- Automatic trans 125

MONTERO 4WD/3.0L-V6 (143hp)

	WS	Ret
Base 4dr Utl	2575	3850
Base 2dr Utl	2150	3350
RS 4dr Utl	3100	4500
Sport 2dr Utl	2675	4000

Add:
- LS trim (RS) 225

VAN RWD/2.4L-I4 (107hp)

	WS	Ret
Cargo Mini Van	1025	1800
Passenger Mini Van	1875	3050

Add:
- LS trim 225

1989 WS Ret

MIGHTY MAX (5sp) RWD/2.0L-I4 (90hp)

	WS	Ret
Base Sbed Pkp	1125	1975
Base ExCab Pkp	1425	2325
Sport Sbed Pkp	1250	2025
Sport Lbed Pkp	1325	2150
SPX ExCab Pkp	1625	2650

Add:
- 4-wheel drive 450
- Automatic trans 100

MONTERO 4WD/3.0L-V6 (143hp)

	WS	Ret
Base 4dr Utl	2525	3775
Base 2dr Utl	2175	3375
LS 4dr Utl	3000	4350
Sport 2dr Utl	2625	3925

VAN RWD/2.4L-I4 (107hp)

	WS	Ret
Cargo Mini Van	875	1675
Passenger Mini Van	1550	2525

Add:
- LS trim 150

1988 WS Ret

MIGHTY MAX (5sp) RWD/2.0L-I4 (90hp)

	WS	Ret
Base Sbed Pkp	925	1775
Base ExCab Pkp	1225	2150
Sport Sbed Pkp	1050	1825
Sport Lbed Pkp	1075	1875
SPX ExCab Pkp	1350	2200

Add:
- 4-wheel drive 375
- Automatic trans 50

MONTERO 4WD/2.6L-I4 (109hp)

	WS	Ret
SP 2dr Utl	1800	2925
Sport 2dr Utl	2175	3375

NISSAN

2001 WS Ret

FRONTIER (5sp) RWD/2.4L-I4 (143hp)

	WS	Ret
SE ExCab Pkp	10425	12700
SE CrewCab (V6) 4dr Pkp		
Supercharded CrewCa 4dr Pkp		
XE Sbed Pkp	8025	10350
XE ExCab Pkp	9625	11725
XE CrewCab (V6) 4dr Pkp		

Check Truck Equipment Table on page 4

Add:

	WS
4-wheel drive	2300
Automatic trans	675
Alum alloys	250
Chrome trim	250

PATHFINDER 4WD/3.5L-V6 (240hp)

	WS	Ret
LE 4dr Utl	22425	25675
SE 4dr Utl	20375	23325
XE 4dr Utl	18675	21375
Add:		
Sport pkg	300	
Bose audio (std LE)	250	
Naviagation System	800	
Entertainment Center	800	
Deduct:		
2-wheel drive	2075	

QUEST FWD/3.3L-V6 (170hp)

	WS	Ret
GLE Mini Van	17775	20575
GXE Mini Van	15925	18425
SE Mini Van	16825	19475
Add:		
Entertainment sys	775	

XTERRA 4WD/

	WS	Ret
SE 4dr Utl	15875	18375
XE 4dr Utl	15200	17900
Add:		
Wheels-alloy (std SE)	225	
Utility pkg (std SE)	400	
Sport pkg (std SE)	450	
6-disc CD chngr	325	

2000 WS Ret

FRONTIER (5sp) RWD/2.4L-I4 (143hp)

	WS	Ret
SE ExCab Pkp	9450	11500
SE CrewCab (V6) 4dr Pkp.	12700	15475
XE Sbed Pkp	7025	9050
XE ExCab Pkp	8650	11150
Add:		
4-wheel drive	1775	
Automatic trans	525	
Sport pkg (incls alloys)	475	
Alum alloys	200	
Chrome trim	200	

PATHFINDER 4WD/3.3L-V6 (170hp)

	WS	Ret
LE 4dr Utl	20425	23375
SE 4dr Utl	18375	21250
XE 4dr Utl	16625	19225
Add:		
Sport pkg	250	
Bose audio (std LE)	200	
Deduct:		
2-wheel drive	1600	

QUEST FWD/3.3L-V6 (170hp)

	WS	Ret
GLE Mini Van	16400	18975
GXE Mini Van	14625	17225
SE Mini Van	15525	18275
Add:		
Entertainment sys	600	

XTERRA 4WD/

	WS	Ret
SE 4dr Utl	14750	17375
XE 4dr Utl	14175	16700
Add:		
Wheels-alloy (std SE)	175	

1999 WS Ret

FRONTIER (5sp) RWD/2.4L-I4 (143hp)

	WS	Ret
SE ExCab Pkp	8700	11225
XE Sbed Pkp	6450	8325
XE ExCab Pkp	7900	10175
Add:		
4-wheel drive	1475	
Automatic trans	425	
Sport pkg (incls alloys)	400	
Alum alloys	150	

PATHFINDER 4WD/3.3L-V6 (168hp)

	WS	Ret
LE 4dr Utl	17350	20075
SE 4dr Utl	15375	18100
XE 4dr Utl	13825	16275
Add:		
Sport pkg	200	
Off road pkg	200	
240hp V6 (1999.5 model)	500	
Deduct:		
2-wheel drive	1325	

QUEST FWD/3.3L-V6 (170hp)

	WS	Ret
GLE Mini Van	15200	17900
GXE Mini Van	13550	15950
SE Mini Van	14400	16950

1998 WS Ret

FRONTIER (5sp) RWD/2.4L-I4 (143hp)

	WS	Ret
Base Sbed Pkp	5025	7000
SE ExCab Pkp	7625	9825
XE Sbed Pkp	5675	7325
XE ExCab Pkp	6950	8950
Add:		
4-wheel drive	1225	
Automatic trans	350	
Alum alloys	125	

PATHFINDER 4WD/3.3L-V6 (168hp)

	WS	Ret
LE 4dr Utl	14950	17600
SE 4dr Utl	13300	15650
XE 4dr Utl	11850	14425
Add:		
Sport pkg	150	
Deduct:		
2-wheel drive	1100	

QUEST FWD/3.0L-V6 (151hp)

	WS	Ret
GXE Mini Van	10725	13075
XE Mini Van	9350	11400
Add:		
ABS brakes (std GXE)	225	

1997 WS Ret

PATHFINDER 4WD/3.3L-V6 (168hp)

	WS	Ret
LE 4dr Utl	12700	15475
SE 4dr Utl	11150	13575
XE 4dr Utl	9925	12100
Add:		
Sport pkg	100	
Deduct:		
2-wheel drive	900	

PICKUP (5sp) RWD/2.4L-I4 (134hp)

	WS	Ret
Base Sbed Pkp	4100	5700
SE ExCab Pkp	6450	8325
XE Sbed Pkp	4725	6575
XE ExCab Pkp	5875	7575
Add:		
4-wheel drive	1000	
Automatic trans	300	
Chrome pkg	150	
Alum alloys	100	

QUEST FWD/3.0L-V6 (151hp)

	WS	Ret
GXE Mini Van	9550	11625
XE Mini Van	8300	10700
Add:		
ABS brakes (std GXE)	200	
Alloy wheels (std GXE)	75	

1996 WS Ret

PATHFINDER 4WD/3.3L-V6 (168hp)

	WS	Ret
LE 4dr Utl	11425	13925
SE 4dr Utl	10125	12325
XE 4dr Utl	9025	11625
Add:		
Sport pkg	75	
Deduct:		
2-wheel drive	750	

PICKUP (5sp) RWD/2.4L-I4 (134hp)

	WS	Ret
Base Sbed Pkp	3450	5000
SE (6cyl) ExCab Pkp	5550	7150
XE Sbed Pkp	3925	5450
XE ExCab Pkp	5000	6950
Add:		
4-wheel drive	825	
Automatic trans	250	
Chrome pkg	125	

QUEST FWD/3.0L-V6 (151hp)

	WS	Ret
GXE Mini Van	7950	10250
XE Mini Van	6825	8800
Add:		
ABS brakes (std GXE)	150	

1995 WS Ret

PATHFINDER 4WD/3.0L-V6 (153hp)

	WS	Ret
LE 4dr Utl	8225	10600
SE 4dr Utl	7125	9175
XE 4dr Utl	6275	8100
Add:		
Sport pkg	75	
Deduct:		
2-wheel drive	675	

PICKUP (5sp) RWD/2.3L-I4 (150hp)

	WS	Ret
Base Sbed Pkp	3075	4475
Base (6cyl) Lbed Pkp	3475	5050
SE 4WD (6cyl) ExCab Pkp.	6025	7775
XE Sbed Pkp	3275	4750
XE ExCab Pkp	4200	5850
Add:		
4-wheel drive	775	
Automatic trans	225	
Chrome pkg	125	

QUEST FWD/3.0L-V6 (151hp)

	WS	Ret
GXE Mini Van	6550	8450
XE Mini Van	5625	7250
Add:		
ABS brakes	125	

1994 WS Ret

PATHFINDER 4WD/3.0L-V6 (153hp)

	WS	Ret
LE 4dr Utl	7525	9700
SE 4dr Utl	6625	8550
XE 4dr Utl	5900	7600
Add:		
Sport pkg	50	
Deduct:		
2-wheel drive	625	

PICKUP (5sp) RWD/2.4L-I4 (134hp)

	WS	Ret
Base Sbed Pkp	2750	4100
Base (6cyl) Lbed Pkp	3100	4500
SE (6cyl) ExCab Pkp	4400	6125
XE Sbed Pkp	2950	4275
XE ExCab Pkp	3725	5400
Add:		
4-wheel drive	700	
Automatic trans	200	
Chrome pkg	125	

QUEST FWD/3.0L-V6 (151hp)

GXE Mini Van	5600	7225
XE Mini Van	4800	6675

1993 WS Ret

PATHFINDER 4WD/3.0L-V6 (153hp)

SE 4dr Utl	5975	7700
XE 4dr Utl	5350	7450

Deduct:
2-wheel drive ... 575

PICKUP (5sp) RWD/2.4L-I4 (134hp)

Base Sbed Pkp	2225	3450
Base (6cyl) Lbed Pkp	2550	3800
Base ExCab Pkp	2925	4250
SE (6cyl) ExCab Pkp	3525	5125

Add:
4-wheel drive ... 625
Automatic trans ... 175

QUEST FWD/3.0L-V6 (151hp)

GXE Mini Van	4800	6675
XE Mini Van	4025	5600

1992 WS Ret

PATHFINDER 4WD/3.0L-V6 (153hp)

SE 4dr Utl	5300	7375
XE 4dr Utl	4750	6600

Deduct:
2-wheel drive ... 525

PICKUP (5sp) RWD/2.4L-I4 (134hp)

Base Sbed Pkp	1925	3000
Base (6cyl) Lbed Pkp	2200	3425
Base ExCab Pkp	2550	3800
SE (6cyl) ExCab Pkp	3050	4425

Add:
4-wheel drive ... 575
Automatic trans ... 175

1991 WS Ret

PATHFINDER 4WD/3.0L-V6 (153hp)

SE 4dr Utl	4550	6325
XE 4dr Utl	4000	5550

Deduct:
2-wheel drive ... 475

PICKUP (5sp) RWD/2.4L-I4 (134hp)

Base Sbed Pkp	1600	2600
Base (6cyl) Lbed Pkp	1850	3000
Base ExCab Pkp	2125	3300
SE (6cyl) ExCab Pkp	2600	3875

Add:
4-wheel drive ... 525
Automatic trans ... 150

1990 WS Ret

PATHFINDER 4WD/3.0L-V6 (153hp)

SE 4dr Utl	4150	5775
SE 2dr Utl	3850	5350
XE 4dr Utl	3725	5400

PICKUP (5sp) RWD/2.4L-I4 (134hp)

Base Sbed Pkp	1425	2325
Base (6cyl) Lbed Pkp	1650	2675
Base ExCab Pkp	1850	3000
SE (6cyl) ExCab Pkp	2250	3500

Add:
6cyl engine ... 100
4-wheel drive ... 500
Automatic trans ... 125

1989 WS Ret

PATHFINDER 4WD/3.0L-V6 (145hp)

SE 2dr Utl	3700	5375
XE 2dr Utl	3325	4825

PICKUP (5sp) RWD/2.4L-I4 (106hp)

E Sbed Pkp	1300	2100
E ExCab Pkp	1675	2725
E (6cyl) Lbed Pkp	1450	2350
SE (6cyl) ExCab Pkp	2000	3100
Special Sbed Pkp	1400	2275
Special (6cyl) Lbed Pkp	1575	2550
Special ExCab Pkp	1775	2875

Add:
6cyl engine ... 75
4-wheel drive ... 450
Automatic trans ... 100

1988 WS Ret

PATHFINDER 4WD/3.0L-V6 (145hp)

SE Sport 2dr Utl	3175	4600
XE Sport 2dr Utl	2900	4325

PICKUP (5sp) RWD/2.4L-I4 (106hp)

Base (4sp) Sbed Pkp	1175	2050
E Sbed Pkp	1300	2100
E Lbed Pkp	1350	2200
E ExCab Pkp	1600	2600
SE (6cyl) ExCab Pkp	1850	3000

Add:
6cyl engine ... 50
4-wheel drive ... 375
Automatic trans ... 50
XE trim (E) ... 125

OLDSMOBILE

2001 WS Ret

BRAVADA AWD/4.3L-V6 (190hp)

Sport Utility 4dr Utl	16150	18675

SILHOUETTE FWD/3.4L-V6 (185hp)

GL Mini Van	15250	17950
GLS Mini Van	17125	19825
Premiere Mini Van	18400	21300

Add:
Traction ctrl (GL) ... 175
Sliding door-pwr ... 250
Wheels-alum (std GLS) ... 200
Wheels-chrome ... 325

2000 WS Ret

BRAVADA AWD/4.3L-V6 (190hp)

Sport Utility 4dr Utl	14650	17250

SILHOUETTE FWD/3.4L-V6 (185hp)

GL Mini Van	13975	16450
GLS Mini Van	15800	18275
Premiere Mini Van	17025	19700

Add:
Intgrtd child seat ... 100
Sliding door-pwr ... 175

1999 WS Ret

BRAVADA AWD/4.3L-V6 (190hp)

Sport Utility 4dr Utl	13475	15875

SILHOUETTE FWD/3.4L-V6 (185hp)

GL Mini Van	13075	15925
GLS Mini Van	14800	17425
GS Mini Van	13225	15575
Premiere Mini Van	15525	18275

Add:
Intgrtd child seat ... 50
Sliding door-pwr ... 150

1998 WS Ret

BRAVADA AWD/4.3L-V6 (190hp)

Sport Utility 4dr Utl	11350	13825

SILHOUETTE FWD/3.4L-V6 (180hp)

GL Mini Van	11325	13800
GLS Mini Van	12925	15750
GS Mini Van	11450	13950
Premiere Mini Van	13550	15950

Add:
Intgrtd child seat ... 50
Sliding door-pwr ... 125

1997 WS Ret

BRAVADA AWD/4.3L-V6 (190hp)

Sport Utility 4dr Utl	10075	12275

SILHOUETTE FWD/3.4L-V6 (180hp)

Base Mini Van	8050	10375
Base Extended Mini Van	8975	11575
GL Mini Van	9750	11875
GLS Mini Van	10325	12575

Add:
Intgrtd child seat ... 25
Sliding door-pwr ... 100

1996 WS Ret

BRAVADA AWD/4.3L-V6 (190hp)

Sport Utility 4dr Utl	8775	11300

SILHOUETTE FWD/3.4L-V6 (180hp)

Van Mini Van	6425	8275

Add:
Intgrtd child seat ... 25
Sliding door-pwr ... 75

1995 WS Ret

SILHOUETTE FWD/3.8L-V6 (170hp)

Van Mini Van	5100	7100

Add:
3.8 Liter V6 ... 125
Sliding door-pwr ... 50
Integrated child seat ... 25

1994 WS Ret

BRAVADA AWD/4.3L-V6 (200hp)

Sport Utility 4dr Utl	5325	7400

SILHOUETTE FWD/3.1L-V6 (120hp)

Van Mini Van	3725	5400

Add:
3.8 Liter V6 ... 100
Sliding door-pwr ... 50

1993 WS Ret

BRAVADA AWD/4.3L-V6 (200hp)

Sport Utility 4dr Utl	4650	6475

SILHOUETTE FWD/3.1L-V6 (120hp)

Van Mini Van	3075	4475

Add:
3.8 Liter V6 ... 75

1992 WS Ret

BRAVADA AWD/4.3L-V6 (160hp)

Sport Utility 4dr Utl	4125	5725

Check Truck Equipment Table on page 4

SILHOUETTE FWD/3.1L-V6 (120hp)

	WS	Ret
Van Mini Van	2550	3800
Add:		
3.8 Liter V6	50	

1991 WS Ret

BRAVADA AWD/4.3L-V6 (160hp)

	WS	Ret
Sport Utility 4dr Utl	3250	4725

SILHOUETTE FWD/3.1L-V6 (120hp)

	WS	Ret
Van Mini Van	1975	3075

1990 WS Ret

SILHOUETTE FWD/3.1L-V6 (120hp)

	WS	Ret
Van Mini Van	1500	2425

PLYMOUTH

2000 WS Ret

VOYAGER FWD/3.3L-V6 (158hp)

	WS	Ret
Base Swb Van	10200	12250
Grand Base Lwb Van	11425	13700
Grand SE Lwb Van	12475	14975
SE Swb Van	11250	13500
Add:		
ABS Brakes (Base)	275	
Integrated child seat	100	
Deduct:		
2.4L-I4 (150hp)	400	
Psgr slider only	325	
No ABS brakes	325	

1999 WS Ret

VOYAGER FWD/3.3L-V6 (158hp)

	WS	Ret
Base Swb Van	8250	10475
Grand Base Lwb Van	9400	11275
Grand SE Lwb Van	10350	12425
SE Swb Van	9225	11075
Add:		
ABS Brakes (Base)	225	
Integrated child seat	75	
Deduct:		
4cyl	325	
Psgr slider only	275	
No ABS brakes	275	

1998 WS Ret

VOYAGER FWD/3.3L-V6 (158hp)

	WS	Ret
Base Swb Van	7725	9800
Grand Base Lwb Van	8725	11075
Grand SE Lwb Van	9575	11500
SE Swb Van	8575	10900
Add:		
ABS Brakes (Base)	200	
Integrated child seat	50	
Deduct:		
4cyl	275	
Psgr slider only	225	
No ABS brakes	225	

1997 WS Ret

VOYAGER FWD/3.3L-V6 (158hp)

	WS	Ret
Base Swb Van	6050	7675
Grand Base Lwb Van	6950	8825
Grand SE Lwb Van	7725	9800
SE Swb Van	6825	8675
Add:		
ABS Brakes (Base)	150	
Rallye trim (SE)	200	
Integrated child seat	25	
Deduct:		
4cyl	225	
Psgr slider only	175	
No ABS brakes	175	

1996 WS Ret

VOYAGER FWD/3.3L-V6 (158hp)

	WS	Ret
Base Swb Van	4475	6125
Grand Base Lwb Van	5250	7200
Grand SE Lwb Van	5950	7550
SE Swb Van	5150	7050
Add:		
ABS brakes (Base)	150	
Rallye trim (SE)	175	
Integrated child seat	25	
Deduct:		
4cyl	175	
Psgr slider only	150	
No ABS brakes	150	

1995 WS Ret

VOYAGER FWD/3.0L-V6 (142hp)

	WS	Ret
Base Swb Van	2600	3825
Grand Base Lwb Van	3250	4650
Grand LE Lwb Van	4300	5900
Grand SE Lwb Van	3875	5300
LE Swb Van	3625	5175
SE Swb Van	3150	4500
Add:		
4-wheel drive	675	
ABS brakes	150	
LX trim (LE)	175	
Integrated child seat	25	
Deduct:		
4cyl	175	

1994 WS Ret

VOYAGER FWD/3.0L-V6 (142hp)

	WS	Ret
Base Swb Van	2125	3250
Grand Base Lwb Van	2725	4000
Grand LE Lwb Van	3575	5100
Grand SE Lwb Van	3175	4550
LE Swb Van	3000	4300
SE Swb Van	2625	3850
Add:		
4-wheel drive	625	
ABS brakes	125	
LX trim (LE)	150	
Integrated child seat	25	
Deduct:		
4cyl	150	

1993 WS Ret

VOYAGER FWD/3.0L-V6 (142hp)

	WS	Ret
Base Swb Van	1575	2525
Grand Base Lwb Van	2000	3050
Grand LE Lwb Van	2700	3975
Grand SE Lwb Van	2425	3700
LE Swb Van	2275	3475
SE Swb Van	1975	3025
Add:		
4-wheel drive	550	
ABS brakes (Base,SE)	125	
LX trim (LE)	125	
Deduct:		
4cyl	125	

1992 WS Ret

VOYAGER FWD/3.0L-V6 (142hp)

	WS	Ret
Base Swb Van	1400	2250
Grand Base Lwb Van	1700	2725
Grand LE Lwb Van	2250	3450
Grand SE Lwb Van	2025	3100
LE Swb Van	1925	2950
SE Swb Van	1700	2725
Add:		
4-wheel drive	475	
ABS brakes	75	
LX trim (LE)	75	
Deduct:		
4cyl	125	

1991 WS Ret

VOYAGER FWD/3.0L-V6 (142hp)

	WS	Ret
Base Swb Van	1200	2075
Grand LE Lwb Van	1850	2950
Grand SE Lwb Van	1650	2650
LE Swb Van	1575	2525
SE Swb Van	1425	2275
Add:		
4-wheel drive	400	
Air bag-driver	50	
LX trim (LE)	75	
Deduct:		
4cyl	100	

1990 WS Ret

VOYAGER FWD/3.0L-V6 (142hp)

	WS	Ret
Base Swb Van	825	1575
Grand LE Lwb Van	1300	2075
Grand SE Lwb Van	1200	2075
LE Swb Van	1125	1925
SE Swb Van	1025	1775
Add:		
LX trim (LE)	50	
Deduct:		
4cyl	100	

1989 WS Ret

VOYAGER FWD/3.0L-V6 (125hp)

	WS	Ret
Base Swb Van	525	1100
Grand LE Lwb Van	950	1800
Grand SE Lwb Van	850	1625
LE Swb Van	800	1525
SE Swb Van	700	1450
Deduct:		
4cyl	50	

1988 WS Ret

VOYAGER FWD/3.0L-V6 (144hp)

	WS	Ret
Base Swb Van	475	1000
Grand LE Lwb Van	800	1525
Grand SE Lwb Van	650	1350
LE Swb Van	725	1500
SE Swb Van	575	1200
Deduct:		
4cyl	50	

PONTIAC

2001 WS Ret

AZTEK FWD/

	WS	Ret
Base 4dr Utl	12250	14925
GT 4dr Utl	13825	16275

MONTANA FWD/3.4L-V6 (185hp)

	WS	Ret
Extended Mini Van	16325	18900
SWB Mini Van	15025	17700
Add:		
CD changer	325	
Sliding door-pwr	250	

Models Include auto trans, a/c, ps, pb, am-fm stereo

	WS	Ret
Traction control	175	
Wheels-alloy	200	

2000

MONTANA FWD/3.4L-V6 (185hp)	WS	Ret
Extended Mini Van	14400	16950
SWB Mini Van	13100	15950
Add:		
Intgrtd child seat	100	
Sliding door-pwr	175	
Traction control	125	
Wheels-alloy	175	

1999

MONTANA FWD/3.4L-V6 (185hp)	WS	Ret
Extended Mini Van	12650	15400
SWB Mini Van	11375	13850
Add:		
Intgrtd child seat	75	
Sliding door-pwr	150	
Traction control	100	
Wheels-alloy	125	
Deduct:		
Psngr slider only	275	

1998

TRANS SPORT FWD/3.4L-V6 (180hp)	WS	Ret
SE Mini Van	9700	11825
SE Extended Mini Van	10775	13125
Add:		
Intgrtd child seat	50	
Sliding door-pwr	125	
Montana pkg	450	
Alloy wheels (std w/Montana)	100	
Deduct:		
Psngr slider only	225	

1997

TRANS SPORT FWD/3.4L-V6 (180hp)	WS	Ret
SE Mini Van	8450	10900
SE Extended Mini Van	9375	11425
Add:		
Intgrtd child seat	25	
Sliding door-pwr	100	
Montana pkg	375	
Alloy wheels (std w/Montana)	75	
Deduct:		
Psngr slider only	200	

1996

TRANS SPORT FWD/3.4L-V6 (180hp)	WS	Ret
SE Mini Van	6150	7925
Add:		
Intgrtd child seat	25	
Sliding door-pwr	75	

1995

TRANS SPORT FWD/3.1L-V6 (120hp)	WS	Ret
SE Mini Van	4675	6500
Add:		
3.8 Liter V6	125	
Sliding door-pwr	50	
Integrated child seat	25	

1994

TRANS SPORT FWD/3.1L-V6 (120hp)	WS	Ret
SE Mini Van	3825	5325
Add:		
3.8 Liter V6	125	
Sliding door-pwr	50	

1993

TRANS SPORT FWD/3.1L-V6 (120hp)	WS	Ret
SE Mini Van	3200	4650
Add:		
3.8 Liter V6	100	

1992

TRANS SPORT FWD/3.lL-V6 (120hp)	WS	Ret
GT Mini Van	3125	4525
SE Mini Van	2675	4000
Add:		
3.8 Liter V6	50	

1991

TRANS SPORT FWD/3.1L-V6 (120hp)	WS	Ret
Base Mini Van	2225	3450
SE Mini Van	2575	3850

1990

TRANS SPORT FWD/3.1L-V6 (120hp)	WS	Ret
Base Mini Van	1875	3050
SE Mini Van	2300	3575

SUZUKI

2001

GRAND VITARA 4WD/2.5L-V6 (155hp)	WS	Ret
JLS (2WD) 4dr Utl	9825	11975
JLX 4dr Utl	11500	14000
Limited 4dr Utl	12400	15100
Deduct:		
2-wheel drive (not JLS)	1150	

VITARA 4WD/2.0L-I4 (127hp)	WS	Ret
JLS (2WD) 4dr Utl		
JLS (2WD) 2dr Utl		
JLX 4dr Utl		
JLX 2dr Utl		
JS (2WD) 4dr Utl		
JS (2WD) 2dr Utl		
JX 4dr Utl		
JX (1.6L) 2dr Utl		

XL-7 4WD/2.7L-V6 (170hp)	WS	Ret
Base (5sp) 4dr Utl	13200	15550
Plus 4dr Utl	14350	16900
Touring 4dr Utl	14900	17550

2000

GRAND VITARA 4WD/2.5L-V6 (155hp)	WS	Ret
JLS (2WD) 4dr Utl	9225	11225
JLX 4dr Utl	10900	13275
Limited 4dr Utl	11800	14375
Deduct:		
2-wheel drive (not JLS)	900	

VITARA 4WD/2.0L-I4 (127hp)	WS	Ret
JLX 4dr Utl	9450	11500
JLX 2dr Utl	8550	11025
JS (2WD) 4dr Utl	7050	9100
JS (2WD) 2dr Utl	6075	7825
JX 4dr Utl	8850	11400
JX (1.6L) 2dr Utl	7925	10225
Deduct:		
2-wheel drive (not JS)	900	
1.6L/I4-97hp	225	

1999

GRAND VITARA 4WD/2.5L-V6 (155hp)	WS	Ret
JLX 4dr Utl	9925	12100
JS (2WD) 4dr Utl	8200	10575

VITARA 4WD/2.0L-I4 (127hp)	WS	Ret
JS (2WD) 4dr Utl	6275	8100
JS (2WD) 2dr Utl	5400	7500
JX 4dr Utl	7900	10175
JX 2dr Utl	7150	9225
Deduct:		
1.6L/I4-97hp	200	

1998

SIDEKICK (5sp) RWD/1.6L-I4 (95hp)	WS	Ret
JS 4dr Utl	4825	6700
JS Convertible 2dr Utl	4525	6300
JX 4WD 4dr Utl	5925	7650
JX 4WD Cnv 2dr Utl	5600	7225
Sport JLX 4WD 4dr Utl	6850	8825
Add:		
1.8L 4cyl-120hp	350	
Automatic trans	300	
ABS brakes (std JLX)	175	
Hardtop	150	
Sport (JS,JX)	200	

X-90 RWD/1.6L-I4 (95hp)	WS	Ret
2-Seat 2dr Utl	3850	5350
Add:		
4-wheel drive	600	

1997

SIDEKICK (5sp) RWD/1.6L-I4 (95hp)	WS	Ret
JS 4dr Utl	3900	5425
JS Convertible 2dr Utl	3625	5250
JX 4WD 4dr Utl	4925	6850
JX 4WD Cnv 2dr Utl	4600	6400
Sport JLX 4WD 4dr Utl	5775	7450
Add:		
1.8L 4cyl-120hp	300	
Automatic trans	250	
ABS brakes (std JLX)	150	
Hardtop	125	
Sport (JS,JX)	150	

X-90 RWD/1.6L-I4 (95hp)	WS	Ret
2-Seat 2dr Utl	3100	4500
Add:		
4-wheel drive	500	
ABS Brakes	150	

1996

SIDEKICK (5sp) RWD/1.6L-I4 (95hp)	WS	Ret
JLX 4WD 4dr Utl	4650	6475
JS 4dr Utl	2975	4325
JS Convertible 2dr Utl	2775	4150
JX 4WD 4dr Utl	3850	5350
JX 4WD Cnv 2dr Utl	3600	5225
Add:		
Automatic trans	225	
ABS brakes	125	
Hardtop	100	

X-90 RWD/1.6L-I4 (95hp)	WS	Ret
2-Seat 2dr Utl	2300	3575
Add:		
4-wheel drive	400	

1995

SAMURAI (5sp) 4WD/1.3L-I4 (66hp)	WS	Ret
JL Convertible 2dr Utl	2425	3775

Check Truck Equipment Table on page 4

SIDEKICK (5sp) RWD/1.6L-I4 (80hp)

Model	WS	Ret
JLX 4WD 4dr Utl	3850	5350
JS 4dr Utl	2525	3775
JS Convertible 2dr Utl	2300	3575
JX 4WD 4dr Utl	3225	4675
JX 4WD Cnv 2dr Utl	3025	4400

Add:
- Automatic trans 200
- Hardtop 50

1994 WS Ret

SAMURAI (5sp) 4WD/1.3L-I4 (66hp)

Model	WS	Ret
JL Convertible 2dr Utl	2050	3175

Add:
- Hardtop 50

SIDEKICK (5sp) 4WD/1.6L-I4 (80hp)

Model	WS	Ret
JLX 4dr Utl	3350	4850
JS 2WD 4dr Utl	2250	3500
JS Convt 2WD 2dr Utl	2075	3225
JX 4dr Utl	2850	4250
JX Convertible 2dr Utl	2675	4000

Add:
- Automatic trans 175
- Hardtop 50

1993 WS Ret

SAMURAI (5sp) 4WD/1.3L-I4 (66hp)

Model	WS	Ret
JA Convt 2WD 2dr Utl	850	1650
JL Convertible 2dr Utl	1525	2475

Add:
- Hardtop 50

SIDEKICK (5sp) 4WD/1.6L-I4 (80hp)

Model	WS	Ret
JLX 4WD 4dr Utl	2725	4075
JS Convt 2WD 2dr Utl	1525	2475
JX 4dr Utl	2225	3450
JX Convertible 2dr Utl	2050	3175

Add:
- Automatic trans 175
- Hardtop 50

1992 WS Ret

SAMURAI (5sp) 4WD/1.3L-I4 (66hp)

Model	WS	Ret
JA Convt 2WD 2dr Utl	750	1450
JL Convertible 2dr Utl	1350	2200

Add:
- Hardtop 25

SIDEKICK (5sp) 4WD/1.6L-I4 (80hp)

Model	WS	Ret
JLX 4dr Utl	2325	3600
JS Convt RWD 2dr Utl	1275	2075
JX 4dr Utl	1900	2950
JX Convertible 2dr Utl	1775	2875

Add:
- Automatic trans 150
- Hardtop 25

1991 WS Ret

SAMURAI (5sp) RWD/1.3L-I4 (66hp)

Model	WS	Ret
JA Convertible 2dr Utl	450	1150
JL 4WD Cnv 2dr Utl	950	1825
JS Convertible 2dr Utl	550	1150

Add:
- Hardtop 25

SIDEKICK (5sp) 4WD/1.6L-I4 (80hp)

Model	WS	Ret
JL Convertible 2dr Utl	1750	2850
JLX 4dr Utl	2050	3175
JS Convt 2WD 2dr Utl	1175	2050
JX 4dr Utl	1700	2750
JX Convertible 2dr Utl	1575	2550

Add:
- Automatic trans 125
- Hardtop 25

1990 WS Ret

SAMURAI (5sp) 4WD/1.3L-I4 (66hp)

Model	WS	Ret
Convertible 2dr Utl	800	1550

Add:
- Hardtop 25

SIDEKICK (5sp) 4WD/1.6L-I4 (80hp)

Model	WS	Ret
JLX Htp 2dr Utl	1800	2925
JS Convt 2WD 2dr Utl	1125	1975
JX Convertible 2dr Utl	1500	2425

Add:
- Automatic trans 100
- Hardtop 25

1989 WS Ret

SAMURAI (5sp) 4WD/1.3L-I4 (64hp)

Model	WS	Ret
Convertible 2dr Utl	750	1450
JX Cnv 2dr Utl	800	1550

Add:
- Hardtop 25

SIDEKICK (5sp) 4WD/1.6L-I4 (80hp)

Model	WS	Ret
Custom Cnv (AT) 2dr Utl	1350	2200
Deluxe Cnv 2dr Utl	1250	2025

Add:
- Auto trans (std Custom) 75
- Hardtop 25

1988 WS Ret

SAMURAI (5sp) 4WD/1.3L-I4 (64hp)

Model	WS	Ret
Convertible 2dr Utl	650	1375
JX Cnv 2dr Utl	750	1450

TOYOTA

2001 WS Ret

4RUNNER 4WD/3.4L-V6 (183hp)

Model	WS	Ret
Limited 4dr Utl	24900	28650
SR5 4dr Utl	20650	23750

Add:
- 4-wheel ABS (Base) 350
- Aluminum wheels (std Ltd) 275
- Wood dash (std Ltd) 175
- 6-disc CD chngr 400
- Sport pkg (incls alum whls) 550

Deduct:
- 2-wheel drive 2250

HIGHLANDER AWD/

Model	WS	Ret
Base 4dr Utl		
Limited 4dr Utl		

LAND CRUISER 4WD/4.7L-V8 (230hp)

Model	WS	Ret
Wagon 4dr Wgn	39625	44650

Add:
- Navigation System 800

Deduct:
- No 3rd seat 775

RAV4 4WD/2.0L-I4 (127hp)

Model	WS	Ret
Base 4dr Utl	14925	17650
L 4dr Utl	15850	18425

Add:
- ABS brakes 325
- Wheels-alum 275
- L pkg 1225

Deduct:
- 2-wheel drive 1800

SEQUOIA 4WD/

Model	WS	Ret
Limited 4dr Utl		
SR5 4dr Utl		

SIENNA FWD/3.0L-V6 (194hp)

Model	WS	Ret
CE Mini Van	17075	19850
LE Mini Van	18925	21775
XLE Mini Van	21075	24250

Add:
- Alloy wheels (std XLE) 250
- Door-pwr sliding 200
- Entertainment System 800

Deduct:
- Psngr slider only (LE) 475

TACOMA (5sp) RWD/2.4L-I4 (142hp)

Model	WS	Ret
Base Sbed Pkp	9125	11175
Base ExCab Pkp	10625	13000
DoubleCab 4WD (V6) Sbed Pkp		
Limited (4WD) ExCab Pkp	16350	19000
Prerunner (AT) Sbed Pkp	12400	15175
Prerunner (AT) ExCab Pkp	14225	16825

Add:
- 3.4L-V6 (190hp)(std Ltd) 600
- Automatic trans 650
- 4-wheel drive (std Ltd) 2400
- SR5 trim 625
- Chrome pkg 175
- Wheels-alloy (std Ltd) 250
- 4-wheel ABS brakes 325
- Off-road pkg 625

Tundra RWD/4.7L-V8 (245hp)

Model	WS	Ret
Base (3.4L V6/190hp) Lbed	13550	16025
Limited ExCab Pkp	19200	22100
SR5 (4WD) Lbed Pkp	16300	18950
SR5 ExCab Pkp	17500	20350

Add:
- 4-wheel drive 2375
- 4-wheel ABS 375
- Chrome pkg (Base) 175
- Wheels-alloy (std Ltd) 300

Deduct:
- 3.4L-V6 (190hp) SR5 475

2000 WS Ret

4RUNNER 4WD/3.4L-V6 (183hp)

Model	WS	Ret
Base (4cyl-150hp) 4dr Utl	16525	19225
Limited 4dr Utl	24525	28225
SR5 4dr Utl	19825	22800

Add:
- 4-wheel ABS (Base) 275
- Aluminum wheels (std Ltd) 225
- Wood dash (std Ltd) 150
- 6-disc CD chngr 300

Deduct:
- 2.7L (4cyl-150hp) 425
- 2-wheel drive 1750
- No ABS 350

LAND CRUISER 4WD/4.7L-V8 (230hp)

Model	WS	Ret
Wagon 4dr Wgn	34050	38375

Deduct:
- No 3rd seat 600

RAV4 4WD/2.0L-I4 (127hp)

Model	WS	Ret
Base 4dr Utl	13375	15825
Base 2dr Utl	11650	14250

Add:
- ABS brakes 250
- Wheels-alum 200
- L pkg 950

Deduct:
- 2-wheel drive 1400

SIENNA — FWD/3.0L-V6 (194hp)

Model	WS	Ret
CE Mini Van	15475	18300
LE Mini Van	17250	20050
XLE Mini Van	19475	22400
Add:		
Alloy wheels (std XLE)	200	
Door-pwr sliding	175	
Deduct:		
Psngr slider only (LE)	375	

TACOMA (5sp) — RWD/2.4L-I4 (142hp)

Model	WS	Ret
Base Sbed Pkp	8025	10400
Base ExCab Pkp	9550	11700
Limited (4WD) ExCab Pkp	15275	18075
Prerunner (AT) Sbed Pkp	11325	13850
Prerunner (AT) ExCab Pkp	13150	15550
Add:		
3.4L-V6 (190hp)(std Ltd)	475	
Automatic trans	500	
4-wheel drive (std Ltd)	1850	
SR5 trim	500	
Chrome pkg	150	
Wheels-alloy (std Ltd)	200	
4-wheel ABS brakes	250	

Tundra — RWD/4.7L-V8 (245hp)

Model	WS	Ret
Base (3.4L V6/190hp Lbed Pkp	11975	14650
Limited ExCab Pkp	17050	19825
SR5 (4WD) Lbed Pkp	14750	17450
SR5 ExCab Pkp	15425	18250
Add:		
4-wheel drive	1825	
4-wheel ABS	275	
Chrome pkg (Base)	150	
Wheels-alloy (std Ltd)	225	
Deduct:		
3.4L-V6 (190hp) SR5	375	

1999 — WS — Ret

4RUNNER — 4WD/3.4L-V6 (183hp)

Model	WS	Ret
Base (4cyl-150hp) 4dr Utl	14925	17650
Limited 4dr Utl	22375	25750
SR5 4dr Utl	18000	20925
Add:		
4-wheel ABS (Base)	225	
Aluminum wheels (std Ltd)	175	
Wood dash (std Ltd)	100	
Deduct:		
2.7L (4cyl-150hp)	350	
2-wheel drive	1450	
No ABS	300	

LAND CRUISER — 4WD/4.7L-V8 (230hp)

Model	WS	Ret
Wagon 4dr Wgn	31825	35850
Deduct:		
No 3rd seat	500	
Std. wheels	200	

RAV4 — 4WD/2.0L-I4 (127hp)

Model	WS	Ret
Base 4dr Utl	11850	14500
Base 2dr Utl	10275	12575
Add:		
Active/Rugged pkg	175	
ABS brakes	225	
L package	775	
Wheels-alum (std L)	175	
Deduct:		
2-wheel drive	1150	

SIENNA — FWD/3.0L-V6 (194hp)

Model	WS	Ret
CE Mini Van	13950	16500
LE Mini Van	15575	18425
XLE Mini Van	17650	20525
Add:		
Alloy wheels (std XLE)	150	
Door-pwr sliding	125	
Deduct:		
Psngr slider only (LE)	300	

TACOMA (5sp) — RWD/2.4L-I4 (142hp)

Model	WS	Ret
Base Sbed Pkp	7175	9300
Base ExCab Pkp	8600	11150
Limited (4WD) ExCab Pkp	13700	16125
Prerunner (AT) Sbed Pkp	10200	12475
Prerunner (AT) ExCab Pkp	11750	14375
Add:		
3.4L-V6 (190hp)(std Ltd)	400	
Automatic trans	425	
4-wheel drive (std Ltd)	1550	
SR5 trim	425	
Chrome pkg	100	
Wheels-alloy (std Ltd)	150	
4-wheel ABS brakes	225	

1998 — WS — Ret

4RUNNER — 4WD/3.4L-V6 (183hp)

Model	WS	Ret
Base (4cyl-150hp) 4dr Utl	13125	15525
Limited 4dr Utl	19550	22500
SR5 4dr Utl	15750	18325
Add:		
4-wheel ABS (Base)	200	
Aluminum wheels (std Ltd)	150	
Wood dash (std Ltd)	75	
Deduct:		
2.7L (4cyl-150hp)	300	
2-wheel drive	1200	
No ABS	250	

LAND CRUISER — 4WD/4.7L-V8 (230hp)

Model	WS	Ret
Wagon 4dr Wgn	28525	32625
Deduct:		
No 3rd seat	425	
Std. wheels	175	

RAV4 — 4WD/2.0L-I4 (127hp)

Model	WS	Ret
Base 4dr Utl	11000	13475
Base 2dr Utl	9650	11800
Add:		
Active/Rugged pkg	150	
ABS brakes	175	
Wheels-alum	150	
Deduct:		
2-wheel drive	950	

SIENNA — FWD/3.0L-V6 (194hp)

Model	WS	Ret
CE Mini Van	12125	14850
LE Mini Van	13600	16100
XLE Mini Van	15350	18150
Add:		
Alloy wheels (std XLE)	125	
Door-pwr sliding	100	
Deduct:		
Psngr slider only (LE)	250	

T-100 — RWD/2.7L-V6 (150hp)

Model	WS	Ret
Base (4cyl) Lbed Pkp	6775	8725
Base ExCab Pkp	8300	10700
SR-5 ExCab Pkp	9525	11600
Add:		
4-wheel drive	1250	
4-wheel ABS	200	
Chrome pkg (DX)	75	
Wheels-alloy	150	

TACOMA (5sp) — RWD/2.4L-I4 (142hp)

Model	WS	Ret
Base Sbed Pkp	6700	8675
Base ExCab Pkp	7925	10275
SR5 (6cyl-4WD) ExCab Pkp	10125	12400
Add:		
3.4L 190hp V6	300	
Automatic trans	350	
4-wheel drive (std Ltd)	1225	
Chrome pkg	75	
Wheels-alloy (std Ltd)	125	
4-wheel ABS brakes	175	

1997 — WS — Ret

4RUNNER — 4WD/3.4L-V6 (183hp)

Model	WS	Ret
Base (4cyl-150hp) 4dr Utl	11550	14125
Limited 4dr Utl	17425	20250
SR5 4dr Utl	13975	16525
Add:		
4-wheel ABS (Base)	150	
Aluminum wheels (std Ltd)	125	
Elite pkg (wood dash)	50	
Deduct:		
2.7L (4cyl-150hp)	250	
2-wheel drive	1000	
No ABS	200	

LAND CRUISER — 4WD/4.5L-I6 (212hp)

Model	WS	Ret
Wagon 4dr Wgn	21100	24275
Add:		
40th Anniv Edit.	225	
Deduct:		
No 3rd seat	350	
Std. wheels	125	

PREVIA — RWD/2.4L-I4 (161hp)

Model	WS	Ret
DX Mini Van	10400	12725
LE Mini Van	11775	14425
Add:		
4-wheel drive	975	
Dual sunroof	375	
Alloy wheels	100	
Deduct:		
No ABS brakes	175	

RAV4 — 4WD/2.0L-I4 (120hp)

Model	WS	Ret
Base 4dr Utl	8875	11500
Base 2dr Utl	8250	10675
Add:		
Active/Rugged pkg	125	
ABS brakes	150	
Deduct:		
2-wheel drive	800	

T-100 — RWD/3.4L-V6 (190hp)

Model	WS	Ret
Base (4cyl) Lbed Pkp	6000	7725
Base ExCab Pkp	7350	9475
SR-5 ExCab Pkp	8450	10900
Add:		
4-wheel drive	1025	
4-wheel ABS	175	
Alloy wheels	125	

TACOMA (5sp) — RWD/2.4L-I4 (142hp)

Model	WS	Ret
Base Sbed Pkp	5450	7625
Base ExCab Pkp	6600	8550
SR5 (6cyl-4WD) ExCab Pkp	8550	11075
Add:		
6cyl engine	250	
4-wheel drive	1050	
Automatic trans	300	

1996 — WS — Ret

4RUNNER — 4WD/3.4L-V6 (183hp)

Model	WS	Ret
Base (4cyl-150hp) 4dr Utl	9650	11800
Limited 4dr Utl	14700	17400
SR5 4dr Utl	11725	14350
Add:		
4-wheel ABS	125	
Aluminum wheels (std Ltd)	75	
Deduct:		
4cyl	175	
2-wheel drive	825	
No ABS	175	

LAND CRUISER — 4WD/4.5L-I6 (212hp)

Model	WS	Ret
Wagon 4dr Wgn	17725	20600

Check Truck Equipment Table on page 4

Deduct:
No 3rd seat 275
Std. wheels 100

PREVIA RWD/2.4L-I4 (161hp)

DX Mini Van 8975 11625
LE Mini Van 10175 12450

Add:
4-wheel drive 800
Dual sunroof 300

Deduct:
No ABS brakes 150

RAV4 4WD/2.0L-I4 (120hp)

Base 4dr Utl 7700 9975
Base 2dr Utl 7125 9225

Add:
Active/Rugged pkg 75

Deduct:
2-wheel drive 650

T-100 RWD/3.4L-V6 (190hp)

Base (4cyl) Lbed Pkp 5100 7100
Base ExCab Pkp 6300 8125
SR-5 ExCab Pkp 7250 9350

Add:
4-wheel drive 850
4-wheel ABS 125
Alloy wheels 100

TACOMA (5sp) RWD/2.7L-I4 (142hp)

Base Sbed Pkp 4800 6700
Base ExCab Pkp 5800 7525
SR5 (6cyl-4WD) ExCab Pkp 7500 9725

Add:
6cyl engine 200
4-wheel drive 875
Automatic trans 250

1995 WS Ret

4RUNNER 4WD/3.0L-V6 (150hp)

SR5 4dr Utl 9100 11150

Add:
4-wheel ABS 125
Aluminum wheels 75

Deduct:
4cyl 175

LAND CRUISER 4WD/4.5L-I6 (212hp)

Wagon 4dr Wgn 15950 18550

Deduct:
No 3rd seat 250

PICKUP (5sp) RWD/2.4L-I4 (116hp)

Base Sbed Pkp 3900 5450
Dlx Sbed Pkp 4325 6050
Dlx ExCab Pkp 5125 7150
SR5 (6cyl) ExCab Pkp 6025 7800

Add:
6cyl engine 175
4-wheel drive 800
Automatic trans 225

PREVIA RWD/2.4L-I4 (138hp)

DX Mini Van 6775 8775
LE Mini Van 7800 10100

Add:
2.4L Supercharged 4cyl 300
4-wheel drive 750
Dual sunroof 275

Deduct:
No ABS brakes 150

T-100 RWD/3.4L-V6 (190hp)

Base Lbed Pkp 4725 6600
DX Lbed Pkp 5075 7050
DX ExCab Pkp 6125 7900

SR-5 ExCab Pkp 6975 9000

Add:
4-wheel drive 850
4-wheel ABS 100
Chrome pkg 100
Alloy wheels 75

TACOMA (5sp) RWD/2.4L-I4 (142hp)

Base Sbed Pkp 4300 6000
Base ExCab Pkp 5225 7300
SR5 (6cyl-4WD) ExCab Pkp 6750 8750

Add:
6cyl 175
4-wheel drive 825
Automatic trans 225
4-wheel ABS brakes 150
SX trim 200

1994 WS Ret

4RUNNER 4WD/3.0L-V6 (150hp)

SR5 4dr Utl 8150 10550

Add:
4-wheel ABS 100
Aluminum wheels 75

Deduct:
4cyl 175

LAND CRUISER 4WD/4.5L-I6 (212hp)

Wagon 4dr Wgn 13825 16350

Deduct:
No ABS 175
No 3rd seat 225

PICKUP (5sp) RWD/2.4L-I4 (116hp)

Base Sbed Pkp 3450 5025
Dlx Sbed Pkp 3825 5350
Dlx ExCab Pkp 4450 6225
SR5 (6cyl) ExCab Pkp 5175 7225

Add:
6cyl engine 175
4-wheel drive 725
Automatic trans 200

PREVIA RWD/2.4L-I4 (138hp)

DX Mini Van 6025 7800
LE Mini Van 6900 8950

Add:
4-wheel drive 675
ABS brakes 125
Dual sunroof 250

T-100 RWD/3.0L-V6 (150hp)

Base (4cyl) Lbed Pkp 4200 5850
DX Lbed Pkp 4750 6600
SR5 Lbed Pkp 5450 7575

Add:
4-wheel drive 775

1993 WS Ret

4RUNNER RWD/3.0L-V6 (150hp)

SR5 4dr Utl 6375 8250
SR5 4WD 4dr Utl 7150 9250

Deduct:
4cyl 175

LAND CRUISER 4WD/4.5L-I6 (212hp)

Wagon 4dr Wgn 12650 15475

Deduct:
No ABS 125
No 3rd seat 175

PICKUP (5sp) RWD/2.4L-I4 (116hp)

Base Sbed Pkp 2975 4350
Dlx Sbed Pkp 3300 4825
Dlx Lbed Pkp 3400 4950
Dlx ExCab Pkp 4025 5625

SR5 (6cyl) ExCab Pkp 4725 6600

Add:
6cyl engine 150
4-wheel drive 650
Automatic trans 175

PREVIA RWD/2.4L-I4 (138hp)

DX Mini Van 4850 6775
LE Mini Van 5700 7375

Add:
4-wheel drive 550
Dual sunroof 225

T-100 RWD/3.0L-V6 (150hp)

Base Lbed Pkp 4050 5625
SR5 Lbed Pkp 4775 6650

Add:
4-wheel drive 700
Automatic trans 175

1992 WS Ret

4RUNNER RWD/3.0L-V6 (150hp)

Base 4dr Utl 5625 7275
SR5 4WD 4dr Utl 6450 8350
SR5 4WD 2dr Utl 6000 7775

Add:
4-wheel drive 575

Deduct:
4cyl 150

LAND CRUISER 4WD/4.0L-I6 (155hp)

Wagon 4dr Wgn 10600 12975

Deduct:
No 3rd seat 125
Steel wheels 100

PICKUP (5sp) RWD/2.4L-I4 (116hp)

Base Sbed Pkp 2675 4000
Dlx Sbed Pkp 2975 4350
Dlx Lbed Pkp 3025 4400
Dlx ExCab Pkp 3600 5250
SR5 (6cyl) ExCab Pkp 4150 5800

Add:
6cyl engine 125
4-wheel drive 575
Automatic trans 175

PREVIA RWD/2.4L-I4 (138hp)

DX Mini Van 4125 5775
LE Mini Van 4950 6925

Add:
4-wheel drive 475
Dual sunroof 175

1991 WS Ret

4RUNNER 4WD/3.0L-V6 (150hp)

SR5 4dr Utl 5575 7225
SR5 2dr Utl 5150 7200

Deduct:
4cyl 150
2-wheel drive 575

LAND CRUISER 4WD/4.0L-I6 (155hp)

Wagon 4dr Utl 8475 10975

Deduct:
Steel wheels 75

PICKUP (5sp) RWD/2.4L-I4 (116hp)

Base Sbed Pkp 2350 3675
Dlx Sbed Pkp 2650 3975
Dlx Lbed Pkp 2700 4050
Dlx ExCab Pkp 3175 4625
SR5 (6cyl) ExCab Pkp 3700 5400

Add:
6cyl engine 100
4-wheel drive 550

Automatic trans 150

PREVIA RWD/2.4L-I4 (138hp)

	WS	Ret
DX Mini Van	3350	4875
LE Mini Van	4025	5625

1990 WS Ret

4RUNNER 4WD/3.0L-V6 (150hp)

	WS	Ret
SR5 4dr Utl	4925	6875
SR5 2dr Utl	4575	6400

Deduct:
4cyl 125
2-wheel drive 475

LANDCRUISER 4WD/4.0L-I6 (155hp)

	WS	Ret
Wagon 4dr Utl	7075	9175

PICKUP (5sp) RWD/2.4L-I4 (116hp)

	WS	Ret
Base Sbed Pkp	2225	3475
Dlx Sbed Pkp	2450	3825
Dlx Lbed Pkp	2525	3775
Dlx ExCab Pkp	2950	4300
SR5 4WD Sbed Pkp	3225	4700
SR5 Lbed Pkp	2800	4200
SR5 ExCab Pkp	3175	4625

Add:
6cyl engine 100
4-wheel drive 500
Automatic trans 125

1989 WS Ret

4RUNNER 4WD/3.0L-V6 (150hp)

	WS	Ret
Dlx 2dr Utl	4025	5625
SR5 2dr Utl	4225	5900

Deduct:
4cyl 100

LANDCRUISER 4WD/4.0L-I6 (155hp)

	WS	Ret
Wagon 4dr Utl	6500	8425

PICKUP (5sp) RWD/2.4L-I4 (102hp)

	WS	Ret
Base Sbed Pkp	2025	3150
Dlx Sbed Pkp	2175	3400
Dlx Lbed Pkp	2225	3475
Dlx ExCab Pkp	2575	3850
SR5 4WD Sbed Pkp	2825	4225
SR5 Lbed Pkp	2425	3775
SR5 ExCab Pkp	2775	4150

Add:
6cyl engine 100
4-wheel drive 475

Automatic trans 100

VAN RWD/2.2L-I4 (101hp)

	WS	Ret
Dlx Mini Van	1800	2950
LE Mini Van	2050	3200
Panel Mini Van	1275	2075
Window Mini Van	1375	2250

Add:
4-wheel drive 325

1988 WS Ret

4RUNNER 4WD/3.0L-V6 (145hp)

	WS	Ret
Dlx 2dr Utl	2900	4350
SR5 2dr Utl	3050	4450

Deduct:
4cyl 75

LANDCRUISER 4WD/4.0L-I6 (155hp)

	WS	Ret
Wagon 4dr Utl	5675	7350

PICKUP (5sp) /2.4L-I4 (116hp)

	WS	Ret
Base Sbed Pkp	1775	2900
Base Lbed Pkp	1800	2950
Base ExCab Pkp	2075	3250
Dlx Lbed Pkp	1925	3000
Dlx ExCab Pkp	2200	3425
SR5 4WD Sbed Pkp	2425	3775
SR5 ExCab Pkp	2375	3700

Add:
6cyl engine 75
4-wheel drive 400
Automatic trans 50

VOLKSWAGEN

2001 WS Ret

Eurovan RWD/

	WS	Ret
GLS Mini Van		
MV Mini Van		

2000 WS Ret

Eurovan RWD/

	WS	Ret
GLS Mini Van	16925	19675
MV Mini Van	17950	20875

1999 WS Ret

Eurovan RWD/

	WS	Ret
GLS Mini Van	15575	18425
MV Mini Van	16250	18900

1993 WS Ret

Eurovan RWD/2.5L-I5 (109hp)

	WS	Ret
Base (5sp/AT) Mini Van	3425	5000
GL (5sp/AT) Mini Van	5250	7325

1991 WS Ret

VANAGON (4sp/AT) RWD/2.1L-F4 (90hp)

	WS	Ret
Base Mini Van	3775	5625
Carat Mini Van	5175	7375
GL Mini Van	4375	6225
GL Camper Mini Van	6750	8925

Add:
4-wheel drive 400

1990 WS Ret

VANAGON (4sp/AT) RWD/2.1L-F4 (90hp)

	WS	Ret
Base Mini Van	3525	5250
Carat Mini Van	4750	6775
GL Mini Van	4050	5775
GL Camper Mini Van	6275	8300

Add:
4-wheel drive 375

1989 WS Ret

VANAGON (4sp/AT) RWD/2.1L-F4 (90hp)

	WS	Ret
GL Mini Van	3525	5250
GL Carat Mini Van	4050	5775
GL Camper Mini Van	5475	7800

Add:
4-wheel drive 325

1988 WS Ret

VANAGON (4sp/AT) RWD/2.1L-F4 (90hp)

	WS	Ret
GL Mini Van	2900	4425
GL Camper Mini Van	4575	6525

Add:
4-wheel drive 300

Check Truck Equipment Table on page 4

VMR® PRICE GUIDES

SUBSCRIPTION ORDER FORM

VMR Standard Used Car Prices is an independent, reliable and up to date source of used car, van and light truck prices direct from today's market.

VMR Canadian Used Car Prices features 10 years of Canadian-specific values direct from the Canadian used car marketplace. The only Canadian guide that uses VMR's exclusive Value-Track® technology.

Collector CAR&TRUCK MARKET GUIDE

Collector Car & Truck Market Guide covers over 70 makes of domestic and foreign vehicles from 1946-1974 (Corvettes through 1982). Coverage includes the most extensive listing of engines and standard equipment of any classic auto price guide, auction reports, investment profiles and market tracking.

2002 Annual Subscription Rates

VMR Standard Used Car Prices (6 issues/year)	**$22.00**
(Canada & Mexico $28.00. Other countries $38.00. US funds only)	(2yrs $38.95)
Collector Car & Truck Market (6 issues/year)	**$18.95**
(Canada & Mexico $24.95. Other countries $36.00. US funds only)	(2yrs $30.95)
VMR Canadian Used Car Prices (4 issues/year) *NEW!*	**$22.00**
(Canada & Mexico $26.00. Other countries $34.00. US funds only)	(2yrs $34.95)

Please check the publications you wish to subscribe to:

- ☐ VMR® *Standard Used Car Prices*
- ☐ VMR® *Canadian Used Car Prices*
- ☐ *Collector Car & Truck Market*

Name ______________________________

Address ______________________________

City ______________ State ________ Zip ________

PAYMENT METHOD:

- ☐ Check or Money Order $__________
- ☐ Mastercard
- ☐ Visa

Card no. ______________________________

Exp. Date: ____________ Signature ______________________________

Please make all checks payable to:
VMR International, Inc.
41 No. Main St.
No. Grafton, MA 01536-1559 USA
or call 800-867-4685. *05/02*

FREQUENTLY ASKED QUESTIONS

VMR's exclusive customer helpline has helped thousands of readers with pricing, content, and other car buying questions. To help all our readers, we've assembled some of the more commonly asked questions below.

Where do you get your pricing?
VMR's pricing data is compiled from several different sources. Auction results, our exclusive Value-Track® database, actual sale reports, government data, and new car inventory levels and incentives are included in our pricing model.

Why do your values differ from the guide the dealer has?
VMR compiles actual market data. Our guides publish numbers the way they really are, not how some guide thinks they should be. Popular dealer guides such as NADA (which is published by the National Automobile Dealers Association - hardly an unbiased source) and Kelly Blue Book, in our view, overstate the value of most vehicles.
This is precisely the reason dealers use these - they lend credibility to inflated prices. Both publish different versions of their guide - one for consumers, one for dealer showrooms, and a wholesale guide for a dealer's car buying purposes. Consumer Editions of dealer guides omit a wholesale price. We believe this makes them incompatible with *your* interests.

Why don't some guides publish wholesale numbers?
The wholesale price is the market's single most important figure. Guides that show trade-in, loan, or only retail figures are dancing around the issue. The wholesale number sets the baseline for all parties - buyer and seller. If you are using other guides in addition to VMR's, or even if you are not using our guide at all, we strongly recommend that you look for market-derived wholesale pricing.

Do I add the option pricing to the wholesale & the retail number?
Yes, you add equipment pricing to both numbers.

Can I call your helpline with questions about cars & car buying?
As long as you have a current edition of our guide, we'll share our knowledge about anything to do with cars.

Do trim packages listed with trucks include power accessories?
No. All van and truck trim packages have been "decontented" so you do not have to worry about figuring out what was standard and what wasn't for the myriad of trim and equipment packages available. The pricing reflects adjustments for the trim only -- you still need to go to the Truck Equipment Table on page 4.

The dealer tells me that your prices are national, and that pricing is higher in our region.
If we had a nickel for every time we've heard this one! It doesn't matter what region the caller is in -- it's always the highest-cost region of the country! Don't buy it. Except in *very* isolated instances, prices fluctuate less than 5% from any one region to another.